CHANGING
WOMAN
CHANGING
*W*ORK

CHANGING
WOMAN
CHANGING
WORK

Nina
Boyd
Krebs
Ed.D.

MacMurray & Beck

Aspen, Colorado

Printed and Bound in the United States of America
Library of Congress Catalog Card Number: 93-077399

Publisher's Cataloging in Publication
(Prepared by Quality Books Inc.)

Krebs, Nina.
    Changing woman, changing work / by Nina Boyd Krebs.
    p.   cm.
    Includes bibliographical references and index.
    ISBN 1-878448-56-0 (hard.)

    1. Vocational guidance for women.   2. Women—Psychology.   I. Title.

HD6057.9.K74 1993   650.1'4'024042
                                         QBI93–659

The passages from Ruth Gendler's *The Book of Qualities* on pages 12-13, and 188, are reprinted by permission from Ruth Gendler, *The Book of Qualities* (San Francisco: HarperCollins, 1988).

Stephanie Ganic Braunstein's "Apology", which appears on pages 210-211, is reprinted by permission of the author.

"Changing Woman Said It So", which appears on page 21 is reprinted from *Meditations with the Navajo*, by Gerald Hausman, Copyright 1987, Bear and Company, Inc., P.O. Drawer 2860, Santa Fe, NM 87504.

THIS BOOK IS DEDICATED TO

ERICA SCHAFER • KAREN FLEMING

*who
ground my energy,
touch my feelings,
fire my heart,
and inspire my love.*

DAVID KREBS

Contents

FIRE

PASSION
AT WORK

AIR

SPIRIT:
A NEW VISION

Preface

September 1987. With our friends Elsa and Rich, my husband Dave and I dipped and swayed along a northern California Highway—the back way to Mendocino—to celebrate their marriage. A few persistent sunbeams penetrated the redwoods' darkness with their mystical optimism. We were all excited. I felt cradled in a rare opportunity to talk about my summer's experience—the intensity of a women's spirituality camp in June and then the Creativity and Madness Seminar in Aspen in August. And the deepening of my commitment to write this book.

I knew the time had come. For several years I had wanted to write another book. I had reflected, strategized, puzzled about ways to capture my profound experience working as an external consultant for a burgeoning family-owned business. I couldn't formulate that experience honestly and still safeguard the trust my client had granted me.

I'd worked over twenty years as a psychotherapist and nearly that long as a consultant. As well as the ever present home/work balancing act all of us do, I constantly wrestled with another—trying to balance my interest in working deeply with individuals with a passion for understanding and having an impact on the organizational systems in which we live our lives. I've heard thousands of stories and dealt with buckets of pain. Much of the pain has been about women struggling to live their lives fully—to honor personal connections and to thrive in workplaces that impose formidable constraints. I wanted to give something back—to share some of what I had learned about life from these women and from my own efforts as well.

In 1986, I was invited to be on a panel with economist Sylvia Hewlett, whose book *A Lesser Life: The Myth of Women's Liberation in America*, had just been released. The panel never happened, but reading the book affected me more than I wanted it to. I practically worship Gloria Steinem and the Women's Movement, but I could see that Hewlett—who takes the women's movement to task—hit the mark in some ways that resonated with my experience. The ordinary, middle-of-the-road woman—who forms a large segment of today's work force—doesn't have a voice or model for feeling powerful in her own right. Outspoken women tend to polarize the feminine by rejecting or minimizing relationships with men on one side or capitulating to the patriarchy on the other. As individuals, we gravitate toward one of these limited models and live it as if it were our own. Or, we muddle around in the middle and feel like we're nowhere in our identities as women.

I began to think about writing a book that would support today's working woman in her efforts to be more of who she really is. I started to feel strongly that the increasing acceptance of women in the work world, including middle management isn't enough. It's time for the feminine—how we think and feel as women, not as man clones—to have a voice. And that's a whole different story.

A major reason many of my clients experience so much pain in their work lives is that, on the job, they're expected to behave like men and/or be seen as inferior and treated accordingly. For too long, they—like me—bought into that model and didn't question it.

It became clear to me that the archetypal feminine invites women to be powerful in ways different from the ones to which we've grown accustomed. Not only can individual women benefit by being true to themselves rather than role playing all day long, but they have significant, as yet unacknowledged, contributions to make to the organizations in which they work. The other side of power—the grounded, connected, passionate, and spiritual feminine—belongs in business, politics, and international relations.

I have written this book about feminine power at work for women. My goal isn't to exclude men, or the masculine. I've felt constant conflict about how to include the masculine balance that is an essential part of life, a key part of any decisionmaking or implementation. Men have suffered as deeply from patriarchal distortion of the masculine as women have. They need to learn about their masculinity as well as to honor their feminine side. In so doing, they can respect the depth and complexity of the feminine in women rather than accepting only those parts that satisfy, or at least don't threaten, the patriarchal power structure. Our view of the masculine is as limited as our view of the feminine. Another book that outlines the archetypal masculine as I have tried to do here with the feminine would be a real contribution. But that is truly another subject. As I wrestled to include both feminine and masculine perspectives at each point, an already elusive subject disappeared in the confusion.

Throughout my work on *Changing Woman Changing Work*, I've tried to honor what I've come to regard as archetypically feminine—non-linearity, receptivity, presence, process, emotion, connection, wholism, nature. I love Marion Woodman's four pillars of the feminine—receptivity, presence, process, and paradox—and have kept them in mind. I've listened to people and taken in what they've given me when it rang true. Sometimes that has drastically changed my views. I've tried to stay present—write the truth as I feel it, hear it, and see it rather than bending for convenience. The process of researching and writing this book emerged from my experience. In addition to my daily work as a therapist, increasing trips to the library and interviews, I attended workshops—both on writing and on gender issues. I gave workshops for working women (and one for men) on "Feminine Power at

Work"—heard and saw their responses to the model that was forming. And I lived with paradox—logical contradictions in the feminine, such as those between solitude and connection, power and openness, passion and containment—and included them, knowing that linear logic says you can't have it both ways.

Living that paradox meant staying connected with the important people in my life while trying to find enough alone time for the book. Throughout my five years' research and writing, my friends' support has been legendary. Phyllis Watts read every word of the early manuscripts and offered supportive, insightful feedback. Mary Bolton gave me gold earrings to wear at my book-signing party when I had only just begun and has been an inspiring friend and consultant throughout. Ruth Ghio said, "Even if this book never gets published, your work has affected me deeply." Phyllis, Mary, Ruth, and Peggy Northup met with me to brainstorm when confusion and overwhelm took over. Karen Davis and Melissa Lawler, in addition to their encouragement and faith in me, generously arranged contacts and interviews in New York and Indianapolis.

Countless other friends and colleagues encouraged me, gave me material and suggestions, and attended or referred women to the workshops that helped me clarify the model. My daughters, Erica Schafer and Karen Fleming, assumed that "Mom's book" was a *fait accompli* from the beginning and offered candid, helpful comments from time to time that kept me in touch with younger women's issues at work. Judy Wavers, my sister and loving friend, also helped me tune in to work groups that I might not typically have access to. These women and too many others to name, create the web, that deep, feminine connection that supports my efforts and keeps me centered when uncertainty and self doubt threaten. They have my deepest love and gratitude.

Clients, individual and organizational, created both the inspiration and the grist for this book. Their pain and joy have shaped me as well as my writing. Over time, I've integrated bits and pieces of their stories that form the patterns of feminine power—both the strengths and the shadows. I feel privileged to have shared the lives of so many people, and I thank them for their trust in me.

The fifty or so people I interviewed in different parts of the country thoughtfully answered my open-ended questions about the feminine presence and expressed their opinions and feelings. Some influenced the structure of the book, while others added color and music. When I started the interviews I was just looking for information. When I finished I knew my soul had been touched. I'm deeply grateful to them all.

I had professional help too. Paul Aikin, my therapist and teacher of many years, taught me to value my own femininity and honor myself as an ordinary woman. Eleanor Vincent validated the conceptual strength of my earliest drafts and launched my interest in learning to write as more than an academic exercise. She told me in all sincerity that anyone could write a book if she were willing to work at it long and hard enough. Those words buoyed me when I nearly sank in the mire in the middle. Marj Stuart's editorial assistance helped me create a creditable proposal and manuscript. Consultant Jennifer McCord, in her succinct way, informed me, "You have three books here; make one chapter for each dimension and take all this other stuff out." That's when I thought I was finished, but I followed her advice, and took another year to integrate her recommendations. Katie Gartner pulled my proposal from the stack at MacMurray & Beck Communications and called me on my birthday to ask if I had sold the book yet. Her grasp of my message and capacity to transport it to the marketplace thrill and amaze me. Fred Ramey's understanding of the feminine dilemma in the workplace, his substantive suggestions, and his editorial artistry transformed the book that was almost there to a finished product.

And through it all, Dave Krebs has been my partner, friend, and confidant, reading and listening to unending versions of the feminine presence at work. Occasionally, he's offered suggestions and feedback, but mostly he's been there—unwavering in his emotional, homemaking, and financial support, understanding that it takes time away from other aspects of a relationship to write a book. His sustaining love has taught me the possibility—reminds me each day of the warmth and joy in true partnership.

It's one thing to live and study feminine process. It's another to name it. Starting with *Melting the Monolith* (too esoteric), living for a long time with *Feminine Power at Work* (too scary), I searched for a title that embraced what I wanted to say. I had pages of brainstorms—ideas from friends and family as well as my own. I felt like Coleridge's ancient mariner with the albatross around his neck. I asked anyone I thought might be remotely interested if they had suggestions for a title. I was thinking of sponsoring a contest. Throughout, I trusted that the right title would appear, but the time had come and it wasn't there.

When I admitted my woes to publisher Fred Ramey, he said, "Why don't you consider something that reflects the Native American theme you've woven through the book?" I shared Fred's suggestion with Dave who, in his own quiet way, started some serious reflection on the title project. At five o'clock one morning, he startled me by sitting up in bed. "I've got it!" he said. "Your title."

That certainly woke me up. "*White Buffalo Woman Roams the World Making Things All Better for the American Working Woman*," he said. Only years of self discipline as a therapist and consultant kept me from saying, "Oh, honey, that's interesting, but it would never fit on a book cover and besides most working women probably won't relate to White Buffalo Woman." Instead we spent the next hour or so musing about Native American spiritual images, including Changing Woman, and how those relate to the feminine and what I was writing about. I happened to have Hausman's book, *Meditations with the Navajo*, by the bedside. When I read "Changing Woman Said It So" (you'll see it in the first chapter), I wondered how finding a title could ever have been so hard.

I could write a book about writing this book. It has taught me, entertained me, challenged me, threatened me, hurt me, and given me great joy. I've had to examine myself in both sides of all thirteen dimensions that you'll find between the covers. I've tried to be honest, both with myself and in the writing, and that hasn't always been easy or pleasant. I've been surprised repeatedly to see the right quote, example, or research material appear when I needed it. That includes this little piece I found at the end of a travel book review in the *Women's Review of Books*:

> We need many more intrepid women who set out to expand both their and our concepts of the world. We need them in writing just as we need them in politics. We need that sense of adventure, of reaching wider, delving deeper, pushing further afield, whether that field be geographical intellectual, political, personal, or all of these and more. Enough with decorousness. Let us risk preconceptions and treasured philosophies, bodies and souls. Let us be big and bawdy and full of courage. Let's go.

Lesley Hazleton's paragraph proclaims what we need to do to give voice to the diverse, archetypal power of the feminine in places that count. *Changing Woman Changing Work* is a map for that brave journey.

—Sacramento, January 1993

Changing Woman Changing Work

The women's movement made it possible for women to charge into the world of business and public service and, to a limited extent, into positions of power. That we've done, with enthusiasm and competence—and with great pain. Strategically, we learned to think and act like men in order to fit in—to compete and win on a level playing field. But now, recognizing that the field will never be level, many women are sick of the charade.

In beauty it is done

in harmony it is written

in beauty and harmony

it shall so be finished

Changing Woman said it so.

Gerald Hausman,
Meditations with the Navajo

A woman who has her own business and makes much less than she did as deputy director for a major state department told me, "The workplace demanded that I sever my relationship with myself to play man. I had aready been ripped off in all the right places to be a good student. I did it well. It took a long time to know that I was losing myself at the same time I was so successful. I made the decision to do without the money. Now I find that I've internalized those patriarchal values so deeply I have myself on a production quota. My loss is greater than I ever would have imagined."

Less bitter, but reflective, a government official who's still in state service said, "I used to spend hours arguing with men friends and colleagues about women's place at work. I asserted, adamantly, that there were no differences between women and men. Women just needed equal opportunity to show what we could do. I made sure that I acted tough and logical to assure my credibility. Only recently have I discovered—much to my surprise—that when I look at things in my own way—which doesn't always fit the tough and logical path I learned in graduate school—and pay attention to all those feelings I work so hard to control, I'm much less stressed. Speaking from this more personal place opens new avenues or adds a different twist to what we're doing. I could have taken better care of my uniqueness all along—and made a contribution—if I had valued my differences as a woman rather than trying to erase them."

Another woman—a psychotherapist who made the transition from a hospital setting to private practice fifteen years ago—told me, "I can't believe I still do things to make men in authority like me, even when I can't stand them. I walk away wondering why I did that. When I left my job and started my own practice, I had hardly anything to do with men. My clients were nearly all women. Most of my colleagues were women. It took a long time not to lose myself—to hold my own around men. I do much better now, but I couldn't stand working in a system where my ways are automatically put down because I'm a woman. Or where I have to cater to men in authority just to do my job."

Not only does the glass ceiling still hang over the heads of women in most companies, but the feminine way—the deep, connective, reflective side of human experience—remains undervalued in our culture. Decision-making is still linear—tough and logical—throughout the business world. Authority in the workplace is almost always hierarchical. And most major government and business decisions are made as though the world were populated only by men like the decisionmakers.

Women are still not routinely heard in ways that count. Even when we get into positions of influence, we lose contact with what we know and value and can't—or

rarely do—express what we know *as women*. Instead, as Rosabeth Moss-Kanter, author of *Men And Women of the Corporation*, has pointed out, our voices and actions echo those of the men around us, though our feelings and perceptions may be in serious disagreement.

What is missing?

If women are truly to have a place other than in the lower ranks of private industry and public service, we have to do more than fit in. We have to know and value the legitimacy of our feminine viewpoint so that we can bring its wisdom to work with us and express it so that others comprehend its depth and importance. Only then will there be a real place for us as women—at the top as well as at the bottom of the pyramid. Only then will it be possible for real change to occur that brings balance to the patriarchal emphasis on power and acquisition.

We need to rethink what we mean by authority—to redefine that concept from a more reflective, feminine position that takes into account the real experience of the female half of the world's population. The bottom line can be very positively affected by feminine approaches that enhance productivity. But that isn't the only determinant of what makes good business. The quality of our lives at work and at home, the condition of our planet, the future well-being of our children and their grandchildren are important factors too.

Women have always been strong and have assumed incredible responsibility for the personal side of life. But women's ways—our focus on relationship, our emotions, our intuition, and our cyclical biology—are deemed unacceptable in the masculine work world. The feminine—mistakenly understood by many to be a prissy, fluffy, sanitized kind of thing—has been second class for so long that we assume the dominant culture is right about how we ought to be. In our attempts to fit in or to get ahead, we squeeze into masculine modes that pinch and hurt us and abandon our good judgment and best interests. In the process, we deprive the world of feminine wisdom. The result is a workplace that continues, out of balance, to follow patriarchal values that benefit the minority and ignore the long-range effects of doing business as usual.

"I can't imagine working again in a setting where men run the show and I have to be careful how I dress and what I do. Tiptoeing around fragile egos takes a tremendous amount of energy that I don't want to put out." This woman's ten-year career as a department store buyer ended abruptly over a disagreement. Recovering from that jolt, she established her own successful business as a consultant and loves the difference. "We should be able to take for granted that we can go to work and be comfortable, able to work in ways that suit us, free of harassment and other gender-related hassles," she continued, "so that we can focus on what we're trying to accomplish."

Hard-won freedom to express ourselves in our work and to be powerful in accord with our talents and interests is an important part of being a woman. But big barriers—**territoriality, sexism, prejudice, intolerance** of "women's issues"—still stand tall at work. Nothing in this book should be interpreted to deny or minimize the existence of those barriers. Collective legal and social confrontation of those long-standing problems must continue. The need for change has yet to be thoroughly digested by those in charge. But necessity is ever so slowly nudging changes into place.

The part of the process that's in the dominion of each individual is self-development. We must energetically uncover, value, and work with our feminine strengths. This happens when we pay attention to ourselves and take our own perceptions and experiences seriously. We have to understand that feminine power and wisdom are as important and necessary as the masculine view of the world. We have much to offer a culture that currently suffers gravely from corporate inefficiencies, decreased national competitiveness, bureaucratic sluggishness, an inordinate concentration of wealth and power, and a crushing national debt.

To be taken seriously, we first have to take ourselves seriously. We must define our personal characteristics in terms of what we know and believe rather than how we've been defined by men who are threatened by our difference. Then we'll be positioned to give up our second-class roles at work, to trust ourselves, to say what we have to say, and to offer much-needed feminine balance to the daily decisions that affect all our lives.

We need to know how to be powerful *as women*—to support ourselves emotionally as well as financially—and to stay well. And we need to know how to deal with the failures that inevitably come when we take risks or push. In our own way, not as Madam Macho or a behind-the-scenes-helpmate, we can offer the strength, connectedness, passion, and spirit of the feminine to the organizations that employ us and the communities where we live.

Women who know, trust, and express their deep feminine presence offer balance to the workplace. We can shift. We can bring harmony. But first, we have to reclaim our feminine birthright.

Deep personal loss occurs when we abandon our femininity or define it narrowly in ways that conveniently support existing stereotypes. The erosion is such a subtle thing, and so culturally common, that it isn't noticeable in the early stages. It's not as if we're giving up anything we've learned to value. But to awaken at mid-life and discover we've traded our feminine souls for someone else's dream aches bitterly.

One of the great stereotypes that haunts the workplace is that to be feminine is to be weak. Little wonder. I checked my 1983 *Webster's* and found "feminine" defined this way: "having qualities regarded as characteristic of women and girls, as gentleness, weakness, delicacy, modesty, etc." The word *feminine*, isn't even listed in a leading computer thesaurus, although *masculine* is strongly and clearly defined. Learning about and expressing feminine strengths empowers us to make a dent, at least, in such limiting, outdated definitions of what it means to support and express a very important life force.

Beyond "gentleness, weakness, delicacy, modesty, etc.," the heartier stereotypes of sex goddess, maternal hearth warmer, office helpmate, teacher, or assistant to the healer only begin to express the depth and variability of the feminine. They're important aspects. But we're also equal partners, leaders, decisionmakers, lawgivers, judges, jokers, artists, and healers. We have our own ways of working that, when we're true to ourselves, differ from our masculine colleagues'. When we honor those ways, we break the roles, stereotypes, and limits we've bought into and redefine ourselves to include the full power of our femininity.

Women inherit a long line of feminine strengths. It is said that before duly recorded history, life centered on the feminine. All creatures were connected with the Earth, Gaia, the Great Goddess. Women were the lawgivers, decisionmakers, judges. It's probably too good to be true, but it is said, at least, that when the feminine principle guided all life, harmony reigned.[1]

In America, as in other parts of the world, pockets of indigenous people whose life patterns follow the cycles of nature, still honor the feminine as a major life force. Balance is central in the mythology of our country's largest group of first citizens, the Navajo. They too, have their struggles with contemporary life, but the old ways haven't been completely lost. Changing Woman, the "most highly revered and dependable" of their deities, holds amazing

We need to know how to be powerful as women— to support ourselves emotionally as well as financially.

7

power in the Navajo creation story. Not only can she be different elements at different times, but she loves and cares for all living things.

> . . . Holy People are powerful and mysterious, capricious and capable of every human emotion. They travel on sunbeams, rainbows, lightning . . . . Changing Woman . . . never harms Earth Surface People and can always be depended upon for aid. From her symbolic image comes the strength of Navajo woman . . . . Changing Woman confers female qualities upon the world . . . . She is the source of life, the giver of sustenance and destiny to all beings.[2]

The typical American working woman has no such symbolic image to support her strength—in part because "female qualities" aren't part of the balance. They just don't have a place at the top echelons of American business. As a result, the everyday lives of women who work away from home are out of harmony. We work in masculine ways in masculine settings. Even "feminine" occupations like teaching and nursing exist only within patriarchal structures. Since, in our culture, men define the feminine, we abandon our female qualities at work and do our best to comply with masculine expectations, as though there really is no difference between women and men.

The American way has been to attempt a blend, to create a "melting pot," rather than to accept and benefit from the rich contributions of differences. The mistaken idea that equal rights means everyone is the same—that there is a "right way," the dominant white male way, to behave and that we just have to know how to do it—leads us to cancel ourselves out. Either we become white male clones or we work hard to please the men in power. As women and people of color we've shrunk our differences to allow this blending. The scary part is that most of us have blended so matter-of-factly that we don't even know what we've lost. But the cost of abandoning our "female qualities" is too high to continue.

This book offers you an opportunity to explore your feminine presence on the job. You can become much more self-supportive and expressive at work as well as in your personal life when you understand the power of the feminine. We have to learn to take our feminine energy to work in such a way that it makes a difference. As changing women in a changing world, we have the opportunity to change work, by being who we truly are.

When she was chair of her university department artist/professor Cornelia Schulz observed that:

> For women in the workplace, the dance is very delicate. We *must* really know what we feel and think. We're not just one of the guys out there . . . .
>
> We as women are operating within a dominant masculine system with feminine bodies and souls. If we continue operating by the same value standard, we mess up in the same way they do. The only way it will be different will be if we have done very significant work on ourselves.[3]

STRENGTHS FOR TODAY'S WORK

Women are not better or worse than men, but we bring some very different qualities to work with us.

The traditional patriarchal approach to work is to maintain a clear chain of command—to know who's at the top. The resultant scramble up the pyramid requires competition and autonomy. Feminine connectedness and creativity flow more freely when women can work in collabo-

rative ways—in "web"—with less importance attached to status or position.

These approaches, of course, are diametrically opposed. Each creates different standards for what needs to happen—and how. The conflicting fears—women's of floating free and unsupported, dropped from the web, and men's of being caught in it—give rise to different feelings and ideas about what is worthwhile. As Carol Gilligan puts it: "Each image marks as dangerous the place which the other defines as safe."[4]

So our perceptions are probably accurate when we feel that we're not being heard or taken seriously. When we suggest something that smacks of collaboration rather than individual competition—a team approach where an individual has done it before, attention to childcare or job-sharing—we're flying directly in the face of an important "difference." When we try to do something in a perfectly reasonable way, the way we might do it at home, it may be unacceptable because it doesn't follow protocol or match the "correct" masculine approach. This could be true even if our way is more efficient, less costly or otherwise "better."

As she recounted a little herstory for the 20th anniversary issue of *Ms.*, founding editor Letty Cottin Pogrebin wrote:

> Trying to choose a single representative anecdote is as impossible as conjuring a soufflé by cracking open one egg . . . The *Ms.* Kids? (My twin daughters and son, along with other employees' kids, spent many a school vacation at the office—surrounded by an extended family of women—crayoning, photocopying their faces, playing in the Tot Lot . . . .) But especially I remember the cramped (donated) space at our first office, where my 'desk' was a large cardboard carton with holes

Think about what we're missing because we censor our energy and creativity until they slide unruffled into environments designed and defined by men.

cut into it for my knees—a far cry from the office I
had had as a book publishing executive. More than
20 years later, I have a clear image of that funky
carton, and a sense memory of the exhilaration I
felt helping to translate a movement into a magazine—surely the most fun a woman could have sitting up.[5]

So, you say, "That's the rarified feminist atmosphere of
Ms. They could do what they wanted. Most jobs aren't like
that." Right. That's the problem. Think about what we're
missing because we censor our energy and creativity until
they slide unruffled into environments designed and
defined by men.

Women who've squelched their feminine styles to succeed in business have as much trouble with webby, cooperative work patterns as men do, sometimes more,
because their sacrifice has been greater. One such woman
said as she walked out in the middle of a seminar I presented, "This is all very pretty, but I want something that
will work!"

It will.

A male attorney who is comfortable with his feminine
side, observed, "Women attorneys deal with secretaries
and legal assistants differently—they don't yell and scream.
They get their work done in a softer way, cultivate loyalty.
When I was administrator at the Court, I worked this way
and felt very effective."

An archaeologist working in an environment that most
would agree is dominated by masculine values, described
to me her experience supervising the rebuilding of an historic cabin: "I greased the wheels—talked on the radio,
made sure we had what we needed—made sure people
had something to do and didn't have to just sit around and
wait for the jobs that took lots of hands. It was an exciting
thing! I don't tell people what to do. I encourage participa-

tion in planning, as well as execution—say thankyou, thankyou, thankyou. My boss said he was amazed at how I get people to work for me."

Teaching space law and policy to Air Force missile and bomber crews in North Dakota, Attorney/Professor Joanne Irene Gabrynowicz (see Wholistic Thinking) stayed very connected with her feminine presence even while she worked with defense personnel. Working tirelessly in Congress and on the campaign trail, Congresswoman Patricia Schroeder exemplifies our rich feminine heritage, the strength and energy that has been channelled through women from past ages. Facing the nation at Senate hearings in 1991, Anita Hill dared to speak about the shadow in public, relying on her core strength to sustain her.

The power of the feminine is not always so obvious, but the strength and stamina required for pregnancy and child bearing provide a physical prototype. Patience and endurance that underlie childcare aren't usually dubbed power, but they are. Finding a way to move into our power as women in a culture where we've been defined as helpmates, or "the hand that rocks the cradle," takes some doing. Poet Ruth Gendler provides imagery on the subtleties of this subject.

> Power made me a coat. For a long time I kept it in the back of my closet. I didn't like to wear it much but I always took good care of it. When I first started wearing it again, it smelled like mothballs. As I wore it more, it started fitting better, and stopped smelling like mothballs.
>
> I was afraid if I wore the coat too much someone would want to take it or else I would accidentally leave it in the dojo dressing room. But it has my name on the label now, and it doesn't really fit anyone else. When people ask me where I found

such a becoming garment, I tell them about the tailor who knows how to make coats that you grow
into. First, you have to find the courage to
approach her and ask her to make your coat. Then,
you must find the patience inside yourself to wear
the coat until it fits.[6]

Think of your feminine presence as a "power coat."
Not a man-tailored number designed to straighten your
lines and toughen your armor, but a "coat that you grow
into," that "you must find the patience inside yourself to
wear . . . until it fits." As with any garment, there will be
times when it's too heavy, pulls in the wrong places, or
just isn't right. But usually it will be warm, comforting,
attractive, and dependable wherever you go. If not water-
proof, it has the capacity to recover from an occasional
drenching.

Since you create your coat yourself, you can experiment with design—vary it with color, texture, weight, and
style. When you finish, you can say with certainty, "It has
my name on the label now, and it doesn't really fit anyone else."

DIMENSIONS OF THE FEMININE PRESENCE

The first step in bringing feminine presence to the
workplace is to name the lost dimensions of our womanly
selves. Then we can reclaim them and rely on them as
resources at work. We have to know clearly who we are,
both our strong sides and our shadows, and embrace the
dimensions of our inner selves so firmly that we don't lose
them, become fabulous fakes, or quietly fade into the
woodwork on the job.

So just what is this "feminine," this way that women
are different? Here are two big factors that make this a dif-

ficult question to answer:

1) "Feminine" characteristics shared by women and girls cover a lot of shifting ground—they change throughout a woman's life. The girl, young woman, mother, and crone (older woman) all present different feminine images. Different aspects of the feminine emerge at different stages of development and in different life situations.

2) Each of us (just as is true with men) is unique. Individually, we create our feminine presence in very different ways, and none of those ways is right or wrong, better or worse. Astronaut Sally Ride, poet Maya Angelou, glamorous star Michelle Pfeiffer, and social activist Delores Huerta are all feminine. Each of these women has emphasized different dimensions of her personality. There is no specific way to be feminine, or to be a woman.

In addition to "gentle, weak, delicate, modest, etc.," "feminine" has been stereotyped as mentally unstable, passive, and self-sacrificing. As Susan Faludi has written, the "feminine" woman has been defined as "forever static and childlike. She is like the ballerina in an old-fashioned music box, her unchanging features tiny and girlish, her voice tinkly, her body stuck on a pin, rotating in a spiral that will never grow."[7]

Does this fit you? It doesn't fit the working women I know. And it doesn't fit me either. People unconsciously confuse "femininity" with "sexuality" and with passivity.

The great archetypal energy of the feminine has had a bad rap. By continuing to define femininity so narrowly, rather than understanding it as half of life's energy in a balanced world, we forfeit our own power. This understanding must be embraced by each individual in her own way.

The measure you'll need to create your new (or refurbished) feminine power coat can be divided into thirteen dimensions. They're intangible, inexact—even contradictory at times. But they offer a framework for self-exploration and new consciousness about your strengths as a working woman.

As you work through the next chapters, you'll get better acquainted with your strengths and weaknesses in each of these dimensions: 1) Body Energy, 2) Persistence, 3) Core Strength, 4) Receptivity, 5) Flexibility, 6) Nurturance, 7) Affinity, 8) Sexuality, 9) Creativity, 10) Aggression, 11) Intuition, 12) Wholistic Thinking, and 13) Wisdom and Spirituality.

You don't have to have all of them to claim and enjoy your femininity. Some may fit better than others. Some may not fit you at all. That doesn't mean that you're not feminine.

Nor are these thirteen dimensions necessarily exclusive to women. Men are certainly intuitive, creative, and persistent, for instance. But they tend to experience and express these qualities differently from women. The thirteen dimensions emerged through my research—reading, interviewing, and working with people as a therapist and consultant for many years. If someone used the same process to identify the components of the masculine, different and similar aspects would make themselves known.

In combination, the thirteen dimensions stretch and flex to hold the complexities of the feminine. I've organized them into four groups—I) Strength and Stamina (Earth), II) Connectedness (Water), III) Passion (Fire), and IV) Spirit (Air)—to make them easier to learn and remember. If you learn to call up and rely on the strong side of each of these qualities, you'll have a firm base of self-support that will help you to move out and express yourself at work.

REAL WOMEN CAST SHADOWS

We take another step when we acknowledge the shadow side of our femininity. Of course women are intelligent, creative, and strong. But we're not all good. Like men, we have our darker aspects, which we need to deal with at work as well as in our private lives. A woman's shadow side darkens and grows when she ignores or denies it. Without the light of exposure, it distorts her vision and stains her whole personality.

All bodies cast a shadow and if we deny this body, we cease to be three dimensional and become flat—without a shadow.

C. G. Jung

Unpleasant as it may be at times, our dark side serves a purpose. As C. G. Jung so aptly put it, "Life is born only of the spark of opposites."[8] When we embrace our shadow, it fills us out. Our shadow energy propels us into contact with who we are. And if we don't take the journey consciously our shadow will sneak up behind us.

While you work to understand each of the thirteen dimensions, look at the shadow side as well as at your strengths. This is a major step in avoiding the "sweetness and light" feminine stereotype that none of us can—or would want to—live up to. We can ground ourselves with our own inner experience and pay attention to what our fear, anger, frustration, or vindictiveness tries to tell us. We don't usually need to act on these feelings, but we do need to listen to them. Here's how my shadow spoke to me one spring day.

Two weeks had passed since I had sent six chapters of a manuscript off to New York for review by a woman I hoped would work with me as a literary agent. It seemed like a major accomplishment when I paid my money at the Parcel Plus counter and, feeling as though I were giving up a body part, handed the stack of neatly printed white pages over to the clerk. Along with a whisper of vulnerability, I felt excited and optimistic—anxious to get a fresh opinion from inside the publishing profession.

I took a little vacation, tended to several long-standing obligations, read Tom Robbins' new novel, and prepared to write about the shadow.

I had collected material to write this book for months (or years, depending on how you look at it). I'd thought of several possible approaches and was ready to get my hands into the goo.

At 2:30 Easter morning I found myself wide awake. Sleep had slipped out the sliding glass door. Plunked on my stomach, right beside Ajax the family feline, was another almost equally tangible weight. It was the presence of the shadow man himself, C. G. Jung, the great psychoanalyst who gave us the shadow concept in its most developed form. For some reason I had chosen this moment to grasp the significance of a passage from his writing that implied that all of Freudian psychology was about the shadow. I got up and reread the reference:

> The result of the Freudian method of elucidation is a minute elaboration of man's shadow-side unexampled in any previous age. It is the most effective antidote imaginable to all the idealistic illusions about the nature of man . . . . [Although Jung did more than any of the early theorists to support the feminine principle, his writing resounds with "man" as the whole human race.]

That didn't help much. I slid back under the covers, tossed, and turned some more. What did I think I was going to do? Write about "the shadow" in a few paragraphs? And deal with the feminine aspects to boot?

As my husband Dave and I walked along the river, a little after the Easter sunrise, I couldn't ignore the pain that was beginning to surface. Out on the river bank with the

17

sun streamers lighting the purple lupine and warming the licorice-fragrant fennel, I felt small and weak.

I admitted my doubts.

"Maybe I can't do this book. It's too hard. I'm not sure that any of what I'm trying to do has any meaning to anybody but me. And how can I write about the shadow? Jung said it's all of Freudian psychology. That's overwhelming. I want to be clear and helpful to women who struggle with these issues at work. They may find this whole idea off the wall, or even repulsive. And now I'm going to try to summarize the equivalent of Freud's life work in one chapter?"

By this time, I felt like a lump of lead. To my embarrassment, tears dribbled down each cheek. Dave put his arm around me but didn't say anything. We just kept walking.

And then somewhere in my awareness a tiny bell tinkled. I was in it—deep in my own murky depths of self-doubt and criticism. I was belittling myself in a mean and sneaky way. Once again I was face to face with my shadow, staring at personal phantoms that I try to keep pushed out of sight. But they creep out and surround me when I'm insecure. I was overwhelmed by a feeling that I had no substance, no power, and that I was very, very small. A familiar refrain dinned in my ears: "I don't count at all."

I realized where I was. I could start.

My anxiety—which had stayed hidden before—about whether the agent was going to like the manuscript had nudged me without my conscious awareness into the abyss of my inner darkness. Feelings that I hadn't let myself feel had taken over. When I realized what had happened, I looked for the message I knew I'd find. It was like reaching behind a mirror.

By opening up to my pain and talking about it with Dave, I found a moment of clarity. Even though this was my unique experience of the moment, I realized it was a very familiar one. This is how my shadow feels to me. I was experiencing what I wanted to write about. That was the message that was waiting for me and what I needed to take home from the river bank. The gift in discovering my shadow—openly admitting and experiencing this hidden part of me—was that I could write about it for you. The shadow is more than theory. It's real.

As modern working women, we're encouraged to reject our shadows. To succeed, we have to be *good*— good to look at, good at our work, and good at getting along. We develop those parts of our personalities that please the people who can reward us—first our parents, later our employers. When feelings from the dark side pour into the open, they terrify or overwhelm us and those around us. We try to push the fear away. We run to the bathroom, hide our tears, or take a sick day and stay home. We can't be small and weak in public—or weepy, angry, out of control. We're simply not supposed to have, or at least display, these feelings. And the more rigid and monolithic the expectations are, the thicker our defenses become. The "woman with the flying hair," that perfect creature who lives on the cover of working women's mag-azines,[9] casts no shadow.

As modern working women, we're encouraged to reject our shadows.

We don't need to act on our shadow urges at work. In fact that's rarely a good thing to do. But we do need to hear what she has to say. It's time to invite this shady lady into the open and view her scary features more clearly—to admit our discomfort, give her a hug, welcome her wis-dom and energy. When you're so mad you see red, or feel like collapsing and throwing it all in, or get rigid and stub-born and won't move an inch no matter what, your shadow is talking to you.

Whether we acknowledge them or not, our shadow aspects are visible to others. Our defensiveness and denial, the subtle and intricate ways we try to fool ourselves, don't fool others. And beyond being visible, the shadow aspects act as magnets—attract the shadow energy of others—just when we need it least. We need to own these parts of ourselves without embarrassment and choose how we want to work with them. The Self-Assessment in the next chapter is a tool that can help.

We can recover from treasures that have almost been lost to modern women and bring the complexity of the feminine tangibly into our everyday lives. We can wear it to work. Before you move on to the Self-Assessment and all that follows, sit with the ancient wisdom of Changing Woman's imagery. Let her beauty and power inspire your journey:

CHANGING WOMAN SAID IT SO

CHANGING WOMAN is not changing her hair
　　　　to suit the times. She wears it long
　　　　when it rains. Her black hair rains down.

CHANGING WOMAN wears her heart where
　　　　her People can see it. She has bled
　　　　for centuries of love, none of it wasted,
　　　　none of it lost. Out of her heart's blood,
　　　　the corn grows green.

CHANGING WOMAN is White Shell Woman.
　　　　She lives in the Pacific
　　　　where Sun Father shines.
　　　　She gives us her blessing,
　　　　these little shells
　　　　we wear on our neck.

CHANGING WOMAN wears white when it is cold.
　　　　In winter we walk softly
　　　　upon her snowy skirt. Those who leave
　　　　hard tracks upon her do not
　　　　receive her blessing. Those who take
　　　　from her, rape her—spoil her
　　　　goodness. Those who steal
　　　　her treasure out of the soil
　　　　cannot know the beauty of

CHANGING WOMAN; nor can they harm her.
　　　　For her loyalty
　　　　is beyond our measure . . .

IN BEAUTY it is done,
　　　　in harmony it is written.
　　　　in beauty and harmony it shall so be finished.
　　　　Changing Woman said it so.

Gerald Hausman,
Meditations with the Navajo

21

Self-Assessment

To do it in beauty and write it in harmony, we need to embrace those qualities in ourselves. A step in that direction unfolds as we broaden our understanding of our feminine presence.

The Self-Assessment scale on pages 26-28 helps you begin your personal exploration in each of the thirteen feminine dimensions. Take a quick look at it. Then return to this page to learn more about how to use it.

The more clear and specific you make your understanding, the more available it will be for you in the future when you want to rely on it.

Changing Woman Changing Work is designed for your active participation. Since our culture rarely provides us with models of the strong feminine, we have to create our own. Like building a house or designing and making your "power coat," this task has many steps. You may first find the materials, then choose the design. Or you may know exactly how to shape your coat and then search for materials to do the design justice. Similarly, after you complete the overall Self-Assessment, you may choose to start with Body Energy and work through all thirteen dimensions in the order that suits you. Or, you may want to dash straight to Creativity or Sexuality or some other dimension that grabs your attention. It doesn't matter, so long as you work through the dimensions in a way that feels right for you.

Whatever your approach, it's important to keep track. The more clear and specific you make your understanding, the more available it will be for you in the future when you want to rely on it. Your imagination is a powerful tool. As you work through the exercises that follow, you'll think of examples—words, pictures, sounds, people—that, pieced together, form your power coat and portray who you really are. This collection of your feminine strengths, rounded by shadows here and there, will grow brighter as you learn more about all thirteen dimensions.

You may prefer working through the exercises individually if you're a person who enjoys solitary soul-searching and reflection. Or it may be easier and richer to do this self-exploration with a friend or a group so that you can discuss and compare notes. Either way (one is not better or worse than the other), the more you participate, the more you gain. Open to your experience and solidify your self-understanding.

A journal is the best tool for keeping track. When you put your thoughts, feelings, or impressions on paper—in either words or pictures—you give them form. You then can look at them and take them back in. The part of your brain that reads them is different from the part that writes or draws. You get to see who you are from a different perspective. You learn something new about yourself.

You will become better aware of your insights or emotions if you will work through the exercises, write or draw them in your journal, and then reread them. In this way, you "handle" the issue at least three times, and that will help you clarify and remember what you've revealed about yourself. As your collection of images grows, you will get to know yourself from different angles. Putting the collection on paper creates a history that will become much more meaningful as its complexity and depth become apparent.

First, though, take as much time as you need to look inward through the lens of the Self-Assessment and map out your own unique patterns. Respond to each item with your most honest intuitive guess. Try to avoid agonizing. You're only trying to put together a rough estimate at this point and will have ample opportunity to rework your views as you proceed through the book.

The left side of the Self-Assessment represents your connection with each dimension as a source of strength. When you get acquainted with each of these parts of you, you'll see that they fit together piece by piece until your coat takes form. You'll begin to see how you share these characteristics with other women. You can learn how each of them fits you and what to expect and trust from each.

The right side, the shadow, will help you pay attention to parts of yourself you attempt to ignore or underplay. When you get them out in the open you can make some decisions about how you want to work with them. The exercises in each chapter will help you with this task.

Remember, these dimensions are clustered into four elements so you can work with them a few at a time: I) Strength and Stamina (Earth), II) Connectedness (Water), III) Passion (Fire) and IV) Spirit (Air). These categories symbolize the dynamic tension and positive contributions of the feminine. Different though they are, together they create a complex whole. They weave the thirteen dimensions of the feminine presence in a sensual way we can comprehend with our bodies as well as our minds. The "elements" provide a matrix, a web within which to explore the dimensions.

The Self-Assessment gives you an introduction to the thirteen dimensions and an opportunity to estimate the intensity of your personal response to each. You may simply want to note your place on the line. Or you may want to use the numbers as suggested. If so, 5 is a strong response and 1 is weak. It's possible to have strong responses on both sides of the continuum, weak responses on both sides, or unbalanced responses.

There is no right or wrong. This simply gives you another way to know yourself.

The most straightforward approach is to base your assessment on how you see yourself at work. But feel free to base it on the way you are at home or to register your impressions as they have been at different times of your life. Just keep your framework of time and place in mind for each completion. You might want to use different colors to record different perspectives.

Here's an example. If you think you are very nurturing in a good way, give yourself a 5 on the *Strength* side of "Nurturance." If, on the other hand, you think you provide those around you with way too much caretaking—or if you reject this quality in yourself and never do anything for anyone—that would warrant a 5 on the *Shadow* side. Work through the scale, one dimension at a time, and see what you add to your psychological self-portrait.

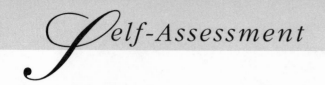

Self-Assessment

EARTH STRENGTH AND STAMINA

	STRENGTH	THE SHADOW SIDE
	5 4 3 2 1	1 2 3 4 5
BODY ENERGY	*Comfortable with my body and feminine cycles, good muscle tone and nutrition*	*Constricted, self-critical about body, out of shape, poor nutrition*

	5 4 3 2 1	1 2 3 4 5
PERSISTENCE	*Able to sustain; determined*	*Stubborn, rigid; distractable*

	5 4 3 2 1	1 2 3 4 5
CORE STRENGTH	*Substantial, solid self-trusting*	*Anxious, expect to collapse*

WATER CONNECTEDNESS

	STRENGTH	THE SHADOW SIDE
	5 4 3 2 1	1 2 3 4 5
RECEPTIVITY	*Open, warm, compassionate*	*Guarded, jealous, rejecting*

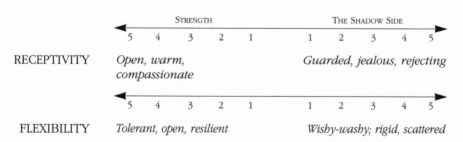

	5 4 3 2 1	1 2 3 4 5
FLEXIBILITY	*Tolerant, open, resilient*	*Wishy-washy; rigid, scattered*

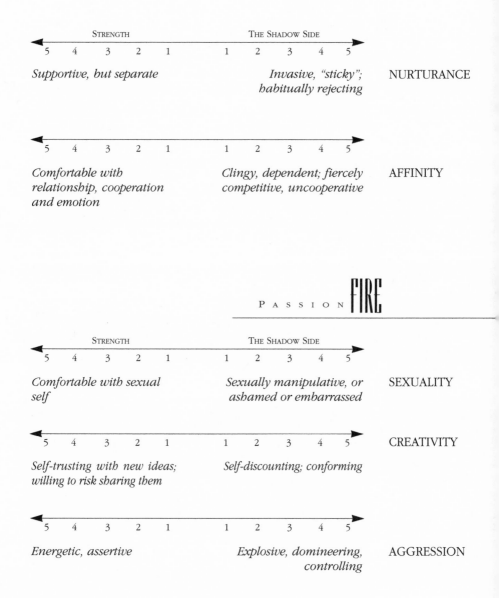

STRENGTH | THE SHADOW SIDE

5 4 3 2 1   1 2 3 4 5

Supportive, but separate — Invasive, "sticky"; habitually rejecting — **NURTURANCE**

5 4 3 2 1   1 2 3 4 5

Comfortable with relationship, cooperation and emotion — Clingy, dependent; fiercely competitive, uncooperative — **AFFINITY**

PASSION FIRE

STRENGTH | THE SHADOW SIDE

5 4 3 2 1   1 2 3 4 5

Comfortable with sexual self — Sexually manipulative, or ashamed or embarrassed — **SEXUALITY**

5 4 3 2 1   1 2 3 4 5

Self-trusting with new ideas; willing to risk sharing them — Self-discounting; conforming — **CREATIVITY**

5 4 3 2 1   1 2 3 4 5

Energetic, assertive — Explosive, domineering, controlling — **AGGRESSION**

 SPIRIT

	STRENGTH					THE SHADOW SIDE				
	5	4	3	2	1	1	2	3	4	5

INTUITION *Insightful, "tuned in"*   *Self-doubting;*
exclusively linear

	5	4	3	2	1	1	2	3	4	5

WHOLISTIC *Futuristic, inclusive,*   *Limited to here and now,*
THINKING *far-sighted*   *nit-picky, critical*

	5	4	3	2	1	1	2	3	4	5

WISDOM AND *Compassionate, congruent,*   *Judgmental,*
SPIRITUALITY *aware*   *self-aggrandizing*

Guidelines for Understanding

The chapters that follow will help you understand each of the dimensions and your experiences with them. But it helps to have an overview. Here are some guidelines for working with your Self-Assessment results. Roll up your sleeves and get started with your journal. You could, but don't have to, have a gorgeous leather-bound "blank book" with goldleaf edges. A spiral notebook works great. So do bits and scraps of paper that you keep together in a box. The notes you take will give you a baseline for future comparison. They'll also help you track your goals. Treat yourself to the slowed-down reflective enjoyment of getting to know yourself in some new ways.

• Make a list of your pronounced strengths by writing down all the dimensions (Persistence, Receptivity, Intuition, etc.) where you have 4s or 5s. These are probably dimensions you rely on without even thinking about it. Does your list of strengths fit the way you see yourself? If not, what are the surprises?

• Now make a separate list of pronounced shadow areas. Any surprises here? These dimensions may be troublemakers for you.

• Did you have all 4s or 5s on the strength side in one or more of the four elements (Strength and Stamina, Connectedness, Passion, or Spirit)? If so, you may feel more secure with these elements—less threatened by events that challenge you. This provides you a base from which to expand.

• On the other hand, if in some elements the shadow side pulled mostly 4s and 5s, you have spotted discomfort or uncertainty. Don't be self-critical. This is useful information as you work to understand some of the trouble you may have being yourself in these elements. Give yourself some time to explore and reflect upon what you have uncovered. It's useful to create a summary. Try something

like, "I am a woman who has experienced deep pain in these dimensions:_____. My fears seem to be concentrated in the (EARTH, WATER, FIRE, AIR) dimensions. I don't want to think about the way I manage my life in (EARTH, WATER, FIRE, AIR) dimensions. The shadow sides of _____ push me into situations I wouldn't consciously choose for myself."

• On dimensions where you have 4 or 5 on both the strength side and the shadow side, you are in conflict. If you have several of those in one element (Connectedness, for instance), you might want to take a look at whether you have to "play a role" in order to get by at work. If so, this probably causes you a lot of stress.

• If you're very high on the strength side in an element (Passion, for instance) when you feel safe, and exactly the opposite when you're vulnerable, you have discovered a problem area. You won't always be able to predict whether you'll feel safe or vulnerable in any particular situation. It will be important for you to avoid making commitments from a strong place that may overwhelm you at another time when you feel less sure of yourself.

• If 1s and 2s are the most frequent numbers on your Self-Assessment, it's hard for you to name and respond to your various inner communications. You will be able to learn more about yourself as you pay more attention to these inner messages.

• Note your overall impressions in your journal. Here's an outline: "I am a woman who feels more substantial with the (Strength and Stamina, Connectedness, Passion, Spirit)_____ element(s) than with the others. I feel strongest in the dimensions of _____. It appears that my least developed element is (Strength and Stamina, Connectedness, Passion, Spirit)_____. My areas of exploration and work (my 4s and 5s on the shadow side) are_____. I seem to have conflicts in these dimensions (4s and 5s on both ends of the same continuum)_____. I have trouble being clear in (1s and 2s)_____ and look forward to exploring these dimensions more. Overall, it appears that my greatest strengths are_____.

A Shift Into the Feminine

In order to know and express yourself, you have to live in all of you, including your femininity. It won't do to hang out in a few safe parts. You can be who you are at work as well as in your private life. That's what this book is about.

This will be something new and different for the American workplace. If you've been working overtime to beat men at their own games, or to please them so that you'll be appreciated, it will be a major shift for you. But when you shift securely into the feminine at work, you'll find that your confidence grows. Your approach might differ from the standard way of doing things, but it will feel right for you. If others criticize you, you'll be able to listen for the constructive parts. Differences won't feel so threatening or demeaning. Compared to your masculine colleagues, you may invest more time and energy in the personal part of work or in solving values conflicts that emerge there—and you'll feel good about doing so. Moving around at work will become easier and help to generate a sense of well-being about your body. You will be able to contribute your ideas, trusting that they are worthwhile and that you deserve to be taken seriously. Your power coat will fit.

For now, you've sketched your feminine strengths and completed a preliminary assessment. The next chapters will take you more deeply into each of the thirteen dimensions and their shadows. Before you continue your exploration, take time to reflect on what you've learned about yourself so far and to write down new ideas that came to you as you worked through your Self-Assessment. There will be more to come, but your early impressions are important ones.

As you read through the rest of the book, return to your Self-Assessment and update it based on the new understanding you acquire with each chapter.

EARTH

STRENGTH AND STAMINA

Earth: The Element

In 78 percent of subsistence cultures surveyed, it is usually women who gather and carry home fuel— usually firewood. In 15 percent, men usually do this work . . .Women are the usual water-carriers in 89 percent, and they usually carry the other burdens in 59 percent.[1]

From the beginning of time, women have done heavy work as the water carriers and burden bearers in most places in the world. We do tasks that require physical strength, persistence, and stamina. "But," you say, "that was then, this is now. That isn't me. That may be true in third world subsistence cultures. But ours is different!"

Take another look. Here's what Arlie Hochschild found in her research for *Second Shift: Working Parents and the Revolution At Home*:

. . . I began with the measurable issue of time. Adding together the time it takes to do a paid job and to do housework and childcare, I averaged estimates from the major studies on time use done in the 1960s and 1970s, and discovered that women worked roughly fifteen hours longer each week than men. Over a year, they worked an extra month of twenty-four-hour days a year. Over a dozen years, it was an extra year of twenty-four-hour days. Most women without children spend much more time than men on housework; with children, they devote more time to both housework and children. Just as there is a wage gap between men and women in the work place, there is a "leisure gap" between them at home. Most women work one shift at the office or factory and a "second shift" at home.[2]

As much as the nature of the work may have changed, the need for endurance seems to stay the same. Where did we get this business about being the "weaker" sex? It doesn't reflect now, and never has in any major way, the experience of any but a few women's lives.

Most women are different from most men in terms of muscle mass and short bursts of energy. But that is not to say we are weak. Feminine strength and stamina are formidable forces, and we can take better care of ourselves when we know how those forces operate in each of us. We can contact and appreciate our own energy shifts, ebbs, and flows, if we understand our *Body Energy.* *Persistence* and *Core Strength* are reliable dimensions we can develop and trust to keep us together in hard times.

Here's one example of a petite, "older" woman, trusting her strength and stamina to accomplish the almost impossible, which made a difference in a lot of people's lives.

Sacramento's Mayor Anne Rudin, in her mid 60s, had been on the City Council for twenty years—in the top spot for eight. Her leadership style evolved over that time and she weathered the pressures of life at City Hall with her integrity intact. When I asked her about some of her accomplishments as a leader,[3] she shared this example of strength and stamina that supported her skill and feminine strategy in solving a very tough problem:

"When the symphony almost went under in 1985, I stepped in between the musicians and the board. Persistence was one of the qualities that helped me. It had been a long, bitter dispute and everyone had nearly given up. We were on the verge of losing one of our city's major assets.

Feminine strength and stamina are formidable forces, and we can take better care of ourselves when we know how those forces operate in each of us.

"My way of doing things is to bring people together. I always see that as mobilizing resources that you need. I knew the right people to call. It happened that our labor negotiator was not busy with other city issues at that time. I called on the Chair of the County Board of Supervisors, Illa Collin, and she agreed to help. We told the players and the symphony management that we were willing to sit down with them.

"We began on a Saturday morning and we met, literally, day and night. There were some nights we got away, but sometimes we met through the day and through the night.

"One morning around 4:00, I was beginning to read the signs, when it was time for pushing, when it was time to hold back—when they had put enough of their demands on the table—the give and take. Anyhow, everybody got angry and the musicians just stormed out. They said we weren't getting anywhere.

"But I could see that we were. I could also see, though, that they did not know how to present what they needed. So at 6:00 A.M. I called a representative of the local musicians union—told him that I needed help. He called the musicians and offered his assistance if they would accept.

"By the middle of the afternoon, we had an agreement. He knew how to present their demands for them and how to give and take a little. . . ."

Mayor Rudin didn't give up. She used common sense and good judgment, creativity, and contacts to make the process work. Her sensitivity to non-verbal communication helped her read participants' emotional reactions and work effectively with the embattled groups.

But the part that all of us can learn from is that she provided leadership by hanging in there. Through the long days and nights of tension and disagreement, she refused to fold. "Women do things differently. It was different to have Anne and Illa involved," she heard later from the sec- retary of one of the men who had participated. The power inherent in the Mayor's position and her skill were cer- tainly factors. But her feminine presence and that of her colleague—the special qualities they brought to the process—also made a difference in the way things went.

The Mayor felt that one of the differences was that she and Illa could see people's reactions—body language and movement. And another was that she asked for help.

When I questioned her about how she sustains herself in the midst of the conflict and controversy that are part of her job, her response reflected what I call core strength. "When I feel like I'm doing the right thing," is how she said it. "And from knowledge. I make it a point to under- stand the issues." She also dips into that deep well of femi- nine power, connectedness: "I do get upset sometimes. But I get strength from other people—from constituents. My public gives me emotional support—moral support— and the feeling that I did the right thing."

Although this example portrays the experience of a feminine political leader, the same strengths that helped her through that long week and through other times of stress can support you in your work life. Manager, line operator, secretary, nurse, executive vice president—what- ever your job—you face intense demands on your physical and emotional energy. The earthy, everyday qualities Mayor Rudin relied on to sustain her—endurance, persis- tence, core strength—along with learning more about how to appreciate and nurture your body energy—are the focus of the next three chapters.

Regardless of the work you do, the power in these dimensions, *Body Energy, Persistence,* and *Core Strength,* is available to you. They provide a solid foundation that differs from stereotypes of the "weaker sex" and from much of what we've learned by imitating the masculine way. They have to do with being grounded and staying in your center, rather than indulging in "learned helplessness" or toughening your shell.

The qualities of vulnerable strength (the capacity to withstand, flex, and not collapse) and endurance are legitimate in the business world, as well as at home, for both women and men. The energy and stamina of the strong feminine in a woman who knows and trusts herself grow from a different center than the facade of macho toughness she has learned to use as armor to survive at work.

Susan Griffin's portrayal of earth and sisterhood symbolizes the strength and stamina of the feminine—the deep connection with nature that sustains the species.

> . . . This earth is my sister; I love her daily grace, her silent daring, and how loved I am, how we admire this strength in each other, all that we have lost, all that we have suffered, all that we know; we are stunned by this beauty, and I do not forget: what she is to me, what I am to her.[4]

The power of this poem calls for images that differ from stereotypes of femininity as weak or passive. It speaks to that part of womanhood that "the woman with the flying hair" flies right past. It does, though, give us a glimpse of the strength and stamina of our feminine presence.

Body Energy

Generations of

working women

have learned to

dress like men,

move like men,

think like men.

But we can't feel

like men.

The feminine presence is physical, and so the atmosphere shifts when women move into settings that have been dominated by the masculine way. Whether it's vibrant, sensuous and earthy, or quiet, calm and airy, feminine energy changes work. The female body brings a basic connection with nature—with birth and death, with moon cycles, and with the continuity of human life. When we know about and value this precious dimension, it energizes our work. It's exciting. And it complicates matters for men who are accustomed to working mainly with other men, or with women as support staff, not as equals.

The mysteries of feminine biology—bleeding and not dying, pregnancy, the end of monthly bleeding in midlife—are profound. The feminine life cycle doesn't fit neatly on the competitive, upward angles of a career ladder. We deal with frustration, shame, blame, and, in our struggles, can come to regard our biology as negative—an inconvenience, a hindrance to our careers. Feminine energy, this connection with life cycles in the workplace, offers a form of rebirth if we can learn to recognize its value and listen to it rather than trying to hide it.

Increasing numbers of women hold positions of responsibility at work as well as at home. The patriarchal establishment can't ignore family needs the way it always has. Now organizations have to take seriously things like childcare, flex-time, family leave, and other so-called "women's issues." Maybe someday in the distant future it will become apparent that the solution is to provide space for these needs in all the places women work, so that birthing and caring for the next generation escape the label "women's issues." But for now, the difficulty and threat of making these changes erects blinding barriers that interfere. It's much easier to expect inconvenience and disruption than it is to grasp the contributions our feminine ways of working can offer. When we regard our biology as negative, we buy into the notion that we are the problem.

One way we've tried to secure our position, and to make ourselves less trouble, is to masculinize—to ignore or reject our feminine bodies. This has been a slow and subtle process and it's causing a lot of damage. (See the Sexuality chapter.) Generations of women have learned to minimize feminine differences on the job—to dress like men, move like men, think like men. But we can't feel like men. And so we develop two personalities, one for work and one for whomever we are without the armor. Men do the same thing, but since the workplace is, by design, usually more compatible with masculine style, the differences aren't as dramatic for them.

There is another way. That is to appreciate our very real, feminine difference and use it to enlighten and inform our work, whatever it is. We have a wonderful opportunity to bring the feminine presence to the workplace. One of the simplest, most direct ways we can do this is to pay attention to what our bodies tell us.

Nancy K. Jungerman, a psychotherapist respected not only for her work with individuals and families, but also as a resource to other therapists, shared this story:

> A therapist in one of my consultation groups became pregnant with her first child in her late thirties. Although she had many years of psychotherapeutic experience in a variety of work situations, she admitted to becoming uncomfortable with her clients and so unsure of how to deal with the reality of her

pregnancy that she found herself pretending that nothing would change. Her denial and self-criticism temporarily blinded her to the creative possibilities that her pregnancy offered in terms of enriching and deepening the therapy.

In the workplace, if you're trying to do something that is not in accordance with your feminine nature, you feel like you're not doing it right—feel inauthentic. We get into self-evaluation that comes from a model that isn't felt as inherent.

The young therapist I mentioned was able to shift—to use what was forming in her to work with her clients. When she didn't get defensive about clients' responses to her pregnancy and planned absence, those feelings became part of the therapy, as they should be.[1]

Whatever job we do, we can use our feminine presence to enrich the workplace. Obviously, since they can't be masculinized, pregnancy, lactation, even premenstrual syndrome (PMS) and menopause, add qualities that change the usual way of doing things. These very feminine conditions may be inconvenient on the job. They may reduce certain kinds of efficiency. But when we pay attention to them, they can also contribute an awareness of the life process that makes a difference in workstyle, policy decisions, the very products that are created. Subtle and not-so-subtle forms of abuse that men have tolerated or perpetuated stand out prominently when pregnant workers are involved.

It's not just the drama of menstruation and childbearing, though, that deserves attention. Whether motherhood is part of our lives or not, women aren't just men with curves. Our bodies, our rhythms, and our energy flows differ from masculine ways of being. Learning to honor our feminine body energy on the job is a function of how we dress, move, and feel about ourselves, as well as of how we go through our cycles. We work best when we know and respect our body energy.

Strength and stamina, the capacity to endure, are very much a part of feminine body energy. Achieving hard-body toughness is a questionable goal for most women, but learning about and appreciating our physical strength and stamina, as well as accepting our vulnerability, is invariably reassuring to us. Childbirth, childcare and other "women's work" have always required physical strength and endurance. As we've shifted to a culture where most women work away from home, while taking most of the responsibility for home and childcare, we ignore our needs for physical exercise. Who has time? But physical well-being and activity help both women and men to develop self-confidence and ease with our bodies.

Care for and trust your physical competence—based on how you feel, not necessarily how you look—and you will establish a strong base for self-reliance. One summer—in the face of a long history of dedicated non-exercise—I trained for and successfully completed a ten-mile run. For a non-athlete, middle-aged at that, the feeling of physical accomplishment provided real support for the long, hard days my work requires at times. My increased physical stamina helped me feel much stronger emotionally—more able to stand my ground, less likely to cave in to manipulation.

You don't have to run ten miles to tune in to your physical strength. But it will help if you create your own physical conditioning program. When you learn to listen to them, your muscles can provide you with potent information about how you are affected by what's going on around you. Through exercise and conditioning, you can know and love your female body, a key to understanding your feminine presence.

Another step requires coming to terms with the ebb

and flow of hormonal cycles. Other than attempting to deny they exist, we haven't dealt with the realities of female biology on the job. To reduce our threatening presence, we've pretended that the mysteries of the feminine don't exist. We make believe that we're just men in skirts.

Painful menstruation or agitating PMS become inconvenient, for some women even difficult, enough to interfere with daily activities. Psychiatrist Lesley Schroeder, a specialist in this area, estimates that 15% of women suffer from PMS that is so disruptive they seek treatment.[2] In a world organized around men's ways, women buy into negative, self-critical views (the popularity of PMS jokes might be a clue) and we reject ourselves at this deepest, cellular level. An alternative is to acknowledge the realities of emotional ups and downs and take special care of ourselves when we need to.

We need to find ways to be practical, productive, and efficient, and to honor our feminine biology as well. If we know ourselves and respect our physical and emotional fluctuations, we can learn to work around the difficulties we have rather than denying them or feeling inadequate. This means taking time off or arranging for a lighter work load if we need to, reducing our work schedule during some times in our lives, knowing the times when we may be particularly vulnerable and when it requires more energy to focus. At times, we may really need to work alone, or really need to work with others. Our strengths fluctuate, too. At times, we may have the energy to "move mountains" or more than usual access to sharp intuition.

Historians tell us that menstruation was seen as magical, valuable in some ancient civilizations. Women took part in rituals where they returned their menstrual blood to the fields to fertilize the soil.[3] This approach probably doesn't have much appeal for today's woman, but we can learn, with new respect for our femininity, to love our bodies and cease to regard our periods as "the curse."

Those menstrual huts we've heard about where anthropologists tell us women went during their periods weren't necessarily about being ostracized from the rest of the group. They were also about women being together to tend to women's interests—education, humor, tradition, and taking a break.[4] What a concept!

Your feelings about your body—your level of self-acceptance or self-rejection—determine whether you relate to others openly or defensively. If you hate your body, you're likely to assume that others hate it, too. Bogged down by your own negative views, you may maintain a defensive stance—expecting to be criticized or ridiculed. If you talk about hating your body, or what you don't like about it, you invite others to think less of you. Each of us is in charge of how we live in our bodies and present them to the world.

Routinely, feelings about our bodies are complicated by the "dress code." The uniform for professional or office jobs has been dresses or suits, high heels, and pantyhose. Some women find this way of dressing comfortable and enjoyable. Many, especially large women, suffer daily in attempts to fit round bodies into the straight (masculine) lines of "business" clothes.

The project was a success if the goal was to design clothing to keep us off balance. Just try to ride your bike to work, pick up your three-year-old, or move boxes in your professional straitjackets. Traditional women's business dress style cramps the healthy nobility of our body energy. It also communicates the feminine in a safe, male-defined way, rather than in a way that feels comfortable or expressive for women. "It's a good idea to wear shoulder pads; they de-emphasize your breasts," her female boss advised one of my clients. Maybe this is necessary protection around some men, but consider what it says about being a woman.

Here's what Catherine Steiner-Adair found in her

To reduce our threatening presence, we've pretended that the mysteries of the feminine don't exist.

research with fourteen- to eighteen-year-old girls.[5] When asked how they think the culture views the ideal woman, they said: She's thin, rich, fit (hard-bodied), youthful, tall, pretty, dressed-for-success, energetic, carries a brief-case. Doesn't this fit the images you see on the newsstand? Except for "pretty," this describes a young, privileged, adult male.

When asked what would make them happy in their own lives—in other words, what do they value?—the young women in the study said: girl friends, a relationship (husband), children, money, career, and home. Their personal goals have more to do with their femininity—with connection and relationships—than with being at the top.

The young women who were grounded in their own values, who didn't buy into the "ideal image," were the ones who felt more sure of themselves. The researchers found that the woman who doesn't realize that her personal values are central and important—regardless of her body shape and size—is much more likely to suffer from one of the most prominent emotional disabilities of our time—eating disorders (anorexia, bulimia, obesity). This sometimes life-endangering form of self-hate is disturbingly frequent among women today. While, on the planet, large populations are starving and others have food stored and spoiling, we have become a culture that is fanatic about what and how much we eat.

The rounded feminine form, the basic female body shape, has become an object for self-hate and for rejection by others. Catherine Steiner-Adair estimates that in the female population 10-15% may be naturally tall and thin. Most of us aren't. Just like men, we're energetic sometimes but not all the time. Unlike men, we're likely to spend the money we make on our appearance—having something done to our hair, skin, bodies or buying clothes.[6]

If, in fact, our culture sees the successful woman as a tall, thin, hard body, then round women—that is most of us—have a harder time with credibility. We need to know how to take care of ourselves in this situation, how to talk about feminine strength and the reality that women's ways make an important contribution. And if we do happen to fit in that tall, thin picture, we may need to be especially supportive and compassionate with our own femininity. In that spot, not only are we more likely to be accepted as one of the boys and supported for our masculine side, we're more vulnerable to the jealousy and suspicion of our rounded sisters.

In some areas, slight changes are afoot. Broader ranges of dress, workstyle, and scheduling are increasingly acceptable. But these shifts need encouragement from all of us. When you're willing to push the limits and create traditions of comfort rather than conformity, you free up your energy and support the powerful feminine—not the stereotype or the male-defined idea of attractiveness.

For some women workers, physical fitness is not an option. Many do strenuous work because that's all they can get. Others choose heavy work to get equal access to high-paying jobs in non-traditional areas or to satisfy a personal preference. Those of us who perform non-traditional work have to be strong emotionally as well as physically. We can learn to deal with taunts and tests in ways that fit our femininity—to connect with others and with our own strength. Then we won't have to prove that we're one of the boys. By teaming with another woman or a supportive man, we can check out our viewpoints and don't have to endure the stress alone.

Women who do non-traditional work are a serious financial threat to the male blue-collar establishment and usually have to deal with harassment. But we are more successful on the job if we avoid attempts to compete in a masculine way. We can learn to rely on our own inner resources—what feels right for us—rather than copying the way the tough guys do it. Feminine strength and stamina are about holding our ground, staying with the task, and weathering it through to completion. There is tremendous power in this approach.

Janet Nielson, an urban police detective with more than twenty years' service, the first officer in her city to get pregnant and the first of her department's women officers to win the Medal of Valor, provides a classic example. Out of uniform, Janet's round, open face and easy manner wouldn't tag her as an officer of the law. She melted the stereotypes I had about women who do this work.

She told me that she learned to develop "a presence" when she was on patrol rather than rely on physical force. Knowing that a tough, intimidating style wasn't right for her, she learned from other, male, officers who maintained authority through body language and de-escalated conflict whenever they could. She found she was taken seriously when she carried herself with authority, maintained eye contact, and spoke in a firm but gentle way. Effective use of humor helped, too. She didn't have to use he-man tactics to be taken seriously.

Janet's realistic, understated approach fits her femininity even though she learned it from her male colleagues. Her strong feminine style has been successful for her in a stressful and sometimes violent occupation. Not that it's been easy. She put up with hazing and rejection from some of the other officers, including some potentially dangerous harassment.

When she was pregnant, she said the only rule was "you were out of uniform, off the street. Pregnant police officers weren't assigned to public duties. They put me in the radio room, treated me as if I were sick, not pregnant. I got swing shift projects and was labeled 'long term disabled.' After a while I changed shifts and went back to running investigations."

"Some women," she continued with a frustrated tone, "have been absolutely confined to office work, not allowed to have any contact with suspects or go out on investigations while pregnant." Pregnant women, like women in all other phases of our lives, are capable of deciding how much and what kind of work to do through-out our terms. Treating pregnancy as illness is discrimina-tory and undermines women at work.

Janet observed that years ago, when pioneering women first joined the department, they tended to mas-culinize themselves so they could fit in. She pointed out that when women go into patrol, many try to become one of the boys. In her view it takes them two to five years to find out that they'll never gain acceptance in that way. The first weeks on patrol, she had to learn to walk differently, with her arms out so she didn't bump them on her gun all the time. All of a sudden she became aware that she wasn't 'feminine' either. Lots of women try to get into manly sports, get really good at shooting, go out hunting ducks or deer, or go drinking after work. It can't work. "Each of us," Janet concluded the interview, "has to earn respect. If you're a woman, you have two strikes to start."

Through it all, Janet created her own effective style in an occupation where masculine toughness and aggression are the standards of comparison. She listened to others, tried different ways of working, and persisted until she found a way to maintain her deep connections with her feminine presence.

THE SHADOW

Body Energy casts its shadow with subtlety for many, cruel obsession for others. We may experience it through the perpetual search for the perfect body—addiction to exercise—the tyranny of the bathroom scale. Some of us attempt to deaden personal pain or fear with alcohol or other drugs. Others experience life from the neck up only—denying the existence of a physical self. We mirror the cultural negativity toward the feminine when we hate our bodies for the inconveniences that are part of PMS, menstrual cramps, pregnancy, or menopause. When we hate our bodies we are living in our shadow.

At work, we may express discomfort with our body energy in different ways. We may be compulsive about how we look, obsessed with having to be perfect. Or we might pay no attention to our appearance. We're likely to be catty about how others look, and feel vulnerable and insecure when something or somebody reminds us of our own discomfort.

All bodies

are beautiful,

contrary to

what many

of us have

learned.

The shadow can restrict movement so that we walk rigidly, stiffly concealing anything that resembles femininity. Insulation becomes thick. No expression leaks through. One woman said to me, "I'm totally asexual at work—don't feel anything. I never get harassed. And it has cost me a lot. I've been doing it for so long, I don't have a clue about how to meet and relate to a man outside work. Either I'm totally discombobulated and fall head over heels for him, or I keep him at such a distance there's not a chance to get anything going." Although she's struggling to contact her feminine presence again, this woman has spent a major part of her career experiencing her body energy as a liability rather than an asset.

We can become so busy—or so sedentary—that we ignore the body's basic need for exercise. "I don't have time, I don't like exercise, I'm not the athletic type," the shadow says to justify neglect. Sleep problems, general sluggishness, and poor muscle tone clue you in to this one.

One of the shadow's meanest forms is illness. One symptom after another grabs the foreground. The body speaks about pain or self-hate you can't deal with directly. You may become preoccupied with physical symptoms; or accidents may happen to you, and happen again. If this feels like your history, consider the possibility that your shadow's trying to say something to you. One of my clients said to me, "My husband must get tired of hearing about all my illnesses. First I have a cold, then I sprain my ankle, then I get a bladder infection. I'm always sick." This basically healthy woman hates her job but doesn't want to risk looking for another. Her shadow is screaming at her.

If you find yourself driving down the street thinking, "If I had just a little accident I could be off work and someone (?) would take care of me. . . ," listen! Get more assertive about asking for what you need. Or, "maybe I'll get the flu and not have to finish the budget by the end of next week. . ."—take a look at your relationship with your body, at how you may be working against yourself. All of us face work crunches from time to time and dive into overwork. But if getting sick is the way you take the time off, create more active strategies for getting the rest you need. The time off will be the same whether it's spent in misery or on scheduled "mental health days."

The shadow side of body energy is a basic rejection of self, so it makes just about everything else problematic. All bodies are beautiful, contrary to what many of us have learned. If this is an area that's difficult for you, as it is for many women, give yourself permission to explore it now, and linger with this dimension as long as you like.

SELF-REFLECTION

Use the following ideas as guides to estimate how comfortable you are with your body energy. Look at your strong points first. Learn all you can about your strengths. Then begin an exploration of the part of yourself that is more difficult to accept—the shadow side. Often, what we learn by delving into the murky, confusing chaos of the shadow helps us understand and become more open to what our darker feelings are trying to tell us.

STRENGTH: I love my body. I exercise regularly and stay fit. I wear comforting clothes to work. I'm comfortable with my feminine cycles. My body is a source of pleasure. I feel grounded most of the time. I trust my body.

SHADOW: I hate my body. I exercise to attain perfection. / I never exercise. I hate my periods. I hate being a woman. / I ignore my body, wish I didn't have it. / I abuse my body with alcohol or other drugs. / I know I have a beautiful body and use it to control men. / My body betrays me.

Take time now to design and commit to a fitness plan that supports your body energy. Work on one that you know you can complete. Avoid fantasies of a total "remake." You may want to select one or two of the exercises that follow as a primary focus. Start today by shaping your routine to pay attention to your body energy. Write this commitment to yourself in your journal, and keep track of how you're doing as time goes on.

TIME FOR YOURSELF

Women aren't just men with curves. Give yourself permission and time to regard your body energy at work as important, even if your job requires little physical exertion. For many of us, just getting to work takes stamina. When you're securely grounded and your energy flows freely, you're in a stronger position to expect others to take you seriously.

Here are exercises—some mental, some physical—that have to do with your body energy. It helps to make clear in your mind what you're trying to accomplish. Select the steps that appeal to you and take notes in your journal. Then stretch, bend, breathe, and enjoy the glory of your body energy!

As you read through the exercises after each dimension, select a few that are most appealing to you. The idea is to experiment and become more conscious of each dimension. If you try to do them all, you may get overwhelmed and stuck—which will do you no good and just may keep you from addressing the other dimensions covered here. Go easy on yourself; sample and enjoy.

• LOVE YOUR FEMALE BODY—whatever its shape or size. If you find yourself being judgmental, see if you can figure out whose judgment you're using. Is it truly your own? Would you trust the source of this judgment in other important areas of your life? In your journal, write a loving statement (a list, a poem, or a description) that honors your body.

• FIND A WAY to take exercise seriously. A regular exercise program that conditions your cardiovascular system and muscles is by far the best for stress reduction and maintaining your strength and stamina. If you're basically healthy, check your bookstore or library for books on basic conditioning. Consultation at the gym or workout center can help you design a program that fits you. If you have physical limitations or health problems, your chiropractor, physical therapist, or physician can help you design a program to meet your needs.

• COMPROMISE if daily exercise is impossible. An option is a 30-40 minute jog or walk, three or four times a week. Coupled with some stretching and deep breathing, exercise also serves as a chance to think your thoughts and feel your feelings.

• IF YOU ABSOLUTELY CAN'T FIND TIME to exercise on a regular basis, use household activities as a way to breathe deeply and stretch your muscles. Exaggerate your stretching movements if you make the bed. Bend from the waist and breathe deeply if you pick up the daily mess. Use deep breathing while loading or unloading the dishwasher. Stretch as you reach into the cupboard. Romp with the kids—yours or a friend's. Use the stairs at work rather than the elevator. Remember, perfection isn't an issue here. Every little bit helps.

• TAKE A CLASS. Yoga, aerobics, and dance classes provide opportunities for exercise, reflection, and social contact. Even learning a few simple yoga positions can make a real difference. "Mountain" pose is great for standing in grocery store lines and the "Salute to the Sun," in just a few seconds, wakes up all your muscle groups to start the day.

• PAY ATTENTION TO YOUR BODY ENERGY AT WORK. If your job requires that you sit most of the time, get up and walk around every hour. Stretch and breathe deeply. If you spend most of your time at work on your feet, find ways to stretch, relax, and breathe.

• WEAR CLOTHES THAT ARE COMFORTABLE—even comforting—things that feel good and allow for easy movement. If you wear a uniform, find some way to be yourself. Treat yourself to underwear that you really like, a special pin that has meaning for you or a scent that you can enjoy all day long.

• STASH A PAIR of walking or running shoes for lunchtime walks. They can be just the ticket to letting go of some tension on an impossible day—even if you use them rarely. Better yet, use them often.

• TUNE IN TO YOUR MUSCLE STATE at work. Are you holding tension in your shoulders? Your jaw? Your back? Exaggerate the tension and then relax. Breathe into the tense places. Pay attention to what the tightness is telling you. Is the location meaningful? The source? What are you holding in—or out? This focused attention requires no extra time and can be done at your desk or work station without drawing attention to what you're doing. If you take notes in your journal, you may begin to identify a pattern that you can work with.

• PAY ATTENTION TO HOW YOU SIT. Think about being grounded—centered. When you let yourself curl over, you squeeze the energy out of your center and become more tired. When you find yourself collapsing of your own weight, get up, walk around, stretch, and breathe deeply.

• FIND OUT whether your nutritional practices help or hurt your body. Eating disorders have become a common way for us to express self-rejection. If you're a junk food junkie or fad dieter, you might want to ask yourself why. Write the answer in your journal in some detail.

• KEEP TRACK of your menstrual cycle if PMS or other symptoms cause you stress at work. Learn when your emotional and physical ups and downs are most likely to happen. Develop a strategy for self-care that reduces your work load at times you can guess are going to be most difficult for you.

• IF YOU HAVEN'T DONE SO already, look into some of the ancient feminine lore that is positive about the feminine body—including the cycles of fertility, reproduction, and old age. *Women Who Run with the Wolves*, by Clarissa Pinkola Estes; *The Crone: Woman of Age, Wisdom and Power*, by Barbara Walker; *The Chalice and the Blade*, by Rianne Eisler; and *To Be a Woman*, by Connie Zweig, all provide different glimpses of this material.

• HERE'S AN EXERCISE for home. Try a body awareness exercise when you have some time to yourself at home. Margaret Fjelstad, Ph.D., suggested this one that takes about twenty minutes and is amazingly grounding and self-loving.

Sit in a comfortable place. Close your eyes. *Slowly* feel your hair, touch your scalp and massage it. Feel your face; stroke it. Give yourself a neck massage. Explore and massage one shoulder and arm and hand. Repeat on the other side. Feel your chest and breasts. Breathe and expand. Explore and massage under your ribs and across your belly. Move your shoulder blades, reach around and massage down the spine with your thumbs. With your hands, squeeze and massage both hips. Lie on your back, explore and massage each thigh, calf, and foot.

We usually don't massage ourselves long enough to get any effect. This helps you see that you can lovingly care for your own body.

Return to the Self-Assessment Scale on page 26. How powerful are the pulls for you on each side of body energy? Are you happy with this? If so, great! Would you mark it now the same way you did when you read through the Self-Assessment the first time? Take a minute to make any adjustments that will make it reflect your self-understanding now. It helps if you make changes in a pen that's a different color from your original markings.

STAYING GROUNDED

In the first two chapters, as you initially worked through the Self-Assessment Scale and explored the thirteen dimensions of your feminine presence, you tuned in to your strengths and weaknesses. You have new possibilities to explore in self-development and new awareness of your shadow side and how you express it. As you gain comfort with both sides of each of your thirteen dimensions and how you experience and express them, new confidence should emerge. How can you live them on a daily basis and bring them into the workplace in a way that supports your feminine power there?

It's one thing to travel inward—to gain appreciation for your feminine presence—in the protection of home with a friend, in a workshop, or in your therapist's office. It's another to take your vulnerable new way of understanding yourself to work.

Ground yourself first by taking stock of where you are. Find a quiet minute or two each day to bring your current state into your conscious awareness. Here's a quick checkup you can do at your desk or while you repair your frazzled hair.

- Are you centered or off balance?
- Are you breathing?
- What old images about how you're "supposed to be" do you hang onto? (For example: thin, rich, hard

bodied, youthful, tall, pretty, dressed-for-success.)
- What is your energy level?
- Are you feeling heavy and loaded down?
- Are you focusing on your inadequacies or short-comings?
- What are your choices?
- Are you feeling mean and hateful—picking at others out of your past or present hurt?

If you're humming along in a centered way, enjoy the flow of your feminine power. If you're off-balance, tune in to your body energy. Let your muscles inform you about where you're tense and need to relax. First tighten and then relax the places your tension has gathered. Give yourself time to take some deep breaths and let the air out slowly. As you grow more confident about your body, no one may notice specific changes, but you will *feel* different. You will be more substantial and better able to feel your strengths and accept your limitations. You'll be able to take on work or stand your ground emotionally in ways that might have been too much for you before.

BODY ENERGY GOES TO WORK

One of the barriers that pops up here is an old familiar one. **Feminine Biology is Inconvenient.** We've been taught that women aren't dependable—can't be trusted with important decisionmaking or responsibilities—at "that time of the month" or when pregnant, lactating, or menopausal. Women, we're told, aren't tough enough.

When you feel strong enough, try fitting your work schedule more to your needs:

"I don't feel well now, but I'll be back and ready to work tomorrow/Wednesday afternoon/Monday morning."

"I'd like to arrange time off to nurse my baby—from

2:00 to 3:00 in the afternoon for the next six months. My co-worker is willing to cover for me during that time while I take a late lunch."

Yes, women's emotions are cyclical—more up and down. Let your supervisor know that you still have the capacity to take responsibility and make excellent decisions. If you're familiar with your own biology and are willing to deal with it, you can guarantee the quality of your work.

It is a reality that feminine biology creates inconvenience at work. But *that* is not the barrier. The barrier is the exaggerated idea that your biology renders you incompetent as a worker or leader.

As you read through the "do's" and "don'ts" below, check the possibility that the "don'ts" describe some of the ways your shadow sneaks out at times. If you act on the "do's," the "dont's" aren't as likely to be the way you choose to express your feelings.

Do	*Don't*
Learn to confront put downs about female biology.	Collude with comments or jokes about female biology.
Keep track of PMS or other symptoms you experience.	Whine or complain about your aches and pains.
Assume you have a right to care for yourself. Arrange time off when you need it.	Assume that male supervisors are knowledgeable about feminine biology.
Admit to limited energy when that's the case. Learn to say, "I'm not in a place where I can do that. I'll do it tomorrow."	Be intimidated about explaining your needs to a male supervisor.

Do	*Don't*
Stay aware of your strengths and limitations if you work while pregnant or lactating.	Expect women who have denied their own needs to be sympathetic to yours.
Teach the long-range view of getting work done. Most crises aren't really crises.	

Protective Males Watch over Little Women is another barrier that relates to body energy. This way of keeping women from being powerful emerges from a loving aspect of masculine energy—the urge to protect the pregnant female or new mother—and from the physical fact that the male body is designed to lift more weight and carry heavier loads. But in the contemporary workplace, what appears to be "helpful" or "protective" can be anything but.

It's hard to sort out truly supportive good intentions from the kind of "protection" designed to keep you in your place. One way to tell the difference is in the response you get if you tactfully refuse help when you don't really need it. If your refusal is greeted with a pout or a jab about "liberated women," you just encountered the protection barrier.

Do	*Don't*
Be realistic about what you take on.	Play "poor damsel in distress" when you need help.
Learn to say, "I appreciate your concern, but. . . ."	Accept help you don't need. If you don't need it, say so.

Do	*Don't*
Express yourself clearly about your strengths and competencies.	Accept physical assignments that are beyond your capacity.
Accept help gracefully when you need it.	Try to be one of the boys.
Be ready and able to express your needs clearly.	Diminish yourself by playing the "daughter" role.
Equate what you do at work with what you do in other parts of your life, i.e. lifting a wiggly young child.	

Through tactful, supportive limit setting, you have the opportunity to demonstrate your competence and help change some stereotypes. "Thanks for your offer to help me, but I've learned to handle this equipment comfortably and safely," is a clear message that respects a good intention if that was the offer.

SUMMARY

Your body energy, including the inconvenience your feminine cycles cause at times, is a rich resource for you at work. Value your feminine body. Let your clothing and the way you present yourself increase your comfort with your body energy. If you need time off to care for yourself, find ways to coordinate with your colleagues to provide this self-care. Listen to the messages your body sends to you about what is right, what is humane about the work you're doing, and how you're doing it.

To whatever extent each of us asserts her body energy as a legitimate, important part of the workplace, she increases the comfort zone for herself and for other women. We can then work in a place that feels good. It's much easier to concentrate on our work and not have to put energy into excusing, protecting, or defending something as basic as our biology.

Being there is a first step in bringing feminine balance to the decisionmaking that affects all of us. The changes that the feminine presence brings to the board room, the engineering department, the inner circle at the White House are positive ones. We make it harder to forget that all humans are connected with families, with the earth, and with future generations. As we learn to care for ourselves, in addition to our personal benefit, we teach others that concern for the feminine is legitimate and important.

Persistence

Grains of sand. The daily effort to hold a relationship together. Type, type, and retype—and retype. An assembly line. A toddler's unrelenting demands for attention. A twelve-hour work day. The repeated practice of an intricate musical passage. Quilting, knitting, crocheting—hobbies that create their wonders stitch by stitch.

We don't think or talk much about persistence in our fast-paced times. It's an old-fashioned virtue. But it's a central part of the feminine, and it's still around. "Women are more persistent," was a comment I heard repeatedly as I asked people about femininity at work. One man put it this way. "What is feminine energy? Persistence. Women will stay with something, just keep plugging away at it, way beyond the point where I would have said forget it." Not a particularly glamourous portrait, but it implies the power to move mountains—like water cracking stone, drop by drop, year after year, century after century, winning the right to vote and changing the course of history. Women have had to knock on closed doors long enough to get a response. And the needs for persistence persist. It's important for you to know how yours works—or doesn't work—for you.

Masculine-style persistence paints with a broad brush; it tends to be aggressive and goal-oriented. It's designed to accomplish something that is clear and obtainable: to win a heart or a game, to solve an engineering problem, to

> *Men may lift the big boulder. But women can move rocks over the course of the day. And they do. Day after day all over the world.*
>
> Chuck Baroo,
> New York City

make a point. When a man is persistent, you know it.

Feminine persistence, by contrast, can be almost invisible, low-key, assertive repetition. Other words that come to mind are patience, tenacity, self-discipline, perseverence. At first, energized by a feeling, not a clear goal, the outcome may be unpredictable, because only the small steps are visible. But the goal may become more obvious as the small steps make their mark.

"I think about my mother, who would do things non-stop, never still, driven," Delores Jimenez, a community organizer, shared with me. "She could have chosen not to live that way, but she had incredible energy related to the family. It's hard to believe the number of things she took care of." Delores continued to describe some of her work with community groups: "And women who don't have children may have this same energy in a different way. I've seen them take on community projects and drive themselves when they feel that it's best for their people. They do insurmountable amounts of work with very little regard for their health and sleep. From men may come a different motivation—more likely to be head commitment not heart commitment. The man says, 'I'm committed to my family, but. . . .' The women sacrifice themselves. The 'buts' aren't as prevalent."

Most women's lives aren't built on great deeds. Watching a young substitute kicker score a field goal from fifty plus yards to win a football game, my husband remarked, "He'll have something to tell his kids!" What we have to tell our kids is something very different. It's, "I'm here for you. You can count on me." Every day, we spin the thread, weave the fabric that holds our lives together. We get good at being consistent, and dependable, because we know it's important and nobody else is going to do it for us. We assume that we'll do what needs to be done. And we take this capacity to work with us.

Persistence is the energy that pushes you to do something over and over and over and over and over and over and over. Or to return to a task after repeated interruptions. You work either until you get it right or you get it done. The drive may not be clearly conscious or thought out, but it's powerful, often in an understated way. Persistence is a quiet dimension that gives us the capacity to endure pain and tedium—to stay with the process, ill-defined as it may be, to make sure the job is done. It's the kind of thing that wins out over time.

Or it can be a well-organized effort toward a clearly defined but distant goal. Although it feels much better when there's some validation, feminine persistence can live a long time with neither recognition nor reward.

Nobel Prize-winning geneticist Barabara McClintock, brilliant and highly trained but unable to secure academic appointments reserved for men, persistently conducted experiments in her own garden for years. She could see that, under certain conditions, genetic strains in her corn samples changed in particular ways. Further complicating her attempts to gain support from the scientific community, her observations didn't fit the theories of the time. But she continued working in her own way, painstakingly crossing and re-crossing strains of corn and studying the results. The will to keep at it came out of her own interest and personal conviction. She was not trying to meet another's needs or get approval; she just believed what she saw and refused to give up.[1]

Basic survival in so-called primitive societies—food preparation, infant care, educating children (the original "woman's work")—all require patience and persistence. "Upingarrlainarkta—Always Getting Ready," was the title of a photographic exhibit I saw at the Anchorage Museum of History and Art, James H. Barker's Solo Exhibition portraying village life in the Yukon-Kuskokwim River delta. Tribesman Walky Charles' comments next to a photograph of his people's time-honored fish-curing process captured both the central importance of this dimension and its invisibility:

> Me and a cousin, we've just finished doing herring. Our aunt's too old to work so we had to do all the fish. I never realized how much work it was. You know, going out fishing and hunting is easy and fun. But we had to sit hour after hour, six hours one day, five another, gutting them and then stringing them up. It is so tiring. There I was, sitting and working all those hours, thinking the same thoughts my mother would think when she was doing fish. Well, it's incredible the amount of work these women do. I'll never eat fish again without thinking about all the work these women do.[2]

And the same is true of feminine survival techniques for our culture and time. We may not be stringing fish, but many of the tasks associated with educating ourselves, getting a job or promotion, finding good childcare and keeping it, demand the same tenacious capacity. Whether it's biological or learned, this ability to persist in small, repeated tasks supports women doing what's necessary in everyday life. It's a force of unmeasured power in the workplace. And it becomes even more potent for each of us when we recognize it for what it's worth. Small, routine tasks then become part of life's foundation. They take on meaning that makes them less tedious.

THE SHADOW SIDE

The shadow of persistence builds a living tomb. We know this when our repeated, stuck, action goes nowhere—too much persistence with too little direction. No matter how carefully done, re-arranging the deck

chairs on the *Titanic* doesn't save either the ship or anybody's life. Persistence provides a distraction, a hiding
place, when fear stops us from plunging into the unknown
and risking change. "As soon as I get my files caught up,
I'm going to apply for a fellowship to teach overseas," a
colleague tells me—and has been telling me for the past
five years. The filing is safer than risking either the rejection of the application or the changes that teaching overseas would really mean.

Persistence that becomes rigid or compulsive shuts out
new information and ignores the feelings of others. Single-
mindedness that doesn't have room for the facts but just
keeps on going is the voice of the dark side. It keeps out
needed feedback so that confusion or conflict won't stir up
all those insecure feelings that flare when we don't know
what will happen next.

Perfectionism—doing something over and over to
reach some ever-elusive state—is another way to spend a
long time in the shadow of persistence. If you can't take
the risk of exposing some flaws, persistence is a good
place to hide.

The shadow side of persistence has been emotional
home base for working women who are trapped in non-
opportunity. Compulsive attention to detail, nit-picking,
and a sense of martyrdom provide some release for feelings of worthlessness and frustration. This has been a survival mode for women who haven't been able to move
beyond detail-oriented, routine jobs that go nowhere. It
contributes to negative feminine stereotypes that women
are drones who don't have initiative and can only handle
minor responsibilities.

Learned helplessness, "Somebody else will do it; I
can't," enlarges the shadow side of persistence. This is a
vicious cycle. By not trying, by giving up, we miss out on
the practice or learning experiences that make us better at
any task or skill. The unrealistic expectation that we

Persistence

is a quiet

dimension that

gives us the

capacity to stay

with the process,

ill-defined as it

may be, to make

sure the job

is done.

should be able to do a tough assignment on the first try or without practice darkens the shadow here: "I submitted a proposal and the boss didn't like it. That's it! I'm not putting myself out again."

Persistence is very powerful in pushing for a goal or learning how to do something really well. On the shadow side, it can mean drudgery, loss of self-direction, and ultimately, defeat. If you're captured by the shadow here, ask yourself what you're hiding from.

Self-Reflection

Look at the way persistence weaves in and out of your work life. Pay attention to how this dimension pulls at you from both sides.

STRENGTH: Persistence is part of me. I trust my capacity to stick with something until it's done. I might not like it, but I can do something over until I get it right. My persistence helped me get my present job. I learned to (sew, play the violin, climb a mountain, etc.) by practicing small steps over and over.

SHADOW: My persistence turns into compulsivity. I get started on something and can't quit until it's finished. I get tunnel vision and persist in self-defeating ways long after it's clear that whatever I'm doing isn't working. / I try once and give up. / I can't stand to redo something I've completed. / It drives me nuts to see someone else do something over and over.

TIME FOR YOURSELF

How do you feel about persistence—in you and in others? Do you like it? Does it bore you or irritate you?

Experiment with this quality in your own work life. Select a few of these exercises and work through them.

• THINK OF SOMEONE you know who has sustained herself at work or in her outside life through patient little steps done over and over. Why was persistence needed? How did it pay off? Would a more action-oriented approach have been effective or was persistence necessary? Answer these questions in your journal.

• HOW MUCH PERSISTENCE do you have? Think of a time when persistence and stamina paid off for you. Were you conscious of being persistent or did you just do it? What kept you going? In your journal, write about ten tasks at which persistence has been or will be productive. (Examples: learning a new computer program, creating a network, building a mailing list, writing in your journal.)

• PERSISTENCE AND STAYING POWER are central to developing any skill, craft, or art form. Think about actions you have done or plan to do over and over to develop skills. Select an example from your experience and list the tiny steps you did to accomplish some part of it.

• LITTLE TASKS MATTER. Contrary to media images of the rich and famous, much of life *is* repetitive or boring, not particularly glamorous or exciting. When you can let go of inflated ideas of how your life ought to be and appreciate your everyday competence, a wonderful thing happens. You can do the small, necessary parts of life—pay bills, run the Saturday errands or fill out insurance forms—with a sense of harmony and centeredness, and with little impatience. Write about one example in which you have found this to be true.

• WHO IS THE MOST PERSISTENT person you know? How do you feel about that quality in her/him? Do you have a tendency to discredit or discount persistence as picky? Brainstorm a list that describes the positive aspects of this person's persistence.

• IS PERSISTENCE ONE OF YOUR STRONG DIMENSIONS? Is it just part of the way you are, or did you learn it? If you learned it, who taught you? What do you admire about that person? In your journal, compare the way your persistence flows with the way this "teacher" persists. What do you need to learn? Write it.

• IF PERSISTENCE ISN'T A STRONG PART of your personality, is it something that would help you feel grounded and secure? The opposites of persistence are impatience and impulsiveness. Do these qualities get in your way at work? Describe ways you undermine your persistence.

• IF PERSISTENCE IS AN AREA of your work style that you want to develop more fully, create a plan to follow through persistently and learn more about this dimension in your life. Identify a particular skill or process that you would like to improve—nothing grandiose; just a little step that needs some work. Make a plan, a time line, for doing this work. Write it down. Do it.

• IF YOU TEND TO SLIP FROM PERSISTENCE into shadowy compulsivity, create some techniques to help you let go. Set a time limit for yourself and stick with it. Stop whatever you're doing, relax, and ground yourself when that time is up. Give your self an imaging break. Imagine a special, peaceful place to which you like to go. Take yourself there in your mind and enjoy it. Stretch and breathe. Give yourself permission to clear your head for a while. Everything worth doing is *not* necessarily worth doing well.

• IF YOU ARE A PERSON WHO HAS TROUBLE with persistence, are you likely to try a task two or three times and then forget it? Think about what gets in your way—what contributes to your self-defeating style. Make a list of these barriers in your journal. Is this what you want? Try again with some different approaches.

• MAKE A LIST OF BLOCKS you face that undermine your persistent efforts. (Example: get caught in perfectionism; easier to repeat than to move on to something new; haven't experienced succeeding as a result of persisting; prefer detail work because you can hide in it.) Underline one or two that you think you can reduce. Explain in writing or pictures how you will do this.

Success in self-development lies in choosing a project that is within your grasp—something that you care about that is really workable. If you have trouble persisting in something that's important to you, look at the messages you give yourself. You need to confront whatever blocks you creatively—and you need to confront it with persistence.

Return to your Self-Assessment on page 26 and see if your rating still fits. Make the adjustments that reflect your persistence as you understand it now.

PERSISTENCE GOES TO WORK

Every parent who first sees a baby walk thrills at the tiny faltering steps. No matter that they are unsure, awkward, and lack direction. No one expects them to be perfect. The image of those little steps as you take your own first steps in learning a new skill or tackling a big project can be a great support. The toddler doesn't give up when she falls down. Mom and others will spend years helping her learn to walk and become competent in thousands of other ways. When you take the long view, when you understand the importance of shaky, repetitive first steps, you can appreciate persistence when things are tough at work.

Tiny steps make a real difference in your learning process. Over time, you see your accomplishments accumulate. Try to find another person with whom to share your small accomplishments. He or she will benefit from hearing about them as much as you will from sharing.

When you can accept and value your own small accomplishments, you can appreciate the work of others in the same way.

Boring, non-glamorous tasks that contribute to getting the work done over time are a major part of life. And women do more than their share of this work. Charles Baroo, a community worker whose travels have taken him into the homes and lives of ordinary people all over the world and whose quote opens this chapter, talked with me about immigrants in New York.

> They're able to transition into this culture mainly because the women persevere at menial tasks much longer than men can—stoop, labor, do domestic work. In one of the Latino communities, the women easily find jobs—do mundane tasks repetitively. The men can't do this. Maybe their expectations are higher. Some of the new-wave Asian groups are having tremendous difficulty adjusting to NYC. I sense this is more true for the men. Black West Indian men in England have an incredible incidence of breakdown, but the women keep on going.[3]

It's important to know how to take good care of yourself emotionally and to take the time out to do so. When you can nurture and encourage your persistence at work, rather than fight it or feel ashamed of it, you open up another way to support your feminine power.

Persistence is feminine strength at work, subtly, and often behind the scenes. Water dripping carves stone, but it takes uncountable drops and a long time. Persistence doesn't require tremendous physical strength or high rank in an organization. The persistent person who's committed to her goal takes small steps—a comment here, a reminder there—but she comes back again and again. She doesn't go away. And because she doesn't make it easy to forget something that is uncomfortable or difficult, she may get put down or characterized as a pain in the butt.

She is just being stubborn may sound familiar if you persist at trying to change things where you work. This popular barrier falls into place if you push a little too repeatedly against the way things have always been done. Or if you try to create conditions that are better for female workers. This barrier is designed to make you doubt yourself or think you're being bad.

"Stubborn"—refusing to yield, obey, or comply, resisting doggedly, determined, obstinate—has some of the feel of the shadow side of persistence. "Stubborn as a mule" catches the essence. It implies rigidity and closed-mindedness and gets applied in a negative way to women when we don't fit the sweet, compliant feminine stereotype. The "nag" is a concept that comes directly from persistence, and is used to devalue women who don't give up easily. When we've grown up thinking it's important to be nice, we don't like to hear that we are "stubborn" or that we "nag." Mayor Anne Rudin, who shared how she persistently worked through a week's round-the-clock negotiations to save the Sacramento Symphony, gets called "stubborn" from time to time, too.

She is just being stubborn is a tough barrier to deal with. It's not likely to be said to your face, but it is, nonetheless, an attitude that others may have toward you that hurts your credibility. It's belittling and it implies you're some sort of robot, that you don't think through what you do: "She is such a pain. She continues to bring up this childcare thing, when she knows it can't work! Why can't she just drop it?"

Here are some suggestions for those times when you realize you've bumped headlong into this hidden but dangerously undermining barrier:

Do	*Don't*
Trust your intuition and stick with your feeling even if your goal isn't clear.	Give in to manipulation like sighs or words like "stubborn."
Work persistently with small steps when bigger ones are blocked.	Get discouraged if others don't understand what you're trying to do.
Develop a sense of the long range. Time passes and new opportunities emerge.	Give up just because you feel uncertain of the outcome.
Give yourself breaks and come back when you feel refreshed.	Expect others to support efforts they can't understand.
Learn the rhythm and flow of your persistence.	Quit until you're quite sure you're headed in a non-productive direction.
Gain comfort with turning down offers that distract (and undermine) you.	Join with your critics in ravelling the fabric you're weaving.Give yourself breaks and come back when you feel refreshed.
Listen to yourself and try to hear what your persistence is telling you.	Learn the rhythm and flow of your persistence.

A PERSISTENT WOMAN AT WORK

Persistence moves one grain of sand at a time and changes the landscape while it appears that nothing is happening. Similarly, Joyce Davis's efforts built an organization contact-by-contact, phone-call-by-phone-call. With compassion and determination over the years, she devoted time and energy, made herself available, and stuck with the small steps that needed attention in a subtle leadership process.

Along with her consulting and therapy practice, Joyce worked as Executive Director for a professional association. Members consult for diverse businesses and government agencies in the greater New York area as well as nationally and internationally. Many travel constantly, keep hectic schedules, and routinely work in high-stress, conflictual situations. They compete with each other for business and benefit from each others' support.

Quietly and persistently, Joyce served as a communication channel, a connector for this group, establishing the groundwork for openness and participation. Through her "connecting" energy, people with similar interests met and found ways to benefit each other. She wove a safety net that promoted interpersonal contact. Then, persistently, she supported people who were willing to tackle the countless details required to establish computer networking as a support tool when the group hosted their national organization's annual conference. She facilitated this complex, time-consuming project and then managed the predictable opposition, disappointments and technical difficulties that came with interfacing with the national group.

Her matter-of-fact openness, compassion and optimism about people grounded her work. She avoided getting stuck in the gooey shadow side of feminine leadership that tends to bog down when receptivity and flexibility aren't balanced by structure, closure, and decisionmaking. By empowering others, she smoothed the rough places in the participative process which relied on group wisdom for direction. Busy people, who can be uneasy with a push for commitment and want a "strong leader" to control and provide structure, increasingly shared responsibility for the process. The successful development of the organization created a sense of identity and connection among competing professionals where the jungle of alienation easily overtakes the cultivated fields of collaboration.

Now this organization provides a resource network, as well as a professional exchange forum, for individuals whose work has broad-reaching impact throughout the world. Joyce's low-key, behind-the-scenes efforts shaped the energy and contributions of willing members. They continue building a home base that serves them professionally and personally.

Creativity, persistence, and nurturance, over several years, supported Joyce's step-by-step efforts. Her style was to work individually but consistently to acquaint people with mutual interests, brokering business connections as well as supportive professional ones. As the group slowly came together, she supported others who emerged as leaders. She then handed over her responsibilities, after a period of transition, and left the group in the hands of a new board which continues an open, participative leadership process.

Subsequently, as a member of the national board for a similar association, using a comparable process, Joyce has heightened a global perspective and influenced the creation of an international focus in that organization. Her wholistic thinking, core strength, creativity, and persistence have been key in connecting consultants, particularly in Latin America, but also throughout the world. Her efforts, energized by her love, persist toward co-creating possibilities for diverse people to work together.

Joyce's example affirms that one persistent person can make a difference and create fundamental change through small steps over time. Working against the constraints of busy schedules and competing motivations, Joyce served as a glue in a loose, unwieldy organization. Now she directs her efforts at doing the same in a fragmented world. When she started her work, she didn't know how it would come together, but she stayed true to her own process. She didn't have, or need, a clear picture of the outcome to be persistent.

SUMMARY

Persistence allows for a gradual unfolding and deep connection with self and others. Let your energy speak to you and inform your actions. When your feelings push you to hang in with an idea, goal or relationship, pay attention to them, whether or not you know where you're headed. If you get stuck, if you feel like you persist only because you're afraid, listen to what your shadow is telling you. Get some help confronting your fear, if you need to.

In our "have it all now" lifestyles, we don't take seriously that it's possible to build something worthwhile over a long period of time. But, in fact, that's what women have been doing for many centuries. Our capacity for taking small steps consistently and endlessly can be very sustaining and reassuring when more immediate goals seem out of reach. The ability to stick with the process when the going gets tough makes a real difference. Those drops, grains, stitches, and small assertions are important parts of your daily life, and they mold your imprint on the world.

Core Strength

Sarah Olds was a Nevada homesteader who, when her son became ill, found it her job to check the trap lines. "On my first trip around the trap line I caught a bobcat," she remembered painfully. "I hadn't expected to catch anything, and now I was faced with the task of killing what I had caught. . . . For a while I stood there and bawled good and loud. . . ." She finally stunned the animal with a tap behind the ear, followed by a death blow to the heart. She also devised her own method of rooting out fleas and lice from hair and clothing. "We all took baths with plenty of sheep dip in the water. . . . I had no disinfectant . . . so I boiled all our clothing in sheep dip and kerosene."[1]

Stamina, hope, conviction, a dash of creativity, determination. Core, underpinnings, not-to-be-messed-with primal center of the feminine. Every woman has it. Glaciers brush off half her soul and she emerges with invented energy for a sick child, one more hour with a dying friend, a finished piece of work that dawn's light welcomes, or the job she really wanted but thought was out of reach. She stands firm when crumbling would be so much simpler.

Core strength is constitution, mettle enlivened by determination and hope. It's the bedrock of feminine authority, the quality that communicates, "I'm in charge of myself. My presence makes a difference. You may disagree, give me a hard time, or love what I have to offer,

but you must take me seriously. I'm not to be ignored."
More importantly, it's the quality that each of us can trust
and reach into when we need to get through hard times.
Core strength is the foundation of the inner self.

It's not the kind of thing you think about or choose.
It's just there. Core strength, endurance brightened by
hope, carried Sarah Olds, the pioneer woman in the quo-
tation that opens this chapter, through the incredible hardships she faced. And it is there for today's women as we
pioneer new paths for our complex lives—giving birth and
caring for our children while we endure the hardships and
challenges of work. Of course, core strength isn't just
about children. Married and "childfree," lesbian, or living
the life of a single person who has total responsibility for
all the details of keeping her life together, including her
work—it keeps us going and nourishes the spirit long after
exhaustion sinks in. This strength is personal and inner-
directed, and it has nothing to do with having power over
someone else.

Core strength is constitution, mettle enlivened by determination and hope.

Do you know your core strength? Do you recognize
and trust it? Is it easy to reach? Or is it subtle and hard to
find? Depending on how you learned about your feminine
self, your core strength may be easy or difficult to contact.
It may or may not be well-developed, but it's there. Use
this chapter to identify this dimension in your personality.
Learn to use your core strength both for self-nurturance
and for confidence. It's yours to rely on.

Nor is inner strength limited to the feminine. But
being strong is one of the stereotypes men live with. Their
struggle more often involves accepting their own gentility
and vulnerability. In our culture, men expect themselves to
be strong, though they're more likely to think about their
strength in external terms like winning and losing, being
the best, being on top. They see a "strong man," as someone who's physically powerful, in charge, perhaps concerned about the welfare of others, but not to be pushed

too far. "The strong, silent type," another masculine stereotype, raises a different image—someone who isn't expressive but will be there for you. Neither concept fits core strength in the feminine presence.

Each of us builds her core strength in a different way by collecting a broad base of information about life, the world, who she is. Hard experiences test us and we grow from them. People who care tell us how we're strong. Information that we trust and believe comes to us from many sources—education, growing up, relationships. We preserve this information in conscious memory as well as in that cluttered and mostly inaccessible emotional storage shed, the unconscious. This lifelong, growing collection reminds us we survive in spite of difficulties and underlies our core strength. Unless we pay attention, we won't catch its full significance as a resource. It's there for us, but we have to learn to believe in it and trust in it.

A sense of being in and of ourselves, a feeling of personal authority, arises when we trust the floor of our inner resolve. It's based on willingness to risk doing what seems right—succeeding some of the time.

Knowing our limits is as important as knowing our strengths. Then our expectations for ourselves are realistic and we can stand firm without collapsing.

Melissa Lawler, an Indianapolis professional, shares her reliance on core strength:

> I know when I'm truly responding to my inner knowing about an issue. I feel calm and open to hearing all the data from others. When I'm defensive and stubborn, I don't want to hear—I want to tell— and tell and tell! I feel an element of anger when others aren't convinced. But when I'm coming from my own centered strength, I usually don't feel angry when others see things differently. I just feel puzzled. I say, "I need to stay open to the possibility

that I'm not right," but I proceed under the assumption that I'm correct, even when everybody else is
saying something different.[2]

Powered by our own energy source, we're more productive than when our actions are attempts to please others. If we placate rather than living in ways that are true to
our core strength, we lose touch with our inner emotional
reality and feel off balance.

The quality of our work reflects who we really are. It
saps our energy when we diminish our judgment or creativity and compromise what we believe is right. Not only
do we have to generate more energy to do it somebody
else's way, but when we undermine our integrity, we do a
real disservice to ourselves and depression may begin to
set in. Then we have to plow through its heaviness to get
anything done. When we spend the day pleasing others at
our own expense, we end up feeling very tired—and very
empty—especially when the person we're trying to please
doesn't notice.

Reaching into core strength is a private and unobserv-
able process. Both male and female leaders appearing in
the media typically present themselves in ways that match
images of power and male-defined success. If they don't
easily communicate this quality, they create such a per-
sona for themselves—or worse yet, have one created with
the help of media consultants. Political candidates of either
gender speaking in sound bytes rarely give us an idea of
their soul searching or inner struggles. CEOs rarely disclose their self doubts, or the process used in decisionmaking.

It's hard to identify public examples of prominent people sharing an honest, centered process that portrays their
vulnerabilities as well as their strengths. We have adopted
the myth that, if a leader does not always look strong,
authoritative, and "together" then he/she is not to be

trusted. And so we are typically presented with the polished exterior, a "finished product," not the unlovely gymnastics all men and women must go through to get there. We miss out on the human tussle with insecurity, vulnerability, and uncertainty. And we get skewed ideas of what it means to be strong.

These public figures are the models that women who aren't celebrities think they have to live up to and struggle to imitate in highly visible or difficult situations. Reading a draft of this book, a sensitive professional woman said to me, "Revelation of lack of certainty, such as in the first part where you're talking about your own shadow, may be a marketing minus. People want to know that 'This woman knows what she's doing, and believes in it'—that it will work for them." The contradictory nature of the feminine allows us to know what we're doing and have doubts. Core strength is about going on *in spite of* the doubts.

Core strength—

power from an

inner source

that sets a limit,

draws a line,

or asks for

reflection—

is a balancing

response to

oppression.

Core strength is something very different from a manufactured image. It grows within; it's not painted on. It acknowledges imperfection, uncertainty, and vulnerability and goes on anyway. Here's an everyday example.

Diana, a woman who had worked several years in health care, described an experience in which a much older, powerful male physician attempted to intimidate her. In her job as Director of Nursing, she confronted him when he ignored an important charting step. He had omitted this step many times before and hadn't ever been challenged because no one was willing to deal with his overbearing style. When she called the omission to his attention, he raged and threatened her.

This capable woman found herself shaking—feeling deeply frightened. Suddenly, from the depths of her being, calmness flowed through her as she realized that she didn't have to tolerate bad treatment from this man or capitulate to his demands. She didn't have to take the attack personally and respond like a scared and powerless child. She reached inward, gained control, and confronted her colleague in a professional, matter-of-fact style.

She looked him squarely in the eye and said, "I know, Dr. Blank, that you're mad about this. And I know that you haven't ever had to chart this step. It's your job, though, not mine. It's hospital policy and your liability. I won't accept the chart without the notation." He slammed the chart on the counter and left. But he came back and completed his work.

Diana wasn't able to deal with this man effectively until she tuned in to her personal authority, her basic right to stand up for herself and for what she knows is right. The "structural" power she had through her administrative role was not enough. Her *personal* power, rising from her core strength, energized her self-confidence. This confrontation of a senior male physician by a woman in her twenties breached the accepted power structure in an industry known for its rigidity and patriarchal traditions.

The masculine way, or more correctly, the patriarchal caricature of the masculine that is prominent in our culture, relies on the hierarchy. The group with the most power controls what happens. The "in-group" uses rules and regulations for support when convenient, but underplays them when they get in the way. Diana enforced the rules by confronting the physician. But she had to have personal courage to do so. Enforcing, or calling attention to, rules that have been long overloooked is one of the ways women break barriers in organizations run by informal trade-offs among the "old boys."

Core strength—power from an inner source that sets a limit, draws a line, or asks for reflection—is a balancing response to oppression. Diana's encounter with the physician gives us an example of core strength in action. Her capacity to hold her ground kicked into gear before she was even aware of what was happening. Core strength helped her make her stand. But, "This very inner strength is most threatening to the rule-bound patriarchal structure," consultant Ed Tamson pointed out to me, "It is often attacked, as in many sad cases of 'whistle blowers.'" The patriarchal structure may be rule-bound, but the old boys' club is even more powerful. Women who challenge the informal power structure, even by following the rules, need all the core strength they can find.

Core strength contains elements of softness and resilience as well as hardness. So it often isn't as obvious as more immediate masculine responses. As with other dimensions of the feminine, the submerged quality of core strength may make feminine ways appear, on first glance, weak or disorganized by masculine standards. We get treated as if we are weak, since weakness is part of the feminine stereotype, making it even harder to break through and stand up for our convictions.

"Feminine" is strong and receptive when we learn to trust ourselves in this dimension. We can be true to ourselves and stay connected at the same time. We have room for negotiation, for hearing the voice of the other without losing ourselves. We don't have to be perfect or to win every time. This complex capacity is strength, not weakness. And it helps even more if we can talk about it.

Those who've learned to trust core strength know that even when it's not apparent to others, they can trust themselves and take the risk of trying to get what they need. Until more men understand and respect this process, it remains necessary to talk about thoughts and feelings that come from this centered place so they can become part of the language of the workplace: "I understand that you disagree, but I feel strongly about this and will stand by it." "I know this is a different way. I believe it will make our company better. It's worth the effort."

We can rely on our inner process, our core strength, for information and support. The next step is to speak about the results in a way that's clear to people who habitually see women as weak: "I've invested five years in this program. We've met our goals each of those five years. It was a struggle all the way, and I'm proud of our work." The emotional intuitive shorthand of women's ways of talking, and our habits of being humble, confuse those who haven't learned to appreciate our strength. We need to explain how we are strong and how we find the strength to do what we need to do.

THE SHADOW SIDE

It's no wonder if the idea of core strength, a feminine quality, is hard to take for granted as the basic design structure for your feminine power coat. In our culture, strength is too often associated with "masculine": "She's as strong as a man" or "She'll have to work like a man to keep that job." "Strong woman," for many, sounds destructive, devouring—someone who walks over people to get what she wants. It isn't a compliment when used in this way. A young minister I interviewed candidly described a "strong woman" this way:

> We have these typical strong domineering mother types—physically big, full of power. She's like a viper for the minister. How do you avoid being devoured by her? Walk a very straight and narrow line. She has the power of a mother. You don't want to be punished by her. She's more moral than we, the ministers, are. We're there, trying to please our mothers. The Church is seen as a "she." We're there worshipping that typical male God, but we don't relate to the devouring mother. We build fences around her so she doesn't hurt us. I don't think we know how to enter into a relationship with

her. We "be-friend" at great personal cost. They show up at all the church functions, and they either tell us that we did a great job, or that we really messed it up. On staff, we do a tremendous number of mother jokes.

Not a pretty picture. A powerful shadow image of the strong feminine. This man clearly and courageously talked about what remains unspoken more often than not. The devouring mother image, in its countless varied forms, raises fear in women as well as men.

We fear our own strength, fear that we'll be perceived as domineering, "too powerful," frightening to the men we would relate to. Generations of women learned to defer, learned even that helplessness was attractive. We are good at diminishing ourselves. Of course, when we do so we miss out on getting to know and trust our own core strength. We need to know as much about our core strength as possible. This major dimension of our central, sustaining femininity gives us both the endurance and the resilience to deal with our lives on our own terms.

Core strength becomes pathetic either as weakness or as stubborn dominance on the shadow side. Both are exaggerated aspects of this dimension that take over when we lose our capacity to be vulnerable and strong at the same time. Remember the example at the beginning of the chapter? First Sarah Olds "stood there and bawled good and loud," and then she killed the bobcat. Her vulnerability surfaced first and then core strength kicked in.

Pathetic weakness gives us permission to hide within our low aspirations. We don't expect much of ourselves and neither does anyone else. Helplessness becomes our style, and so we act and get treated like a victim.

It's time to take a look when we find ourselves feeling victimized.

• How am I making myself look inept?
• What do I fear?
• What am I avoiding?
• How am I denying my core strength?

The answers to the questions give us direction about where we need to make choices and be assertive.

Attempts to control the behavior of others substitute for a feeling of inner confidence on the stubborn dominance side. We may appear "strong," but in fact we've developed ironclad defenses that block personal contact with our inner selves and with others.

At work, this stubborness or hardness makes for the unapproachable "iron maiden" style. What many people think of as "strong women" are stuck in this impenetrable frozen shadow. The old-style "organizational" man or woman fits here. When we're in a place like this, it's very hard to recognize our vulnerabilities, but that's just what needs to happen.

Feelings of tightness, frantic desperation, and cynicism are clues that can lead us to examine our hardness. If we're truly operating from core strength, we're not "brittle"—we're not easily defeated when our armor is pierced. We also have the capacity for vulnerability and softness.

We can be overwhelmed by our shadows when we mistake being strong for taking responsibility to do it all. We criticize others who don't do enough, according to our standards, rather than monitoring our own tendency to over-extend. When we find ourselves in this place, our shadow may be suggesting that we take a look at why. How are we abusing ourselves? How can we be more self-nourishing? How can we get better at setting priorities and limits?

Because our culture tends to see strength as masculine, the shadow side of feminine core strength is seen as typical feminine behavior. Woman as victim and even as iron maiden are stereotypes that may not be loved, but they're tolerated. When we slip into these robes, we're not likely to get feedback about it. Our own shadow, in that case, is our best informant.

Perhaps the main shadow quality of core strength is that age-old feminine process of holding back. We defer, don't live in our power, because we're afraid of being too visible, too far "out there" or more powerful than our companions. We hold back from taking risks or enjoying our strength. We opt for what's easy or available rather than facing up to challenges that are important to us. Then we project our dissatisfaction onto our partner and blame him or her for not being enough.

Our shadow is trying to get our attention when we blame our partners, children, or colleagues for being less than we think they should be. It's time to take a look at how we're holding back—being less *ourselves* than we want to be.

We can get into this same process with people on the job. Holding back gets to be a way of life and we defer rather than going after what we really want. Our shadow speaks to us through blaming or bitterness. When we're wise enough to listen, we can move into our core strength and out of the darkness.

SELF-REFLECTION

Grapple with your personal concept of core strength. Let the following items suggest ways to estimate your position on both ends of this continuum.

STRENGTH: I know and trust my center. Under stress, I can tune into my inner strength. Sometimes I'm surprised at my calm in difficult situations. I can rely on myself to stand firm. I have the capacity to sustain myself in difficult or painful situations when I need to.

SHADOW: I feel frightened most of the time, even when things are going OK. I hardly ever say what I really think if I believe others will disapprove. / I keep order in my world by attempting to control those around me. I'm seen by others as a "strong woman." / I hold back because I don't want to seem more powerful than my (partner, boss, friend).

TIME FOR YOURSELF

The capacity to contact and rely on your core strength allows you to be self-supportive in tough or frightening times. And core strength supports your confidence in complex situations. Here are some ways to dig into this dimension and expand your capacity for self-support on the job. Read through them and select several for deeper exploration.

• MAKE A PICTURE of your own core strength. When you think about "core strength," what comes to mind? Sexuality? Physical strength? Endurance? Intelligence? Emotion? Draw it in your notebook. Your symbol might be a mountain, a deep canyon, a rock, a generator, a favorite building, a tree, or anything that comes to mind. Let your thoughts drift until you find an image you like.

• MOVE WITH YOUR CORE STRENGTH. Imagine yourself as an energy source that moves with nature. You are in tune with all of nature and all of time. As you let yourself fill up with this image, move around. Buzz, hiss, sizzle, hum. Let your body be a container for this energy that you can use as needed. In your journal, write the key words that describe your experience.

• CLOSE YOUR EYES and visualize your core strength symbol now. Make it become very clear for you. Practice pulling it into your awareness easily. Learn to reach it. When you're in a difficult situation, you can rely on this symbol to remind you of your core strength.

• LIST FIVE TIMES in your life when your core strength emerged for you in a tough situation (a job interview, a confrontation, a board exam, personal loss, conflict with someone you love). These may be small or large events in your life. The key is that you relied on your inner resources in some stressful situation and were true to yourself in a centered, non-defensive way. The outcome may not have been what you wanted; it might even have been painful. But you know your process was right for you. How did your core strength make itself known or grow stronger in each case? Write about it in your journal. The greater your understanding of how your core strength works for you, the more consciously you can nurture it. Self-support grows over time as you learn to trust your track record.

• LEARN WHAT METHOD YOU USE to contact your core strength. (Your symbol, a certain feeling, or self-talk like, "This is hard, but I know I can do it.") If you really understand how you do this, you can readily start the process when you're under stress. If not, work to create a consistent method as you become better attuned to this dimension of your feminine presence.

• LIST IN YOUR JOURNAL five times in your life when you have purposefully or without any conscious awareness gone against your core strength. As you look back on those events, do you understand how and why you betrayed yourself? Are you in a better position now to stand your ground? If not, what needs to change for you? Name and note this needed change. List the steps you will take to make it happen.

• LEARN TO BELIEVE in your inalienable *right* to your feelings, perceptions, and experiences. They are resources that reflect your own truth. And that truth is worth expressing. Your way has value. List three important feelings or beliefs you want to trust more.

• CREATE OPPORTUNITIES for personal reflection, meditation, or guided fantasy. Make room in your life for quiet time that allows you to make contact with your grit and bedrock at a deep level. As you get to know more about who you are, write about what is really important to you.

• WHAT VALUES ARE MOST PRECIOUS to you? Are they violated at work? What prevents you from expressing your concerns about what is happening at work? (WARNING: If you decide to speak up, your style and timing are important. Good judgment and communication skills are essential if you are to be heard and taken seriously. In some places, there can be no hope for change and your only choice is to walk—speaking up as you go—or deal with the ever-deadening consequences of work in an emotionally toxic environment where you get little or no support and validation.)

• LEARN TO DEAL WITH hearing "no." Others also have rights to their truth, which may differ from yours. When you can accept disagreement or rejection without collapse, you communicate your strength to others and invite trust.

• WHEN MANAGEMENT TRAINING or personal growth opportunities are offered at work, take advantage of them to learn more about yourself. If they teach compliance or conformity rather than leadership and creativity, pay attention to the strong part of yourself as it resists. Ask yourself, "Can I help create change here? Can I accept what's going on? Or do I need to get out?"

Rely on your deepest personal strength to know and interpret your world. Your inner awareness provides a significant balance to what others have to say as a new rhythm emerges between the inner and outer flow of information. Learn to look inside first, to trust your intuitive process; you will gain a sense of centeredness and self-confidence that can't be obtained by imitating someone else. Of course, it's important to be responsive to what others have to offer, but know and trust your own position as part of your response.

Now return to your original Self-Assessment on page 26 and update your rating. You should have better understanding of both sides of your core strength. Add this new data to your Self-Assessment, using a different colored marker than the first time you completed it.

CORE STRENGTH GOES TO WORK

Core strength in the feminine presence is different from more masculine styles that emphasize territoriality or competition. It's the strength to know who you are and to act on your integrity. It provides you the courage to say no when something doesn't feel right or to set a limit when you need time to think. Talking about core strength combats the prejudice that women are weak either emotionally or physically. Say things out loud like:

"I know this is a big assignment, but I have the stamina to carry it through."

"It's true a woman hasn't done this job before in this company. I can understand it might feel a little strange to you to think that I'm taking over this responsibility. Let me tell you about my qualifications. . . ."

"You seem worried about whether I can finish this work. Tell me your *specific* concerns, and I'll tell you how I plan to address them."

Old stereotypes are hard to change. As you rely on your core strength over time, you begin to trust yourself more and more. It may still be necessary, with those who expect women to collapse under stress, to point out your track record, your ability to come through in the crunch.

Two barriers have a lot to do with recognizing core strength on the job. One, **She Can't Do It; She's Too _____**, tunes in with the negative messages you've always heard about your femininity. The other, **She Can Do Anything; Assign It To Her**, jumps up as your competence becomes evident.

Since it vibrates so well with your inner experience at

those times when you doubt yourself, **She Can't Do It;
She's Too** _____ is most likely to fall off the cliff and land
on you when you already feel overwhelmed. When that's
the case, you feel like the weakest, dumbest, most inept
person who ever did a job like yours—or maybe any other
job. The whole idea that women are too something (sensitive, weak, volatile) to do challenging or desirable work is
a very old one. What it really implies is that we're too feminine, which of course is not an acceptable way to be at
work. It's designed to scare us into not being very daring,
and it has worked too well. Here are some things to think
about when you find yourself confronted with **She Can't
Do It; She's Too** _____:

Do	*Don't*
Ask for what you want.	Be manipulated by thinking you have to do it perfectly.
Confront sexist ideas that women shouldn't travel.	Collude by calling other women too _____.
Talk about your strengths and interests.	Feel inferior because you have emotional ups and downs.
Agree that you're sensitive and have limits	Cave in when others "power trip" you.
Learn to mend fences.	Agree with others if they call you too _____.
Learn to negotiate for time when others "power trip" you.	Think you have to win every time.
Get good at being assertive.	

The twin brother of **She Can't Do It** is **She Can Do Anything; Assign It To Her**. In an attempt to gain acceptance and survive sexist attitudes at work, competent women learn to be super-competent. It doesn't take long for this process to reach monstrous proportions. This barrier has risen too high when you've become so buried in responsibility you can't finish what you start or make choices about where you want to devote your energy. Deep in this ever-growing pile is the need to please and to get approval. Although it may look like you're being honored and rewarded with responsibility, you're being exploited. Your core strength can support you in saying no as you get selective about your pace and direction. Here are some guidelines for dealing with **She Can Do Anything; Assign It To Her**:

Do	*Don't*
Understand that your purpose is to get to be who you are.	Be manipulated by attempts to inflate your ego.
Respect your personal limits and vulnerabilities.	Feel obligated to accept assignments just because you can do them.
Learn to set and maintain your priorities.	Buy into the idea that you're indispensable.
Learn to share your expertise with others who are less skilled than you.	Take responsibility for implementing an idea just because you have it.
Protect your personal time and nurture your personal life.	Expect your colleagues to be sympathetic when you get over-extended.

It takes courage to honor your feminine presence at work, especially if you are in an environment where women and human issues are put down. Learn to stay connected with yourself—with your experience and perceptions. Don't give in to those who imply, or say outright, that you're wrong, you don't count, or you're not enough. Contain your energy until you're ready to release it. Create your own way of being at work.

Recognize core strength in your female colleagues. Talk with them about it—about how they sustain themselves over the long haul. Acknowledge their efforts and let them know that, even though they don't flaunt it, you know they are strong.

Your energy system is yours. As you rely on your own worth, it becomes easier to create your own personal boundaries and take yourself seriously so that you will not be invaded and exploited.

Another Kind of Pioneer

I met Mary Bolton in the mid 1970s. Her amazing wit and brilliant capacity to understand the complexities of the feminine struggle were the first things that grabbed my attention. She is present, up-front, and warm. A nonconformist, she says outlandish things and gets away with them. Passionate about life, she notices beauty and comments on it.

Mary's energetic approach to life was instantly appealing to me. But it took a while for me to understand the core strength that powered that approach.

We started working together soon after we met and continued for the next fifteen years. Both of us were committed to doing something about the flagrant abuse experienced by many working women. We worked as independent organizational consultants, tackled some hard projects, and learned hard lessons. I started to catch on.

Rather than being defeated, Mary would say, "That didn't go over too well, let's try this. . . ." And she'd be ready for another attempt. We gave up our first effort to break into working with women in non-traditional jobs after bruising our knuckles on closed doors for a year. Our second effort, in the same general area, was a success, technically. But we were deeply disappointed that the agency which had hired us didn't implement our recommendations. The operation was a success, but the patient died.

We learned from the second project that you need real support—not just consent—from decisionmakers at the top of an organization for any change effort to succeed. That painful lesson gave us the stamina to hold out for what we needed in the negotiations and contract setting we did from then on. We knew where we stood and that we couldn't be successful unless our conditions were met.

Mary knows about doing things the hard way. As a child she had asthma. "After I got over being very frightened, I began to understand I wouldn't die—it would go away. Then I began to *hope* it would go away. When the attacks came late at night, I was too scared to get up and ask for help. If I could stay awake and be brave, it would soon be daylight.

"I learned about endurance, hope—and later—creativity. I think core strength combines those three. I had two strong grandmothers who were good models for me. One of them endured a lot of death. She had eleven children. Lots of them, I don't know how many for sure, died. And the other grandmother was physically strong. She'd get out and work hard—sweat would pour off her and her hair would curl—and get a lot done. She gloried in it. She'd say, 'Look at all those peaches we canned,' or 'Look at all the wash we did,' and be obviously pleased about it. They were both helpful and supportive to me—models for my real self."

She also learned to be responsible for more than her share and to protect her younger brother and sister. As the oldest child, she learned self-reliance. And, "In order to avoid blame, I saw that things got taken care of."

Responsibility for others continued as a central theme for Mary. Sorting out what to hold and what to release in order to make room for her many talents and interests has been an ongoing dilemma. Mary walks this tightrope better than most.

About the same time that she divorced, Mary finished a Master's degree in Medieval English. She moved her four teenage daughters and multi-handicapped son from the suburbs of Detroit to California. It took nearly a year to find a job—clerical work that didn't begin to use the skills her new degree provided, but a job as an administrative assistant at a university counseling center. When I met her, Mary had wound her way out of the clerical ranks. She'd written a grant and was Assistant Director of the university's Learning Assistance Center. Shortly after we began working together, she left the university—once again facing the void of absolutely no job security. Her telling comment was, "I haven't starved yet!"

I learned about endurance, hope—and later— creativity. I think core strength combines those three.

Our consulting work increased. We grappled with the intricate human relations problems our major client presented to us. We dealt with rejection, conflict, distrust, and skepticism. Mary never wavered. We drove thousands of miles together, providing training and consultation to our major client's widely scattered business sites.

Mary's first angina attack seized her in the middle of a training session in Modesto. Neither of us knew what it was. We were both terrified. As we left the hospital later that day, she said, "You don't need to worry. There's no way I'm going to die in this client's bathroom!" And then, six months later while caring for her daughter and infant twins who had hepatitis, she contracted that disease.

Time passed and Mary slowly recovered. She learned what she could about her heart condition. It was scary for her, but she dealt with the frustration of limited energy and having to be selective about her activities. She kept on keeping on. Our client continued to grow and we became more and more deeply involved in the organization's processes.

That wasn't enough. Mary's difficult, aging, and ailing mother moved in with her. Various daughters and now, grandchildren required assorted levels of support. Her disabled son continued to live at home. She patched together a support system of part-time caregivers who could lend a hand when she was out of town. And she continued to live her life.

Mary worked with our mutual client after I left. Her last project there was to help them institute a childcare program for employees.

Over the years, Mary has personified core strength, the inherent authority of the feminine, for me. She matter-of-factly deals with her responsibilities, disappointments, and personal pain. And she finds life very much worth living. Late one afternoon as we were driving along, I was particularly aware of how burdened she must be. We were talking away, but the other track in my brain was focused on the many stresses that fill her life, wondering, once more, how she does it. Suddenly, she lifted both hands upward toward the glowing, backlit leaves of the giant sycamores that arch the downtown Sacramento street we were on. "Look at that light," she said. "Isn't that glorious? I feel like the luckiest person alive!"

Core strength is more than being tough or hard or strong. It also has to do with appreciating the light.

Summary

The dimensions you've worked through in this section provide a solid base for moving on to the next chapters. As you allow yourself to understand and appreciate your strength and stamina, your grounded self-trust becomes realistic and solid.

Spend some time with your journal now to create a personal summary for this section. Describe yourself in terms of *1) Body Energy, 2) Persistence,* and *3) Core strength.* Make three columns on a page, one for each of these dimensions. List the ways that you rely on each of them at work. You can add to the lists as you learn more about each dimension on the job. Write the specific ways you intend to concentrate your attention on one or more of them. Tell a friend what you plan to do.

Before going on to the next section, which swirls and bubbles through water's connective dimensions, get up and move around. Feel the floor beneath your feet and appreciate your connection with the Earth. Walk hard and feel securely grounded in your *body energy, persistence,* and *core strength.* Better yet, take the opportunity if you can to go for a walk outdoors. Concentrate on the way you place your foot for each step. Think about connecting with the very center of our planet—about yourself as a part of the earth. A sense of being well centered in the Earth dimensions is a strong base for moving on. You can swim from that base without losing yourself. Go for your walk. Relax. And then dive in.

Water

The Flowing Connection

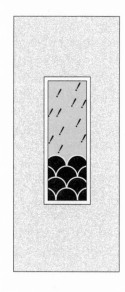

Water: The Element

As one male vice president said to me, "Whether she makes it or not is determined by a woman's ability to kick ass." It has become O.K. to be a woman in more and more places, but getting along in womanly ways remains taboo for the most part. "Feminine" isn't a positive label in the business world. In order to survive the standard work environment, the feminine takes a deep dive out of sight.

It's time to find ways to get the work done that honor rather than violate relationships.

Energy for closeness—contact and caring—flows from the heart of the feminine presence. Can we create pathways that permit and foster connectedness in corporate life and politics? How can we use this energy to ease stress and work together productively? The previous section focused on individual strength and stamina. This one explores the dimensions that thrive in relationships.

Understanding your own personal experience is first. What is your way of being receptive or flexible? How does each dimension in this section help you or get in your way? How can you find these strengths in yourself when you need them? How does your shadow side express itself? When your inner experience seems clear, you can speak out and be self-supportive on the job.

For many centuries, masculinity has had center stage to solidify the patriarchal values of law, order, form, and science. The flow of connection brings feminine balance to these important contributions.

Concern and caring wash through this element. It's the

aspect of the feminine that is most different from the masculine, and it's the part that suffers most at work as women move into positions of authority. It's where women sacrifice themselves beyond reason in jobs that provide support or care—secretarial work, teaching, nursing, social work.

To elevate the qualities of caring into the decisionmaking aspects of work life—into management and executive board rooms—is to change the way business is done. That can happen only if women value staying connected and climb the ladder at the same time, a very tricky maneuver that requires highly developed balance and skill.

In an office where "winning at any cost" is emphasized, feminine needs for connection lose out. Who wants to compete with someone she cares about for a promotion or stab her work partner in the back to get preferred hours? Research tells us that girls learn to hang back rather than hurt a friend's feelings by beating her,[1] and this style goes to work with us. Flowing connection is the power of the feminine that is most undervalued on the job.

When the company's priority is to move in a straight line—to observe order—then feeling-based logic falls behind. Women's ways of knowing, personal and experience-based as they are, don't fit. We need to be secure enough to recognize the ways we think and feel as legitimate tools for getting work done.

But it's also important to look at the other side. The organization bogs down of its own weight when structure and power needs are ignored and connection is overvalued. Talented, productive artists can't support themselves with their art when they don't develop the structures necessary to finish or market their work. Groups that can't progress for fear of hurt feelings over disagreements *don't function*. There has to be a way to "cut the losses" and move on to a decision. A balance between masculine structure and feminine unboundedness is most effective.

Part of feminine sensitivity is knowing when to make the shift and having the flexibility to do it.

Work relationships, and then work practices, can change only when we're each secure in our womanhood. We have to be willing and able to lower our Superwoman shields and risk a different kind of honesty and vulnerability in our work relationships. This is asking a lot. So, understandably, we hide our feminine needs and feelings and move over to the dominant masculine mode in systems that run with strict attention to rules and protocol. For short-term, high-pressure situations, this approach may be the most direct and efficient. But as a lifestyle it has a very high price. Alice's story provides a case in point.

THE VERY FAMILIAR STORY
OF LOST FEMININE CONNECTION

Alice checked the last item on the agenda and closed her briefcase as the meeting ended. She had run the planning session by the book. Assignments were clear and complete. Everybody had eventually agreed to do her or his part. Sparks had flown over whether simply to inform the supervisors who would be responsible for carrying the project forward, or to ask for their input and consent. Alice had put a lid on the discussion when she said, "In the interest of efficiency, I prefer that we just let the supervisors know what we expect of them." The energy in the room slackened as tired staff members complied. After all, the supervisors would *have* to cooperate. It was their job.

Alice knew the ropes. She'd been with the company for fifteen years. After college, she had captured a stellar job in aerospace with one of her present company's competitors. She had known it would be a challenge, that she was a "token woman," but she was very skilled at being one of the boys. She felt good about her style: "In college

I was a top seeded tennis player," she told me, "I spent days on end travelling and kibitzing with men. I speak their language." She could talk sports with the best and clearly understood the importance of "chain of command." And, more importantly for her new job in middle management, she could glide through "administrivia" without ruffling feathers.

Alice's education in human relations had started early. She was her father's daughter. She learned how to get his attention by doing a "good job." She could see clearly that he knew how to get things done and she learned to do the same to earn his praise. When he told her to do something, it didn't occur to her to hesitate.

In high school and college Alice didn't have much patience for her classmates who "questioned authority." She could be the life of a party and knew how to have a good time, but she most enjoyed her reputation for competence, leadership, and not rocking the boat.

At one point, she had thought seriously about marriage. But Stan couldn't ever get it together in a way that seemed secure for her. She knew he loved her, and at times she could imagine being very happy with him. They lived together for a while, but she found work more exciting—more stimulating than Stan's less than ambitious lifestyle. She couldn't take time for "doing nothing," as she put it. She could rely on her own efforts, her career, for fulfillment. She'd never been particularly interested in any other partner.

When I met Alice, she was 45 and her career, now that she was a VP, was no longer either stimulating or fulfilling. Her company loved her. She could run a meeting and get the company's work done with talent and skill. But still, as she said, "I'm the woman who has everything, and my life is a wasteland. I don't have time to turn around, but I'm bored to death. I wonder why I stick around."

A LOOK AT THE SPIN-OFF

I'm not implying that marriage and children are the ways to fulfillment for women. On the contrary, I'm saying we need to bring the feminine along with us to work. We all also need the challenge and stimulation we find in the bigger world. But, like many of us who bought those grey pin-stripes with an air of excitement—"I'll show 'em"— Alice deadened some important dimensions of her feminine presence, and she had no conscious awareness of her loss. The fluid, complex, feminine needs, feelings, and vulnerabilities that are the focus of this chapter are the ones she worked hardest to cover up.

Oh sure. She could rely on them when she wanted to tune in to nonverbal communication and other "people" parts of work—or to move around men who followed more linear paths. But as for indulging them in herself, nurturing them, or expressing them in public, forget it.

At work, Alice had wrung herself dry in her flight from the ill-defined, boundless depths of the feminine. But could she have found a richer, more self-nourishing way to work? What other options did she have?

WATER, THE FEMININE METAPHOR

What better reminds us of both the constructive and destructive feminine urges toward connection than water? Water supports life, cuts canyons through hard stone, bubbles up in virgin springs, destroys everything in its course, or putrifies in brackish sloughs. Variable and boundless, it goes where it flows. Like connection, it's necessary for life but can be unwieldy to manage. On the job, it's tempting to build dams and reservoirs for control and forget about the wild beauty of white-water rivers.

Our capacity to live in our womanhood at work, to

find comfort in the ebb and flow of relationships, can grow as we discover ways of attending to rather than ignoring our connections—R*eceptivity, Flexibility, Nurturance,* and *Affinity.* When we respect and promote these qualities, we can successfully nurture ourselves as well as others on the job.

To get into a watery frame of mind, let your imagination float freely for a moment. Imagine that you can splash yourself with sparkling bubbles. Bathe in water's mysteries. Allow other water images to pour in. A clear Rocky Mountain lake mirrors a summer day. A flood swallows half of Georgia and leaves thousands homeless. April showers, thunderclouds, icebergs, steam, rolling Pacific waves. Water isn't a simple element. It's surface calm hides riptides and dangerous currents. Water's soothing, reassuring qualities are legendary. Our bodies are full of it. We depend on it for life itself. It can cleanse us, buoy our spirits, sustain us, engulf us, or wash us away.

But it's hard to take to work.

Feminine eddies such as the secretarial pool support organizational work but don't direct its course. As a result, moving into the mainstream is still difficult for many of us. Women who have been "left behind" in the more "feminine" parts of the organization are often resentful and can be the toughest critics of women moving up. And women who have achieved power often did so at great personal cost. So they aren't inclined to welcome and nurture their sisters. And in a competitive system, they have no model for doing so. Their lives are further complicated by the fact that work at the management level isn't easily observable, which leaves ample room for projection, prejudice, and stereotyping. They easily become objects of suspicion or chronic attack. In the struggle to survive under such strenuous conditions, many set down the water jug and just climb the ladder.

To "live our feminine presence at work" we need to

To elevate the qualities of caring into management and executive board rooms is to change the way business is done.

communicate effectively that we feel comfortable and capable with who we are. We need to get the message through in ways that allow people to relax the unconscious barriers they maintain.

We also need to find language that portrays the subtleties and strengths of connectedness. We need to let men—and women who downplay their femininity—know that they can take us seriously even though we don't conform to masculine ways of working. Our communication can be indirect, through our actions rather than our words. For instance, when manager Shauna Granger enters a room, her presence is noticeable. And, even in her man-cut uniform jacket, her warm personal style, invites connection. She walks without self-consciousness, smiles directly, and hears your conversation. It doesn't take long to discover she says what she means and admits her mistakes. At the same time, it's clear that she is not someone to mess with.

To change things at work, we have to find ways to translate what we've learned about our feminine strengths into behavior. We can wear our own coat, unless the "corporate uniform" really fits.

Not everybody is going to appreciate a feminine, connected approach. Barriers that protect the status quo may become even more prominent in relation to this element. We need to know how to deal with those barriers when we encounter them—whether to go through, over, or around them, or simply sail our ship on friendlier seas.

You can truly appreciate your tendency to make connections as you wade in the water of the feminine presence at work. Net weaving is a legitimate, effective way to work that has increasing acceptance in the corporate world.

Companies such as Hewlett-Packard and Volvo have built their advanced organizational systems on the principle of cooperation in team-building, planning, and quality control. These concepts are difficult for men and women who've moved up in competitive organizations. They fly in the face of rugged American individualism. And to move from competition to cooperation requires a significant redirection of underlying assumptions—a paradigm shift. When this occurs, everything changes. The values, culture, and style of the organization may shift. Sometimes even the reason for being in business is different. The old assumptions are out the window.

But participative management, a collaborative, non-competitive approach to getting work done, is much more effective for running complex organizations than is the traditional "chain of command." The flexibility of the matrix (shifting centers of authority and control) increases confusion but ultimately handles modern work challenges better than the top-down pyramid can.

As Marilyn Loden points out in her book, *Feminine Leadership, or How to Succeed in Business without Being One of the Boys,* " . . . there is a growing recognition of the need for more people-oriented skills—a heightened sensitivity to nonverbal cues, creative problem-solving, intuitive management, participatory leadership—the same skills that women have been taught to cultivate since they were little girls."[2] All of these spring from flowing connection.

Inroads are starting to appear in noticeable ways. Joan Konner, Dean of the Graduate School of Journalism at Columbia University, made these observations:

> The female sensibility is growing everywhere in our culture today, in literature, in art, in history, politics, the media. There seems to be a great hunger for values that we associate with the private sphere of home, family and spiritual life. We see it in the concern for the environment, in the search for a collective spirit and relationships based on the awareness of the interconnectedness of all life.

> Some believe that women, as they succeed in the marketplace, are retaining what is valuable in what used to be considered the domestic sphere and bringing that broader, more life-supporting perspective into view. On a threatened Mother Earth, some—women and men—are calling into question the efficacy of the instinct for the jugular. . . . [3]

As an individual working in an organizational system, you know about making connections. What you have to offer is valuable. But, because it rocks the status quo, problems accompany a personal, feminine style at work. The dimensions in this section offer some of the qualities that can help you stay afloat. Explore each of them, and keep your focus on how you can bring the gifts of each one to your job.

Receptivity

isten. Hear the music. Absorb the subtleties. Sense the emotion that flows behind the words. Open up.

The capacity to take in, to "allow" a connection, forms a significant dimension of the feminine presence. Receptivity is the quiet dimension of the feminine that receives—a lover, a child, a friend, an idea. It's the part we want from our partner or our boss when we say, "I just want her or him to *hear* what I'm saying!" It's quiet. But it's not passive.

The receptive feminine has been misinterpreted as "passive." So, we need to make conscious decisions about when to receive and when to shut the gate.

In making a connection, it's as important to receive as it is to reach out. Receptivity provides the fertile moment in which the seed is planted—the open gate that invites the visitor and welcomes the unknown. When the door is closed, there can be no invasion. But new thoughts and feelings are shut out, too.

Openness and gentleness reside here: a teacher who hears a student's pain and confusion about a late assignment, a nurse who truly understands the terror a pre-operative patient isn't talking about, a manager who remembers that her secretary's son collects baseball cards and brings one to him from a business trip.

Receptivity allows differences, even confusion. Because no immediate action is necessary, listening should come easily. The focus is on the other, not the self. The capacity to be there is enough.

Receptivity controls the sluice gate through which nurturance flows. If the gate's always closed, we dry up. We can't take in support, affection, love.

In the business world, time pressures and competitive relationships tend to squeeze receptivity dry. On the other hand, sitting around being receptive can get us exploited if we're seen as weak. The receptive feminine has been misinterpreted as "passive." So, we need to make conscious decisions about when to receive and when to shut the gate. And that's not an easy thing to do. Sacramento's former Mayor Anne Rudin (see pages 37 – 39) spoke of some of her struggles:

> In the development of North Natomas, I've been criticized as being unflexible, unwilling to support growth in this community. The opposite is true. We should have taken four years, not one, to plan that area and we would have been able to learn about the flooding before committing large tracts of land for development. The planning process has to unfold like the petals of a flower.

The capacity to say no or to set a boundary when we've had enough—and to make it stick—ensures our ability to be receptive. The receptive feminine is safe only when it can't be overrun. Many women who don't know how to set a boundary feel they have to submerge this part of themselves for fear of being seen as weak.

But receptivity is such a central part of us that its annihilation hurts after awhile. The absence of conscious receptivity is hard to detect. But when we work with our guard up all the time, we deaden our ability to accept a genuine connection. Relationships with others begin to be based on what works, an economy of trade-offs, rather than on honest human feeling.

Alice's story in the opening pages of the "Water" section (pages 106 – 107) demonstrates how a lack of receptivity and the fear of being overrun blocked her openness to the concern that her staff members expressed. They wanted to involve the supervisors—to be receptive and take in their advice rather than just inform them of a set decision. But Alice skipped over this information in the interest of "efficiency," and the people with whom she worked gave in to her authority. As a result, their energy collapsed, and Alice deadened herself a little more.

If Alice had been receptive to the concerns of her colleagues, things would probably have turned out differently. To invite and use input from the supervisors would certainly have taken more time and trouble up front. But the time spent listening to the supervisors and using their input would likely have been more than repaid in results. As it was, the policy was passed along and the supervisors had to make do. Order was maintained, but the messy richness of creativity was lost.

In today's complex organizations, the capacity to listen to others is a valuable asset. As organizations shift from clear chains of command to project-based management or other less clearly defined structures, our capacity to take in information, both content and emotional messages, helps us stay tuned to the constant processes of change. By paying attention, we can make decisions based on what's really happening or needs to happen.

THE SHADOW SIDE

A quagmire hides in receptivity's shadow. Generations of disempowered women live half-lives here. There are no boundaries, no solid places to take a stand. It's a terrible place to get lost.

The "doormat" is stuck here. She doesn't say no and she gets walked on. The shadow says to give in and conform, to pay more attention to the views of others than to your own. Years of habit make it hard to stand up for one's own view, or to know for sure what that is.

Closed-mindedness and rigidity are other ways the shadow forms this dimension. If it's too scary to be receptive, nothing new or different can enter. Only information that fits with preconceived ideas is allowed in. Alice lives in this place.

The ultimate "yes woman" also lurks on the shadow side of receptivity. She fits the feminine stereotype of "weak, passive, dependent." She lives in all of us and emerges when we are too frightened or overwhelmed to stand up for ourselves. She whispers, "Oh, I can't do anything about it anyway," and collapses when it's too hard or too much work to set a limit.

Receptivity's shadow opens the door for any and all ideas, suggestions, projects. *Just because something is worth doing, it's not up to you to do it.* If you find yourself distracted by more input than you can manage, look here. Give yourself permission to build a dam, to say no, to choose. Create a system for making priorities based on choices that are good for you.

Have you ever had the feeling that you have spent the whole day working as hard as you could and that you haven't done one single thing that has any meaning to you? Receptivity's shadow may be the culprit here. Glance over your shoulder and see if she is directing you in the service of others so much that you've lost yourself.

A finely tuned ability to receive, to hear, and take in, sensitizes the feminine presence to important information that waters all the other dimensions. If you feel you've taken in too much, that you're stuck in a quagmire of too many yesses, reach for the one word that shines light on receptivity's shadow: No.

SELF-REFLECTION

Where does receptivity fit in your personality make-up? Be as honest as you can when you estimate where you fit on both sides of this continuum.

STRENGTH: Listening is easy for me. I'm comfortable with differences. I like being emotionally close to others. I'm comfortable being quiet while others talk. I can hear feedback that I don't like and work with it. I can take compliments. I can hear my own inner voice.

SHADOW: I believe others' opinions of me more than my own. My feelings are easily hurt. I let other people walk all over me. / I shut out opinions that differ from mine. I keep to myself and avoid close relationships at work. / I will do anything to avoid hurting someone's feelings.

TIME FOR YOURSELF

Receptivity can be a frightening dimension because it has to do with letting go. The best way to understand how it works in your personality is to wade in and take a look.

If you want to spend more time on the Earth dimensions before receptivity becomes your focus, just list the ideas that come to you while you read through this section. Your first impressions will be useful to you later. Take your time and proceed through the following steps in a receptive mood. Choose a few of the exercises to explore in depth, either now or later.

- IN YOUR JOURNAL, describe your "receptivity" in a positive light. What does receptivity mean to you? Being passive? Exploited? Vulnerable? Having the capacity to hear another? Create your own *positive* definition that affirms this feminine dimension for you.

• THINK OF AN EXAMPLE of your "inner voice" trying to communicate with you in the past week. Receptivity includes the capacity to hear yourself as well as others. Self-confidence grows as you learn to allow your inner experience to inform you. Take that information seriously. It provides balance to what you receive from the outside.

• TAKE TIME TO LEARN more about your own receptivity. Is there someone at work with whom you feel comfortable in this dimension? How do you relax your guard with this person? Can you feel your muscles relax?

• WRITE DOWN THREE THINGS you've seen other women do that seem appropriately receptive. Do they differ from your own typical way of being receptive? Do you know another woman who can be open and receptive without getting pushed around? Ask her how she does it.

• TAKE A LOOK AT YOUR SHADOW. Think of the most passive "yes woman" you know. What about her behavior do you find most disgusting? Are these things you do yourself or are afraid you might do? We can usually see our shadow side more easily in others than in ourselves. Write about the ways you say yes when you really mean no. What is your shadow trying to tell you?

• LEARN TO LISTEN really well. It's safe to take in what other people say when you are secure in your self. You can be in sync with another person's feelings without abandoning your own point of view. You don't have to agree with what others say to be a good listener. Think of a time you've been able to do this, and describe it in your journal.

• LEARN TO BREATHE DEEPLY and relax when you're trying to receive. Your body energy sends information to your mind. Pay attention to your patterns of tension in various situations. Let your muscles tell you whether you feel safe enough to be open, vulnerable, and compassionate, or whether you need to be careful. Draw a stick figure in your journal. Highlight in red the places your tension increases when you block your receptivity.

• LEARN TO RECOGNIZE OVERLOAD so that you can speak clearly when you want to set a boundary. Develop skill at assertive limit setting. When you say something like, "I've taken in as much as I can for now. I need to think about what you've said," you set a clear limit that requires no immediate action or work overload on your part.

• BE CONSCIOUS OF WHETHER or not a particular person or situation deserves your receptive vulnerability. This dimension calls for an ability to say both yes and no—an ability to open and close by choice, not just by reaction. How you choose to share this dimension is up to you.

• TRY BREATHING INTO YOUR TENSION when you find yourself erecting blocks. Say to yourself, "I can relax and open up, because if I get overwhelmed, I know I can set a limit"—and *then* listen. Have you observed women like Alice at work who block their receptivity? Are you aware when you put up blocks unnecessarily? When you intentionally set a limit, you're making a choice. But when a block emerges without your knowledge, your shadow is in charge. Write about an example of each that you can remember.

• IMAGINE YOURSELF AS A POWERFUL, open listener who can deal with another and set limits when needed. What images come to mind when you think of powerful, feminine receptivity? Making love? Holding an infant? Listening to a friend? These feelings are so personal they're difficult to transport to the workplace, but you can do it. Write a brief scenario that describes both your receptivity and your limit setting at work.

• TRUST YOURSELF TO STAND your ground. Core strength and receptivity work together. The woman whose resolve is clear doesn't get thrown off course by criticism or differing opinions. If you trust your core strength, you can afford to open up, take in what's useful, and discard the rest.

Now, turn back to page 26 and make any necessary adjustments to your Self-Assessment Scale. Mark it with a different color than your first note so you can easily compare your original beliefs with your more educated response.

FLOW WITH YOUR CONNECTION

You've had the opportunity to get to know both sides of your receptivity dimension in a personal way. Now let's move from personal experience to the work environment and explore what happens to this part of you on the job. Why do we work so hard to veil this dimension? Why is it so hard to benefit from this finely tuned instrument at work?

Research with young children as well as studies of adult group communication patterns,[1] provides help in understanding some of the negative aspects of receptivity in the workplace. If we follow the path of least resistance, get stuck in the shadow side of receptivity, we do more than our share of receiving. If we don't balance it with good limit setting and solid assertive communication, we run smack into a barrier: **Men Don't Listen To And Aren't Influenced By What Women Say.**

Women in business have dealt with this barrier by learning to behave and communicate like men. But in doing so, they dilute their ability to bring feminine influence to work. To get through this barrier rather than become a part of it, work constantly to improve your communication skills in ways that support your feminine presence. Say it in "feminine." Then translate to "masculine" if you need to. "Something about this just doesn't feel right. I can't say what" becomes, "I think we need to evaluate _____ and determine whether it's really feasible."

Do what you can—organize workshops or other educational experiences—to increase the numbers of people

---

who support and accept feminine influence. People who are simply inexperienced are often willing to accept new views, and a lack of information just adds to gender bias.

Use feminine language that communicates feminine emotions—attitudes of caring and responsibility—rather than emphasizing more masculine passions toward domination and territoriality. Avoid language that is loaded with violent metaphors from war and male team sports, even though that may be the accepted mode of communication where you work. Use language that portrays your own interests and values. Be receptive to your inner voice and express it.

Patriarchal communication practices affect men as well as women because they address "position" rather than "person." It may not be an easy process, but it's worth it to try to find others with whom you can talk about their emotional experiences. If you can find a male co-worker who is open to this possibility, a conversation about what happened is a way of softening this barrier and building an alliance. For instance, check in with him when bad things happen: "When the vice president told us he didn't think we were doing a good job, how was that for you?" If he glosses over his pain, try a gentle confrontation: "That doesn't seem to fit with the amount of effort you've invested in this project. I'm surprised to hear you take it lightly."

If you know that this powerful barrier, **Men Don't Listen To Women**, is a reality where you work, you can learn to deal with it effectively. If you're tuned in to your own receptive capacities, you're in a good position to help others develop theirs.

Do	*Don't*
Make sure that your listener is giving you his or her full attention.	Participate in putting down your efforts or those of others.
Assert your wish to finish any sentence or thought you have started to say.	Consistently interrupt other women speakers.
Ask for the listener to say back to you what he or she has heard from you.	Expect that you will automatically get your "turn" in a mixed-sex group discussion.
Counter subtle or overt put-downs of your communication style.	Hesitate to point out that another woman's comments have been cut off or ignored.
Explicitly state that you expect to be taken seriously.	Let other people tell you how you should feel about issues at work.
Confront overt sexist comments or actions.	Assume that you will be heard and taken seriously.

The other side of this barrier is that women *do* tend to be influenced by men. This takes a tremendous amount of awareness and self-confidence to work through. It is so well-learned, unconscious, and deeply imbedded that it has the capacity to shut out feminine influence without your even knowing that's what happened. Your best efforts can be negated and you'll get no feedback to let you know why. Conscious, open communication with your male colleagues about this issue is very important.

When you can trust yourself, your own worth and power, you can stay open—receive—and you can relate to other women with openness and trust. You create the possibility of sharing information and knowledge, of contributing to a network of mutual trust and support. When you nurture this sharing, it can energize the best of your feminine presence at work—open and holding, contained and energetic.

Publicly acknowledge those who receive well, those who are good listeners. Call attention to the fact that you are listening, taking in information. Receiving is an active process that requires skill and concentration. It's a way of connecting.

Listen to other women. Your own self-hate and disrespect may run so deep that you not only discount yourself but also put down the contributions of other women. Try to listen between the lines for the music that sings beneath the surface. Hear what others are saying, what their feelings and concerns communicate. Support, share, learn to cooperate. Validate. Acknowledge. Corroborate.

The often unconscious patriarchal strategy of divide and conquer is a negative force for all women at work. When you compete for the attention of men you may win the "victory," but you defeat yourself and other women in vicious, destructive ways. The shadow side of the water dimensions invades the workplace and gives force to the patriarchal view that women are shallow and can't get along.

A Feminine Leader at Work

Ellen Steele, an executive officer in a New York manufacturing firm, told me a story that portrays the power of receptivity at work. At the time of the incident she described, her job as Vice President for Human Resources included responsibilities for organizational design, as well as other human resource functions. The more experienced of two women in the executive group, she was deeply involved in the company's massive efforts to reorganize.

The CEO wanted to improve the company's way of getting work done—to integrate historically different businesses within the organization, including a new acquisition. He looked to Ellen for help in making a major shift. As part of this effort, he proposed an off-site retreat that would involve the thirty top people.

Ellen dived in. She was excited about the opportunity and threw herself into designing a retreat experience. The company's business was to create experiences that involved learning. The retreat design would experiment with the ways people learn—physical, mental, emotional processes that address the whole person—as well as the hard-core business-oriented planning and development goals.

Ellen was well aware that many of the people involved felt threatened and would dig their heels in at the prospect of the unusual intimacy of a retreat experience. She put together a plan she felt would respect their needs and still provide opportunities for growth and change. The stakes were high. As an experienced, competent professional, she felt challenged, excited, and nervous about this major risky responsibility.

On a Friday two weeks before everyone was to leave for the retreat site, the CEO cancelled it. He said it wouldn't work. People—particularly the most senior members—didn't want to go. Ellen had expected resistance from the group but was dumbfounded by the CEO's announcement. She was hurt and furious. The CEO had *wanted* the retreat. She had supported the project and planned for it. More than anything, she felt betrayed. What had happened? Why?

Ellen confronted the CEO about his decision. He agreed to hold an emergency meeting of the top eight decisionmakers the following Monday.

Ellen's emotions swirled. What in the world could she

do? She was convinced that this event was necessary to get the diverse group together in one location to plan their joint future. It was a potential turning point for the organization. Not a person who is easily thwarted, Ellen became immobilized. She didn't know if she wanted to, or could, do anything to neutralize the resistance to this event.

Ellen's angry shadow loomed large, growled, and drooled. Conflict gripped her as she vacillated between giving in to company pressures and sticking to her own beliefs and feelings. Her struggle portrays one woman's efforts to stay in her feminine presence while contributing to her company.

She considered gearing up to create a presentation for the emergency meeting—logic, notes, pages of overheads designed to persuade them that this was the thing to do— good, solid, masculine logic to make the listeners change their minds. She also considered quitting.

Ellen worked. She agonized. She fumed and felt depressed. It wasn't right. Somehow, she was taking responsibility for convincing people to do what she believed was a necessary move. She knew this was against her principles. It pushed against everything she was trying to embody in her life and her organization to respond in this way. But she was at a total loss for an alternative.

Ellen began saying things to herself like, "Trust your wisdom." This was a little comforting but didn't have much form or provide security when she thought about the Monday meeting. She went to church and prayed . . . no answers. She returned to her apartment and plopped on the couch. She picked up a copy of Lao Tzu, searching for an eastern alternative, and even found herself looking through the Bible. No tangible help there either. She only continued to hear the faint refrain: "Trust your wisdom."

There were no peers or role models to hear her cry for help. She had to work her own way to an approach. After hours of confusion, reaching in and wondering what her wisdom and experience were going to offer, clarity emerged. Ellen began to feel calm as she understood what she would do. She would let go—give up investment in the outcome. If she didn't hold a position, it wasn't her retreat. She would not have an agenda. She would walk into the meeting empty.

Feeling centered and in herself, an open if somewhat uncertain vice president, did just that. As people arrived and settled themselves, she waited. When time came for her presentation, she said, "I understand nobody wants to go. What do you want to do?" Her executive colleagues began talking to each other. For three hours they talked to each other.

Ellen held the space—listened, stayed receptive. She maintained a truly open hand, neither pushing nor pulling. She served as a resource and support while the decision-makers, through their own heated discussion and in their own wisdom, became clear about *their* needs for the retreat and the importance of supporting it. It became their event, a company retreat, not Ellen's or the CEO's.

Ellen would most likely have been able to convince the group to hold the retreat through direction and persuasion. But two things would have been different. The group would not have owned responsibility for the decision, and she would have been less true to her feminine self. Ellen's personal experience was important. But the real difference for the group had to do with whose retreat it was going to be. No longer was a retreat being imposed on resistant participants, or cancelled by a frightened and frustrated CEO. The executives had responsibly taken ownership of the decisionmaking process. They would work *with* Ellen rather than giving in to the company's power to require their attendance. Now the participants would be present in a real way, not just making an appearance.

First, Ellen was receptive to her own inner experience—hurt, anger, confusion. She listened to her unhappi-

As organizations shift to project-based management, our capacity to take in information helps us stay tuned to the constant processes of change.

ness about doing a high-powered persuasive presentation. She used that information to guide her decisionmaking. Then she had the courage to be receptive to the needs and opinions of others who disagreed with her. She walked into the executive committee meeting "empty." She was a vessel ready to receive.

But her receptive process was far from passive. She was open, vulnerable, capable. Although it may have appeared that she was doing nothing, that was not the case. Holding and supporting is active, not passive, and at times can require tremendous psychological effort. To sit by, stay out of the fray, may require more energy than to get involved, especially in our culture where non-directiveness is often interpreted as inept or weak.

Summary

Receptivity is the underlying dimension for all connectedness. It fits so much devalued and stereotyped feminine behavior in the business world that it may be difficult to see it as a powerful resource. But it's 50% of every relationship. The fact that women have done 95% of the receiving and are trying to turn this habit around sometimes gets in the way of developing and appreciating receptivity's gifts. For the record, they include the ability to hear, to have empathy, and to predict intuitively what's going to happen next.

Being receptive takes courage. It isn't being passive. It's agreeing to hear new information, differing viewpoints, someone else's pain.

Develop your receptivity as an equal partner with your core strength. By doing so, you take in what's available from the outside world, combine it with your own feminine wisdom and experience, and create a new mix that adds feminine sensitivity to what happens at work.

Flexibility

When

transferred to

the work

environment,

flexibility

delivers small

miracles.

S–t–r–e–t–c–h, b–e–n–d, t–w–i–s–t. Feel your muscles relax and tingle. Now do it all over again. And keep doing it. No, it's not aerobic exercise. It's just life. This magnificent quality of flexibility runs throughout the feminine presence. It lets your attention flow to wherever it's needed and changes directions with little notice or awareness in order to keep you connected with your surroundings. If receptivity is working well, flexibility follows.

Both genetics and learning influence feminine flexibility. Your body may be in one state or another, depending on the time of the month or the time in your life. You learn to ride the hormonal roller coaster and go about your business. When you're a mom or a person who works with babies and small children—not to mention adolescents—flexibility is the key to maintaining a sense of personal balance. A basic feminine strength is your ability to take care of children while you cook dinner, plan a schedule, watch TV, and think through tomorrow's meeting. At the office, this translates into the ability to take a phone call, work on the computer, talk to someone who walks into your office, and respond to a crisis, all within a few minutes. "Women are more flexible," I heard over and over as I asked people around the country questions about the feminine. "Women can do a lot of things at once, and it doesn't seem to bother them too much." This is one of the advantages confirmed by Sally Helgesen in *The Female Advantage: Women's Ways of Leadership*.[1] She found that women executives expect and flow with interruptions—see them as part of their job, not something outside the job—rather than getting upset by them.

The capacity to attend to conflicting needs of several different people and relate to each of them is a part of this, too. This quality is often under-appreciated, even ridiculed as fickle or two-faced. Men, and women who have adopted masculine standards, sometimes find flexibility threatening and diminish it by calling it "flaky." Other women who identify with this evaluation often reject their own gifts in this dimension.

When transferred to the work environment, flexibility delivers small miracles. Secretaries who type letters while they answer the phone, manage an appointment schedule, and keep track of who is who and who is where, develop their flexibility to a fine art. Supervisors who have a sixth sense about what's going on, or account executives who move from one client's problem to another's at a rapid rate, rely on this dimension without giving it a thought.

And it is revolutionizing such major industries as healthcare. A physician with whom I spoke pointed to ways that the flexibility of female physicians allows them to find ways of practicing medicine and managing their complex lives:

> Women physicians see their work differently than Western-trained male doctors. We're willing to work fewer hours. Involvement in our private lives is important to us. We take different jobs. Many women work in situations where they can count on regular hours—in agencies, HMOs [health maintenance organizations], part time, in government positions. Benefits and flexible hours are priorities.
>
> Usually, women-centered health care networks are all women—a team. They provide alternative referrals to nurse practitioners and chiropractors, and for acupuncture and therapeutic massage.
>
> Women physicians take time out for maternity

leave and child care. But they practice longer, live longer, survive the profession longer.

New ways don't come easily. This same physician described a professional meeting focused on "Women in Medicine." About half the male physicians walked out after the first twenty minutes. "You are ruining medicine!" one of them said to the speaker as he exited.

Misunderstandings between women and men happen when we take our male colleagues' ability to be flexible for granted. In working with groups of men, I learned after a few uncomfortable confrontations that it was important to *announce* a change in direction if I shifted a meeting agenda. Admittedly, that's good practice with any group. But I've noticed that women "go with the flow" much more easily. Minor adjustments or shifts are less likely to throw us off track.

A good, clear, straight line to the goal has become the accepted way to get work done. Men seem to have a more difficult time shifting their attention from task to task and prefer a focused approach. They experience darting from item to item as disconnected and upsetting. Seen through their eyes, this "flightiness" isn't flexibility but lack of focus. If we look to these men for their stamps of approval, we are likely to agree that our way is inferior and reinforce this misconception. We need to know about our flexibility and speak up on its behalf.

Even if your job requires concentration and focus rather than flexibility, getting along with your co-workers is easier with the help of this dimension. Flexibility, like persistence, is one of those qualities that you probably take for granted unless, for some reason, its absence is called to your attention.

THE SHADOW SIDE

Of course, a darker side shadows flexibility. That wonderful radar that tunes in to nearby activity can distract you too easily. You can be so flexible that you automatically pick up on work items that fall through the cracks as if they're discarded and forgotten toys. Soon you're doing everybody's work but yours.

One of the hardest things women who have been at home have to learn to do in the work environment is to build personal boundaries and stay within them. At home, especially doing the work of mothering, *everything* is your responsibility. Mom is usually the person who keeps track of the toddler while folding the laundry and helping the eight-year-old with her homework. It doesn't work to say to the toddler, "Stay in one place, now, I'm focused on helping Jenny with her story." For those who are accustomed to taking responsibility for whatever presents itself it takes self-discipline to walk by and leave the toys on the floor.

Old-time practices in the office assume that men do the "important" work and women "pick up after them." And without giving it a thought, many women fall into the trap. This can change only when we look our flexibility in the eye and say, "No. I see that needs to be done, but I'm not the one."

Flexibility gets shadowy when we slip into another's emotional space and get stuck there. It's great to have the capacity for empathy, but we need to stay on our own side in emotional relationships. We can get so flexible that we lose our ability to take care of ourselves and try to be all things to all people in situations where others need a lot. In the helping professions, many women struggle with this shadow until experience or burnout helps them learn about setting limits clearly, if not comfortably.

Rigidity is another aspect of flexibility's shadow. Fear

of being overrun stiffens the response before any bending can be allowed. A colleague said to me once, "I always say no. Then I can change my mind if I want to." This practice protected her, but it also made her a tough person to work with.

Self-Reflection

Take a few moments to estimate how your flexibility works for and against you. Focus on how this dimension serves you at work (strength)—or gets in your way (the shadow side). The following ideas can help you with your self-assessment of this dimension.

STRENGTH: I can shift from one activity to another with ease. When my attention is disrupted, it's not difficult to return to what I was doing previously. I can deal with opinions that are different from mine. I can change direction when I get information that lets me know it's important to do so.

SHADOW: It's hard for me to stay focused on anything. My attention is easily diverted, and I constantly skip from one thing to another. / I'm fairly rigid and can't take in ideas that differ from my own. Changing direction is very difficult for me once I get going on something.

If flexibility is a dimension you want to develop further, the first step is to heighten your awareness of ways you find yourself being either rigid or wishy-washy. After you get better acquainted with this dimension, identify one or two areas at work and experiment with flexibility in a conscious way. For now, make a note or two in your journal about what these areas are, and how you can go about working with them. Then sample a few of the exercises for greater self-understanding and a chance to work in this dimension.

TIME FOR YOURSELF

As you think about yourself in this dimension, see if you're as psychologically supple as you might hope. Here are some ways you can experiment. Try to determine the degree of flexibility that's comfortable for you. Think about whether you need to s–t–r–e–t–c–h your capacity or work to define your boundaries more clearly.

• LIST IN YOUR JOURNAL the things that are happening around you right now. Music, machinery noises, other people? Were you aware of them as you were reading? Is it difficult to shift your attention from the book to your journal to your surroundings and back to the book again?

• NOW SHIFT YOUR ATTENTION back to your immediate environment. Do you find it difficult or easy to shift your thoughts and focus on your surroundings? You can choose either concentration or scanning. Pay attention to whether or not you resist change—whether previous thoughts trail into the present activity. Then shift your concentration back to your reading.

• GIVE YOURSELF PERMISSION to focus on your own flexibility for a moment. List the ways you are flexible at work. Can you shift easily from task to task? Do you deal with differences well? Are you able to relate to people who disagree with each other? And you?

• THINK OF A RECENT EXAMPLE in which you dealt with conflicting information and kept or modified your own position. Write about it in your journal. If you trust your own capacity to sustain your beliefs, you can afford to hear conflicting information and selectively change your views without losing your sense of self. Do you accept information or ideas that differ from your own view? Can you put your preconceived views aside and evaluate the relevance of someone else's opinions?

• LOOK AT YOUR SHADOW SIDE. Think of the most wishy-washy person you know—first she's on one side and then the other. Write down what you like least about her exaggerated flexibility. Which of these character-istics are part of you? Or are there some you work overtime to keep under control? Listen for the message under your urge to comply too readily. What are you frightened about? Write it in your journal. What's a more direct way to deal with your fear than giving in?

• LEARN TO RECOGNIZE whether you're following your own inner direc-tion or doing another's bidding in order to avoid rejection or anger. Co-dependency, getting your needs met by taking care of others, contributes to hyper-flexibility for women who haven't been powerful in their own right. The capacity to bend to another's needs as a way of maintaining control is a dark side of this dimension that has trapped many a woman. If you hear yourself saying, "If I don't do this for so and so, she or he will be mad at me," you're in your shadow. List examples of co-dependency in your relationships at work.

• LIST SOME EXAMPLES OF PATHS you haven't followed. How do you capi-talize on flexibility without being either wishy-washy or co-dependent? The down side of flexibility means that you never follow a job through to the end. In order to trust your flexibility, you must also trust your capacity to concentrate when that is your task.

• PAY ATTENTION to how you express yourself when you're with an all-female peer group at work. Experiment with using "feminine" expression at work. Be ready to translate into "business language" when you need to. In their book, *The Feminization of America*, authors Elinor Lenz and Barbara Meyerhoff point out that women are much more able to adopt masculine language style than men are to communicate in feminine lan-guage.[2] Do you find yourself shifting from feminine to masculine lan-guage in order to be understood or taken seriously at work? List some examples.

• IF YOU WOULD LIKE TO increase your flexibility at work, get in touch with your fears. If you tend to be somewhat rigid, you have probably been hurt in ways that make it difficult for you to tolerate enough openness to move easily in your environment. Identify an area in which you feel secure at work and stretch your flexibility there by relaxing your guard and risking less perfection. Then move on to another area that might be just a little scarier and do the same thing. Keep track of your progress in your journal.

• ASSERT THE BENEFITS of your flexible style if someone alludes to it as "flaky" or disconnected. "Yes, I have the ability to deal with a lot of things at once," or "this may look 'flaky' to you, but I'm tracking the issues we're talking about while I'm sorting through these files. I can pay attention to both things at once."

Return to your Self-Assessment on page 26 and update the information about your flexibility that you recorded there earlier.

LET FLEXIBILITY WORK FOR YOU

You've examined your own flexibility and have a sense of how it works for or against you. How can this dimension benefit you at work? What can it contribute to getting work done?

Whatever your skill or craft, your level of performance can only be what it is at any given time. When you can accept your skill level with its flaws and imperfections, you can be flexible and open to hearing about needed improvements. Flexibility helps you benefit from feedback, use suggestions, and change your approach when needed.

Even though you may work in a rigid system, flexibility is a part of your personality that you can nourish and support. If you stay conscious of it, you won't give in to the rigidity of the environment and lose your own form. You can bend when you need to while taking care to *choose* where you do the bending.

Use your flexibility where it counts. Doing several things at once can work to your advantage, but it's important to communicate clearly about what you're doing. That *you* know you're tracking several different projects doesn't make it obvious to others who may become anxious about their parts of those projects.

When you take in information that is new or contradictory and make adjustments accordingly, communicate about that, too. Otherwise people assume you're still headed in the same direction you started. Shifting gears may be relatively easy. The cumbersome work of explaining the process is tedious, but equally important. You make life easier for your colleagues if you give them a roadmap.

Avoid unconscious acts of rebellion like being late or demonstrating your flexibility in other self-defeating ways. If you work where rigid organizational limits frustrate and inconvenience you, find ways to be flexible within the limits of your control and responsibility. If organizational rigidity continues to thwart you, look for another place in your company, or maybe even another job that is more compatible with your style.

Learn to identify negative comments or attitudes toward feminine flexibility. Talk with other women about this. Learn to tell the difference between flexibility and irresponsibility. Point out the positive aspects of flexibility when they are part of the work process.

Avoid using "flexibility" to mask incompetence or lack of knowledge. If you're late or unprepared, just say so rather than implying that others might not be as flexible as you if they're upset.

Flexibility gives you new eyes for looking at the way things are done. Eight o'clock Thursday morning staff meetings might have been the best arrangement once upon a time. Now that it conflicts with childcare connec-

We no longer have to squeeze ourselves into rigid work patterns that were designed by men to fit what were once men's needs.

tions for two staff people, some other time might be better. Research the possibilities and propose a change.

Openness to working in different ways offers other options. Cross-training, making sure several people know how to do each job, is an important part of team-based management. Your flexibility as you participate in or support this process can help it flow more smoothly.

Staffing flexibility supports the needs of working women. Flex-time, job-sharing, and parental leave programs are all easier when people can fill in for each other. The ups and downs of menstrual discomfort that some women experience can be easily worked around if scheduling and work assignments are flexible.

We no longer have to squeeze ourselves into rigid work patterns that were designed by men to fit what were once men's needs. (These are changing, too, as more men take family life to heart.) With attention and consciousness, we can translate our inner flexibility to change the way work is done. By doing so, the place where we spend most of our waking hours becomes much healthier and more enjoyable. We can create balance so that feminine needs are taken seriously, too.

A Woman In Her Time

Sponsored by Women's Alliance, a group of serious-minded women and a few men gathered for a two-day seminar on the UC Berkeley campus in early spring 1991 to hear *Women's Voices in Troubling Times.*[3] Winona LaDuke had finished her formal presentation and moved from side to side on the stage so she could see the speakers behind the microphones in each of the auditorium aisles. Speaking from her background as a Chippewa Native American and a skilled change agent, she had outlined some of the economic and social issues that native people in our country and others contend with. Obviously under the weather, the much recognized leader had spoken just above a whisper, her voice ravaged by the flu. Conference participants asked Winona and the other nationally prominent presenters tough questions about motives, strategies, and future plans.

She had spoken in Los Angeles the day before, made the long trip to Berkeley by car with her two-month-old son, and now patiently listened and responded with clear, thoughtful answers.

One woman asked, "How do you find the energy to do all this? You have a new baby, another child, and you're actively working on political and economic issues on many different fronts?"

Winona must have been sorting her answer with each step as she walked to the mike at the center stage podium and said, "When you're clear about who you are and what you want to do, the energy comes." And then she spoke into the dark corner of the auditorium where her baby's voice had been heard a few minutes before. "You can bring the baby up here." It took a while. The woman who was taking care of the infant had slipped out an exit. But she returned with a very young man who appeared quite happy to see his mother.

Winona sat down in a chair, reached to take the microphone off the stand. A female sound technician appeared from nowhere to supply a chair-level mike on a boom. Winona smiled, lifted her blouse, offered the baby her breast and continued answering questions. She didn't apologize, she didn't make a joke and she didn't miss a beat. When spontaneous applause erupted from time to time, she gently covered the baby's ear with her hand.

The beauty of this woman, framed by a huge vase of blooming fruit sprays—her dark skin, purple blouse, turquoise necklace, and the baby nursing—communicated the essence of feminine strength and tenderness. Her capacity to sit in the bright lights and field technical and philosophically challenging questions and comments without losing connection with her feminine core spoke of an age-old flexibility that can serve us all very well. Winona seemed very grounded in what was right for her. She responded to the demands and needs of those around her from her comfort zone.

"Very nice," quipped one woman who read this vignette, "but she'd be *fired* if she were a vice-president at ____ and did this!"

The corporate world may not be ready to embrace the feminine at this level. But think about what might be possible when the feminine presence is seen as a legitimate half of that world. If women who choose to have children are flexible enough to manage microphones and breast feed at the same time and wish to do so, more power to them.

SUMMARY

Flexibility from a centered place is neither flaky nor co-dependent. It's a feminine strength that provides us the resilience to deal with life's hassles without losing ourselves in the process.

On the shadow side, women get so good at being flexible we forget to stand up for ourselves. This has been seen as "feminine" in the past and makes boundary-setting hard for many of us. The key is to know about and appreciate our flexibility but not feel required to bend at every pressure. Choice makes the difference. *You* choose when to be flexible, when to be firm. And *you* determine whether you're being flexible, or being flaky.

Nurturance

other's love, the milk of human kindness—nurturance. Women encourage, support, foster, warm, heal, teach, feed and comfort. We connect with others by giving and caring. And we feel good about ourselves in the process. What exciting gifts to bring to the workplace!

But in our lopsided culture where men are powerful and women serve, the joy of nurturing can expire from sheer exhaustion. In generations past, we carried more than our share of this dimension, but in trying to shift the weight of the burden today, we're in danger of losing the whole load—of sacrificing a precious part of ourselves. To give up the capacity to nurture on the job in order to maintain a tough, competitive stance is to block a major feminine connective path.

But how in the world can we nurture without losing ground at work or being stuck with all the caretaking responsibilities at home? Do we give away our hard-earned positions to support our competitors and co-workers? Do we refuse to nurture as a matter of principle? The struggle for balance has been going on for a while.

Nearly forty years ago, Anne Morrow Lindbergh wrote about her attempts to contain the rapture of a wonderful day alone at her beach hideaway. Her words betray the tension between her sense of personal richness and her tendency to give herself away as the hub of family activity:

> Is this then what happens to woman? She wants
> perpetually to spill herself away. All her instinct as a
> woman—the eternal nourisher of children, of men,

of society—demands that she give. Her time, her
energy, her creativeness drain out into these channels if there is any chance, any leak. Traditionally we
are taught, and instinctively we long, to give where it
is needed—and immediately. Eternally, woman spills
herself away in driblets to the thirsty, seldom being
allowed the time, the quiet, the peace, to let the
pitcher fill up to the brim.

—*Gift from the Sea*

We need to find a middle ground between withholding and giving too much. In our private lives, the nurturing
flow is dependent upon our resources and the levels of
need around us. A mother's milk appears at feeding time.
In the more structured work environment, where the need
is great—and constant—different rules apply. For many
people, work substitutes for personal life. If we unconsciously respond to their emotional needs then we can be
depleted without having done a bit of work. Many
women, especially in their early stages as managers, get
mired in this trap.

It helps to nurture and support others *in ways that
will get the work done.* Hours listening to the pain of someone else's difficult personal relationships probably will not
help very much. In such situations, a tactful referral to the
employee assistance program might be in order. But support and direction about setting limits, learning new techniques, or developing additional skills will help your co-
workers.

One of the hardest things for many women to learn is
to take care of themselves by ending a conversation while
the other's need is still intense. A pressured public relations director who spends an hour on an unscheduled
phone call educating a reporter about her client's product
has given too much. Twenty minutes and a referral to
other resources is enough. This is essential learning for

survival on the job.

Some women handle this dilemma by not giving anything. They buy into the "dog eat dog" philosophy and become simply unapproachable. But this leaves them to operate in a masculine style that serves neither them nor the people around them. It's worth it to learn about your own nurturing style so that you can negotiate the shades of grey between giving too much and not giving enough.

In recent years, the flowering of the Twelve Step programs, Alcoholics Anonymous and other Anonymouses, has made co-dependency a household word. The idea that we take care of people in order to be taken care of ourselves—a shadowy form of nurturance—has been explored from many directions, which has brightened possibilities for many otherwise hopeless lives. But it's hard to sort out what's co-dependency, what's nurturance, and what's generosity.

Jean Baker Miller is a pioneer psychologist whose groundbreaking 1976 book, *Toward a New Psychology of Women,* opened a new era of understanding. In a later publication, Miller talks about women's traditional roles as fostering the growth of others—that we empower others through our own power by increasing their resources, capabilities, effectiveness, and ability to act. She points out that a major component of nurturing "is acting and interacting to foster the growth of another on many levels—emotionally, psychologically, and intellectually." She asserts that what women have been doing all the time is a very powerful thing to do, but "no one is accustomed to including such effective action within the notions of power."[1]

And Janet Surrey carries the idea a step further as she describes "one of women's particular sources of strength—the power to empower others, that is, to participate in interaction in such a way that one simultaneously enhances the power of the other *and* one's own power."[2]

Now we're talking! All this giving we've been doing gives us something back. And that's neither sick, selfish, controlling, nor self-denying. Giving something to someone because you want her to have it, or taking care of someone, not out of guilt or obligation, but because you're concerned about him, is a very powerful act. As contemporary working women, we get to express ourselves, live our birthright as nurturers and empowerers, and empower ourselves in the process. So let's learn to make it work for us.

We need to find a middle ground between withholding and giving too much.

Traditional work environments don't foster generosity and sharing. Nurturance is contrary to the competitive expectation that we need to hold onto whatever we can grasp. Of course, women continue to do it anyway, even so.

Frustrated by the failure of female candidates to get elected, Ellen Malcolm found a way to turn her ability to nurture into a powerful political force. Recognizing that female political candidates have a chance only if they're well funded early, she created EMILY'S List (Early Money Is Like Yeast). She and her colleagues simply wove a network that collected donations from people (mostly women) interested in supporting female candidates for office. This campaign chest tipped the scales in the election of Governor Ann Richards in Texas and for a number of women in the 1992 congressional races, women who are now positioned to make a real difference in our country's future.

Strategic nurturing, selecting where to put your nurturing energy, helps you to stay conscious of when to give and when to withhold. In my work as a therapist, a job that makes significant demands on this dimension, I've determined that I can see a few clients on a sliding scale and one person for no fee at all. Over the years, I've worked out a loose formula that works for me. When those spaces are full, I don't accept any more clients on a sliding scale. I know what I'm comfortable with and when I start feeling drained. At work, you can choose whom you're going to help and how much. Understanding your limits makes it easier to say no when you need to.

In the past, unbounded nurturance was the expected organizing dimension of women's lives. We perpetually spilled ourselves away. Now we have more choices. As we learn to rely on all of our dimensions, not just the traditionally "feminine" ones, we can nurture knowing that we can also ask for what we want and set firm limits. We can enjoy the richness of this important dimension rather than either freezing it when we walk through the office door or subjecting ourselves to rampant exploitation.

Marion Vittitow, whose creativity has nurtured many women and men, gives us these thoughts:

> The Native American Spider Woman expresses all-pervasive feminine creative energy. A spider can move any way that it wants to, and can do so by creating its own path into that space. It goes after and gets what it needs in terms of nurturance or excitement by putting itself out.
>
> Although Spider woman's energy includes destruction, it's not willful. Disintegration is necessary for integration to emerge. Her energy honors this part of relationship, allowing people to find their own way—even through the dark times—to renewal and regeneration by offering support and encouragement.[3]

This is feminine power. Power with. Renewal rather than power over.

"Honoring relationship . . . allowing people to find their own way . . . by offering support and encouragement. . . ." Marion's words create a roadmap for nurturing on the job. It's about honoring relationships, not caretaking.

Because relationships are reciprocal, it feels good to nurture. We get something back if we have a hand in advancing someone's growth: a warm feeling, a sense of connection, validation of our worth. Even though it's against the unspoken rules in many business environments, we benefit emotionally when we help a colleague, support a new effort, lend a hand. And we change the way it feels to be at work. Here's a story a woman told me about some healthy nurturing she did at her office.

A "re-entry woman," Suzanne began her professional career in her late 40s, after finishing her mid-life college education. And she did it with finesse. She's a success in her industry and continues to flourish with the same commitment and integrity she relied on as a mother and homemaker. Hard work, honesty, and concern for other people are her stock in trade.

In discussing current issues at work, Suzanne shared a great example of appropriate nurturance in what is often a viciously competitive industry. She laughingly acknowledged that she doesn't much like the people at her office in her age group ("mostly men who tend to be old-fashioned chauvinists"), so she hangs out with the younger crowd. Several of them, both women and men, rely on her as a confidante, and she likes the role.

Several of the brighter stars let her know that they were preparing to go to work for a competing company. They didn't really want to go, but they had tried to talk to the chief and he had rebuffed them..

Suzanne listened for a while and offered to talk to the CEO. He had accepted some of her recommendations before "because I'm part of his generation. And he's not used to working with women who talk back to him. He really doesn't know what to do with me."

The crusty, highly-competent, but self-centered CEO wasn't about to listen to a bunch of "kids." But this mature (by now mid-fifties) woman, who had given him some very useful feedback in the past, set him down and told him what he needed to know to save his company from drying up in its own rigidity. He listened to her and became more open to hearing what the younger employees had to say.

Suzanne not only nourished her young colleagues, she "nurtured up." She supported the boss, the "kids," and herself in a typically homey, feminine way. This is a woman who knows what she wants and works to get it. The "mom" stuff is so much a part of her that there's no way to stop it in her relationships at work. And it works for her in a relaxed and natural way. The feminine focus on relationships encourages a free and easy nurturing style for women like Suzanne. But that style doesn't fit everyone. We each need to come to terms with how we express this dimension.

"Nurturance" popped up most quickly and most often when people I interviewed shared their thoughts about femininity at work. Women are expected to be nurturing—that is, caring, open, warm, and giving. But when we're that way in formal business environments, we're seen as naive or unprofessional. On the other hand, when we don't fit this pattern because it just isn't our style—or because we're stressed or focused on something else—we're seen as cold and unfeminine. It's hard for corporate life to relate to femininity, whether we fit our stereotypes or not.

Mothering experience isn't a requirement. Although stereotypes of nurturing often include motherhood, the generous connections that many people make with friends and colleagues at work express this dimension, too. Relationship and social contact form a central part of satisfying work life. Personal support, sharing, and celebrating special occasions are all nurturing ways we connect with each other.

When both women and men can support each other

It helps to

nurture and

support others

in ways that

will get the

work done.

in this way, it makes work a happier, healthier place to be. Easy contact and sharing are possible if cut-throat competition isn't an issue. Unfortunately, that's not always the case.

If you work in a setting where every move is competitive, nurturing others is likely to be a problem. Take a close look to understand the nature of the competition. Is it necessary? Or is it a way that insecure people protect their turf and make themselves feel better by exerting power over others? Good-natured competition can add interest and excitement to work if mutual respect and trust are part of the process. The cut-throat variety is toxic and destructive, and rarely, if ever, contributes to the overall health of the organization.

Suzanne knows how much money she wants to make, trusts she'll meet her production goals, and isn't driven by greed. She loves making a big sale and gets excited about being the top producer once in a while. But her self-esteem doesn't depend on it and she doesn't go for the jugular to make it happen. And so she can nurture others with no fear of loss to herself. In fact, it makes her happy to do so.

THE SHADOW SIDE

The shadow side of nurturance taints both giver and receiver. Distrust, guilt, and resentment grow in its darkness. Here's where co-dependency comes in.

The cloying, controlling, caretaker who lives through others is a painful example of nurturance's shadow. Generations of women grew up believing they deserved nothing for themselves. Mere survival depended on taking care of a spouse—nurturing grown men bought us a meal ticket. It hasn't been too long since women were treated like chattel, legally and in every other way, and this history's had a profound effect on the way we see ourselves.

In the past, our culture has taken for granted that as women we put the needs of others before our own. The part about taking care of ourselves, too, got left out. Many of us took that message literally for a long time and spent our lives "nurturing" out of guilt and obligation. Others rebelled and refused to nurture anybody. "I don't take care of kids at home; I'm not going to baby sit at work," is the way one manager put it. This approach casts another kind of shadow. It limits the give and take that's central to any personal relationship. Prima donnas are lonely people who wonder why their competence doesn't make them happy.

Modern day misers, women who withhold on general principles, can't give. They're frightened to death of being overwhelmed and of having to give more than they can spare. Or they're fearful that their generosity will be used against them. Miserliness sets an extreme boundary if assertiveness isn't well enough developed. It seems easier to keep the gate completely shut than to have to set a limit when the demands outweigh the resources. So these folks hold on tightly and suffer profound loneliness.

Nurturing is sharing that flows from generosity of spirit. If your resources are limited and you don't feel like sharing, give yourself permission to be *self*-nurturing. All of us have times when we have nothing to give. That's the time to *ask* for nurturance. If you find yourself strategically nurturing in order to accomplish some goal or another, take a second look.

The self-sacrificing martyr whose boundaries are so leaky she keeps nothing for herself fits here too. In order to nurture others, we first have to take care of ourselves. If you habitually give yourself away, rather than taking responsibility for nourishing your own growth, a little self-talk is in order. An excerpt from Carol Lynn Pearson's poem, "Millie's Mother's Red Dress" might help. It captures the pathos of a dying woman's conversation with her daughter as she shines some light into the shadow of nurturance. On an impulse, the mother bought the beautiful red dress for herself, but never wore it:

"And I'm telling you, Millie, if some miracle
Could get me off this bed, you could look
For a different mother, 'cause I would be one.
Oh, I passed up my turn so long
I would hardly know how to take it.
But I'd learn, Millie.
I would learn!"

It hung there in the closet
While she was dying. Mother's red dress.
Like a gash in the row
Of dark, old clothes
She had worn away her life in.

Her last words to me were these:
"Do me the honor, Millie,
Of not following in my footsteps.
Promise me that."

I promised.
She caught her breath.
Then Mother took her turn
In death.

As you explore your shadow in this dimension, pay attention to the rules you've made for yourself about how you're supposed to nurture. Look for those secret trade-offs you make without getting informed consent. If you find yourself being self-critical, your shadow may be trying to teach you a new rule, "If you don't feel it, don't give it."

Self-Reflection

Nurturance is an area of great conflict for many women on the job. Estimate where you fit on the nurturance continuum. Keep in mind that it's your work-related behavior that you're measuring here.

STRENGTH: I find it easy to support others at work. I take care of myself. I often provide training or suggestions for others. Co-workers seek me out when they need support, and I can say yes or no depending on my resources at the time.

SHADOW: I have so much responsibility for the welfare of others at work, I can't focus on my job. I'm the only one who remembers special occasions and instigates a celebration. I'm frequently involved in helping a "wounded bird" at my office. / I expect others to take care of themselves and don't provide support for anyone. It's not my job to nurture.

Time For Yourself

What is your nurturing style at work? Is this dimension one you've learned to underplay? Do you feel comfortable supporting others whether they are "above" or "below" you? Are you aware of ways others have nurtured, or failed to nurture you in your growth?

The following tips provide some steps you can take to dive into this dimension of your feminine presence. Choose a few for more exploration.

• NURTURE AT WORK by taking good care of yourself. (Take your lunch break and eat something that's tasty and good for you; stay home when you're sick; make your physical environment as comfortable as possible.)

When you take care of yourself first, you have energy to nurture others genuinely. List some ways you nurture yourself on the job or in relation to your work.

• Name the feelings you've had if you've been the object of invasive caretaking at work. Write them in your journal under the heading "How it feels to be suffocated by co-dependent behavior." If you have the feeling that you're always in debt to someone for her or his supportiveness, you may be on the right track. Many women are much more comfortable giving than taking. Caretaking can creep into places where it doesn't belong. The shadow side of the nurturer feels invasive and sticky as uninvited "help" imposed at work. Do you know someone whose behavior I just described? This is co-dependency, not nurturance. How do you feel when you're around this person? Write about these feelings in your journal.

• Learn to talk clearly about your nurturing behavior. "I want to do this for you and I expect nothing in return," might be a good place to start. If you can't honestly say this, determine what you do want and ask for it directly. In the competitive work world, men may interpret your attempts at nurturance as manipulative ploys to "get something" you're not asking for directly. The "good ol' boy" system works on trade-offs, which differs from nurturing. It's a challenge to communicate new ideas about feminine nurturing.

• Support other women in nurturing ways. This can be done very simply by kind comments or by creating space for them. If you find that your female colleagues are consistently interrupted by men, or can't get a word in edgewise, you can say things like, "I don't think Janet had a chance to finish her thought," or, "Cindy, what do you think about that idea?"

• Include others in activities that have been assigned to you when that's possible. Everybody benefits. They get training and credit. You get help. Make a list of ways you might do this in the near future.

• Women make a real difference in the work environment by attending to birthdays or other special occasions that their masculine counterparts have ignored for years. This is tricky business because it can become a sexist drag. The goal is to make the environment one everyone likes to work in. Little kindnesses can transform a work site. Women may be the mentors here, but men can assume equal responsibility.

- USE YOUR CAPACITY FOR NURTURANCE to understand and appreciate differences in others. List some times this has worked for you.

- THINK ABOUT THE WAYS you take care of others on the job. List five things you've done during the past week that seem like healthy nurturance. Write about what it felt like to do these things.

- IDENTIFY WAYS YOU MAY be "strategically nurturing." Think about your motivation for doing these things. Is your behavior manipulative or co-dependent? If you asked directly for what you want, what would it be? Does something feel too scary for making a direct request? Write about how you learned to relate to people in this way.

- WHEN YOU CHOOSE TO NURTURE, maintain awareness of what you're doing so that you don't move into unconscious co-dependence. Recognize the difference between nurturing and a co-dependent attempt to control. Write about an example of each.

- CLEARLY ACKNOWLEDGE appropriate nurturing tendencies in others, especially men.

Nurturance is a powerful and constructive dimension that women who are in touch with their feminine power can promote in the workplace. But it doesn't usually translate directly from home to work without some conscious thought about what's appropriate and what results in exploitation or uninvited caretaking. Write your thoughts about this dimension in your journal. Think of at least one example where you have expressed it well and one where you wish you had done it differently. Do you like the way you offer nurturance now? If you think some fine tuning is in order, clarify your thoughts by writing them in your journal.

Check the Self-Assessment on page 27 and update your rating.

Nurturance Goes to Work

In our culture, women are the designated nurturers. As we go to work in masculine environments, we can bring this dimension with us if we haven't abandoned it in ourselves. If you've shelved this dimension as part of surviving and succeeding, now is a good time to take a second look. You have a great opportunity to make a positive difference where you work if you can find ways to share the wealth rather than continuing in your role as primary nurturer.

In order to nurture others, we first have to take care of ourselves.

This means teaching men who have customarily operated in competitive, non-nurturing ways that a different approach has merit. Participative management, team building, and informal communication networks all require nurturing skills. These "new" management skills, which experts see as solutions to our current business crises, require the open give and take of connected relationships. Nurturance is already "in." We need only put into words the importance of this feminine gift at work. Talking about nurturance as a legitimate part of business interaction takes it out of the realm of motherhood and cookie baking. And we can learn to ask for nurturance in return.

This process may begin as "trade-offs," which men understand very well. But nurturance is an emotional connection, not just a mechanical one. It can provide a basis for mutual trust when the give and take is balanced, but when women do all the giving, the old exploitive patterns continue.

For men to feel comfortable nurturing, they have to know they're not going to be asked to give everything up. When asking for support and nurturance, you can say things like, "I'd like your support with _____, but I don't need it with _____."

Or, "Give me a hand with _____ and I can take responsibility for _____."

The teaching mode can be useful at times. You can clue in a male colleague with something like, "So and so is having a tough time with her new assistant. Some coaching from you about how to deal with him could help her out." Giving and receiving nurturance is a legitimate need for both sexes. For women to take most of the responsibility for this process doesn't work at the office any more than it does at home.

As you try to create ways to nurture yourself and find a balance in nurturing others, you're likely to confront two powerful unconscious barriers that are rugged but elusive.

Woman = Mother is the first of these two. The feminine presence grows out of female biology—our child-bearing capacity. Mothers shape our sense of who we are and have a lot to do with how we relate to authority figures. Even though you don't always, or even usually, wear your mother hat to work, you may be seen in a "mother role" by others. Whether you like it or not, if authority is part of your job, people's responses to you are colored by the quality of their relationships with their mothers.

Your feminine presence stirs up feelings in others that are unresolved in their relationships with their mothers—hatred, resentment, and fear on the negative side; yearning, admiration, and love in a more positive vein. And this is before you even *do* anything. No wonder the presence of women prompts agitation and discomfort in some. These feelings bubble around outside awareness and may be expressed as disagreement or resistance to something you say which, if proposed by a male colleague or superior, would be heard and accepted as routine.

"Watch out! The bitch is on the rampage again!" is not a serious response to a female manager's attempts to work with her staff. When you experience automatic resistance to your ideas, especially those involving authority, it is useful to wonder whether "mother issues" are lurking in the listeners. You can help clear up some of the hostility projected onto you in two ways: 1) try to avoid getting hooked by your own anger, and 2) talk plainly about what you're trying to accomplish, providing as much information as possible so that others can share responsibility.

"Dads," male authority figures, certainly create authority issues for co-workers to deal with as well, but they are different. Men are expected to be in charge at work—as women are expected to be in charge at home. For women to be in charge in both places disturbs some men deeply. It helps if they can see you as someone trying to get a job done—not as another mother.

Do	*Don't*
Learn to use authority with comfort and clarity.	Create or add to images that the work group is a "family."
Confront assumptions that you are in charge of nurturing (mothering) at work.	Allude to other women as "mom types."
Be clear in asserting the limits and boundaries of your responsibilities.	Habitually take on "wounded birds" or "ride to their rescue."
Acquire sensitivity to others' fears about you as an authority figure.	Rely on other women to take care of you.
Allow yourself to be as powerful as you are.	Assume that other women are like your mother.

Men Are Powerful—Women Are Silent Caretakers is the second of the nurturance-related barriers. The arrival of a woman on the management team is disturbing at many levels. Do you lower the value of the real estate on this block? What can a man expect? He knows the rules with the guys; will you know how to play?

You probably do, or you wouldn't have made it to this level. But whether you choose to or not is a whole different story. It's at this point that your core strength can serve you best and when you are least likely to hear it or be able to reach in to it. The pressure to act in masculine ways, rather than simply to cooperate with masculine energy, is overwhelming.

Our views are colored by traditions that portray men as powerful and women as obedient—or at least silent—caretakers. What may have started as partnership for survival when most people lived on the land has become lopsided in a way that overloads the masculine and devalues the feminine. This way of looking at the world doesn't take into account individual differences, feelings, values, talents, or needs. It is reflected in an economy in which male high school dropouts make more money than women high school graduates with some college. One percent of women are in the top income bracket that encompasses 20% of white male earners. Even with increased emphasis on equal rights, women's incomes are still significantly below those of men, approximately 62 cents on the dollar. The fact that more single women head households than ever before has had little impact on the American image that men are—or should be—the breadwinners.

The assumption is that men are the powerful, competent ones simply by virtue of their masculinity. Many men believe this and act accordingly. The image is even more potent because women buy into it. We've catered to it by learning to be helpless or by avoiding appearing smarter or more competent than men. Middle-aged women can recall advice like, "If you have a romantic interest in a man, don't let him know when you get the answer before he does," and "Men aren't attracted to women who are smarter than they are." Early this century, satirist Dorothy Parker said it simply: "Men don't make passes at girls who wear glasses!"

Carol Gilligan's research with young women tells us that this process continues as part of our culture. Eleven-year-old girls who were outspoken about their feelings and opinions blur out and become indefinite at sixteen. By junior high, they're sophisticated about seeming less intelligent than they really are.[4]

Growing awareness of the feminine presence in business magnifies the insecure man's fear of losing control. What will happen if this new, different entity becomes powerful? Attempts to prevent this scary possibility show themselves in countless "innocent," seemingly rational ways. To deal with these blocks:

Do	*Don't*
Expect to exercise your authority with confidence.	Collude with the "women serve" mentality.
Confront expectations that you will defer to males who have less authority than you have.	Expect men to be as skilled at personal communication as you are.
Learn to deal with masculine vulnerability to women in authority.	Be manipulated by masculine ineptness at traditionally feminine tasks.
Look at assignments you're given to be sure they're right for your work level.	Take the path of least resistance as a way of avoiding conflict.
Confront unspoken expectations that you'll do the caretaking.	Make the coffee unless everyone shares equally and/or it's your turn.

The feminine urge to do what will stir up the least trouble—to avoid conflict—is a powerful one. (Making coffee is a classic example.) Coupled with masculine expectations that men should be in charge, it contributes to an almost impenetrable barrier at work. If you need to, take an assertiveness training course to learn to confront unspoken expectations that you will defer to males and provide caretaking services. Learning to do this is a skill, not an inborn talent. The more conscious you become of how this barrier slides into place for you, the better you can be at trying to neutralize it. Nurturance doesn't mean staying in second position.

Nurturance does include saying "Hello," in the morning or inquiring about someone's health or family. You have many opportunities during the day to offer support to a co-worker, your boss or others in your organization. You can do this by listening or by "reflecting"—saying in different words—a feeling they've expressed: "I know you're really (stressed, angry, hurt) about that. I'm sorry to hear it."

Your emotional presence is more important than "doing" nurturing things. Learn the difference between "merging" into someone else's space—unconsciously taking on a task or an emotional load that isn't really yours—and connecting in a supportive, intentionally nurturing way. You can be supportive and at the same time communicate to others your confidence that they can manage their own business. When you do this, the interaction between you empowers you both.

Some things to keep in mind as you work with this dimension include these guidelines for nurturing on the job:

- Know where you're going. Suzanne was free to nurture because she knew her goals and how she would reach them. Helping others only added to her ability to take care of herself.

- Be explicit about what you're giving and what you do or don't expect in return.
- Take the risk of being "had" once in a while. You're not a fool if that happens to you.
- Don't give more than you want to.
- If one of your gifts backfires, try to understand why. Do you need to confront or clarify?
- Take care of yourself before burnout hits.
- Learn to tell the difference between real need and manipulation. One clue is whether you feel good about helping someone out, or whether you feel exploited.

SUMMARY

Nurturance is intricately woven through many aspects of your feminine presence. It's so much a part of feminine behavior that it is taken for granted. As you become more conscious of how you nurture or how you get stuck in your co-dependent shadow, you can learn better ways to take care of yourself. If you're a person who long ago gave up on nurturing as a bad bet, it may be possible for you to revisit some possibilities. Choosing to nurture is easier if you're comfortable setting limits when you've done enough.

Business has much to gain if we can learn to work in ways that are self-nourishing as well as supportive of those around us.

Affinity

Strength is assumed to be a singular thing. Standing alone. Autonomy. The ability to make it on one's own is the standard of success in our male-dominated culture. But competition does violence to connections. You can't compete and cooperate at the same time, and connections are rarely the same when there's been a winner and a loser. Sometimes, it's hard not to be seduced into the fray.

But femininity is about connectedness and relationship—affinity. In her poem, "For strong women," Marge Piercy lays it out very clearly:

> What comforts her is others loving
> her equally for the strength and for the weakness
> from which it issues, lightning from a cloud.
> Lightning stuns. In rain, the clouds disperse.
> Only water of connection remains,
> flowing through us. Strong is what we make
> each other. Until we are all strong together,
> a strong woman is a woman strongly afraid.[1]

For the feminine, strong doesn't mean alone. *Our* strength is in relationship. And this strength grows when others affirm us. When cooperation rather than competition channels the work flow, we can give and receive support and encouragement and feel nourished rather than depleted. At some time or another, everybody seeks the recognition and satisfaction that personal success brings. That success is sweeter when we can hear the applause from friends and colleagues, and know that we didn't sacrifice our personal connections to achieve it.

Janet L. Surrey offers these basic elements as central to the self in women:

1) We're interested in and pay attention to others, which forms the base for emotional connection and the ability to empathize.

2) We expect a mutual process in which *both* people have empathy. The sharing of experience leads to a heightened development of self and others.

3) We expect relationships to be mutually sensitive and responsible. This reciprocity provides the starting point for the growth of empowerment and self-knowledge.

Emphasis on individuality, competing, and getting ahead collides with our needs for connection. At work, we often learn to sacrifice our tendencies toward togetherness and forge on "professionally," regardless of our reticence. And we get ulcers, headaches, and bad temper in the process. If we decide it's not worth the trouble, then we are left to feel isolated. But if we value connection too greatly, we settle for less than we really want so as not to hurt our friends and colleagues on the way up.

As women, we tend to define ourselves in our relationships with others. What we get from and give to each other enriches or threatens our sense of well-being. And so our emotional antennae scan a room to check the climate. Without thinking about it consciously, we sense the emotional vibes—whether others are mad, tense, excited, or open. Comfort, trust, and security rest in the give and take of our relationships.

This isn't weakness or a lesser way of being than the more visible male model that touts autonomy and separateness. It is only different. As we get to know and value this dimension, we can encourage affinity as a contributor to our work life rather than feeling ashamed of its presence in our make-up. Closeness isn't a whim. It's central.

And we need to be assertive that connective values can be valuable in a work environment.

In general, affinity includes these ideas:

• Relationships are important, not just convenient. Interconnection feels good—it's reassuring and valuable. Choices may be based on who's doing something rather than on the task itself. How things turn out for both people makes a difference. It matters that relationships continue, that we live with our actions and their impact on others who are important to us. There is no expedient goal—like profit or promotion—that justifies acts and decisions regardless of their personal consequences.

Closeness isn't

a whim.

It's central.

• Cooperation is comfortable and almost always preferable to competition. The price of winning (often the torn fabric of relationship) leads to fear of abandonment, of disconnection from the defeated one who might be a friend or close associate. It's enjoyable to collaborate even when that means sharing the rewards. Of course, this doesn't mean all the time, or for every woman. Individual work is important and meaningful too.

• Emotions—our own and others'—are an important part of life, including worklife. Empathy, "feeling" someone else's feelings, is an important part of our make-up. In our relationships at work, we acknowledge the emotional aspect as significant rather than pretending we're robots. Even though we need to use judgment about what we choose to express, it's unreal to think that we leave our emotions at the threshold on our way in the office door.

• Children and family life are important. The workplace has responsibility to make it possible to pace one's job or career to produce, nurture, and train the next generation. Even though many men shoulder shared responsibility and commitment to family life, most working women continue to take primary responsibility here. Consequently, work decisions tend to take second place to heartfelt family needs and priorities at times in women's

lives. This may be true even when work feels more interesting and rewarding than dealing with the never-ending
responsibilities at home.

This isn't an exhaustive list. And it's not exclusive to
women. But it offers the flavor of affinity in contrast to the
status quo assumptions of autonomy, competition, and
hierarchical order.

Handed down through unending generations of
women who've been excluded from power, the gifts of
affinity have much to offer today's chronically shifting
workplace. Although connection appears to get in the way
of expediency at times, it can make for much more
humane decisions. Personal communication, trust, and
openness where they are warranted weave organizations
together when hierarchies aren't flexible enough to bend
with new complexities.

Decisions that seem simple and logical at the executive level can have far-reaching effects on both personal
and work relationships. In a Sacramento Valley manufacturing company that operates under seasonal pressure, an
executive decision to add an hour to both ends of the
workday would have been handled very differently if
attention had been given to how personal connections
help the company work. The decision was made and
announced two days before the longer work day was to
begin. Apparently, little if any thought was given to the
impact on the workers—on their childcare arrangements,
carpools or other issues related to personal support systems.

In addition to the immediate personal stress and strain
it caused employees, most of whom were women, the
new schedule negatively affected important work relationships. Adding an hour to the end of each day required
rescheduling for management coverage. It wiped out the
brief period during the week when all management personnel could be on site at the same time to meet with

each other. A year's work in team building—a conscious focus on affinity—was undermined overnight. If this had been a response to an emergency and had been announced as such, employees would have taken it in stride. It wasn't. There was plenty of time for input and prior planning by the management teams, and to allow adequate lead time for employees to make the shift.

It wasn't the decision that was bad. Many people were delighted about the possibility of more work. It was the lack of attention to personal impact that was insensitive. When confronted with the morale implications of this move, the executive director had a hard time understanding. "Surely the managers can work this out with their people," he said, "can't they?"

The need for connection has been seen as a problem rather than an asset in traditionally organized businesses, even though among support staff or service providers, affinity clearly makes the office run more smoothly. The office wife/secretary who knows everybody on the floor can get things done through her connections that wouldn't happen otherwise. Research about work shows that social needs are a primary reason that people work, but this factor still doesn't rank high with decisionmakers. The bottom line typically takes precedence over all other factors when organizational decisions are at stake—a very short-sighted view that neglects feminine strengths.

Secretaries have greased organizational skids for years, intuitively operating through affinity. They quietly maneuver organizations with their own cooperative networks to find unorthodox, feminine solutions to all kinds of problems, while bypassing formal power structures. Traditionally, the bosses receive credit for the success and the secretaries end up invisible and underpaid in the support staff ranks.

Since it's contrary to a traditional competitive style, getting things done cooperatively doesn't necessarily gain positive attention in an authoritarian organization. It may even be seen as "weak." When this feminine process blossoms at the management level, people begin to notice and may become critical of unpredictable, non-hierarchical approaches. "I believe in hierarchy!" a female CEO whose style was quite traditional said to me. When her mid-management group attempted to use informal, connective pathways to work through knotty conflicts in her company, their easy way of getting along threatened her sense of order. It was not an acceptable way to do business there, even though the chief was demanding "better communication." That situation was not likely to improve— because the CEO was unable to see her own conflict.

Hierarchy is essential in military organizations and in families where parents need to take care of young children. But in situations that require collective creativity and effort, "flatter" organizational models work better. The art of management is in knowing which model works better for which task. Here again, balance is the key.

Shauna Granger, the first woman promoted into the all-male management ranks of her organization, described her move into a difficult situation. After getting her feet wet, she found herself repeatedly propelled into the role of troubleshooter. She described one particular assignment that had caused the company difficulty for some time. "I knew that those folks weren't going to trust anyone. The only thing I could do was work with them one on one— each in a different way according to their personality, until I could get them to communicate with me. I decided to emphasize training and worked with each person on whatever skills they wanted to develop."

This very personalized, feminine approach, based on sensitivity and excellent communication skills, worked beautifully where less personal, power-oriented approaches had failed. Shauna's affinity and honest concern for the well-being of the employees helped her to move into the situation in ways that other managers hadn't chosen. She was low key and cooperative and relied on her capacity to relate to each individual—which she took the time to do.

Shauna had no need to emphasize that she was the boss. Everybody knew it. Her manner supported the emotional well-being of the workers, mostly women. They had stymied several control-oriented male managers by stonewalling and endless bickering. Because this manager dealt with them individually, they were much more willing to cooperate. Although she spent lots of time and energy working individually with people, the investment paid high dividends in the long run.

Women who are willing to speak out for their feminine needs can be strong agents for change.

Our femininity expresses that part of us that holds and nurtures a deep sense of women as the carriers and protectors of new human life. In the workplace, this can simply mean taking the time and energy to relate to people, taking their emotional well-being seriously. The patriarchal struggle to get to the top of the heap often dams the flow of concern for the importance of the interpersonal connection.

Strong feelings for children and family life feed working women's nightmares as we try to balance home and work. We're torn between our connections at home and our responsibilities there and the demands and challenges at work. We live with impossible schedules and painful emotional stretches that perpetuate a chronic guilt state. We adapt to work patterns that were designed for male workers with stay-at-home wives, although this pattern now fits only a small percentage (I've seen figures that spread from 7% to 20%) of all families. Men's needs have changed, too, without wives at home. The work schedule has to change for them, as well. It's in this area that traditional attitudes toward working people have to shift, but change will happen only if it's pushed.

In the meantime, it helps if we honor our feelings and

talk about them. Responsibility for the well-being of the next generation doesn't belong to you alone. Calling attention to the hardships imposed on family life by company decisions raises awareness of decisionmakers. Even small things, like rules about whether or not it's O.K. to have photos of your children in your workspace—which you might or might not choose to do—communicate an attitude about affinity.

Women who are connected with their inner experience and are willing to speak out for their feminine needs can be strong agents for change. Men who are or have been active parents are excellent allies. Affinity, working cooperatively together to inform employers of the need and suggest solutions, is one way to make a difference.

THE SHADOW SIDE

Affinity's shadow hopelessly confuses our loving, loyal connections with feelings of guilt and obligation. When that happens, we disconnect from our centers and live by our efforts to win approval. It becomes second nature to be more in tune with someone else's priorities than our own.

Our needs for connection are so powerful, we sometimes lose track of who we are in attempts to meet them.

Marie's story is a familiar one. She shared this with me in her struggle to return to her own center. The shadow side of affinity had overtaken this competent woman's emotional life. Abuse of her capacity for flexibility permitted her to bend and twist, adapt—and deny herself. She hated the thought of becoming another statistic. She couldn't tolerate subjecting her children to the predictable wounds from the divorce that would end her unhappy marriage.

Marie had organized her life around her husband and

children and tried to will it into being all right. This pattern had moved beyond healthy concern and nurturance. For several years she had negated her deep personal pain, shut down receptivity to her inner feelings. The shadow side of affinity had intruded to the exclusion of her other feelings that were just as valid.

One morning, Marie was abruptly awakened by a phone call. She finished the call and replaced the receiver. Even while she stuck her head under the pillow, images of her sensual mauve and seafoam bedroom, light streaming through the shutters to caress the satin coverlet, wouldn't go away. She and Dan had worked for years to create their beautiful home. It was her pride and joy.

She hoped the phone didn't rouse the kids. She needed a few minutes to contain the wild roar in her brain.

Dan had left for work an hour ago. Now he was coming home.

"I rolled the car. It's totalled," his shaky voice said on the phone.

When she heard Dan's voice, she tried to sound awake, as though she'd stayed up after he left. She replied with whatever people say at times like this. "Oh, honey. How awful! Are you O.K.?"

She had gone back to bed that morning, and nearly every morning for the previous month. She was depressed, not tired. And she couldn't believe her internal response to Dan's accident. She had to admit the truth to herself. She was disappointed that he hadn't been killed. And she was mad at him for wrecking "her" car. She wanted to throw up—to purge herself of her vicious thoughts. She was horrified by her own feelings.

The shock of Dan's accident brought Marie's shadow into the light. Her wish that her husband had been killed oozed from darkness through her denial. She knew she had to do something about her life—to give up pretending that this relationship would work, to admit that her need for connection imprisoned her. Ugly, brutal, terrifying as it was—that revelation was a gift from her shadow. She could not continue to live the lie that if she just worked at it hard enough this marriage could survive.

Affinity casts its shadow at work as well as in our personal lives. Anne loved her job as executive secretary. She had mastered it years ago and from time to time she considered moving on to a management track. In fact, her friends who had done the same encouraged her, brought her announcements of job openings, and one even offered her a job. She knew her boss depended on her. He had been generous with her when she was struggling to make ends meet after her divorce. She didn't ever ask him how he would feel about her leaving, but she felt that would put him in a real bind. When he asked her to move over so he could promote a younger woman to her position she was devastated. She blamed him. It took a long time for her to look at her own part in this bitter tale.

Immobilized in her feelings of appreciation and loyalty for her boss, Anne ignored her own inner promptings. She squelched her needs and didn't risk checking out what her boss had in mind. Even if he had not wanted her to leave, she could have prepared for an exit in such a way that it wouldn't have been abandonment. This relationship wasn't reciprocal, but Anne didn't know it. *Affinity is not servitude.*

At work, when we live on the shadow side of affinity, we find ourselves doing all those stereotyped feminine things that lead to self-hate. We're nice to people we don't like, say "yes" when we mean "no," and bend to things we disagree with in order to avoid conflict.

As we try to move from work situations that are familiar but limiting, this shadow casts a dark obstruction in our way. A friend shared with me recently that she needed to look for new office space to set up her own business but had been fiddling around for several weeks, having a hard time shifting into action. She acknowledged her hesitancy: "I'm afraid to stand on my own in my business where I've always shared office space. It's time to move on, and I'm very reluctant to look for space downtown because I don't know anyone I can share with. It's scary!"

Need for connection is so powerful, we sometimes lose our individuality to it. Chronic self-denial of this sort creates physical symptoms—such as headaches and gastro-intestinal distress—as the true self screams for release. Depression is a predictable byproduct too. When affinity's shadow hovers indefinitely, we begin to hate our jobs and everybody there, as well as ourselves.

Affinity is not servitude.

Dealing with people who are in this place is very frustrating because it's impossible to know what they really think or feel. Their niceness or care-taking seems like it should be comforting, but being around them feels more like drowning than being nurtured or supported.

If you find yourself immobilized so that you have a hard time initiating a move or a project on your own, your shadow side is lurking. Relationships are important and we grow by working within them. But we also need to be able to move on our own. If everything you do has to be done in connection, it's worth asking yourself what feels so frightening for you.

The shadow side of affinity is particularly dangerous because it enfolds the feminine stereotype with great comfort. It makes room for timid, indecisive, inexpressive women who are too frightened to look at their own feelings. We can live our whole lives here and never upset anybody.

SELF-REFLECTION

Affinity is a complex dimension affecting several different issues. The main focus includes all those things we feel and do to honor human connections at work. It could be the simple gesture of saying "Hello" in the morning or the complicated process of organizing a childcare center. All flow from the center of femininity and are likely to go against the grain in many work environments.

Where do you fit on this dimension? Use the following suggestions to help you make this self-assessment.

STRENGTH: I'm comfortable with the way I deal with connection at work. I shift without too much stress from home to work and back again. I deal with my emotions well at work and express them when I need to. I can compete as needed and cooperate with others easily.

SHADOW: I'm almost always in conflict between "business-like" ways of relating and how I really feel. I feel like a wooden woman most of the time. / I'm constantly torn between home and work and hate the pain of it. / I can't work independently. I collapse under individual responsibility.

Time For Yourself

If you live fully in your womanhood, issues of affinity create constant conflict in work environments that elevate individualistic values. As you understand this more clearly, you can make conscious decisions about how to deal with the chronic stress that results. For one thing, it helps to know that it's not just you. You may not be able to change much of what happens in the work setting, but you can change the expectations you have for yourself about how to manage.

• NOTE IN YOUR JOURNAL the situations at work in which you find yourself in conflict about affinity. (Examples include: Pain about having to confront someone who's a friend; competing with a friend for a promotion; deciding to refuse a promotion to spend more time with the kids; returning to work shortly after giving birth.)

• MAKE A LIST OF DECISIONS you've dealt with that hurt or supported your affinity dimension. List the connected approach on one side and the separatist approach on the other (part-time work so you can be with your kids vs. full-time so you don't get left behind on your career track; honesty about your feelings vs. voicing the party line; involving co-workers in doing a project vs. doing it yourself for all the credit).

• LIST WAYS THAT YOU COLLABORATE rather than compete at work (serve as co-chair rather than chair, include others in important decisionmaking steps even though their job titles might not be equal with yours, job-sharing).

• LIST WAYS YOUR CONNECTIVE NEEDS and feelings support your effectiveness at work (ease of relating to others, capacity for empathy, good communication skills, etc.).

• OBSERVE WHETHER OR NOT men and women in your office behave differently in this dimension. If so, how? Name the feelings that come up for you when you ignore pulls toward affinity because they don't fit your work environment (sadness over loss, feelings of hyprocrisy, emotional numbness).

• DESCRIBE IN YOUR JOURNAL two occasions at work when strong emotions have interfered with your ability to work. How did you handle the situation (cry in the bathroom, leave work, explode, stuff your feelings)? Think about ways you could honor your feelings, support yourself, get support from others. Write some suggestions in your journal.

• IN YOUR JOURNAL, describe as many ways as you can that your shadow side comes to work with you in this dimension. How do you find yourself being compliant rather than dealing with conflict in a work relationship? Are you immobilized in some way because if you make a move you'll hurt someone? Do you give too much value to a relationship that may or may not be reciprocal?

• LIST THREE WAYS you organize your work life to accommodate family needs (career choice, flexible scheduling, delaying a promotion, part-time work). Include in each item a statement that describes how you feel about doing this—both the strong side and the shadow side.

• WRITE YOUR FAVORITE self-support technique for neutralizing work-home conflict stress (assertiveness about sharing childcare responsibility, enough good childcare, acknowledgment that you're a good-enough parent). Ask a co-worker what her favorite self-support technique is. Write it down if you like it, and see if you can add another as well.

• NOTE IN YOUR JOURNAL three things you've learned from someone you know who is able to be effective at work and maintain her relationships in a positive way. If you can, take the opportunity to talk with this person about how she does this and what issues arise for her.

As you work to sort out where you fit in this dimension, give yourself time to reflect on how you really feel about these issues. It's hard to sift through how much is really you and how much has to do with adaptations you've made to get by at work. You may want to come back to this dimension after you've finished all the others. If that's the case, make a note in your journal to remind yourself.

Now that you've explored the affinity dimension, return to page 27 and see if your Self-Assessment needs to be brought up to date.

AFFINITY GOES TO WORK

Most of the organizations in which we work are patterned after the military. Hierarchies and bureaucracies evolved to remove the personal element from tasks—especially to dehumanize the military business of killing or being killed. The feminine presence threatens this leftover, stubborn attempt to sterilize the business environment. If the needs of individuals are taken seriously, the old rules about "disinterest" are no longer adequate guidelines for decisionmaking. Increased participation blurs right and wrong.

Women's ways are different, and that can be a contribution, not a barrier, at work as well as at home. Do what you can to bring the differences out in the open and show how they balance the equally important contributions that men make. The goal is to work in partnership, to benefit from the new energy and creativity that combined resources can generate.

Organizations that welcome and support feminine contributions increase their flexibility and resilience. In doing so, they improve their chances to survive today's chaotic business challenges. Characteristics that such organizations value include:

- Participative management
- Cooperation over competition
- Job-sharing
- Flexible scheduling
- Shared rewards and responsibilities
- Shared decisionmaking
- Personal development
- Concern with family well-being
- Environmental concerns

When you work in an organization that routinely relies on the above strategies, a different basis of support is available for you than when you work in a traditional hierarchical company or agency. In either case, it is to your advantage to develop to their fullest your communication skills and your capacity to work collectively with others. This is a lifetime project, but every little bit helps. Learn to confront supportively, to deal with differences and conflicts in a personal, rather than a rule-based way. Look for, point out, and accept opportunities to work *with* others, to share rewards as well as responsibilities. Initiate suggestions for shared projects or responsibilities.

In response to a barrier that can be called **Women's Ways Are Different (And Therefore Unacceptable)**, here are some guidelines.

Do	*Don't*
Pay attention to your responses to what's happening, even if they don't match the majority's.	Assume that men work the same way you do.
Work at affirming what you want and need.	Jump to closure too quickly just because that's what is expected.
Speak. Talk about what you want and need associated with work style.	Capitulate because linear logic seems so clear that it must be right.
Team with other women.	Be embarrassed because you see and say things differently.
Hold other women in high regard. Support them when you can.	
Acknowledge and suppport men who support women.	

Support others who are trying to work collectively—in job sharing or team approaches. It's especially important to support "new men," those who are willing to risk the rejection of their peers to work in partnership with women. Tell them that you appreciate their trust and openness—that it makes a difference. Sharing increases the complexity of the workplace by doing away with the fantasy of "clear lines of communication." But it humanizes work at the same time.

Support other women. Stay in contact with your own prejudices about bimbos, airheads, and flakes. When your shadow side wants to take over and elevate you or your friend at another woman's expense, take a look at what's motivating you. Find ways to let your gentler aspects connect with women who have hardened themselves as a way to survive the rat race.

The goal is to work in partnership, to benefit from the new energy and creativity that combined resources can generate.

Find ways to speak out about "women's issues"— childcare, flexible scheduling, parental leave, and comparable worth. Why are the life-and-death issues about the well-being of the human race and the planet called domestic (women's) issues? Stop acting like children are the special province of women and include fathers more when they're present. Most men have kids. Appeal to them: "Would you want the mother of *your* kids gone ten hours a day?" Read Arlie Hochschild's *The Second Shift: Working Parents and the Revolution at Home* and share it with others, especially your male colleagues. Promote the idea that we're all in this together and that the welfare of our children is of highest importance.

Create a substantial support network for yourself and others at work and outside work.

Alice's way (pages 106-107) of freezing her needs for connectedness was a survival tactic used by many women who broke new ground in the work world a decade or more ago. It hurt her and limited the people she supervised. However, as more women assume more authority at work, the richness of the feminine can pour into our corporate world more freely.

Your interest in closeness, in making connections, brings powerful feminine energy to the place where you work. As you become comfortable and feel strong in these aspects of your femininity, you can master turning them into contributions where you work. Your gift for relationship will feel like strength, not weakness or inadequacy or something to be ashamed of. As you understand more about yourself, you can learn to rely on these dimensions for self-soothing and comfort. You can share this part of yourself with others who value the productive energy of relationships at work.

The increasing complexity of today's work scene makes the need for "high touch"—the personal connection—ever more relevant. As you embrace this part of you, you can stay afloat with good support. It will no longer be necessary to submerge the feminine principle.

SUMMARIZE YOUR INNER WORK

Each of the dimensions in this "water" section has been outlined individually. As you worked through them, you could see that they are most meaningful in relation to other people. In order to be receptive, someone else must give you something. To nurture, another must receive your care and support. As you continue your exploration of these dimensions, ask other women how they recognize and support these qualities in themselves at work. Heighten your awareness of constructive ways to express this part of your womanhood in your daily work life. Acknowledge others when they flow from this element.

Marge Piercy's image of strong women is that "Only water of connection remains, flowing through us. Strong is what we make each other. . . ." Janet Surrey tells us that ". . . it becomes as important to understand as to be understood, to empower as well as to be empowered."[2] Anne Rudin, Ellen Steele, and Shauna Granger, women whose stories fill this section, know that working through the water of connection is powerful and fulfilling. Getting things done in ways that empower others—rather than tearing the feminine web by violating the connected ways women work—feels much more fulfilling than getting the job done at any cost.

Take some time now to review each of the flowing dimensions in this section and highlight areas for future attention. In your journal, describe how each lives in you—both as strengths and shadows. A brief verbal description or drawing for each of the four dimensions will help you focus your thoughts and feelings.

You're now half-way through the thirteen dimensions. This is a good time to review all the writing you've done in your journal. Take your time. Add notes or drawings where you've gained more understanding. Highlight places where you still have questions or loose ends.

Linger in the water as long as you like. Bathe and soothe your harried soul in the richness of feminine connection. It is a healing element, one to reach for when the intensity of the next fiery section blazes too hotly.

FIRE

PASSION AT WORK

Fire: The Element

olten energy roars beneath all that forms at the surface of the earth. Feminine passion, individually speaking, is just as powerful. With some skill and finesse we can nourish, rather than suffocate, the energy that glows in *Sexuality*, *Creativity*, and *Aggression*. That way, we neither smother the fire inside us nor reduce ourselves to burnout before our time.

A woman with drive and commitment doesn't do well with restrictive comments like, "This is the way we've always done it."

We all know that the potentially destructive power of feminine passion scorches sensitivities at work very easily. In fact, it is so frightening that we've learned to keep it under control—turned down so low we freeze ourselves. Male bosses may be known, and excused, for their rages, or have reputations for being bastards to work for. But they're tolerated, even respected. The same behavior quickly raises hackles and earns a woman outright rejection—as well as the label "bitch," or worse. Feminine fire is so hot to handle that when it flares, it's likely to be quickly doused.

The fiery, passionate feminine doesn't fit neatly into bureaucratic structures or stay quietly within arbitrary boundaries. A woman with drive and commitment to make something happen doesn't do well with restrictive comments like, "This is the way we've always done it."

Containment, peacemaking, and collaboration are part, but not all, of the true nature of the feminine. The fiery side is equally important. Of course we can, and need to, manage our inner fires. But we've over-controlled them for so long that we've nearly extinguished them in attempts to create a safe climate at work. It's time to ask "safe for whom?"

ANCIENT VIEWS AND MODERN PHYSICS

Fire fascinated our ancestors. Evidence tells us that in prehistoric times fire had god-like status. It danced on altars reflected in admiring eyes. Its mystical value came first; practicality for warmth and cooking occurred later.

This safe and reassuring connection with hearth and home feels warm and comfy. It's O.K. to associate heat with the security of the maternal feminine. The more primitive, more dangerous fascination with the flame is the one we shy away from. But it flickers still, somewhere in each of us.

In *Myths to Live By*, Joseph Campbell portrays some of that power.

> . . . Fire has the property of not being diminished when halved, but increased. Fire is luminous, like the sun and lightning, the only such thing on earth. Also, it is alive: in the warmth of the human body it is life itself, which departs when the body goes cold. It is prodigious in primitive traditions, it has been frequently identified with a demoness of volcanoes, who presides over an afterworld where the dead enjoy an everlasting dance in marvelously dancing volcanic flames.[1]

Wow! We'd better be careful.

Fair enough. It makes sense to be careful. It's not functional for wild demonesses to prance around the office or sexual sirens to run rampant. But it's important for each of us to know how this energy glows as part of our life force. It's unreal to think that the OFF switch is flipped forty hours a week. Where's the balance?

Three conditions permit fire to burn: 1) fuel, 2) high enough temperature to ignite it, and 3) oxygen to feed it. An explosion occurs when rapid burning causes a sudden increase in the volume of hot air. Spontaneous combustion flares when oxidation occurs in fuel. Not all substances burn in the same manner. Fire is a catalyst that changes one substance to another—sand to glass, iron to steel. Materials are fireproof when they have combined as much oxygen as possible—or when they won't unite with oxygen at ordinary temperatures.

The rules of physics that describe the conditions and properties of fire also apply to our relationships at work. It takes heat to ignite a flame, fuel to keep it going, and air to feed it. Excitement about a project, adequate support, and breathing room for creativity energize work. When inner fires don't have enough space, explosion results. Too much pressure—or not enough time and resources—leads to intense frustration and volatility. Unpleasant though it may be, explosive aggression may serve as a catalyst for change. The explosion may clarify the need for priorities. Or it may destroy the project, the organization, the process. On the other hand, suppressed over time, heat burns us out. Human energy sputters and dies when inner fires burn too fiercely or too long. When we run out of fuel, when the air supply is exhausted, we give up.

The ancients appreciated, even worshipped fire as a core element. It still is. Life is the crucible of the human spirit—and work is a central part of that life. Let's see how we can fan our personal fires—reach a kindling point, find adequate fuel and oxygen—but neither explode nor burn out in the process.

Sexuality

S hort skirts, long jackets, great legs. Passion, the life force. Excitement, magnetism, flashing eyes, a woman full of herself. A Pandora's box. Along with all our other attributes, we bring our sexuality to the workplace. We are competent and sexual, bright and sexual, responsible and sexual, moral and sexual. Sexuality is part of who we are and of how we are.

Whatever else it is—whatever else might be more convenient or less threatening—feminine sexuality is the most outward indication of the difference we bring to the places where we work. Whether we know it or not, we "think" with our bodies. A woman's sexual presence in the office is the promise of a separate way of seeing things, of solving problems, and of setting priorities. It can promise creativity and a more open agenda than masculine managers and workers may have allowed. Cancelling that sexuality—asking her to deny her curves and her fluidity—is to deny a woman her identity. One woman told me she learned to walk as if she had a steel rod in her spine and steel rods in both legs, just so that she wouldn't be "suggestive." In the context of work, transforming a woman into a configuration of steel rods deprives the office of her comfort and her talents and threatens the workplace with sameness.

> *Sensuality does not wear a watch but she always gets to the essential places on time. She is adventurous, and not particularly quiet. She was reprimanded in grade school because she couldn't sit still all day long. She needs to move. She thinks with her body. . . .*
>
> Ruth Gendler, "Sensuality"

Gender difference promises long-needed balance for male-dominated environments that diminish or deny the feminine—but only if we resist defining our sexuality as a liability. We need to understand clearly that sexual approaches, sexist dismissals, and sexual conquests are the most direct ways to maintain patriarchal control and to undermine the promise that we bring to an office.

A woman who is comfortable in her desirability can be confident in her ability, too, and will not be easily sidetracked or intimidated into abandoning her complexity in order to be just a sex object. And the men she works with can grow to respond to that confidence with the desire for proximity, cooperation, and investment in the new work vitality her difference promises.

Only the half-man who lacks confidence in his own sexuality will choose to throw all that away by reducing feminine presence to an opportunity for another meaningless sexual encounter.

Comfort and confidence are part of the same package. But let's not kid ourselves. Comfort with fire takes some doing. Most of us have received negative messages about our sexuality from childhood on, and that can make comfort in our desirability an elusive quality. We must first give ourselves permission to make that comfort a personal goal; then, we just might find that our sexual energy can be the basis for a whole new way of working.

Sensuality, sexual expression, and sexual security are central to our feminine identities, whether or not we choose to believe, as Freud did, that behavior is motivated by sexuality and aggression. How we experience these fiery intensities in our personal lives is private. But if we feel that we have to shut this part of us down, to become gender-neutral, at work, then we lose a major source of energy.

School and work are places where we've learned, sometimes the hard way, to say no to our sexuality. We've been carefully taught that we're responsible, not only for our own sexuality, but also for the sexual responses that men have to us. We've been so injured by images of feminine sexuality as shameful or dirty—and by our treatment by half-men—that healthy, energetic ways to live the promise of our difference elude us. There is something radically wrong with this picture.

Sexual issues always get the biggest response in discussions or workshops on women at work. The idea that sexuality—erotic fire—is a legitimate part of our energy even on the job invites uproar. The power of the patriarchy, the ghosts of our Victorian grandmothers, invariably scream out: "You have to pay attention to what kinds of messages you're sending." "You can't expect men to work if you're wearing a skirt up to your tokus." "You'll never be taken seriously if you're sexy," and the biggest threat of all, "You don't want to be one of those women who uses her sexuality to get ahead."

And we've all had experiences that validate these warnings. Here's an example that's still vivid two decades after it happened to me in my stint as a university counseling center director:

With more involvement than they wanted, the other therapists on the staff offered up pieces of the annual budget, and I assembled the whole. Financial planning was part of my job that I didn't like. My stomach hurt as I worked the calculator and maneuvered staff needs, represented by dollar figures, into artificial categories defined by specific, frequently confusing university regulations.

Strong, mixed feelings zinged through me on the day of the presentation. I was scared to death and felt overwhelmed with responsibility. But I was also a little exhilarated with the anticipation of wheeling and dealing with a campus-wide committee. I believed that campus psychological services—always subject to budget cuts in an academic environment—would lose much needed support if I failed in my efforts. And I couldn't wait to get the whole thing over and done with.

Nearly rigid with performance anxiety, I made it through the presentation. The all-male committee broke for lunch after I finished. They hadn't asked many questions. I had no idea what they thought or felt.

As I walked back toward my office, one of the members caught up with me. "Well, Dr. Krebs, I'll bet you're glad that's over!" he said as he smiled at me.

I was. I was very relieved. He continued, "In case you're wondering why the committee didn't respond very much, it's because we were ogling you while you presented all those boring facts and figures."

"Ogling?" It took a minute for the word to sink in. Needless to say, I was flabbergasted and spent the next few days creating clever retorts. The man thought he offered a compliment. I was appalled and furious. The budget came out O.K., but I felt bad that, at least according to this professor, the committee had discounted my efforts just because they saw me as someone they didn't have to take seriously.

Virtually every working woman can tell stories about her efforts' being ignored or seen as less because she was perceived sexually, to the exclusion of her work abilities. If she's "attractive" that has gotten in the way of her being taken seriously. If she doesn't fit the accepted standards for "looks," she may have been disregarded as unwomanly.

But it doesn't have to be that way. Granted, men have a lot to learn about treatment of women in this department. But we're in charge of our side of the equation. Our comfort with our own sexuality supports us in our ability to be whole women and makes it possible for us to deal with off-balance remarks or behavior.

In the glossary of her book, *The Passion of Being Woman*, Mary Hugh Scott defines sexuality to include "the

A woman who is comfortable in her desirability can be confident in her ability, too.

enjoyment of life moment by moment" and sharing that enjoyment with others. Our fire energy is much more than the narrow interpretation the patriarchal fathers would have us believe. As Scott asserts, it *excludes* "sexual duty in marriage, obsequious behavior, pornography, and obsession with cultural idols."

This chapter is not about being seductive or overtly sexual at the office. Nor is it about exploiting your sexual allure as a promotional strategy. It's about claiming the fire in your sexual energy unashamedly, in a self-supportive way.

Becoming a man clone, or worse yet, a sexless robot, denies a very real part of a woman's identity—and that's certainly no long-term ethical way to respond to sexism. We have to learn, from a centered place, to trust and assert our right to be who we are. And, unfortunately, this includes acquiring the necessary skills to deal with people who choose to isolate this dimension as the only one they want to see.

Although men and women increasingly share power on the job, dealing with the issue of sexuality in a real way is a new frontier. Legislation has been passed in an attempt to protect workers from sexual discrimination and harassment. In fact, the laws have made such a difference that my daughters take for granted opportunities that weren't open to me. But, unfortunately, the laws can only hold the space. They can't begin to deal with the intricate emotional relationships between women and men at work in ways that create respect and safety for the feminine presence to step into the open. As a result, both of my daughters have experienced the kind of harassment that many people think doesn't happen anymore.

Our society, especially the world of work, has changed rapidly, but traditions for relationships between women and men lag behind. Until very recently—the past thirty years—any woman in the workplace who wasn't a nun, a teacher, or a nurse was considered by many men as fair game for sexual exploitation. Customs of equal treatment and regard are still evolving, and men who've had little experience working with women as equals or superiors are still having considerable trouble with the change.

Since we humans are sexual creatures, all our relationships, including those at work, have sexual components, large or small. For the most part, these feelings aren't particularly strong and we ignore them—or perhaps note them and consider them no big deal. We can treat them as we would any other feelings: anger, fear, compassion. We don't have to act on them—but, as with any other intense feelings, we have to have confidence that we can handle them. In terms of our own feelings, the fire can flicker and flare, but we have a choice about whether or not to fan it—whether to use that energy to build a working relationship or a romantic one.

One of the reasons this subject is so volatile is that it has been unacceptable to speak of our sexual reactions. Even if we don't discuss our grief, anger, pain, or joy openly on the job, we can talk about them with our close associates and family. This is not so with sexual feelings; we don't have many outlets for this fiery energy. We feel outrageous or guilty for having them and so we hide them (or act on them impulsively).

Gaining comfort with the idea of yourself as a sexual person increases your options. If you accept your sexuality as part of your normal range of feelings, you can discuss it with a close friend, partner, or therapist without feeling like a bad person. Giving these feelings a voice helps to ground you so that you can appreciate their energy and contain the fire.

Comfort grows from a sense of pride or excitement about your sexual self, rather than embarrassment or shame. How you feel about this has to do with how you've learned about your sexuality. It's a developmental thing. All those growing-up messages and experiences are still saying their piece. If they were positive, you have a solid foundation in this dimension. If they were negative, you face more of a challenge.

Still, it's never too late to learn a different way of thinking and feeling about ourselves. Although we can't change our emotional histories, we can do some significant repair work. When women get together to talk, many share similar stories. Our right to our sexuality—how to be sexual and taken seriously, too—are important topics for these discussions. Talking with others, in women's groups, in therapy, or with friends, can enrich us and clarify ways to be comfortable with this dimension.

Maintaining a victim's stance gets us nowhere fast. And hiding our femininity is only a last resort. It doesn't work well as an everyday approach, and it doesn't carry the process beyond the status quo.

Many men are the victims of our cultural tradition that exaggerates male sexuality. When they're not in control, they feel personally and economically threatened by women at work. Attempting to maintain their equilibrium, they come on or make off-color jokes or comments aimed at keeping us in our place. They work to prove their importance—or is it their potency?—to female colleagues (and their heterosexuality to other males) by casting a sexual glow on everything.

The old way of looking at things was that a woman was responsible for a man's sexual response to her. Some men (as well as some very adamant women) have had difficulty moving from this point of view into a more personally responsible one. Today, just as in the example from my counseling center days, we work with men who don't quite know how to experience us as work partners. So we need to be clear and comfortable with our sexuality.

If I had been more confident when the "ogling" professor came on to me, I could have said something like,

Men have a sexual presence at work which is held as their right and isn't neutralized by organizational traditions. Feminine energy is no more or less.

"Dr. _____, I trust you mean what you're saying as a compliment. If you're really interested in knowing me better, in working with me, I'd be glad to talk with you more about my budget proposal. Your support could make a difference."

Women don't have to be masculine or neutral to succeed in business, though that's basically what we've been asked to do (except in secretarial or other support positions where feminine sexuality is often exploited). But we do need to be sensitive to our sexual presence and have a good working knowledge of our sexual fire. Men have a sexual presence at work which is held as their right and isn't neutralized by organizational traditions. Feminine energy is no more or less. But many men are still ill at ease with that energy in the workplace. We can expect to have to deal with their discomfort and sometimes with the offensive behavior or withdrawal that results from their lack of experience or their wrongful assumption that they are *naturally* in charge. When we feel good about our own sexual presence, we are not thrown off balance by someone who gives us a hard time. And we may have more capacity to reach out in a reassuring way to a man who withdraws.

THE SHADOW SIDE

Sexuality at work offers energetic resources and poses a powerful threat *because it's a reality*. That doesn't mean that everybody at work chooses to be sexual with someone there, but it does mean that sexuality's fire and richness smoke and smolder on the dark side, whether we choose that or not.

Unfortunately, the feminine shadow has often been blamed for the destruction of men—beginning with Eve and carried throughout the Judeo-Christian mythology.

Navajo mythology also provides an unforgettably negative image of feminine sexuality. In her book, *Changing Woman and Her Sisters*, Sheila Moon describes an evil deity named Snapping Vagina. After being manufactured from the marrow of dead persons and Earth Grease, Snapping Vagina mated with other evil forces, producing an array of new monsters.

> All these monsters now began to destroy the people and the Snapping Vagina went her evil way, committing her adulteries, and was the wickedest thing ever seen. . . .

Analyst Moon expresses the depth of the evil evoked by this monster:

> To hear this story . . . in the cadences of Navajo language is to feel a full impact of the negative Feminine. Each of these various monsters issuing from monster matings had its own particularized method of destroying victims. Snapping Vagina's method was to sit down beside and engulf her victim.[1]

No wonder the shadow side of this dimension is so scary. All she has to do is sit down next to her unsuspecting victim and engulf him.

Fantasies of the idealized feminine encourage us to deny our shadow—especially in the sexuality dimension. Eve, the temptress, is a cultural ghost—a long-standing image of woman as evil so potent that we pretend it doesn't exist, especially at work. We don't want negative feminine stereotypes glued to our images.

But this myth is still powerful in the business world. Witch mother, castrating bitch, iron butterfly, and dragon lady are a few of Snapping Vagina's everyday labels that float through corporate hallways on the wings of this mythology. But the deadliest labels have to do with sexuality or sexual practices. These labels attach easily to those of us who don't comply with the "acceptable" feminine stereotypes. They are damaging and dehumanizing—and they turn their target into an object of scorn and rejection. As a way of protecting ourselves against being caught in this negative light, we choose to see ourselves as somehow above sexuality. In doing so, we deny our own shadows. If someone else gets caught in hers, we tend to run away from her rather than reaching out.

In his book, *The Dangerous Sex: The Myth of Feminine Evil*, H. R. Hays weaves an incredible tapestry—the history of the feminine shadow. Awesome power flows from feminine sexuality, from the ability to give birth, nurture, and even destroy life. So great is this power that from ancient times onward, tough taboos and traditions have been designed to keep it under control. And one of the ways has been to interpret feminine sexuality as evil.

On the one hand, all human beings are dependent and fear being left alone. On the other, we have an equally powerful fear of being trapped and suffocated. For men in relation to women, these feelings can get very confusing. In order to deal with their mixed emotions, some men either try to control us or simply disregard us at work—because we're too sexual.

Sexual shadow qualities are perceived by both women and men as so powerful—"the wickedest thing ever seen"—and as containing so much potential to get us rejected that we learn to smother them. With the dread—and reality in experience—that if we're not "good" we'll be alone, we've learned to stuff the shadow: either to avoid its inner heat or to use tremendous energy in denying its presence. At work, this part of our personalities often gets projected onto other women. We see them reflecting our own weakness or power hunger, and we hate them for it.

Sexuality's shadow is particularly troublesome at work

if our style is to seek value as a sex object—to invite sexual attention, mainly for the attention, not for the sex. Men who haven't learned that this is just another smoke screen to cover insecurity reach toward the warmth and get burned. Other women are threatened and put off by this style.

When we use sexuality to control others or to get what we want, we're living in this shadow. From this place, we see men as objects and women as the competition. The workplace becomes a hunting ground and we grow more interested there in proving our power and prowess than in anything else. Work takes second place to our needs for knowing that we're attractive and desirable.

This is defensive behavior designed to hide real problems with self-esteem. It's a smoky, stuck place that's quite different from the energizing fire of sexuality for a person who's comfortable with herself. And it's a dangerous place with a long history.

We each need to know how Snapping Vagina lives in us—how she seduces us into power trips, addiction, dependency on others for our happiness, or mating with other monsters. The shadow side of feminine sexuality is about control. When we dare to look into the "maw of uncreative possessiveness and thus of destructiveness,"[2] we gain valuable information about ourselves. This part of our shadow reveals hidden power motives that are hard for us to own. As we come to understand what we really want, we can use our strengths, not our sexual shadows, to go after it. And we stand a much better chance of maintaining our gains.

Sexuality at work offers energetic resources and poses a powerful threat because it's a reality.

SELF-REFLECTION

Take a moment to estimate your level of comfort with your sexual presence at work. Since this is a very complex subject, you might not arrive at a black-and-white answer. You probably feel differently with different people at different times. Just do the best you can to clarify where you are. Then you'll have a better idea where you might focus your growth efforts.

STRENGTH: I'm comfortable with my sexuality. When men make sexually colored comments to me, I deal with them easily. I enjoy my sexual feelings. I don't flirt at work. I've had a crush on so and so for a long time, but I keep it to myself.

SHADOW: I feel very vulnerable at work because I'm a woman. My boss makes passes at me that embarrass me. / I taunt my female supervisor by flirting with her boss. I get what I want because I'm attractive. / I feel dirty and ashamed much of the time.

TIME FOR YOURSELF

As with any of the other dimensions, this one provides you with information about your feminine presence at work. In some ways, it is at the center of the difficulty women have had in being accepted in the power structure, and usually it has absolutely nothing to do with how you do your job.

It's an art to appreciate your sexuality. Let it add fire to your activities (including work) and know yourself well enough that you can state limits if and when others invade your boundaries. Here are some ideas to work with toward achieving that goal. Scan through all of them and then select a few to concentrate on.

• THINK OF A WOMAN YOU KNOW, either personally or through the media, who seems comfortable and confident about her sexuality.

Describe her carefully in your journal in writing or drawing. What characteristics lead you to conclude that she is relaxed and confident about her sexuality? How are you similar or different? Write the advice you imagine she might give you about this ever so interesting and sensitive subject.

• KNOW YOUR OWN COMFORT LEVEL with your sexuality and relationships with others on the job. List any areas where you feel insecure, uncertain, or under attack. (For example: I don't know how to deal with my boss's compliments; I'm not sure if my dress style is right for work; I want to go out with so and so, but it could cause problems if it doesn't work; my male co-workers put me down because I'm a woman.)

• LIST FIVE STEPS you can take to make the situation(s) in the previous item better for you. If you have trouble coming up with these steps for yourself, think of someone you can consult and get some help.

• OPEN YOUR JOURNAL so that you have two blank pages available to you. Draw a line horizontally across both pages. Create a time line, from day one of your life to the present, that portrays the creation of your image of yourself as a sexual person. List important events, comments, memories. (First knowledge of yourself as a girl, discovery of the "facts of life," traumatic sexual experiences, first menstruation, times in your life you felt exceptionally good about your sexuality.) Write items that contribute to your positive self-image in red or another fire color. Write items that reflect your negative self-image in shadow tones.

• SELECT AREAS FROM THE TIME LINE to revisit so that you can work with them. Write a strategy for expanding a positive item or confronting a negative one. Strategies might include seeking more information, talking with a friend, joining an incest survivor's group, drawing or writing different endings for scenarios that you create.

• FROM A POSITIVE VIEWPOINT, describe yourself in writing or drawing, or both, as a sexual person. Include comments that clarify your feelings about yourself in this dimension.

* WORK AT COMING TO TERMS with your sexual feelings. Everybody has them—whether they are obvious or hidden. If you fit in the "blatantly present" category, use your sexual fire as energy. That energy can fuel a lot of productivity on the job. If you're more inhibited, get acquainted with how your sexual feelings express themselves indirectly. On a scale of one to ten, with ten being completely relaxed, how comfortable are you with your sexual self at work? Why? Answer this question in your journal.

• DOWN ONE SIDE OF A PAGE in your journal, list sexual innuendos, comments, or behaviors that have hurt you in the past at work. Opposite each one, write a response that you would like to make from a comfortable, confident, centered position.

• PRACTICE MANAGING your sexual feelings. If you have a crush on someone who isn't available for a relationship for whatever reason (including just because you work together), allow yourself to enjoy the fire of your sexual feelings. These feelings are part of the richness of human experience and nothing to be ashamed of. You can enjoy them and keep them to yourself. They will slow down of their own accord as you get to know the real person rather than the fantasy you have created in your imagination.

• EXPLORE YOUR SHADOW. Pay attention to your tendencies to relieve tension by making sexual jokes or innuendoes or by being seductive with male colleagues. Granted, this is one way to break up the office routine. But when you do so you shift the unconscious focus of your co-workers from the business at hand to much more interesting thoughts of primal pleasure. Describe a time when your sexual shadow went after something you wanted. What was the outcome? Write about options you had and a possible different ending.

• LEARN TO DEAL WITH MEN who misinterpret your warmth and openness as a sexual invitation. You can talk with such a person about your intentions in a way that supports him as well as yourself. If someone makes this mistake with you, you can say, "I think that when I offered to help with such and such (or I was interested in your hobby, etc.), you mistook my support for personal interest. I am interested in being supportive to you at work. I'm not interested in a relationship outside work."

• SCHOOL YOURSELF IN WAYS to confront undesired overtures from men who have difficulty respecting your personal boundaries. Three books that deal with this issue in detail are: *Working with Men: Professional Women Talk about Power, Sexuality and Ethics,* by Beth Milwid; *On Your Own Terms: A Woman's Guide to Working with Men,* by Kathryn Stechert; and S*exuality in Organizations: Romantic and Coercive Behaviors at Work,* edited by Dail Ann Neugarten and Jay M. Shafritz. Know your rights related to sexual discrimination and harassment.

The goal is for you to be comfortable with your sexuality and to integrate its energy as part of your way of working. In order to feel whole and safe at work, it's important to know how to confront effectively when you receive unwanted sexual attention. The more comfortable you are with your sexual energy, the more comfortable others will be with you.

Now that you've explored this dimension in more depth, return to page 27 and change your Self-Assessment Scale if you need to.

FEEL YOUR FIRE

You've explored your personal feelings and concerns in this dimension; now let's get more specific about how to deal with them at work. The true art of the working woman is to find ways to enjoy the energy of passion while maintaining clear boundaries.

Your sexuality, creativity, and aggression fire your ambition and productivity. When your sexual energy is high, get a lot done. Be creative. Have fun with your work—where you can. If it aids your creativity, give yourself permission to be beautiful in your own way. If you wish, push the envelope by wearing clothes and colors that announce your womanhood.

You, your employer, and your colleagues will love the products of your fire if you learn to regulate its heat. Create open agendas. Invite participation. Use your influence to set priorities and solve problems in ways that feel right for you. Discuss differences. Drop the pretense of sameness. Take the opportunity to talk about:
  • Feminine connections with life,
  • Nature and future generations,
  • Capacity for collaboration,
  • Brightness of intuition,
  • Strength and stamina for getting things done.
Find other women and men of good will who support your efforts and work together.

Of course, as we all know, sexuality invites both barriers and invasion. Of all the barriers that complicate your life at work, the most primitive is **Sexuality Provokes the Raging Beast**. It's unrealistic to ignore the reality that insensitive chauvinists like the "ogling" professor on the budget committee still roam the hallways and byways of working life. But the idea that women at work stimulate raging male hormones and are so distracting that men can't work provides a rationalization for excluding women from shared power positions: "I'm such a virile, horny man, how could I be expected to contain myself—to concentrate—around an attractive female?"

Interestingly, this dynamic doesn't appear to be such an issue if women are in support positions. It's acceptable to be turned on by one's secretary because, in a hierarchical system, she isn't a colleague with whom one must negotiate. She triggers no fear of loss of power. But in professional or management positions, women have been taught that to be taken seriously it is important to avoid looking either feminine (brainless) or sensual (distracting). And so, they have learned to keep their sexuality contained, disguised, covered in tailored suits with high collars and neckwear. Clearly, the issue isn't sexuality but authority.

The delusion that the workplace is a sterile environment free of human emotion is a relic. The feminine presence invites responsibility for a broad range of human emotion, including sexual feelings. The workplace has always been sexual. The difference now is that women are actually present, no longer just the conversational objects of he-man chest beating and imaginary conquest. Now, they have to be dealt with face to face rather than under defenseless scrutiny on the porno pages. This creates real problems for men who are not secure in their masculine identity or who have trouble dealing directly with women.

Do	*Don't*
Identify who the culprits are.	Take it personally.
Talk with other women about your concerns.	Let someone else's immature behavior define you.
Get help if you choose to confront. Any confrontation should be private after you have created your strategy.	Engage in sexual banter as a way of gaining acceptance.
Inform yourself of legal protection against sexual harassment and discrimination. Know the definitions for both.	Mistake sexual attention for admiration of your work. Make idle threats about harassment and discrimination. Do give thought and planning to consequences of such action.
Make it clear in your own mind that you will not tolerate sexual harassment or discrimination.	

A related but more sympathetic barrier is Women Complicate Play at Work. Yes, play! The social aspects of work are where women really mess things up. The presence of women in power positions creates problems with informal office atmosphere and work-related social occasions. The all-male getaway now has to include you. When "the girls" were all in the background, leaving them behind was the logical thing to do. Somebody had to tend the store! And of course "the wife" would stay at home and take care of the kids. Women on a golf weekend completely change the nature of the event.

Stag movies, dirty jokes, sexual language, and pornography are still parts of male social life, business seminars, and meetings. Some women have survived these events by "going along with the guys." They endure humiliation and hold their own. This tactic may succeed in the short run, but it is a real violation of womanhood. Comments or activities intended as put-downs, even as informal talk and play, get in the way. If the prevailing atmosphere is sexist, any attempt to set a limit—such as not laughing at sexist comments—is likely to draw negative attention. Unless you are very self-confident, it feels like the choice is either to go with the flow or to feel even more like an outsider.

Do	*Don't*
Attend recreational functions.	Go along with behavior that degrades women.
Be sensitive to the loss men experience.	Let them get your goat.
Confront sex-role stereotypes.	Take on guilt for being included.
Take care of yourself.	Abuse alcohol.

Do	*Don't*
Team with other women.	Try to be one of the boys.
Regard recreational events as work time even though they're supposed to be fun.	Get into situations where you have no emotional support.
Explore your own capacity to have fun.	

As you gain comfort and confidence in yourself as a sexual person, you will learn to sustain your fire at work and the barriers will be less threatening. You will no longer need to masquerade as a robot or a man to cool the fear your sensual presence stirs in the once masculine management ranks. Your colleagues will feel your power, but they'll know you're not available.

For many of us, this is the most difficult dimension to integrate at work. Either we try to be neutral or we feel extremely vulnerable and threatened. A good middle ground is to know that your sexuality is your business and your energy and that other people's reactions to you don't define you.

"I don't appreciate personal comments about my appearance," is a relatively gentle way to set a boundary for unwanted compliments or suggestive comments.

"I see our relationship as a work relationship, not a personal one," responds to sexual innuendos or invitations.

"Your non-verbal messages suggest that you have a personal interest in me. You need to know that I don't return that interest," provides a way to bring gestures or looks into the open for discussion.

Continued, persistent, unwanted comments or invitations are sexual harassment. When you're confronted with this situation, get help and deal with it. You're not responsible for the unwanted behavior of others.

But if you choose to build a personal relationship with someone where you work, make it a project for your partnership to decide the best way to manage. Decide ahead of time how you will handle work if you break up, and try to be as realistic as you can. Think about the potential impact of your relationship on your colleagues. Will they feel shut out? Are issues of fairness involved?

As you truly grow more comfortable with your sexuality, and your feminine power in general, you can appreciate and contain your sexual energy without acting in seductive ways that confuse your male colleagues. Remember that you are responsible for *your* behavior, not theirs. When you can deal with this highly charged dimension in a self-supportive and constructive way, you offer your male co-workers a new level of security and partnership.

SUMMARY

Feminine sexuality is a fiery topic about which there is a great deal of myth and misunderstanding. The tendency is to blame the victim: "If she hadn't been wearing that outfit, she wouldn't have been raped."

Women will be the ones who change this attitude, but we have to be comfortable with our own sexuality and willing to voice our rights to be *all* of who we are. As more wives and daughters enter the workplace, more men are willing to hear about what really happens there and to take a look at their own ways of relating to women. "Would you want someone to say that to your daughter?" can be a powerful confrontation.

Feminine sexuality has been so dangerous and taboo on the job that working women have cloaked their sexuality by adopting masculine styles or pretending robotism. This makes things safer, but it eliminates vital feminine fire.

If we know ourselves well in this dimension and can own both our strengths and our shadows as sexual creatures, we will be in a position to educate those who misinterpret our warmth or animation as an invitation. At times, it's possible to turn the sexual approach that really says "I want to know you better and to be close to you" into a strong working relationship. It's also important to be skilled at handling sexual approaches that aren't sexual at all, but are power trips designed to disempower their target.

This chapter has only brushed the surface of this most complicated subject. Take as much time as you need to write in your journal about related issues you intend to pursue or resources you will seek. Now is the time!

Creativity

I should have been a great dancer,
but, like my mother before me,
I mopped small spills from freshly waxed
kitchen linoleum

> instead.

I could have been an interior designer,
but, like my mother before me,
I rearranged the musty linen closet one more time.

I might have been a writer of novels,
but, like my mother before me,
I scrawled a note: "please excuse my son's absence . . ."
on the back of last week's grocery list

> *Passion fruit*
> *papaya nectar*
> *pickle relish (sweet)*

I should have been a fashion designer,
but, like my mother before me,
I matched the shoes with the bag
with the hose with the scarf.

Creative juices flow
onto oilcloth,
commingling with the stains
spilled from last night's supper,
> only to be
> absorbed by a green and

yellow sponge; the green side
purposely abrasive, making it
easier to eradicate any stubborn residue.

But I still might be a poet;
Perhaps it's not too late.
I don't know.
My mother is gone, I have
no daughter,
I'm all that's in the way.

Stephanie Ganic Braunstein, "Apology"

irginia Woolf called it "the match burning in the crocus." Feminine creativity—the flash of insight, spark of genius, spirit of play—shapes the raw material of everyday life. At home, we generate meals with ingredients we have on hand, or beautify our surroundings with more talent than money. We substitute, compromise, do what's necessary to feed the multitudes and weave life's fabric in color and beauty for ourselves and for those we love. As workers in our own new businesses, we piece together intricate steps, do what needs to be done. If we're in charge, we're not confined by the limits of other people's standards. We're breaking new ground.

The uncontained feminine kindles the flame. Creativity finds its own way best where expectations are unclear or unknown and a protected space exists.

In everyday life, unfortunately, the stubborn residue of our creativity tends to get eradicated with little notice. We whisk it aside, underplay it. Woven into the fabric of other people's lives—a gift here, a party there, a new way of getting the work done—it rarely results in a major product. We have little time and less belief in ourselves. We sacrifice our dreams and get in our own way. The fire flickers from time to time, but it rarely blazes. And, because we live in a world attuned to the products of masculine creativity, we miss the significance of our own creative work.

Nevertheless, accomplishments emerge bigger than life in those for whom creativity burns fiercely—Georgia O'Keefe, Maya Angelou, Alicia de la Rocca, Barbara McClintock, Martha Graham. These women, with unnumbered less known sisters, indelibly brighten the world with their colors. Boundless energy, daring and dedication, as well as talent, fueled their contributions. Each found her way. But they all stand out as exceptions. Small spills, musty linen closets and notes to the teacher, seemingly tiny interruptions, use up the little fuel there is for more tentative fires. With our efforts divided by relational responsibilities, women rarely find or create the sheltered environment that supports world-class creativity.

We have trouble with what qualifies as "creative" in our own minds. A mistake, a coincidence, an "accident" occurs that opens new possibilities. We get a sense of what we want to do and figure out how to do it. We need to expand our definitions to include marketing design, a teaching unit, software, a therapeutic intervention, running a household adequately on too little money and too little time.

Suzanne, a woman who moved from home to a career in the financial world after age forty, explained to me one day in all seriousness that she really isn't a very creative person.

Surprised, I said, "What are you talking about? Look what you've done! You've translated your ability to do fifteen things at once as a mother and homemaker into a successful career in a dog-eat-dog industry. And you maintain your integrity in the process. You use creativity in your work every day with your clients—not to mention the way you went about getting your education and shaping your career. That in itself was a very creative process."

This is a woman who returned to college while she

managed her household, worked, and mothered three teenagers. After college, she created a niche for herself in an environment that wasn't supportive to women by marketing herself as someone who could relate to older clients—and to divorced women. She finds, or invents, ways to meet her clients' needs, sincerely keeping their best interests at heart. They love her and refer their friends. All this requires more than time management. Suzanne can see the big picture, determine where she fits, and create a unique spin in a highly competitive business.

"I think of creative as the ability to do all those art and craft things that I've never liked," she said. "But I guess I do have to use some original thinking in my work. It makes me feel good to think of that as creativity."

We're used to a male-oriented view of creativity. We look for a product, a creative work. But women are incredibly creative in ways that don't end with a product. The creative feminine is much more likely to be involved in *process*—the way something happens. These contributions are often taken for granted—the kind of thing that doesn't get recognition, but is missed if it's not there.

For many of us, "creative" describes somebody else. But, in all its forms, creativity is *really* the human capacity to see the world through fresh eyes and express what we see in new and different ways. It's not limited to genius-level art or invention. It certainly can't be owned by the feminine. But feminine sensitivity, emotion, and expressiveness can fuel the creative spirit.

Maria Martinez,[1] a Native American of the Tewa tribe, lived her ninety-plus years on the high desert near Santa Fe at San Idelfonso Pueblo in New Mexico. This woman, who at an early age stood out as the best potter in her village, is in many ways the model of the creative feminine. She did produce a product—her wonderful pottery pieces are now in museums and worth tens of thousands of dollars. But, as much as her stunning art, the way she lived

Creativity entails not only fluent and original thought, of which women are very capable, but also the ability to tailor ideas to practical problems.

her life was a work of great creativity.

This woman's art is of the earth. The way the fire treated it made it magic. She collected her clay from the New Mexico landscape by hand, painstakingly screened it, and carefully conditioned it for use. She and her artist husband, Julian, discovered that adding cow dung to the kiln fire turned the pottery's natural reddish color to deep black. Tedious hand polishing made it glow.

Maria's pots, decorated by Julian, her daughter-in-law, Santana, and others, were recognized and valued from the 1920s on. But her way was to support other women of the pueblo in their art and their efforts to earn money from it. She taught them how to do the special firing and made no attempt to "patent" the process. She helped other potters sell their wares, sometimes displaying theirs and holding hers back—even signing a friend's pot from time to time in the early days, to help with sales.

Although she was known and respected internationally in the art world, she made decisions about her life from her feminine center. Her choice was to stay at the pueblo, to live in very simple circumstances, in conditions that most would call "primitive" by Twentieth Century urban standards. She and Julian were central to the spiritual life and government of this intimate but complex native community. Later, their sons and their families shared responsibility for supporting and maintaining the Tewa tradition at San Idelfonso. Intellectually brilliant and with an unusual memory for detail, Maria lived her life in the midst of her family. In her 90s she still molded pots extracted from the high desert clay, tempered with just the right amount of water and shaped to a perfect roundness that contrasted with her gnarled but seemingly clairvoyant fingers.

Maria's simple, non-materialistic way has little in common with the rat race that many of us pursue. But her capacity to stay connected to her own process and her loved ones, and to fuel her creative fire, portrays feminine creativity at its richest. She worked closely with the earth as she scanned the color and texture of the soil around her to find just the right clay, patiently waited until it appeared, and then conditioned it for days until it was ready to use. The image of Maria walking the desert sustains me when I think things are difficult or are taking too long.

But the secret was in the fire. The fact that she and her partner found a way to transform shit into art speaks to the practicality of their creative process.

The fire of the creative feminine is key to understanding, nurturing, and supporting feminine power at work. The creativity of everyday life vitalizes any work site where it sparkles. Innovation, bringing a new view from a feminine perspective, adds a real difference. But there are lots of problems associated with getting this dimension out in the open.

Water elements, which are such a central part of the feminine—receptivity, flexibility, nurturance, and affinity—are often the wellsprings of creativity. But unless they flow in a fairly sheltered environment, they drown creativity in two ways: 1) Creative production is often isolated work—relating takes time and energy—and 2) the need to please someone else gets in the way of risk-taking. Fear of hurting or displeasing another invents artificial limits. "I was going to wait until my parents died to paint the pain of our family life," an artist shared with me, "but I'm so full of it, I can't do anything else." We worry about disrupting personal connections by telling the truth, taking the next step.

It's hard to push the limits if financial survival is at stake. Leaving my tenured job at the university to start a private practice took a huge leap of faith. I couldn't know if I could make it work, because I had never done it before. A creative move often has to make it across the chasm in one bound—with little or no safety net. A new product, a new market, or a new way of doing business is, by definition, untested—unproven. The feminine, which seeks comfort in connectedness, may hesitate too long at the brink while old self-doubting messages echo loudly.

Visible support on the other side helps.

The creative feminine is a tentative commodity on the job where expectations are set and rules are rigid, and it may take longer to gestate than its more masculine counterpart. Harsh conditions smother any quality that's understated or not too well identified. In its fragile, underdeveloped form, it evaporates before it's born. It slips into the mold of existing structures—subtle and too willing to defer. And (it took me a while to figure this out) there are organizations that don't want employees, especially female employees, to be creative. It's just too threatening. So new ideas are actively squelched, or women aren't given credit. How many times have you heard, "I know I can make it work, I just have to get him to think it's his idea"?

New ideas don't always work out. The freedom to fail, security in the face of criticism, is essential. It takes a strong woman or a protective environment to fuel this fire in typical work environments. But when those conditions exist, the results speak for themselves.

Men occupy center stage in the history of art and creative thinking. This lopsidedness speaks to the politics of women's lives, not to any lack of feminine creativity. Creativity entails not only fluent and original thought, of which women are very capable, but also the ability to tailor ideas to practical problems. In the past, the practical problems of women have been home-oriented and mostly invisible, rather than in the public realm. Presently, women who work away from home while taking most of the responsibility for home and childcare have only enough energy left to hear the noisiest of their creative urges. They squeeze the nectar from stolen moments to

The creative feminine is much more likely to be involved in process—the way something happens.

bring their creations to life.

Some researchers tell us that creative individuals are those who have the capacity to use the feminine side of the self. Here's how Donald MacKinnon stated it in his classic research study:

> The evidence is clear: the more creative a person is, the more he reveals an openness to his own feelings and emotions, a sensitive intellect and understanding self-awareness, and wide ranging interests including many which in the American culture are thought of as feminine. In the realm of sexual identity and interests, our creative subjects appear to give more expression to the feminine side of their nature than do less creative persons. . . . [2]

Michael Dues, a songwriter, makes a similar point: "My friends are the fathers of the songs. I am the mother."[3]

The ultimate feminine creativity carries and delivers new life. Though this process is often life-endangering and warrants endless commitment, it gains neither Nobel Prizes, financial rewards, nor social status. A mother's creative product is somebody else's life. Even if she dedicates most of her energy to nurturing and training this child, her job isn't finished until she can let go—rightfully give credit for growing up to the child, not herself. The maternal analogy fits well for all forms of feminine creativity, regardless of our choices about parenthood.

Fertile feminine mulling is so biological and so ordinary. Its richness and profundity are easily overlooked, by ourselves as well as by those who take us for granted. The creative feminine asks questions, takes on unpopular projects, isn't satisfied with the status quo. But she can quickly begin to feel like the odd-woman out—it's not a comfortable place. Translated to the office, issues that engage the creative feminine—energy for life, concern for its quality and for the well-being of the species—shrink into the background as the daily pressures of business take over. How we learn to support this leading edge of the feminine presence is key to creating feminine balance at work.

THE SHADOW SIDE

The shadow of creativity looms dark and powerful. Rot, decay, and decomposition are necessary aspects of creativity. The old has to disintegrate to make room for the new. That's what makes this dimension so threatening. Light turns to dark turns to light.

And since we're frightened of the dark, we have a hard time seeing it as part of the creative process. In this dimension, maybe more than any other, we have to be willing to dive into our shadow rather than pushing it away.

In her great feminist sourcebook, *The Woman's Encyclopedia of Myths and Secrets*, Barbara Walker provides some background for the dark side of creativity. She borrows from mythologist G. M. Neumann to describe Kali, the major goddess of ancient India:

> "Dark Mother," the Hindu triple goddess of creation, preservation and destruction; now most commonly known in her Destroyer aspect, squatting over her dead consort shiva and devouring his entrails, while her yoni sexually devours his lingam (penis). Kali is "The hungry earth, which devours its own children and fattens on their corpses. . . . It is in India that the experience of the Terrible Mother has been given its most grandiose form as Kali. But all this—and it should not be forgotten—is an image not only of the Feminine but particularly

and specifically of the Maternal. For in a profound
way life and birth are always bound up with death
and destruction."[4]

It's worth noting that this one goddess represents
three major feminine (maternal) processes: Creation,
preservation and destruction. Kali represents both the light
and the dark side of the creative feminine. But the dark
side is so scary, it's the one for which she is best known—
the dark side of the maternal.

How this darkness forms in our own personal shadow
is important information. We eat up our own creative
works before they're born. The destruction can be subtle
or out in the open. It's the quiet voice that says, "Nobody
will like it." Or the loud voice that says, "Who do you
think you are? Can't you just do it the way everybody else
does?" Unfortunately, work environments often provide
real life voices that corroborate these shadowy sentiments,
making it doubly hard to avoid getting overwhelmed.

We create socially acceptable diversions of many kinds
to avoid facing our creativity straight on. Staying too busy,
supporting other people's creativity rather than our own,
over-involving ourselves with our children's projects.
(How many science projects have you done?)

Writer's block, performance anxiety, test anxiety, and
failed confidence in our ideas all speak the shadow's language. Exploring the dark pathways to the roots of these
evils helps you untangle the knots that prevent you from
expressing yourself. Who says you shouldn't be able to
write, perform, excel, create? Diving into these shadows
helps you find the permission and self support you need
to move forward.

The dark side of creativity, in one of its most identifiable forms, indulges in "retail therapy," overspending on
clothes or other things that meet a creative need. "Retail
therapy" appears to require less time and energy than

doing our own creative work. And we get instant recognition for our efforts. If you look at the vicious cycle of overwork, stress reduction through retail therapy, and more overwork to pay for overspending, you can see the false economy.

Darkness deepens when we generate more ideas than we can use and feel victimized when we can't bring them to life. The creative fire burns out of control—with little capacity to organize well enough to carry projects forward. We get grandiose, believe that we're so creative we shouldn't have to do the mundane work to make the projects happen. Or creativity suffocates, becomes cynicism, fueled by frustration, and a pained anonymity.

Creative tension, thwarted and turned inward, provides just the right conditions for the pseudo relief of substance abuse or assorted sexual addictions. Unreleased creative energy fuels a tension state that burns for expression. An extra glass of wine or mood-shifting chemicals in one form or another seem innocent enough antidotes to bitterness and self-hate. Pursuit of the perfect adoring lover, this week's partner in escape from everyday life, fits here too. If these are your coping strategies, listen to your shadow screaming at you and perhaps you'll find more creative outlets for your life energy. Heed her screams and risk looking for help.

Destruction of the creative work or ideas of others is a vicious aspect of this destroyer mother. Unable to birth her own children, she eats other women's kids. This fits a negative feminine stereotype—that women can't work together. When we operate on the shadow side, often in competition for masculine recognition or rewards, the stereotype fits.

We're likely to smolder when we live on the shadow side of our creativity at work. Nothing is just right. We feel frustrated, blocked. Ideas don't flow. We may blame others or ourselves.

The variable and unpredictable direction of feminine creativity can be threatening to those who prefer straight lines.

When that happens, we need to give ourselves time to get back inside and regenerate. It helps to look at how we have failed to take responsibility for our work situations.

The shadow side of creativity speaks loudly. Hearing her can give you permission to take care of this dimension, which has been so oppressed in the feminine. Dive in. Encounter her darkness and learn from her gold. She'll help you to understand what form your creativity takes. Trust that it exists, whether or not you've recognized it yet. Make some decisions about how, when, and where you'll express it.

SELF-REFLECTION

Contact your creative fire. Is it bright? Barely flickering? Hard to find at all? This dimension exists in all of us and may be more or less intense, depending on current circumstances. When you hardly have time to breathe and stress is at the max, the creative glow fades.

Estimate your place on the continuum for creativity.

STRENGTHS: I trust my creative energies. Often I put things together in ways that haven't occurred to others. I try new things with relative ease. I can tolerate failing when I try something different. I feel good about my efforts even when others reject them.

SHADOW: I see so many options, I can't focus on one. / I get super-frustrated with my routine job. / I'm afraid to try new things. When I fail, I'm devastated. / My talents are irrelevant to my job. / I know I'm not creative.

TIME FOR YOURSELF

Creativity is sandwiched between two other fiery dimensions in this book for a special reason. If those two are suffocated, creativity usually sputters out! As you get better acquainted with your fire dimensions, find ways to support your creativity at work as well as in other parts of your life. Time flies when you can express yourself through your originality and inventiveness—and work becomes a lot more exciting. By taking a risk here and there, you may be able to create a more interesting and rewarding environment for yourself. The following tips provide some ways to help you fire up your own creative process at work. Choose several for deeper exploration.

• IN YOUR MIND, transport yourself to work. List three things you've invented or started up in the past month that help with your work. Think of steps, processes, or relationships you've created that seemed obvious to you, but hadn't been done before. This is your creativity in action. Acknowledge it by writing about it in your journal.

• THINK OF OTHER PEOPLE at work whose innovative approaches flavor their work. List three unpredicted steps or events you've observed within the last month that resulted from co-workers' creativity. How did they establish permission to take those steps? Did they have to deal with resistance and criticism? How did they support themselves or gain support from others? Or did they just "do it?"

• LOOK AT A BLANK PAGE in your journal. Fill it with colors, lines, or shapes—as many or as few as you like—in whatever form seems right for the moment. Don't judge it.

• ON THIS PAGE that you have glorified with color and with line—or on another one—list several words that spark your creative spirit. These may be ideas, objects, people, artworks—whatever inspires you. Add a drawing if you feel like it. Remember that this is just for you. It's not headed for the Museum of Modern Art.

- LIST YOUR CREATIVE STRENGTHS in your journal. What personal qualities spark your creativity? Do you find better ways to do your work or combine activities in unusual ways? Do you challenge the way things have always been done? Do you ask questions that make other people stop and think?

- LIST SEVEN WORDS that describe what support for your creativity has meant to you. Who in your life has supported your creativity? How did she or he encourage you? Write a letter in your journal (or to that person if possible) expressing your thanks.

- LIST THREE EXAMPLES of your own creativity in everyday life outside work. How can you translate the joy of these activities into your work environment? Write about some steps you can take, and then take them.

- IDENTIFY THREE AREAS at work where your creativity could find more expression. What blocks you there? Can you do something about the blocks? List several steps that might help.

- FIND OPPORTUNITIES to be assertive on behalf of others' creative attempts. Creativity needs a safe environment in which to flourish. What can you do to make your workplace supportive to creative efforts?

- WHOM CAN YOU ASK to support you in your efforts? List their names in your journal. Talk with one or more of these people about creative next steps that interest you.

- YOUR CREATIVE EFFORTS at work have to be open to the scrutiny of others in order to thrive and grow. They won't all be successful. Learn to keep the creative fire burning despite the cold water of criticism. Give yourself a little time to recover from the pain. Then see if there is something to be gained from the critique. Sift through what is helpful and use it to your advantage.

• IDENTIFY ONE creative work-related project you would like to pursue in the coming months. For instance, if you're working on your business writing, find a current magazine with a related article. Read it and follow any tips it suggests. Or, if you're trying to increase your client base, read a novel or biography of a woman who is an inspiration to you and see what you can learn from her. Write in your journal when you plan to commit time and how you plan to proceed.

The workplace benefits when the warmth of the creative feminine is fueled. Its fire brings fulfillment and satisfaction to your everyday life. Its shadow darkens the door when the press of business and glamorized images of the creative life make it easy for us to underrate ourselves in this dimension.

Return to your list of creative strengths and underline them in your journal. Write them in neon lights in your awareness. Now, review your Self-Assessment on page 27 and make whatever adjustments are needed. If you've worked through the exercises in this chapter, you probably have expanded your definition of creativity to cover more of you than it did before.

CREATIVITY GOES TO WORK

Learn to support your efforts and those of others who are willing to challenge the system.

This is the way we've always done it, especially if "we" are the masculine molders of the organization, tends to deaden creativity in even the most self-assured employee. This killer phrase stifles everybody's creativity. And the message can be loud and clear even if the words are never spoken. It's especially deadly if the implication is that the traditional masculine way is the right way and that any variation is inferior. The variable and unpredictable direction of feminine creativity can be threatening to those who prefer straight lines.

Many years ago, working in a special reading program, my job was to order several thousand books to be distributed to teachers in fifteen different elementary schools. I pondered this task with great seriousness and, predating the personal computer by a few years, created various systems to limit the potential for unbridled confusion. I settled on an approach that relied on charts and color coding. It made good sense to me. On paper, I grouped the books in color-coded sections and could cross-reference them in the necessary different directions. I knew which school needed which books and, efficiently from my point of view, proceeded to construct the orders. My supervisor, an enormously overworked man who was glad for any help he could get, approved the plan.

But his boss, the superintendent, blew his stack at me. "I don't know what you're trying to do here. This is the silliest thing I've ever seen." Bypassing my creative endeavor, he personally instructed me on how he wanted the orders physically collated, and even stapled in a certain way. It took much longer and added nothing to accuracy or ease of recordkeeping. It was simply his way. Today, I would respond to that kind of pathetic power move by asserting the positive pay-off my method offered. "Yes, this may appear to be a little unusual. But, see, here's what it offers. . . ." At that stage of my career, I was hurt and infuriated. My insecurity and anger scrambled any possibility of an effective, self-supportive response.

This is the way we've always done it, tends to be well entrenched in traditional work sites, and in some non-traditional ones as well. It's a fast-growing virus. Bureaucracies are famous for it. Here are some suggestions for supporting your creative fire in a suffocating environment.

The creative feminine asks questions, takes on unpopular projects, isn't satisfied with the status quo.

Do	*Don't*
Express your ideas tactfully and repeatedly.	Take criticism personally.
	Undermine yourself.
Ask questions.	
	Put down the ideas others express.
Push the limits a little at a time.	
Learn by your mistakes; critique, don't criticize yourself.	Give up because your efforts aren't appreciated.
Reality test with someone you trust about whether you're "off the wall."	Expect to be affirmed for something that threatens to change the way things are.
Make sure support is in place when you try to make big changes.	Lose your sense of humor.
Trust your inner voice.	

Research shows us that, contrary to popular belief, competition curtails creativity.[5] If your eye is on winning, or protecting your backside, your energy slips from the task at hand. You are likely to become more rigid and less able to let your imagination roam freely. In competitive environments, you need to secure the space in which to be creative. Know the areas in which you are safe enough to express your creative energy and those in which you have to be more guarded and self-protective. If you don't expect yourself to be competitive and creative at the same time, you'll be less likely to be self-critical about your limitations.

Barriers to your creativity at work may exist in the

restrictions and limitations of your job or workplace. But they are even more likely to be internal blocks—attitudes *you* cling to, like "This isn't any good—So and so won't like it—It's not that important." Draw a circle around that one and put a line through it.

Maintain contact with your creativity—the creativity of everyday life—at work. Protect some private time and space so that your creative process can form and emerge. "Something's cooking here; I need some time to think about this," can become your theme song. Support your efforts even when they "fail" or don't meet with the approval of others: "That didn't work, but here's what I learned from it. . . ." Support the creativity of others. Stay tuned in to ideas that seem different or new—thoughts that don't slip neatly into the well-worn groove. Don't be afraid to acknowledge a co-worker: "I noticed that you got us hooked into a new resource network. I hadn't thought about using that approach. It will help a lot."

Support your creativity by taking risks. What you perceive as your weirdness may be your unique contribution to the vitality of your workplace. Choose supportive women or men you trust and talk with them about your process for "reaching in." Or let them in on some of your intuitive flashes. Propose an intuitive, non-linear solution for some problem that your work group is struggling with.

Stay in touch with your process—the ways you personally create your job on a daily basis. In even the most structured job you have choices about what you do first or how you choose to approach certain tasks. Use your ingenuity to make your job work for you in as many ways as you can.

If you have a lot of control over your work and how you do it, let your intuition guide you. Move beyond the realm of what's been done before. Bring your individuality and creativity to bear on your work in as many ways as you can.

And for the most fun of all, feminine creativity heats up in group form. If you want to see feminine power at work, get a group of women together who share values and goals and are dedicated to making something happen—a party, a seminar, a political action, or an artistic endeavor.

Photographer Catherine Busch-Johnston[6] spoke of her experience this way:

> I'm producing 8, half-hour shows on older women. I have two women as my crew. They're always doing their best. They assume their responsibility plus a little more. I'm making a video. It's a collaborative effort—very feminine. Everyone depends on everyone's efforts. People on crews usually work together—cover for each other. Everybody helps carry equipment.
>
> The women I'm videotaping are amazing. Nellie Red Owl, an 85-year-old Lakota Sioux Elder; Betty Kazosa, a woman who was in one of this country's concentration camps and has used her experience to enter politics as a catalyst for helping others appreciate the differences in people. I received a Laurence Rockefeller grant and was able to raise matching funds. Four shows are taped—one edited off-line. The vision is there and I can't not do it.

Catherine's creative fire provided her with energy, not only to create and carry forth her vision, but to hustle the resources she needed to make it work. Although working independently at the time I interviewed her, Catherine had spent years in film, TV, and publishing.

"How would corporations be different if women were in charge?" I asked her. We were sitting on a boat dock at a lake near Nevada City, California. She gazed off across the water and let it roll:

Day care, warm environment, paintings, lighting, rugs, layout. An environment creates another way of thinking and feeling—builds trust. If people felt that they were heard—human provisions—they would be happier and more productive. Women would have concern for the well-being of people and provide time to take care of themselves. When workers realize people are spending on them they have incentive to work harder. Flexible hours. When you work with women, you don't have to tell them what to do—don't need a task master, a production manager.

Given time and resources, and the opportunity to work together, the combination of connectedness and creativity can produce stunning results. Create this opportunity for yourself and others at work whenever you can.

And don't take it all too seriously. Your sense of humor is part of this dimension. Creativity and humor have several things in common: 1) the ability to see and appreciate unusual relationships, 2) the ability to combine ideas that don't usually go together, and 3) the intuitive ability to cut through layers of defensiveness to the unconscious truth. Feminine humor, which of course has been around forever as a subversive art, is coming of age. Regina Barreca writes:

We have had to learn to embrace the idea of ourselves as striving for our goals, as aiming for success, as willing to set our sights for the very top. We have learned to love the thought of our own ambition. And we are learning to love our own laughter, to see that our sense of humor makes sense and can help us make sense of the world around us, which means relearning to trust our instincts and to stop

checking whether the guy sitting next to us is laughing before we laugh. If it's funny, we should let ourselves laugh, loud and clear.[7]

Barreca's book, *They Used to Call Me Snow White . . .
But I Drifted: Women's Strategic Use of Humor,* and another
one, *What Mona Lisa Knew: A Woman's Guide to Getting
Ahead in Business by Lightening Up—The Bold New
Strategy for Less Stress and More Success on the Job,* by
Barbara Mackoff, provide fun reading, refreshing insights,
and validation. And, as Barreca points out on her book
jacket, "She who laughs, lasts."

FEMININE CREATIVITY—A PROCESS

Andrea is an administrator, a therapist, and a consultant. She's sensitive, talented, and highly skilled.

She had weathered the stress of early conflict resolu-
tion with the decisionmakers in the software business
where she's an external consultant. She dealt with them in
a centered, confrontive, calming way that moved them forward rather than further into the flames of their strong personal conflicts.

Reorganization of the company demanded restructur-
ing of the technical staff. Women who had worked directly
for one boss since the founding of the company would no
longer be identified with a particular person or job. Two
teams, each supervised by a coordinator, would handle the
heavy work flow. Typical rivalries and personality conflicts
zinged among these women. Solid alliances with previous
bosses made this shift hurtful. It felt like a demotion. The
whole idea was experimental and nobody was particularly
happy about it.

Andrea had worked with the coordinators through
several training sessions. These women were technicians,

not skilled leaders, but the success of this organizational transition depended on their capacity to lead their new "teams." The coordinators and their immediate supervisors were beginning, tentatively, to form a team.

They looked to Andrea for the answers. A two-hour "team building" session was scheduled for each of the groups. It would be the first time the new teams met with their fledgling leaders.

"What would you like from me?" Andrea had asked them.

"Teach us to do what you do. Help us feel secure. Bring your bag of tricks."

Andrea was floored. She'd spent nearly twenty years learning to do what she does. Her work is grounded in solid knowledge of herself gained through years of personal therapy and self-development, plus technical skills gained from three different career paths. The naiveté of their request threw her.

"What can I possibly do in two hours that will make any difference?" she asked herself. And, "We have to start somewhere," she answered.

She had Saturday morning to create her strategy. Optimistically, she tripped upstairs to her home office. She pulled together some books and other materials on team building. Very familiar with this material she mostly stared at the covers while she thought about the contents. She mentally rehearsed a dozen different approaches. None seemed right. Three hours later, she returned downstairs for lunch, not one bit closer to what she'd do than when she started.

She drifted through her heavy weekend schedule distracted—preoccupied. This shouldn't be such a hard problem. She wanted to deal with these women in a real way, not do some canned exercise that might feel good for the moment and make little if any difference later.

Sunday, after dinner, shouldering the bruskness of her

Given time

and resources,

and the

opportunity

to work

together, the

combination of

connectedness

and creativity

can produce

stunning

results.

partner's disbelief, she headed upstairs again. She pulled out her professional bag of tricks—personality inventories, warm-ups, communication-skill-building exercises. "Not enough time. Not right. Too structured." She discarded each.

"These are all women. They're scared, vulnerable. Some are angry and defensive. What if I get them to talk about their strengths and weaknesses as women working together?"

It was all there. She pulled out her sample copy of my Self-Assessment Scale. Her design fell into place. This wasn't going to be a typical team-building process. It was going to be straight from her heart. Either it would work or it wouldn't, but it would be real.

The next morning, as she walked toward the room where the first group was waiting, the office manager approached and said, "Oh, Andrea, I hope you won't mind, but the boss decided to include two more people. Joe will be in this group and Harry in the other."

Andrea blinked. "Fine," she said.

A design focused on the feminine, and now one man would be present in each group. "It's the feminine," she said to herself, "not necessarily women," and she walked on down the hall.

A rack of jitters shivered lightly through her, but, mostly centered, she greeted the waiting group. Each sat as if in her own plexiglas cubicle, separated from the others. Joe looked as if he would rather be anyplace else.

Andrea talked briefly about the purpose of the meeting and the idea of shifting to a team.

She asked them to describe how they felt about this shift. They were honest. The answers boiled down to, "We don't like it."

She asked for their cooperation, just for the two hours. They agreed.

"We know a lot more about being separate than we

know about being together. To work as a team, we have to have some way of connecting with each other. When we're connected, we give energy to each other and we receive energy from each other. Each of us is then more powerful than any of us could be individually."

She invited them to a meditation in which, lightly holding hands, each would visualize his or her heart energy and in turn, with a gentle squeeze, would pass it on to the next person. Not a typical beginning for a corporate team building.

They knew Andrea and they liked her. They'd had enough previous contact with her to trust. Whatever their feelings about their colleagues, they were willing to try what Andrea asked. Following her guided imagery, they opened themselves to meditation. The mood in the room shifted.

More talk about connection.

"We connect better with each other if we know who we are and we know who they are—and if they know who we are." She distributed copies of the Self-Assessment. The next hours flew as each person extracted her (and his) strengths and began to grapple with their shadow patterns. They were honest with themselves and with each other. They were excited. They began to understand more about their problems with each other. And they began to comprehend that their similarities far outweighed their differences.

"You asked me to bring my bag of tricks," Andrea reminded them. She fished a purple silk pouch from her neatly ordered brief case. The chatter quieted. "I tried to think of techniques I could teach you in just a little time. Even the most basic group skills require understanding and practice. We'll work with those along the way. For today, though, here are some things to think about as you work together."

"The turtle symbolizes courage, vulnerability, and persistence for me." A small black onyx fetish sat in her hand. Tiny turquoise, long a symbol of healing in Native American lore, studded each section of the turtle's shell. "She doesn't move fast. She makes decisions about when and how far to stick her neck out. When she does, she can be incredibly vulnerable. She's tough as can be when she retreats into her shell. She gets to where she's going in her own time."

Move beyond the realm of what's been done before.

The foggy glow of a smoky quartz crystal emerged from the bag next. Andrea held it up to the light. "I brought this because, for me, its darkness and lack of clarity represent woundedness. We're all wounded. When we accept that about ourselves we can be much more open to others. We don't have to pretend to be perfect."

Now the soft pink of a rose quartz crystal shimmered as Andrea held a new "trick" up to the light. Its vitality sparkled in amazing contrast to the smoky quartz. "This rose quartz symbolizes healing. The light of life shines through it. Its color communicates hope."

"The green in this tiger's eye marble radiates heart energy—the vitality, courage, essences of life. When we're connected at this level, we have the stamina and flexibility to struggle through our differences. You'll notice a slender rosy thread of color that appears here. For me, its beauty symbolizes femininity—a connection with internal, personal power."

Andrea shifted from linear problem solving—imposing a masculine solution where it just wouldn't fit—to her own feminine connection with the women on the teams. At that point, her creative fire blazed. She gave herself permission to do what made sense to her rather than following the "rules." She created a process that allowed the team members to view working together as a gain rather than a loss.

SUMMARY

Creativity, as with most other subjects researched by psychologists until very recently, has been defined by masculine standards. Research subjects tend to be male, though generalizations are made to cover everybody. When I started looking for material on feminine creativity, it was slim pickings. Research in this area will open up exciting possibilities.

For now, what we need to do, in all phases of our lives, is pay attention to our own creative urges, express them, and value them. We can then appreciate our creativity and validate that of other women. By doing so, we have the capacity to bring a significant shift to the places we work—aesthetically, interpersonally, in the way we do our work, and in the values that underlie the products we produce.

Aggression

How do you feel when you're mad? Or when you're totally committed to pushing toward some goal? Do you see red? Is your body energized? Do you feel solid and strong or shaky and splattered all over the place? What does it take to fire up your aggression?

Feminine aggression isn't usually for territory or position. It's aggression that supports self-sufficiency, not control over someone else.

"*Feminine* and *aggression* are contradictory terms. You can't be aggressive and feminine too." This sentiment, expressed by nearly a third of the people I interviewed—some women, some men—is a fairly common one. Does it fit your experience? In my own life, I feel the hot breath of feminine rage. Occasionally, her blazing eyes glare at me from the face of another. Her fire, energizing or destructive, also flares inside me. I don't always welcome the feelings, but, at times, they crackle with insistence.

Your own slow burn, anger, or rage kindles your feminine aggression. It comes from deep within you. As you read this section, test it. See if you can clearly identify your fire as it flickers or flares. Recognize energy that is different from the masculine-style aggression many of us have adopted as a survival skill.

Well trained to be a nice woman, I've had a hard time getting to know and trust my fire. As with many of us, this dimension was nearly snuffed as I was growing up. And so it tends to erupt as tears, not heat. But it has sustained me at times. I've gloried in achievements won by long slow fights, fueled by outrage and commitment. I've felt the coldness of defeat when my battle failed. I've worked and fought hard to achieve goals that seemed impossible. I've been accused of being ambitious. All that feels like aggression to me—aggression of a feminine kind.

Most women don't fight to dominate others. Feminine aggression isn't usually for territory or position. It has more to do with personal survival than with power. It's aggression that supports self-sufficiency, not control over someone else.

The raw energy of combative aggression is more masculine than feminine. It's the main way boys' play differs from girls'. Masculine aggression has more to do with taking over, with defeating another. Men appear to enjoy aggressive actions much more than women do. Sports fans admire a bone-jarring hit in a football game. They see combat as a sport—and sport as combat. Women may attend prize fights, but usually as supporters, not fight enthusiasts. Few women experience joy in watching two people knock each other into oblivion or thereabouts.

Feminine aggression lurks in corners—comes out in the open for a cause. Or it presents itself indirectly—in sneaky ways—not for the hearty fun of it. Frank Lawler, a human relations professional in Indianapolis, confessed: "I'd much rather have a man angry with me than a woman. Men are more predictable with their anger. You know where they're coming from. With women, aggression is hidden, malicious—difficult to get a handle on. It's very tricky—a knife behind the back and lots of sideways movement."

Christine Newsom, a rural California physician whose male colleagues outnumber her ten to one, expressed her opinion heatedly: "A hell of a lot of feminine aggression exists in our country—stemming from women's tremendous frustration with their lot. I think more times than not, it's unrecognized. Most women wouldn't come out and say it. Frustration leads to anger and self-hate—which is another form of aggression—self-aggression."

Pure feminine aggression is the energy that harangues until the school crossing is secured, pushes for a defined relationship, organizes a peace march, fights to save the life of a condemned criminal. It's assertion, ambition, and willingness to take on a cause. It forges connections with others, rather than using people as stepping stones to power.

We can handle masculine aggression at work without getting hooked into blowing up or giving in when we're comfortable with our own anger. We can protect our personal boundaries and fight to be taken seriously. We can stand firm to protect opportunities for soft or creative expression.

It's important for us to honor the feminine side of our aggression openly and completely. Here's a story about some consultants who paid dearly for not giving enough attention to their inner fires. They could have made a stronger case, but didn't take the risk.

The woman who told me this story opened by saying, "I don't know whether to laugh or cry!"

Until shortly before she shared this tale of woe, she and another woman had worked many years for a medium-sized manufacturing company.

> For close to a year, we talked with the decision-makers about the importance of reorganizing a particular department, internally as well as the way it served the total organization. We could see that they were headed for trouble. It would have been a major change, requiring big expenditures.
>
> Since our contract ended, the company has hired "Mega Masculine Consulting Firm," for at least four times what they were paying us. The new consulting firm looked at this problem area and saw the administrative failure that we had predicted. The decisionmakers had all but sneered when we called attention to the problem and recommended big changes. Mega Masculine Consulting Firm came up

with recommendations revoltingly similar to those we had made repeatedly. And the decisionmakers went for it.

We were furious. We really wanted to say "I told you so!" It was maddening. We had horrible green-eyed monsters—ferocious images of mayhem and worse.

These women felt their aggression. After the fact. Contained aggression—not acted upon—but aggression, nonetheless, felt too late to do them any good. The same amount of energy firing their early recommendations might have won the decisionmakers' attention.

This event provides a great example of how the feminine presence is exploited in typical work settings. Healing feminine energy was O.K. for keeping the peace and making the organization work better. But when it came to really changing the structure, the way things worked, feminine voices landed on deaf ears. It's O.K. for women to "help," but not to move aggressively into new products or new ways of doing business.

The story might have unfolded differently if these women had taken their own aggressive energy more seriously. They can be angry with the decisionmakers and feel put down, but they can't blame the company executives. Their low-key style was a big part of their defeat. From here, it's easy to see what they *should* have done. More heat and considerably less fear of being seen as pushy— more energy in confronting the way women were treated in that company—would have served them, and their client, well.

Possibly, they could have held the space to move in and do the work that needed to be done. But to do so, the fire had to burn. Their aggression early in the process—in the form of clear, supported assertion and confrontation— could have energized them to fight, to say clearly and directly what needed to happen and why. The consultants hadn't risked fighting hard enough for what they believed—and were put off. The results felt terrible.

Here's a story with a happier conclusion. Although it concerns a single afternoon, not a long process, the principle is the same.

At the time of this event, Peggy worked as a staff assistant to an elected state official.

For some people, it was just another scorching summer afternoon. For Peggy, it was another day of legislative hearings—hours and hours of detailed material that would eventually shape the state law. She hadn't thought there would be a problem with the testimony she had to offer. But as her presentation unfolded, she found herself surrounded by hostile witnesses.

"I find it hard to see this item worth talking about," one staffer bantered.

"I concur," another drawled.

Much to her surprise, the legislative staffers, friends of hers she thought, were belittling the issues at stake. They were playing political games, bantering and exchanging verbal barbs with no apparent commitment to get the work done. A strong but quiet person, Peggy shifted without even thinking about it from routine participation into the energy of her own aggression.

Her voice rose. She fought for eye contact.

"Here's a crucial section . . ." she asserted, and launched into the details.

As the afternoon's dialogue wore on, her agitation grew. The seriousness of the situation hit her. A little panic set in. She was feeling picked on. A slow burn heated her cheeks. She feared tears. "I just can't cry," she thought. "These guys are acting like jerks. I'm not going to let them get to me."

Instantly, she could feel her calm increase and her strength grow. Resolve replaced irritation. This typically soft, gentle woman found that she had abundant fire to counter their smart comments and to squelch the nitpicking that threatened her proposal. She couldn't stop all the damage singlehandedly, but she avoided serious losses. She didn't "win," but she held the space so she could return another day.

The feminine side of life isn't all sweetness and light, but many of us keep this idea going. We douse our internal fires and adopt a smiling face to cover the pain. This smothering process adds to the high frequency of chronic depression among women. As we live in our powerful feminine experience, more of us are better able to care for ourselves in the world. Smiling masks drop and the female depression index slopes downward.

In addition to having it stomped out of us by centuries of male-centered history, we have our own needs to quiet scary aggressive feelings. As the physically weaker sex in terms of mass and muscles, it's dangerous to be aggressive in situations where we're not in control and don't have the power to win. But we duplicate this condition at work, where men hold the organizational power. In typical work situations they still have institutional muscle mass—financial control, decisionmaking power, the right to hire and fire. We need to learn psychological Aikido—the ability to fend off aggression without countering it directly. Our own aggressive energy supports us in knowing we have the right to go after what we want.

On the job, we have to be willing to deal with the defensive and angry reactions that aggression provokes. If we dish it out, we have to be willing to take it. Sometimes it's not worth it.

Most little girls are discouraged when it comes to feeling and exploring aggressive feelings. We learn that these feelings are "bad"—that people won't like us unless we're nice. We find ways to blend with the environment rather than assert our differences. By the time they're in the fifth

As the physically weaker sex, it's dangerous to be aggressive in situations where we're not in control. But we duplicate this condition at work, where men hold the organizational power.

grade, girls have given in to what Catherine Steiner-Adair has dubbed "The tyranny of kind and nice." They've learned to say, "Do you want to know what I think? Or do you want to know what I *really* think?"[1] Since we don't typically accept and explore our own feminine aggressive patterns, we find ourselves tying on boxing gloves that are oversized and weigh too much. We struggle with masculine tactics that don't really fit who we are.

During the 1970s, "assertiveness training" became very popular—a major force that supported women's efforts to get out into the world and get their share. Assertiveness training teaches skills and builds confidence to go for more of what we want and need. When my colleagues and I taught assertiveness skills, we were very careful to accent the difference between "assertive" and "aggressive." To assert was fine—to aggress, a no no. But we need to go further, to understand and express aggression that is an important aspect of our womanhood.

The path is in our most primitive feelings. We need to connect with the energy that fires a mother bear to defend her cubs. We need to reach for Warrior Woman's righteous rage. Individual access to this personal power is a strong, protective force when we know it and can contain it. All humans have primitive feelings. Our choice is to deal with them consciously or lose a vital connection with a prime energy source. Use them to fire assertion, persistence, creativity. In getting to know these very basic feelings, we can honor our feminine aggression, expand our self-understanding, and grapple with who we really are.

Too often, we understand aggression in the ways we see leadership—in masculine ways. They fit us about as well as a jock strap. Because our aggressive feelings have been so unacceptable to us, many of them have been stuffed deep into our shadows. When we have the courage to plumb their depths, the experience is a rich and necessary one—but not a particularly pretty sight. The smiling mask cracks and falls off. We feel exposed.

To copy the masculine style doesn't really do it either. When we learn to play men's games—to go for the jugular or win for the sake of winning—we lose contact with our own feelings. That route leaves us empty and guilty, one more example of acting rather than being. We need to feel our own fire and find ways to channel our hot feminine aggression.

To ignore this part of our existence, though, means that unexpressed aggression simmers and flares in unpredictable ways. It blocks access to our love energy. We can't be mad and loving simultaneously. If we don't know how to get mad and get through it, we just deaden ourselves a little bit. Over time, we feel more numb than anything else. Dealing with anger in close relationships is very hard for most women. It brings up deep fears of loss of connection. But learning how to do this is essential for keeping a real relationship over time—at work or at home.

THE SHADOW SIDE

"Hell hath no fury like a woman scorned." This phrase deals with the shadow side of aggression—pure, raw, unbridled rage—anger spewing with no concern for the consequences. Destruction is the goal, plain and simple.

Aggression comes from the dark. Fiery anger flares in the open. In less obvious ways, carping, cattiness, and mean withholding are also the shadow side of this dimension. When we feel trapped, we splatter our anger, even without intending to do so, on those who are closest and dearest to us. Or we stuff it.

The shadow side of feminine aggression is also familiar as self-hate. It boils when women compete for masculine approval or attention. It appears as getting even, deceitfulness, and cruelty—as destructive explosiveness.

Headaches and depression are often the shadow side of aggression that is too frightening to express directly. Our shadow tries to inform us. When we don't pay attention, or can't, it doesn't just go away.

For some, unexpressed aggression is hungry. Food soothes; eating subsitutes for fighting. Getting fat seems safer than expressing anger toward someone else. The anger is still there, of course, but now self-hate is piled on. You can be mad at yourself. No contest. Anorexia and bulimia are about feminine anger too. They are complex expressions of rage that don't yield to simple solutions but can be successfully treated.

Every working person is familiar with the shadow side of passive feminine aggression—being aggressive without saying anything—at work. We know her tight lips, averted glance, burning eyes. The woman who won't deal with her aggression directly fumes. She isn't fun to be around.

Women in authority have another shadowy option. We can be impossible to satisfy. We use criticism as a weapon, pick on people who don't have the power to fight back, and control others in destructive ways. When we find ourselves in this place, we need to figure out what we're angry about and handle it directly.

One of the most damaging forms this shadowy dimension takes is gossip—"trashing" other people, especially other women, but men get their share, too. We learn to do this as little girls and get even better at it as teenagers. It is a "safe" way to dump aggression, because the target isn't around to fight back.

Smoke, the shadow side of this fiery dimension, is dangerous at work. Flames can burst out at the slightest, irrelevant, provocation. When we find ourselves in a state of chronic low burn—hostile, sarcastic, cynical—it's time to figure out some better ways to take care of ourselves.

Shadowy aggression is not to be ignored, but it is complex to try to understand. We need to be able to sort out the roots of our anger. Are we responding to unrealistic, childish expectations that have been stomped out? Or are we reacting in self-supportive ways to real danger?

By ourselves, we can't do a very good job of sorting out whether our own anger is grounded in present reality or the unresolved past. Outside feedback helps. If trying to manage the shadow side of aggression consumes a major part of your energy, a guide—friend, therapist, or trusted colleague—can be very helpful.

SELF-REFLECTION

Aggression is an important dimension in your feminine power at work. It's your backbone and your fighting spirit. The fire of your aggression protects you in the dark night of exploitation or oppression. But you have to be in charge, not whirling about, out of control, in its smoky heat.

Is your aggression a familiar driving force for you, or can you barely feel it? It's not so much that you should have it in great abundance. It's more that you need to know what to do with it when it arrives. If your fire in this dimension has died or been smothered, other areas are likely to suffer as well.

Now, think about how you see yourself in this dimension. Use these suggestions to guide your assessment.

STRENGTH: I get angry at times and can deal with those feelings. I have a hot temper, but I've learned to contain myself. Sometimes I get so mad I can't see straight, but I can go for a walk and cool down. I don't particularly like to fight, but I won't back down from something that's important to me. I don't let people exploit me.

SHADOW: My rage overwhelms me at times, and I

don't care what I do or say. Sometimes I get physical if I'm really mad. I'll get even, no matter what. / I never get mad. Nothing is worth a fight, as far as I'm concerned. I'm afraid of my anger and never let it out.

TIME FOR YOURSELF

To live in your world with authority, you have to be highly visible at times and take actions that may be unpopular. Expressing your aggression means being ready and able to handle any backlash that comes your way. When you can trust and express your aggressive feelings with confidence and clarity—using good communication skills—your fire energy fuels your inner support system. You know who you are. You know that you're being true to yourself.

It's time to make a place for this frightening dimension of the feminine. Then you will not be so likely to collapse and subject yourself to being used. Here are some ways to practice:

• THINK OF ANY TIME in your life when your aggression has served you well. If you have several examples, you might choose just one to work on for now. Write a few sentences about that time in your journal.

• IF YOU CAME UP WITH no examples in the step above, look for a situation that irritates or offends you in some way. Your aggression may be deeply buried—inaccessible to your conscious search. It is possible that your aggressive fire burns somewhere in that situation. List the ways you might be angry.

• WRITE ABOUT HOW your feminine aggression (fierce, protective, solid, goal-oriented rather than win-oriented) emerged in the incident you described above. Or were you relying more on your masculine style (combative, territorial, need to win)? Neither is right or wrong, good or bad. But it helps to know which is which. If you're relying primarily on masculine-style aggression—fighting to be sure the rules are enforced—you may have more centered fire under that. Aggression that comes from your core, from your own subjective sense of what is right, provides more solid guidance than something you've copied as a survival skill.

• MAKE A LIST of ways you express your healthy feminine aggression. (Push for childcare services where you work; confront inappropriate sexual remarks at work; write letters to the editor.) Think about things you can add.

• DIG OUT YOUR ART SUPPLIES and find some fire-colored pens, crayons, whatever. In your journal, experiment with their brightness. Color a fire if you're so inclined. Or just put the colors on the page. Write words over the colors that name your aggressions.

• THINK OF A TIME AT WORK when your aggressive energy could have energized you to function more effectively. Write about that time. How would you do it differently now?

• DO YOU CRY when you're mad? Next time you have the opportunity, talk through the tears. Concentrate on your fire energy and support yourself with your anger.

• KNOW WHEN AND WHERE you choose to make a stand. Know, too, what you want from the effort. Many of us work in environments that spark aggressive fires on a regular basis. If this is your situation, be selective about which battles you choose to engage in. It makes sense to fight battles you have a chance to win. If there is one brewing now, list steps you might take, supported by your aggression, to make things better.

• PREPARE TO DEAL with the results you don't want that inevitably accompany aggression. Try to estimate the direction and intensity of backlash that any aggressive action entails. Know ahead of time how you plan to handle it. Write about what you predict and how you intend to respond for the example in the previous exercise.

• PAY ATTENTION TO YOUR HUMOR. Much humor is hostile, covering more direct expression of aggression. Think of an incident where you have used hostile humor recently. Write a few lines in your journal about what you think your shadow was trying to say to you.

• KNOW THE DIFFERENCE BETWEEN venting—letting off steam—and making a stand. Pure discharge of feeling is likely to be destructive. It helps if you can say, "I need to let off steam!" When you take a stand, your goal is clearly in mind—something that you have a chance to achieve. Write briefly about one example of venting and one example of fighting for a goal.

• ANGER IS OFTEN A COVER for hurt which neither seething nor venting can heal. Such a hurt needs to be dealt with directly and assertively. If you find that you are chronically hurt, take steps to determine whether you are taking things too personally. If you are being mistreated, make a list of steps you can take to leave what is for you an abusive situation.

• IF YOU HAVE A REALISTIC FEAR of losing control, learn about rage-reduction techniques. People who are fairly inhibited often feel that any show of emotion is loss of control. It's not. On the other hand, if you are explosive and lose contact with how your actions affect others, look at this issue closely. Being able to turn your aggressive heat up or down requires knowing yourself well. List some techniques you can use to contain your anger—keep it under control—so that you can sort out which parts you choose to express directly.

• CHRONIC, OVERWHELMING RAGE that indiscriminately smokes up the environment is a form of feminine aggression that needs special attention. If you're a person whose usual mood state is a low burn subject to ignition by a short fuse, you face a different task from the one this chapter emphasizes. First, you have to learn to integrate and contain your aggression so that explosions don't blow you and your co-workers away. Ultimately, it's important to do some internal fire-fighting. Some places to start include books such as: *The Angry Book*, by Theodore Rubin; *Dance of Anger*, by Harriet Goldhor Lerner, and *The Intimate Enemy*, by George Bach.

• Using the last time you exploded as an example, write some ways that you could have expressed your anger without losing control. It's important to know the difference between using aggression to energize yourself and dumping it. The latter is destructive to others and to you. List some consequences you have suffered from dumping your aggression—or from being the target of somebody else's dump.

Turn to page 27 and make whatever changes you feel would sharpen your rating on aggression. Use a red pen.

Living with Your Aggression on the Job

Did you ever notice how your boss thinks your fire is wonderful if you're aggressively seeking new clients but not so great if you're angry about something she or he has done? Aggression at work is tricky business. Unless you have the perfect job, more of your aggression is likely to get stirred up than you can express safely. Plan your strategies well. Although your aggressive feeling comes from the depths of your feminine soul, if you dump it thoughtlessly at work the fallout can really hurt you. Be sure that you're centered and able to handle the consequences you trigger.

It's important to learn to stay in touch with your aggression at work. Let it surface and inform you. You don't have to act it out. If you're mad as hell about something, look for the shadow aspects first. What parts of yourself are you trying to reject in the other person or the situation? After you identify these and work with them, figure out what you need to do either to change the situation or to get out. Psychosomatic illnesses—ulcers, some headaches, hypertension—clue you in to the possibility that you're burying your aggression. Listen to your body.

Learn to confront from a centered place when you need to do so. If you haven't already, take an assertiveness training workshop or find one of the many good books on this topic and equip yourself with basic skills in assertive communication.

Whether it's biological or a learned response to crushed feminine aggression, many of us cry when anger flares. If you dissolve into tears when you're mad, it's important to be able to say, "I'm crying because I'm angry. And I want to keep talking about this until we finish the conversation." Your tears aren't a sign of weakness and they don't have to stop you. Let others handle their own discomfort with the situation.

On the other side, any time you push the system, compete, or assert something that threatens the way things are, you're likely to become the *target* of aggression. It's important to know how to protect yourself when aggression is aimed at you. If you do this from a feminine perspective, your stance may be simply to hold the line—without reacting outwardly. Sometimes you "win" if you can stay centered without getting hooked into the fight. Images from Aikido or other martial arts, where the attacker is defeated by his or her own force, are helpful. If you genuinely know your position, you can flex one way or the other so that your antagonist flies right past you. You won't be hurt.

It helps to know, too, if your "opponent's" aggression is based in fear. If that is the case, it may be possible to offer reassurance directly or indirectly to reduce his or her anxiety: "Look. We both have a job to do here, and we're both trying to get ahead. Let's see if we can figure out some ways to work together rather than working at cross purposes. Let's determine exactly where we disagree and see if we can divide up the territory." Remember, the more prickly and nasty a person has to be to protect his or her territory, the more insecure and frightened he or she is inside.

Regardless of how clear you are or how competent

you have become in living with your own strong feelings, there will be times when you have to deal with people who don't play by the rules—when there is no way to "win" fair and square. There are people in the world who have been so psychologically wounded that they have developed no conscience or capacity to care about others. And because of their willingness to hurt or exploit others, many of them are highly "successful" in positions of power. When you have to deal with someone like this, open honest encounters are not effective. Open communication requires some trust. If you're sure this is the kind of person you're dealing with, your choices are to join them in a dirty fight, shut them out, or leave.

Most of your colleagues, though, have their own struggles with aggression and other strong feelings. Wherever people live, work, or play together, conflict is bound to erupt. Trust your resilience and learn to come back and work together or fight another day. Learn to resolve issues through negotiation, neither placating nor dominating. It helps to say things like, "I disagree with you, and I'm angry with you, but I'm willing to work on this until we get it cleared up."

As you speak out against the male-centered tradition of your workplace, the first part of learning to work together may look and feel more like conflict, intimidation, resistance, and explosion. Trust your staying power—your core strength. It is quieter but just as strong as the explosion. Bringing conflict out in the open doesn't have to mean humiliation and defeat. If you have the resources to rebound with honor, you may be able to understand and use your communication skills to talk about the conflict in a workable way that brings new energy to the job.

If you have the resources to rebound with honor, you may be able to talk about a conflict in a workable way that brings new energy to the job.

251

FEMININE AGGRESSION AT WORK

The huge state department where Ginny worked as a manager directing a statewide project had slashed, cut and squeezed until there was no more give. Budget cuts had become routine, first 10% across the board and then 20%. Now it was just a matter of "how much," not "whether" there would be another. Paranoia was rampant. Managers guarded their territory like starving tigers. Morale sagged.

Ginny stared at the memo in disbelief. She had heard rumors, but didn't think there was a chance it would really happen. With no consultation, the decisionmakers cut the whole category of temporary help from the budget. This way, no permanent people would have to be laid off and no particular programs would be drastically affected. An imperfect, but highly logical solution.

Stunned and furious, Ginny asked around. "How many people does this involve? Who are they? How much does it save? How will it impact programs? What other options are being considered? Nobody really knew the answers to these questions. And it appeared that no one really wanted to know.

Ginny was well aware that her 23-year-old, single-mother secretary, Rosa, fit in this category. She'd hired Rosa after interviewing several candidates for the important, but low-paying clerical job. Rosa's quick wit and dedicated efficiency kept the under-staffed office from bogging down completely. Ginny didn't even want to think about what she would do without her.

Ginny was well aware of political in-fighting among department leaders. As she began to get more information about how their power-brokering was going to affect peoples' lives, she became increasingly outraged. At the top of the department, deputies, directors, and managers, all men, were supported by executive secretaries and office personnel in full-time, permanent positions. When work overload poured in, they hired from a pool of regular employees who were known as permanent part-time, to get the work out the door. These employees worked for specified periods of time and received advance, formal notice when their time was up.

Ginny searched out the information she needed with persistence fueled by her anger. This cut would affect at least forty people. The savings would be hardly noticeable after "exceptions" were made for those managers who successfully protected their "temporary help" from layoff.

Ginny's hunch was right about who would be affected. Newer program managers who didn't have the clout to acquire new positions, mostly women, used temporary help as a resource. Using their creativity and flexibility, they patched together the staff they needed for projects that might last from months to several years. This way, in addition to clerical staff, they could hire people with special skills to do the specific things they needed. Although individuals who took the positions were warned that they were temporary, they took their jobs seriously and depended on them for basic support. In fact, that had been a workable arrangement in the past. Nearly all of the temporary staff were women. Many worked part time around precariously balanced childcare.

Despite her backbreaking workload, Ginny dropped everything and moved into warrior mode. She had never fought for an issue in the open, and she had never taken on something that seemed like a foregone conclusion. But she was so mad at the lack of caring and responsibility involved that she could hardly see. For three days straight, her red-hot aggression fueled her search for information, her creativity in putting together a plan, and her courage to fight hard for an unpopular issue.

She wrote a two-page memo to the decisionmakers: "When budget cuts became a way of life with this department, we agreed that the first priority was our people. Our commitment was to work relentlessly to achieve our main goals and to avoid putting our people out on the street at any cost. I guess we have forgotten that commitment. . . ." Her opening statement set the stage for facts and figures that clearly outlined the impact of the proposal. She finished by urging a reversal of the plan.

The deputies flared.

They were mad at her and she knew it. Not only because she had sent the memo up to the chief, but because they were embarrassed that their insensitivity was showing. This was a first. Sparks had flown in the past, but nothing like this. They didn't quite know how to do battle with this nice woman they'd worked with all these years.

But they couldn't deny the truth she had brought to them. Her willingness to search out the details and provide a clear statement of who was going to be hurt and how little it would really save made the difference. They could no longer eliminate temporary help in the fuzzy haze of ignorance.

The decision was reversed. The decisionmakers found a way to make the shift gracefully enough. Without Ginny's challenge, the initial proposal would have slipped through with no awareness of the sexism involved. Her willingness to bring the issue into the open and fight for it had saved 38 women's and 2 men's jobs against almost certain extinction. Her effort nourished the department's battered morale. She shared a moment of quiet pride when she said, "I'm exhausted and have a lot of work stacked up on my desk. But I feel wonderful about the outcome."

This woman's contained, focused aggression burned to sustain her efforts to help people who couldn't help themselves. It didn't explode all over the place, and she didn't try to smother it. She let it energize her.

Summary

Two of the dimensions in this section on passion, *Sexuality* and *Aggression*, don't fit the ways we have learned to think about feminine behavior at work. But they do provide powerful energy for the woman who knows how to contain and channel them. *Creativity* tends to sit around in the wings, under-appreciated by all concerned. But she's there for you if you invite her into the open.

Spend as long as you like with your journal summarizing how you connect with some of the suggestions in this chapter. If you've identified ways you can appreciate your aggression—or establish more effective methods to manage some of your explosive tendencies—clarify your thoughts by writing them down. Before flying off into Spirit's higher altitudes, use these moments to capture and record any insights or future steps the last three chapters have brought to you.

AIR

SPIRIT: A NEW VISION

Air: The Element

ig questions, questions about what it means to be a person, waft into our awareness at work as well as in more meditative moments. What's right? What's fair? How do we deal with work challenges to our personal integrity? This section explores *Intuition, Wholistic Thinking,* and *Wisdom and Spirituality,* the dimensions of the feminine that juggle those cosmic questions on the job.

At work, I think about matters of the spirit "simply" in terms of personal integrity—how we stay true to our human spirits.

We can connect with our strength and stamina, live in the ups and downs of our relationships, and feel our passion. Air, the invisible element that surrounds us—that we can't do without—symbolizing ethics and personal integrity, is more elusive. It evades our grasp and our sight. Like the wind, we hear its passage sometimes—feel its gentle warmth on our faces or its gritty dust in our eyes. But we have trouble pinning down the issues, because our experience doesn't fit the patriarchal world in which we work.

We breathe in and process this world in a personal, connected way. We get by. But a lot of what we do or how we do it doesn't make sense to us. We need to give ourselves permission to notice our conflicts and think our own thoughts about how we want to manage our inner tugs and pulls. We can still wonder and explore—feel our world with our own hearts and minds.

I can remember, as a kid, lying on my back beneath the sparkling dome of Arizona sky stuffed with blue. I reveled in its unending depth. Supported by the warm earth, covered by that blanket of blue, I felt full and safe—a real sense of what it was to be me.

I thought about the sky, beyond the sky, beyond the sky—tried to pierce its heights with my bare eyes. Explanations for its vibrant color fell short—didn't satisfy me. If the air between you and me is colorless, and the sky is air—why's it blue? I wondered where heaven was in relation to what I could see. And how did the angels stay up there?

Sprawled on the scratchy bermuda grass of my front yard, I could see the San Francisco Peaks, sixty miles away. Lavender against that infinite space that looked blue, their lofty volcanic pinnacles offered a sacred home to the kachinas, legendary Hopi spirit guides. From where I sat, the mountains appeared within easy reach. When the hot pink and purple sunset (this was before "mauve") converted them to silhouettes, it was easy to see that any self-respecting god would call them home.

I'd heard stories of the power and wisdom of the kachinas. Some of the tales of their attitudes toward child development were enough to keep me in line when the off-limits cookie jar called to me. But I was in way over my head when I tried to resolve what I understood about the Native American way I knew at home with what I heard about God at Episcopal Sunday School. To my way of thinking, each view had its plusses and minusses. No way could I reconcile their massive contradictions with each other. I had friends who were Mormon, Catholic, or Baptist—and some who seemed quite nice to me but had no truck with God at all. Their actions all seemed about the same amount of good or bad, right or wrong, based on what was happening—not necessarily on their religious preferences.

When I was twelve or so, Meme died. This woman who had lived in my home from before my birth and had provided major TLC for my sister and me was a Papago who had converted to Catholicism as a child. I was too sad to go to her funeral. But later I overheard my mother telling someone that the service was part Catholic, part Mormon, part Papago. And as their special blessing for her spirit journey, her Hopi friends made offerings of piki bread at the grave site. In its own way, each group expressed love and concern for Meme's earthly departure. I felt a little reassured. Lots of people cared about her. And I understood now that grown-ups had trouble with those choices that always seemed so clear to whoever preached the sermon, but not to me. Somehow Meme, in her spiritual equanimity, had lived them all.

Today, that brilliant Arizona sky that reached forever greys with smog. I'm not sure you can see the home of the kachinas from sixty miles away. And the elms that shaded that scratchy patch of lawn and others along the street that bore their name have long since succumbed to disease and been cut down. The natural haze of the Grand Canyon, its trademark from before time, now binds with impurities that clog the view so that on many days the throngs of tourists no longer see from rim to rim. Pollution particles intensify the sunset, but deaden the daytime sky.

Our environment is in trouble. The human environment of the workplace suffers too. We sabotage the atmosphere on an individual basis. We settle for less than clean air when we lose our connections with our inner selves. More and more of us live in technical, urbanized settings, cut off from our connections with nature. We shutter the authenticity and richness of the human spirit and conform to the expectations that surround us. We focus on survival—play the roles in which we've been cast. We can do terrible damage to our personal air quality and not even know it. There's no immediate visible feedback.

At work, I think about matters of the spirit "simply" in terms of personal integrity—how we stay true to our human spirits. And if we extend the feel of it a little, how we respect, support, and connect with the deep humanity of others on the job. It seems as though this should be fairly simple, but for many reasons the air at work, symbolic or real, can be polluted or in short supply.

We can take more of our blue-sky gazing to work with us than we ever thought possible. In fact, as time goes on, our capacity to stay in touch with and support our own spirituality on the job—to honor who we are at a deep personal level—enriches our lives and keeps us healthy.

Though it provides no answers, each of the following sections offers support for your journey inward, contact with your human spirit as a working woman. The self-discovery that unfolds in these dimensions inspires all the others and can only grow throughout your life.

Intuition

Sit down to write a letter to a friend. She calls.
Wake up understanding perfectly how to do something that's been puzzling you for weeks.

Take a different route home from work, only to find that the regular one was blocked by an accident.

Start concentrating on a project and remember a phone call you were supposed to make three days ago.

Look at someone you've never seen before and know what he's going to say before a single word forms.

Greet a customer and know, within a few seconds, what she's going to buy.

Intuition, the morning breeze of subjective truth, refreshing and unconventional, vitalizes business when we know how to hear, respect, and communicate it. Our own truth, the quick breath of insight, a shifting current within, alerts us. We get wind of something—without the support of tangible data. A hunch pushes us to action. We look at a new situation or problem and know what it's about in a quick, automatic way. Or we look at an old problem for the hundredth time and suddenly see a way through it, without understanding how the solution came together.

As Marilyn Loden has pointed out,

> like other qualities associated more with women, intuition in problem-solving was not regarded as a skill to be taken very seriously by organizations. In fact, evidence suggests that because of its association with women, intuition was under-

valued, misunderstood, and regarded as virtually useless in many businesses.[1]

But times are changing. We have to deal with so much complex information in so little time these days that we can't always wait for step-by-step data analysis. In some situations, knotty problems can't be untangled in orderly ways. "Just woman's intuition," is an understatement in serious need of revision. We need ready access to our intuitive processes. And we need to know how to support and express what we find there.

Whether or not women are really more intuitive than men, feminine body energy, receptivity and flexibility are sensitive to intuitive messages in ways that make them useful. In his book, *Intuition in Organizations,* Weston Agor credits Frances Vaughn with "the best-known theoretical treatment of intuition to date." She believes that intuition functions on four distinct levels:

- Physical—bodily sensations that send us messages about people or situations for no apparent reason,
- Emotional—signals transmitted in the form of feelings,
- Mental—recognition of patterns in seemingly unrelated facts, and
- Spiritual—direct, personal perceptions or feelings that reveal the underlying oneness of life.[2]

We are channels for non-linear information from many inner resources.

"I just had a great idea!" precedes an intuitive statement that something new and different is on the way. Fun, colorful, irrational, intuition's unpredictability breezes through us.

In "Five Ways Women Are Smarter than Men about Money," *Money Magazine* writer Gary Belsky says that women do their homework: "Men are much more likely to

Whether or not women are really more intuitive than men, feminine body energy, receptivity and flexibility are sensitive to intuitive messages in ways that make them useful.

act first and think later. Women pay attention to hunches too but then tend to follow with careful research."[3] Not having to know it all, the ability to ask for help, and the persistence to go after needed information are powerful partners for "woman's intuition."

Dreams, fantasies, and shielded memories all expand our view of reality. Intuition invites a shift in our everyday routine. A whirlwind through the rich scramble of the unconscious supplies us with images and information to which no one else has access—our own personal mythology for decoding the world. When current experience connects with this material in a meaningful way, a mini-tornado spins by with insight or information. The form it takes may be visual, incomplete, seemingly unrelated to anything at hand—but its meaning can be expanded if we give it room to breathe.

An inner voice may speak to us in unexpected ways when we are deeply connected with a subject or another person. "I just had a hunch that I should check on Jonathan," a young mother wept with relief as she shared a terrifying experience. She had intercepted her two-year-old just as he tumbled over the edge of the family swimming pool. "Suddenly, I felt uneasy and went to check him," she told me, "When I got up to go outside, I gave myself a bad time for being silly and overprotective. He was playing in a little area we had enclosed for him. I couldn't believe he had opened the childproof gate. I'm glad I acted on my hunch. I saved his life!"

The same process fans our work. Intuition is what we have that computers don't. When we're filled with information and experience, we synthesize and analyze it at a level beneath our awareness. We know, or at least have a good hunch, about what needs to happen even before we step through an item-by-item analysis. We guess what the problem is, what the market's like, what the audience will respond to. Given the overload of information that storms us and the impossibility of dealing with it all, this is a handy asset to have easily available. It makes sense to develop and use it.

At work, an inner riffle to double check my appointment book has saved me from scheduling errors innumerable times. The ability to say "Something just doesn't feel right about this . . . " has opened conversations that led to clearing up conflicts that hadn't yet come to light. Sales people, managers, buyers, psychotherapists, teachers all rely heavily on intuition, whether they identify it as such or not. Scientists, lawyers, inventors, and physicians do to.

Dreams with full-blown problem solutions or sudden ah-ha's come to people who have been working on complex challenges over a period of time. Deena Metzger dreamed the title of her book, *Women Who Sleep with Men to Take the War out of Them*. She also quipped in a talk about feminine spirituality that when she asked her dreams for the rest of the book, she didn't get it.[4]

An early step in all of the organizational analyses that Mary Bolton and I conducted was the "intuitive take." We relied on feelings and hunches to create form where there was none. As we began work with a new organization, we listened very carefully to the workers at many levels. We tried to hear their emotional communication as well as the facts. Often the words didn't match the music. What they said didn't seem to make much sense, or fit too well with the obvious conflicts involved. As we began to collect preliminary information, we would discuss, feel, explore everything we knew about the situation. We walked in a windstorm of mythological ideas, characters from fiction, dreams, and examples, or scraps of previous experience until a graphic "map" would present itself.

Images of Knights Templar, roaring lions, pleasure seekers, and a serving class of indentured women surprised us with their presence in one case. We guessed at how the dynamics of the groups or individuals within each cluster in this medieval scenario might play out. Tentatively, we trusted our guesses as guidelines for next steps. Most of the time, data of a more linear, "reliable" type fell into place to support our intuitive insights—even though initially they seemed absurd or irrelevant.

If you're a person who works intuitively, you'll have other techniques to add to this list. In their research for *Women's Ways of Knowing*, Mary Belenky and her colleagues found that, for women, many of whom rely on subjective experience for knowledge and understanding, truth is an intuitive reaction—not thought out—felt rather than constructed.[5] This truth arrives in many different forms.

What *is* remarkable is the low regard that business and academia hold for subjective experience. Although men can have "gut reactions," it's dangerous for women to admit them. Marilyn Loden and others attribute this to the fact that intuition has been closely associated with the feminine and therefore discounted. In their research, the Belenky group found that women who rely on their own subjective experience as a source of knowledge are at a special disadvantage when they go about learning and working in business and industry. It's the public, rational, analytical voice, not the intuitive, that receives the corporation's attention, respect, and rewards. The product that emerges from intuition's inspiration receives the praise. In "For the young who want to," poet Marge Piercy laments:

> Genius is what they know you
> had after the third volume
> of remarkable poems. Earlier
> they accuse you of withdrawing,
> ask why you don't have a baby,
> call you a bum.

This speaks to the difficulty we have trusting intuition

as a resource. The masculine format of the public culture isn't fond of the feminine "intuitive take." "Logical" or "scientific" approaches may use intuition as a starting point but, until recently, didn't cop to it. This is so much the case that many of us labor under the impression that we're not very intuitive. If indeed we're not, the condition isn't necessarily permanent. Those intuitive zephyrs may be stifled and still, but if you invite them, the air flow will increase.

The blockage didn't start with work. Typical school experiences stamp out intuitive wanderings early and replace them with linear focus. Off-the-wall ideas disrupt classroom conformity and order. We learn to keep our ideas to ourselves if they don't fit in, or if we can't support them with "logic." And so our unique contributions fly out the window as we learn to conform. Of course, this happens to little boys as well as to little girls. Everyone loses.

Intuitive understanding threatens people who relate to the world mostly in terms of what they can see and touch. "How do you know that?" they ask with amazement. It's scary for them if you jump to a correct conclusion without going through the data step by step. And they reject or belittle what they don't understand.

Demands for conformity and "efficiency" in the educational system, bureaucracies, and corporate life dull our intuitive capacities. It's hard to nurture intuitive flashes on a deadline or hear new ideas that don't fit the curriculum guide. We've become very good at ignoring information that doesn't move us toward our goals—goals that, in many cases, have been established without much conscious choice or insight.

Invite intuition to stay in your house and open her gifts. Let her whisk the stale air out of your life. She may not be particularly orderly or predictable, but she is colorful, poetic, and honest. When you listen to her, you hear the music of your soul, sparkling melodies that tune you

What is remarkable is the low regard that business and academia hold for subjective experience.

in to what's important and meaningful for you. Despite her artistic appearance, her high-tech scanning capacities offer you complex information summaries in mere seconds. She can clue you in to the subtleties of your environment. And more than anything, she will advise you about relationships, yours and those you manage. Intuition brings the fresh air of unique personal insight to the mundane strivings of public life. Getting to know her well may bring some painful conflicts into the open, but it's worth it to learn to trust her.

THE SHADOW SIDE

Intuition's shadow harbors dark premonitions and suspicion. You may be afraid of being wrong or afraid of being right. When we've been hurt or abused, we see darkness whether it exists or not. If our internal information is grounded in pain, that pain intuits more than necessary caution and a constant sense of foreboding follows us through our lives. Or our intuition shuts down and we relate only to what we can see or touch. We need proof at every step and can't trust our capacity to "know without knowing." Fright and insecurity rush in when others share their intuitions.

Feeling something strongly but refusing to recognize it expands intuition's shadow. The attempt to resist being who we really are because it's painful or inconvenient blocks receptivity to our intuition. Seeing things we don't want to see may be a disruption from the shadow side of this dimension, and not always welcome, but when we reject these offerings time after time, we deaden ourselves and become less conscious.

Intuition's ability to know things before they happen or predict events with some accuracy can be upsetting if the events are negative. What do you do with "unfounded" information that predicts dire consequences? Is your strong feeling that the plane you're about to step onto will crash intuition, fear of flying, or a death wish? The shadow keeps you stuck here rather than recognizing that each possibility deserves looking into.

Chasing intuitive whirlwinds without other kinds of reality testing can carry you off into impulsive actions that you may regret later. The shadow says, "I'm enough. Act now and check later!" Remember that your intuition is subjective data. Give yourself a chance to see how it fits with the rest of your world so that you're not off tilting at windmills.

Pictures from your intuition don't often come neatly framed. They may be abstract scribbles, blurred and difficult to understand. The shadow whispers, "Ah, that's not worth anything." You can trust, though, that if you look closely enough, you'll find something budding, if not yet quite definable. Stay with it rather than being sidetracked because it feels different.

Similarly, fragmented intuitive information in its raw form may be hard for others to follow. Another kind of shadow reaction, an exaggerated sense of self importance, mistakenly expects to be understood without efforts to order, clarify, and communicate. The shadow says, "Well, if they don't get it, that's their loss." Your intuition is important, but it's just a first step. Bringing it into the open to share with others requires some work.

The unique, self-centered nature of intuition, when not balanced with the ability to test our perceptions, can trap us in an inner whorl filled with distortions and crooked thinking. Bad dreams and other scary images disturb our sense of personal security.

Strong as it is, intuition isn't always "right." We need a way to respect both internal and external input. Sorting out what to pay attention to and what to ignore can be very confusing. It's always worth considering what your intuition offers. Your process of deciding what to keep and what to discard is one you develop over time by finding ways to test what works for you.

Even intuition's shadow side—exaggerated subjectivity—offers rich information. It highlights areas of your unconscious that are begging for attention. Make the scary characters in your dreams your allies. Get outside input from someone you trust about coded messages that are trying to surface. If you find yourself consistently ignoring or making light of your intuitive flashes, whether they're bright inspiration or terrifying nightmares, you're cutting off a major source of information about your inner life.

SELF-REFLECTION

Your intuition never sleeps. It fills your dreams as well as your waking hours with information from your unconscious and from the environment around you. As you learn to give it your conscious attention, you reach toward yet another powerful internal resource.

Take a few moments to reflect on your intuitive processes. Where do you tune into the continuum in this dimension?

STRENGTH: My intuition is alive and well. I recognize and value flashes of insight or awareness that come to me at various times. My "off-the-wall" ideas are a valuable resource to me.

SHADOW: I have no intuition. I hate it when other people offer silly ideas for consideration. I discard illogical thoughts that come to me. I want hard data to support anything I have to suggest.

Time For Yourself

The personal, scrambled, intuitive richness of the feminine offers honesty that brings a new level of human contact to work situations. Whether you decide to talk about intuitive information openly or not depends on how safe you feel. If an off-the-wall idea will get you clobbered, enjoy it in silence or find a safe place to share it. But don't put it down as stupid or silly in your own mind.

Your intuition is an important part of you if you're true to yourself. If it feels weird or meaningless that's likely to reflect the rigidity of the environment, not craziness on your part. If your intuitive channels are open and flowing, you can provide support for others whose feminine power is blocked on this point. If your channels are clogged, some of the exercises that follow may help.

• IN YOUR JOURNAL, make a list of hunches—things you knew without knowing—that you followed and that worked out for you. Do they have anything in common? Write about how much you value and trust your intuition.

• LIST THE FIRST FIVE WORDS that come to you that describe your intuitive process. Don't censor. (For example: quick, bright, funny, morbid, sarcastic. . . .)

• CHOOSE ONE OF THESE WORDS. Mull it over. Think about it in as many ways as you can for about ten seconds. Now write as many related words as you can that positively describe your intuitive style. Use some of these words to write a few lines in support of your intuitive process.

• THINK ABOUT A WORK-RELATED ISSUE that perplexes you at the moment. Write about it in your journal. Choose several words from your list and use them as guides over the next day or so. Just let the perplexing issue float around in the back of your mind without trying to organize it in step-by-step fashion. When ideas or thoughts breeze through, jot them down immediately. Record them in your journal when you have a moment, and then see if a pattern starts to form.

- WRITE ABOUT A WORK EXAMPLE where you intuitively knew something was going to happen and it did. Did you express your concern or excitement? If so, what helped you do so? If not, what got in your way?

- WRITE A BRIEF SUMMARY of a dream you had last night or one you can remember from some other time. Now read it as if it were someone else's story. What parts stand out? Is something asking for attention? What's your best guess about what this dream is saying to you? Write the answer in your journal as something to think about.

- IF YOU GENERALLY ACCEPT intuitive blips that come to you, intensify and expand them. Take them seriously before you decide whether or not to discard them. Listen to them. See if they become a part of you. Tell a friend about an intuition you've had recently.

- IF YOU TEND TO REJECT ideas that come to you—assume others will laugh or make fun of them—try being kind and supportive to yourself instead. Catch the thought before it goes away. Nurture and embellish it. It may not be usable in its present form, but if you work with it, meaning will emerge.

- FIND SOMEONE ELSE at work who is interested in paying more attention to her/his intuition. Share your thoughts and insights. Are you in touch with information that isn't being used or acknowledged? Is it useful to be expressive about your insights? Why or why not?

- FROM A CENTERED PLACE, try sharing your intuitions from time to time as suggestions or ideas to be considered. Don't expect immediate acceptance or appreciation. Differences are threatening to people who don't understand where they're coming from. Over time, as your "off-the-wall" truths are borne out, they will gain more credibility—with yourself and others. If your insights don't always pan out, this is valuable information for you also.

• DRAW THE SHADOW SIDE of your intuition. Is it tiny or huge? Where are its darkest splotches? Write words around the edges of your drawing that describe how your shadow works in this dimension. Does it scare, inhibit, worry, or confine you?

• DESCRIBE A NIGHTMARE or bad dream that you've had recently, or even sometime earlier in your life. If you look at it as a message from the shadow side of your intuition, what do you think it's trying to tell you? Use Ann Farraday's *Dream Power* or another method you know to work with this dream.

• WRITE THREE THINGS you say to yourself to diminish your intuitive flashes. ("It won't work," "It's too weird," etc.) Then write ways to counter each of these internal messages—to test and support your intuition.

• WRITE THREE EXAMPLES of times you've had dark premonitions and what happened to each. Was your "knowing" accurate? Or was the shadow side of your intuition blocking you in some way? Write about what you learned in each of these experiences.

• LOOK FOR EXAMPLES of intuitive thinking by others at work. Do you have a colleague who relies on this dimension extensively? Talk with her or him about how to rely on intuition as an inner guide. Write about what you learn.

• THINK ABOUT HOW YOUR INTUITION and your creativity work together. In the last week or so, what flashes have you had that have led to a creative effort on your part? Describe the moment of insight. How did you expand it to bring it to life?

Take a moment or two to check your initial Self-Assessment on page 28. Was your intuition clear the first time? Make whatever adjustments seem right.

INTUITION GOES TO WORK

Research tells us that women have more connective tissue between the right brain, which is thought to deal with non-verbal input, and the left brain, which seems to organize language. It may be easier for women to translate feelings and hunches from the right-brain into words.[6] To whatever extent this is true, women have more access to right-brain functions, which seem to include non-verbal, non-linear thinking—i.e., intuition. "Woman's intuition" may, in fact, be more than a survival skill developed to cope with living in a one-down situation. There may be biological reasons it is associated more with the feminine than with the masculine. Given this access, it makes sense to become supportive of the gifts intuition has for us on the job, rather than discounting them as unscientific.

Until femininity is more accepted as a legitimate work style, here are some ways to respond to a familiar and intimidating barrier: **Just Woman's Intuition:**

Do	*Don't*
Trust your feelings; they've been right before.	Discount or ignore your hunches.
Risk expressing your ideas.	Let propriety keep you from exploring.
Talk about your idea as data of a different kind.	Be quick to reject someone else's intuitive take.
Try it to see what happens.	Be overwhelmed by "logical" arguments or "scientific" data.

Do	*Don't*
Draw it, dance it, paint it to get it into words if you need to.	Be stopped by the argument "It's never been done before; it won't work."
Check out your hunches.	
See if your dreams are telling you anything about work.	Give up because you have a hard time getting it into words.

The first step is to get intimately acquainted with your intuition—with what it contributes as well as the conditions under which it flourishes. If you're an intuitive type, you probably already know these things. If you're not, which is true of about half of us according to the Myers-Briggs researchers,[7] the task is a little tougher. But it's worth pursuing.

Here are some ways your intuition can inform you on the job:

Let it tell you how the inner you connects with what's happening around you. When you can forget the expectations of others or how something is "supposed" to be done, your full concentration can focus on your task. You realize suddenly that something you're struggling with is clear and accessible when you can relax and see it from your own perspective.

You have more information than you can process. Give yourself time to sift and sort—to find the words you need to communicate what you know.

Earlier experiences, things that you may have done in some entirely different context, that you're not currently aware of but that you're processing at a level that's unclear to you, connect with work. The feeling you had when you were in the toughest part of a ten-mile hike may come to you as you grapple with an unwieldy marketing plan.

Now you know how hard it is and you can settle in to work it out step by step.

You may look at the same balance sheet you've been working with for a week and start to think of the color blue, which somehow lets you see where you can make the cuts you need to make.

You may be driving on the freeway and find yourself humming "Ding, Dong, The Witch is Dead" before you realize you have to have a conversation with your boss about how angry you are.

Or, you may realize, seemingly out of nowhere, that "this is like when Mara was cutting teeth—it's just going to be difficult for a while."

When you and your intuition are in trusting dialogue, you have the capacity to project into the future rather than being limited by what's provable. Based on your best guesses, you can create action plans to move in the direction you want to go. Then you can organize to make them work.

You can "reframe" or look at problems in contexts entirely different from the way in which you typically see them. A power struggle with a colleague becomes a challenge to your creativity rather than a measure of your strength or importance.

Intuition tells you whether a place is good for you— whether it "fits" or not. If for no logical reason, an apparently wonderful job possibility doesn't feel right, months later you may find out why. Perhaps the company will prove to be on shaky grounds; perhaps all the new hires will be on the street.

Given a chance, your intuition can tell you a lot about other people. Pay attention to how you feel when you're with them, not necessarily what they're saying about themselves. If you feel intimidated or insecure, they're probably making themselves feel important at your expense. If they're making promises that sound too good to be true, they probably are. You have more to work with than meets the eye when you trust your intuition.

Getting along with others is the area where intuition, knowing without tangible data, serves us best. Even a simple conversation goes on at many levels, most of them unspoken. If more than two people are involved, the situation gets even more complicated. Since it's impossible, for all practical purposes, to understand relationships in a linear way, other ways of knowing are a real asset.

Combining experience, knowledge of human behavior, and the way we feel when we're with someone gives us the information we need to make judgments about relationships. This is true for personnel decisions we make at work, as well as for the more personal decisions we make in our private lives. For most of us, the hard part is developing enough self-discipline to listen to our intuition when it's saying something we don't want to hear.

Since intuition is a subjective experience, not something that anyone else knows just the way you do, it's easy to back down when you're challenged. It helps to be able to restate your idea in several ways and to allow others to have a chance to mull it over. When ideas are new, they often get rejected first but accepted later.

If you happen to be a strongly intuitive person, you may find yourself becoming impatient with people who have a hard time following you. It's not because they're dumb or slow. Different people just have different ways of taking in and expressing information. When you know your intuitive process well, you can listen to it, integrate the information, and translate so that others can understand.

Earlier experiences that you may not be currently aware of but are processing at another level connect with work.

Summary

Intuition has been associated, sometimes negatively, with the feminine. It's a non-scientific, non-linear way of knowing—instantly, without much data—what's happening, what's about to happen, or what could happen. When it works well, it offers insight into complex situations or knotty problems that are unwieldy to study in more orderly ways. Under shadowy conditions it can lead us into dark subjective places that float away from what we know as external reality.

Intuition's reputation as a problem-solver is improving as organizations become more complex. Brainstorming and other techniques that rely on this dimension are commonplace as part of today's management tool kit. By giving more attention and respect to this part of your personality, you learn more about who you are. You also intensify your contact with what's happening around you. You then have more choices about how to initiate action and how to respond, both at work and at home.

Wholistic Thinking

> But there is another kind of seeing that involves a letting go. When I see this way I sway transfixed and emptied. The difference between the two ways of seeing is the difference between walking with and without a camera. When I walk with a camera I walk from shot to shot, reading the light on a calibrated meter. When I walk without a camera, my own shutter opens, and the moment's light prints on my own silver gut. When I see this second way I am above all an unscrupulous observer.
>
> Annie Dillard, *Pilgrim At Tinker's Creek*

A friend shared an example that illustrates a difference in the two views: "My husband fixes coffee every morning and brings it to me while I'm getting ready for work. I love him for it. It's a nice way to start my day. When we run out, he's off to the store to replenish the supply. If I ask him, he'll bring back whatever I put on a list. It would never occur to him, though, to look around and notice that we also need toilet paper, laundry soap and toothpaste."

On the other hand, the wholistic* thinker—an "unscrupulous observer" unrestrained by ideas of right and wrong or by how things *ought* to be—can take it all in.

---

* For the purposes of this book, Rollo May's concept of *wholistic*—integration of form with passion to make sense out of life—better describes the archetypal feminine capacity to comprehend and value the complexities and contradictions of the

We embrace big-picture thinking when we become parents. The baby needs to be fed, the toddler needs attention, and the rent has to be paid. It doesn't much matter if it's in the job description or whose job it is. We organize around making it happen. Although immediate needs may limit us to the most basic tending and caretaking, we remain very concerned about the world in which the child will live.

Receiving the world "on my own silver gut" describes the three-dimensional feminine view that includes the emotional impact of information. The "unscrupulous observer" sees it all, unrestricted by anybody's sense of right or wrong, good or bad. A single "snapshot," plucked from its surroundings, doesn't substitute for the truth that only the whole picture can reveal. And it can't work for us to continue to fit ourselves into a work world (or a home life) that is wholly defined by men. We have our own important ways of seeing.

Wholistic thinking blows in from all four directions. This special way of seeing—a broad view that encompasses the many parts of life, unrelated and contradictory though they may seem. Circular and illogical according to traditional "objective" standards, it may treat time and space as irrelevant. It sees with imagination—the opposite of short-term, focused, practical thinking. This dimension, our knowing that the aftereffects are as important as the event, has been sleeping for a long, long time. It's time for us to pay attention to it.

We know that it's not enough to "walk from shot to shot, reading light on a calibrated meter." Psychotherapist Nancy Jungerman says it this way, "In tune with our inner

---

whole scene than *holistic*, which means only that an organic or integrated whole has a reality independent of and greater than the sum of its parts. Rollo May, *The Courage to Create* (New York: Bantam Books, 1976), p. 158.

environment, our monthly cycles, we bring to our work an experience of tidalness. When we can be true to our femininity we ride these cycles in some kind of way—stay connected with the universe."[1] In addition to our technical knowledge and personal sophistication, we're integral parts of a natural whole. As the carriers of new life, we're concerned, not just about our own, but about the well-being of future generations. We need to be in tune with the "big picture." What is safe? What is healthy? What will best preserve the future?

Stephanie Johnson, a corporate executive in an eastern state, talked about wholistic thinking this way: "Women invest more energy in thinking through the full impact of an action—learning to anticipate the next immediate step. Men, including my husband who I love and respect a lot, don't seem to do this—they don't think big picture." This pattern doesn't fit everybody. Some of us are detail-oriented and don't relate to the big picture at all. But at a deeper level, it fits the feminine connection with nature and concern about future generations.

Women tend to see many sides to an issue and take them into consideration in making decisions. While men certainly have the capacity to do the same thing, the traditional masculine approach relies more on rules, the law, or agreed-upon steps to arrive at a solution. If the rules don't seem adequate to getting the job done, women are less likely to stick to them. Balance is important here. As Boston-based creativity consultant Marcia Yudkin pointed out to me, "Certainly a good Supreme Court Justice needs to be able to use both."

Wholistic thinking isn't about creating a great plan and fitting yourself into it any more than it's about fitting into someone else's master plan. It is about taking in the totality of your environment on your own silver gut and holding it there. In time, you digest it, make it your own, and turn it into energy. This energy allows you to express yourself from a centered place based on your view of the world and your place in it.

When I asked Joanne Irene Gabrynowicz[2] what came to mind when she thought of "feminine presence," her first words were, ". . . wholistic—the difference between being the parts of something and the totality that the parts create. The feminine aspect tends to relate to the whole by nature, whereas the masculine relates to the parts of the whole."

Joanne is an attorney who moved from New York City to North Dakota to teach space law and policy in the Space Studies Department at the University of North Dakota. She moved because it seemed right at the time and would do it again, she says. The thoughts she shared with me when I asked her about the feminine touched me deeply. They bring to life the feminine connection with wholistic thinking—how our "silver gut" collects and digests the world around us:

"Many of my students, members of missile and bomber crews, are the people who wait for the President to call. At any given time, one-third of them are on alert— in class in war gear. [Since the time of the interview this ratio has been reduced.] The bomb or missiles are right down the block. I teach on base—see the instruments of war—missiles and bombers.

"The way this first started to emerge in me was that I found myself worrying about my health. Cancer—my mother died of cancer—AIDS, death. I never had done this before. What was happening was that mortality—fear of death—was growing in me. What came fully to consciousness in the face of seeing those symbols—the life force burst forth in me—fear of my own death. Past that, this feminine force said 'life shall be preserved!' To call it maternal is trite. It would be feminine—like Sigourney Weaver in *Aliens*—protecting her baby at all costs. It's important to differentiate—very archetypal. I shared this with my students as well as another experience that affected me deeply.

"We have mammoth bombers here—the newest strategic bombers. If you've ever heard one, you don't forget it. They don't sound like commercial aircraft. One morning lying in bed before the sun came up, I heard one of them flying low toward the air base. As it flew over I started to think—Where did it go? What was its mission? Why did it have to be back by dawn? I told my students. Some of them laughed nervously. After the class some came up and asked if I was O.K. I realized they knew the process I was going through. They live with it.

"These experiences have influenced the content of the classes I teach—policy and law. I have actively begun to teach about the policy of fear. We have many policies based on fear. The driving force behind a lot of Cold War policy decisions was fear. This has to be brought to the surface—recognized for what it is. There may be perfectly reasonable reasons why we should be frightened. We have to know it and say it—recognize the force that it plays in our policies—the role that it plays in our policies. I don't think that many of my male counterparts see it this way. They would say that 'You are a professional, and there is no room for emotions.' My view is that if you are going to be a professional you have to recognize those emotions right up front."

Joanne took in the big picture and told it the way she saw it. She couldn't ignore it or push it away. She listened. She took the truth of her terror seriously—and believed it. Then, in a way very different from her male colleagues', she expressed it. She didn't follow the unwritten rules of silence. Instead, she named the issue—"The driving force behind a lot of policy decisions is fear"—and brought it into the open. Rather than separating her insight as "just an emotional response," she integrated it as a central focus of her teaching.

The feminine takes in, flexes, integrates and compre-
hends in ways that differ from masculine tradition. Our
self-esteem and sense of well-being center in our relationships, so we learn early to understand and care about how
we affect others. In the give and take of relationships, we
learn that self-interest isn't enough. We understand that
what we put into the atmosphere touches us all.

Philosopher Sara Ruddick writes:

> . . . A child's acts are irregular, unpredictable,
> often mysterious. A child herself might be thought of
> as an "open structure," changing, growing, reinter-
> preting what has come before. Neither a child nor,
> therefore, the mother understanding her can sharply
> distinguish reality from fantasy, body from mind, self
> from other. The categories through which a child
> understands the world are modified as the changing
> world is creatively apprehended in ways that make
> sense to the child. If there are comfortably sharp def-
> initions, they are ephemeral. A mother who took one
> day's conclusions to be permanent or invented sharp
> distinctions to describe her child's choices would be
> left foundering.[3]

Not all women are mothers, and Sara Ruddick writes
about "maternal thinking," but her point is a good one. If
we took care of children the way we run our businesses, it
wouldn't work. We can do better by bringing to work
what we know about nurturing kids—the capacity for
melding and molding, for responding and taking things in
context. Why would we follow short-sighted procedures
and planning at the office? How is it that we buy into limiting or destructive practices and products because they
are represented to us as more "professional" or business-
like?

We know, consciously or not, that we can't make decisions about life in small, discrete sections. We all breathe the same air. This is an important asset to bring to the business world, not only for influencing the way work gets done, but also for determining the goals we work toward. Wholistic thinking brings balance to the often misguided attempts at efficiency or profit that artificially chop work into small sections and severely limit connection with the big picture.

The "unscrupulous observer" sees it all, unrestricted by anybody's sense of right or wrong, good or bad.

But looking at life wholistically isn't an easy thing to do. In the rush to complete everyday business, wholistic thinking can be quite upsetting. We get so accustomed to tunnel vision we lose sight of how the parts fit with the whole. Taking an overall view, my consulting partner, Mary Bolton, would say impractical things like, "We need to get these guys together (warring factions who did not *speak* to each other) and have them look at how their short-range, instant, profit-focused actions are hurting the long-range well-being of the company." We didn't always necessarily make that intervention; our intuition and judgment balanced our wholistic thinking. But we used the idea to create a step in the direction of healing open wounds.

Long-range, wholistic thinking may work toward the preservation of the species and the planet, but it doesn't fit well with work deadlines. Keeping a focus on priorities—what's important in the never-ending spiral of birth, death, and transformation—makes a weird juxtaposition with deciding what to wear to work or whether or not the sales meeting goes well. The ability to see many contradictory facets—and to value them—rarely slides smoothly into the competitive business mode. It's contrary to the business-style focus on short-term goals that makes it difficult to support or explain the global view. Taking time to evaluate a situation and consider the implications of various courses of action on the future may appear inefficient or unfocused to those who need to get a product out the door today. And yet, wholistic thinking has much to offer today's suffering business and government.

In fact, the long-range view and extra time invested in making decisions can improve the quality of outcome and reduce the time needed to untangle and revise the results of hasty, "logical" decisionmaking.

Wholistic thinking presents a challenge. To meld this gift with more expedient approaches requires yet another balancing act. It's relatively easy to support and justify clear, specific, short-range goals in terms of profit and loss. And it can be overwhelming to look at the long range. The art of problem solving is in knowing when to shift from the feminine overview—holding, mulling, creating—to a more immediate "masculine" focus.

Since wholistic thinking tends to be non-linear, it's often hard to organize and communicate in a way that makes sense to those thinking in a sequential mode. We can feel crazy and confused about our own thoughts and, at the same moment, know they're solid and worthwhile. It's difficult to let yourself think and care about, let alone say, "I know that our new multi-million dollar plant in Korea is state of the art and will reduce our production costs. But it's hard for me to get excited about it when I know that we have high unemployment here and that the company will exploit the Korean workers as much as possible." Your wholistic view is likely to be seen as "disloyal," even though, in addition to your humanistic concerns, you're forseeing your company's difficulties in selling its products in the sliding economy where unemployed workers have reduced purchasing power.

THE SHADOW SIDE

Wholistic thinking gets shady when we become so overwhelmed by the big picture that we're immobilized.

We shut down and can't deal with anything but the most immediate detail. Anxiety rolls in and dancing dust particles obscure the distant view. We stumble blindly, directing our energy toward short-term solutions. When this happens, we need to get help in managing and understanding the anxiety. The shadow is letting us know that we've over-extended and need to pull back and regroup.

An exaggerated sense of self-importance can hide in the shadow of wholistic thinking. We can use this dimension to feel superior and put down those who don't see the world in the same way. Arrogance, or feeling superior because we can't be bothered with the details, alienates those who have to work with us. But sooner or later, if we are tuned in at all, we will get the picture that we can't do it all alone.

Oversight also creeps out of this shadow. When I first learned to drive, I was concentrating so hard on the stop light two blocks away that I ran through one that was right in front of me. That was a scary but potent lesson. We can get so concerned with a long-range goal that we lose touch with present reality. The overall plan is certainly important, but positive, day-to-day contact with customers, clients, or colleagues is what makes work flow smoothly.

The shadow side of wholistic thinking threatens to reduce us to total insignificance. Take any area of needed social change. If we look at the full scope of problems and think about what needs to be done in education, social services, mental health, highway improvement or health care—let alone all of them together—we can feel so small and helpless that any effort we might make seems useless. When this happens we need to get back to home base and find a level where we can make a difference. Very often, that will be in taking care of our own personal business.

The long-range view of our own self-interest also thrives on the shadow side of wholistic thinking. Greed is the shadow side's main component here. In the darker reaches of this dimension, our egocentric blinders slip into place and the big picture fades out of sight. The major push of our culture is to throw ourselves into a money-making or pleasure seeking frenzy and forget about everything else. It's no accident that a series of very slick, expensive beverage commercials, many of which subtly equate women with their product, repeat "Why ask why?" on the family television set. It's easy to get stuck here.

SELF-REFLECTION

Where do you fit on the wholistic thinking continuum? Like the other dimensions, this one isn't good and bad. Think about the shadow side, especially your vulnerability to being overwhelmed by too many possibilities, as you work with this dimension. If you get stuck in the big picture, it's hard to focus or know where to start. If the shadow takes over, you can become immobilized or headed in a direction that is not satisfying.

STRENGTH: Typically, I absorb a lot of information that helps me relate one thing to another. I don't have much trouble integrating contradictory information. I like to understand the relationship of one thing to another. Long-range outcomes concern me deeply.

SHADOW: I get impatient with others who are short-sighted. / I get overwhelmed with too many possibilities. I can't focus. If I can't do the whole thing, which is usually the case, I'm immobilized. / I want what I want now and know how to get it.

TIME FOR YOURSELF

This dimension has to do with how you take in and organize information from your environment. Are you aware of how you experience and express this dimension? As you select a few of the following steps to explore in some depth, reflect on ways you use information in a wholistic manner.

• LIST THREE EXAMPLES of times you've seen "the big picture" at work but didn't say anything because you thought others surely must know better.

• THINK OF A TIME you expressed concern about a long-range impact and were laughed at or received some other negative reaction. Who laughed?

• THINK OF A TIME you expressed concern about a long-range impact and your recommendation was accepted. Write about the outcome and how you felt about it.

• LIST SOME OF YOUR CURRENT CONCERNS about decisions at work that may have negative long-range outcomes for your workplace or for the environment. Would your organization be better off if they attended to the things on your list? Do you think they will? If the answer is no, what gets in the way? Write about values conflicts this brings up for you.

• WHEN AN IDEA FORMS or an image emerges, when you have an insight about the big picture, share your thoughts with someone you trust. Allow yourself to feel comfortable talking about your ideas even though you can't support them "logically." Support yourself, no matter what the reaction is. You've made a contribution.

• TUNE IN TO EXPRESSIONS of wholistic thinking by others. Whether you agree with them or not, support their right to their concerns. Be assertive.

Support yourself and others in expressing this dimension of the feminine presence at work. Big-picture thinking by women is threatening to those who are desperately attached to the status quo, and they often deal with this threat by belittling women who express big thoughts.

• Do you know a woman whose wholistic thinking you admire? How does she express this part of her feminine presence so that others understand? Talk to her about this aspect of her feminine power. Write down three steps you learn from her that can help you be more expressive.

• Write four feeling words that describe your emotional state at a time when you have felt overwhelmed by the number and complexity of details you have to manage. List three steps you could take to ground yourself if this happens again.

• Describe your shadow in this dimension. Does it grow and become grandiose so you have no patience for details or the short-sightedness of your colleagues? Or does it intimidate you so that you shrink to insignificance and hang on to the most obvious immediate step you can take? It may do both at different times. As you write your description, exaggerate it a little so that your shadow can stand out even more clearly.

• Think about a time when you focused so hard on the long-range goal that you failed to tend to your immediate business. Write about the lessons your shadow taught you with this experience. What would a more balanced approach have been?

• Draw a picture or diagram that illustrates how your job relates to someone in another country.

Wholistic thinking is nonlinear—not "logical." Through its wide-ranging rambles, the long-term relationships of one thing to another become apparent. It often provides a starting point, a brainstorm, for more practical steps. If you didn't experience strong pulls one way or the other doing these exercises, your thinking style may not fit this model. That doesn't reflect negatively on your intelligence or your femininity.

Did you identify areas where you might want to be more supportive or expensive of yourself at work? Were there some shadow feelings that popped out at you? Write in your journal about the steps you want to take for future work in this dimension.

Wholistic thinking is one of the more difficult dimensions to grasp. Return to your initial Self-Assessment on page 28 and adjust your rating to fit any new understanding you have gained.

WHOLISTIC THINKING GOES TO WORK

The world is shrinking. Multinational corporations are bigger and more powerful than governments. Decisions made by government and industry have life-and-death influence over countless individuals. What we do in our jobs has potential impacts for people on the other side of the globe, as well as in our immediate environment.

Air quality makes a real difference to people on a daily basis in the thriving city where I live in Northern California. Autos by the hundred thousand puff out their toxins as we busily transport ourselves from one end of the city to the other and back again. The Air Pollution Index fits neatly in the newspaper as part of the weather report. Citizens, particularly those with respiratory problems, plan their outdoor activities based on how "good" or "bad" the air is on any given day. Each year it gets more dense.

The newspapers also describe another kind of pollution, a political system clogged with vested interests. That, too, is the focus of this chapter—the deeply personal exploration of the place of a whole person in a whole world.

The state is the single biggest employer in Sacramento. Airtight office buildings where thousands of people spend their days are well-defended against a basic life support that I used to take for granted—fresh air. As city dwellers, we grow accustomed to this deprivation and numb to its consequences. We dull our senses a little to get by, just as we dull our sensitivity to our own feelings and those of others at work. There's no blue sky of any shade inside an office building, no fresh air in a factory, a hotel kitchen, or a warehouse. We survive on the recycled substitute. At work, we have dulled, recycled relationships, too—not too personal, not too real.

The "air quality" in many contemporary organizations is none too good. Demands for short-term profit, productivity, or the basic struggles for financial survival whirl us along like tumbleweeds in a dust storm. As we explore elusive ethical dimensions in the feminine presence, let the symbolism of this murky condition emerge as an image that screams for attention. Self-contact and healthy relationships occupy deep second place in those unnatural environments where we spend most of our waking hours. Concern for the impact on "air quality," symbolic or real, are swept aside by the goals of the existing power structure.

This dimension can make a major difference in how our corporations and governments operate and in the goals they work toward. It's part of us all.

We have to be practical after all. We can't lie on our backs and gaze at the sky and be productive workers—or feed our families, or buy the latest goodies. And who has time to practice four different religions at once?

But we can make room for some other images as well. How would the world be if feminine balance had a voice at work? Can we open the windows, let in the fresh air as we speak out clearly on issues that affect women's ways of working? Can we make our voices heard?

This dimension can make a major difference in how our corporations and governments operate and in the goals they work toward. It's part of us all. But we're so accustomed to fitting in rather than taking our own views seriously that we discount our wholistic view and don't give it an opportunity to grow. In the impersonal atmosphere of the workplace, it's easy to underrate our feminine power and see wholistic thinking as something that other people—those who have real power—do.

The capacity to form an overview and to see how the organization relates to the world at large puts your work in context. Wholistic thinking may be more or less welcome, depending on your company and level of responsibility. But in your own business, it's crucial. You deserve to take your self, including a wholistic view of your life, seriously. Regardless of where you work or your company's philosophy, you are the central creative force in your own life. Looking at your worklife wholistically will help you to keep things in perspective as you manage your own time and energy. No man is an island, and for sure, no woman is.

Step One is to understand fully how work fits into your life—how it is part of the whole. Since work is structured and the demands can be neverending, we find ourselves organizing around work at the expense of everything else. Women tend to blend work and home responsibilities much more than men do. But with constant pressures to deal with work in a masculine way, we can lose ourselves along with our wholistic views, our personal connections with the universe.

Dealing with how work fits into your life, not how your life fits into work, includes looking at how balanced your home responsibilities are. Research and everyday conversations tell us that many women, even though they're working away from home full-time, are still taking most (by far) of the responsibility for home management and childcare. As a result, the depression, burnout, and bitterness rate among working women is out of sight.

If you're single, or a single parent, networking and sharing with others can be important support for you. It can be nearly impossible to keep a full-view perspective when you're burdened with the day-to-day responsibilities of keeping things together. It's unrealistic to think you can do it all. When you can create a good overview for yourself, based on your feelings, intuition, and the practical realities of life, you can make decisions about what's necessary and what's not.

Here's what Joanne Gabrynowicz said when I asked her how she takes care of herself:

"I find other women—in the community. The first year was very difficult. Moving from Wall Street to North Dakota was a shock. In the beginning, I wouldn't have articulated that it was the absence of women that was bothering me. It took a couple of months. In New York, I had a strong spiritual community. I was ripped away from that. I'm a philosophically driven person, and I missed being connected with people who share that. There are men here who are understanding of philosophical and spiritual aspects, but it is not the same.

"The first winter was very hard. If you're not socially established, winter isn't a time you get to know people in North Dakota. It is 40 degrees below zero and people stay home. They don't go for walks.

"When spring came—I made a point of getting out and meeting people—a strong community at the university—very active network of women. It was like a drink of water in the desert.

"The college that I'm in—Aerospace Sciences—is perceived by many in the rest of the university to be a military-oriented institution. This includes the women on campus. It has been interesting to see how they find me. They were receptive when I approached them. I was accepted. They accept me, but I can't talk to them about my institution." Joanne found personal support even though she couldn't share her professional concerns with her women friends.

If you have a partner, figuring out how to look at your responsibilities and make a plan for sharing them is key to honoring this dimension. Working together, you can man-

age home and work in a balanced way. This includes consciously looking at and determining how much of your life
energy each of you chooses to devote to work. Otherwise,
traditional feminine responsibilities on top of a job wear
you down very quickly.

Step Two is to express your wholistic views at work.
Balancing work and home is a lifelong task. As you work
toward it, you can contribute at work by growing increasingly assertive about human issues on the job. How does
your company manage childcare? Flex-time? Job-sharing?
Parental leave for pregnancy, birth, or adoption? Time off
for managing family concerns? What are the company's
attitudes toward pollution, war, world trade? Your voice on
these topics makes a difference.

Many companies today solicit input on company mission and goals, quality of work life, and other core issues
from employees at all levels. Quality Circles or other work
groups directly seek opinions and ideas from workers.
These are ready-made opportunities for you to share your
wholistic thinking. The more you have brought it into your
awareness, the clearer you can be.

Courage in expressing your wholistic views can make
a difference if you work at policymaking levels. Whether
or not your ideas are adopted, their expression changes
the context. Next time around they will sound more familiar. In positions of less authority, talking about your
wholistic views may not change policy but it may start
other people thinking and open up new possibilities. If
you take yourself seriously, you become credible to others
who are willing to open their minds.

Give yourself permission to think and talk about
what's best for you and your family, what's best for the
company, what's best for the world. These thoughts are
part of all of us, but sometimes we lose sight of them or
get overwhelmed. Since this isn't the usual way that people at work think about their jobs, it can seem weird to

When you can create a good overview for yourself, you can make decisions about what's necessary and what's not.

talk about the big picture.

A process to work with as you explore wholistic thinking on the job includes these ideas:

- Pay attention to your own cyclical nature.
- Give yourself permission to look at and think about the whole picture.
- See what needs to be done.
- Express what you see.
- Talk about the relationship of your work to the world at large.
- Talk about the importance of balancing personal life with work.
- Find other people who are willing to share their wholistic thinking and talk about issues that require being "unscrupulous observers."

For the past two years, I've been part of a group of professional people who get together once a month or so to talk about emerging feminine energy in our culture, a wholistic topic if ever there was one. Following principles of wholistic thinking, the process stirs the group's energy to explore what comes along with no particular direction in mind. We agreed that, as a group, we wouldn't work on "causes" or support political actions.

Personal, relevant discussion enlivens us each time a topic emerges and develops over the evening. Now something else is beginning to form. Various individual members are undertaking projects—some small, some large—but each something that expresses that person's way of supporting the feminine in our culture. The energy for these activities comes from each individual as group support nurtures her or him.

Shared wholistic thinking allows individuals to support their own efforts. It becomes possible see your work—and your life—in more than its most immediate steps. Look for ways you can provide this kind of support for yourself.

SUMMARY

Wholistic thinking moves us beyond the details of our daily lives. It gives us the perspective we need to guide our most significant decisions. Our materialistic culture has distanced us from this part of the feminine for a long time. And so we easily lose sight of what we know—of the big picture—and get stuck in spending our good energy to meet goals and expectations that we've grabbed because they were obvious or within reach.

Taking this dimension seriously can connect us with our deeper selves and, consequently, with our archetypal feminine presence. As "unscrupulous observers," we can see the world as it really is, not distorted through convenience or what others want us to believe. Learning to live with our wholistic views is a lifelong task that takes trust in yourself and the courage to speak out about what "the moment's light" prints on your "own silver gut."

Wisdom and Spirituality

> . . . here in the skin of our fingertips we see the
> trail of the wind." And then she made a circular
> motion to indicate the whirlwind that had left its
> imprint in the whorls at the tips of the human finger.
> "It shows where the wind blew life into my ances-
> tors when they were first made. . . . It was in the leg-
> end days when these lines happened. It was the leg-
> end days when the first people were given the
> breath of life.
>
> Jamake Highwater, *Kill Hole*

The "trail of the wind" rushes through each of us, connecting us with each other and with the universe—
before us and yet to come. We take in the breath of life
and let it go.

The idea of "medicine"—spirit, specialness, the
uniqueness of each fingerprint—reaches us from ancient
times. Each baby is herself alone from day one. If you've
had children or experience with tiny infants, you've seen
it. She is someone special, similar to others in many ways,
but different from everyone else in the world.

Even in this high-tech era, our individual fingerprints,
"where the wind blew life into my ancestors," follow us as
singular identification throughout our lives. Maybe souls
are spiritual fingerprints. Each makes its own mark. This
chapter is about treasuring that uniqueness, following the
trail of the wind and letting it breathe in you deeply and
fully—even at work. A certain amount of wisdom is
required for this task, and each of us carries that wis-

dom—if we can hear it whispering within us.

In her book, *Psychotherapy Grounded in the Feminine Principle*, analyst Barbara Stevens Sullivan writes about feminine wisdom. This treasure is profoundly undervalued in the business world, although each of us harbors it in some way. Sullivan says it is knowledge that comes from experience and is the "product of feminine immersion in life":

> . . . We call this feminine consciousness wisdom
> . . . the intelligence of the heart, even of the stomach, the wisdom of feeling. It comes with age and maturity . . . only with years of deeply savored and suffered life. It is knowledge of oneself and of the world attuned to one person, to a unique incident. It is never guided by universal, abstract truths.[1]

Feminine wisdom is personal, heartfelt—wisdom of the uterus, of the breast, of the ovaries. It carries on its winds everything we learn from men as well as from other women. Old women have more of it than young women. It grows from life's lessons—losses, joys, pain, progress.

Where are these old women in business and government? Does anyone listen to them any more? How do we learn to hear and value this dimension in ourselves? And speak it with confidence?

Old woman! The crone of times gone by. Like the goddess Hecate at the crossroad, she peers into the future as well as the past—the carrier of life experience that produces wisdom. What a concept. It's so far removed from our youth-oriented way of being that it's almost guaranteed to produce a shudder.

A sign in a department store's personnel office reads: "We do not discriminate against those aged 40 to 70." It doesn't say: "We welcome those whose life experiences contribute to their value as employees."

Our ageist culture rejects old women. We reflect that view when we reject the old woman in ourselves—and her wisdom and accumulated life experiences along with her. We apologize for our age and our life seasoning. Instead, we can look at our own aging faces with love, rather than with horror and dismay. We can embrace and value the crone in each of us who understands that our life experiences count for something. We have learned from them and should trust ourselves with the depth they've given us. And we can use our personal wisdom to guide our work lives.

But wisdom isn't reserved for the old. Each of us is enough if we take the time to honor what we know—and to speak it.

Feminine spirit breathes life into wisdom. It isn't knowledge about a particular thing, but it is knowing. Of the earth, of nature, curled into life's cycles, the spirit wind murmurs through our connections with each other and the universe.

Sherry Ruth Anderson and Patricia Hopkins' book, *The Feminine Face of God: The Unfolding of the Sacred in Women*, discusses feminine spirituality as ordinary, everyday practice. Men go on spiritual quests. Women stay home to find their spiritual practice in their ordinary lives.

The Greek word for soul, mind, or spirit is *psyche*, self. A woman's spirituality includes all those images and feelings around which she organizes her inner life and understands her place in the universe. Whether it's well developed or not, we all have some sense of how we connect with our own life and our own death. As we become more conscious of our feminine heritage, we welcome, seek, and create feminine images that fit our own experience. We no longer have to bend our feelings to fit images we've inherited from our masculine culture.

Wise men have taught us that pursuing our spiritual essence takes hard work and discipline. For those of us who scramble just to manage our worldly responsibilities, such pursuits are what other people do. Although we can enrich ourselves by learning about its history and practices, feminine spirituality isn't something that can be learned separate from our daily struggles. It is just who we are. Wise women learn to honor that feminine spirit of the here and now, the precious quality that feels, lives, and breathes everyday life. We can live in our bodies, do our work and honor our feminine spirit simultaneously. Each of us is enough.

Do you think of your job as a path to spiritual enlightenment? Most of us don't. But things happen sometimes that wake us up. We're expected to do something destructive or dishonest that rubs us the wrong way. We find ourselves lying or cutting corners. Or, on the other side, we breeze along, work flows, and we feel like we're perfectly in tune with the universe.

As we pay attention to our inner experience, we have a basis for thinking about and feeling these conflicts. At times, we're especially tuned in; we know who we are and have a sense of how we fit in the great scheme of things. We trust that what we think and feel has value.

When we don't have this sense of inner direction, we try to fly on automatic pilot—not exactly a feminine concept—at work. At such times, it's hard to pay attention to some of the things we see or feel. So we aim straight ahead with limited sensitivity to our personal values or those of our colleagues. We put on our blinders and drone numbly through whatever turbulence or balmy air surrounds us. We don't take our own flight pattern seriously, because it's just too painful.

Our materialistic culture splits the spirit off into particular days or times—if this untouchable part of our living is acknowledged at all. All we have to do is read the daily paper to see that the feminine spirit is not much of a priority. God has the face of a man we go visit on the week-

Power and strength evaporate when we punch the automatic pilot button and travel along pre-defined directions at work.

end. Except when someone at work dies, or a tragedy of some sort pulls us up short, feminine wisdom and spirituality seem far away. At those exceptional times we find ourselves grasping to understand, comfort, or be comforted.

And yet, if we delve into this dimension, each of us has the choice to walk into work any day as a whole person. We may not always be able to influence what happens, but our inner guides will help us know how we feel about it. And when we do have a chance to say something or decide about an outcome, we can do so in a way that feels solid.

What are we doing to ourselves? How can we stay on the trail of the wind while we work? Can we avoid punching the automatic pilot button? Is it possible to fly with greater attention to the journey?

Feminine spirituality honors the uniqueness and worth of each individual. It breathes with the ongoing circle of life and death. Spirit enlivens woman's connectedness with her inner self at all ages. In ancient times, it was symbolized by the triple goddess—virgin, mother, and crone. Each stage had its own power, with the greatest wisdom living in the crone. How does this trinity apply to today's working woman? Such power and strength evaporate when we punch the automatic pilot button and travel along pre-defined directions at work.

Feminine spirituality has a way of whistling to get our attention if we give it the slightest chance. We have moments when we feel deeply connected with those around us. Or we feel especially in tune with the earth or the sky on a beautiful spring day. A friend points out a truth we've spoken. Or we realize the simplicity of something that's been puzzling us.

When we're just too busy to notice, nighttime delivers unbidden gifts in our dreams and not-quite-conscious wanderings. These momentary glimpses don't substitute for deeper study, but they do provide a starting place.

One of these offerings, a dream, came to me shortly after my 49th birthday. It was different from dreams I commonly remember and so real that I had to pay attention. Here's what I recall:

It was a soft, sunny day. I was outdoors somewhere in the foothills. In the wondrous liquidity of the dreamworld, my movements weren't limited to the conventional. My upturned moccasined toes stretched for sunlight. With my back scrunched on a little wooden chair, I joyously relaxed into an unorthodox upside-down, backwards-reaching posture, feeling open and free.

"It's time for the meeting!" A woman's voice intruded through the warm pleasure of my reverie.

"Do you have the form?" Her tone held accusation.

Irritated, I brought myself to reply, "No, I forgot about it."

"You have to have the form!" she persisted.

"I can finish it when I get there." I was beginning to put it together. One more time I had agreed to attend some gathering that I didn't really want to take time for.

She pushed again. "They won't let you in without it!"

In the dream, my stomach clutched. I noticed that my breath was tight. My shoulders sagged, but I was determined to enjoy myself.

I gathered my energy and said to the woman, "Come on. I'm going anyway. I can't believe the form is so important."

"You can't go looking like that!" she admonished me.

"I'm fine," I insisted, but I didn't really feel fine by this time.

"You have to wear a shirt!"

My confidence slipped, melted into a puddle of ineptitude as I recognized my semi-nudity.

"I'm going like this." If they won't let me in, I'll deal with it when I get there," I insisted.

Her warning echoed many I had heard before. "I'm afraid you'll be sorry."

We followed the bike path over a rise and saw green hills unfolding. The sun felt reassuring.

Music! Women singing. There they were!

Goosebumps jumped onto my arms as the marching troop formed in my vision. Yellow and white serpent-crested flags, standards held formally aloft, flanked the first row. The women inspired images of a medieval throng in their contemporary full-length dresses of green and white print. They looked so strong! I wondered if they were witches. They seemed so sure of themselves.

Each of us has the choice to walk into work any day as a whole person.

Old visions of my own unacceptability blipped into my thoughts . . . dirty fingernails at my piano recital . . . slip showing at graduation . . . hair dishevelled.

Awareness dawned. My brain clicked away: "I'm not prepared. I can't get into this group the way I am. I didn't do my homework and I wore the wrong thing.

I would never be part of this group.

The sun rubbed my back as I sat crosslegged on the hill and watched while two women planted the standards. The group appeared to prepare for a ritual. Interesting. I remembered rituals in which I'd participated without belief.

I felt a little sadness . . . I didn't fit in. I watched as the women milled around. An odd scene.

And then slowly, warmly, still in the dream, relief radiated through me. I would hate being part of that. It didn't fit me. That wasn't my group . . . and not the only group.

This dream happens to be mine. But the themes are familiar ones. I hear them all the time from others as they try to fit in, when they think someone else knows the way, and whenever they degrade themselves and their own competence and experience.

Sometimes, I also hear the hope.

As this healing dream gusted in and out of my aware-ness, I wondered what it meant to me. I felt inspired to get off automatic pilot and become more connected to my own flying patterns. I understood that feminine presence is different for each of us. Some dimensions fit neither the cultural stereotypes nor what is commonly seen as a "femi-nist" point of view. They go beyond traditional views of femininity and are different from commonly accepted mas-culine views. We can identify, embrace and own these dimensions as parts of ourselves that enrich our personal sense of well-being. They empower us and enhance our relationships with other women and men.

I decided to begin a project that I had fiddled with in dim awareness for a long time. I wanted to write a book about women and spirit and work. I was ready to devote serious time and effort. I wanted to share what it means to be a regular, ordinary woman at work—not the woman with the flying hair—not radical—not subservient—but just an everyday person trying to do her job and maintain her sense of personal integrity in the process. I knew it was a big, hard job. People want to be glamorous, not ordinary. We want to be "successful" in the eyes of the masculine world.

I had no idea that it would take years and that I would do it over and over until it was finished. Nor did I have a clue about how I would wander and dig or about the lessons I'd learn along the way.

But I did learn about my own feminine spirit. When I jotted notes so I could remember my dream, I wanted to leave out the part about the snakes on the yellow flags. They seemed so icky to me, a gruesome symbol. Imagine my surprise to find, as I began exploring feminine mythol-ogy, that the serpent represented the Great Goddess of ancient times and had been a symbol of the feminine way before it became associated with evil in the Garden of Eden.

Learning about the feminine beyond my own experience, trying to get a sense about how women could really live in the feminine presence at work, began to feel like a search for the Holy Grail. I knew that somehow I would find a way to work with the idea, but it seemed impossible to grasp. Whenever I would think, say, or write "search for the Holy Grail," in my attempts to describe what I was going through, it felt wrong. But I couldn't quite come up with the feminine equivalent of the masculine spiritual search—the hero's journey.

I didn't journey or have epic conquests; I meandered. Even though I'm a well-organized person, I wasn't going in a straight line. I'd start out that way and then find myself wandering. I would look for something, fail to find it, be frustrated, and find what I wasn't looking for. This happened over and over. I gathered bits and pieces, and had small, rich encounters along the way. I suffered defeats and disappointments, and I kept going.

Naomi Newman helped. As the Jewish mother character in her one woman show, *Snake Talk: Urgent Messages from the Mother*,[2] she explains the whole thing. Here's what I learned: We dig. We go outside and we dig. We don't dig in a straight line. We dig here; we dig there. We take three steps and we fall-down-and-get-up. Fall-down-and-get-up is one move. And we do it some more. Pretty soon we find some, not all, of what we're looking for. And we dig some more. And we each do it in our own way.

I gave up looking for a grand metaphor.

When we invite our spirits to work, we trust the part that goes outside to dig and fall-down-and-get-up. We experience a sense of personal power and integrity on the job. We have a personal basis for making our decisions rather than just doing what is common practice in the work environment. We give our inner guides a louder voice.

THE SHADOW SIDE

The shadow side of wisdom and spirituality harbors some mean women—the cynic, the holier than thou, the know it all. And some sad ones too. If you find them lurking in you, try to discover what fears they're helping you avoid taking a look at.

The cynic, the bitter woman who rejects her feminine presence and everyone else's, makes light of what she can't see or measure. It's hard for her to allow her own feminine wisdom and spirituality much opportunity to grow. She focuses on the material side of life for fulfillment: "she who has the most toys wins."

Another shadow form is the woman who suffers from the holier than thou syndrome. This person has her head in the clouds and has a hard time being present or productive. She may feel intellectually or spiritually superior to others, but this self-deception is a way she avoids confronting her doubts or feelings of insignificance—the scariness her shadow side represents.

She who has found the answer knows it all and has no room for uncertainty or groping lack of clarity. She terrorizes herself when she can't live up to her own unreal expectations about how to be a person. Watch out for her. She'll eat you up. She tries to shut you down when your uncertainties frighten you or your human fallibility disappoints you.

The spiritual junkie moves from one guru or practice to another, drawn to someone else's answers. Last year's solution fades as this year's sparkles brightly, only to dim as it grows apparent one more time that there really are no magic answers. Commitment to the hard work of self-development is hard for her.

Spiritual impoverishment, lack of attention to our inner life, and the absence of soul searching, are major by-products of late Twentieth Century life. We lose ourselves because we don't have time to weigh and consider the values choices we make every day. Emptiness, meaninglessness, a hollow feeling stays with us in what should be our happiest moments.

Wisdom and spirituality are personal matters that each of us encounters and manages in her own way. If we believe we've "found the way" and try to impose it on others, we operate from the shadow. Instead, we need to be expressive without putting others down for their beliefs or lack thereof.

This dimension contains great potential for abuse. What Joseph Campbell called the "institutionalization of mythology," usually in the form of organized religion, is one of the biggest dangers. All groups of people create living myths to explain the unexplainable in their lives. When any group selects part of the myth and consciously tries to foist it off on others as a form of social control, the vitality of the myth, the spirit, is lost and the shadow takes over. In our excitement about our own spiritual discoveries, we can come to expect others to be equally enthusiastic. When they're not, it's important to respect that response. Each of us has to find her own way.

At work, the shadow side of this dimension gets played out in destructive ways. People belonging to one religion or spiritual group feel justified in supporting each other to the exclusion of those who differ. This can affect every part of work life, from hiring and promotion to the way individuals are treated on a daily basis. Since the behavior and decisions are covert, this is a kind of discrimination that's very difficult to confront.

A shadow side of wisdom is activated by people who consider themselves wise just because they've been around a long time or hold high position. Autocratic behavior from a self-appointed "wise man" or "wise woman" leaves little room for negotiation. Lacking the true wisdom to benefit from others' knowledge and experience, such people believe it's their way or no way.

On an individual basis, the shadow side of this dimension deepens when we're so much into our own trip that we don't really hear those around us, or if we assume a sense of personal superiority for one reason or another. The shadow ignores the personal worth of others, and is even more critical and punishing to the imperfect, vulnerable spirit of an ordinary person.

SELF-REFLECTION

Now that you're in this philosophical place, take a moment or two to see where you fit on the Wisdom and Spirituality dimension. Remember, this is not a bigger-than-life kind of thing. None of us does it perfectly. It simply has to do with how you live your authenticity at work—the very human process of being real wherever you are.

STRENGTH: I know my values and have no trouble living them at work. I don't always agree with my co-workers but I respect them for who they are. I try to stay connected with my inner experience while I'm at work. I take time for my spiritual practice.

SHADOW: I associate only with people of my own spiritual persuasion. I know what's best. / I have no patience with people who are off on some mystical trip. All this woo woo stuff has no business at work. / What could a bunch of old women know that would help me get ahead?

TIME FOR YOURSELF

You can reach ever-greater understanding of what's important to you—where you're willing to compromise and where you choose to stand firm. When this wisdom comes from inside you, not from an external authority, you're the same powerful person at home and at work. You're in touch with your feminine spirit, and the gift of self-confidence is yours.

Here are some steps for expanding contact with this dimension at work:

• IN YOUR JOURNAL, list three non-negotiable values, things you really believe in that are deeply important to you. Describe how you live each of these at work.

• WRITE ABOUT WAYS you are asked to compromise your non-negotiable values. What conflict does this cause for you? How do you work it through?

• ARE THERE SOME OLDER WOMEN where you work? Do they hide their wisdom? If you have a relationship with one of these women, have a conversation with her about life's lessons. Write about the feelings that get stirred as you talk with her (fear of getting older, a wish to be taken care of, tenderness, scorn).

• ARE YOU AN OLDER WOMAN? Do people seek your counsel? Do you offer it? Take yourself and your experience seriously. Write in your journal about crone wisdom and how it grows in you.

• MAKE A TIME LINE THAT ILLUSTRATES your spiritual development. Start with early childhood and break it into sections that help you remember—grade school, middle school, jr. high, through to wherever you are now. Or break it into the places you lived, if you have moved around a lot. Or you can organize it around significant people who influenced your spiritual growth. On the time line, write or draw (or both) key events, ideas or people that influenced you.

• Find ways to meditate or be in touch with your spiritual center or with images related to your spiritual self while you are at work. It was the practice of Mayor Anne Rudin to close her door for a half hour every day to meditate. You owe your employer your time, your energy, your best efforts, *but not your soul.* List five ways you stay connected with this dimension at work.

• Make a good clear fingerprint in the middle of a piece of white paper. Using a copier that enlarges, blow the fingerprint up as much as you can. Write a story between the lines that describes your spirit journey following the trail of the winds. Color and decorate the trail story with symbols that are meaningful to you.

• Honor your connection with nature. Go for a hike. Go to the park. Look at a tree. Find ways to be in nature whenever possible. Redwoods, mountains, deserts, canyons, ocean waves, and plains put work conflicts in perspective. So does the incredible yellow of a daffodil.

• Find someone at work who likes to talk about matters of the spirit, such as the unbroken chain of women since the beginning of time, the idea that your internal state influences whoever stands next to you, the sense that we're all part of a global community. Write down what you learn from these conversations.

• Take your own spiritual search seriously outside work. What are the ways you open up to your feminine wisdom and spirituality? Religious practices, meditation, yoga, reading, art, nature, a woman's group? Take time to draw or write in your journal a brief sketch of this part of your life.

• On a blank page in your journal, color, scribble, or draw your shadow in this dimension. Write ten words that name it (hopelessness, greed, cynicism, judgmentalness, a general tendency to know it all, self-doubt).

- MOVE A LITTLE FURTHER into your shadow. What is it trying to say to you? What fears might you be trying to cover up? Write something that begins, "When I look at my dark side in this dimension, I fear. . . ."

- PAY ATTENTION to what enlivens you at work. Write down three ways your work energizes you and connects with who you are.

- FOR ONE WEEK, briefly summarize any dreams you can remember. Can you find a pattern? Is there something you're trying to tell yourself about who you are and what's important to you?

- READ ABOUT THE EMERGENCE of the feminine and how others are working in this area. Some places to start include: *The Chalice and the Blade: Our History, Our Future*, by Riane Eisler; *The Crone*, by Barbara Walker; *The Song of Eve: An Illustrated Journey into the Myths, Symbols and Rituals of the Goddess*, by Manuela Dunn Mascetti; *When God Was A Woman*, by Merlin Stone; and *The Feminine Face of God*, by Sherry Ruth Anderson and Patricia Hopkins.

Now you have explored all 13 dimensions. Return to page 28 and make any adjustments that seem to fit for wisdom and spirituality.

WISDOM AND SPIRITUALITY AT WORK

Find ways to support your human spirit, your real self, at work. Take seriously the way you respond to things you're expected to do—or decisions you make to get ahead in your own business or career. The way you feel about your connection with the universe and with nature is not something that you drop at the door as you go to work each day. Without having to sit around and contemplate the meaning of life, you can tune in to this dimension in bits and pieces as a rich personal resource.

A very powerful myth about the importance of work exists in our culture. It has two sides. On one side, you give up your identity, your individuality, your soul when you go to work. The company owns you. For women who have felt disempowered in their private lives, this is nothing new.

On the other side is the idea that you *are* your job. This way of identifying with work has been very powerful for men and is now creeping into feminine culture. When men meet, the first question they ask is "What do you do?" You're not so much a human being as a human doing.

This idea fills people up; it provides a sense of self when the inner self hasn't been very well nurtured or developed. But it isn't enough to sustain a real person. It is, in fact, very dangerous. You may have known men who dumped their lives into their jobs or women who "lived through their children" and crashed into emptiness and isolation when they could no longer work or the nest emptied. When you sustain your inner self, your spirit, along with your work life, you live from your center. You can make the daily shift from your personal life to your work life without losing yourself in the process. When your work years come to a close, retirement is a transition, not loss of identity.

As you expand into your feminine presence at work and maintain focus on your emotional presence—your spiritual self—the breeze of your existence brushes those around you. Your presence becomes a threat to a way of life that has been a stronghold for men since the industrial revolution. When you try to progress upward in the organization, **Masculine Identity Is Work** is one of the barriers that comes forward to stop your progress. Here's how:

The deep threat that a man is less than a man if somehow "under" a woman is probably the single strongest barrier to the routine promotion of women to positions of power and responsibility. It's hard for many men to maintain self-esteem if they aren't in control. They may imply that "strong leadership" is needed and that women can't lead. Their fear of loss is hardly ever stated openly. It is more often expressed indirectly by putting down the ability of women to handle power and responsibility. Or by saying that we're unstable or not strong enough.

Some men are supervised by women, but these women may pay a terrible emotional price unless they are unusually centered and secure individuals. Our culture idealizes masculine power in an unrealistic and exaggerated way. Men are under phenomenal pressure to live up to images of potency, strength, and protectiveness. Psychologist/writer Sam Keen and the men's movement are beginning to register protest against these crippling assumptions.[3] Nonetheless, comfortable acceptance of one's ordinary limits and graceful cooperation with a woman in authority don't fit for most American men.

Men too often fight for traditional organizational survival and exclude or diminish their feminine colleague unless she is able to communicate that she is "one of the boys." But when a woman adopts the masculine style, she doesn't do herself any favors. Instead, she distances herself from her core strength and steps into a role rather than enhancing her authentic position. She may be welcomed as a fake man, but not as a real woman who lives and trusts in her feminine power.

Here are some suggestions for dealing with the idea that **Masculine Identity Is Work.**

When we invite our spirits to work, we trust the part that goes outside to dig and fall-down-and-get-up.

Do	*Don't*
Maintain sensitivity to the depth of the threat women bring to work.	Puff up or harden.
	Disparage men directly or indirectly.

Do	*Don't*
Learn to see through bravado and support vulnerability.	Accept statements about "women" as applicable to you.
Describe yourself as another worker, regardless of status.	Go out of your way to show up male co-workers.
Learn to assert your competence to do your work.	Try to be one of the boys.
Articulate the feminine way of doing things as another way, not the right way.	

Support your wisdom and spirituality on the job. Work and identity issues for men have been brewing for a long time. You can be sensitive and supportive, but you can't protect them from their own pain. As you allow yourself to maintain self-contact and be expressive of who you really are at work as well as in the outside world, you provide a model for men who are struggling to do the same thing.

SUMMARY

Wisdom and spirituality form an important feminine power dimension that isn't typically acknowledged as part of the work environment. How you live this dimension is deeply individual and personal. When you can let the spiritual breezes blow through the stuffy air of your workplace, your contact with your deep inner self supports you and makes you strong.

This growing process happens from the inside out—not from "image polishing" or beating men at their own games. It includes working things out directly, interpersonally, rather than relying on rules or tradition to settle conflicts and differences. When you know who you are as a woman and can trust the complexity and power of your feminine self, you are in a good position to offer partnership to your male colleagues.

Feminine values that have been central to our foremothers for centuries—care and responsibility, the importance of life, the well-being of children, respect for emotion—come to work with us. When we take those values seriously, listen to them and believe their worth, we can be true to our connection with our place in the golden chain. As we live this feminine legacy at work, the purity of the air that future generations will breathe is part of our daily thinking. Deep connections with nature, with the phases of the moon, the changing of the seasons, the ebb and flow of our own monthly cycles, become assets that we trust and rely on. We no longer need to treat our femininity as a liability.

Take a few minutes to look at the skin of your fingertips and trace the trail of the wind.

Feminine Power at Work

Holding my tired body and flattened spirit into the car one evening after a long day at the office, I turned on the radio. I was just in time to hear former Congresswoman Bella Abzug respond to an NPR reporter's question. The discussion was about women in politics and whether or not the women's movement has had any impact on world leadership. The reporter's question was the proverbial one: "Do you think power will change the nature of women?" Bella's clear strong response brought tears to my eyes and raised goosebumps on my arms. "No," she said, "Women will change the nature of power."

I hope Bella is right. But before that change becomes visible we have some important work to do.

Changing power means knowing who you are, trusting that you're enough, and taking the risk to speak from your heart about things that are important to you. If you're the CEO, your voice affects the lives of many people. If you spend your days at a computer terminal, your colleague who sits next to you hears your voice. It can inspire and energize her to know herself, and you too, in a whole new way.

There's more to breaking the glass ceiling than hard work and legal battles against sex discrimination. For women to reach the heights and live there happily, the feminine—the rich treasure of our inner depths—must reveal itself. We have to know who we are, support ourselves, and be able and willing to talk about our feminine power. Then our voices can affect those who assume that the masculine way is the only way to do business.

Understanding is the first step. Support is the second. Expression and interaction, the final steps, bring your femininity to life in the world.

You've had an opportunity to explore your feminine presence, to mull it over, to think and feel from 26 different directions. With practice, you can contact your core strength, respect your intuition, and dance with your creativity. You know about your shadow and can hear some of what she has to say. Now it's time to put all the pieces together. Are your colors bright and flashy or subdued? Is the coat you've stitched bulky or flowing? Is the texture rough or smooth? Is it reversible so it looks one way in the sun and different on a rainy day?

Review your journal as you read this last chapter. Reflect on how you've learned to value your femininity by understanding more about assets that, until now, have often been defined as liabilities in the business world— nurturance, affinity, wholistic thinking. And think about how you're energized by dimensions you previously thought you had to leave at home—sexuality, aggression, wisdom, and spirituality.

Knowing and trusting your femininity gives you a strong base for understanding and relating to others. Think in terms of your thirteen dimensions. Expand your consciousness about how every one of them lives in you. Polish them like fine jewels so that when you want or need their energy they sparkle for you. Each adds its own light and color. The better you care for it, the more accessible it becomes.

Sexism exists at an unconscious level. By confronting your own negative attitudes toward feminine ways, you're less likely to echo a negative cultural bias toward yourself or other women. By embracing your strengths and accepting your vulnerabilities, you can feel secure. Your relationships with men can be grounded in a sense that you're worthwhile if imperfect, just like they are, and that your ways are valuable.

Self-knowledge—exploring and clarifying the thirteen dimensions—will open new vistas for you at work. As you become more secure in each of them, you can take better care of yourself. When you know where you're coming from and can trust what you feel as valid, it's easier to stay with your impressions and believe in yourself. You can feel comfortable, or at least not scared to death, saying things that differ from traditional masculine views. And you can trust your internal base for expressing values that support the feminine.

Expression and interaction in our male-dominant culture are a challenge. The strong, flowing, passionate, spiritual feminine has been degraded for so long that putting her in plain view feels dangerous, and sometimes it is. Doing so in a way that doesn't simply mirror the masculine isn't easy. Fortunately, you don't have to go on a campaign or do it all at once.

The more you grow into your feminine power, the easier it is to use opportunities to self-define. It will become habitual to say, "My intuition, which I've learned to trust, tells me we need to pay attention to this," or, "I'm receptive to your comments and will get back to you with a response." Ultimately, you can assert, "Let's look at our options. This plan seems highly profitable, but it has a lot of negative side effects. I don't support it."

Remember, paternalism doesn't just affect women. Its constraints and demands shackle men, too. As you become more confident and expressive of your feminine differences, you model for men the possibility that they can be real with no sacrifice to their competence. There's more to life than competing and achieving. As you risk expressing what you really think, some people can hear your truth and then take their own more seriously. When even a few people in a work environment are willing to be honest with each other and dedicate their efforts to taking care of themselves, it changes the feel of the place.

It's important to remember that both feminine and masculine ways are necessary. Part of feminine receptivity and flexibility is knowing when it's time to move from the reflective to the active—from circular to linear logic. In order to make the move in a conscious way, you first need to be grounded in the feminine. Then you contribute to balance rather than abandoning half of all human experience.

Breaking the glass ceiling is a worthy, but not necessarily the only, valuable goal for working women. The quality of your life, at work and off the job, is important. Nobody gets to have it all. The excruciating emptiness of painfully achieved "success" hurts when we abandon our inner selves—our femininity—along the way. The task is to be true to yourself, nurture your relationships, and compete and achieve in the process. It can be done, but only if you're willing to take your own feelings and needs seriously.

Get to know how your dimensions interact with each other, how core strength supports receptivity and flexibility, how aggression fires creativity, how wisdom and spirituality inform nurturance. Your own moving, shifting patterns are familiar to you at an unconscious level. You can use them for firm support by highlighting them in your awareness. When you can trust that creativity will follow anger, you can express your rage without having to act it out. Or, if you know that your core strength moves into place when it's time to set a limit, you can listen with an open mind.

Despite the fact that our culture still views women as objects and defines us as successful only when we meet masculine standards, you can develop new ways of trusting your femininity. As you understand the depth to which your persistence, flexibility, aggression, and wholistic

There's more to breaking the glass ceiling than hard work and legal battles against sex discrimination.

thinking are assets, you value and rely on them more. You're not as vulnerable to manipulation as you might once have been. You can deal with the implication that you're wishy-washy or impractical by asserting clearly the value of your flexibility or your wholistic thinking. Your own self-understanding and confidence will support you.

Winning at any cost isn't an option. As you trust your feminine power, you value your relationships without feeling ashamed or weak. You won't be willing to stab your friend in the back for a promotion or even to ignore her needs or feelings to get ahead. This doesn't mean that you'll become a doormat or abandon your own hopes and dreams. As you feel confident in recognizing the importance of your relationships, you can be honest and assertive with your friends and colleagues. And then you will feel less manipulated by others' need for you to be tough or to "kick ass." When you rely on your feminine strength and stamina, you can be very powerful and caring at the same time.

We live in a high-tech, throw-away society that values image over substance. The fledgling men's movement is starting to question whether the sacrifices of self-abandonment are worth the rewards of material gain. Women who have been "doing it all" talk about burnout, the pain of self-neglect, and what they've missed with their children and other loved ones. It's unreal to think that a back-to-nature movement is the answer. But we do need to come up with some next steps that balance the wonders of our technological gains with our simple basic need for connection with others and the universe.

At least part of the answer is in learning to treasure our ordinariness, to value our human qualities—including the desire for personal connections—and to give voice to the feminine side of life. We don't have to be "special" or masculine to be worthwhile. We need to listen to our personal experience and inner truth and consider it important. And we need to share that truth with each other and with the men in our lives. This will lead us to challenge the basic structures of our culture that talk about valuing the family but finance just about everything else before getting to childcare, parental leave, adequate education, or medical care.

Regardless of where you work in your company, school, or agency, you have only as much power as you give yourself. Women have typically used their energy to support and empower others. We don't think of our efforts to accomplish that as powerful. We're accustomed to thinking about "power" as authority or dominance, concepts that don't fit well with women's ways of working. But there is another way of looking at it.

When you say, "I'm concerned about how this decision will affect our employees' childcare arrangements," that is a powerful statement. "We can produce a better quality product if we use teamwork," has clout too, when you can support it with evidence. "Let's get together for an hour and brainstorm solutions to this mess," empowers others and opens the way to creativity. That's power. It isn't power over anyone, or dominance that makes you look big and important. It's, as Jean Baker Miller defines it, "the capacity to produce a change," the power to get work done. That is feminine power at work. It's persistent, nurturing, aggressive, and wholistic.

Defining power in feminine terms gives you a different way to look at how you're valuable at work. It also calls into question what work is worth doing. If every woman in the United States talked about what needs to happen to make this a better place for the next generation, change would occur. If each of us felt that her perceptions and ideas were worth expressing, our voices would be heard. Power isn't about dominance. It's about feeling whole and substantial—free to talk about and act on how we understand ourselves, the world, and what's important.

Time For Yourself

Take time now to meander back through the thirteen dimensions, smoothing here and reshaping there.

Start by rereading the poem, "Power," in the very first section, "Changing Woman Changing Work." It's time to stitch together the pieces you've been working with to complete at least the most recent version of your feminine power coat. Move around in it. Make sure it fits and will provide you with comfort and warmth, even as you keep remodeling it in the future.

This is a good time to rework dimensions you've left unfinished. Spend more time on those that were hard to deal with on first reading. To review what you've learned about these many aspects of yourself and how they relate to each other takes time and energy. *There's no need to hurry.* Take as much time as you need to hear both sides of each dimension and receive as much as you can.

These final exercises will help you to integrate your new learning with what you already know about yourself. By reviewing the material, you make it yours. Over time, as you work consciously with all thirteen dimensions, you can return to any section and refresh. Add your own insights and exercises.

Look for colorful threads that wind through your journal writing—growing self-acceptance, needs for closeness, a willingness to say what you want, the trust that you will get to be you. Pay attention to the darker hues that define your doubt and vulnerability. What recurring themes travel through several dimensions? Highlight them as important information about your self.

Summarize your understanding one dimension at a time. Treat yourself to the luxury of writing about both sides of each dimension in your journal, if you're so inclined. Or you might simply reflect on each without writing, and select a few for concentrated journal attention. Here's a format to organize your review:

- I trust my (*body energy*) to let me know_____.

- I know I've undermined my (*body energy*) when_____.

- My (*body energy*) shadow takes over when _____.

- (*Body energy*) is most helpful to me when _____.

- (*Body energy*) empowers me at work when _____.

After you finish a section, such as Strength and Stamina, it's worth it to go through and summarize the section as well. For example:

- I trust my (*Strength and Stamina*) to let me know _____.

Avoid temptations to rush through the exercises. If you can allow time and space to let this rich mixture steep, you will become aware of some of the work your unconscious has been doing all the time you've been reading.

Whatever your review process, this is a place of beginning, not ending. Reading this book and working through the exercises are steps in your discovery of the uniqueness and beauty of your feminine presence. Only you can make those discoveries, and this is just one window into that wondrous territory. Look for other books. Talk with your friends. Form or participate in a group to delve into and support your feminine power. Because it comes from your inner truth, your feminine power grows as you explore it, and it spreads to others.

For the past several years, I've spent most of my "free" moments reading, collecting, thinking, and feeling about this material. Now that it's time to say goodbye, my feelings have erupted all over the place. I feel like I'm parting with a dear friend. My deep hope is that I've communicated some ideas that spark your connection with your feminine power and all that means. I've imagined you working as a welder, a secretary, a manager, a drug clerk, a nurse, an executive, or a psychotherapist, like me. As I've worked, I've heard the voices of the people I interviewed. I've thought about Shauna, Ellen, Joyce, Marie, Suzanne, Alice, and the others whose stories brighten these pages.

And through it all, I know that my own meanderings and diggings are just that. I've received much more than I can ever express or acknowledge. Thanks for coming along with me. I keep the coda of the Changing Woman chant taped to my computer cabinet next to a list of words I have a hard time spelling and an inspiring quote from Georgia O'Keefe. It's a small card that says:

> In beauty it is done
> in harmony it is written
> in beauty and harmony it shall so be finished
> Changing Woman said it so.

I hope it will keep you company as you continue your journey.

Thirteen Ways to Live Your Feminine Power at Work

1. Regard your **body energy** as a natural resource and care for yourself accordingly. Dress in ways that are comforting to you. Honor your feminine cycles. Breathe, ground, center, and relax.

2. A journey of a thousand miles begins with one step. Honor and support your **persistence**.

3. Trust your **core strength**. Learn the ways that you are strong and resilient. Develop channels to this inner resource.

4. Listen; take in. Make room for **receptivity**. Allow support and positive energy to enter. Hear your inner voice as she guides you.

5. Honor the **flexibility** with which you go about your daily life. You determine whether you're being flexible or flaky.

6. **Nurture** yourself. Choose when and how much you want to nurture others. Structure your work so that it nurtures you.

7. Assume that your needs for **affinity**—your feelings and values—are valid. Express your concerns about work decisions that affect the quality of human life.

8. Value your **sexuality**. It's yours. Take steps to become comfortable with your sexual feelings. Learn to use your sexual fire as energy at work.

9. Let your **creativity** emerge and unfold. Invite its presence. Don't panic when it hides in the back alleys.

10. Heed the fire of your **aggression**. Listen to its roar before you douse it.

11. Open your inner channels to **intuition** as your guide.

12. Appreciate your capacity for **wholistic thinking**. Enjoy your world view and share it with others.

13. Remember that you're enough. Your **wisdom and spirituality** go to work with you and touch those around you.

Notes

CHANGING WOMAN CHANGING WORK

1. Rianne Eisler, *The Chalice and the Blade: Our History, Our Future* (New York: Harper and Row, 1987).

2. Gerald Hausman, *Meditations with the Navajo*, (Santa Fe: Bear and Company, 1987), p. 13.

3. Cornelia Schulz, Personal interview, Nevada City, CA, June 24, 1988.

4. Carol Gilligan, *In a Different Voice: Psychological Theory and Women's Development* (Cambridge, MA: Harvard University Press, 1982), p. 62.

5. Letty Cottin Pogrebin, "*Ms.* Family Album," *Ms.*, Sept. 1992, p. 48.

6. J. Ruth Gendler, *The Book of Qualities* (San Francisco: HarperCollins, 1988).

7. Susan Faludi, *Backlash: The Undeclared War Against American Women* (New York: Anchor Books, 1991), p. 70.

8. Carl G. Jung, *Collected Works, Volume 7, Two Essays on Analytical Psychology*, Bollingen Series XX (Princeton University Press, 1953), p. 53.

9. Arlie Hochschild, with Anne Machung, *The Second Shift: Working Parents and the Revolution at Home* (New York: Viking, 1989), p. 1.

EARTH—STRENGTH AND STAMINA

1. Anne Campbell, *The Opposite Sex* (Topsfield, MA: Salem House, 1989), p. 190.

2. Hochschild, pp. 3-4.

3. Anne Rudin, Personal interview, Sacramento, CA, May 12, 1991.

4. Susan Griffin, *Woman and Nature: the Roaring Inside Her* (New York: Harper and Row, 1985), p. 219.

BODY ENERGY

1. Nancy Jungerman, personal interview, Davis, CA, July 25, 1988.

2. Lesley Schroeder, M.D., personal interview, Sacramento, CA November 18, 1988.

3. Betty De Shong Meador, "Thesmophoria: A Woman's Fertility Ritual," in *To Be a Woman*, Connie Zweig, ed. (Los Angeles: Jeremy Tarcher, 1990), pp. 173-180.

4. Clarissa Pinkola Estes, *Women Who Run with the Wolves* (New York: Ballantine Books, 1992).

5. Catherine Steiner-Adair, "The Body Politic," in *Making Connections: the Relational Worlds of Adolescent Girls at Emma Willard School*, edited by Carol Gilligan, Nona P. Lyons and Trudy J. Hammer (Cambridge: Harvard University Press, 1990), pp. 162-182.

6. Catherine Steiner-Adair, "Feminine Development and Eating Disorders," workshop, California School of Professional Psychology, Alameda, CA, April 20, 1991.

PERSISTENCE

1. Evelyn Fox Keller, *A Feeling for the Organism: The Life and Work of Barbara McClintock* (New York: W.H. Freeman and Company, 1983).

2. James H. Barker, "Upingarrlainarkta: Always Getting Ready," photography exhibit, Anchorage Museum of History and Art, August 1992.

3. Charles Baroo, Personal interview, New York City, November 19, 1988.

CORE STRENGTH

1. Cathy Luchetti, with Carol Olwell, *Women of the West* (St. George, UT: Antelope Island Press, 1982), page 31.

2. Melissa Lawler, Personal interview, Indianapolis, March 20, 1989.

WATER—THE FLOWING CONNECTION

1. Martina S. Horner, "Toward Understanding the Achievement — Related Conflicts in Women," *The Journal of Social Issues* 28, No. 2, 1972:157-176.

2. Marilyn Loden, *Feminine Leadership, or How to Succeed in Business Without Being One of the Boys* (New York: Times Books, 1985).

3. Joan Konner "Female sensibility starting to influence what's in the media," *Sacramento Bee*, May 18, 1990.

RECEPTIVITY

1. Eleanor Maccoby, "Gender and Relationships: A Developmental Account," *American Psychologist*, April 1990.

FLEXIBILITY

1. Sally Helgesen, *The Female Advantage: Women's Ways of Leadership* (New York: Doubleday/Currency, 1990).

2. Elinore Lenz and Barbara Meyerhoff, *The Feminization of America: How Women's Values are Changing our Public and Private Lives* (Los Angeles: Tarcher, 1985), pp. 34-36.

3. Women's Alliance seminar, *Women's Voices in Troubling Times*, Berkeley, March 1-2, 1991.

NURTURANCE

1. Jean Baker Miller, "Women and Power," in Judith V. Jordan, et al. (eds.), *Women's Growth in Connection: Writings from the Stone Center* (New York: Guilford Press, 1991), page 199.

2. Janet L. Surrey, "Relationship and Empowerment," in Judith V. Jordan et al. (eds.), *Women's Growth in Connections: Writings from the Stone Center* (New York: Guilford Press, 1991), p. 164.

3. Marion Vittitow, personal interview, Seattle, WA, October 1987.

4. Carol Gilligan, Nona P. Lyons, and Trudy J. Hammer, eds., *Making Connections: The Relational Worlds of Adolescent Girls at Emma Willard School* (Cambridge, MA: Harvard University Press, 1990), pp. 10-18.

AFFINITY

1. Marge Piercy, "For Strong Women," *The Moon is Always Female* (New York: Alfred A. Knopf, 1986), p. 57.

2. Janet L. Surrey, "The Self-in-Relation: A Theory of Women's Development," in Judith V. Jordan et al. (eds.), *Women's Growth in Connection: Writings from the Stone Center* (New York: Guilford Press, 1991), p. 59.

FIRE—PASSION AT WORK

1. Joseph Campbell, *Myths to Live By: How We Re-Create Ancient Legends in our Daily Lives to Release Human Potential* (New York: Viking Penguin, 1972), p. 35.

SEXUALITY

1. Sheila Moon, *Changing Woman and Her Sisters* (San Francisco: Guild for Psychological Studies Publishing House, 1984), pp. 92, 93.

2. Moon, p. 102.

CREATIVITY

1. Susan Peterson, *The Living Tradition of Maria Martinez* (Tokyo: Kodansha International, 1977 and 1989).

2. Donald MacKinnon, *In Search of Human Effectiveness: Identifying and Developing Creativity* (Buffalo, NY: Creative Education Foundation, Inc., 1978), p. 61.

3. Michael Dues, Personal conversation with Virginia Kidd, Sacramento, CA, 1989.

4. Barbara Walker, *The Woman's Encyclopedia of Myths and Secrets* (San Francisco: Harper and Row, 1986), p. 488.

5. Catherine A. Martin and Karen L. DeMoss, "The Development of the Woman Child Psychiatry Researcher: A Review," *Journal of the American Academy of Child and Adolescent Psychiatry*, vol. 30, no. 6 (Nov. 1991), pp. 1009-1014.

6. Catherine Busch-Johnston, Personal interview, Nevada City, CA, June 22, 1988.

7. Regina Barreca, T*hey Used to Call Me Snow White . . . But I Drifted: Women's Strategic Use of Humor* (New York: Viking, 1991), pp. 4, 5.

AGGRESSION

1. Catherine Steiner-Adair, "The Body Politic," in Carol Gilligan et al. (eds.), *Making Connections: The Relational World of Adolescent Girls at Emma Willard School* (Cambridge: Harvard University Press, 1990), p. 162-182.

INTUITION

1. Marilyn Loden, *Feminine Leadership, Or How to Succeed in Business without Being One of the Boys* (New York: Times Books 1985), p. 182.

2. Weston Agor, *Intuition In Organizations: Leading and Managing Productively* (Newbury Park, CA: Sage, 1989), pp. 12, 13.

3. Gary Belsky, "Why Women Are Often Smarter than Men about Money," *Money Magazine*, June 1992, pp.76-82.

4. Deena Metzger, "Her Voice, Our Voices," lecture, Women's Alliance Camp, Nevada City, CA, June 1988.

5. Mary Belenky, et al., *Women's Ways of Knowing: The Development of Self, Voice, and Mind* (New York: Basic Books, 1986), p. 69.

6. Anne Campbell, *The Opposite Sex* (Topsfield, MA: Salem House, 1989), p. 224.

7. David Kiersy and Marilyn Bates, *Please Understand Me* (Del Mar, CA: Prometheus Nemesis Book Company, 1978).

WHOLISTIC THINKING

1. Nancy Jungerman, Personal interview, Davis, CA, July 25, 1988.

2. Joanne Irene Gabrynowicz, Phone interview, November 9, 1988, from Grand Forks, ND.

3. Sara Ruddick, *Maternal Thinking: Toward a Politics of Peace* (Boston: Beacon Press, 1989), p. 96.

WISDOM AND SPIRITUALITY

1. Barbara Stevens Sullivan, *Psychotherapy Grounded in the Feminine Principle* (Wilmette, IL: Chiron Publications, 1989), p. 24.

2. Naomi Newman, *Snake Talk: Urgent Messages from the Mother*, Seminar, "Women's Voices in Troubling Times," Women's Alliance, Berkeley, CA, March 2-3, 1991.

3. Sam Keen, *Fire in the Belly: On Being a Man* (New York: Bantam Books, 1991).

Bibliography

Agor, Weston H., ed. *Intuition in Organizations: Leading and Managing Productively.* Newbury Park, CA: Sage, 1989.

Arrien, Angeles. Talk at "Her Voice, Our Voices," Women's Alliance Camp, Nevada City, CA, June 26, 1988.

Astin, Helen S. and Carole Leland. *Women of Influence, Women of Vision: A Cross-Generational Study of Leaders and Social Change.* San Francisco: Jossey-Bass, 1991.

Astrachan, Anthony. *How Men Feel: Their Response to Women's Demands for Equality and Power.* Anchor Press, Doubleday, 1986.

Bagby, Rachel. Campfire comment, "Her Voice, Our Voices," Women's Alliance Camp, Nevada City, CA, June 26, 1988.

Baroo, Chuck. Personal Interview, New York, November 19, 1988.

Barreca, Regina. *They Used to Call Me Snow White . . . But I Drifted: Women's Strategic Use of Humor.* New York: Viking Penguin, 1991.

Belenky, Mary, with Blythe Clinchy, Nancy Goldberger, and Jill Tarule. *Women's Ways of Knowing: The Development of Self, Voice, and Mind.* New York: Basic Books, 1986.

Bennis, Warren. *Why Leaders Can't Lead.* San Francisco: Jossey-Bass, 1989.

Bolen, Jean Shinoda. *Goddesses in Everywoman: A New Psychology of Women.* New York: Harper and Row, 1984.

Bolton, Mary. Personal Interview, Sacramento, CA, July 2, 1991 as well as conversations over fifteen years.

Braunstein, Stephanie Ganic. "Apology," *Poet*, Vol. 1, No. 5.

Broverman, Inge K., et al. "Sex Role Stereotypes: A Current Appraisal." *The Journal of Social Issues* 28, No. 2, 1972: 59-78.

Brownmiller, Susan. *Femininity.* New York: Fawcett Columbine, 1984.

Busch, Catherine. Personal interview, Nevada City, CA, June 22, 1988.

Campbell, Anne. *The Opposite Sex.* Topsfield, MA: Salem House, 1989.

Campbell, Joseph. *Myths to Live By: How We Re-Create Ancient Legends in our Daily Lives to Release Human Potential.* New York: Viking, 1972.

Davis, Karen J. Personal conversations over many years, New York City.

Dillard, Annie. *Pilgrim At Tinker Creek.* New York: Harper and Row, 1974.

Dinnerstein, Dorothy. *The Mermaid and the Minotaur.* New York: Harper, 1976.

Doyle, Michael and David Strauss. *How To Make Meetings Work.* New York: Jove Books, 1976.

Dues, Michael. In personal conversation with Virginia Kidd, Sacramento, CA, 1989.

Eisler, Riane. *The Chalice and the Blade, Our History, Our Future.* New York: Harper and Row, 1987.

Faludi, Susan. *Backlash: The Undeclared War On American Women.* New York: Anchor, 1992.

"Fire, Our Friend and Enemy," *World Book*, Chicago: Field Enterprises Educational Corporation, 1976, Vol. 7, p. 116.

Forbes, Beverly. "Transformational Leadership Model Based on Theory F," publication pending, Seattle, 1990.

Ford, Bonnie L. "Women, Marriage and Divorce in California, 1849-1872," dissertation, Davis, CA: University of California, 1985.

Friedan, Betty. *The Second Stage.* New York: Summit Books, 1981, 1986.

Gabrynowicz, Joanne Irene. Phone interview, Sacramento/Grand Forks, ND, November 9, 1988.

Gendler, J. Ruth. *The Book of Qualities.* San Francisco: HarperCollins, 1988.

Gilligan, Carol. *In a Different Voice: Psychological Theory and Women's Development.* Cambridge: Harvard University Press, 1982.

Gilligan, Carol, Nona P. Lyons and Trudy J. Hammer, eds. *Making Connections: The Relational Worlds of Adolescent Girls at Emma Willard School.* Harvard University Press, 1990.

Goldhor, Harriet Lerner. *The Dance of Anger.* New York: Harper and Row, 1985.

Gray, Barbara. *Collaborating: Finding Common Ground for Multiparty Problems.* San Francisco: Jossey-Bass, 1989.

Griffin, Susan. *Woman and Nature: The Roaring Inside Her.* New York:

Harper and Row, 1978.

Gutek, Barbara A. *Sex and the Workplace: The Impact of Sexual Behavior and Harassment On Women, Men, and Organizations.* San Francisco: Jossey Bass, 1985.

Hancock, Emily. *The Girl Within, Recapture the Childhood Self, The Key to Female Identity.* New York: Dutton, 1989.

Harragan, Betty Lehan. *Games Mother Never Taught You.* New York: Warner Books, 1977.

Hay, Louise. *Love Your Body: A Positive Affirmation Guide for Loving and Appreciating Your Body.* Santa Monica: Hay House, Inc. expanded edition, 1988.

Hays, H. R. *The Dangerous Sex: The Myth of Feminine Evil.* New York: Pocket Books, 1966.

Heider, John. *The Tao of Leadership: Leadership Strategies for a New Age.* Toronto: Bantam New Age, 1985.

Heilbrun, Carolyn G. *Writing a Woman's Life.* New York: W. W. Norton and Company, 1988.

Helgesen, Sally. *The Female Advantage: Women's Ways of Leadership.* New York: Doubleday/Currency, 1990.

Hewlett, Sylvia Ann. *A Lesser Life: The Myth of Women's Liberation in America.* New York: William Morrow and Company, 1986.

Highwater, Jamake. *Kill Hole.* New York: Grove Press, 1992.

Hochschild, Arlie Russell, with Anne Machung. *The Second Shift: Working Parents and the Revolution at Home.* New York: Viking, 1989.

Horner, Matina S. "Toward Understanding the Achievement-Related Conflicts in Women." *The Journal of Social Issues* 28, No. 2, 1972:157-176.

Janeway, Elizabeth. *Powers of the Weak.* New York: Alfred A. Knopf, 980.

Jardine, Alice and Paul Smith, eds. *Men in Feminism.* New York: Methuen, 1987.

Jimenez, Delores. Personal Interview, Sacramento, CA, November 22, 1987.

Johnson, Robert. *Femininity Lost and Regained.* New York: Harper and Row, 1990.

_____. *He: Understanding Masculine Psychology.* New York: Harper and Row, 1974.

_____. *She: Understanding Feminine Psychology.* New York: Harper and Row, 1976.

Jordan, Judith V. et al. *Women's Growth In Connection: Writings From the Stone Center.* New York: Guilford Press, 1991.

Jung, Carl G. *The Practice of Psychotherapy.* (Volume 16 of the Collected Works) Bollingen Series XX. Princeton University Press: 1954, 1966.

_____. *Two Essays on Analytical Psychology,* (Volume 7 of the Collected Works) Bollingen Series XX. Princeton University Press: 1953, 1966.

_____. *The Structure and Dynamics of the Psyche.* (Volume 8 of the Collected Works) Bollingen Series XX. Princeton University Press: 1960.

Jungerman, Nancy. Personal Interview, Davis, CA, July 25, 1988.

Kanter, Rosabeth Moss. *Men and Women of the Corporation.* New York: Basic Books, 1977.

Keller, Evelyn Fox. *A Feeling for the Organism: The Life and Work of Barbara McClintock.* New York: W.H. Freeman and Company, 1983.

Kiersy, David and Marilyn Bates. *Please Understand Me.* Del Mar, CA: Prometheus Nemesis Book Company, 1978.

Krasek, Robert and Tores Theorell. *Healthy Work: Stress Productivity and the Reconstruction of Working Life.* New York: Basic Books, 1990.

LaDuke, Winona. "Indigenous Perspectives on Feminism and the Environment," Women's Alliance Seminar, *Women's Voices in Troubling Times,* Berkeley, CA, March 1-2, 1991.

Lawler, Frank. Personal Interview, Indianapolis, IN, March 19, 1989.

Lawler, Melissa. Personal Interview, Indianapolis, IN, March 20, 1989.

Lenz, Elinore and Barbara Meyerhoff. *The Feminization of America: How Women's Values are Changing our Public and Private Lives.* Los Angeles: Tarcher, 1985.

Lindbergh, Anne Morrow. *Gift from the Sea.* New York: Pantheon, 1955.

Loden, Marilyn. *Feminine Leadership: How to Succeed in Business Without Being One of the Boys.* New York: Times Books, 1985.

Luchetti, Cathy, in collaboration with Carol Olwell. *Women of the West.* St. George, UT: Antelope Island Press, 1982.

Luke, Helen. *Woman: Earth and Spirit, Feminine in Symbol and Myth.* New York: Crossroad, 1984.

Maccoby, Eleanor. "Gender and Relationships, A Developmental Account," *American Psychologist,* April 1990.

MacKinnon, Donald. *In Search of Human Effectiveness: Identifying and Developing Creativity.* Buffalo, NY: Creative Education Foundation, Inc.

1978.

MacLean, Adam. *The Triple Goddess: An Exploration of the Archetypal Feminine*. Grand Rapids, MI: Phanes Press, 1989.

Malloy, John T. *The Woman's Dress for Success Book*. New York: Warner Books, 1977.

May, Rollo. *The Courage to Create*. New York: Bantam Books, 1976.

Meador, Betty De Shong. "Thesmophoria: A Woman's Fertility Ritual," in *To Be a Woman*, Connie Zweig, ed. Los Angeles: Jeremy Tarcher, 1990, pp. 173-180.

Metzger, Deena. Talk at "Her voice, Our Voices," Women's Alliance Camp, Nevada City, CA, June, 1988.

_____. *The Woman Who Slept with Men To Take the War Out of Them* and *Tree*. Berkeley: Wingbow Press, 1983.

Miller, William A. *Your Golden Shadow: Discovering and Fulfilling Your Undeveloped Self*. New York: Harper and Row, 1989.

Moon, Sheila. *Changing Woman and Her Sisters*. San Francisco: Guild for Psychological Studies Publishing House, 1984.

Neugarten, Dail Ann and Jay M. Shafritz, eds. *Sexuality in Organizations: Romantic and Coercive Behaviors at Work*. Oak Park, IL: Moore Publishing Company, Inc., 1980.

Newman, Naomi. *Snake Talk: Urgent Messages From the Mother, Seminar,* "Women's Voices in Troubling Times" Women's Alliance, Berkeley, CA, March 2-3, 1991.

Newsom, Christine. Personal Interview, Nevada City, CA, March 19, 1989.

Owen, Harrison. *Leadership Is*. Potomac, MD: Abbott Publishing, 1990.

Pearson, Caroline. *The Growing Season*. Salt City, UT: Bookcraft, Inc.

Perera, Sylvia Brinton. *Descent to the Goddess: A Way of Initiation for Women*. Toronto: Inner City Books, 1981.

Peterson, Susan. *The Living Tradition of Maria Martinez*. Tokyo: Kodansha International, 1977, 1989.

Piercy, Marge. *The Moon is Always Female*. New York: Alfred A. Knopf, 1986.

Pinkola Estes, Clarissa. *Women Who Run With The Wolves: Myths and Stories of the Wild Woman Archetype*. New York: Ballantine Books, 1992.

Pogrebin, Letty Cottin. "*Ms.* Family Album," Ms., Vol. III, No. 1, Sept. 1992, p. 48.

Rich, Adrienne. *Blood, Bread, and Poetry, Selected Prose, 1979-1985*. New York: W. W. Norton and Company, 1986.

Robbins, Tom. *Even Cowgirls Get the Blues*. New York: Houghton Mifflin, 1976.

Rubin, Theodore Isaac. *The Angry Book.* New York: Macmillan, 1969.

Ruddick, Sara. *Maternal Thinking: Toward a Politics of Peace.* Boston: Beacon Press, 1989.

Rudin, Anne. Personal Interview, Sacramento, CA, May 12, 1991.

Schaff, Anne Wilson. *Women's Reality: An Emerging Female System in a White Male Society.* San Francisco: Harper and Row, 1985.

Schroeder, Lesley, M.D. Personal Interview, Sacramento, CA, November 18, 1988.

Schulz, Cornelia. Personal Interview, Nevada City, CA, June 24, 1988.

Schwartz, Felice. "Management Women and the New Facts of Life," *Harvard Business Review,* January-February 1989, pp. 65-76.

Scott, Mary Hugh. *The Passion of Being Woman: A Love Story From the Past For the Twenty-First Century.* Aspen: MacMurray and Beck Communications, 1991.

Shallcross, Doris J. and Dorothy A. Sisk. *Intuition: An Inner Way of Knowing.* Buffalo, NY: Bearly Limited, 1989.

Starhawk. *Truth or Dare: Encounters with Power, Authority, and Mystery.* New York: Harper and Row, 1987.

Stechert, Kathryn. *On Your Own Terms: A Woman's Guide to Working With Men.* New York: Vintage Books, 1987.

Steinem, Gloria. *Outrageous Acts and Everyday Rebellions.* New York: Holt, Rinehart and Winston, 1983.

Steiner-Adair, Catherine. "The Body Politic," in *Making Connections: the Relational Worlds of Adolescent Girls at Emma Willard School,* edited by Carol Gilligan, Nona P. Lyons and Trudy J. Hammer. Cambridge: Harvard University Press, 1990, pp. 162-182.

Stewart, Felicia, M.D., and Felicia Guest, Gary Stewart, M.D., and Robert Hatcher, M.D. *Understanding Your Body: Every Woman's Guide to Gynecology and Health.* Toronto: Bantam Books, 1987.

Stipek, Deborah and Jacquelyn McCroskey. "Investing in Children, Government and Workplace Policies for Parents," *American Psychologist,* 44:2, February 1989.

Stone, Merlin. *When God Was a Woman.* New York: A Harvest/HBJ Book, 1976.

Suib-Cohen, Sherry. *Tender Power: A Revolutionary Approach to Work and Intimacy.* Addison-Wesley Publishing Company, 1988.

Sullivan, Barbara Stevens. *Psychotherapy Grounded in the Feminine Principle*. Wilmette, Illinois: Chiron Publications, 1989.

Tamson, Ed. Personal Interview, Sacramento, CA, April 1992.

Vaill, Peter B. *Managing as a Performing Art*. San Francisco: Jossey-Bass, 1989.

Vittitow, Marion. Personal Interview, Seattle, WA, October 1987.

Wagner, Jane. *The Search for Signs of Intelligent Life in the Universe*. New York: Harper and Row, 1986.

Walker, Barbara. *The Skeptical Feminist: Discovering the Virgin, Mother and Crone*. New York: Harper and Row, 1987.

_____. *The Woman's Encyclopedia of Myths and Secrets*. New York: Harper and Row, 1983.

Waring, Marilyn. *If Women Counted: A New Feminist Economics*. San Francisco: Harper Colophon, 1988.

"Women Allege Sexist Atmosphere in Offices Constitutes Harassment," *Wall Street Journal*, February 10, 1988.

Woodman, Marion. *The Owl Was A Baker's Daughter: Obesity, Anorexia and the Repressed Feminine*. Toronto: Inner City Books, 1980.

Woodman, Marion, with Kate Dawson, Mary Hamilton, and Rita Greer Allen. *Leaving My Father's House: A Journey to Conscious Femininity*. Boston: Shambhala, 1992.

Yudkin, Marcia. Personal Interview, Taos, NM, July 1992.

Zweig, Connie, ed. *To Be a Woman: The Birth of the Conscious Feminine*. Los Angeles: Tarcher, 1990.

Index

Order Form

(For credit card orders, please call 1-800-233-3792)

Quantity

Changing Woman, Changing Work
by Nina Boyd Krebs, Ed.D.,
ISBN 1-878448-56-0
_____ Hardcover ($22.95 x number of copies) $ _____

**For Men Only: How to love a
woman without losing our mind**
by Joseph Angelo, ISBN 1-878448-53-6
_____ Paperback ($9.95 x number of copies) $ _____

Some Mid-night Thoughts
by Mary Hugh Scott, ISBN 1-878448-52-8
_____ Paperback ($12.95 x number of copies) $ _____

The Passion of Being Woman
by Mary Hugh Scott,
_____ Hardcover ($19.95 x no. of copies), $ _____
1-878448-50-1
_____ Paperback ($12.95 x no. of copies), $ _____
1-878448-51-X

Subtotal $ _____

Shipping ($3.00 for 1st book, $1.00 for $ _____
each additional book to same address)

Colorado residents add 3.3% sales tax $ _____

Total $ _____

Name _____

Address _____

City, State, ZIP _____

Phone_____ (for order clarification only)

Make checks out to MacMurray and Beck and send to:
PO Box 4257, Aspen, CO 81612.

2

245-258

298-312 ∧ media on man

334-350

/ 7 people

hist 65-78

medium

in message

57 Darwin

sKim Beco

Molders of Modern Thought

Molders
of Modern
Thought

Edited with an Introduction by

Ben B. Seligman

◊ a New York Times Book

Quadrangle Books
CHICAGO

Contents

2. The Twentieth-Century Philosophers

3. Contemporary Psychology and Anthropology

Molders of Modern Thought

Introduction

Antecedents of Modern Thought

The contemporary mind is the product of extraordinarily diverse influences. Isaiah, Plato, Aquinas, Descartes, Copernicus, Montesquieu, Locke—these and many other thinkers have poured their thought into the mainstream of Western consciousness. The turbulence created by the conflict of Platonist and Stoic, Nominalist and Realist, Romanticist and Classicist, Positivist and Existentialist still troubles man as he struggles with a world he did not make but wistfully hopes to control. By that control man believes he will come to know himself and his milieu. Always a mindmaking creature whose main business was to transform himself, man has become what he is by creating social organization and philosophy; by evolving ritual and religion, revealing a concern with ultimate matters; and by constructing a wide-ranging symbolic universe which has encapsulated his whole cultural existence.

It may be argued that the men discussed in this selection from the *New York Times*—ranging from Giambattista Vico, a crotchety Italian philosopher and jurist, to the advocates of the New Left today—have all cultivated a complex of symbols and metaphors. In its poetic intensity, this complex has often reached the hidden sources of the human soul. As philosophers, psychologists, economists, historians, anthropologists, and activists, these writers have sought in the final analysis to interpret *man in society*. The task is as fascinating as it is difficult.

There were always beginnings. While we may seek to mark off boundaries in history, the further we go back the more we see it as a seamless web. Vico drew on Bacon and Descartes, though their conception of man and nature was transformed in his tortured prose—as Sir Isaiah Berlin so well demonstrates in his essay that begins this book. Bacon and Descartes illustrated the increasing preoccupation with nature and science in the seventeenth century, a preoccupation that presaged a revolution in human thought. Man was displaced from the center of the universe by Copernicus. He became instead "a tiny speck on a third-rate planet revolving about a tenth-rate sun drifting in an endless cosmic ocean." Teleology and will were set aside by Cartesian mechanical process and the Copernican solar system. Man was now alone. If there was an Ultimate Being, He was so distant that only faith could make Him relevant.

Descartes had cast doubt on the usefulness of history and other humanistic studies because they could not be reached through mathematics. Vico rejected this attempt to depreciate everything external to nature, insisting that man's experience could still be understood scientifically. As society was made by man, it was entirely possible for the mind to grasp social principles. Here Vico anticipated Karl Marx, for Marx also knew that men make themselves. For Vico, as for Marx, penetrating the past had to be done in the same manner as it had been constructed, that is, from within. Thus economic and social position could go far in explaining the relation of classes to each other, whether in ancient Greece or medieval Florence. Clearly, such a procedure demanded empathy with the past and the realization that the world always had been filled with sensitive beings.

There are parallels also between Vico and Sigmund Freud. Both men saw social development as a recapitulation of individual development. Both accepted the universality of symbolism. Both understood that individuals projected their feelings onto the world about them. Both located social origins in a primitive trauma that created a sense of guilt. Vico, however, viewed history as a process of recurring events that was providential. The occasional optimism implicit in this notion was lacking in Freud.

Vico's contemporaries had a less complicated view of the universe. For them nature displayed a Copernican simplicity that lent order to existence. To be sure, complexities had been introduced by Tycho Brahe and Johannes Kepler, who modified the Copernican harmony by studying actual data: mathematics alone did not complete the world picture. The emphasis was now placed on experiment, and its importance was highlighted in the work of Galileo. Though the Inquisition might force the aging Galileo to recant, he had so firmly rooted the Copernican view of the universe in men's minds that no amount of theological hostility could falsify it.

But if the world was to be a perfect Cartesian machine, then man ought to be able to control it. Here was a Pandora's box, for man began to tinker with that machine in the hope that it would do his bidding. He did not know that by acting on nature he assumed the risk of creating new processes that, once initiated, moved by themselves, and often to the detriment of human existence. It was an experience that even social scientists, who should have known better, attempted to replicate: they assumed that the ability to manage nature implied the ability to manage men. It is such thinking that culminates today in the fallacies of behaviorism and is celebrated in that strange cacophony known as McLuhanism.

The philosophic implications of eighteenth-century science suited the rising middle class quite well, for such views offered a frame of human relations appropriate to its ideological needs. Newtonian celestial mechanics completed the Cartesian revolution: the world was now truly a mechanism embodying the fundamental precepts of natural law. John Locke then transferred these ideas to the political arena, lending support to the middle class in its struggle for liberty. Newton had epitomized the ideals of natural science just as Locke was the harbinger of the new social science. The attainment of truth was assured by mathematics and experiment, while the rational and the natural were merged to form the basis of a society of science and a science of society. Reason and mathematics prevailed for all men of intellect.

Calculus was invented (by Newton and Leibniz independently), and algebra and geometry were fused to facilitate the measurement of motion. Mathematics was employed to establish the laws of the solar system, so that what was true on earth held as well for the heavens. Mathematics revealed the principles of action that moved the world machine. So striking was the new method that men began to apply it to all human affairs. Rousseau could begin with the proposition that all men are free and deduce from it his politics; and the Classical economists, basing themselves on Locke, could derive economics from the axioms of private property.

The construction of a science of man was a most significant achievement of the eighteenth century. An intellectual atmosphere was created in which such creative thinkers as Vico could flourish. But the understanding of man had to concur with the harmony established by the laws of the universe. For some thinkers this was nothing less than a social physics that specified a deductive and mathematical method for social science. Even Locke, who disliked mathematics, thought like a geometer, devising a model of society along methodical lines that eminently suited the sort of man he had fashioned. Thomas Hobbes had also built a precise image of man, but one that was to justify a monarchical politics. In all of these theories, knowledge was based on combinations of elementary components, the sensations, thus paralleling the Newtonian scheme of things. For Locke, sensations came from the outside to impress themselves on the blank tablet of the mind; hence all men initially were created equal. The different situations in which men found themselves in later life were entirely matters of environment. Therefore, inequities could be corrected only through politics. The middle-class demand for freedom to do as it pleased could find no superior justification than such a philosophy.

That these beliefs were used to sustain the political demands of the middle class seems undeniable. English economic success was vindicated by a system of natural rights that was as inviolable as the laws of physics. To secure claims to property was consequently a proper function of the state. Hobbes might view society as a war of all against all, necessitating a social compact enforced by a king, but Locke knew that man was social by nature and had no need for a powerful central government. But when the state failed to protect the most natural right of all, property, then a revolution was permissible—provided it was a middle-class revolution.

These principles rationalized the action of the American colonists against the British crown and underpinned the ideals of the Constitution. The Founding Fathers wanted a government that would normalize business relations and protect them against both the tyranny of an absolute ruler and the tyranny of a mob. Differences were compromised so that a national government could be founded on a delicate set of balances guaranteeing equilibrium in politics. The distribution of power seemed reasonable, accommodating as it did all of the interests of the middle class. Thus politics, too, reflected the Newtonian universe.

But in the nineteenth century a discernible shift in thinking took place, moving the emphasis from nature to society. Jeremy Bentham weighed institutions by a pragmatic test and was ready to discard those that failed. The mainspring of action was the pleasure-pain nexus, a criterion that led to the elevation of community interest as the sum of individual happiness. The belief in the greatest good for the greatest number—a Benthamite principle —is still persuasive enough to move many persons, though we know now that human nature is infinitely more complex than what the net sum of pleasures and pains would indicate.

If all men have a right to happiness, however, then no one may deprive another of that right. Thus middle-class doctrine could support general rights, lending a tone of humanitarianism to political theory. Writers began to praise the universality of toleration and a spirit of accommodation that would transcend national boundaries. Progress became a natural phenomenon, inherent in society, always moving upward, and totally self-sufficient. But social scientists were unaware that they were offering an egocentric doctrine rooted in the belief that middle-class careers always ascend in rising spirals. They made history predictable and beneficent, and men happy subjects of a kindly fate. It was as mechanical as any piece of Cartesian clockwork.

The reaction was inevitable. Clockwork missed the emotional side of man, and mathematical uniformity failed to uncover the true richness of the human personality. Reason was insufficient, for man was also a biologic being possessed of a soul. Everything that man felt and witnessed testified to the complexity of experience. Nature was more than reason could describe, and once we had understood human sentience even religion could make sense. Above all, the individual was supreme; the object of life was self-expression and the development of man's uniqueness. Man had ideals and he needed a way of expressing them. Such was the Romantic protest, one that was flexible enough to support religion, revolution, individualism—and political reaction.

Embedded in such thinking was the idea of growth. Applied to the world of man, it meant the use of foresight to counteract the loss of energy. It meant renewing the climb to perfection. Transferred to biology, the idea of growth placed man in a natural setting and gave him a new understanding of his origins. But a puzzle remained: was growth a matter of chemical transformation, or was there an *élan vital* at play? Most biologists continued to explain life processes in purely chemical terms, although some dissenters argued that it was necessary to search for a vital life-principle. Yet the filiation between the chemical and the mechanical once more revealed the influence of the Cartesian outlook.

It was Charles Darwin—discussed in some detail here in Paul B. Sears's centennial article—who drew attention to the importance of a causal analysis of growth. It became important to know how the process took place and to investigate patiently the cumulative effects of increments of change. The result was the theory of evolution, which despite fundamentalist hostility has continued to exert a mind-blowing effect. Increasingly, the social sciences were forced to see man as an animal that interacted with his environment. Man adapted himself to his surroundings continuously, even as he tried to reshape them. Yet nature was complex enough to allow for infinite variations in response, thus allowing man to satisfy both whim and curiosity. For a long while nature was still the master; today, man calls the tune and he is often a poor musician.

By responding enthusiastically to evolution, modern man has continued to display an invidious egocentricity. He has always preferred the later stages of the process, denigrating that which came earlier as "primitive." It is against such value schemes that Claude Lévi-Strauss has inveighed, for to judge by contemporary experience it is surely difficult to say for certain that one culture is superior to another.

The point is that evolution is a theory of change, not a theory of progress. In no way does it suggest a movement toward perpetual wholesomeness. Nor is there any promise in evolution for better or worse: there is only continuity. That is to say, evolution is a process of becoming, though governed by biological "laws" that offer many alternatives. The direction seems to be a question of happenstance, and often enough the direction has turned out to be a blind alley. Such a conception contrasts sharply with Cartesianism, in which the universe rigidly unwinds itself. And who is to say that we may not have now entered upon one of those blind alleys—like the dinosaur and the saber-toothed tiger—and by having evolved so highly specialized a brain may not be on the verge of self-extinction?

A significant outcome of evolutionary theory was to highlight the idea of the unconscious. Since beliefs appear to be a matter of adaptation, there seems little basis for thinking that they must conform to an unchanging Platonic Ideal. Hence a study of beliefs must take account of the process of adaptation, in which the irrational has an important role. Men do habitually conceal the real reasons for their beliefs and in doing so fill the unconscious with a jumble of motivations, wishes, loves, and hates.

The unconscious was known before Freud. As Leonard Engel demonstrates in his article, "Philosophers, poets, and novelists have long been aware that mental activity is not confined to the level of consciousness." One can discover intimations of the unconscious in Shakespeare, Rousseau, Coleridge, and above all, Dostoevsky. But none of this diminishes Freud's remarkable achievement; for the first time, man's hidden mind was mapped and the possibility of its exploration revealed. Critics have complained that Freudian theory is "not operational"; perhaps so, but one can learn more about the human mind from it than from all the clinicians combined.

But Freud ranged far beyond his theory of the individual mind, extending his discoveries to an analysis of society and its history.

To be sure much of his social analysis has remained bold speculation, but its main point cannot be ignored—an understanding of
present social neurosis may be achieved by introducing an awareness of a buried past. Thus mythology, philosophy, and even poetic
insight were as important to a diagnosis of man's personal and
social ills as were biological and physiological data. As in Vico,
individual development seemingly recapitulated historical development. Freud wanted to grasp the *meaning* of mental phenomena,
for they were not purely biologic; such phenomena stemmed from
an unknown relationship between unconscious thought and overt
action, comprehension of which required knowledge not only of
the "how" but the "why" as well.

Implicit in Freud was a theory of society based on tension. For
it seemed evident that social institutions circumscribed sharply the
areas in which the powerful instinctual drives of man could function. The ensuing conflict posed the threat of an explosion in the
human being. Yet cultural advance could be achieved by re-
directing instinctual energies to create art, music, and other
products of man's spirit.

The idea of tension as a prime mover in history was central in
the system of another giant of nineteenth-century thought—Karl
Marx. The corpus of Marxian doctrine is considerably vaster
and more complex than Sidney Hook is able to describe within
the compass of his article. One wishes to stress especially Hook's
reference to Marx's humanistic outlook. A few years ago a heated
debate emerged among intellectuals concerning the relevance of
Marx's early philosophical papers. On one side were such commentators as Daniel Bell and Lewis Feuer who argued that
Marx's youthful humanistic perceptions had been displaced by
the more stiffnecked views of his later years; on the other were
writers like Erich Fromm and Michael Harrington who saw no
fundamental contradictions between the burning pages of *Das
Kapital* and the insights of the earlier discussions. A full exploration of Marxist thought would show that the latter are closer to
the truth of the matter.

Understanding Marx's philosophic development does require
starting with Hegel. He suggested a sort of idealism that fused

external and internal reality in human consciousness as a realization of Absolute Spirit. But in Marx, consciousness is placed in the center of social institutions, making them the dominant reality. Thus Marx demonstrated that Hegel's idea of the culmination of the spirit in the Prussian state was mistaken. In Marx state and society were clearly distinguished; moreover, the concept of alienation was rooted in social and economic origins. With the introduction of private property, politics was subordinated to the social relations that emanated from property institutions; the interests of the state became a "cloak for class interests," and concern with the immanent development of human beings was submerged.

If there is anything in the Marxian view that displays immediacy it is the concept of alienation. In historical terms, it reflects the particularity of man's relationship to a world in which the prospects of creativity have been suppressed. At this point it becomes possible to join Marx to Freud, one starting from society, the other proceeding from the individual. Marx located the alienating process in the capitalism of his day. His economics—a grand and rough body of thought that continues to impress scholars despite its patent errors—is essentially a formal statement of the concept of alienation. The analysis of pre-capitalist societies, their transformation into capitalism, the labor theory of value, commodity fetishism, and the human impact of capital accumulation revealed the social forms through which alienation was generated.

Needless to say, alienation is reflected through social and individual consciousness, philosophical concepts that became the focus of later phenomenological writers. Here the reader's attention must be called to several of the subsequent essays in this book, particularly those on Jean-Paul Sartre, Martin Buber, and Herbert Marcuse. The similarity between the Marxian view and that of the phenomenologists should be obvious. This is hardly surprising, as both schools can trace their intellectual ancestry to Hegel. But whereas the phenomenologists assume that objects are illusory and created by consciousness, Marx insisted that a necessary condition for consciousness was the natural and material substratum. Since that substratum was comprised largely of sociological elements, it was an aspect of reality subject to human control.

Marx moved from the potentiality of change to practice, the only mode through which change could be achieved. Inherent in practice was the anticipation of the idea of community, one that would replace the contemporary collective ant heap of social reality. To be sure, such anticipation provided the teleological thrust and utopian character of the Marxian system, but from a philosophic standpoint it all hangs together. It is a remarkably relevant body of thought in which economics, sociology, and politics comprise integral categories of analysis.

The section on antecedents closes with the late Irwin Edman's article on Friedrich Nietzsche, a much misunderstood philosopher. The Nazi regime in Germany had clasped Nietzsche to its ideological bosom, although it is more than likely he would have rejected their embrace. As Edman says, the Nietzschean "will to power" simply emphasizes the quality of excellence that man is capable of. It was a psychological concept, suggesting that power rested in self-control, not in subjugating others. If men seek power in this sense, it is because they search for self-expression and self-determination. The man of power was he who creatively deployed his passions for higher ends. Once again, comparisons may be drawn with Freud, for both men were exploring hidden drives to action. Further, said Nietzsche, as men give meaning and sense to existence, they are obligated to become "creators instead of remaining mere creatures." Only thus can they escape the deadly fate of being what they were.

Nietzsche's influence was widespread. The Nazis mutilated his work, savagely tearing ideas out of context: he would have treated them with the utmost contempt. His influence on literature was enormous, as evidenced in the work of Thomas Mann, André Gide, Bernard Shaw, and André Malraux. His impact on Sartre and Camus, as well as on Buber to some degree, was significant. Nietzsche clearly had a seminal mind: his work was most important among the antecedents of modern thought.

Twentieth-Century Philosophies

Of all the philosophies in the history of ideas, none has had more effect on the present era—for good or for ill—than positivism. The roots of this style of thinking go back, of course, to Descartes, but in their modern garb they begin to flower in the writings of Saint-Simon and Auguste Comte. In their work, positivism was an expression of a hope that all forms of valid knowledge would reveal an intimate relationship to something called science. Facts, it was argued, are the sole objects of knowledge, and awareness of their existence could be achieved through a method that was common to all the disciplines. Beyond the fact, nothing was intelligible; hence it was fruitless to attempt to cross the border of the realm of fact. These views were related to nineteenth-century conceptions of progress, which were, as we have noted, embedded in the idea of a rising spiral reaching heights of human perfection. Yet no such movement was "progressive" if it violated the "permanent" features of life, one of which was, of course, private property.

The positivist mentality refused to speculate on *why* events moved as they did, but asked rather *how* they moved. It was only necessary to collect the "facts" of social and economic life in order to demonstrate "how." From such a procedure one could readily distill all the universal laws that governed the natural order of things. Comte's positivism was a kind of scientism, a belief that all of man's social ills could be cured by the *method* of science. This belief permeated all later forms of positivist thinking and created strict criteria by which discourse in philosophy and social science was to be evaluated.

These doctrines became the touchstones of social science. They included a complete submission to facts, whatever they might be; a belief in a rather rigid determination of events and phenomena, enabling experiment and inquiry in human affairs to be conducted "scientifically"; the insistence on insufficiency of mere confirmation by which to judge the usefulness of an hypothesis; and the eradication of all metaphysical, indeed all philosophical, questions. In short, human thought seemed capable of reduction to brute physical fact. Phenomena were to be explained solely by an observer recording all the uniformities he could detect in nature, specifying such uniformities as descriptions of nature's handiwork. A scientific law became an expression in abstract form of a natural principle operating through material objects. It did not occur to positivists that social "laws" operated through human beings, creating what Alfred Schutz has called problems of intersubjectivity—the realm of conscious personal relationships. These were questions to which positivists and their close affiliates were unwilling to address themselves. Economists, for example, were reluctant to view the act of choosing as a problem involving intersubjectivity, being quite content to accept choice as a revealed act. Had the distinction been taken seriously, it is conceivable that economists would have acknowledged choice as culturally conditioned, as much a matter of responding to others as it is a search for individual want satisfaction.

The unwillingness to take such complexities into account, and the anxiety to be a thoroughgoing positivist in one's thinking, to slash with Occam's razor, appear to have generated considerable difficulties. Overconcern with economy of thought has too often led to the use of mental bulldozers, leaving the intellectual landscape barren. To remove a few trees that obscured their view, positivists frequently leveled entire forests. To drop the image, it may be argued that a good deal more than what positivists would retain may be necessary for perceptive and meaningful analysis.

The debate that ensued enveloped in part such American philosophers as Charles S. Peirce and William James. Peirce argued that no qualities were so hidden as to be unavailable to the scrutiny of science, a view whose relation with positivism was evident. James insisted that the meaning of a statement was revealed in its practical outcome, lending a utilitarian character to the determination of truth.

These trends found fullest expression in the philosophy of logical positivism, a system of thought that was fostered by the so-called Vienna Circle in the early decades of this century. The scientific philosophy that stemmed from logical positivism had its sources in mathematical logic and physics while maintaining science as a description of experience. Metaphysics was rejected as a pursuit that perpetually posed meaningless and unanswerable questions. Metaphysical questions violated the principle of verifiability, a precept that was central to the logical positivist's effort to clear philosophy of useless lumber. Yet a metaphysician could simply ignore their rules of investigation, carrying on philosophic discourse in his own terms. Moreover, was it not possible that positivist rules of verification were themselves based ultimately on metaphysical notions? Even more fundamental, if certain propositions were ruled out as meaningless, then the task of deciding their truth or falsity could not be logically carried through. Such decisions required more than the severely restricted criteria of the positivists.

Since verifiability seemed to become untenable as a criterion of meaningfulness, the positivists retreated to the possibility of disproving propositions as an alternative criterion. Thereafter, philosophy was reduced to the precise and logical analysis of language. While such an approach appeared to imply that language *per se* would reveal the nature of experience, it did not dawn on the positivists that language and experience might not be in tune with each other. Since experience is antecedent to language, one is confronted by the task of addressing both realms rather than concentrating solely on language. Such a confrontation stems from the close and intimate relationship of language and experience. Although it may be difficult to unravel these interconnections, it is nevertheless essential for clarity and meaning. General propositions that pose problems of meaning and language may be abstractions and basically language formulations, but they are related to events experienced through human action. Thus, while events and abstractions take place at different levels, there is always the problem of relating one to the other.

The positivists insisted that social scientists have been laggard and backward as a consequence of their allegedly crude methodology and their unwillingness to adopt a "scientific" posture. But this is hardly an acceptable stricture. The social sciences have many more variables to contend with, are concerned with subjective interpretations, must confront the question of problematic verification, lack exactness and precision, are frequently unable to obtain basic data or to establish numerical constants, and often cannot match the predictability of the laboratory world. None of this makes them inferior; it all simply means that the basic properties of investigation in social science require alternative approaches with attributes quite distinct from those of the natural sciences.

There would seem to be degrees of explanation in social science, as contrasted to, say, physics, that have nothing to do with backwardness. In economics, for example, the construction of a model may be a way of providing an orientation to a problem, or providing a guide to research, rather than specifying in detail the way in which the component variables actually move. Such a procedure may not be quite as precise as the positivist would like, but at least one is involved with substantive content rather than with linguistic purity alone. To be sure, language may set the limits of particular problems, but it seems essential that the work be done.

Let us, however, return to the question of verifiability. We have noted that verification *per se* appeared inadequate as a scientific criterion. The dilemma of the positivists was nevertheless seemingly resolved by the alternative formulation of Karl Popper. His substitute procedure, labeled "defeasibility," was based on the possibility of disproving a proposition. In other words, a statement was deemed to be an empirical one if it suggested some method for making it disconfirmable. We should be able, it was argued, to indicate how empirical reality differs from the reality in which the proposition would be false; confirmation by itself does not lend empirical content to a statement or a theory, said Popper. The social scientist, therefore, must think of ways in which his model might be disproved. The difficulty with this approach is that asserting the existence of certain conditions may itself not be disconfirmable, hence not empirical by Popper's standards. Perhaps the way out is via the route of probability and contingency, for in human affairs nothing is really certain.

But such an approach tends to eliminate all interest in the origins of the problems of social science. Generic origins and the way in which questions may have evolved seemed to the positivists to be quite beside the point. They were not concerned with motivations or historical relationships, insisting that all knowledge consisted of empirical statements, the tautologies of which were to be unraveled through the logic of linguistic usage. Consider the circle into which the positivist would take us: having defined his terms by what his propositions may achieve, he takes his premises as granted and then asserts that his enterprise is indeed "scientific." As Abraham Kaplan once remarked, rather wryly, "It does not matter much what we do, if only we do it right," thus creating what he dubbed the "myth of methodology."

Nowhere has this myth been perpetuated more effectively and with more serious consequences than in that variant of positivism that goes under the name of "operationalism." This version of the philosophy of science stemmed from the practical work of the physicist Percy Bridgman. The properties of phenomena, according to Bridgman, were to be described only by the operations necessary to disclose those properties; hence any concept must be defined by the operations implicit in it. But, since some operations may be superior to others, one would seemingly require some metasystem through which one could establish criteria for making judgments of superiority or inferiority. Moreover, it is obvious that a concept may have but the loosest of relationships with its operations, a criticism that led Bridgman to modify his earlier rigid position. There would seem to be a parallel between such criticism and Gödel's second theorem, which held that the consistency of a formal system in arithmetic cannot be proved within the system. The implication was that a hierarchy of assembled hypotheses or a metasystem was needed, for the idea of a self-contained deductive set of ideas was insupportable.

Bridgman consequently placed himself in the same difficulty as that confronting the logical positivists, since the operations provided in a direct manner ultimate *verification* of their concept. It seemed that Bridgman wanted to be sure that the business of formulating a theory was related in some way to the subject of the theory, to that which was being scrutinized. If no such relationship could be established, then the theory would have to be rejected. Such a link seemed essential in order to establish a theory's meaning. One notes at this point the impact of the pragmatic posture, for Bridgman really implies that truth is not independent of the operations stemming from practical work. Such a view seems troublesome, for in the social sciences, operations are themselves variables altering the meaning of the situations subjected to study. Essentially, Bridgman has told us merely to check a solution before accepting it—not a very striking principle of investigation.

Escaping from the positivist impasse requires a broader reach. To be sure, some philosophers have retreated to more modest operationalist perceptions. There is a reasonableness in their approach that acknowledges the devilish complexity of reality. Here one thinks of the important work of Abraham Kaplan or Ernest Nagel, for they have indeed recognized that reality may be so complex that the best we may be able to do is to devise a set of "reasonably acceptable constructs" that describe a situation. We may be able to provide explanations of social phenomena in many instances only through the general principles of a rough model. Clearly, the model's implications are subject to testing. There needs to be a method to establish whether reality can be reconciled with the model. Yet it would seem that the criteria for judging such a reconciliation must be drawn from a broad metasystem. Hypotheses are embedded in a large set of social phenomena stemming from the entire system; hypotheses and phenomena are not only all related in some way to each other, but also form a kind of hierarchy.

Another difficulty one has with the positivist or operationalist approach stems from an excessive concern with technique. For example, the way in which scarce resources are allocated is often culturally determined. If that is the case, then economists ought to know both the how *and* why of the allocative mechanism. Ignoring the why leads to such strange anomalies as the latter-day focus on the size of the gross national product without regard to the quality of its composition.

An extreme consequence of positivism is the cult of quantification. Its adherents argue that all forms of human behavior can be known only if they are measured, counted, and weighed, lending a scientific aura to numbers. So ingrained has this belief become in some circles that it generates a fervent hostility if subjected to question. Anything not amenable to the mathematical approach is to be ignored and deemed unworthy of rational attention. Besides, numbers offer a superb defense against the complexities of the human condition—much of which is, unfortunately, still qualitative. The quantifying habit is now so well established that it leads precisely to scientism—a fascination with form and a faith in the values of only that which is objective. That so much of existence and behavior is qualitative does not seem to be very troublesome to the quantifiers. Under the regime of the objective, feelings and sensations are reduced to the irrelevant, and what is human is of little account.

Bertrand Russell was an important contributor to the positivist ethos, though he was more than a technical philosopher, as Charles Hussey underscores in his article. In a long life that almost reached the century mark, Russell was a mathematician and logician, a historian of philosophy and philosopher of language, a writer on ethics and religion, an astute commentator on politics and education, the author of some seventy volumes, and a caustic critic of mankind. In his scientific work he was determined to create a philosophy that would be founded on neutral inquiry devoid of the irrelevancies of moral belief. The object of philosophy, he once said, was "to give an account of the world of science and daily life." His logic was employed to establish a system of analysis that stripped phenomena to their bare "atomic propositions" thus reducing experience to its simplest elements. In this sense, Russell developed the tradition of British empiricism, and thereby of positivism, to its ultimate.

One must also note the contributions of Ludwig Wittgenstein, an Austrian philosopher who did his critical work in England, where he was for a while a student of Russell's. Wittgenstein's ideas were known at first in a kind of oral tradition, as he published little in his lifetime. It is most difficult to summarize them without distortion. The *Philosophical Investigations,* issued two years after his death in 1951, seems little more than jottings in a notebook. One thing was clear, however: Wittgenstein's conception of language, the study of which became his primary philosophic preoccupation, had changed since the publication of his *Tractatus Logico-philosophicus* in 1922. Like Russell, he had connected language and experience through the relation between "atomic" or elementary propositions and their corresponding facts. But the second book was actually a rejection of the first. Whereas the 1922 work argued that any proposition presupposed language in general, the posthumous study conceded that a particular proposition could presuppose but a small part of language. The *Tractatus* had imagined that language could be accorded a universal form: the *Investigations* discovered nothing common in language forms, only overlapping relationships that *suggested* common qualities, but which could not be identified.

Such studies might have led to specifying rules of language, and might have provided certain psychological insights, but they left everything else in philosophy mere collections of trivia. The resulting arrogance was unbelievable. Realms of being were said to be misbegotten products of ancient scribblers who failed to realize that a good philosophy was a purgative, ridding us of all our ailments. In essence, misunderstanding was merely a matter of semantical comprehension. If the mind of man was troubled, an analysis of language would set it right.

West European philosophers, aside from the English, have by and large rejected this approach. Struggling for a suitable way of looking at man and his works, they are convinced that positivism and linguistic analysis are concerned more with form than with substance and are therefore sterile. For them, thought and being do not inhabit unbridgeable realms; it is possible to connect them. Rationality may be discovered in being as well as in thought, and there is ground for sensible discourse in both. Even if there is no initial awareness of experience, that does not imply that consciousness and feeling generate only non-sense. The world of experience can be explored rationally, for philosophy should be able to transcend the boundaries of scientific discourse. That is to say, the scope of philosophy is broad, limited only by its own meta-philosophical frontiers.

If such an argument is acceptable in defining the proper limits of philosophy, then the rehabilitation of Marxism, in particular, appears feasible. Following such leads, Continental philosophers have been reviving Hegelian and Marxian ideas in their contest with positivism. By extending consciousness to social and political issues, it is felt, one avoids the methodological strictures imposed by Anglo-Saxon traditions. The social sciences, for example, cannot be said to be *wertfrei,* for as Gunnar Myrdal has demonstrated, a social scientist brings with him value-laden luggage from which troublesome demons are always escaping. The problem is to keep these demons under control, not to deny that they exist.

Whatever else might be said of pragmatist filiations with positivist thinking, there is no question but that a deeper concern with public issues was manifested by Charles Peirce, William James, and especially John Dewey. While Peirce was primarily a logician, he also wrote on ethics, history, phenomenology, and religion. James, who was a physician and psychologist, addressed his philosophy to the general public. His conception of the truth took account of the feelings of the man in the street, and he included everything derived from experience. And Dewey, who achieved pre-eminence as America's major philosopher, quickly developed a sense of the interdependence of things and the dynamism with which they are infused. As Irwin Edman points out in his essay, Dewey's influence was enormous. Wherever he taught, whether at Chicago, Columbia, or in Japan, students were entranced, even though he was not a particularly good lecturer. But they knew they were in the presence of a great mind. In Chicago, Dewey came to know workers and trade unionists, and was thoroughly familiar with the social and economic problems they had to face. Although his writing was often opaque, he was widely read.

While Edman emphasizes Dewey's conception of freedom and intelligence, one must also underscore the key notion of experience rooted in naturalism. Thus, whatever empiricism there is in Dewey, it does not display the disembodied character of positivism. He sought rather a fusion of solid knowledge and scientific method. There may be distinctive levels of interaction between man and nature—ranging from the physical and chemical to conscious awareness—but there are gradations that signify continuity. The most complex level is that of experience, where consciousness itself is manifest.

Concentration on consciousness is most intense among the phenomenologists, existentialists, and affiliated thinkers, whose challenge to a desiccated positivism has been thus far the most serious. Here the giants are Edmund Husserl, Martin Heidegger, Jean-Paul Sartre, Maurice Merleau-Ponty, Alfred Schutz, and, tangentially at least, Martin Buber. This book includes articles on two members of this loosely defined group—one on Buber written by Meyer Levin, and a perceptive portrait of Sartre by John L. Brown.

Buber, a religious existentialist, may be said to have been at the periphery of this rich philosophic movement, yet in many ways he overlaps it. Buber distinguished between relationships to things and relationships that are impregnated with personal content. One may be "objective" or impersonal with people as well as things, but when one addresses another person to establish genuine contact—an "I-thou" relationship rather than an "It" relationship—both individuals are affected, shaped, and reshaped by that nexus. "I-thou" relationships can exist only in the present, and impinge on immediate existence. The "It" relationship moves always into the past, as objective knowledge displays a temporal character.

Phenomenology—literally a study of phenomena in contrast to things-in-themselves—relies heavily on intuitive insights, a feature of existentialism as well. Kant had conceded that, in general, phenomenological investigation was needed as an antecedent to metaphysics. Hegel later emphasized the priority of subjectivity in philosophical pursuits, a point accepted by Husserl. Before World War II, phenomenology was primarily a German movement, fostered mainly through the efforts of Husserl and his students, who sought a philosophy with rigorous investigating techniques. Earlier, during the 1930's, French thinkers had begun to respond to phenomenological tendencies; eventually they were to "socialize" it by replacing Husserl's extreme subjectivism with a deep concern for man's fate in a world where consciousness displayed a dialectical relationship with social environment.

Yet Husserl's philosophy was a radical challenge to standard modes of thought. Its stress on subjectivity highlighted the centrality of consciousness and led to a sense of wonder that there could exist a being aware of itself as well as others. Psychology was criticized for specifying rules of thinking that emanated from itself as a discipline, rather than from a broader parametric realm. In essence, Husserl argued that guidelines had to be derived from a wide range of phenomena. Consciousness also revealed the attribute of intentionality, a concept that was most significant for both phenomenologists and existentialists. Intentionality described the objectives of consciousness, identified them, and established expectations and connectibility. On these grounds alone, the assumption of the positivists that there is nothing beyond sense data appears factitious.

Martin Heidegger, who departed somewhat from Husserl's subjectivism, is an extraordinarily difficult philosopher to understand. His personalized use of language and special terminology repels the reader. Yet his concepts of existence (or standing in the midst of being in the sense of having access to being), of the burden of being, anxiety, and the thrust to escape from nothingness, have had a powerful impact on contemporary thought.

Sartre began with Husserl and Heidegger, but evolved in quite different directions. In his most recent work, *The Critique of Dialectical Reason,* he has attempted to fuse his earlier philosophy with Marxist insights. Some commentators have charged that Sartre has abandoned existentialism to embrace a leftist outlook. But it does seem possible to interpret his philosophical development as a struggle to move from the level of intersubjective analysis to more complex sociological investigations. The Sartrean view now links knowledge and action (often realms in conflict, as with André Malraux), making subjectivity simply the starting point. As Sartre has said, one begins with interior experience not related to exterior experience, but the blows of reality reshape the interior to make it respond to the exterior. Hence, for Sartre, Marxism seemed to provide the necessary pretext for constructing a system in which the facts of the human situation could be grasped and in which courses of action could be clarified. The fundamental factor of subjectivity was always present and could not be obliterated, even in Marxism where consciousness is that of a class or group, rather than an individual. For where there is opposition or resistance there is an Other, and the mutual responses comprise subjective materials. Yet while the world creates consciousness, it is subject to alteration through reciprocal action. History makes men insofar as they make history. In a recent interview, Sartre explained that the inspiration for his *Critique of Dialectical Reason* could be traced to wartime experiences when he discovered that human reality existed among things. "Man always makes something out of what is made of him," he says. Such is the context of a dialectic of action yielding an increasing recognition that the Other is also a social being. To acknowledge that subjective and objective are functions of each other produces a shock of awareness.

An even more attractive version of the new philosophy has been suggested by Maurice Merleau-Ponty, a one-time associate of Sartre's who eventually was to break away. In 1955, Merleau-Ponty leveled sharp criticisms against Sartre over the issue of communism. Merleau-Ponty further charged that Sartre employed a truncated dialectic in which the contradiction or antagonism between the self and the Other seemed irreconcilable. For Merleau-Ponty, it seemed essential that the connection between subject and object be established, and, he insisted, this could be done: there was more, he argued, to the conditioning milieu than Sartre was ready to concede. In his early psychological investigations, Merleau-Ponty moved quickly from Cartesian egocentricity and behaviorism to a Gestaltist position, giving his philosophy a powerful sociological center. He recognized that a mechanistic approach to behavior was inadequate.

Contemporary Psychology and Anthropology

Much of the intellectual attraction in phenomenology and existentialism stems from their direct confrontation with psychology as refracted through the human situation. Unfortunately, those psychologists who prefer laboratory instruments and statistical computation do not reciprocate this interest. All they have provided is a "welter of isms"—to employ Suzanne Langer's phrase. Thus we have been subjected to reductionism, physicalism, introspectionism, environmentalism, behaviorism, and others. Dubious formulas are concocted which yield little in the way of concrete results. Jargon is invented to disguise commonsense conclusions. And the primary goal of objectivity displaces anything that might be deemed to be subjective. The outcome is that mathematical abstractions substitute for useful generalizations about events in the life of man. For humans are beings infused with feelings, and it should be the purpose of psychology to say something meaningful about it. As Langer has said: "The basic need [in psychology] is for powerful and freely negotiable concepts in terms of which to handle the central subject matter which is human mentality."

The dominant trend in psychology, however, is a contrary one. At best it fills its conceptual tool kits with borrowed beliefs; at worst, it keeps the kits shut tight with the language of behaviorism. The work of B. F. Skinner presents an extreme version of behavioristic psychology: it is described here in a not unsympathetic article by Berkeley Rice. The reader should easily recognize the mechanistic conception of the human being that this system represents. And, as Skinner acknowledges with appropriate expansiveness, his approach has had an important influence. Noam Chomsky once asked whether it was an influence that helped us to understand man and his society. The question was not an unfair one.

Ludwig von Bertalanffy has described modern psychology as "sterile and pompous scholasticism." One suspects that he may have had Skinnerism in mind. It is a scholasticism that still uses the vacuous notion of stimulus-response, an idea that should have been relegated to a museum for archaic scientific theories. Significantly, Skinnerism contains the seeds of a technocratic impulse, one that would have society's fate determined by engineers and managers, who with modern machines and technology would reshape man to comply with the criteria inherent in that technology. One does not fear the new machine: one fears, rather, those who will control it. For the fact is that the effort to manage man inevitably excludes the responsibilities of consciousness and leads to the belief that this is the best of all possible worlds—or that the best world is what the technocrat thinks it is.

Skinner's psychology was preceded by the behaviorism of John B. Watson, who developed his theories in the 1920's. Watson believed that human behavior could be controlled if it could be measured, and that the only aspect of behavior worth studying was that which could be measured. He was concerned only with control and predictability—and predictably enough he eventually became an advertising executive. For him, as for all behaviorists, consciousness and mind were meaningless concepts, thus precluding any consideration of the richness and complex variety of human action.

According to the behaviorist, only the observable is meaningful, and only those external acts of behavior which are presumably subject to control are observable. The totalitarian potential of such a psychology has been consistently ignored by its advocates. This was no problem for Watson, nor is it one for Skinner. Given Watson's commitment to pecuniary standards, it was inevitable that behaviorism should be most useful for an outlook in which the standards of Madison Avenue were dominant. Consciousness has no place in such a body of thought, for it would only inhibit the smooth functioning of the machine; behaviorism denies the motive force of intention, making a man a robot responding to the stimulus of a toothpaste advertisement.

Jean Piaget, the noted child psychologist, viewed behaviorism as a way of reducing conceptualization to mere conditioning. Piaget has always put concept formation in a totally naturalistic setting. Forty years of studying child behavior convinced him that intellectual growth proceeds through a series of stages that are closely related. The emphasis of Piaget's studies has been on logical procedures that stem *naturally* from a child's perception of the world. Although Piaget's method, like the behaviorists', is based on observation, there is little in his work that can be called mechanistic. He has emphasized rather the adaptive qualities in behavior and a kind of intelligence that has little in common with the conditioned reflex. Moreover, his method is basically clinical; thus Piaget can see clearly the mutual interplay of biologic growth and experience in the formation of human thought.

Erik Erikson has also emphasized a thoroughgoing naturalism in his investigations of human behavior. Erikson's attention was early drawn to the question of identity, a concept that might be interpreted by an existentialist as the problem of consciousness. The "trust-mistrust" nexus in Erikson might be expressed in terms of an "I-thou" relationship or a confrontation with the Other. But Erikson went a step beyond the existentialists by examining the *development* of these relationships, an understanding of which is of momentous importance to the very idea of man. Moreover, the definition of the eight stages of life in Erikson's work has expanded and enriched the Freudian progression from oral stages to puberty and has given to psychoanalysis a depth that is lacking in the efforts of other neo-Freudians. And throughout Erikson's work, the cultural rootedness of personality formation is so clear that one wonders how it could have been slighted by so many other writers.

That Bruno Bettelheim sees the world as hell is understandable, for he knows the totalitarian mind only as one who has faced it can. If he has no use for "permissiveness" and its consequences, it is because he grasps better than most the illusions of power and grandeur that have stemmed from utter lack of restraint. Fundamentally, he wishes individuals to *work* to fulfill themselves, rather than leap into the closest mass movement as a way of conquering a pervasive sense of loneliness. But David Dempsey has allowed Bettelheim largely to speak for himself in his article. Critical views of Bettelheim's theories are not lacking. It has been said that he does not really understand the need for change, that what he wishes is accommodation to what is.

This criticism has been leveled at most post-Freudian psycho-analysts. While Alfred Adler pointed to the drive for power and domination, certainly a crucial issue in contemporary society, his theories were labeled superficial for failing to note how a sense of inadequacy is generated within society. Karen Horney's emphasis on sociological factors tended to submerge the biologic; hence she was unable to discover how the somatic was involved in a dialectical interplay with the social. Erich Fromm, who has not hesitated to call on Aristotle or Spinoza for sustenance, seems to have confused the internal structure of character with its intersubjective expression. And Harry Stack Sullivan slighted the power of a culture to submerge the individual. All of these criticisms can be reduced to a single observation—that too many contemporary analysts have sought the easy way via the advocacy of accommodation.

Anthropologists are perhaps the least ethnocentric of social scientists. They can ill afford such luxury, for, as they insist on telling us, and rightly so, there are no superior societies. The idea is a salutary one, especially in a world dominated by Western man. To be told by Lévi-Strauss that gift exchange is as significant to a Polynesian as the law of supply and demand to a stockbroker ought to make the latter more humble. Yet there are troublesome implications in Lévi-Strauss's structuralism: he insists that man "obeys laws he did not invent" and that these laws reflect "the *mechanism* of the human brain" (italics added). As Sanche de Gramont says in the article included here, the whole humanist tradition disappears, as man is placed once again in a fixed, pre-determined environment, now called a structure. Insofar as Lévi-Strauss affiliates himself with the Cartesian clockwork of a Watson and a Skinner, he has stripped man of self-awareness. As Paul Samuelson says, the new algebra of cookery will not survive. It may be well to seek out uniformities, but what is important are the differences among men, their unique qualities, not their likenesses. The very process of inventory taking in which Lévi-Strauss engages serves to create a homogenized conception of man and culture, a conception that is patently false.

Alternative insights in anthropology are available in the work of the late Ruth Benedict. The idea of searching for uniformities was alien in her approach. Although a culture casts up dominant personalities, she said, it does differentiate among individuals by altering potentialities. Thus it becomes possible to explain character and human drives in the context of an "historically shaped cultural style." This is a far cry from the static structuralism of Lévi-Strauss. Or one may consider the contributions of Bronislaw Malinowski, whose study of the Trobriand Islanders led to the idea of cross-cultural comparison. Here again there is a recognition of differences in cultures and an emphasis on continuity. A culture derived its functional purpose from the needs of human beings, said Malinowski. There was a perceptible dialectical relationship between man, the biological specimen, and the artifacts that he created—that is, his culture. Paul Radin, another anthropologist of stature, viewed primitive man's experience as a central factor in history. To Radin, the individual was always the center of an evolving culture. There is a particularity in this concept that structuralism evades, thus escaping from the plasticity of consciousness.

It is such plasticity that Margaret Mead has always emphasized, as suggested in David Dempsey's article. In searching for national character, Mead has said, the anthropologist seeks to uncover the connection between childhood learning and adult behavior. But as that behavior leads one directly to interpersonal relationships, what Sartre has called the problem of the Other, or in Buber's terms, the "I-Thou" relationship, is again highlighted. In Mead's approach, however, one must also examine the sanctions that a culture imposes in order to obtain particular behavior patterns. She asks how such sanctions achieve consistency and how they may be absorbed and internalized by individuals. Finally, Mead wishes to know how one society measures up against another— the problem of cross-cultural comparison.

Mead's analysis of variations in sex behavior among South Sea Island groups underscores the potent influence of culture on personality. Male and female behavior patterns are so powerfully conditioned by the culture that what Western man believes to be the normal biological role is frequently reversed. And, Mead has argued, health is often a matter of the relation of man to his environment: somatic and psychic disturbances may be occasioned by a lack of "continuity" between the individual and his soil. Readers may note the closeness of these ideas to the thinking of several other molders of thought included in this book.

Trends in Economics

When Alfred Schutz, the phenomenological philosopher, spoke of multiple realms of reality, the most immediate of which was working activity, he came close to the borders of economics. Yet this is one field that has been fertile ground for the cultivation of the positivist persuasion. This is most evident in the work of Milton Friedman, although the article included in this reader does not touch on this issue, describing mainly his political and monetary theories. It would not be difficult, however, to show an intellectual connection between the politics and the positivism in Friedman's views.

Friedman has always distinguished lines of demarcation between positive or purely scientific economics, and normative economics that are concerned with social goals. He has asserted that the former can be as objectively scientific as any of the physical sciences. And he has refused to reject the conclusions of positive propositions because they clash with normative standards. Nor does he believe that values are necessary to any positive analysis of economic questions. Yet, as Gunnar Myrdal has demonstrated, a belief in the existence of scientific knowledge in social science independent of value systems does reflect a rather naive empiricism. Facts, Myrdal has told us, are organized through concepts which are fundamentally expressions of human interest and particular points of view: these can be described only as valuations. Nor are such value systems arbitrary, for they stem from the society in which we live and work. Of course, since it is possible for several schemes of valuation to coexist in a single society, intellectual conflict does arise. But it seems fallacious to assume that values can be suppressed: in fact, the various models developed by Friedman and his students reflect certain well-defined values when they urge that free, unbridled competition is worthwhile because it ensures individual freedom. The difficulty is that the character of such freedom generally remains an abstraction: rarely are its attributes and limitations defined. Consequently, Friedman's contention that progress might be made only on the basis of a positive analysis collapses, for policy decisions clearly require some consensus in the area of normative standards.

The validity of an hypothesis, Friedman contends, must be judged solely by its predictive powers. Conversely, if a prediction is not contradicted by subsequent events, the initial hypothesis is fully acceptable. That is, direct verification is not essential. Thus any consideration of the "realism" of one's assumptions in economic theory becomes irrelevant. The argument is indeed ingenious: there is no need to examine one's assumptions because in any theory which abstracts from a complex reality they will be so far removed from real conditions that little information about them will be forthcoming.

It would appear reasonable to suggest that evidence should be brought to bear on any point in an economic theory, including its premises. It was certainly a scientific oddity to suggest absolution for one's preconceptions and premises. A search for "congruence with reality" is essentially an attempt to explore the relevance of a set of assumptions for the problem at hand. Paul

Samuelson once refuted Friedman's contention in a powerful attack that virtually destroyed the Chicagoan's theoretical approach. Samuelson employed set theory, and related esoteric mathematics to demonstrate that consequences are contained in antecedent theorizing, which in turn is implied by certain premises. By violating this sequence, Friedman improperly admitted invalid propositions into analytical discourse. In essence, Friedman's approach merely insists that a theory is a theory.

Yet Friedman cannot escape the impulse to check his own assumptions. An hypothesis, he has remarked, must be consistent with the evidence at hand. Certainly, if one's assumptions facilitated even an indirect test of a theory, there was room for judging the relevance of premises. Friedman seeks to substantiate his argument by analogy with physical science in which "laws" are derived from certain given conditions. But in economics such conditions are essentially fictional and exist only in "as if" situations, with the result that their predictive powers are constrained and limited.

Friedman's monetary theory has a soft underbelly, as George Garvy, a Federal Reserve Board economist, has demonstrated— it makes light of the factor of the velocity at which money circulates. Monetary injections into the economy might not affect it as much as Friedman believes if velocity is sluggish, that is, if there is an insufficient turnover. Garvy has shown that velocity may be affected by alterations in the method of settling debts, especially when the need for large bank balances is obviated; or corporations may invest excess cash which they can afford to "sterilize" temporarily, as in the movement of cash into European money markets; or consumers may expand the use of charge accounts or increase their savings. All of these have important effects on money velocity. To alter one's definition of money, as Friedman will on occasion, simply obfuscates the issue. Velocity is a consideration that the Friedman school has not attended to with the same intense investigation they have applied to other terms in their money equations. One awaits further study. As for Friedman's politics, Milton Viorst's article speaks for itself.

Clearly, the greatest economist of the twentieth century was John Maynard Keynes. There is little one can add to what John

Kenneth Galbraith, himself an important figure in economics, has written in his classic review of Keynes's masterpiece, *The General Theory of Employment, Interest, and Money*. The empathy between author and critic stems from a deep concern both have displayed with the state of the *real* world. Keynes was a dissenter from orthodoxy; so is Galbraith. Keynes sought solutions for depression and poverty; Galbraith confronts prosperity and affluence. Keynes was dubious about neo-classical theory; Galbraith contends with contemporary economics and economists. Keynes knew as Galbraith knows that reform and change are essential if civilization is to survive. While Galbraith has conceded that technical developments such as national income accounting, input-output matrices, and the refinement of index numbers have been useful, he has chided economists for failing to accommodate their perfect market-wage doctrine to the existence of trade unions, or to assimilate the modern corporation into the main body of economic theory. Indeed, when some economists, for example, Edward H. Chamberlin or Joan Robinson, sought to develop theories of imperfect or monopolistic competition, theories that would analyze more realistically modern market structures, many economists resisted on the ground that such modifications would destroy economic theory!

For Galbraith, much of the reluctance on the part of economists to confront the real world stems from their perpetual desire to imitate the precision of the physical sciences. By attempting to avoid the impact of institutional change, Galbraith charges, economists can construct, for example, elegant theories of consumer demand without reference to the world of advertising. Further, concentration on principles of scarcity in a world of affluence denies that choice is less meaningful and seemingly rescues the calculating economic man from oblivion. Or, to take a more recent illustration, unshakable faith in an inverse correlation between prices and unemployment—the Phillips curve—supports a policy of controlling inflation by putting people out of work.

Galbraith has argued that economic theory is not always the source of wisdom. He has noted that during the Great Depression of the 1930's many persons urged the government to remedy the lack of aggregate demand through deficit spending, much to the consternation of academic economists. Later Keynes proved there was much to commend in the commonsense view of the day. Galbraith has also argued that the idea of consumer sovereignty should be relegated to the same dust-bin in which older academic views of business cycles were deposited.

Galbraith's conception of the modern economy, which he has offered in such persuasive and graceful ways as to cause his peers much intellectual anguish, rests on the patent fact that the large corporation is a good deal more powerful and has more impact on the market than orthodox theory will admit. Such power is inherent, he says, in the well-organized, complex, and highly technical productive apparatus that these corporations have created. Consumer sovereignty has been displaced by corporate sovereignty.

These large corporations, producing an ever-increasing flow of goods, are not guided in their decisions by consumer demand in a perfect market; rather, they "administer" their prices, that is, establish them on the basis of costs and profit targets and then persuade the consumer what to buy. Thus, wants do not originate in the consumer but are stimulated by the producer. Repeat purchases, essential for a continuous outpouring of goods, are induced by producers through fads, fashions, and built-in obsolescence. And the need to acquire more goods encourages the consumer to forgo leisure time in favor of more work and more income in order to sustain the productive efficiency of the large corporation. As Galbraith says, the consumer has "the myth of power on his side, but [the corporation] has the reality of power."

The institutional patterns implicit in Galbraith's vision also go far to explain the enormous accumulation of external diseconomies that have been inflicted on society. Thus the consumer must continue to suffer the ills of environmental despoliation—air pollution, water pollution, roads clogged with autos, and a host of other deficiencies—because the decision to roll more autos onto the city streets or to dispose of industrial wastes in fresh-water lakes is a matter of corporate policy, not consumer action. But economic theory reverses the responsibility, making the consumer indifferent to his surroundings whereas responsibility rests in the producer's determination to work his will. Indeed, as Galbraith argues with great forcefulness, much consumption—cigarette smoking or pesticides, take two cases—has become not merely harmful but irrelevant. Standard economic theory has continued to deny this at the risk of becoming itself irrelevant.

Galbraith's analysis of the modern corporation is predicated on the widespread distribution of stock holdings, a phenomenon that has occasioned the separation of ownership and control. This separation was noted in the 1930's by Adolf A. Berle and Gardiner C. Means in their pathbreaking study of the modern corporation. Stockholders no longer behave like nineteenth-century entrepreneurs, directing the affairs of the enterprise. These are tasks delegated to a corps of managers. The stockholder focuses his attention on the price of the shares on the exchange, and feeling no sense of loyalty to the corporation, he can always sever his connection with it simply by selling his holdings. Participation in annual stockholders' meetings is minimal; further, considering the thousands of corporate stockholders, it would be a most difficult logistical problem to hold a meeting with all shareholders present. Hence most stockholders simply turn over their voting rights to incumbent managers through the proxy device. And it is this device that often enables managers to perpetuate their control of the corporation.

With the accumulation of funds from long-term profits, managers have had less recourse to the capital markets, thus avoiding the need to establish strong relationships with financiers. At times, contests for control will break out among the managers, and great political campaigns will solicit proxies from stockholders. Again, the stockholder does not effectively participate in the management of corporate affairs: he is merely expected to sign a proxy for one contending managerial group or another.

Nor does the stockholder take part in the decision-making process. Determination of production goals, questions of technological mix, or matters relating to market and advertising all fall within the exclusive province of the managers—the controlling group in the corporation which is labeled by Galbraith as the Technostructure. With this term Galbraith seeks to emphasize the fact that managerial control permeates the corporation at all levels of decision-making. The nature of modern technology demands such control, for production has a time structure which becomes more technical and more complicated and requires extensive capital investment. New technology also requires specialized manpower, making the system less flexible and less responsive to small shifts in the market. All this demands coordination and careful planning if the corporation is to survive.

But planning implies displacement of the market as a guiding and allocating mechanism. Planning in the corporation becomes a way of either superseding the market (through vertical integration) or of controlling it through monopsony on the buying side and advertising on the selling side. What has happened, argues Galbraith, is a shift in the locus of power from the market to the corporation. Hence it comes as no surprise that key prices in the economy—say, steel or autos—are "administered" or predetermined by the Technostructure. Increased wage costs are absorbed and passed along in the final price bill. In a period of inflationary pressures, the use of wage-price controls, as in war-based economies, is thus, according to Galbraith, not an unreasonable device.

Further, manpower requirements are altered by a changing technology, a consideration quickly recognized by the Technostructure. Industry has less need for those with minimal skills as a more advanced structure of production calls for a work force that brings with it higher levels of technical education. In essence, Galbraith has recognized that the economy does undergo significant structural change.

Galbraith addresses himself to *strategic* corporations and their impact on the economy and society. To assert that he believes *all* corporations to be dominated by the Technostructure would be a gross misreading of his analysis. That the individual has become an instrument of large private—and sometimes public—bureaucracies that plan his life now seems undeniable. For, to use more technical language, these strategic firms do affect the slope of their demand curves, and do thereby seek to stabilize market response. And by doing so they influence the utilization of resources, savings, the trade-off between work and leisure, and the level of output. To be sure, such industrial tactics are deployed in the face of countermeasures taken by other firms and at times by the resistance of consumers (the unfortunate experience of the Edsel automobile being a case in point). Yet none of these responses diminishes the fact that Galbraith's analysis seems accurately to reflect the nature of the economy today. Addressing himself not so much to his professional colleagues as to a wider general audience, Galbraith has been an astute practitioner of *political* economy.

New Intellectual Trends

Although we are unable to include in this anthology articles on sociologists or historians, we can present a group of thinkers who strikingly exemplify contemporary intellectual trends—André Malraux, a rare man of action and thought; Marshall McLuhan, unclassifiable expert on the worst of modern technology; and the enigmatic, nihilistic, and sometimes infuriating philosophers of the New Left.

André Malraux is discussed here in an article by Theodore White. Author, revolutionist, and politician, Malraux's work is infused with a restlessness and an intensity that were rooted in experiences which often confronted violence. He participated in the Chinese Revolution of the 1920's; he explored the Cambodian jungles and the arid wastes of Arabia; he was involved in the Spanish Civil War of 1936; he was a leader of the French Resistance; and he has been an important figure in the Gaullist movement. The central focus of his intellectual concerns has been the fate of civilization, and he has been able to bring to this concern an enormous erudition in art, literature, and history. For him, man has never been a detached observer: thus he has had to define what a man does by commitment and action. And through writing, the experience of that action was transformed into consciousness. According to Malraux, man's search for a comprehensible image of himself was destined to be frustrated by the attenuation of values. The outcome was distraction from the task of constructing an appropriate image, and a descent into nihilism.

No one today celebrates that distraction more than Marshall McLuhan: it is symptomatic of the state of civilization that such a writer should be accorded so much attention. McLuhan's continuous ode to electricity converts the new technology into a vehicle for "cosmic humanism." It makes the dynamo an object of veneration and promises a new paradise of eternal peace. The millennarian character of McLuhanism justifies Leslie Fiedler's remark, cited in the article here; McLuhan gets too close to Dr. Strangelove for comfort. The fusion of the animate and the inanimate is illustrated in the comment of a McLuhan admirer who said of electricity that "[it] is anti-machine. . . . It's more organic than anything. It unites everyone." It can only be hoped that we shall quickly recover from the assault on our sensibilities carried on by McLuhan.

The syndrome of McLuhanism is mirrored in that other form of contemporary nihilism—the New Left. That Herbert Marcuse may have touched on crucial matters in his early work is undeniable. The conflict of the individual and his society *is* an important issue, and change *is* an urgent question on the agenda. But change demands a political strategy into which immediate tactics must fit. This is what Marcuse and his young admirers fail to grasp. It is a sad story: grounds for complaint are manifold, yet the complainants behave as though in an historical vacuum. History teaches them nothing; they believe that a frantic lashing at the world will bring about revolutionary change. They do not know that their elders, a good deal shrewder than youth is willing to admit, are giving them soft pillows to strike. The blows merely push the feathers into the pillow's corners, accomplishing nothing. Youth—students and nonstudents alike—are being contained and deflected because they do not know, nor do they care to know, the art of politics. It does not occur to them that politics demands more critical thought than can be generated by an escape through hemp and other substitutes for sotweed.

In their frustration, youth has become a *lumpen*-intelligentsia, hostages to a nihilism on which no serious politics can be built. For a while it seemed possible to do so, at least in the short days of Eugene McCarthy; but, alas, all that is past now. How can today's "revolutionary" youth be the carriers of social change? Workers look at them with contempt, and their tactics are expressions of the same disorder they wish to correct. If much in Western civilization is irrelevant—and much is—then what the New Left does, says, and thinks, is part of that irrelevance.

Thus the tragedy of the West has come full circle. It began with the collapse of the Greek polis, and each succeeding attempt to achieve full civilization has been frustrated. We now face disarray in our own polity. We have a magnificent technology, but we have not learned to direct it for human purposes. We have a splendid body of science that moves from one dramatic achievement to another, but we cannot use it to elevate the human spirit. We have philosophies—not philosophy—and we chatter at each other uncomprehendingly. If anyone questions these melancholy observations, he is invited to read the articles that follow, and especially those at the end.

Part 1

ANTECEDENTS

The five figures discussed in this first section were all innovators in intellectual history. Vico insisted that it was possible to study history scientifically in reconstructing the past. His *New Science* suggested that sociological and anthropological techniques could lift the opaque curtain of time that separated man from his ancestral heritage. He knew that our forefathers were neither gods nor monsters but men like ourselves, involved in an adventure of life quite like our own.

Charles Darwin turned a speculative theory—the notion of evolution dated back at least to the Greeks—into a scientific one, supported by irrefutable evidence. Men finally realized that all things had their antecedents, and confronted with the fact that as a biological specimen there was nothing special about *Homo sapiens* they became somewhat less egocentric.

Sigmund Freud may have very well felt that the future of psychology was his, even though his concepts were metaphors rather than pure scientific constructs. No longer could human consciousness be a matter of mere awareness, for the darknesses of the unconscious now shaped the mainsprings of action. Freudianism became a new reality that lent poignancy to the ancient aphorism, "Know thyself."

Though Karl Marx built his formidable system of thought out

of blocks supplied by German philosophers, English economists, and French social theorists, it was nevertheless an original body of doctrine that anyone concerned with history could ignore only at his own peril. That Marxism has had a profound impact on the world is self-evident.

And Nietzsche—easily misunderstood and easily attacked—had a greater sense of where Western civilization was heading than any other writer of his time. He wanted human perfection and he knew that it was not forthcoming.

One of the Boldest Innovators in the History of Human Thought

by Isaiah Berlin

GIAMBATTISTA VICO died two and a quarter centuries ago, and since then has remained a peculiar figure in the history of thought. Famous in the country of his birth, his name is scarcely known outside its frontiers. As for his ideas, they are seldom mentioned even among professional philosophers, at any rate in English-speaking countries. Yet he is one of the boldest innovators in the history of human thought. Jules Michelet, who said of him towards the end of his life, "I had no master but Vico. His principle of the living force of humanity creating itself made both my books and my teaching," * and the philosopher, Benedetto Croce, who celebrated his genius tirelessly throughout his own long and productive activity. Nevertheless, Vico was in his own time, and he remains in ours, at the periphery of the central philosophical tradition. He has not entered the canon; he remains

From the *New York Times Magazine,* November 23, 1969, copyright © 1969 by The New York Times Company.

* From the admirable introduction to the "Autobiography of Giambattista Vico," translated by M. H. Fisch and T. G. Bergin. Cornell University Press, 1963.

among the apocrypha—a queer, isolated figure, of interest to specialists in the philosophy of history or in Italian thought and literature, or to students of the early 18th century. Like Berlioz, half a century ago, among composers, or Piero della Francesca in the 19th century, among painters, he is a master passionately admired by a small minority, but dismissed with a few sentences by the majority of writers on the subject.

Yet Vico's achievements are astonishing. He put forward audacious and important ideas about the nature of man and of human society; he attacked current notions of the nature of knowledge of which he revealed, or at least identified, a central, hitherto undiscussed variety; he virtually invented the idea of culture; his theory of mathematics had to wait until our own century to be recognized as revolutionary; he anticipated the esthetics of both romantics and historicists, and almost transformed the subject; he virtually invented comparative anthropology and philology and inaugurated the new approach to history and the social sciences that this entailed; his notions of language, myth, law, symbolism, and the relationship of social to cultural evolution, embodied insights of genius; he first drew that celebrated distinction between the natural sciences and humane studies that has remained a crucial issue ever since. Yet, unlike the philosophers of classical antiquity, unlike Descartes and Spinoza, Leibniz and Locke, Berkeley and Hume, Kant and Hegel, he has remained outside the central tradition. After being discovered by this or that champion of his thought—by Coleridge or Leopardi or Michelet—he fell into oblivion once again; rediscovered later in the last century, he was again forgotten save in the land of his birth.

Today, new interest in him is being taken, but it seems unlikely to last—Vico will surely be ignored once more, only to be disinterred again by thinkers made indignant by his lack of recognition. The principal reason for this destiny is probably the obscurity and chaotic nature of his writing—his thought is a tangled forest of seminal ideas, recondite allusions and quotations, sudden excursuses and divagations—rich, strange, confused, arresting, immensely suggestive, but unreadable. Too many novel ideas are jostling to find expression at the same time; he is trying to say too much about too much; the ideas conflict and obscure each other, and although this communicates a kind of turbulent vitality to all that he writes, it does not make for lucidity or elegance. The reader tends to be buffeted, bewildered and exhausted; no idea is properly presented or developed or organized into a coherent structure. It is a very punishing style. As Heine said of Berlioz, he had not enough talent for his genius. Yet much of what he has to say is of cardinal importance—original and convincing.

Vico's life somewhat resembled his writings: ill-organized, frustrated, without adequate recognition. His father was a poor bookseller in Naples, and he probably owed his considerable but unsystematic erudition in large part to the opportunities offered by the books and conversations with his father's clients. An accident in his early youth made him a cripple and undermined his health. He was always poor, his life was one long struggle to keep himself and his family alive, he found it difficult to interest scholars in his work, although towards the end of his life his fame grew. He became professor of rhetoric at the University of Naples, but the post was ill-paid, and he was forced to supplement his income by constant hack-work for various notables upon whose favor he depended. He was, in short, a poverty-stricken, irritable, somewhat pathetic scholar, who wrote when and as he could, in a society which did not recognize his extraordinary gifts. And yet, despite his constant craving for recognition, he knew, when he had conceived the central ideas of the New Science, that the standard cliché of entering a land where no man's foot had trodden before, was, in his case, genuinely valid: he knew he had made a discovery of genius, and this sustained him.

What was this discovery? The heart of it is this: that men were able to understand their own history in a fashion different from and, in Vico's view, superior to, that in which they understood the works of nature; and, as a corollary of this, that to understand something, and not merely to be able to describe it, or analyze it into its component parts, was to understand how it came into being: its genesis, its growth, that its essence consists in coming to be what it is; in short, that true understanding is always genetic, and in the case of men and their works, always historical, not timeless, and not analytic.

Historical studies were by no means neglected towards the end of the 17th century. Indeed, learned antiquaries, both within and outside the church, were laying the foundations of modern historical science. Nevertheless, historical study was viewed with suspicion by the real intellectual masters of his time, the mathematicians and the natural scientists whose achievements were the glory of the age. Descartes and his disciples dominated thought in Vico's youth, and Descartes had made it plain that true knowledge rests on clear and irrefutable axioms and the application of rules whereby conclusions may be rigorously drawn from such premises, so that a system can be constructed that is logically guaranteed in all its parts.

Only upon such adamantine foundations could a genuine structure of true knowledge be built. Where were the transformation rules, the demonstrative conclusions of history? What historical theorems had been proved beyond possible doubt? History might be like travel, an agreeable pastime, but the most minute researches into the ancient world did not yield new knowledge in the sense in which the magnificent progress of the natural sciences was clearly doing. In the sciences men build on the work of their predecessors: a later generation can see further or deeper than an earlier one, for it is lifted on its shoulders; but in the humanities—in recovering the knowledge of the past—we can at best know only what they knew. About nature we know far more than the ancients; but what, Descartes inquires, could the most erudite student of Rome discover that was not known to Cicero's servant girl? Is this progress? Moreover, the methods used by historians were anything but scientific, neither demonstrative nor experimental, and therefore unworthy of respect: their conclusions might be entertaining, but could not be important. No serious man capable of advancing knowledge would waste his time upon such inquiries.

There was another quarter also from which an attack upon history was made. Since the middle of the 15th century skeptics had pointed out that there was little reason to trust historians: they were apt to be subjective, biased, and even when not actually venal or corrupt hacks, liable, out of vanity or patriotic pride or partisan spirit or sheer ignorance, to distort the truth. All history in the end rests on an eye-witness testimony—if the historian was himself engaged in the affairs he was describing he was inevitably partisan; if not, he would probably not have direct access to that vital information which only participants possessed and were hardly likely to divulge, so the historian must either be involved in the affairs he describes, and therefore partisan, or uninvolved and liable to be misled by those who had an interest in bending the truth in their own favor; or, alternatively, remained too far from the true sources of information to know enough. Hence the notorious fact that historians contradict each other freely, and that opinions alter from age to age and almost from historian to historian.

What then was the value of systematized gossip of this kind? If one attempted to get away from literary sources and use only surviving monuments, these did not provide enough evidence of the real life, the motives and purposes and acts of the human beings whom the historian was attempting to describe and explain. Monuments could be fitted into almost any theory; they were too bare, too uninformative.

Vico was at first impressed by this—not so much by the skepticism of the Pyrrhonists (as they were called), as by the frontal onslaught of the Cartesians. The success of the natural sciences, above all of mathematics, was too vast and arresting to be denied, and yet his own interests lay elsewhere. He was by temperament an antiquarian and a jurist steeped in the history of law, of institutions, especially of the Roman world; he was devout, intuitive, literary, imaginative, sensitive to nuances of style, outlook, expression—not to the structure of abstract systems or to the quantifiable properties of the external world. He belongs to the tradition of those who respond to the impalpable and unanalyzable characteristics of experience, rather than to that which alone is measurable, definable, capable of fitting into a transparent, logically organized scientific system.

He raised the banner of revolt: he conceded that all that Descartes had said about mathematics was true, demonstrable, wholly clear and irrefutable; but this was so because mathematics conveyed no information about the world. Mathematics was a system created by the human mind, like a game whose moves are invented arbitrarily, so that they are wholly intelligible because they have been constructed for this very purpose. Mathematics was a human construction: it was not a transcript of reality. He boldly denied what had been believed since Pythagoras or Plato, that mathematical propositions embodied perfect, eternal truths, lifted high above the world of change, and corresponding to the most general characteristics—the bony structure, the permanent skeleton—of reality. The real world, unlike mathematics, was not transparent at all: it was opaque. He went back to an ancient Christian truth according to which one could understand fully only what one had oneself created. If, like God, one created something out of nothing (for God knowing *was* creating) then one understood what one had made because one had made it—it was the product of one's free creative will. Only God understood the world wholly, for He alone created it. As for man, external nature could not be fully intelligible to him, because he had not created it; we understood geometry wholly because we made it; we would understand the material universe wholly if only we could make it, but we cannot. There was in the science of physics something that was impenetrable to us, namely, matter itself, which we could only know, as it were, *ab extra,* not as God knew it, who had willed it to be—whose thought in a sense it was. We understand only what we have made: mathematics, works of art, legal systems, constitutions, which, because we have created them, we can know, as it were, from within.

This, originally medieval, doctrine developed by Hobbes in his own fashion, was used by Vico to draw a line between two types of knowledge; his fully fledged doctrine of this appeared in 1710. As God knows men, so Shakespeare, say (though Vico uses no such example), knows what it is to be Hamlet because he made him, but does not know what it is to be a rock or a tree, because he did not make them. We can say what a tree looks like, what happens to it, i.e. what it is for an external observer, but we cannot "understand" it, because we cannot *be* a tree, and we cannot make one. Something in the world of nature must forever remain opaque to us, for we cannot create matter. Descartes does indeed talk of knowledge by means of clear and distinct ideas; this works in the case of mathematics because mathematics is not "in Nature" but "in us," and is indeed knowable, but offers no information about the world.

As for external matter, clearness and distinctness are not enough. "When I suffer, for instance, I cannot recognize any form in my suffering, nor set a limit to it . . . yet it is bright and vivid beyond others, so bright indeed that it can be observed only through a darkened glass." * Am I to say that it is not real because it is not definable, measurable, analyzable into uniform atomic constituents? Are qualities not real because they are not susceptible to Cartesian categories? We know more about mechanics than we know about physics, because there, as Hobbes had learned, we can manipulate the parts at will. We understand our own manipulations, for we do it ourselves; but external nature obeys laws that we have not made, that we can only record and describe but not understand, as only He who has made them with a purpose of His own can understand them. Hence, mathematics, physics and natural sciences in general are not the vaunted paradigm of knowledge that they have been represented as being from the time of the Greeks to the Renaissance and after it.

But there is one province where I can know more than this, where I need not confine myself merely to recording uniformities —what happened next to what, after or before or simultaneously with what—but can ask a further question, "Why did it happen?" or "With what end in view?" If I explain my own conduct I do not merely describe it, but give my motive, my reason for acting, the plan of which this action forms an element. I convey the form of life in which it plays a part—something which, at any rate in theory, I can alter at will, adopt or discard, something for which I am responsible. There is clearly a sense in which I invent my own conduct, at least when I am acting consciously; and here I can ask not merely what my body is doing, but also what I am *at,* what my movements are intended for, or meant to achieve. This is precisely what I cannot do in the case of trees or rocks or indeed animals, into whose motives, if they have them, I cannot pretend to penetrate.

If I can introspect and explain my own conduct in terms of

* From the "Autobiography of Giambattista Vico."

purpose—in terms of hopes, fears, wishes, decisions, doubts, love, hatred, self-interest, principle and the like, then I can do this also in the case of others, for in the very process of communication I assume them to be creatures like myself: and if I can do this for the present, I can do it also for my own past, through memory and imaginative re-creation; and do it also for those with whom I am linked, my family, my tribe, my city, my class, my profession, my nation, my church, my civilization, humanity at large. I do not know others merely by observing their bodily movements and inferring causes, as a biologist might. I understand them by immediate analogy, by the response they give to me, by the sheer phenomenon of interaction. Creatures similar to myself speak to me, and I understand them. In civilized times they use developed language, but men can speak to each other in other ways also—by means of gestures, by hieroglyphs, by song and dance; writing may well precede spoken words. They speak to each other, and they speak also to the unseen powers that they believe to be greater than themselves, the powers by which they believe themselves to be governed—the gods of earlier civilizations, the nymphs and the dryads of the Greeks and Romans, the true God of the Jews and Christians. To them they speak by acts of worship.

Man's institutions are molded by such efforts to communicate, express themselves, create a common structure responding to their beliefs, their hopes, their desires, their fears, their fantasies. Because we are men we can enter into the experience of other men; we may make mistakes—such knowledge is not infallible. But the very possibility of such intercommunication, based, as it is, on the understanding of motives, outlooks, ways of life, rests in principle on something different from the knowledge that we have of the external world which can never, in the end, be more than a recording of what occurs, or how, without knowledge of why it occurs, or indeed whether such a question makes sense at all. This kind of understanding is different, too, from the formal disciplines—mathematics, logic, the rules of games, which we can indeed know through and through, because we have made them ourselves, but which (unlike our knowledge of ourselves) do not give knowledge of reality, news of what is there. This is the kind of knowing that re-creates the past in our minds.

This was Vico's great move. He reached it in about 1720, when he was overwhelmed by the fascinating vista of re-writing the history of mankind in terms of the acts of men based on insight into their monuments, the frozen relics of such acts: relying not upon the writings of historians which may indeed be inadequate or mendacious, but on what men have made in order to communicate with others—men or gods—artifacts, words, works of art, social institutions, which can be understood by other men because they are men, and because these communications are addressed by men to men.

When I read a book or hear a man speak I understand what he is saying, i.e. I understand what he is at. Nature is a book only for God; but human institutions—myths, fables, structures of language, rites, poems, works of art, laws, customs—men have made these to express themselves with, and therefore other men can by imaginative sympathy grasp them. To know that one tree is taller than another, or that water extinguishes fire, or that Caesar conquered the Gauls, or how to count, or ride a horse, are very different kinds of knowledge from knowing what it is to love one's country, fear God, be jealous of a rival, resist a tyrant, pray, starve, exert authority, defend a principle, be a traitor, make a revolution.

Vico's ambition was to create a truly new science—a science based on an examination of what men have made, been, done, suffered, from an "inside" point of view, that of a participant, not an observer, by means of a process which, he insisted, was possible, though at times exceedingly difficult—the "entering" by means of *fantasia*—imagination—into the minds of men remote from one's own society in space or time. This can be achieved by letting their works speak directly to one, by seeking to understand how they saw the world, what they wanted to do in it and with it, how it appeared to them and how they tried to make themselves at home in it, understand it, mold it, dominate it, dominate each other, enter into new relationships, create, express themselves, act. Vico had read Lucretius in his youth. Lucretius was a pagan and, worse, an Epicurean atheist, and Vico therefore did not, being a timid member of a highly authoritarian and powerful church, emphasize this; nevertheless he was deeply influenced by him, and in particular by his description of mankind as rising from brutal barbarism toward more civilized modes of living. It is only by the most appalling efforts, Vico tells us, that we can enter the imaginations of those gross, cruel and primitive men, who are very different from us; nevertheless they are men and, therefore, communicators, doers; and if we try hard enough, we can, at any rate to some degree, reconstruct their world. As they approach our own times, they become easier to understand by "empathetic" insight.

The central principle is still that men can truly understand only that which they have made; they understand best what they have made themselves, but they can understand also what others have made, because creation is collective, most of all in primitive times. Hence myths, so far from being false stories about reality spread by wicked priests, imposters seeking to bamboozle the foolish masses, or artificial embellishment created by poets to entertain and delight, or by philosophers to put their truths in more attractive guise, are, in fact, ways of conceiving and ordering the world natural to early man, the concepts and categories that govern his vision. When the Roman poet says that everything is full of Jove, what can he possibly mean? On the one hand, Jove is a bearded thunderer, the father of the gods; yet he is also the sky. It means nothing to us to say that the thunderer is at the same time the illimitable sky; but it must have meant something to those primitive men who articulated the vision of their society, and the task is to transpose oneself into a condition where one can begin to have some inkling of what the world must have looked like to those who expressed themselves in this fashion— by means of what Vico calls "credible impossibilities"—to whom such metaphors, images, similes were a natural way of description and expression.

To the Greeks Poseidon is both a god wielding a trident and all the seas of the world, Cybele is both an enormous woman and the whole earth, Herakles both a single hero, and yet multiple too: there is an Argive and an Athenian and a Theban Herakles; he is many and also one. The fact that this is unfamiliar, indeed unintelligible, to us now, does not mean that it was always so. It must (Vico believes) be possible to enter into the consciousness of those remote savages, to see the world as they saw it, and then, and only then, will their poetry, their myths, their institutions, their rites, their entire society whence we ourselves originate, become intelligible to us.

To understand is to enter into the outlook of those who speak to others, and whom we too can overhear. By tracing the history of words we can trace the altered attitude toward, the sense of, the things that words denote, the part that they played in the lives of those whom we seek to comprehend. Hence the crucial importance of the history of languages. Vico's etymologies are sometimes wildly fanciful, but the idea is new and fertile; the growth of a language is not merely evidence for, it is part of the very essence of, the growth of consciousness of which the language is an expression, with which it is one. So too with the history of myth and art and law and religion. The history of mankind is the history of the activities of men building their worlds, and the histories of their constituent stages are the histories of successive attitudes toward these worlds, of the collective lives in which men play one, and then another, part. Art is not mere embellishment —it is a voice speaking, an effort to embody a vision in a concrete material form.

Vico believes that all nations are destined to pass through the same cycles of culture: from savagery to barbarism and stern oligarchy, followed by plutocracy, democracy, freedom of speech, skepticism, decadence; from piety, severity, discipline, through growing permissiveness and luxury to collapse. This is followed either by the conquest of the soft and degenerate peoples by some more vigorous society still at an earlier phase of its own development, or by a return to a firmer morality reimposed by a powerful ruler bent on the regeneration of his society (Augustus, for example; Vico in the main thinks of Rome when he thinks about the past); or by total disintegration, and return to the caves: after which the entire cycle begins again.*

---

* One of Vico's most brilliant formulations is of what he calls "the second barbarism"—the condition into which a society falls when mounting luxury, materialism, egoism, have destroyed the social bonds to which he thinks religious authority indispensable. When this has taken place, men "though they still throng together, live like wild beasts in a deep solitude of spirit and will, scarcely, any two of them, able to come to understanding . . . base savages under soft words and embraces." (From the "Autobiography of Giambattista Vico.") Modern critics of the dehumanizing effects of "postindustrial society" could hardly better this description of "alienated" man.

The Jews alone are exempt from this, for to them the true word of God was vouchsafed, and they could pursue a conscious path, instead of an evolution which God (or Providence) imposed upon all other men without necessarily revealing His purposes to them. It is only because we lack historical imagination that the poetry of the ancients and their myths seem mere childish errors to us. We shall never understand the magnificent poetry of primitive times, the Homeric poems, for example, if we do not understand the society of which this was the natural vision and expression. Homer for Vico was not a single author who created his poem arbitrarily out of his head as a later poet might have done at some other time; he was the entire Greek people celebrating its heroic forms of life, as Dante did at the corresponding stage of the second cycle—the second Middle Age of mankind.

The notion of a predetermined order of civilizations each of which has its own quality, its own central style, its own life, all the aspects of which are intertwined by a unitary structure, so that to certain kinds of economic organization there must always correspond certain types of linguistic usage, of visual art, of religious belief and forms, certain types of poetry or prose—in fact the notion of a culture unified by some central pattern that determines all the activities of its members—this new idea is one of Vico's most original and pregnant conceptions.

Armed with it, he argued, for example, that the accepted tradition according to which the Romans derived their earliest laws—the Twelve Tables—from Solon's Athens, was patently absurd. Such transmission was historically impossible. He based this on the fact that the kind of Latin idiom characteristic of Rome at that time—the language of the Twelve Tables—together with what we know of early Roman customs as embodied in legends (which always have some "ground of truth," i.e. sense of reality in them—these forms of life and the language which is their vehicle, are totally incompatible with the culture of Solonian Athens as, in its turn, expressed by its language, laws, habits, literary monuments, and are not translatable from or into it. The cultural chasm is too wide.

This art of historical periodization and attribution, whereby one is enabled to say not merely that a given poem or vase or type of warfare not only did not belong to some given age or culture, but could not have belonged to it, because it does not fit in with other manifestations of the age—the kind of knowledge of the structure of a civilization on which the histories of art, technology, economic activity—to take only a few instances—today are based, was virtually invented by Vico. The fact that no one outside Italy read him with any understanding (and, for that matter, not many in Italy) is a sad and curious fact. Vico's immediate influence may have been limited to the Neapolitan jurists, but his originality is not thereby diminished.

That historical understanding is different from the way in which we know or have beliefs about the external universe, from scientific method, whether deductive, or hypothetical-deductive, or inductive; from metaphysical "intuitions" or conceptual analysis (however these may be defined) and from the methods of the formal sciences, logic, mathematics, game theory, heraldry and the like—this thesis, whatever its degree of validity, is one of Vico's claims to immortality. So is the notion that nature is not static, but a flow: that human nature is not a permanent kernel, identifiable as such in all men at all times, as maintained by the advocates of Natural law, but a constant process of growth, *nascimento,* a coming to be, whence *natura* is derived; that all that occurs in the history of mankind can take place only at its appropriate place in the great cyclical pattern.

Hence Polybius's lament, some 19 centuries before, that men might have avoided their errors and follies if only philosophers (and not priests) had presided over their beginnings, is absurd. Vico answers Polybius and the rationalists by saying that philosophy not merely does not, but cannot, occur except at an advanced stage of culture. The order of development is unalterable: magic must precede rational thought. Men see the world in the various ways that they do; these ways depend on the stage reached: to each stage its own mode of vision and expression. Thus the beauty and power of the Homeric poems belong uniquely to the barbarian society, governed by cruel, ambitious and avaricious oligarchs, from which they sprang, and cannot be re-created in an age of legal disputations, philosophy, prose, bereft of those vivid and spontaneous metaphors and images which conveyed the vision natural to an earlier, far less sophisticated and self-conscious culture.

If myths are one door through which the movements of men's minds can be traced, their vision of the universe "entered into," metaphors are not, as they are in modern times, a conscious, artificial, baroque embellishment attacked by those French critics of Vico's time who contrasted such luxuriance unfavorably with the classical plainness and clarity of the great writers of the Grand Siècle. Metaphor, simile, at the times in which they begin, are a natural mode of expression. If the poets of the heroic age spoke of blood boiling round their hearts, it was because the condition of rage literally seemed to them to resemble the physical condition of inner boiling more closely than anything else in the world with which they were familiar. When men of this "age of heroes" speak of mouths of rivers, lips of vases, necks of land, veins of mineral, the bowels of the earth (or of the heavens as smiling, the waves as murmuring, of willows as weeping), they do it not to heighten language, or to be consciously poetical, or to convey mysterious, esoteric truths, but as a natural and spontaneous expression of what the world felt to them.

Animism and anthropomorphism are types of collective consciousness which belong to, and pass away with, their own type of social organization; the poetry that springs from it and is the voice of a particular stage of civilization, has a power and a sublimity that will never recur in the history of the world until the same type of development is again reached in the ever cyclical movement of human history. To expect primitive men to describe their universe in what we should call literal terms, is to lack all sense of how humanity develops, and therefore of what men are, for men *are* their coming to be, rise, apogee, decline. What seem conscious metaphors to us are our ancestors' natural mode of expressing what they saw, felt, heard, feared, of all that they were bound up with. All art must be understood in this way—as a form of natural reaction and expression. It is, for that reason, a direct door to the past.

The very notion of one perfect way of knowing what is true or right, the idea of natural law as being something that any man can, in principle, get to know at any time, anywhere, as implied by Aristotle and maintained by the Stoics long ago, and by Grotius in Vico's century, struck him as wholly untenable. Primitives do not, and cannot, live their lives according to unvarying, timeless principles, for then there would be no growth, no historical change, only eternal repetition, as in the lives of animals. Man is a self-transforming creature, the satisfaction of each set of needs alters his character and breeds new needs and forms of life: he is a perpetual growing, directed by Providence working through his passions, through his very vices. There is no fixed, unalterable "core" common to all men at all times; everything in human life and history can be understood only as a function of a process. This process can be known because it obeys an intelligible pattern of which he, Vico, has discovered the eternal principles, a pattern in which spiritual, economic and social factors are interwoven.

Like other innovators of genius, possessed by a new vision, Vico tends to overstate his case. Euclid and even Thucydides were the children of their age, but their words can be understood (if not fully understood) even by those who do not see them in their proper cultural context. Nevertheless Vico's ideas are transforming. He is the true father of historicism, of the sociology of culture, of the notion of the validity of each form of art or culture for its own time and, consequently, the earliest opponent of what Wyndham Lewis once called "the demon of the idea of progress in the arts." Above all, he distinguished the notion of what it is to understand a joke, a poem, a character, an outlook, a system of values, an entire civilization, from mathematical and scientific knowledge, practical skills and ordinary knowledge of facts. Yet he is most famous for the least original and plausible of all his doctrines, the cyclical theory of history. The ill luck that dogged him during his life pursued him after death.

The great lights of his time largely ignored him. A handful of Italian scholars did what they could; disciples—Duni, Cesarotti, Filangieri—tried to spread his fame. But the most celebrated thinkers of his time remained largely unaware of his work. Even if an editor of a learned journal, and one or two minor German scholars, took some notice of his writings (he circulated them tirelessly to the luminaries of his time), there is no evidence that

Montesquieu, for example, read him. (The assertions of one or two later commentators to show that he echoed him, seem without foundation.)

Italian jurists and critics derived a good deal from him and maintained that some French writers did too. But there is no evidence that either Voltaire or Fontenelle, either Christian von Wolff or Hume had, so far as we know, ever heard of him. Yet he anticipated some of the most brilliant achievements of German classical scholarship of the next century. "If Pythagoras recalled that in a previous life he had fought beneath the walls of Troy," Michelet wrote in 1931, "these illustrious Germans might have remembered that they had all formerly lived in Vico. All the giants of criticism are already contained, with room to spare, in the little pandemonium of the New Science." * Neither the great Homeric scholar F. A. Wolf, nor the equally eminent Roman historian, Niebuhr, showed much pleasure when this fact was brought to their reluctant notice.

Coleridge and Thomas Arnold, Marx and Dilthey, Yeats and Joyce ("Finnegans Wake," for example, is full of Vichian echoes and allusions) recognized his genius. But he remains unread outside his native land save by specialists in the history of literature of ideas. The philosophers and the historians of philosophy, with rare exceptions, ignore him still. Evidently it is the fate of his writings, like that of human culture in his own theory of *corsi* and *ricorsi,* to be forgotten, then to rise again, achieve brief glory, then again fall into oblivion, till the next cycle, and so on forever.

---

* From the introduction to the "Autobiography of Giambattista Vico."

Darwin—and Evolution—
a Century Later

by Paul B. Sears

ON THE AFTERNOON of Dec. 27, 1831, a three-masted brig of
242 tons burden weighed anchor in the British harbor of Devon-
port, near Plymouth, bound for the Southern Hemisphere. In
command was a trim Royal Navy captain in his early twenties,
a superb seaman and a gentleman whose name, Fitzroy, gave more
than a hint of his descent from kings. He was charged by the
Government to make chronometric, hydrographic and other scientific studies around the coast of a great continent—South America.

The name of his 100-foot ship was H.M.S. *Beagle*. Her voyage
was destined to change the thinking of mankind, for with her
sailed a quiet, slender, 22-year-old naturalist named Charles Darwin. His observations during the trip led him, after years of study,
to the theory of evolution, which challenged the accepted belief
in the Biblical account of the Creation by declaring, in effect, that
man and all other animals are descended from a common primordial ancestor.

This year marks the centennial of the first public announcement
of Darwin's theory of evolution, or the transmutation of species,
as he called it, in his paper read to the Linnaean Society in Lon-

From the *New York Times Magazine,* March 23, 1958, copyright © 1958
by The New York Times Company.

don on July 1, 1858. The paper, expanded into a book, was published the following year as "The Origin of Species." This year and next, learned societies the world over will hold commemorative meetings, symposia will be organized, books and papers published to mark the double anniversary. The Royal Society of London is sponsoring a special expedition to the Southern Hemisphere.

Darwin's role aboard the *Beagle* had nothing to do with the physical and mathematical observations for which the voyage was planned. Instead, he was there because the captain had requested a naturalist who could study the land. Darwin was not hampered by any obligation to produce practical results. So far as I know, he did not add any product to the world economy. He was free to observe, collect, study and record. That Captain Fitzroy not only tolerated, but actually encouraged, such activity is a tribute to his intelligence.

Curiously enough, the captain's advisers had nominated a youngster without formal training in natural science. More than that, they recommended an individual who might not have done too well in the Graduate Record Examination, now so widely favored as a screen to determine fitness for advanced study.

Throughout his boyhood, young Darwin had been an ardent collector, sportsman and lover of the out-of-doors. This preoccupation distressed his father, a busy, successful physician at Shrewsbury in the Midlands. Although Dr. Darwin was a kind and generous man, he once exploded to Charles, "You care for nothing but shooting, dogs and rat-catching. You will be a disgrace to yourself and all your family."

I have never seen any record of the elder Darwin's opinion of his own father. Perhaps the fact that he was also a physician took some of the curse off the fact that he, like his grandson Charles, wasted a good deal of time. He wrote poetry and speculated on the origins of life. For he was the famous Erasmus Darwin who rhymed out a theory of evolution in his book "Zoonomia." Charles' other grandfather was famous, too—and must have been something of a dreamer to boot, for the pottery he made is prized to this day. But since his dreaming paid off handsomely, it was, of course, respectable. He was Josiah Wedgwood, and from his son of the same name, uncle of Charles, the young naturalist was to receive the confidence and encouragement that his father was slow to give.

Unpromising schoolboy though Charles was, family pride demanded that he be trained for a respectable profession. His elder brother, Erasmus, was to enroll as a medical student at Edinburgh and so Charles, aged 16, was sent along with him. Medical teaching of that day had more in common with school drill than with the adventure of the laboratory and evidently had no great appeal to Charles. But it was the gruesome experience of watching operations without anesthetics or antisepsis that finished him off. He wanted no more of medicine.

His father solved the problem of respectability by entering him at Cambridge to prepare for the Anglican priesthood. He seems to have accepted this assignment in good faith, although none of the required studies aroused his enthusiasm. Yet Cambridge was a lucky choice. On its faculty were Adam Sedgwick in geology and John Stevens Henslow in botany. Young Darwin became acquainted with both and they in turn became interested in him, encouraging him to accompany them in the field. These activities were strictly outside his curriculum, but no less effective on that account. Under the guidance of these two masters he became a naturalist, and when they learned of the opening aboard the *Beagle,* they put his name in for it.

Darwin was intrigued by the resemblances and differences whereby living things can be arranged into families, genera and species. This problem of form had challenged students of nature since ancient times. The wing of a bat and the foreleg of a horse, for example, are very different, yet both are limbs, with the same basic bony structure. In the bat, the bones nearest the body are greatly prolonged, those of the "hand" vastly lengthened, while the reverse is true of the horse, whose hoof represents the nail of his middle "finger" or toe. What meaning lay behind such facts?

Sailing with the *Beagle,* Darwin had the peculiar advantage of viewing these matters in the double perspective of space and time. Ranging widely as he did, he saw that differences within groups of insects, birds and mammals increased with distance and across such barriers as water, desert and mountain.

In some respects, the high point of Darwin's intellectual adventure came with his study of the Galapagos Islands some 600 miles off the Pacific Coast of South America. Here he found that reptiles—turtles and lizards of an ancient type—were the leading vertebrates. He found, too, that the birds and other animals, although related (as we would now say) to those of the continent, were distinctive and even differed from one island to another. Why, he wondered, should so much creative force be wasted on these bits of barren island? Surely the answer lay in geological change and isolation through the long course of time. It was here, as a brief entry in his journal reveals, that he definitely broke with the idea that species had been stable since the Creation.

He was as careful to note seeming exceptions as to record items that fitted his slowly growing theories. This exceedingly meticulous, conscientious observation of details, pro and con, was one of the secrets of his genius. Another was his capacity for enthusiasm. One must not be misled by the cloaked, bearded, crag-browed, Olympian portraits of the aged Darwin. Instead, one should read his own favorite book, "The Voyage of the Beagle"; his life as written by his granddaughter, Lady Barlow; or the recent lively, brief biography by Ruth Moore. In these one may glimpse his bubbling, infectious excitement, tempered with prodigious knowledge, common sense and good-natured skepticism.

The ship's mission required frequent stops, so that Darwin spent much time ashore, with occasional long trips into the interior. Wherever he went he took notes, which he shipped back to England along with collections of rocks, plants and animals. The value of this material built his scientific reputation long before his return in October, 1836, after almost five years aboard the *Beagle*.

Darwin published "The Voyage of the Beagle," in 1839. The same year he married his cousin and childhood companion, Emma Wedgwood. They lived in London for the next three years while Charles worked over his collections, but the confusion of that great city and the demands upon his time, multiplied by his growing reputation in scientific circles, taxed his always poor health.

In 1842 he purchased a country home at Down, in Kent, where he lived and worked for the next forty years.

Life at Down, despite recurring illness, was idyllic and highly creative as well. It is a somber reflection, in this day of enforced egalitarianism, that such an existence would have been impossible without the leisure conferred by personal wealth. How, in the future, can genius find expression if it must rely solely upon official recognition, favor and subsidy, no matter how generous, to say nothing of scrutiny of one's habits of work and recreation?

Darwin had already, in 1837, begun to collect notes on the transmutation of species. What troubled him (and the troubled mind is a necessary prelude to creative effort) was to find a process that could explain how a multitude of organisms, each so remarkably fitted to its mode of life, could have developed from simple beginnings through the operation of natural laws.

The hint he needed came when he happened to read for diversion the essay by Thomas Malthus on population. Actually, Malthus had been preceded some thirty-nine years by Benjamin Franklin, who wrote in 1751, "There is, in short, no bound to the prolific nature of plants and animals, but what is made by their crowding and interfering with each other's means of subsistence." Malthus was primarily concerned with human beings, but his theory of population growth—and checks—supplied the missing step that Darwin needed to explain his observations of plants and animals. The result was the theory of the origin of species by natural selection. (He later regretted that he had not called it "natural preservation.") In brief, it holds that:

Variation is the rule among plants and animals—no two are exactly alike. Yet among different species there are degrees of resemblance that suggest relationships.

Organisms reproduce beyond their offspring's capacity to survive—large numbers of individuals are eliminated.

Some variations are better adapted to their environments, and hence must be better fitted to survive, than others.

The individuals so favored tend to survive and to transmit their characteristics to their descendants.

In this way new species have arisen by a process of natural selection of favorable variations.

Instead of announcing his theory at once, Darwin spent many years testing it—laboriously searching for evidence against as well as for it. He took a few close friends into his confidence. By 1858 they agreed that the time had come for an announcement. Just then Darwin received a paper from Alfred Russell Wallace, one of his correspondents who was then in the East Indies, outlining the theory of natural selection quite as Darwin had worked it out in two decades of painstaking effort. Darwin never hesitated. He announced to his friends, the geologist Sir Charles Lyell and Sir William Hooker, director of the Royal Botanical Gardens, his wish to withdraw his own paper and present Wallace's. But these two, who had stood at his shoulder throughout, would have none of it. At their insistence, both papers were read before a session of the Linnaean Society by its secretary. The audience of scientists was too stunned to make any comment.

The storm gathered rapidly, however, reaching full force in November, 1859, when "The Origin of Species" appeared. Abuse of Darwin and his ideas knew no bounds. Such a bald contradiction of the common belief in creation as a six-day miracle was more than outrage: it seemed to threaten the very foundations of order and morality. "It contradicted the revealed relation of the Creation to its Creator," thundered one journal, and "was inconsistent with His Glory." Darwin's emphasis on the length of geological time challenged Bishop Usher's generally accepted computation of 4004 B.C. as the date of Creation.

Worst of all, he seemed to have denied man's special role in the universe, for he wrote, "We must * * * admit that all organic beings which have ever lived on this earth may be descended from some one primordial form." Not until "The Descent of Man" in 1871 did he go so far as to declare, "Man is descended from a hairy, tailed quadruped, probably arboreal in its habits * * * For my own part I would as soon be descended from [a] baboon * * * as from a savage who delights to torture his enemies, * * * treats his wives like slaves * * * and is haunted by the grossest superstitions."

The main body of scientists was against the new theory, but Darwin himself took no part in the roaring controversy. He was content to let facts, friends and foes all speak for themselves.

Chief among his defenders was Thomas Huxley, who called himself "Darwin's bulldog." Huxley's most famous clash was with Bishop Wilberforce at a meeting of the British Association which broke up in a riot. The Bishop, known generally as "Soapy Sam," asked Huxley on which side of his family he claimed descent from a monkey. The jubilant Huxley replied, in effect, that he would rather have as ancestor a monkey than a literate and gifted man who talked about things he did not understand and took advantage of religious prejudice to do so. Times have changed, and today a majority of intelligent theologians seems to take the theory of organic evolution in stride, although some reserve opinion as to the origin of the human soul.

The publication of the "Origin" was, in my judgment, the climax of the Darwinian epic. The remainder of Darwin's life was spent quietly at Down with his family, working on variation and heredity, on plant behavior, on the expression of emotion in man and animals, and in writing. The honors which came to him at home and abroad he took in all modesty. Though knighthood for him was impossible in Victorian England, at his death in 1882, he was buried among the immortals in Westminster Abbey.

Darwin would have been among the first to admit that his ideas might be modified by further knowledge. His notion that acquired characteristics, such as the muscles of a blacksmith's arm, might be inherited has not been substantiated and is, indeed, gravely doubted. Questioned, too, is his idea that evolution is the cumulative result of a long series of minute changes. Instead, the immense gap between man and his primate ancestors may have been leaped abruptly. Yet the main outlines of Darwin's theory stand substantially as he gave them. Two sciences were implicit in his finds: genetics, the science of variation and inheritance, and ecology, the science of environment and organism. The former has developed brilliantly since 1900. The latter, so essential to the future welfare of mankind, has progressed more slowly.

Because his findings have often been misinterpreted as a justification of ruthless competition, let us remember that Darwin saw the absolute necessity of collaboration and mutual aid in nature. He viewed man's moral sense not as something thrust suddenly upon a newly emerged and reluctant higher mammal, but as something deeply rooted in our long biological past.

Let him be judged by his own words—"disinterested love for all living creatures [is] the most noble attribute of man." And let the centennial of his theory remind us that the highest function of science is not to devise weapons or serve luxury, but to enable man to learn about himself and the earth which is his home.

The Nietzsche the Nazis Don't Know

by Irwin Edman

THE WORLD hardly has time at the moment to celebrate the birth-day of a philosopher. There are not many who would be inclined to mark with jubilation the hundredth anniversary of a thinker like Friedrich Nietzsche, who has, though falsely, been regarded in some quarters, Nazi ones chiefly, as a Nazi ahead of his time.

The Nazis have done all they could to popularize the teachings of Nietzsche in Germany, as though the Nietzschean philosophy expounded all that was best in Nazi teachings. Hitler, who once sent to Mussolini a privately printed and elaborately bound set of Nietzsche's works, called Nietzsche "a pioneer of national socialism."

One of the most egregious of Nazi cultural propagandists writes in what purports to be a summary of the philosopher's teachings: "Cruelty pervades the core of culture. Generation, life and murder are one. The gorgeous beauty of culture is upheld by the gory hands of the conqueror. What a barbarous, amoral, truly Nietzschean image!" Rather, what a perversion of nearly everything the philosopher stood for!

The Nazis have used and misused sentences and phrases of

Nietzsche as they have used and misused anything they could lay their hands on of European thought and culture.

There are, to be sure, sentences in Nietzsche that are ready made for such misuse, sentences like these: "Democracy has in all ages been the form under which organizing strength has perished. * * * Modern democracy is the historic form of the decay of the state. * * * Ye shall love peace as a means to new wars—and the short peace more than the long."

There are phrases of Nietzsche that have lent themselves to a brutalitarian point of view—phrases such as "The Will to Power," "Beyond Good and Evil," "The Superman," "The Transvaluation of All Values."

From a philosopher like Nietzsche, who writes in the oracular utterances of a lyric poet, it is possible to select isolated apothegms or enthusiasms and to frame a fancy picture to suit one's tastes or purposes.

But whatever disagreements there may be among scholars as to Nietzsche's residual teachings, there is almost no one, I think, who would for a moment identify him with the dishonesty and the brutality of Nazi propaganda.

By "power" Nietzsche meant a man's own inner being, excellence, virtue, as one might speak of the virtue of an herb or the quality of a gem. By "will to power" he meant will to excellence, not (or not alone) will to mastery over other men. By reaching "beyond good and evil," he meant the reaching beyond the conventional good and evil of timid, middle-class, provincial households and of village mentalities, the counterpart of those among which he had been brought up.

Nietzsche saw a possible new glory for humanity; the development of a type that should by its own excellence constitute a new standard of values, a model to which all mankind should repair. He said: "Live dangerously"—an admonition which Mussolini used to love to quote. But he was thinking of the compromises, the softnesses, the evasions of stuffy and cautious lives. Certainly he was not speaking the language of political brigands. He talked melodramatically of compassion as a weakness. But he was harder on self-pity even than on pity for others.

All these things must be seen in the general context and temper of his thought, and of the mind in which that thought was bred. Nietzsche was a pan-European, not a Pan-German, and nothing remotely resembling a Nazi leader. Georg Brandes, the celebrated nineteenth-century critic, called him an aristocratic radical. The aristocratic ideal toward which Nietzsche thought mankind was moving and should move was nearer to that of Plato's philosopher-king than to anything remotely Hitlerian in nature.

Nietzsche's reputation has suffered for other reasons than because he has been glibly identified with a German tradition of arrogance and chauvinism that he himself despised. His talents were not those of a systematic philosopher. Only one early work of his, "The Birth of Tragedy," might be said to be really completed, or to have a genuine order and system in the more conventional scholarly sense. He was a lyric poet in the romantic tradition who wrote some of the finest prose poetry in the German tongue.

Nietzsche's mind was one fed on a love of Greek tragedy and of music, out of which, he alleged, tragedy grew. His temper was that of a man contemptuous of the triviality and vulgarity of the bourgeois life of the nineteenth century, and particularly of the Germany of his time, with its grossnesses and the mask of grandiosities set over its grossnesses. He speaks out forcefully against the imperial regimentation, the timid little hypocrisies of his age, especially, be it noted, in Germany.

"The Germans," wrote Nietzsche, "are responsible for everything that exists today, the sickliness and stupidity that oppose culture, the neurosis, called nationalism, from which Europe suffers; they have robbed Europe itself of its meaning and its intelligence. They have led it into a blind alley.

"The Germans are like women. You can never fathom their depths; they have none. What is called 'deep' in Germany is an instinctive uncleanliness in one's self. Might I not suggest that the word German as an international epithet be used to indicate this psychological depravity? The Germans have no idea of how vulgar they are, which is itself the very acme of vulgarity. They are not once ashamed of being merely German.

"The Germans persist in nourishing themselves with contradictions, Christian love and, at the same time, anti-Semitism, the will to power (to the 'empire') along with humility.

"Not only have the German historians completely lost the broad view, which is banned by them. First and foremost, according to them, a man must be 'German,' he must belong to the 'race.' 'I am a German' constitutes an argument, 'Deutschland ueber Alles' a principle."

There is just enough rhetorical exaggeration in Nietzsche to have made him for a time the idol of the cheap rebel and the perpetual adolescent. His flaming denunciations of conventional Christianity, his robustious assertions of sheer will have often made him the favorite of little men with delusions of grandeur.

But it is worth seeing what Nietzsche, rather than the cultists of Nietzsche, was saying and was driving at, and what were the conditions of his life and psyche that were factors in his taking the particular lines he did. It is dangerous to dismiss what a philosopher says in terms of his biography, but one cannot help looking into the life of this tempestuous poet for the source of some of the tempests and the course those tempests took.

Friedrich Nietzsche was born on Oct. 15, 1844, in a small town in Prussia. He was the son of a minister. His father died early and left him surrounded by women. At 18 he became an atheist, and the whole of the rest of his life may be said to have been a search for new gods. Sensitive and delicate, he early displayed an almost pathological desire for the marks of strength and masculinity. One well authenticated story concerns his lighting some matches and letting them burn in the palm of his hand until they were burned out. He attended the universities at Bonn and Leipzig and had a brilliant career as a student, and tried and failed to lead with satisfaction the sensual life of the undergraduates of his day in Germany.

He early discovered Schopenhauer, and even though later he was to denounce the pity and self-pity in Schopenhauer's writings, his own philosophy was in essence a celebration of the will, as over against the intellect, in man. He briefly served in the army and ever after cherished a romantic notion of the soldier as hero.

He turned from soldiering to a university career, that of professor of classical philology at Basle, in Switzerland. He served briefly again in the German Army in the Franco-Prussian War, and on his way to the front had a sort of apocalyptic vision on seeing a troop of cavalry. The image became for him "an image of will to war, will to power, will to overpower."

The academic philologist who wished he might have been a musician, and who described life without music as a mistake, cherished a vision of the man of power that Freudians today might well call a masculine protest. But the musician in him idealized something quite different, which for a time he found exemplified in the music of Richard Wagner. Greek tragedy, he wrote in "The Birth of Tragedy," had grown out of the spirit of music, and the Dionysian spirit, the assertion of passion and life, was finding its life again in Richard Wagner.

But when Wagner wrote "Parsifal" to renounce the assertion of passion by the enunciation of saintliness, Nietzsche was through with him. He had other business. It was on the mountaintops, where there was life and feeling, and he spoke through an imagined Zarathustra who told him of a dancing god.

In 1876 eye and nervous troubles caused him to take a leave of absence from the university. In 1879 he was pensioned and lived for the next ten years in various health resorts. Toward the end of 1888, after recovering from an earlier attack, he was declared hopelessly insane. He lived on, cared for by his sister, Frau Foerster Nietzsche, until 1900. Some of his most brilliant writing was done in the ten sick years between his retirement and his complete insanity.

It was this sickly, effeminate and yet affirmative soul, this solitary neurotic, who dreamed of a human being of a new mold, shattering all the conventional patterns. It was this delicate child bred in a pious provincial home who sought in imagination to shatter the shibboleths, the conventional Christian slogans and the creed of the bourgeois democracy of his time—a Greek classical scholar celebrating the passion below the harmonious forms of Greek literature and art.

It was this idol smasher who in turn created a new idolatry, the superman. It was this shatterer of the accepted tables of the law who dreamed of new tables of moral values set by a new heroic type, all harmonious vitality, poetry and splendor.

Nietzsche's philosophy must be understood not only as the product of his temperament and its difficulties but also as a reflection of his time and its despairs. He was reacting against the romantic pessimism of his day. He was, like Carlyle, rebelling against the "nay sayers" to life, against those who counseled humility and made a cult of their own weaknesses and their own fears. As over against the Christian "flight from life" he preached a "yes" to life, an acceptance of all life's intensities, a pagan ruthlessness in living, and he romanticized war as an image of life at its intensest. It is the image of war indeed that a Nazi commentator like Alfred Baümler in his book on Nietzsche can most happily seize upon.

Nietzsche rebelled too against what he held to be the "necessary regimentation" of democracy. Nietzsche was content to think some people are by nature slaves. But he conceived evolution dramatically as a process in which eventually there would emerge at some distant day a new heroic type. This new type, the superman, at once poet and saint and ruthless as a warrior in his dedication to perfection, would be an example to all mankind and would rule by the sheer contagion of his excellence.

Nietzsche's "will to power" was really the will to aristocratic greatness. It was vulgarized by many of his later readers into a will toward brutal domination. The "yea-saying" to life eloquently uttered by the chronic invalid was debased into mere brute strength. The transcending of mere negation was reduced to mere idol-smashing and cheap atheism.

Nietzsche at his best is the exponent of a delicate intensity and an aristocracy of art and passion rather than a brutality of wealth or strength or intellect. He is to be associated with the dreamers of dreams, and with the music makers rather than with the analysts. Morally he is a belated and lyric pagan making a cult of the poet's passion.

Nietzsche is the fastidious rebel against barbarism, as far as could be from being its voice. A half-dozen sentences from him about the cruelty and bloodiness of the state, or the killing of the

German spirit by the German Empire, would have been enough to have official Germany denounce him.

Only by borrowing from Nietzsche out of context phrases war-like and cruel, the romantic images of a poet, could the Nazis claim him as one of their own. He predicted that some day, after great wars and revolutions, the "good European" would appear and become universal. It is perhaps an auspicious irony that his centenary should occur when a "master race" he would have despised is meeting its doom.

It is very difficult not to escape dogmatism in trying to present briefly the temper and meaning of a poet-philosopher singularly unamenable to systematic exposition. It is hard not to go too far in whitewashing the moral ideas of a philosopher who has been misused by the Nazis.

Nietzsche's language seems frequently to identify power with good, might with right. In the interest of a new heroic type he seems to countenance ruthlessness, if not brutality. He seems too easily to identify the democratic process with mere leveling down, without any awareness that democracy itself may breed distinction and individuality. He seems too ready, too content, to assume that, in addition to the Superman and the Free Spirits, there might be men who are slaves by nature. He seems to be too willing to smash the ideal of tenderness and brotherhood of Christian idealism, and too eager to dismiss saintliness as a form of disease rather than to recognize it as a human aspiration.

All these are the exaggerations of a hysterical mind. Yet it was also a lyric mind. As over against the Leviathan of the Nazi (or of any other idolatry of the state) Nietzsche preached with extraordinary candor and intensity the Individual—a lonely, severe and aristocratic Individual. It was really the conception of the haughty artist.

Nietzsche needs correction, but so did and so does the world which has inherited his strident criticism.

An Analysis of Sigmund Freud

by Leonard Engel

For one who lived among enemies so long;
If often he was wrong and at times absurd,
To us he is no more a person
Now but a whole climate of opinion.
(W. H. Auden on Sigmund Freud after Freud's death in 1939.)

SIXTY YEARS ago this fall, two Viennese physicians published a modest paper describing their success in treating several cases of hysterical paralysis by uncovering painful emotional experiences of many years before, seemingly forgotten but actually buried in an unconscious part of the mind.

One of the physicians, Josef Breuer, soon returned to his regular medical practice: his name is merely a footnote in the story of medicine. The other, Sigmund Freud, went on to explore the Unconscious, the strange submerged part of the mind pointed to in their study. It led him to a revolutionary theory of human personality and a new method of treating mental and emotional illness, to which Freud gave the name psychoanalysis—which may be described as a method of treating mental illness, involving a theory of psychology based on the struggle between man's instincts and

From the *New York Times Magazine*, October 4, 1953, copyright © 1953 by The New York Times Company.

the demands of society. And it made him, in a few short years, one of the most controversial figures in history.

After six decades Sigmund Freud and psychoanalysis are still matters for dispute. Though the Catholic Church, speaking through the Pope, has officially accepted part of psychoanalysis, religion remains suspicious of it, because it seems to depart from traditional moralities. Communism is also hostile: psychoanalysis looks inside man for the force that makes him go and not to an economic system. Many of Freud's specific teachings, moreover, have never been or are no longer accepted by his professional colleagues and heirs. Still, few men can claim a wider or deeper influence on their age.

Because of Freud we think differently about ourselves, about sex (see the Kinsey report on sexual behavior in women), about foibles like the forgetting of names and slips of the tongue. Paintings, poetry, novels, jokes and women's magazines have borrowed ideas and language from Freud. Social scientists have gained new insights from him. The "permissive" upbringing of today's children and many current educational practices likewise stem from the Viennese pathfinder; it was Freud's pioneer psychological studies of children that got modern child psychology started.

Finally, modern psychiatry began with Freud. Before him, psychiatry was concerned only with the "insane"—roughly, those suffering from schizophrenia, manic-depressive psychosis and other severe mental ailments often requiring hospitalization. Freud turned the attention of psychiatry toward the neurotics—the much larger number of persons who, though sane, cannot be happy with the world or themselves. Moreover, though few psychiatrists now call themselves psychoanalysts, the whole of psychiatry is permeated with ideas and concepts first elaborated by Freud.

What are the principal doctrines of psychoanalysis? How have they been modified by one-time collaborators who broke away from him and by post-Freudian psychiatrists? Just where do Freud's ideas stand today?

In a series of brilliant studies, mostly about the turn of the century, Freud showed that the human mind can appropriately be compared to an iceberg. As with an iceberg, most of the mind is out of sight, hidden away in the Unconscious. Philosophers, poets and novelists have long been aware that mental activity is not confined to the level of consciousness; they understand well that much goes on below the surface. Freud not only documented and deepened this insight but mapped the kinds of mental activity at each level.

Freud divided the mind into three parts, which he named the Id, the Ego and the Superego. The Id, which he located in the Unconscious, he described as the seat of primitive instinctual drives, harking back to man's animal past. The Ego, which is situated in the conscious level of the mind, adjusts desires arising in the Id to reality; the Ego learns the rules of society and decides whether and when the Id's desires can be fulfilled. The Superego is the still, small voice of conscience and tells the Ego whether its decisions are morally right. The Superego is back in the Unconscious; essentially, it represents idealized rules of behavior taught so strongly and so early in life as to have penetrated far below the conscious mind.

Dr. William C. Menninger, one of the famous psychiatrist Menninger brothers, compares the working of the mind to the fake-horse clown act. When Id, Ego and Superego pull together the individual moves steadily along, just as the fake horse when the man in back and the man in front are going in the same direction. Trouble is likely, however, if the Id, Ego and Superego come into conflict, just as the horse gets nowhere if the men inside go off in different directions. For instance, if the Ego, in response to a desire arising in the Id, makes a decision counter to the Superego, the Superego exacts punishment in the form of guilt feelings, worry or the equivalent.

There is no argument among psychiatrists over the existence of the Unconscious or of something that might be called Id, Ego and Superego. People do have deeply buried desires; they do have mental apparatus for making decisions, and they are equipped with censorious consciences. Nor is there serious disagreement over such Freudian discoveries as the symbolic character of dreams or the phenomenon of repression, the "forgetting" or burial deep in the Unconscious of feelings too painful to be borne in the conscious part of the mind. Or over Freud's demonstration that experiences early in childhood have a profound influence throughout life and that the child is truly psychological father to the man.

The historic disputes that repeatedly split psychiatry into a confusing Babel of pro and anti Freudian camps centered mainly about Freud's identification of a kind of generalized sexual instinct (located in the Id) as the main force in unconscious mental life. A second area of disagreement has involved Freud's technique for treating mental disorder—recall of offending "forgotten" experiences and desires by "free association" stream-of-consciousness talk on the psychoanalyst's couch.

Let's take up the debate over sex and the psyche first. In nearly all his early patients, Freud noted a close correspondence between their symptoms and their histories and unconscious sexual desires. Many men patients, for example, told stories reflecting a repressed childhood desire to displace the father and possess the mother (a wish Freud termed the Oedipus complex, after the Greek hero who unwittingly slew his father and married his mother).

Freud promptly came to the conclusion that unfulfilled or unfulfillable sexual desires were responsible for all neuroses. He also concluded that satisfaction of sexual desires was man's chief (if most deeply hidden) object in life. His several theories of personality, accordingly, all made libido or sexual instinct the principal force in psychic development; and the terms libido and sexual instinct always had a strongly sexual content, though he later broadened them to take in other forms of pleasure-seeking as well, from a liking for food to love of music.

Freud's elevation of sexual instinct to a central position in the shaping of personality and the origin of neurosis stirred up a fury of protest on all sides. The storm continued right up to his death in 1939 in London, a refugee from Hitlerism.

Most of Freud's attackers were merely outraged at his lifting the curtain on a side of man that had been passed over in silence too long. A number of his colleagues, however, had rather different objections. The latter, though put forward in many different guises by various individuals at various times, boil down to two.

First, Freud was accused of ignoring other, equally powerful forces in psychic development. Thus, one of Freud's early collaborators, Alfred Adler, found a potent source of the power drive and other forms of neurosis in feelings of inferiority. Another early associate of Freud, the Swiss physician C. G. Jung, a figure almost as controversial as Freud himself, pointed out the decisive role of relations between parents and between parent and child in forming the psychological character of the child. Jung also emphasized influences from the "collective unconscious" (unconscious memories going back to man's primal past); and he contended that the Unconscious holds a distinct, non-sexual creative instinct as well as a sexual instinct.

The second objection to Freud's concept and use of sexual instinct was that he had turned man into an instinct-ridden animal, foredoomed to perpetual misery by inner desires he could never satisfy. According to Freud—who was a strong traditional moralist, for all the charges of promoting immorality made against him—man's libido had to be suppressed in the interests of society. Consequently, Freud's critics pointed out, if Freud was right about the psychic role of libido, man was doomed to eternal frustration.

This objection to Freud's doctrines was raised explicitly by the so-called cultural school of psychoanalytic thought. The latter grew out of the generation of work in anthropology and other social sciences, as well as psychiatry, and came to fruition in the United States in the Nineteen Thirties. Its prime movers were Erich Fromm and the late Karen Horney, who came here from Europe, and the late Harry Stack Sullivan, director of the Washington School of Psychiatry.

The cultural school takes a more hopeful view of man's psychological destiny. According to this school personality is shaped primarily by social and cultural forces which can and constantly are being changed. Man, these psychiatrists hold, has fewer instinctual patterns of behavior at birth than any other animal; he can develop along many different lines, depending on the society he is born into.

To give a simple example, in our society it is quite all right for babies to cry when they want something, but older children behaving in the same way get stern disapproval. Neurotic and "healthy" traits both originate in such social pressures. Thus a child may be made deeply anxious by a parent who demands too much from him, or he may be led to odd attention-seeking behavior as a result of having been denied attention he needed and should have had.

In its denial to instinct of any important part in personality the cultural school represents a sharp break with Freud. The great majority of psychiatrists today do not go that far, however, any more than they accept Freud's exclusive emphasis on libido. They feel that there is truth on all sides of the question. "It is obvious that the sexual instinct plays a considerable role everywhere in life and thus also in neuroses," says Jung, who, with Ernest Jones of England, is one of the last survivors of the original group around Freud and who is living in retirement in Zurich. "But it is obvious that the power drive, the many forms of fear and the individual necessities are of equal importance."

What about the other major area of disagreement over the value and place of the couch and the analytical technique of treatment? When Breuer and Freud first began digging into the Unconscious, they got patients to recall "forgotten" experiences by putting them into a hypnotic state and telling them to talk. Some of their patients, though, could not be hypnotized. Freud hit upon a couch in a partially darkened room, with the analyst out of sight behind the head of the couch, as an alternative.

The couch and the dim light help the patient to relax. He is then asked to talk of anything and everything that comes to mind. With occasional help from the analyst, he dredges up more and more from his Unconscious. In theory this not only gives the analyst insight into the patient's difficulties but gives the patient the relief of confession. It is also supposed to make the patient less sentimental and more grown up about himself—that is, better able to live with his neurosis, if not do away with it.

There is no doubt that the analyst's couch furnishes a powerful tool for peering below the surface of consciousness; modern psychiatry wouldn't exist without it. But psychiatrists (including Freud himself) agree it is no panacea.

To begin with, analytic therapy is most useful in the treatment of neuroses, which are mental or psychic disorders characterized by a distorted view of reality. But it has proved of little value in the psychoses, or more severe forms of mental illnesses in which the patient has so far departed reality as to be living in a dream world of his own—though recently a group of analysts on the West Coast has claimed success in treating schizophrenia analytically.

Second, patients seem to need above-average IQ's.

Third, like any other form of medication, analysis can harm as well as heal. There are patients who can't take what they might discover about themselves and who would emerge from analysis sicker than when they entered it. And there are patients who, with a sort of perverse ingenuity, make examination of their past a means of ducking their present problems.

Finally, psychoanalysis is long drawn out and expensive; sessions may go on daily for two years or more.

As a result, most psychiatrists, including many who are analytically inclined, make use of shorter forms of treatment for most neurotic patients. Most often they depend on face-to-face talks at the psychiatrist's desk on the patient's immediate difficulties and on his "goals"—the direction in which he is moving. They try to give him some understanding of his problem and to turn him in a direction which will at least make him happier with himself. The full analytic treatment is resorted to only when necessary. (Electroshock, surgery and similar means of treatment are employed only in psychoses.)

"The changes and developments of sixty years, however," a working psychiatrist recently observed, "have in no way diminished Freud's stature or influence. He opened up the realm of the Unconscious. He showed us how it helps to make us what we are and how to reach it. Many of his ideas and concepts have had to be modified by his successors in the light of further experience. You might say they have been writing a New Testament for psychiatry. But Sigmund Freud wrote the Old Testament. His work will remain basic."

The Communist Manifesto 100 Years After

by Sidney Hook

A HUNDRED YEARS ago this month there appeared from an obscure printing shop in the Bishopsgate section of London, England, a twenty-three-page pamphlet. Its dark green title page did not carry the name of the author, the then comparatively unknown "Citizen Karl Marx," as the fiery, full-bearded young man of 29 was called by his fellow-exiles. Instead it bore the legend "Workers of the World, Unite!" Although entitled "Manifesto of the Communist Party," it was issued under the auspices of the educational Communist League. This was a propaganda group consisting of a handful of Socialists banished from their own countries. Their temporary headquarters was London, the great city of political asylum in the nineteenth century for the harassed and persecuted of all nations.

The league had been organized in 1847 and was formally disbanded in 1852. Actually it never functioned as a Communist party. It played hardly any role in the revolutionary events of 1848. It was a faction of a splinter group of a much larger movement of democratic refugees from Germany whose members shuttled from Paris to Brussels to London and back while waiting for Germany to catch up with her Western neighbors.

From the *New York Times Magazine*, February 1, 1948, copyright © 1948 by The New York Times Company.

The Communists in whose name the author thundered against bourgeois society, pronounced sentence of doom on all its works, and laid down an international program and strategy of action, numbered at most, a few score persons. Of these precisely two subscribed to all the doctrines expressed—Marx himself and his alter ego, Frederick Engels.

No matter how one evaluates the intrinsic merits of the Communist Manifesto, it is undoubtedly the most influential political pamphlet of all time. Its style is dramatic, its ideas bold and synthetic. Written with prophetic passion which gives buoyancy to its erudition, it includes in its historic sweep challenging judgments on the past, present and future of human culture. No one can read it without being stirred by its rhetoric, its striking figures of speech, and its Promethean defiance of the powers that be. Its very exaggerations give it force. Only the Bible has been translated into more languages, but the Manifesto has won converts in communities that Judaism and Christianity have barely touched.

For a time it had no influence upon those for whom it had been written. Forty years elapsed before the first authorized translation appeared in English. But as working-class movements acquired political consciousness throughout the world the principles and slogans of the Manifesto won universal currency except in the United States, Great Britain and the Dominions. What is truly astonishing is the extent to which the Manifesto, after a century, reads like a contemporary document. It has a fresh and powerful impact despite the fact that the ten items in the concrete program laid down for adoption in "the most advanced countries" have in great part been realized.

There are two reasons, aside from its prophetic vehemence and sense of urgency, why the Communist Manifesto does not date.

The first is that Marx is describing a historical process, the development of capitalism, which is still going on before our eyes. The social phenomena he is writing about we too are still very much concerned with: economic centralization and monopoly, the cycle of boom and depression, unemployment and the effects of technological change, political and economic class wars, excessive specialization and division of labor, the triumph of materialistic and money values on the rest of our culture.

The second is that we unconsciously identify the Communists about whom Marx is speaking with the Communists of today even though the similarities are more terminological than substantial. When Marx writes: "A specter is haunting Europe—the specter of communism," the reader naturally imagines that this is the same specter, somewhat larger and more bloated, which now threatens to take over all of Europe, Asia and more.

These reasons will bear examination.

Marx's thumbnail sketch of the development of capitalism from its infancy to what he prematurely regards as its senescence is a miracle of compression. Many details are out of focus. Some are clearly wrong. In the main, however, it is a plausible account of the history of capitalism from its period of triumph to its time of trouble. The whole is presented as a chapter in a philosophy of history according to which human advance is always the bitter fruit of class struggles between those who own and control the instruments of production and those who live by their labor. These classes replace heroes, royal dynasties, exalted ideals as the chief protagonists of progress in history.

Few critics of the evils of capitalism—and Marx lagged behind none in his moral fury—have paid such handsome compliments to capitalists as benefactors of humanity:

"The bourgeoisie has been the first to show us what man's activity is capable of achieving," he wrote. "It has accomplished wonders far surpassing the Egyptian pyramids, Roman aqueducts and Gothic cathedrals; it has conducted expeditions surpassing by far the tribal migrations and the Crusades.

"During its reign of scarce one hundred years, the bourgeoisie has created more powerful, more stupendous forces of production than all preceding generations rolled into one."

Nor is this all. Capitalism receives credit for the growth of democracy, the applications of science to industry and the emergence of an international culture and mind.

None the less, according to Marx, its heyday is over. It functions like a machine run amuck. It periodically generates unemployment although men are willing to work and there is an acute social need for their product. Marx makes much of the paradox that for the first time in human history men have gone cold and hungry because they have produced too much food and clothing. He charges that capitalism has dehumanized man by subordinating him to the impersonal mechanisms of the market. He criticizes it because it is a brake upon the further development of technological productive forces which can be released only by substituting production for social use in place of production for private profit.

When Marx wrote the Manifesto he expected the early collapse of the capitalist system. The ironical fact was that it stood on the eve of its greatest period of expansion. However, many of his predictions were fulfilled, albeit late. The most notable were the concentration of capital, the emergence of giant monopolies and the choking off of free competition, the recurrence of economic crises of increasing intensity.

Not so fortunate was his prediction of the absolute pauperization of the working class and the disappearance of the middle classes. The application of science to industry, the growth of trade unionism, the effect of belief in, as well as fear of, the Marxist solution raised the standard of living of the working class beyond that of many dominant classes in earlier societies. Nor did he envisage the possibility that the reaction to economic distress might take a Fascist rather than Socialist form.

Yet when all these items are corrected and balanced the challenge of the Manifesto to capitalism remains as strong today as in the past. It is a challenge that capitalism can meet only by doing what Marx to the very end of his life believed impossible, viz., provide opportunity for profitable capital investment, guarantee a continuous high level of employment and a civilized standard of living for all. The real weakness of Marx's argument lay not in his critique of capitalism but in his assumption that complete laissez-faire and complete collectivism exhausted the alternatives, and in his underestimation of the dangers of totalitarianism.

That the Communists of the Manifesto were of an entirely different breed from the Communist parties of today is evident in many ways. The first were honest revolutionaries, not conspirators hiding behind anonymity and false fronts. "The Communists," writes Marx in the concluding paragraph of the Manifesto, "disdain to conceal their views and aims. They openly declare that their ends can be attained only by the forcible overthrow of all existing social conditions."

The small band of Communists a century ago risked much greater dangers and penalties for their ideas than do their presumed namesakes today. For in most countries they could not appeal to due process and the protection of a Bill of Rights. Yet they scorned evasion and deceit to escape the consequences of holding unpopular ideas. They never infiltrated into other organizations under the pretense of being what they were not. Not a single one of Marx's band is known to have denied his beliefs or refused to answer questions about them.

An even greater difference between the Communists of the Manifesto and the totalitarian Communists of today is the fervent belief of the former in personal and civil freedom. This is revealed in the official journal of the Communist League published in September, 1847.

"We are not among those Communists," it declares, "who are out to destroy personal liberty, who wish to turn the world into one huge barrack or into a gigantic workhouse. There certainly are some Communists who, with an easy conscience, refuse to countenance personal liberty and would like to shuffle it out of the world. * * * But we have no desire to exchange freedom for equality." The same issue proclaims what Marx and Engels were to repeat several times later, that in the United States and England it was possible to achieve the goals of socialism through peaceful processes.

Why, then, did Marx call his Manifesto a Communist Manifesto rather than a Socialist Manifesto? Engels explains the reason. At the time the word "socialism," in the public mind, designated the views of two groups from both of whom Marx and his friends wished to differentiate themselves. The first sought to achieve the ultimate ideals of a collectivist society by appealing to philanthropic sentiment, to benevolent rulers, and to principles of religion which were more universally professed than practiced. The second were "multifarious social quacks" with cure-alls guaranteed to do anything but remove basic causes.

Neither group believed that the working class could become the instrument of its own liberation. This was the sticking point between Marx and all the other Socialists of his day. It is typified in his insistence that the slogan "Workers of the World, Unite!" replace the earlier one, "All Men Are Brothers," current among Socialists before his time.

Just as soon as political parties arose in Germany and France which recognized that the emancipation of the working class could be accomplished only by that class—an over-simple view—Marx and Engels dropped the term "Communist" for "Socialist." When Engels wrote the preface to the German edition of 1890, he asserted that "Continental socialism has become the almost complete embodiment of the principles laid down by the Manifesto." Present-day Communist parties whose program depends upon the shifting exigencies of the foreign policy of the Soviet Union cannot be regarded as the heirs of the Communist Manifesto.

As with all great historical writings that have influenced events, the way in which the Manifesto is interpreted as a guide to political activity depends more upon what the reader brings to it than on the mere text. Revolutionary Socialists who wish to collectivize society at one fell swoop can quote it in justification. So can moderate, evolutionary Socialists who emphasize Marx's recommendation that the process of socialization be carried out "by degrees."

One need but list the measures proposed in the Manifesto for "the most advanced countries" to see how far Western countries have come toward realizing them. The list shows how necessary it is to distinguish between Marx's basic principles and his program of short time demands which vary with historical conditions:

(1) Abolition of property in land and application of all rents of land to public purposes.

(2) A vigorously graduated income tax.

(3) Abolition of all rights of inheritance.

(4) Confiscation of the property of all emigrants and rebels.

(5) Centralization of credit in the hands of the state, by means of a national bank with state capital and an exclusive monopoly.

(6) Centralization of all means of transportation in the hands of the state.

(7) Extension of factories and instruments of production owned

by the state; cultivation of waste lands and improvement of soil generally in accordance with a common plan.

(8) Universal and equal obligation to work; organization of industrial armies, especially for agriculture.

(9) Agriculture and urban industry to work hand-in-hand, in such ways as by degrees to abolish the opposition between town and country.

(10) Free education for all children in public schools. Abolition of factory work for children in its present form. Education to be brought in closer connection with the processes of material production.

More fundamental than Marx's economic theories is his philosophy of society and man which underlies them. This philosophy is rational and humanistic in outlook. It has faith in men as the architects of their own social order, determining by the power which common knowledge and common consent give, the direction of human history. No one can reasonably doubt that Marx thought of himself as a democrat—not in the style of the new Eastern despotisms but in line with the French and American Revolutions with their emphasis on civil and personal rights as fundamental to any good society.

It was Marx who said of the proletariat that it needs "a sense of personal dignity and independence, even more than it needs daily bread." In the Manifesto, he describes the working-class movement as "a movement of the overwhelming majority in the interests of that majority." The first step in its revolution is "to win the battle for democracy." He was a resolute opponent of all Communists who conceived of the political rule of the working class as a dictatorship of a political party *over* the working class. His Socialist ideal was a society in which "the free development of each is the condition of the free development of all."

Today many Socialists are not so certain as Marx was that a completely planned collectivist society is the best way to extend democracy. In so far as they follow him they test all measures of socialization and planned control by their consequences in strengthening democratic processes and in enriching the personal lives of all citizens in the community. Whether one accepts or rejects Marx's ideas, they constitute a critical part of the critical tradition of the West.

Karl Marx today is a minor figure in the state religion of Russian Communist pan-Slavism. He is well on his way to being completely eclipsed by the ikons of Ivan, no longer the Terrible, but the Great, Peter the Great, Lenin the Great, and Stalin the Greatest. It would be tragic to surrender a thinker whose favorite motto, *de omnibus dubitandum* (doubt everything), breathes the spirit of free inquiry, to the new Byzantine authoritarianism of the East. His permanent insights, as well as his errors, have grown out of and fed the sources of Western democracy.

Part 2

THE TWENTIETH-CENTURY PHILOSOPHERS

Philosophy, in the words of John Herman Randall, Jr., is an expression of the judgments and aspirations of men. A great philosophy clarifies, perfects, and stirs the mind, and in that stirring there is a search for truth. But in the history of mankind one's truth was not always another's; social, political, and religious conflict impelled men to pit their ideas and their truths against one another in a sometimes successful but often fruitless attempt to see the universe in comprehensible ways. The Greeks viewed philosophy as a justification of the good life, that is, the ethical life; the Romans paid it less mind, except for the resignation urged by the Stoics. But that resignation did help the early Christians hold fast in hostile surroundings, and when they had won the hearts of men, philosophy was made to serve theology.

In the sixteenth and seventeenth centuries, science rescued philosophy with the Cartesian world-view and Newtonian celestial mechanics. Philosophy became an application of reason and understanding for building the foundations of scientific knowledge; it became a matter of methodology and a search for *how* one discovers truth. But such explorations, as we have sought to demonstrate in the Introduction, threatened to produce arid discussions of logic that left out of account the one problem philosophy always ought to consider—the place of man in a world he never shaped. For human experience is universal, and the fundamental fact of that experience is man's confrontation with his fellowmen. To be sure, the form this question assumes varies from era to era, and in that sense philosophy is a culturally determined enterprise. Hence questions philosophers have asked always mirrored the society they lived in—and so it is today.

Earl, Philosopher, Logician, Rebel

by Charles Hussey

BERTRAND RUSSELL, often called the world's greatest living philosopher and the greatest logician since Aristotle, will be 90 this Friday. He is as frail as a famished bird and when he appears on television, viewers see a mass of white hair, a glittering eye and a bony finger. The snowcap of his hair surmounting the long tubular neck has reminded some people of the mushroom cloud that follows a nuclear explosion.

Yet, though Lord Russell's body is becoming ethereal and his dry, precise voice seems to be disembodied, his mind shows no loss of sharpness and clarity. Throughout his eighty-ninth and ninetieth years he has been the Gandhi-like leader of that section of British nuclear disarmers which reinforces its arguments with civil disobedience — the militant Committee of 100, which sprang from the more sedate Campaign for Nuclear Disarmament.

Surrounded by young beatniks, fashionable stagefolk, and anxiety-ridden young London Mums, the third Earl Russell has himself sat in protest on London's damp pavements before the Ministry of Defense. On that occasion the authorities were disappoint-

From the *New York Times Magazine,* May 13, 1962, copyright © 1962 by The New York Times Company.

ingly kind. They brought him a cup of tea (which he refused) and offered him sticky tape (which he accepted) to attach his petition to the Ministry's door.

Though Russell is Britain's greatest citizen after Churchill, he is so controversial a figure that the owners of the Albert Hall, London's biggest concert hall, have refused to let the building for his ninetieth-birthday party, "in case fighting breaks out." There was to have been a musical work written in his honor and presentations from the many organizations in which he has taken part. At the moment of writing, a marathon two-day celebration is being planned, but no details are available.

It is only a few months since Earl Russell, Fellow of the Royal Society and holder of the Order of Merit, the highest non-titular honor Britain can confer, served a week in jail for refusing to pledge to keep the peace. He was put in a private cell in the prison hospital and he said that everybody was very kind to him. In World War I he had spent six months in the same prison but could not see why the warders were so proud of the improvements. In fact, he had a complaint to make against a new severity of prison life: "The wireless seemed to be on nearly all the time." (It interfered with his reading of the life of Madame de Staël.)

The most serious act of nonviolence staged by Russell's Committee of 100 was the attempt to invade an American nuclear airbase at Wethersfield, Sussex. Half a dozen young people have been sentenced to eighteen months imprisonment for this offense and many people feel that they were led astray by the elderly sage. He himself deliberately incriminated himself at the time of the trial and was disappointed not to be charged.

Russell's view is this:

Britain derives no security from nuclear weapons. Russia could destroy her in half an hour and there is no reason to believe that if she were attacked, America would be involved in the war. So Britain has nothing to gain by being armed and everything to lose. But she has everything to gain by being an unarmed neutral. No one would attack her, and—not being engaged—she could draw up a treaty of disarmament for America and Russia. Russell visualizes, in fact, Britain leading a neutral bloc of states.

It is not this kind of assertion, woolly and question-begging though it is, that has antagonized so many people in Britain, but statements like this: "We used to call Hitler wicked for killing the Jews but Kennedy and Macmillan are much more wicked than Hitler." And Russell has criticized British justice for resembling that of Buchenwald because anti-bomb demonstrators were not allowed to argue in court at length that depriving Britain of nuclear strength, far from being prejudicial to the safety of the realm, actually increased its safety.

The old logician is far from scrupulous when he turns propagandist. He himself has said—many years ago—the last word on his present conduct: "The opinions that are held with passion are always those for which no good ground exists; indeed the passion is the measure of the holder's lack of rational conviction."

All his life the rational side of Bertrand Russell has been at war with powerful mystical influences. The seeds of the conflict were almost sown in him. Both his parents died when he was a baby. His father, a Deist, was the author of a skeptical work "Analysis of Religious Belief." He appointed in his will two freethinkers to be Bertie's guardians (one of them was the philosopher John Stuart Mill). But the court set aside the will and the boy was educated in the Christian faith.

"I am afraid," says Russell, "that the result was disappointing but that was not the fault of the law. . . . A parent has the right to ordain that any imaginable superstition shall be instilled into his children after his death but has not the right to say that they shall be kept free of superstition."

Russell's childhood was lonely and unhappy. Freudians may discover the source of his protest in his governesses, a series of German women who imposed an iron discipline. In protest against the nursery regime he has never eaten green vegetables since he grew up.

The religious upbringing succeeded almost too well. In his teens he was not far from religious mania. One of the influences which helped to rescue him was John Stuart Mill's "Autobiography." Its rational clarity—perhaps also its parallel of adolescent depression and breakdown—made Russell decide to abandon the uncertainties of God and sin for the certainties of Euclid and mathematics. He has confessed that he has sought for mathematical certainties as other people seek for religious faith. But he has had to keep a tight rein on his religious proclivities.

Some of his friends see Russell as an inverted priest. Never has this image appeared sharper than during a series of B. B. C. discussions with Father Coplestone, a noted Jesuit, on the existence of God. "A darling man," said Russell, "another minute and I would have converted him." Coplestone said exactly the same about Russell.

I myself have heard Russell say about another priest who seemed to be suffering spiritual doubt: "I wanted to take him in my arms and comfort him and assure him all would be well." Russell has written in his book "Mysticism and Logic": "The greatest men who have been philosophers have felt the need of both science and mysticism."

Russell is, and looks and acts like, an aristocrat. He comes from one of those old English families that have never been afraid of expressing eccentric views or indulging in eccentric conduct. The head of the family is the Duke of Bedford. Their stately home is Woburn Abbey, which, with the aid of jukeboxes, an occasional nudist colony and a zoo, earns more gate money from summer sightseers than Blenheim Palace, the seat of the Churchills.

Russell is the great-grandson of the sixth Duke of Bedford and the grandson of the first Earl Russell, better known as Lord John Russell, the statesman who pioneered democracy in Britain with the Electoral Reform Bill of 1832. On his mother's side, Russell belongs to another historic and noble line, the Stanleys.

His elder brother, the second Earl, became a Buddhist, a Liberal politician and was convicted of bigamy—though only on the technical ground of an American divorce being judged invalid by an English court.

But the main influences on Russell were not aristocratic. They were intellectual. He went to Cambridge at a period when it was seething with ideas. Alfred North Whitehead, G. E. Moore and G. Lowes Dickinson were preparing the great philosophical and ethical revolt against Victorianism.

The most decisive influence was Whitehead's. Whitehead took Russell to a philosophic conference in Paris and as a result Russell was inspired to write what is probably his most important book, "The Principles of Mathematics," and (in collaboration with Whitehead) the three-volume "Principia Mathematica."

They laid the foundations of the mathematical logic of this century. These works alone would ensure for Russell undying fame as a great and original thinker. His work, it is said, took the mystery out of mathematical knowledge and destroyed any connection that might be supposed to exist between numbers and mysticism.

The school to which Russell belongs—modern analytical empiricism—improves on Locke, Berkeley and Hume by incorporating mathematics and by developing logical technique. To some problems it can give definite answers—though the answers are scientific rather than "philosophical."

But, Russell says, there is a vast field of so-called philosophy where scientific methods cannot be applied to ultimate questions of value. Science alone cannot prove that it is bad to enjoy the infliction of cruelty. Matters of feeling lie outside the province of the sciences.

Philosophy, says Russell, has always consisted of an inharmonious blend of (1) theory about the nature of the world and (2) an ethical or political doctrine about the best way of living.

The failure to separate these two with sufficient clarity has been a source of much confused thinking. Throughout the ages philosophers have allowed their opinions about the nature of the world to be influenced by their desire for moral improvement. Supposing they have known what beliefs would make men virtuous, they have invented arguments to prove these beliefs are true.

Philosophers of Russell's school say that the human intellect cannot find conclusions to many questions of profound importance to mankind. They refuse to believe that there is some "higher" way of discovering truths which are concealed from science and the intellect. Nevertheless, they have found that many questions obscured by the fog of metaphysics can or will be precisely answered by objective methods—questions such as: What is number? What are space and time? What is mind? What is matter?

It was back in the time of his association with Whitehead and the others that Russell experienced an agnostic equivalent of a religious conversion. He became suddenly aware that most people live in loneliness and he developed a passionate desire to find ways in which this tragic isolation might be diminished. This quest inspired the torrent of popular writing which has brought Russell an enormous readership far beyond anything his philosophical works could have obtained—books like "The Conquest of Happiness," "Marriage and Morals," "Roads to Freedom" and "Education and the Social Order."

Russell has been caught in the contradiction between his empiricist view of man, as a mere bundle of perceptions, and his political hopes for mankind. Like the signers of the American Declaration of Independence, Russell has an optimistic view of mankind.

"We need," he has written, "a morality based on love of life, upon pleasure in growth and positive achievement. * * * A man should be regarded as good if he is happy and glad when others are happy."

Thus Russell is devoted to the American ideal of the pursuit of happiness, but empirical philosophy allows no place for the Good Man upon which it depends.

The Founding Fathers and Locke fell back on a belief in God, but this Russell has always denied himself. (Hume, of a more skeptical turn of mind, found consolation in beef and backgammon.) Perhaps the contradiction in which Russell finds himself explains much of his permanent love-hate relationship with America, which is one of the clues to his character.

Two of Russell's four wives have been Americans: the first, Alys Pearsall Smith, sister of the critic and essayist, and the last, Edith Finch, a former teacher at Bryn Mawr and daughter of a New York doctor. His two children by his second wife were married to Americans—the son to a daughter of the poet Vachel Lindsay (this marriage is now dissolved), the daughter to an Episcopalian clergyman.

It was an attack on the American Army that got Russell his first prison sentence. During World War I he was a conscientious pacifist. Again and again he invited prosecution by attacking the British Government, but it was only when he turned upon the

Americans that he was given six months in jail. It was not, however, his pacifism that involved him in trouble and bitterness with the American authorities during the Second World War.

By that time he had abandoned an idea he had once held that Britain should treat invading Nazis with kindness, as if they were tourists, and had announced that if he were young he would fight.

In 1938 he had gone to the United States to teach, first at the University of Chicago, then at the University of California. Then, early in 1940, he was appointed to the philosophy faculty at the College of the City of New York. Immediately Bishop Manning denounced him as a "recognized propagandist against religion and morality who specifically defends adultery."

Russell denied that he preached adultery, but a mob of mothers gathered outside the college and threatened to run Russell out of town. The mother of two students at the college filed a taxpayer's suit and the New York State Supreme Court abrogated the appointment. Despite this, he gave the William James lectures in philosophy at Harvard that fall.

With a wife and three children to support, Russell by 1942 found himself penniless at a time when it was very difficult to get money out of Britain. It was sheer economic pressure that drove him to write a book which many people regard as one of his masterpieces: "The History of Western Philosophy."

Russell has been very much a family man in spite of his unconventional views on marriage and morals. His love of children has been one of the guiding passions of his life—perhaps because to be a parent is the agnostic's nearest hope of immortality. His first marriage, which in its early days looked idyllic, was undermined by childlessness.

Russell was 48 when he became a father for the first time, after his marriage to Dora Black, a bluestocking reformer who had been a Fellow of Girton College, Cambridge. Largely for the sake of their own children, she and Bertrand founded a famous experimental school, Beacon Hill, where the pupils' intelligence was measured by their curiosity, and freedom was the rule: "Complete freedom as to all bathroom activities, intermingling of sex in bathing, showering and answering the calls of nature."

Dora Russell announced in 1933 that her third child had been fathered by another man. Burke's Peerage does not mention the child. The marriage foundered shortly afterward.

The third Lady Russell was 26 when she married Russell, who was then 65. The child of this marriage was sent, more conventionally, to Eton.

Though Russell has changed his mind on many issues, on one he has been remarkably consistent. He has been steadily hostile to communism. He visited Communist Russia in 1920 and met both Lenin and Trotsky. Impressed by the crudity and cruelty of what he saw, he did not hesitate to take a strong anti-Communist line. This early and fearlessly critical attitude toward Communist excesses earned him the distrust of many of his Left-Wing friends. The Communists described him as a "philosophizing wolf with all the brutal instincts of the beast."

So great was Russell's hatred of communism that he declared soon after the end of World War II: "Anything is better than submission" to Soviet dictatorship. He declared that the democracies should be prepared to use force if necessary, and even advocated an immediate preventive war against Russia unless it agreed to internationalization of nuclear weapons.

Russell has, in fact, rejected the two most fashionable "isms" of our time. He has rejected Marxism; he has also rejected Freudianism. Brooding and passionate as he is, subject to long fits of melancholia, even to contemplating suicide, Russell might have welcomed the escape routes offered by Freud and Jung with their acknowledgment of the dark side of the soul. But the horrors that lurk in the unconscious have been coldly denied by the archrationalist.

Russell's career has been marked by three recurring phases of happiness and social hope, followed by periods of rebellion and despair.

The first happy years were at Cambridge and in the early days of his marriage before World War I. Looking back, those palmy Edwardian days seem a halcyon time, with leisure, reading, mathematics, conversation with like minds, croquet and traveling in Italy. The Fabian Society was in its heyday. It brought the companionship of Russell's fellow prophets, Bernard Shaw and H. G.

Wells, as well as of that brilliant pair, Sidney and Beatrice Webb. Everybody believed in progress and perfectability.

Then, unforeseen, World War I brought disaster; the unhappy period of Russell's pacifist protest was followed by imprisonment and social ostracism.

Peace, a new marriage, and children opened a new phase of hope. Much of this new life centered around a remarkable woman named Lady Ottoline Morrell, with whom Russell had a long attachment. Lady Ottoline, the daughter of a duke, had married a wealthy brewer. Her home, Garsington Manor, a golden-colored seventeenth-century mansion near Oxford, became a sort of Temple of the Muses for Russell. Frequent names in the guestbook were John Maynard Keynes, Augustus John, Virginia Woolf, T. S. Eliot. Aldous Huxley described these parties somewhat caustically in his novel "Crome Yellow."

Once again the idyll was destroyed by the growth of Nazism, the threat of war and, finally, war itself. Russell went off to the misery of his contentious life in the United States.

The third phase began when Russell returned to Britain in 1944. He became a sort of national hero. In 1948 he inaugurated the famous B. B. C. Reith Lectures, the apotheosis of established respectability. He won world-wide admiration and a new lease on life when he saved himself by swimming in icy water after a plane accident off Norway in which nineteen people died. In 1949 he received the Order of Merit from the hands of King George VI. In 1950 he was awarded the Nobel Prize for Literature.

In 1952 he married his fourth wife, a gentle lady in her fifties, and settled down on the outskirts of London to write fiction. More recently, they have made their home in Wales. His stories, though they showed no understanding of human character, displayed a keen Voltairean bite.

With tragic inevitability, this happy period produced its antithesis of revolt. Russell threw himself into the Campaign for Nuclear Disarmament, and then into the civil disobedience of the militant anti-bomb movement.

It would be wrong to say that Russell is the father of the "Better Red than Dead" school. It existed before his Committee of 100. Many of his followers do have this crude belief, but not all of them are defeatists. They believe that a moral triumph by the West would have a moral effect upon the East, but only a portion of them are in the movement for political ends. Others are Utopians engaged in a cause which—as it has been put—they know is probably unattainable to avoid a fate which is unimaginable.

Far more dangerous than Russell's lawbreakers is the Campaign for Nuclear Disarmament, which succeeded in getting its neutralist views approved by the Labor party conference eighteen months ago. Only the stubborn courage of Hugh Gaitskell, the Parliamentary Labor party leader, in defying this decision of the conference, and the loyalty of two thirds of the members of the Labor party prevented British Labor from advocating a course which must have led them to oppose the American alliance.

But England was in no peril. Had the Labor party adopted neutralism, the party would have been reduced to insignificance at the next election.

The English people regard these movements, led by Russell and others, as a rather healthy sign of idealism and morality, to be tolerated and even admired—on the strict condition that they remain a minority with no hope of success.

Through most of his life, Russell seems to have been moved by an almost pathological hatred of mankind's wickedness and stupidity; and with an equal passion he wishes to save mankind. As long ago as 1901 Beatrice Webb commented: "Bertrand is almost cruel in his desire to see cruelty revenged. * * * He is a good hater."

Russell's latest book, "Has Mankind a Future?", begins with a frenzied indictment of the beastliness of the human race; it ends lyrically: "No limit can be set to what [man] may achieve in the future. I see in my mind's eye, a world of glory and joy * * * and what is noble is no longer condemned as treachery to this or that paltry aim. All this can happen. It rests with our generation to decide between this vision and an end decreed by folly."

Keynes noticed the contradiction in this double vision of Russell's many years ago. He wrote: "Bertie sustained simultaneously a pair of opinions ludicrously incompatible. He held in fact that human affairs were carried on after a most irrational fashion, but that the remedy was quite simple and easy, since all we had to do was to carry them on rationally."

Whatever the end of the present controversy may be, "The Principles of Mathematics" remains a work of original and unchallenged greatness. Russell's ninetieth birthday is celebrated by the whole Western world with pride and love.

America's Philosopher Attains an Alert 90

by Irwin Edman

JOHN DEWEY is 90 years old. Such a feat of survival is always impressive, especially when the survivor is eminent. But what is even more impressive is that at the age of 90 John Dewey should be as active intellectually and as influential as when, over half a century ago, he first became famous as a fresh voice and a liberating energy in American philosophy and education.

With the exception of William James, there is no name within the last century that has become throughout the world so inseparably associated with American thought. Both Dewey's disciples and his critics regard him as this nation's most characteristic intellectual expression, notably in its emphasis on practical reasons for ordered change.

For over a generation now John Dewey's writings have influenced professional philosophers so that even those who disagree with him basically have had to meet the challenges his new thinking has put before them. But he has challenged more than professional philosophers. His theories of education have affected the whole perspective and practice of teaching, both elementary and

From the *New York Times Magazine*, October 16, 1949, copyright © 1949 by The New York Times Company.

advanced. Long before the term "progressive education" had become a label of something to defend and to attack, Dewey and a group of colleagues had started an experimental school—and an experimental point of view—at the University of Chicago that at the turn of the century was to initiate nothing less than an educational revolution in which the child and not the subject was to be the chief concern.

The point of view stated in general terms as an experimental philosophy was also soon to affect the legal thinking of such eminent jurists as Oliver Wendell Holmes and Benjamin Cardozo and all those who felt that legal institutions should be measured by their human consequences, not by a priori conceptions of justice and right.

Relatively late in life (at 70) Dewey turned attention to a consideration of art, in which he found experience most fully and radiantly fulfilled. His point of view in esthetics has already had deep repercussions on the thinking of art critics and art historians.

Nor has Dewey's influence been confined to this country. His works have been translated into every major language, and in France particularly his philosophical influence has been strong. When the new Turkey was being reorganized and Europeanized after the first World War, Dewey was called in as an educational adviser. The liberal movement in China a generation ago, now unhappily in eclipse, was spearheaded by Hu Shih, a pupil of Dewey's at Columbia a generation ago, and Dewey himself visited China as an honored guest and educational leader in the Nineteen Twenties. Wherever democratic movements have sought to express their basic convictions, Dewey's philosophy and frequently the man himself have been welcomed.

The widespread power of Dewey's thinking is all the more remarkable to look back upon when one considers its modest personal source. John Dewey is a homespun, almost regional, character. To this day, on meeting him, one would imagine oneself talking with a Vermont countryman, as seven generations of his forebears were. At many an academic gathering over the last fifty years, those who had come a long distance to hear and see the great John Dewey have been pleasantly discomfited to find that he was none other than the modest, gray-haired, stoop-shouldered man with a Green Mountain drawl and a chuckle and a grin to whom they had been speaking for the past ten minutes.

In other ways, too, he belies conventional conceptions. In classroom lectures, his drawling voice, his abstracted air, his colorless language would have seemed calculated to make his lectures dull —as they were to the dull. Yet for two generations, almost, his university classes were crowded with raptly attentive students. They soon found it exciting to have the experience (rarer in academic circles than one might think) of *hearing* a man thinking creatively as he lectured.

In his books and articles he showed none of the obvious picturesque persuasiveness of William James or the elegance of Santayana. Yet, despite the difficulties of his style, he became celebrated as a philosophical writer. His readers discovered that one of the reasons he was difficult was that he was saying things that had never before been said in philosophy. He was trying to enunciate fresh and liberating things honestly and precisely, "mopping up objections" on the way—as he once said to this writer—often in one sentence a page long.

His origins and his experience go far toward explaining John Dewey. He was born in Burlington, Vt., on Oct. 20, 1859. There is a symbolic coincidence in the fact that this was the year of the publication of Darwin's "Origin of Species." One of Dewey's important essays is entitled "The Influence of Darwin on Philosophy," and the key to the understanding of his thought is the fact that man is continuous with animal life and that thought is a biological instrument of adjustment and survival.

There is significance, too, in the fact that Dewey grew up in a nineteenth-century New England small town where, in a homogeneous pattern of culture, individuality was cherished and where civil liberties and spiritual and social independence were a deep part of the current mores. Dewey's lifelong concern for the rights of everyone as a man and a citizen, his simplicity of manner, his freedom from any kind of snobbishness or obeisance to mere wealth or mere power or social prestige stem from this early background which is ingrained in his manner and in his preferences.

Dewey's early academic career was spent in the Middle West

at the Universities of Minnesota, Michigan and Chicago. He developed in the Middle West—in a society still with traces of the frontier and still patiently creating its own future—the theme of creative intelligence, of the notion of ideas as hypotheses for reconstruction of life and society, of philosophy as the projection of social ideals and as a generalized program of progressive activity.

Creative intelligence is, indeed, the key theme of Dewey's philosophy, the whole of which may be conceived of as an exploration of the ways in which mind functions in a world consisting humanly of a succession of problems to be solved, of difficulties to be clarified, of situations to be improved.

As students and readers came to realize, Dewey was suggesting a reconstruction in philosophy that was both an emancipation proclamation and an emancipation program. What was the nature of the emancipation, from what and to what? What was the program envisaged? Dewey's philosophy has been called—and by foreigners it has not always been meant as a compliment—characteristically American. In many respects it is. It is a conception of philosophy in terms of enlightened practicality; general ideas, moral principles, theories of logical methods are only important in so far as they are useful in solving human and social problems.

Dewey's philosophy is in some sense, too, an analogue in philosophy to the American Revolution in our political history. It constitutes to some degree a revolt against the European tradition, but a revolt against Germany, rather than England; Dewey in his youth had been greatly influenced by nineteenth-century metaphysics, especially that of Hegel. Hegelian metaphysics up to the end of the nineteenth century had dominated American academic philosophy. For the Hegelian, the universe is an unchanging unfolding of reason. History is a ruthless, dialectical development of alleged cosmic rationality.

From Dewey came the revolutionary notion that reason is not something timelessly existing in the nature of things but is simply a development, fortunate and complex, of human behavior. Thinking occurs in the individual when habit and impulse are inadequate to the solution of problems in a world always precarious. Thinking is an exploration of the possibilities of experience through what in practical life are called "hunches" but in science are called "hypotheses" or "ideas." The procedure of science is simply the careful and controlled development of a hunch or an idea. The most elaborate hypothesis, like the simplest guess, must be tested in action. But however elaborate scientific thinking becomes, it is essentially simply refined common sense, the development and testing of suggestions.

And from Dewey also came one of the first enunciations of what the atomic bomb has spelled out for everyone—that the method of free intelligence has produced miracles in the way of control of our physical environment but in the field of moral and social relationships we are still the victims of our own fantasies, superstitions and slogans. We exalt Natural Law or Free Enterprise or the Constitution; we take for granted some changeless entity known as the Family or some changeless principle called the Right. Until we learn to develop and test our moral and social ideas with the same objectivity, candor and care with which we develop and test ideas in the laboratory, we shall be on the brink of chaos and disaster.

Dewey is aware that there are special difficulties in having free and objective thinking about human and social problems. Ideas become *idées fixes;* principles become sacrosanct and through emotion become untouchable. The customary ways of our society, our traditional laws, become fixed social habits.

If we are to keep human intelligence abreast of the changing human situation, we need to develop very early the habit of criticizing habit, the custom of questioning and correcting customs. We are living in a world where we split the atom but in which we act socially by outworn emotional formulas of sovereignty or nationalism or honor. We are, as James Harvey Robinson (a close colleague of Dewey's at Columbia) said, seventeenth-century tradesmen riding around in twentieth-century Rolls-Royces.

Dewey has always regarded and to this day regards the whole realm of education as a nursing and testing ground of philosophic attitudes. Conventional education, he thinks, is too preoccupied with the handing down of alleged final knowledge about a changeless world. Dewey's deepest conviction as a philosopher is also a reflected statement of a familiar American credo: that we are living in a world where change and not fixity is the deepest fact.

To Dewey the important thing about education is not to hand down finalities but to inculcate the habit of reconstructive criticism of all our social habits, which include the processes of government and law and industry. Education is the training ground for the development of the habit of creative intelligence on the part of the younger citizens in a democratic society, the development of attitudes of relying neither on impulses nor on dogma but on the free, disciplined operation of thinking.

Dewey at 90 still impresses his friends and colleagues most by his exhibition of these traits, the constant alertness to change and fruitful growth.

A year or two ago he came back to Columbia to address a group of post-graduate students in philosophy on his present hopes and fears for philosophy. Looking at the contemporary world, he developed somewhat sadly the theme that too many philosophers had retreated to purely technical and trivial questions and that, meanwhile, the great world was given over to violence and dogmatisms of the political extremists. The cultivation of socially responsible individuals through the development of creative thinking is becoming rarer and rarer. It is, he pointed out, a discouraging time to be a philosopher. Then, after he had sat down, the venerable teacher and sage rose again and said, as nearly as I can remember the words, "But now I am talking to the young and I am afraid I have sounded discouraging. In a very important sense it is a wonderful time to be a philosopher. The old slogans, the old formulas are obviously not working. It is a challenge to new and creative hypothesis, some bold and imaginative venture in thought." Then he added, "All it requires is some ideas, imagination and, I warn you, guts." I have rarely seen an academic audience more deeply moved, for this was a call to intellectual adventure and experiment by a man nearly 90.

It is clear why Dewey's whole philosophy—so strong an affirmation of freedom and creative intelligence—should lead its author to be equally an enemy of both the dogmatic right and the dogmatic left. Social democracy has been his chief political theme and he has viewed with natural alarm the resurgence of totalitarianism, authoritarianism of both Communists and Fascists.

Dewey's philosophy remains in the author's old age the fresh voice of the philosophy of a young country and a youthful spirit, the voice of liberal intelligence seeking to rely on intelligence, and not on dogma or passion or violence, for the solution of those problems which face all of mankind today.

Dewey is in no orthodox sense a theologian, but he is in a deep sense a religious man whose "common faith" is in mankind and in its native resources of good-will and intelligence in promoting the realization of each man and the mystical community of all men. It is a generous faith and, as John Dewey at 90 shows, one calculated to keep a man young.

Sage Who Inspired Hammarskjold

by Meyer Levin

SCATTERED in the African underbrush, amid the wreckage of the plane in which Dag Hammarskjold died, were a few books and papers. The Secretary General of the United Nations, on his last urgent peace mission, traveled light. Yet there were two copies of the same book, a German volume called "Ich und Du" by Martin Buber, and its English translation, "I and Thou." There were twelve typewritten pages, the beginning of Dag Hammarskjold's translation into Swedish of Buber's masterwork.

Indeed, Hammarskjold's last known words, spoken to an associate, Dr. Sture Linner, concerned Martin Buber's ideas. Before the fatal aircraft took off, a letter from Dr. Linner to Buber relates Hammarskjold "referred to your work and to the medieval mystics. 'Love, for them,' he said, 'was a surplus of power that they felt completely filled them when they began to live in self-forgetfulness.' "

Thoughts of universal love and self-forgetfulness linked the Swedish man of goodwill to the octogenarian Sage of Jerusalem. Dag Hammarskjold, a connoisseur of art and literature, often gave copies of Buber's books to his friends, for in avant-garde circles

From the *New York Times Magazine,* December 3, 1961, copyright © 1961 by The New York Times Company.

Martin Buber's "I and Thou" philosophy is regarded as the next step after existentialism.

As relaxation, Hammarskjold had translated from French the little known poems of St.-John Perse (the pseudonym of Alexis Léger), soon afterward awarded the Nobel Prize. It was doubtless in his mind that by translating Buber into Swedish he might make Buber, too, more accessible for this highest of literary honors, for which Nobel Prize author Herman Hesse had nominated him in 1949 as "not only one of the few wise men living on earth, but a master who has enriched world literature as has no other living author."

Translating Buber was far more than a literary relaxation for Hammarskjold. He shared in Buber's philosophy of the open-hearted approach, the last hope for mankind. After twelve pages of "I and Thou," he might well have been working on the passage that declares, "All real living is meeting."

In Jerusalem in 1959, the Secretary General had sought out Martin Buber. The Sage of Jerusalem is in many ways a paradoxical figure. A Zionist from the start of the movement, Buber is a thorn in the side of Israeli nationalists. Though profoundly religious, he does not observe Jewish customs and virtues and will teasingly ring up his close friend Prof. Ernst Simon, who is observant, on a Sabbath when telephoning is avoided. A refugee from Nazism, Buber was among the first to resume active cultural contact with Germany by accepting the Goethe Prize in 1951.

He is equally difficult to classify in his work. It is even a question whether his first occupation is creative writing, though, counting translations into fourteen languages, some 860 volumes bear his name. That name became renowned in Germany in 1907 for the poetic retelling of the unique, mystical folktales of a then unknown sect with wonder-working rabbis, called Hasidim. Buber has also written a Hasidic novel, "For the Sake of Heaven." Far more numerous are his studies in sociology, education, psychology, philosophy and religion. All this work is crowned by a new translation into German of the Bible, carried on over thirty years, and so perfect that Hebrew scholars actually refer to Buber's German version to clarify difficult passages.

To meet Buber, Hammarskjold came to a modest house with a

vine-shaded porch, on "Love of Zion" Street. The door bears a brass plate with the name Martin Buber in Hebrew and English. It does not say "Prof.," much less "Herr Dr. Prof."

The door is likely to be opened by a sturdy housewife, Buber's granddaughter, Mrs. Barbara Goldschmidt. A widower since 1958, he lives with the Goldschmidts and their two youngsters— his great-grandchildren, Tamar, 11, and Gideon, 9. Barbara tactfully watches over him, so that he does not give himself too readily to the tourists and admirers who feel that a visit to the Sage of Jerusalem comes with a trip to Israel. She has a loving humor about the great man, and relates how, lately, she had to whisk him to the barber's because, she noticed, he had let his hair grow until the side ringlets gave him the look of a Hasidic rabbi!

Buber's study opens off the wide, old-fashioned central hallway with its round family dining table. He is unexpectedly quite short, like David Ben-Gurion, and with a small paunch, permitted to his 83 years. The sunlight from the room's single window streams through his white hair and beard; one looks directly into his warm golden eyes, as one may look, late in the day, directly into the sun, feeling peace.

His hands are very small, unwrinkled, pink. He uses them in quick gestures. He can talk three or four hours at a stretch, unwearied. Indeed, he confesses that he has always liked to talk rather than write. His talk is not mere discussion. Buber feels "a deep readiness to respond with his whole life," in every confrontation.

Young people, some of them former students, and German students on visit to Israel, seek him out. "I must take upon myself the life problem of each one." There happens, in such a discussion, the "dialogic moment." This is not the one-way wisdom-giving of a saintly Hasidic rabbi, a saddik. Buber's is the "I and Thou" attitude in which the "I" strives always to respond to the other person as a very special person, a "Thou" rather than a "he," "she" or "it."

Prophet? One of his closest followers, Prof. Hugo Bergman, says: "No; the prophets spoke with the word of God. But he is in the tradition of the prophets. Perhaps most like Jeremiah."

Like Jeremiah, Buber has never hesitated to sound unpopular views. Instead of showing himself warningly in the streets of Jerusalem with a yoke on his shoulders, he is more likely to issue a mimeographed statement. Today, it will probably be sponsored by Ihud, the group that speaks for unity with the Arab world. With its professorial élite, Ihud is listened to as the voice of idealism, though Buber, like all idealists, maintains that his program is plain realism.

He has cried out for such unity since his membership on a Zionist political commission in 1923. While still in Germany he joined the movement for a bi-national state, headed by the president of the Hebrew University, Dr. Judah Magnes. Though contact with Arabs has become almost hopeless, Buber at 82 journeyed to the Mediterranean Colloquium in Florence; there he met the Egyptian delegate, George Henein. "It was a real talk, in which we tried to pierce the hard core of the political sphere. Yes, I say it is still, it is always, possible in human terms."

Recently, when Ben-Gurion declared there could be no return of Arab refugees to Israel, Buber promptly issued an Ihud declaration calling for a softer attitude, though conceding that security had to be observed. Ben-Gurion is sensitive to Buber's opinions. Last year a large number of professors signed a statement warning of Ben-Gurion's dictatorial attitude in refusing to accept his Cabinet's decision in the controversial "Lavon affair." Ben-Gurion is said to have reacted only after Martin Buber had signed. "He, too!"

Piqued, he withdrew from an important educational committee on which Buber is still active, selecting classics for translation into Hebrew. Members of this committee, incidentally, testify to Buber's intense practicality. "He is the only one who is down to earth when it comes to such things as printing costs and quality of paper." Indeed, if any one role sums up Buber's life activities, he is an educator—in the highest sense.

His "I and Thou" teaching stresses the creative bond between person and person, between man and God. His precise meaning for each word must be understood. A person is not merely an individual, but someone who has found and freed his true self. Nor, Buber tells us, is this self the same as in Kierkegaard's conception of the individual as "the single one," who seeks to free himself from all human entanglement so as to address himself only to God.

To Buber, each person attains his single identity in order to relate to other beings. A baby, he reminds us, does not know itself as an "I" until it reaches out to others. Each person becomes responsible for finding and freeing himself, so that he may offer a genuine relationship, a true "dialogue," to all within the universe. The "I" exists only as it exists with another being.

The word "with" is important, for it means a community of existence rather than the encounter of two isolated beings. Curiously the modern expression "to be with it" perfectly picks up Buber's meaning. "I and Thou" is easier to understand in its original "Ich und Du," since *"du"* is the special pronoun for the loved or exalted one. "Thou" has become archaic in English; but perhaps, in using "you" for everyone equally, we can come closer to Buber's ideal of treating every relationship fullheartedly as a "Thou."

Martin Buber was born in the Vienna of Sigmund Freud and Theodor Herzl; he, too, came from a middle-class Jewish family. The unfortunate divorce of his parents sent him, a child of 3, to live with his grandfather in the Polish city of Lvov.

Salomon Buber, while president of the Chamber of Commerce, was also a Talmudist, the first to apply the methods of modern scholarship to this wisdom literature. But while studying the Talmud with his grandfather, Martin also avidly read the poetry and novels gathered, in defiance of pious custom, by his grandmother. Thus, at 13, instead of presenting his *bar mizvah* synagogue dissertation on the scriptural portion of the week, Martin Buber offered a talk on Schiller.

A year later he gave up the daily prayer ritual, with its winding on of phylacteries. But on the Day of Atonement he is said to have prostrated himself in the synagogue, in guilt. That same year he came close to suicide because of a "mysterious and overwhelming compulsion" to visualize the "limiting brink of time— or its limitlessness." He was saved from this devouring mental conflict by reading Kant and coming to the idea of "an eternal far removed from the finite and the infinite."

It was this philosophy-riven boy who, at 17, returned to Vienna to enter the university. A few years later he wrote his doctor's thesis in Berlin, on Christian mysticism, the subject of Dag Hammarskjold's last known conversation.

But the spiritual Martin Buber was equally attracted to the active world of Zionism. A wave of pogroms in Russia had stirred the famous Viennese playwright, Theodor Herzl, to sound the call for a Jewish state. Buber, scarcely turned 20, hurried back to Vienna to edit the movement's paper, Die Welt. One of his writers was a brilliant aristocratic Catholic, Paula Winkler. Converted to Judaism on their marriage, raising their two children, she was to remain at his side for sixty years, becoming, meanwhile, a successful novelist under the name of George Munk.

In the Zionist movement, a tragic split developed. Buber was in the spiritual faction, believing a Jewish revival even more urgent than political nationhood. But Herzl, impelled by the needs of the refugees, urged immediate nationhood, if only in Uganda, a territory offered by the British as a "stopover" before Palestine. Buber was among those who cried, "No!"

Feeling bitterly misunderstood, Herzl died not long afterward. Martin Buber suddenly disappeared from his literary haunts. He went "home" to Poland. In the remote Jewish villages lived the Hasidim, whose grassroots Judaism had attracted him as a child. They worshiped with joy, with wordless song, with ecstatic dance. Each Hasid had his saddik, a rabbi whose purity of soul gave him divine wisdom. Miraculous, iridescent tales were told about the founder of the sect, Rabbi Israel ben Eliezer Baal-Shem— the Master of the Good Name.

Buber returned with these tales. Their profundity is glimpsed in the tale of the good Jew whose son, rather simple-minded, was set to herding sheep. On the Day of Atonement the boy, though unable to read the prayers, was brought to the synagogue. It was a dark, evil period. The Baal-Shem strove before the Ark in deepest concentration. For hours, the congregation prayed.

The shepherd boy nudged his father. He, too, wanted to pray. Suddenly he took his reed pipe from his pocket: a pure melody burst forth. The congregation cried out in horror, but the Baal-Shem turned, his face shining. "The boy's song has pierced the clouds of the Evil One," he declared, "and carried up our prayers directly to heaven!"

Buber's Hasidic tales had an amazing effect. They became a part not only of Jewish but of European culture. Judaism had a new respectability. Living in the Berlin suburb of Seelendorf, he founded Der Jude, a lofty magazine that attracted such writers as Jacob Wassermann and Arnold Zweig.

It also attracted a young religious genius, Franz Rosenzweig, who scored the "superficial atheistic theology" of Martin Buber. And one day, made sensitive by this criticism, Buber came to a turning.

Given to trancelike Hasidic absorption, he had become known as the Saddik of Seelendorf. Troubled souls brought him their problems. That day Buber was visited by a young man whom he knew only slightly. He felt that the young man had something to tell him, but he had just emerged from hours of absorption; he listened, politely enough, but contact was not established. The young man left without having spoken what was on his mind. Later Buber learned he had committed suicide.

Overwhelmed, Buber felt he had not "turned to the other." Franz Rosenzweig was right. What he practiced was religiosity, not religion. A new seeking began. The result was "I and Thou," the philosophy of responsibility.

Published in 1923, "I and Thou" was slowly to penetrate world thinking. His "dialogic" approach even faced the danger of becoming an intellectual fad when a London group advertised sessions devoted to "Buberian dialogue." But today, his philosophy stands out clearly as the credo of the individual responsibility in a world where people tend to abdicate before the monolithic will of the party, the corporation, the state.

A Hasidic tale epitomizes this point. The aged saddik Rabbi Susya became fearful as death drew near. His friends chided him, "What! Are you afraid you'll be reproached that you weren't Moses?" "No. That I was not Susya."

The responsibility to be one's self means that there is no rigid fate. Thus, mutable "dialogue" stands in opposition to immutable "dialectics." Where Marx's dialectic materialism declares that economic laws are inevitable, Buber's human dialogue declares that change is possible. The argument doesn't concern capitalism versus communism, for Buber himself was an early organizer of the Socialist labor-pioneering movement in Palestine. The argument reaches from dialogue and dialectics to community and collectivism.

"Collectivism is based on the organized atrophy of personal existence," he wrote in "Between Man and Man." "Massed, mingling, marching collectives, individuals packed together, and armed and equipped in common, with only as much life from man to man as will inflame the marching step * * *." In contrast, "Community is the being no longer side by side, but with one another."

With the emergence of his "I and Thou" philosophy, Buber was appointed professor of the philosophy of religion at Frankfurt University. Then he began, with Franz Rosenzweig, their monumental translation of the Bible. Whereas Luther's translation had sought to make the Hebrew as German as possible, they sought to make the German as Hebrew as possible, rendering the very cadence and sound of the original. Suffering from paralysis, Rosenzweig died in 1929; Buber carried on.

In 1933, as the Nazis came to power, he was dismissed from the university. But when German schools were closed to Jews, Buber was burdened with the sudden task of creating an entire Jewish school system. During the ensuing five years his role was heroic. Many German Jewish survivors ascribe to Buber's efforts their ability to resist madness and suicide. Steadfastly, Buber with the late Rabbi Leo Baeck, continued the Jewish adult-education program begun by Franz Rosenzweig, instilling self-respect into a community labeled subhuman.

Daringly, in 1935, he lectured in the Berlin Philharmonic on "The Power of the Spirit," knowing two hundred S.S. men were present. Then, barred from speaking at public functions or before Jewish organizations, he spoke to groups assembled in the home of a Frankfurt Quaker, Rudolph Schlosser. But finally, in 1938, utterly silenced, he agreed to be brought out, to Palestine.

The rescue committee at the Hebrew University pondered whether to give him a chair in sociology, religion or philosophy, as he was qualified for all. He became professor of social philosophy and entered at once into polemics.

Palestine had for three years suffered from raids and murders by the Mufti's Arab terrorists. Young Jews had begun to retaliate. "If we cannot save ourselves from the wolves, let us not become wolves ourselves!" the newcomer, Buber, wrote in a flaming appeal. "It is for us to instill courage into the well-intentioned Arabs."

He went to live in an Arab house in the exposed quarter of Dir Abu Tor. With fervor, he still recalls the dawn view of the purple hills of Moab from his balcony. When years of meditative effort proved futile, and the Arabs attacked newborn Israel, the Bubers were evacuated by a Christian minister. Buber's invaluable library had to be left behind. His Arab landlord protected it from looting by Iraqi troops. "Are you barbarians? This is the library of a great, wise man!" he cried.

Shortly afterward, the area was retaken by Israelis, and Buber's granddaughter, with a unit of Hagana boys, brought out the 20,000 volumes, including the world's largest collection of Hasidic material.

Becoming professor emeritus in 1951, Buber embarked, past 70, on a lecture tour of America. Some say he is ostentatious in his simplicity. He travels in Israel by public bus and, in the United States, friends found him in a walk-up student hotel in Boston.

Old age, he says, has taught him much, "Of course, life is more difficult, but one learns to know an entirely new dimension of being. In the last five or six years I have learned things in a sphere I didn't know before."

Our greatest problem is to confront the urge to self-destruction. "We must not feel hopeless. If every man of goodwill will do what is in his power, then there is no dark fate. I think about this atomic situation all the time, every day." His eyes suddenly attain an other-worldly clarity, and one feels one's self indeed a Hasid, sitting before his saddik.

"Here, in Hammarskjold—he sat where you sit—I saw a man of goodwill who tried to do something, but he was abandoned. Doing his utmost, Hammarskjold still lacked the technical means to carry out his peace mission, and so he was martyred in his death."

The master's words sink to a whisper, but suddenly he raises his head, having divined a last, unuttered question. Only the thread of unspoken dialogue links one subject to the other. "I have told myself if they condemn Eichmann to death, I'll have to ask for commutation, one way or another."

On what basis?

His eyes open wider. He springs up. "Under the commandment 'Thou shalt not kill.' This remains in power, not only for the individual but for society. Society is composed of men; it has the right to defend itself, but not to kill."

His voice becomes almost plaintive. "The spirit of man is in a tragic situation today. The right thing is to know this, and to go on working because—a surprise may come. After so many bitter surprises—a good one!" His eyes light. "As long as I have force in myself, I am ready to help."

Chief Prophet of the Existentialists

by John L. Brown

BY MIDAFTERNOON every day the offices of Modern Times (Les Temps Modernes), the Existentialist monthly on the rue Sebastien-Bottin, start filling up. There are students from the Sorbonne, wearing full beards and threadbare overcoats; literary ladies who bring along their knitting; a sprinkling of notorious Left Bank dead beats, bent on borrowing a few hundred francs; journalists looking for interviews; visitors from abroad, speaking French with a variety of accents—Anglo-Saxon, Scandinavian, Balkan.

They all want to see M. Sartre.

By 5 there is not an empty chair in the place. Even the tables are occupied. The air is heavy with smoke, buzzing with intellectual discussion. Around 5:30 or 6, a short, hatless figure—beginning to grow bald, a man pale, blondish, blinking behind horn-rimmed glasses—slips into the room. The conversation halts for a moment, everyone rushes over to greet the newcomer and tries to catch his eye or ear. It is Jean-Paul Sartre, Existentialist-in-

From the *New York Times Magazine,* February 2, 1947, copyright © 1947 by the New York Times Company.

Chief. Five years ago he taught philosophy in a Paris lycée. Today he is the most discussed intellectual and literary man in France.

Sartre's glance is sharp, analytical, responsive. He is bundled up in a coat acquired during his lecture tour in the United States and in an enormous knitted scarf of a type that is a uniform along the Boul' Mich'. His coat pockets bulge with papers. As he talks, rapidly and well, he gestures with his pipe. Since he became an international celebrity, equally known for his philosophical writings, his plays and his novels, he is bombarded with all sorts of requests. In the midst of the hubbub he has retained a vaguely professorial manner, good humor, a willingness to listen and a rare accessibility.

In the office Sartre takes time to shake hands with his friend—fresh, handsome Simone de Beauvoir—like himself a philosopher-novelist. She is preparing to leave on a lecture tour of the United States. With her is Michel Leiris, poet and anthropologist, who came to Existentialism by way of Surrealism.

About 7:30 Sartre and his friends adjourn to the near-by bar of the Hotel Pont-Royal. Notes are taken, manuscripts scrutinized. An enormous amount of handshaking goes on—for in this most literary of Parisian bars, everyone knows (or would like to give the impression of knowing) everybody else.

Sartre, with a drink before him, can calmly proceed to the correction of an article, apparently undisturbed by the buzzing about him. This faculty comes from long practice. Sartre's life has been that of the unattached intellectual of the Left Bank, a life divided between the hotel room where he sleeps and the cafe table where he reads, writes, drinks, receives his friends. It is a classic pattern that permits almost complete intellectual liberty and detachment and affords a freedom from social and family obligations that is rarely possible elsewhere. It has left an indelible mark on the life and productions of Sartre.

His philosophical career began at the Ecole Normale Supérieure, behind the Panthéon, which has the reputation of being one of the "toughest" schools in France. There he prepared to take the competitive state examination, the "agrégation" required for all those who wish to teach in the lycées. The majority of the candidates fail. Sartre took first place in the agrégation in philosophy in 1929. Simone de Beauvoir was second.

He was immediately appointed professor of philosophy in the lycée at Le Havre. He remained for several years, reading prodigiously, laying the foundations for future philosophical and literary works, studying the German philosophers like Husserl and Heidegger (then almost completely unknown in France).

He didn't like Le Havre. He wanted to get back to Paris. By the mid-Thirties he was teaching at the Lycée Condorcet, near the Gare Saint-Lazare. He happily resumed his existence as an unattached intellectual of the Latin Quarter. His teaching duties were not heavy, he had time for reading and writing, for discussions with friends. He lived in a small hotel on the rue de Seine, one of the most picturesque of Paris streets, filled with book stores, antique shops and art galleries. A few years hence this rundown, unpretentious Hotel Louisiana may be marked with an official plaque designating it as "the cradle of French Existentialism."

From the rue de Seine to the cafes of Saint-Germain-des-Prés is only a step. In French literary history of the twentieth century, the cafe has the same importance as the salon in the eighteenth. The Deux Magots, Lipp's and the Flore serve as library, study, open forum, reception room for the "men of letters" of the neighborhood. Any number of "isms" have been born on their *terrasses* in the past three generations. Indeed, the Latin Quarter cafe is as sacred a thing as an English club. Chosen after deep reflection, it demands undivided fidelity. Sartre and his friends chose the Flore, just beside the Deux Magots, as their headquarters. He could be found there at almost any hour of the day or night, writing away at his table in the rear.

Sartre was seriously scholarly; but his life did not resemble that of the learned recluse or the retiring professor. He was the type of professor that would have disturbed boards of education. For he haunted the night clubs of Montmartre and Montparnasse; he studied not only the German Existentialists but also the curious forms of life that exist on the fringes of intellectual and artistic Paris—prostitutes, amateur and professional, pederasts, barmen, bums, traffickers in "coco." They all appear in the pages of his novel, "The Age of Reason."

"The Age of Reason"—like Simone de Beauvoir's "The Invited" (L'Invitée)—might almost be regarded as a *roman à clef*. It is said to be freely inspired by the activities of that eccentric group known to connoisseurs of social phenomena of the quartier Saint-Germain-des-Prés as "the band of the Hotel Louisiana." Sartre and his disciples lived at the Louisiana together, shared ideas, money, emotions and mistresses. Summers they sunbathed *en slip* on the roof, while listening to American jazz records. Winters they danced at the *bal nègre,* did the night clubs, dreamed of writing novels that would rival Faulkner and Caldwell in violence. Sartre himself did an essay about Faulkner for the Nouvelle Revue Française in 1938. His admiration for American novelists—especially Dos Passos, Faulkner and Caldwell—is clear from the tone and technique of his own fiction.

It was the heroic, Bohemian period of Existentialism. No compromise with convention was permitted. Simone de Beauvoir circulated in an original costume, half Alpine, half Boul' Mich'—heavy hiking shoes, rolled wool stockings, a scarf tied about her head. Sartre roamed the neighborhood chewing his pipe, clad in an ancient sheepskin.

But that was quite a while ago. Sartre is now a pontiff, Simone de Beauvoir a well-groomed literary lady who has abandoned hand-knitted hose for the sheerest of nylons. And the wild and unconsidered teen-agers of the band of the Louisiana win literary prizes and movie contracts.

Now that they are respectable and well heeled, the old defiance and desperation are going out of them. Steam heat and modern plumbing have lured them away from the cold and not very clean Louisiana. The age of scandal is over, they are making their peace with society, and who knows but that Sartre may end up in the French Academy and Simone de Beauvoir in the Collège de France?

But it was during the disordered and faintly disreputable period of the Louisiana that both of them were composing the books that have made their reputation. Sartre, in addition to his purely philosophical works, was beginning to write, in the mid-Thirties, fiction which "illustrated" his abstract ideas. His collection of short stories, "The Wall," made something of a stir when it appeared. Even more remarkable was his first novel (if novel it can be called) entitled "Nausea."

When the war broke out, Sartre was mobilized as a private. He was taken prisoner, spent several months in a PW camp, was released, returned to the Paris of the Occupation. He took up his old round of life, returned to the Louisiana, went back to his old table at the Flore. In avant garde circles people began to discuss Existentialism, and the publication in 1943 of Sartre's principal theoretical work, "Being and Nothingness" (L'Etre et le Néant)—720 dense, often confused pages—consecrated him as a "serious thinker."

It was dedicated to "Castor," the name by which Simone de Beauvoir was known in the band of the Louisiana. Although much talked about, it remains largely unread even by his admirers, who prefer his novels and his plays. Reviewers, intimidated by its bulk and its professional jargon, passed it over in silence. Some scholars tend to discount its importance, rating it as a French adaptation of Heidegger's "Being and Time" (Sein und Zeit) rather than as a deeply original contribution.

Ever since "The Wall" and "Nausea," discerning critics had singled out Sartre as the most promising newcomer in the Gallimard publishing stable. But his name did not become known to the general public until the production of his play on the Orestes theme, "The Flies" (1943), which, under its mythological trappings, was an eloquent appeal for human liberty. At the same time he was collaborating with clandestine papers like Les Lettres Francaises and Combat. One of the best accounts of the liberation of Paris is Sartre's reportage in the first "overground" numbers of Combat. Another of his plays, a one-acter, "No Exit," was presented at the Vieux Columbier during the war. It is still running there. In New York, on the other hand, "No Exit," while praised by the critics, ran for only a matter of weeks.

In Paris, by 1944, Existentialism had ceased to be the property of a few philosophers and literary men and became a public possession, the theme for sermons on the evil of our times, a subject of popular controversy. Lectures by Sartre occasioned fisticuffs and the intervention of the police. Everyone talked about Existentialism, but very few had any notion what it was.

Even today, the number of those who can define Existentialism are few compared with those who talk about it. Existentialism is a vision of a man as a stranger in the universe—a stranger to himself and to others. The Sartre brand of Existentialist is an atheist who sees man as helpless, flung without knowing how or why into a world he cannot understand, endowed with liberty ("Man is liberty," says Sartre flatly) which he may betray but which he cannot deny, to make his way as best he can in fear and trembling, in uncertainty and anguish.

"Anguish," which to Sartre is interchangeable with "nausea," is a key word in the Existentialist vocabulary. Much emphasized, too, is the belief that man cannot achieve an objective, certain understanding of this world he never made. Thus "Existentialist man" asserts that there is no general philosophic system which can explain the universe and no such thing as human nature, "since there is no God to conceive it a priori." Existentialism holds that the problem of "What is man?" can only be approached subjectively, and that each man defines himself in action.

Sartre does not claim that Existentialism sprang full-born from him. On the contrary, all good Existentialists point to ancestors. They note that Socrates employed a subjective approach to the question of human existence in distinction to the formalized methods of the Sophists. They note that the seventeenth-century Frenchman Blaise Pascal questioned the reality of philosophic systems.

In the "Pensées," Pascal set down a passage that sounds like good Existentialist doctrine: "When I consider the brief span of my life, swallowed up in eternity past and to come, the little space that I occupy, lost in the immensity of space of which I know nothing and which knows nothing of me, I am terrified and I am astonished that I am here rather than there, that I am now rather than then. By whose order and by whose action have this place and this time been destined for me? Everyone has at some time shared this anguish. But he usually succeeds in stifling it in business, or pleasure, or the daily routine."

The real genealogy of Existentialism, however, begins with the nineteenth rather than the seventeenth century, and with a mystical Danish pastor, Sören Kierkegaard, rather than with the French Pascal. Kierkegaard could not accept the rational abstractions of a philosopher like Hegel. To Hegel's objective and systematic logic Kierkegaard opposed a vision of the human condition as essentially tragic and lonely, of the world as absurd, of reason as weak and fallible.

Where Sartre and his followers break with Kierkegaard—and, for that matter, with Pascal—is over the question of Christianity. Pascal, believing in salvation, spoke of "the wretchedness of man without God." Kierkegaard passionately insisted: "Christianity came into the world as an absolute and not, as human reason would like to imagine, as a consolation."

The atheistic Existentialists rejected Kierkegaard's belief in God but accepted his conception of life as disorder. In Nietzsche they found another master. The German philosopher's apocalyptic sense of desolation and despair fitted in very well with their vision of the world and experience.

Today, as Sartre pointed out in a pamphlet written in 1945, "there are two kinds of Existentialists. The first are Christians, and among them we may situate Jaspers [Karl Jaspers, professor of philosophy at Heidelberg] and Gabriel Marcel [Parisian playwright and composer]. The others, atheistic Existentialists, such as Heidegger [Martin Heidegger, who made his reputation as a professor of philosophy at Freiburg] and myself. Both groups believe that existence precedes essence or, if you wish, that you have to start with subjectivity."

From the moment that Existentialism won popular attention it was attacked from both the Left and the Right. Communists found Existentialism the expression of a decadent bourgeois culture, the philosophy of a hopeless, unhealthy world.

Conservative Christians attacked Sartre's brand of Existentialism because of its uncompromising atheism, its denial of transcendent values, its obsession with perversion, and moral and physical ugliness. Clerics called his doctrines "materialistic."

Sartre denies that his philosophy is one of blank despair. He maintains that Existentialism inspires man to positive action, in giving him the full measure of his liberty and in refusing to permit refuge in false security. Sartre's thought, however representative it may be of shattered post-war Europe, by no means constitutes a closed and finished whole. It is in constant development and consequently full of contradictions. At the heart of his thought is the concept of man as liberty, man who has full freedom to create himself and his values as he wills. Yet simultaneously he insists on total responsibility, total "engagement," which automatically curtails this liberty.

Sartre's spiritual drama is by no means yet played out. He is just over 40, in vigorous production, and it will be interesting to see how he will resolve this contradiction between total engagement and total liberty, between positive action and the non-existence of positive values. Is human life possible in a world of unrelieved nausea? Is man capable of hope and action in a world of despair?

As Sartre develops, as he continues to live and write, he seems to be moving away from the sterile nihilism of Heidegger. He has interested himself deeply in the problems of our time, insists that the artist and the writer must commit themselves, that they cannot hope to remain neutral.

His trip to the United States in 1945 had immediate repercussions in his work. On his return he wrote "The Deferential Prostitute," now playing on the same bill at the Théâtre Antoine with his drama about the French Resistance, "The Unburied Dead." "The Deferential Prostitute," an examination of the race question in America, has aroused a good deal of controversy.

He has also devoted a special number of Modern Times to the United States. "In America," he notes, "the myth of liberty coexists with a dictatorship of public opinion; the myth of economic liberalism with monster corporations which embrace a continent, which finally belong to no one, where everyone works from top to bottom, like employes in a nationalized industry. The respect for science, for industry, for positivism and a fanatical delight in the gadget go hand-in-hand with the grim humor of The New Yorker, which makes bitter fun of a mechanical civilization and of the 100 million Americans who try to satisfy their need for the marvelous by reading the incredible adventures of Superman or Mandrake the Magician. * * * Nowhere else in the world does there exist such a contrast between men and myths, between real life and the collective representation of it."

Unlike many Frenchmen who have visited America, Sartre does not find that the United States is capable of offering a solution to Europe's problems. Nor does he see a solution in Russia. Sartre feels that the new synthesis capable of restoring war-shattered Europe has not yet manifested itself.

Part 3

CONTEMPORARY PSYCHOLOGY AND ANTHROPOLOGY

It may very well be that the difficulties inherent in modern psychology stem from its self-conception as a "life," or biological, science rather than as an offshoot of philosophy. That psychologists have forgotten their roots in philosophy may be deplored, for they might have otherwise retained a sense of humility about the nature of man instead of adopting an omnipotent arrogance more appropriate to a primitive shaman. Or the difficulties may simply come from failure to agree on what the subject matter of the discipline really is—mind, or instincts, or physiological responses, or perhaps how animals behave. The great failing among many psychologists is the assumption that human consciousness can be reduced to biological responses, an assumption that could only have been employed because they were baffled by the self and the human mind. The mind may be difficult to study, but that hardly supplies a reason to run off into the laboratory to study an "animal display of hustle and pep."

The work of the anthropologist is important as a framework

for comprehending the whole of a culture. If work, ritual, play, and leisure once made up an integral whole, it is important to contrast that early experience with man's present fragmented existence. The concept of culture enables us to make such a comparison. It casts up the centrality of language, symbols, and custom and reveals that we were thinking animals *before* we became tool-making ones. Even more important, anthropologists have been in a sense liberators, teaching us to respect the total experience of man.

Skinner Agrees He Is the Most Important Influence in Psychology

by Berkeley Rice

ON A Sunday afternoon some weeks ago, Burrhus Frederic Skinner and 50 million other American football fans sat in front of their television sets as the Green Bay Packers mauled the Oakland Raiders in the Super Bowl. Like most of his countrymen, Skinner drank a beer as he watched the game, and had little to say to his wife. But unlike the rest of us, who were following nothing more complex than pass patterns and linebackers, Skinner was musing upon the contingencies of reinforcement that govern our behavior as watchers of football games. In layman's terms, reinforcement is the excitement or pleasure one gets from watching a football game. The contingencies of this reinforcement are the arrangement of the events of the game in such a way as to cause the most excitement and thereby hold the viewers' attention.

"It's beautiful," exclaimed Skinner, who is a connoisseur of such art. "They have all these events scheduled just the way we do in the laboratory."

Burrhus Frederic Skinner's thoughts on the contingencies of

From the *New York Times Magazine,* March 17, 1968, copyright © 1968 by The New York Times Company.

reinforcement and human behavior may not interest the average football fan, but they are of such interest to psychologists that in a recent survey of department chairmen at American univer· sities Harvard's Professor Skinner was chosen overwhelmingly as the most influential figure in modern psychology. The magazine Psychology Today goes further, predicting that "when history makes its judgment, he will be known as the major contributor to psychology in this century." Skinner, whose business is making predictions, considers this one accurate.

Skinner's contribution consists of turning the study of behavior into an objective science. By experimenting with positive and negative reinforcement on laboratory animals, he has learned to predict and control their behavior. His "Skinner box," in which the experiments were carried out, is now standard equipment for most studies of animal behavior, and his books on the subject are standard reading for most psychology students. Nor are Skinner's contributions limited to the world of pure science. His novel, "Walden Two," about a utopian society based on the "scientific" control of human behavior, has sold nearly a half-million copies. As the "father" of programed instruction and the inventor of the teaching machine, both of which are based on his studies of the learning process, he is responsible for what many experts are calling a revolution in American education.

Like most revolutionaries, Skinner has his critics, for while his contributions to psychology and education have brought him the respect of scientists around the world, they have also brought him the enmity of many humanists. They look on him as the archetype of the cold-blooded scientist for whom man is simply a machine that can be trained to do his—or anyone's—bidding. Skinner's followers endure such criticism with patronizing tolerance and dismiss it as ignorant and naive. With the reverence and devotion of disciples, they claim that Skinner will never be fully understood or appreciated in our time.

In the beginning, psychology was a vague mixture of metaphysics and philosophy. It did not emerge as a separate discipline until late in the 19th century, and even then it was not a science in the modern sense of the term. William James's studies of human consciousness and Sigmund Freud's investigations into the subconscious were fruitful but relatively subjective. For them and their followers psychology was the study of the inner processes of the mind, and since these processes were, and still are, invisible and unquantifiable, speculation on them is necessarily subjective and, in this sense, unscientific.

Today, although there are still many Freudian psychologists around, most psychologists are trying to discover the inner workings of the mind through the study of external behavior. In an attempt to achieve the respectability of the physical sciences, which deal with visible or at least measurable data, psychologists have turned their attention to man's behavior, which is at least visible, if not always measurable.

The father of "behaviorism," as this new science became known, was John B. Watson, a professor at Johns Hopkins who in 1914 declared that psychology should be a "purely objective," experimental branch of science. He rejected the subjective concepts of intelligence, thought, purpose, emotion and personality as unscientific, claiming that man's behavior consisted only of physical reflexes to environmental stimuli. (In this view, he was drawing upon Pavlov's studies in conditioned reflex.) To Watson, the goal of psychology was the prediction and control of behavior. By 1924 he was so confident of achieving such control that he claimed: "Give me a dozen healthy infants, well-formed, and my own specified world to bring them up in, and I'll guarantee to take any one at random and train him to become any type of specialist I might select—doctor, lawyer, artist, merchant chief and yes, even beggarman and thief. . . ."

This sort of talk did not endear Watson to the mothers of America, but it did attract the attention of other psychologists. One of them was B. F. Skinner, as he is known to the trade, who established himself as one of the country's leading behaviorists with the publication of "Behavior of Organisms" in 1938. But unlike other followers of Watson, who studied behavior in order to discover the workings of the mind, Skinner restricted himself to the study of external behavior. As he explains today, "I never make any conclusions about what is going on inside the organism, either mental or physiological. I don't mean to say there may not be internal processes going on. They're simply not needed for a study of behavior."

What is needed, according to Skinner, is merely his "operant conditioning apparatus"—his Skinner box, containing a food dispenser operated by a lever. A rat kept in a Skinner box gradually learns that by pressing the lever he will receive a pellet of food. A "cumulative record" charts his responses on a graph and thus makes his behavior and—according to Skinner—his learning process "visible" to the researcher. By experimenting with deprivation, satiation and other variables, the researcher can learn to control the rat's behavior by a system of positive and negative reinforcement.

Since the nineteen-thirties, the Skinner box has evolved from simple relays, timers and counters to an elaborate electronic apparatus utilizing solid-state circuitry and computers. In increasingly complex experiments, Skinnerian researchers have examined the behavior of rats, pigeons, monkeys and other small animals. They have worked with multiple and occasionally conflicting stimuli and multiple responses. Skinner himself claims that such laboratory environments can now approach the subtlety and complexity of conditions to be found in the human environment at large. Of course, most of this research has been conducted with rats and pigeons, since few human beings are willing to subject themselves to life in a Skinner box or any other suitably controlled environment. Because of this limitation, many critics doubt that Skinner's theories of animal behavior can be applied to human beings.

One of the most vocal of these critics is the popular philosopher Arthur Koestler, who accuses Skinner of "the ratomorphic fallacy"—attributing to man only those mental processes that can be shown to occur in lower animals.

Skinner scoffs at such criticism. "It's not a question of getting people to subject themselves to proper laboratory conditions. The world at large is a laboratory. Take the people in Las Vegas, pulling levers on slot machines. They are in a laboratory situation, and very willingly. The slot machines simply use a schedule of conditioning and reinforcement similar to those we use in the laboratory—with money dropping down the chute instead of food. Of course, pigeons aren't people, but it's only a matter of complexity, and we're learning the differences now."

"But can you *prove* that the contingencies of reinforcement work in society the same way they do in your laboratory?" I asked.

"Well, we have used them successfully with mental patients and programed instruction," Skinner replied, "but you don't have to prove all this. If you've studied contingencies long enough in the laboratory, you get to the point that you can see them operating in society. You don't need proof. Just as the physical scientist doesn't need proof of the theories of trajectory, elasticity and gravity each time he sees a tennis ball bouncing."

"Have you run experiments on human beings in which you also had control groups who were not conditioned?"

"Well, with the teaching machines we've been able to compare their effect with the performance of similar classes who have not used them, but the whole idea of control groups is silly in research like this. You don't need them. The success of such experiments is immediately obvious. When you get a new washing machine, you don't wash the clothes by hand every other week as a control test on the efficiency of the washer, do you?"

The performance of a washing machine may not be perfectly analogous to the performance of a human being, but some recent social applications of behavioral techniques have definitely been striking successes. One such took place in a psychiatric hospital where the attendants were having an increasingly difficult time getting the patients to come for meals—it was taking nearly an hour to herd the stubborn psychotics out of their wards and down to the dining hall.

A group of behavioral psychologists solved the problem without the aid of any attendants. They began by waiting 20 minutes after the dinner bell, and then locking the door to the dining hall. The first time only a few patients made it. The rest went hungry. After a few days, everyone was arriving in the dining hall before the door closed. Then the time was gradually cut down until after a few weeks everyone was in the dining hall five minutes after the bell rang.

"What happened there is quite simple," says Skinner. "People in psychiatric wards are generally bored and ignored, and they have almost no control over their environment. When the dinner bell rings, it gives them a chance to annoy the guards. It's simply an opportunity to get attention. Once you realize this, it's easy to correct the situation. You simply shift from one kind of reinforcement—annoying the guards and getting attention—to another— eating when you're hungry. This could be criticized as a form of sadism, but it's really not. The patients are going in quickly now because they want to. And they're walking in with dignity, rather than being pushed in like cattle."

Getting people to respond to bells, even for worthwhile purposes, may seem to some humanists alarmingly similar to Pavlov's conditioning of dogs to salivate at the sound of a bell. Skinner is accustomed to such fears, and resents those who confuse him with the stimulus-response school of psychology. Both Skinner and "the S-R boys," as he calls them, claim that behavior consists only of physical responses to environmental stimuli—but Skinner's concept of the relation between behavior and environment is far more complex. By experimenting with various schedules, or patterns, of reinforcement, he has developed a sophisticated analysis of response based on a system of probabilities. Armed with this methodology, the Skinnerian psychologist can predict the probability of response to any given stimulus and use this knowledge to condition and control behavior to a degree beyond the dreams of Pavlov.

About Freud, Skinner says: "He made some marvelous discoveries about the effects of childhood incidents on later behavior, but he had to invent a complex mental apparatus—the id, ego and superego—to connect the early stimulus to subsequent behavior. All this was really unnecessary. It's all governed by the same laws of positive and negative reinforcement."

Skinner realizes that behavior is the result of genetic as well as environmental influences, but since he cannot observe and control genetics the way he can environment, he is willing to leave genetic research to biologists.

Because of his refusal to consider the internal processes that accompany behavior, many psychologists who do so have a low opinion of Skinner's research. This does not bother him particularly. "Their approach simply destines them to inadequacy and failure," says Skinner. He is understanding about their unwillingness to adopt his own approach. "That's to be expected, of course. They have invested a great deal in certain lines of research, and you can't expect them to admit that they have been wasting their time and have thrown away their lifework." No one has ever accused Skinner of excessive humility. Asked what he thinks of several current movements in psychology besides his own, he replies, "Well, I don't really see much of anything interesting going on."

With such attitude toward the work of his peers, it is only natural that their criticism is also of no interest to Skinner. I asked one of his graduate students whether his professor suffers criticism gladly. "He receives criticism," replied the young man, "but I don't think he suffers much." When M.I.T. linguistics professor Noam Chomsky wrote a scathing review of Skinner's book "Verbal Behavior," causing considerable commotion in academic circles, Skinner did not deign to reply. "I read a bit of it," he says, "and saw that he missed the point, so I never read the rest. I never answer any of my critics. I generally don't even read them. There are better things to do with my time than clear up their misunderstanding."

In his seventh-floor office in William James Hall, overlooking Harvard Yard, Professor Skinner does not encounter much criticism. He receives a steady stream of visitors and telephone calls in search of advice, interviews, or simply the chance to meet someone who has achieved historical greatness in his own time. As a result of this stature, he carries on a voluminous correspondence with scientific societies, other psychology professors, former students (many of whom are now full professors themselves) and people in public life.

At the age of 63 (he will be 64 on Wednesday), Skinner measures his time and energy carefully, for he has had a lifetime of research and there is much he wants to get down in writing. He stopped active research a few years ago, and since then has given only occasional seminars at Harvard. His seminar this year in "verbal behavior" was limited to about a dozen graduate and undergraduate students. "They're a marvelous group," says Skinner of his students. "They're doing things in the laboratory that I can't even follow."

Though he speaks of them with the pride of a father, Skinner subjects his students to the same rigid discipline that he applies to himself. When they gave oral presentations of their final reports, a few weeks ago, he kept them to precisely 15 minutes each. To insure their compliance he used a timer whose quite audible ticking was so disconcerting they complained about it. "They find it abusive," said Skinner, "so I've stopped using it. But I still use the wall clock. I think the pressure's good for them."

Whenever a student approached the end of his time without approaching the end of his report, Skinner smiled and held up his hand. "You have one minute left," he told a nervous young man who was speaking on the confusion of verbal stimuli in free-association word tests. The student stopped short, and looked up unbelievingly at the wall clock. "All right," said Skinner, "I'll make it a minute and a half, since you have spent a half-minute looking at the clock." This generosity did not help much, and the student finished in disarray. In case he was in doubt about it, Skinner told him as he sat down, "I don't think you got around to making your point."

Despite such classroom methods, Skinner's genuine interest in and respect for the work of his students have earned him their devotion. After class I found several of them engaged in a bull session in a room down the hall from his office. Gerbils rustled among the shavings of their wire cages, and a dartboard on the wall displayed a baleful, pock-marked visage of L.B.J. Asked about Skinner's concern for precision in class, one student said, "He's often painted as the cold-hearted scientist, but in fact, he's one of the most humanistic men I've ever known."

"Do you like being called Skinnerians?" I asked.

"Sure. His theories are very adaptable. And besides, he's right, and the others are wrong."

Prof. Richard Herrnstein, a former graduate student under Skinner and now chairman of Harvard's psychology department, does not feel the "others" are wrong, but he does feel that Skinner's work is of awesome importance. "He's amazing," says Herrnstein. "He really is. I think he's a genius. His contribution is gigantic—one of Copernican dimensions."

"What exactly is his contribution?"

"Skinner did what no one had done before. He made the study of behavior objective. Watson changed psychology from the study of the mind to the study of behavior, but Skinner changed it to a science of behavior. The trouble with Fred, though, is he keeps skipping over from basic science into technological applications of his theories like teaching machines. Even 'Walden Two' is just engineering—human engineering."

Fred Skinner's excursions into technology may have offended the sensibilities of his fellow scientists, but they have also brought him a popularity—or infamy, depending on your point of view—that few scientists ever achieve. He first came to public attention in 1945, through an article in the Ladies' Home Journal in which he described an invention he calls the "aircrib." When Skinner and his wife Yvonne decided to have a second child, she told him that she did not mind bearing children, but that taking care of them during the first two years required an unreasonable amount of attention and menial labor. Skinner's reaction, as it is to any problem involving behavior he considers inefficient or unreasonable, was that he could design a way to do it better.

His aircrib is a large, air-conditioned, temperature-controlled, germ-free, soundproof compartment in which a baby can sleep and play without blankets or clothing other than a diaper. It allows complete freedom of movement, and relative safety from the usual colds and heat rashes. It has a sliding glass window and an easily removed plastic sheet. Skinner claims that its time- and labor-saving features assure that mothers will be in a better humor when they remove the child for play.

Skinner raised his second daughter in the aircrib with what he terms complete success, but despite his confidence and its satisfactory use by several hundred adventurous parents (including his older daughter), the mothers of America have not adopted it. One reason may be that it has often been confused with the Skinner box of the animal lab. Many have written letters denouncing him for separating mother from child. Such response does not bother him, since he is willing to let time prove the worth of his creation.

"There is nothing natural about the ordinary crib," says Skinner. "It will probably disappear soon. It's only a small jail. At least the aircrib has a clear view, without bars."

Skinner does not feel that the aircrib solves all the problems of raising chilidren. "It only solves some of the simple physical problems. I despair of teaching the ordinary parent how to handle his child. They spank him when he does something wrong, instead of praising him for doing something right. They have no idea of the proper use of reinforcement. I would prefer to turn child-raising over to specialists." (In his utopia, "Walden Two," he does just that.)

Skinner's concern for using proper reinforcement in raising children led to his best-known invention—the teaching machine. Based on the results of his laboratory research, it is merely the application to education of his theory that the learning process can be controlled—and considerably speeded up—by a system of immediate positive and negative reinforcement. As with the aircrib, Skinner came to the teaching machine through personal experience. He was visiting his daughter's fourth-grade class, and was appalled by the way mathematics was being taught. "It's absolutely horrible," he told an associate who found him later that day, cutting holes in sheets of manila paper. "They're ruining minds over there. I can do something much better." And he did.

His teaching machine, as well as programed instruction in book form, allows a student to work on his own, and at his own pace, learning immediately whether his answers are right or wrong. Many teachers—usually before they see a teaching machine in use—have accused Skinner of trying to mechanize the classroom, but advocates of programed instruction argue that, like it or not, much necessary classroom work is tedious and mechanical. Skinner's machine lets the teacher devote her energies to more subtle forms of instruction such as discussion, enabling her to be a teacher instead of a machine.

Teaching machines of various kinds are in use all over the country today. But many educators have strong reservations about them. Douglas Porter, director of Harvard's Office of Programed Instruction, says, "Programed instruction is definitely the wave of future, but there's still a great deal of confusion. Most of the techniques have been developed, but they have not been properly applied. Most of the programs published commercially today are inadeqate."

Some educators blame Skinner for this state of affairs, but the blame is misplaced. With an extreme shortage of well-trained, competent program designers around ("Less than two dozen in the country today," according to Porter), commercial publishers find it much cheaper to produce mediocre programs than good ones. Since most public school administrators cannot tell the difference between a good one and a mediocre one, the publishers continue to produce and sell the latter.

The fact that Skinner has become known as an inventor would not surprise those who grew up with him in Susquehanna, a small town in northeastern Pennsylvania. As a youth, Skinner built the usual tops, blowguns, kites, model airplanes, scooters and wagons, but he also produced such marvels of engineering as a steam cannon, made from a discarded boiler, with which he could shoot plugs of potato and carrot over his neighbors' roofs. He revolutionized the gathering of elderberries among his comrades with a flotation system which separated the ripe ones from the green ones. And he designed an apparatus out of an atomizer bulb with which he blew hygienic smoke rings.

Skinner recalls his family with the same objective scrutiny that he devotes to any other subject. He describes his grandfather as an Englishman "who had not found just the work he wanted when he died at the age of 90." His father was a small-town lawyer who "suffered from his mother's ambitions all his life." Home for Skinner was warm and stable. He lived in the same house until he went to college, and graduated from the same high school his mother and father had attended.

At Hamilton College, in upper New York State, Skinner "never fit into student life." He found little intellectual companionship and felt the college was pushing him around with unnecessary requirements. An English major, he wrote articles, poetry and short stories. At a summer writing school in 1925, two of the short stories came to the attention of Robert Frost, who later wrote young Skinner that his stories contained "real niceties of observation" and "the touch of art," and that he was "worth twice anyone else I have seen in prose this year."

Such praise from Frost was enough for young Skinner. After finishing college with a Phi Beta Kappa key, he decided to become a writer. He spent two unfruitful years at this trade, including a six-month stretch in Greenwich Village, and made the unpleasant discovery that he had nothing worthwhile to say about human behavior. Hoping to remedy this situation, he embarked upon graduate study in psychology at Harvard.

At Harvard, Skinner acquired the rigorous self-discipline which still governs his life today. For two years, he rose at 6 A.M., studied until breakfast, went to classes, studied until 9 P.M. and went to bed. For two years he saw no movies or plays, had no dates and read nothing but psychology and physiology. After gaining his Ph.D. in 1931, he stayed on at Harvard under various postdoctoral fellowships and continued his research on animal behavior. In 1936 he moved to the University of Minnesota, and during the war he worked on a missile guidance system that utilized pigeons trained in his laboratory. (In more frivolous times Skinner has trained pigeons to play table tennis and the piano.)

In 1948, Skinner came to Harvard, and 10 years later he succeeded the venerable Edwin Boring as Edgar Pierce Professor of Psychology. Today, he works under a career grant from the National Institute of Mental Health. Though no longer engaged in active research, he is involved in a number of different applications of his theories in fields ranging from education to the care of psychotics. Last month he patented a new method of teaching writing, called "Write and See," using a special workbook and an ink that becomes visible only when a child draws a letter or word properly. The workbook offers a choice of several characters, only one of which is properly formed. Only when the child runs his special pen over this character does the ink in it become visible. This assures instant correction and thus positive reinforcement.

Skinner does his own writing in a large, well-ordered study in the basement of his modest modern house in Cambridge. In some ways, the house is similar to an aircrib. Its air is processed by an air-conditioner, a humidifier and a precipitator (a kind of air filter), and one wall of the living room is a large window with a sliding glass door. Skinner leads a life in keeping with his home. "Fred is the intelligent man taking care of himself," says an admiring friend. "He gets up early, eats a good breakfast, walks to work, does regular isometric exercises, drinks very little and goes to bed early. He takes care of himself as if he were a valuable object—which he is."

For relaxation, Skinner reads novels and mysteries (he follows the exploits of Simenon's Inspector Maigret, in French) and plays his piano, clavichord and electric organ, on all of which he is a competent amateur. He and his wife Yvonne have two daughters. Julie, the older, is married to a sociologist and is working toward her Ph.D. in education; Deborah, who was raised in the aircrib, is now working with monkeys in a behavioral research laboratory.

Whether relaxing or working, Skinner always has a notebook near him—in his office, living room, study, briefcase and jacket pocket—in which he records his daily thoughts, on everything from the art of fiction to the contingencies of a football game. For nearly 40 years now he has been carefully saving these notes and his correspondence. For someone of lesser significance all this meticulous preservation might seem a bit much, but not for Skinner. "He thinks of himself as an event in the history of man," says a colleague, "and he wants to be damned sure the record is straight."

Not willing to leave the writing of the record to posterity, Skinner is planning an autobiography, and he has already published a collection of papers entitled "Cumulative Record." The choice of this title, with its overtones of the laboratory, was not accidental, for as Skinner himself admits, "I treat myself exactly the way I treat my rats." His study is his Skinner box—it contains a thermometer, a barometer, a metronome for isometric exercises and two clocks, one of which is a timer that records his daily work input.

Skinner turns out lectures, articles and books at a slow but steady pace. (He keeps a careful record of his words-per-minute rate.) He is currently at work on a second collection of scientific papers and a major book to be called "Freedom and Dignity," which he describes as his answer to "the so-called humanists" who look on behaviorism as denying man his humanity. He comments: "These people are in love with the mental apparatus. They like to believe in free will, and accident, for then they can get credit for controlling themselves. This is absurd. If behavior is determined by genetic endowment and environment—and it definitely is—then man can take no credit for his own actions. Besides, we are being controlled anyway—by parents, teachers, advertising, government—but in an inefficient manner by people who have no idea what they are doing. The guidelines of control must be designed by the scientist."

"Why the scientist?"

"Because he's the only one who knows how to design an environment and how to condition behavior. The scientist may not know more about happiness than others, but he's certainly no worse off than anyone else. At least he's in a position to do something to achieve it."

If this kind of talk sounds like something out of "Brave New World," it is not surprising, for Skinner's "Walden Two" strikes many readers as frighteningly similar to Aldous Huxley's utopia. But whereas Huxley intended his novel as a satirical warning against a controlled society, Skinner wrote his as a serious argument for one. This led one reviewer to suggest that Skinner may have read "Brave New World" and missed the point.

As described in the novel, Walden Two is an economically self-sufficient rural community in the Midwest, run on Skinnerian principles of inducing desired behavior by positive reinforcement. Its 1,000 members work four hours a day, experience no intellectual or moral struggles and lead lives of relatively uninterrupted happiness. Everyone is physically fit, intelligent and interested in the arts. Children are raised, or "conditioned," by professional nurses and teachers to behave in a manner that will insure their own happiness and the continued stability of the community. Their personalities are "shaped" by design, rather than in the haphazard manner of the outside world. A board of "planners" oversees the operation of the community, constantly experimenting with ways to improve the quality of its life, and psychologists keep a close check on the resulting happiness of its residents.

When it was published in 1948, "Walden Two" created an uproar—mostly negative. Joseph Wood Krutch called it "an ignoble utopia," Life magazine attacked it, and someone suggested that "incipient dictators might well find in this utopia a guidebook of political practice." Despite all this concern, "Walden Two" never sold more than a few thousand copies a year until, around 1960, sales began to pick up sharply (according to a graph on which Skinner plots its progress). Last year the sales were nearly 80,000. Asked to explain the current surge of interest, Skinner suggests, "It gives young people a chance to speculate about government and political behavior in a nonpolitical way. I mean, what else can a young man do if he wants to dream about a better world—become a Republican?"

To some of Skinner's followers, Walden Two is not merely a dream. In the summer of 1966 they held a National Walden Two Conference, attended by the master himself, and today there are small, experimental groups near Cambridge and in Virginia, California, Illinois and Michigan that have formed communities based on his theories.

The prospect of living in a society in which one's behavior is controlled from birth does not appall Skinner's followers, perhaps because they envision themselves as doing the controlling. "It is true," one of them admits, "that someone who is sufficiently in control of the contingencies of reinforcement can control your behavior. The fact that this knowledge could be misused is simply a fact of life. Sure, it's a threat, but somebody's going to develop it anyhow, and if we do it first, we can prevent some kind of Hitler from doing it. It all depends on what kind of society you want. You could have 'Mein Kampf' or you could have Walden Two."

Skinner realizes that his controlled society would conflict with many traditional notions of freedom and individual responsibility, but he feels that these notions "have not made us conspicuously successful in dealing with human affairs." To those who fear that man would lose his freedom in a Walden Two, he argues that, on the contrary, only by learning to control and manipulate his own environment and genetics can man achieve real freedom.

To many behavioral psychologists, the argument over whether

man can be controlled is silly. According to Harvard's Herrnstein, "the real issue is not, can you be controlled? Of course you can. There's no question about it. The real issue is one of determination and free will. Are we machines? Because if we aren't, there can be no science of human behavior."

"What do you think we are?" he was asked.

"I feel we are machines. I couldn't be a behavioral scientist if I didn't. But not a machine like a wind-up toy. More like a leveling device on a ship. We are goal-directed machines, and this is something I think Fred doesn't understand. But then, Fred is a visionary, and visionary people are visionary partly because of the very great many things they don't see."

Burrhus Frederic Skinner considers himself a man of goodwill, rather than a visionary. He merely wants a society in which people live together more effectively and more happily than they do today, and he believes he has discovered a technology of behavior that would enable them to do just that.

Giant in the Nursery
—Jean Piaget

by David Elkind

IN FEBRUARY, 1967, Jean Piaget, the Swiss psychologist, arrived at Clark University in Worcester, Mass., to deliver the Heinz Werner Memorial Lectures. The lectures were to be given in the evening, and before the first one a small dinner party was arranged in honor of Piaget and was attended by colleagues, former students and friends. I was invited because of my long advocacy of Piaget's work and because I had spent a year (1964-65) at his Institute for Educational Science in Geneva. Piaget had changed very little since I had last seen him, but he did appear tired and mildly apprehensive.

Although Piaget has lectured all over the world, this particular occasion had special significance. Almost 60 years before, in 1909, another famous European, Sigmund Freud, also lectured at Clark University. Piaget was certainly aware of the historical parallel. He was, moreover, going to speak to a huge American audience in French and, despite the offices of his remarkable translator, Eleanor Duckworth, he must have had some reservations about how it would go.

Piaget's apprehension was apparent during the dinner. For one

From the *New York Times Magazine,* May 26, 1968, copyright © 1968 by The New York Times Company.

who is usually a lively and charming dinner companion, he was surprisingly quiet and unresponsive. About half way through the meal there was a small disturbance. The room in which the dinner was held was at a garden level and two boys suddenly appeared at the windows and began tapping at them. The inclination of most of us, I think, was to shoo them away. Before we had a chance to do that, however, Piaget had turned to face the children. He smiled up at the lads, hunched his shoulders and gave them a slight wave with his hand. They hunched their shoulders and smiled in return, gave a slight wave and disappeared. After a moment, Piaget turned back to the table and began telling stories and entering into animated conversation.

Although I am sure his lecture would have been a success in any case and that the standing ovation he received would have occurred without the little incident, I nonetheless like to think that the encounter with the boys did much to restore his vigor and good humor.

It is Piaget's genius for empathy with children, together with true intellectual genius, that has made him the outstanding child psychologist in the world today and one destined to stand beside Freud with respect to his contributions to psychology, education and related disciplines. Just as Freud's discoveries of unconscious motivation, infantile sexuality and the stages of psychosexual growth changed our ways of thinking about human personality, so Piaget's discoveries of children's implicit philosophies, the construction of reality by the infant and the stages of mental development have altered our ways of thinking about human intelligence.

The man behind these discoveries is an arresting figure. He is tall and somewhat portly, and his stooped walk, bulky suits and crown of long white hair give him the appearance of a thrice-magnified Einstein. (When he was at the Institute for Advanced Study at Princeton in 1953, a friend of his wife rushed to a window one day and exclaimed, "Look, Einstein!" Madame Piaget looked and replied, "No, just my Piaget.") Piaget's personal trademarks are his meerschaum pipes (now burned deep amber), his navy blue beret and his bicycle.

Meeting Piaget is a memorable experience. Although Piaget

has an abundance of Old-World charm and graciousness, he seems to emanate an aura of intellectual presence not unlike the aura of personality presence conveyed by a great actor. While as a psychologist I am unable to explain how this sense of presence is communicated, I am nevertheless convinced that everyone who meets Piaget experiences it. While talking to me, for example, he was able to divine in my remarks and questions a significance and depth of which I was entirely unaware and certainly hadn't intended. Evidently one characteristic of genius is to search for relevance in the apparently commonplace and frivolous.

Piaget's is a superbly disciplined life. He arises early each morning, sometimes as early as 4 A.M., and writes four or more publishable pages on square sheets of white paper in an even, small hand. Later in the morning he may teach classes and attend meetings. His afternoons include long walks during which he thinks about the problems he is currently confronting. He says, "I always like to think on a problem before reading about it." In the evenings, he reads and retires early. Even on his international trips, Piaget keeps to this schedule.

Each summer, as soon as classes are over, Piaget gathers up the research findings that have been collected by his assistants during the year and departs for the Alps, where he takes up solitary residence in a room in an abandoned farmhouse. The whereabouts of this retreat is as closely guarded as the names of depositors in numbered Swiss bank accounts; only Piaget's family, his long-time colleague Bärbel Inhelder and a trusted secretary know where he is. During the summer Piaget takes walks, meditates, writes *and* writes. Then, when the leaves begin to turn, he descends from the mountains with the several books and articles he has written on his "vacation."

Although Piaget, now in his seventy-second year, has been carrying his works down from the mountains for almost fifty summers (he has published more than thirty books and hundreds of articles), it is only within the past decade that his writings have come to be fully appreciated in America. This was due, in part, to the fact that until fairly recently only a few of his books had been translated into English. In addition, American psychology and education were simply not ready for Piaget until the fifties. Now the ideas that Piaget has been advocating for more than 30 years are regarded as exceedingly innovative and even as avant-garde.

His work falls into three more or less distinct periods within each of which he covered an enormous amount of psychological territory and developed a multitude of insights. (Like most creative men, Piaget is hard put to it to say when a particular idea came to him. If he ever came suddenly upon an idea which sent him shouting through the halls, he has never admitted to it.)

During the first period (roughly 1922-29), Piaget explored the extent and depth of children's spontaneous ideas about the physical world and about their own mental processes. He happened upon this line of inquiry while working in Alfred Binet's laboratory school in Paris where he arrived, still seeking a direction for his talents, a year after receiving his doctorate in biological science at the University of Lausanne. It was in the course of some routine intelligence testing that Piaget became interested in what lay behind children's correct, and particularly their incorrect, answers. To clarify the origins of these answers he began to interview the children in the open-ended manner he had learned while serving a brief interneship at Bleuler's psychiatric clinic in Zurich. This semiclinical interview procedure, aimed at revealing the processes by which a child arrives at a particular reply to a test question, has become a trademark of Piagetian research investigation.

What Piaget found with this method of inquiry was that children not only reasoned differently from adults but also that they had quite different world-views, literally different philosophies. This led Piaget to attend to those childish remarks and questions which most adults find amusing or nonsensical. Just as Freud used seemingly accidental slips of the tongue and pen as evidence for unconscious motivations, so Piaget has employed the "cute" sayings of children to demonstrate the existence of ideas quite foreign to the adult mind.

Piaget had read in the recollections of a deaf mute (recorded by William James) that as a child he had regarded the sun and moon as gods and believed they followed him about. Piaget sought to verify this recollection by interviewing children on the subject, and he found that many youngsters do believe that the sun and moon follow them when they are out for a walk. Similar remarks Piaget either overheard or was told about led to a large number of investigations which revealed, among many similar findings, that young children believe that anything which moves is alive, that the names of objects reside in the objects themselves and that dreams come in through the window at night.

Such beliefs, Piaget pointed out in an early article entitled "Children's Philosophies," are not unrelated to but rather derive from an implicit animism and artificialism with many parallels to primitive and Greek philosophies. In the child's view, objects like stones and clouds are imbued with motives, intentions and feelings, while mental events such as dreams and thoughts are endowed with corporality and force. Children also believe that everything has a purpose and that everything in the world is made by and for man. (My five-year-old son asked me why we have snow and answered his own question by saying, "It is for children to play in.")

The child's animism and artificialism help to explain his famous and often unanswerable "why" questions. It is because children believe that everything has a purpose that they ask, "Why is grass green?" and "Why do the stars shine?" The parent who attempts to answer such questions with a physical explanation has missed the point.

In addition to disclosing the existence of children's philosophies during this first period, Piaget also found the clue to the egocentrism of childhood. In observing young children at play at the *Maison des Petits,* the modified Montessori school associated with the Institute of Educational Science in Geneva, Piaget noted a peculiar lack of social orientation which was also present in their conversation and in their approaches to certain intellectual tasks. A child would make up a new word ("stocks" for socks and stockings) and just assume that everyone knew what he was talking about as if this were the conventional name for the objects he had in mind. Likewise, Piaget noted that when two nursery school children were at play they often spoke *at* rather than *to* one another and were frequently chattering on about two quite different and unrelated topics. Piaget observed, moreover, that when he stood a child of five years opposite him, the child who could tell his own right and left nevertheless insisted that Piaget's right and left hands were directly opposite his own.

In Piaget's view, all of these behaviors can be explained by the young child's inability to put himself in another person's position and to take that person's point of view. Unlike the egocentric adult, who can take another person's point of view but does not, the egocentric child does not take another person's viewpoint because he cannot. This conception of childish egocentrism has produced a fundamental alteration in our evaluation of the preschool child's behavior. We now appreciate that it is intellectual immaturity and not moral perversity which makes, for example, a young child continue to pester his mother after she has told him she has a headache and wishes to be left alone. The preschool child is simply unable to put himself in his mother's position and see things from her point of view.

The second period of Piaget's investigations began when, in 1929, he sought to trace the origins of the child's spontaneous mental growth to the behavior of infants; in this case, his own three children, Jaqueline, Lucienne and Laurent. Piaget kept very detailed records of their behavior and of their performance on a series of ingenious tasks which he invented and presented to them. The books resulting from these investigations, "The Origins of Intelligence in Children," "Play, Dreams and Imitation in Children" and "The Construction of Reality in the Child" are now generally regarded as classics in the field and have been one of the major forces behind the scurry of research activity in the area of infant behavior now current both in America and abroad. The publication of these books in the middle and late nineteen-thirties marked the end of the second phase of Piaget's work.

Some of the most telling observations Piaget made during this period had to do with what he called the *conservation of the object* (using the word conservation to convey the idea of permanence). To the older child and to the adult, the existence of objects and persons who are not immediately present is taken as self-evident. The child at school knows that while he is working at his desk his mother is simultaneously at home and his father is at work. This is not the case for the young infant playing in his crib, for whom out of sight is literally out of mind. Piaget observed that when an infant four or five months old is playing with a toy which subsequently rolls out of sight (behind another toy) but is still within reach, the infant ceases to look for it. The infant behaves as if the toy had not only disappeared but as if it had gone entirely out of existence.

This helps to explain the pleasure infants take in the game of peek-a-boo. If the infant believed that the object existed when it was not seen, he would not be surprised and delighted at its re-emergence and there would be no point to the game. It is only during the second year of life, when children begin to represent objects mentally, that they seek after toys that have disappeared from view. Only then do they attribute an independent existence to objects which are not present to their senses.

The third and major phase of Piaget's endeavors began about 1940 and continues until the present day. During this period Piaget has studied the development in children and adolescents of those mental abilities which gradually enable the child to construct a world-view which is in conformance with reality as seen by adults. He has, at the same time, been concerned with how children acquire the adult versions of various concepts such as number, quantity and speed. Piaget and his colleagues have amassed, in the last 28 years, an astounding amount of information about the thinking of children and adolescents which is only now beginning to be used by psychologists and educators.

Two discoveries made during this last period are of particular importance both because they were so unexpected and because of their relevance for education. It is perhaps fair to say that education tends to focus upon the static aspects of reality rather than upon its dynamic transformations. The child is taught how and what things are but not the conditions under which they change or remain the same. And yet the child is constantly confronted with change and alteration. His view of the world alters as he grows in height and perceptual acuity. And the world changes. Seasons come and go, trees gain and lose their foliage, snow falls and melts. People change, too. They may change over brief time periods in mood and over long periods in weight and hair coloration or fullness. The child receives a static education while living amidst a world in transition.

Piaget's investigations since 1940 have focused upon how the child copes with change, how he comes to distinguish between the permanent and the transient and between appearance and reality. An incident that probably played a part in initiating this line of investigation occurred during Piaget's short-lived flirtation with the automobile. (When his children were young, Piaget learned to drive and bought a car, but he gave it up for his beloved bicycle after a couple of years.) He took his son for a drive and Laurent asked the name of the mountain they were passing. The mountain was the Salève, the crocodile-shaped mass that dominates the city of Geneva. Laurent was in fact familiar with the mountain and its name because he could see it from his garden, although from a different perspective. Laurent's question brought home to Piaget the fact that a child has difficulty in dealing with the results of transformations whether they are brought about by an alteration in the object itself or by the child's movement with respect to the object.

The methods Piaget used to study how the child comes to deal with transformations are ingenuously simple and can be used by any interested parent or teacher. These methods all have to do with testing the child's abilities to discover that a quantity remains the same across a change in its appearance. In other words, that the quantity is conserved.

To give just one illustration from among hundreds, a child is shown two identical drinking glasses filled equally full with orangeade and he is asked to say whether there is the "same to drink" in the two glasses. After the child says that this is the case, the orangeade from one glass is poured into another which is taller and thinner so that the orangeade now reaches a higher level. Then the child is asked to say whether there is the same amount to drink in the two differently shaped glasses. Before the age of six or seven, most children say that the tall, narrow glass has more orangeade. The young child cannot deal with the transformation and bases his judgment on the static features of the orangeade, namely the levels.

How does the older child arrive at the notion that the amounts of orangeade in the two differently shaped glasses is the same? The answer, according to Piaget, is that he discovers the equality with the aid of reason. If the child judges only on the basis of appearances he cannot solve the problem. When he compares the two glasses with respect to width he must conclude that the wide glass has more while if he compares them with respect to the level of the orangeade he must conclude that the tall glass has more. There is then no way, on the basis of appearance, that he can solve the problem. If, on the other hand, the child reasons that there was the same in the two glasses before and that nothing was added or taken away during the pouring, he concludes that both glasses still have the same drink although this does not appear to be true.

On the basis of this and many similar findings, Piaget argues that much of our knowledge about reality comes to us not from without like the wail of a siren but rather from within by the force of our own logic.

It is hard to overemphasize the importance of this fact, because it is so often forgotten, particularly in education. For those who are not philosophically inclined, it appears that our knowledge of things comes about rather directly as if our mind simply copied the forms, colors and textures of things. From this point of view the mind acts as a sort of mirror which is limited to reflecting the reality which is presented to it. As Piaget's research has demonstrated, however, the mind operates not as a passive mirror but rather as an active artist.

The portrait painter does not merely copy what he sees, he interprets his subject. Before even commencing the portrait, the artist learns a great deal about the individual subject and does not limit himself to studying the face alone. Into the portrait goes not only what the artist sees but also what he knows about his subject. A good portrait is larger than life because it carries much more information than could ever be conveyed by a mirror image.

In forming his spontaneous conception of the world, therefore, the child does more than reflect what is presented to his senses. His image of reality is in fact a portrait or reconstruction of the world and not a simple copy of it. It is only by reasoning about the information which the child receives from the external world that he is able to overcome the transient nature of sense experience and arrive at that awareness of permanence within apparent change that is the mark of adult thought. The importance of reason in the child's spontaneous construction of his world is thus one of the major discoveries of Piaget's third period.

The second major discovery of this time has to do with the nature of the elementary school child's reasoning ability. Long before there was anything like a discipline of child psychology, the age of six to seven was recognized as *the age of reason*. It was also assumed, however, that once the child attained the age of reason, there were no longer any substantial differences between his reasoning abilities and those of adolescents and adults. What Piaget discovered is that this is in fact not the case. While the elementary school child is indeed able to reason, his reasoning ability is limited in a very important respect—he can reason about things but not about verbal propositions.

If a child of eight or nine is shown a series of three blocks, ABC, which differ in size, then he can tell by looking at them, and without comparing them directly, that if A is greater than B and B greater than C, then A is greater than C. When the same child is given this problem, "Helen is taller than Mary and Mary is taller than Jane, who is the tallest of the three?" the result is quite different. He cannot solve it despite the fact that it repeats in words the problem with the blocks. Adolescents and adults, however, encounter no difficulty with this problem because they can reason about verbal propositions as well as about things.

This discovery that children think differently from adults even after attaining the age of reason has educational implications which are only now beginning to be applied. Robert Karplus, the physicist who heads the Science Curriculum Improvement Study at Berkeley has pointed out that most teachers use verbal propositions in teaching elementary school children. At least some of their instruction is thus destined to go over the heads of their pupils. Karplus and his co-workers are now attempting to train teachers to instruct children at a verbal level which is appropriate to their level of mental ability.

An example of the effects of the failure to take into account the difference between the reasoning abilities of children and adults comes from the New Math experiment. In building materials for the New Math, it was hoped that the construction of a new language would facilitate instruction of set concepts. This new language has been less than successful and the originators of the New Math are currently attempting to devise a physical model to convey the New Math concepts. It is likely that the new language created to teach the set concepts failed because it was geared to the logic of adults rather than to the reasoning of children. Attention to the research on children's thinking carried out during Piaget's third period might have helped to avoid some of the difficulties of the "New Math" program.

In the course of these many years of research into children's thinking, Piaget has elaborated a general theory of intellectual development which, in its scope and comprehensiveness, rivals Freud's theory of personality development. Piaget proposes that intelligence—adaptive thinking and action—develops in a sequence of stages that is related to age. Each stage sees the elaboration of new mental abilities which set the limits and determine the character of what can be learned during that period. (Piaget finds incomprehensible Harvard psychologist Jerome Bruner's famous hypothesis to the effect that "any subject can be taught effectively in some intellectually honest form to any child at any stage of development.") Although Piaget believes that the order in which the stages appear holds true for all children, he also believes that the ages at which the stages evolve will depend upon the native endowment of the child and upon the quality of the physical and social environment in which he is reared. In a very real sense, then, Piaget's is both a nature *and* a nurture theory.

The first stage in the development of intelligence (usually zero to two years) Piaget calls the sensory-motor period and it is concerned with the evolution of those abilities necessary to construct and reconstruct objects. To illustrate, Piaget observed that when he held a cigarette case in front of his daughter Jaqueline (who was eight months old at the time) and then dropped it, she did not follow the trajectory of the case but continued looking at his hand. Even at eight months (Lucienne and Laurent succeeded in following the object at about five months but had been exposed to more experiments than Jaqueline) she was not able to reconstruct the path of the object which she had seen dropped in front of her.

Toward the end of this period, however, Jaqueline was even able to reconstruct the position of objects which had undergone hidden displacement. When she was nineteen months old, Piaget placed a coin in his hand and then placed his hand under a coverlet where he dropped the coin before removing his hand. Jaqueline first looked in his hand and then immediately lifted the coverlet and found the coin. This reconstruction was accomplished with the air of an elementary form of reasoning. The coin was in the hand, the hand was under the coverlet, the coin was not in the hand so the coin is under the coverlet. Such reasoning, it must be said, is accomplished without the aid of language and by means of mental images.

The second stage (usually two to seven years), which Piaget calls the preoperational stage, bears witness to the elaboration of the symbolic function, those abilities which have to do with representing things. The presence of these new abilities is shown by the gradual acquisition of language, the first indications of dreams and night terrors, the advent of symbolic play (two sticks at right angles are an airplane) and the first attempts at drawing and graphic representation.

At the beginning of this stage the child tends to identify words and symbols with the objects they are intended to represent. He is upset if someone tramps on a stone which he has designated as a turtle. And he believes that names are as much a part of objects as their color and form. (The child at this point is like the old gentleman who, when asked why noodles are called noodles, replied that "they are white like noodles, soft like noodles and taste like noodles so we call them noodles.")

By the end of this period the child can clearly distinguish between words and symbols and what they represent. He now recognizes that names are arbitrary designations. The child's discovery of the arbitrariness of names is often manifested in the "name calling" so prevalent during the early school years.

At the next stage (usually seven to eleven years) the child acquires what Piaget calls concrete operations, internalized actions that permit the child to do "in his head" what before he would have had to accomplish through real actions. Concrete operations enable the child to think about things. To illustrate, in one study Piaget presented five-, six- and seven-year-old children with six sticks in a row and asked them to take the same number of sticks from a pile on the table. The young children solved the problem by placing their sticks beneath the sample and matching the sticks one by one. The older children merely picked up the six sticks and held them in their hands. The older children had counted the sticks mentally and hence felt no need to actually match them with the sticks in the row. It should be said that even the youngest children were able to count to six, so that this was not a factor in their performance.

Concrete operations also enable children to deal with the relations among classes of things. In another study Piaget presented five-, six- and seven-year-old children with a box containing 20 white and seven brown wooden beads. Each child was first asked if there were more white or more brown beads and all were able to say that there were more white than brown beads. Then Piaget asked, "Are there more white or more wooden beads?" The young children could not fathom the question and replied that "there are more white than brown beads." For such children classes are not regarded as abstractions but are thought of as concrete places. (I once asked a preoperational child if he could be a Protestant and an American at the same time, to which he replied, "No," and then as an afterthought, "only if you move.")

When a child thought of a bead in the white "place" he could not think of it as being in the wooden "place" since objects cannot be in two places at once. He could only compare the white with the brown "places." The older children, who had attained concrete operations, encountered no difficulty with the task and readily replied that "there are more wooden than white beads because all of the beads are wooden and only some are white." By the end of the concrete operational period, children are remarkably adept at doing thought problems and at combining and dividing class concepts.

During the last stage (usually twelve to fifteen years) there gradually emerge what Piaget calls formal operations and which, in effect, permit adolescents to think about their thoughts, to construct ideals and to reason realistically about the future. Formal operations also enable young people to reason about contrary-to-fact propositions. If, for example, a child is asked to assume that coal is white he is likely to reply, "But coal is black," whereas the adolescent can accept the contrary-to-fact assumption and reason from it.

Formal operational thought also makes possible the understanding of metaphor. It is for this reason that political and other satirical cartoons are not understood until adolescence. The child's inability to understand metaphor helps to explain why books such as "Alice in Wonderland" and "Gulliver's Travels" are enjoyed at different levels during childhood than in adolescence and adulthood, when their social significance can be understood.

No new mental systems emerge after the formal operations, which are the common coin of adult thought. After adolescence, mental growth takes the form—it is hoped—of a gradual increase in wisdom.

This capsule summary of Piaget's theory of intellectual development would not be complete without some words about Piaget's position with respect to language and thought. Piaget regards thought and language as different but closely related systems. Language, to a much greater extent than thought, is determined by particular forms of environmental stimulation. Inner-city Negro children, who tend to be retarded in language development, are much less retarded with respect to the ages at which they attain concrete operations. Indeed, not only inner-city children but children in bush Africa, Hong Kong and Appalachia all attain concrete operations at about the same age as middle-class children in Geneva and Boston.

Likewise, attempts to teach children concrete operations have been almost uniformly unsuccessful. This does not mean that these operations are independent of the environment but only that their development takes time and can be nourished by a much wider variety of environmental nutriments than is true for the growth of language, which is dependent upon much more specific forms of stimulation.

Language is, then, deceptive with respect to thought. Teachers of middle-class children are often misled, by the verbal facility of these youngsters, into believing that they understand more than they actually comprehend. (My five-year-old asked me what my true identity was and as I tried to recover my composure he explained that Clark Kent was Superman's true identity.) At the other end, the teachers of inner-city children are often fooled by the language handicaps of these children into thinking that they have much lower mental ability than they actually possess. It is appropriate, therefore, that pre-school programs for the disadvantaged should focus upon training these children in language and perceptions rather than upon trying to teach them concrete operations.

The impact which the foregoing Piagetian discoveries and conceptions is having upon education and child psychology has come as something of a shock to a good many educators and psychological research in America, which relies heavily upon statistics, electronics and computers. Piaget's studies of children's thinking seem hardly a step beyond the prescientific baby biographies kept by such men as Charles Darwin and Bronson Alcott. Indeed, in many of Piaget's research papers he supports his conclusions simply with illustrative examples of how children at different age levels respond to his tasks.

Many of Piaget's critics have focused upon his apparently casual methodology and have argued that while Piaget has arrived at some original ideas about children's thinking, his research lacks scientific rigor. It is likely that few, if any, of Piaget's research reports would have been accepted for publication in American psychological journals.

Other critics have taken somewhat the opposite tack. Jerome Bruner, who has done so much to bring Piaget to the attention of American social scientists, acknowledges the fruitfulness of Piaget's methods, modifications of which he has employed in his own investigations. But he argues against Piaget's theoretical interpretations. Bruner believes that Piaget has "missed the heart" of the problem of change and permanence or conservation in children's thinking. In the case of the orangeade poured into a different-sized container, Bruner argues that it is not reason, or mental operations, but some "internalized verbal formula that shields him [the child] from the overpowering appearance of the visual displays." Bruner seems to believe that the syntactical rules of language rather than logic can account for the child's discovery that a quantity remains unchanged despite alterations in its appearance.

Piaget is willing to answer his critics but only when he feels that the criticism is responsible and informed. With respect to his methods, their casualness is only apparent. Before they set out collecting data, his students are given a year of training in the art of interviewing children. They learn to ask questions without suggesting the answers and to test, by counter-suggestion, the strength of the child's conviction. Many of Piaget's studies have now been repeated with more rigorous procedures by other investigators all over the world and the results have been remarkably consistent with Piaget's findings. Attempts are currently under way to build a new intelligence scale on the basis of the Piaget tests, many of which are already in widespread use as evaluative procedures in education.

When it comes to criticisms of his theoretical views, Piaget is remarkably open and does not claim to be infallible. He frequently invites scholars who are in genuine disagreement with him to come to Geneva for a year so that the differences can be discussed and studied in depth. He has no desire to form a cult and says, in fact, "To the extent that there are Piagetians, to that extent have I failed." Piaget's lack of dogmatism is illustrated in his response to Bruner:

"Bruner does say that I 'missed the heart' of the conservation problem, a problem I have been working on for the last 30 years. He is right, of course, but that does not mean that he himself has understood it in a much shorter time. . . . Adults, just like children, need time to reach the right ideas. . . . This is the great mystery of development, which is irreducible to an accumulation of isolated learning acquisitions. Even psychology cannot be learned or constructed in a short time." (Despite his disclaimer, Piaget has offered a comprehensive theory of how the child arrives at conservation and this theory has received much research support.)

Piaget would probably agree with those who are critical about premature applications of his work to education. He finds particularly disturbing the efforts by some American educators to accelerate children intellectually. When he was giving his other 1967 lectures, in New York, he remarked:

"If we accept the fact that there are stages of development, another question arises which I call 'the American question,' and I am asked it every time I come here. If there are stages that children reach at given norms of ages can we accelerate the stages? Do we have to go through each one of these stages, or can't we speed it up a bit? Well, surely, the answer is yes . . . but how far can we speed them up? . . . I have a hypothesis which I am so far incapable of proving: probably the organization of operations has an optimal time. . . . For example, we know that it takes nine to twelve months before babies develop the notion that an object is still there even when a screen is placed in front of it. Now kittens go through the same sub-stages but they do it in three months—so they're six months ahead of the babies. Is this an advantage or isn't it?

"We can certainly see our answer in one sense. The kitten is not going to go much further. The child has taken longer, but he is capable of going further so it seems to me that the nine months were not for nothing. . . . It is probably possible to accelerate, but maximal acceleration is not desirable. There seems to be an optimal time. What this optimal time is will surely depend upon each individual and on the subject matter. We still need a great deal of research to know what the optimal time would be."

Piaget's stance against using his findings as a justification for accelerating children intellectually recalls a remark made by Freud when he was asked whatever became of those bright, aggressive shoeshine boys one encounters in city streets. Freud's reply was, "They become cobblers." In Piaget's terms they get to a certain point earlier but they don't go as far. And the New York educator Eliot Shapiro has pointed out that one of the Negro child's problems is that he is forced to grow up and take responsibility too soon and doesn't have time to be a child.

Despite some premature and erroneous applications of his

thinking to education, Piaget has had an over-all effect much more positive than negative. His findings about children's understanding of scientific and mathematical concepts are being used as guidelines for new curricula in these subjects. And his tests are being more and more widely used to evaluate educational outcomes. Perhaps the most significant and widespread positive effect that Piaget has had upon education is in the changed attitudes on the part of teachers who have been exposed to his thinking. After becoming acquainted with Piaget's work, teachers can never again see children in quite the same way as they had before. Once teachers begin to look at children from the Piagetian perspective they can also appreciate his views with regard to the aims of education.

"The principal goal of education," he once said, "is to create men who are capable of doing new things, not simply of repeating what other generations have done—men who are creative, inventive and discoverers. The second goal of education is to form minds which can be critical, can verify, and not accept everything they are offered. The great danger today is of slogans, collective opinions, ready-made trends of thought. We have to be able to resist individually, to criticize, to distinguish between what is proven and what is not. So we need pupils who are active, who learn early to find out by themselves, partly by their own spontaneous activity and partly through materials we set up for them; who learn early to tell what is verifiable and what is simply the first idea to come to them."

At the beginning of his eighth decade, Jean Piaget is as busy as ever. A new book of his on memory will be published soon and another on the mental functions in the preschool child is in preparation. The International Center for Genetic Epistemology, which Piaget founded in 1955 with a grant from the Rockefeller Foundation, continues to draw scholars from around the world who wish to explore with Piaget the origin of scientific concepts. As Professor of Experimental Psychology at the University of Geneva, Piaget also continues to teach courses and conduct seminars.

And his students still continue to collect the data which at the end of the school year Piaget will take with him up to the mountains. The methods employed by his students today are not markedly different from those which were used by their predecessors decades ago. While there are occasional statistics, there are still no electronics or computers. In an age of moon shots and automation, the remarkable discoveries of Jean Piaget are evidence that in the realm of scientific achievement, technological sophistication is still no substitute for creative genius.

Erik Erikson's Eight Ages of Man

by David Elkind

AT A RECENT faculty reception I happened to join a smaller group in which a young mother was talking about her "identity crisis." She and her husband, she said, had decided not to have any more children and she was depressed at the thought of being past the child-bearing stage. It was as if, she continued, she had been robbed of some part of herself and now needed to find a new function to replace the old one.

When I remarked that her story sounded like a case history from a book by Erik Erikson, she replied, "Who's Erikson?" It is a reflection on the intellectual modesty and literary decorum of Erik H. Erikson, psychoanalyst and professor of developmental psychology at Harvard, that so few of the many people who today talk about the "identity crisis" know anything of the man who pointed out its pervasiveness as a problem in contemporary society two decades ago.

Erikson has, however, contributed more to social science than his delineation of identity problems in modern man. His descriptions of the stages of the life cycle, for example, have advanced psychoanalytic theory to the point where it can now describe the development of the healthy personality on its own terms and not merely as the opposite of a sick one. Likewise, Erikson's emphasis upon the problems unique to adolescents and adults living in today's society has helped to rectify the one-sided emphasis on childhood as the beginning and end of personality development.

Finally, in his biographical studies, such as "Young Man Luther" and "Gandhi's Truth" (which has just won a National Book Award in philosophy and religion), Erikson emphasizes the inherent strengths of the human personality by showing how individuals can use their neurotic symptoms and conflicts for creative and constructive social purposes while healing themselves in the process.

It is important to emphasize that Erikson's contributions are genuine advances in psychoanalysis in the sense that Erikson accepts and builds upon many of the basic tenets of Freudian theory. In this regard, Erikson differs from Freud's early coworkers such as Jung and Adler who, when they broke with Freud, rejected his theories and substituted their own.

Likewise, Erikson also differs from the so-called neo-Freudians such as Horney, Kardiner and Sullivan who (mistakenly, as it turned out) assumed that Freudian theory had nothing to say about man's relation to reality and to his culture. While it is true that Freud emphasized, even mythologized, sexuality, he did so to counteract the rigid sexual taboos of his time, which, at that point in history, were frequently the cause of neuroses. In his later writings, however, Freud began to concern himself with the executive agency of the personality, namely the ego, which is also the repository of the individual's attitudes and concepts about himself and his world.

It is with the psychosocial development of the ego that Erikson's observations and theoretical constructions are primarily concerned. Erikson has thus been able to introduce innovations into psychoanalytic theory without either rejecting or ignoring Freud's monumental contribution.

The man who has accomplished this notable feat is a handsome Dane, whose white hair, mustache, resonant accent and gentle manner are reminiscent of actors like Jean Hersholt and Paul Muni. Although he is warm and outgoing with friends, Erikson is a rather shy man who is uncomfortable in the spotlight of public recognition. This trait, together with his ethical reservations about making public even disguised case material, may help to account for Erikson's reluctance to publish his observations and conceptions (his first book appeared in 1950, when he was forty-eight).

In recent years this reluctance to publish has diminished and he has been appearing in print at an increasing pace. Since 1960 he has published three books, "Insight and Responsibility," "Identity: Youth and Crisis" and "Gandhi's Truth," as well as editing a fourth, "Youth: Change and Challenge." Despite the accolades and recognition these books have won for him, both in America and abroad, Erikson is still surprised at the popular interest they have generated and is a little troubled about the possibility of being misunderstood and misinterpreted. While he would prefer that his books spoke for themselves and that he was left out of the picture, he has had to accede to popular demand for more information about himself and his work.

The course of Erikson's professional career has been as diverse as it has been unconventional. He was born in Frankfurt, Germany, in 1902 of Danish parents. Not long after his birth his father died, and his mother later married the pediatrician who had cured her son of a childhood illness. Erikson's stepfather urged him to become a physician, but the boy declined and became an artist instead—an artist who did portraits of children. Erikson says of his post-adolescent years, "I was an artist then, which in Europe is a euphemism for a young man with some talent and nowhere to go." During this period he settled in Vienna and worked as a tutor in a family friendly with Freud's. He met Freud on informal occasions when the families went on outings together.

These encounters may have been the impetus to accept a teaching appointment at an American school in Vienna founded by Dorothy Burlingham and directed by Peter Blos (both now well known on the American psychiatric scene). During these years (the late nineteen-twenties) he also undertook and completed psychoanalytic training with Anna Freud and August Aichhorn. Even at the outset of his career, Erikson gave evidence of the breadth of his interests and activities by being trained and certified as a Montessori teacher. Not surprisingly, in view of that training, Erikson's first articles dealt with psychoanalysis and education.

It was while in Vienna that Erikson met and married Joan Mowat Serson, an American artist of Canadian descent. They came to America in 1933, when Erikson was invited to practice and teach in Boston. Erikson was, in fact, one of the first if not the first child-analyst in the Boston area. During the next two decades he held clinical and academic appointments at Harvard, Yale and Berkeley. In 1951 he joined a group of psychiatrists and psychologists who moved to Stockbridge, Mass., to start a new program at the Austen Riggs Center, a private residential treatment center for disturbed young people. Erikson remained at Riggs until 1961, when he was appointed professor of human development and lecturer on psychiatry at Harvard. Throughout his career he has always held two or three appointments simultaneously and has traveled extensively.

Perhaps because he had been an artist first, Erikson has never been a conventional psychoanalyst. When he was treating children, for example, he always insisted on visiting his young patients' homes and on having dinner with the families. Likewise, in the nineteen-thirties, when anthropological investigation was described to him by his friends Scudder McKeel, Alfred Kroeber and Margaret Mead, he decided to do field work on an Indian reservation. "When I realized that Sioux is the name which we [in Europe] pronounced "See ux" and which for us was *the* American Indian, I could not resist." Erikson thus antedated the anthropologists who swept over the Indian reservations in the post-Depression years. (So numerous were the field workers at that time that the stock joke was that an Indian family could be defined as a mother, a father, children and an anthropologist.)

Erikson did field work not only with the Oglala Sioux of Pine Ridge, S. D. (the tribe that slew Custer and was in turn slaughtered at the Battle of Wounded Knee), but also with the salmon-fishing Yurok of Northern California. His reports on these experiences revealed his special gift for sensing and entering into the world views and modes of thinking of cultures other than his own.

It was while he was working with the Indians that Erikson began to note syndromes which he could not explain within the confines of traditional psychoanalytic theory. Central to many an adult Indian's emotional problems seemed to be his sense of uprootedness and lack of continuity between his present life-style and that portrayed in tribal history. Not only did the Indian sense a break with the past, but he could not identify with a future requiring assimilation of the white culture's values. The problems faced by such men, Erikson recognized, had to do with the ego and with culture and only incidentally with sexual drives.

The impressions Erikson gained on the reservations were reinforced during World War II when he worked at a veterans' rehabilitation center at Mount Zion Hospital in San Francisco. Many of the soldiers he and his colleagues saw seemed not to fit the traditional "shell shock" or "malingerer" cases of World War I. Rather, it seemed to Erikson that many of these men had lost the sense of who and what they were. They were having trouble reconciling their activities, attitudes and feelings as soldiers with the activities, attitudes and feelings they had known before the war. Accordingly, while these men may well have had difficulties with repressed or conflicted drives, their main problem seemed to be, as Erikson came to speak of it at the time, "identity confusion."

It was almost a decade before Erikson set forth the implications of his clinical observations in "Childhood and Society." In that book, the summation and integration of fifteen years of research, he made three major contributions to the study of the human ego. He posited (1) that, side by side with the stages of psychosexual development described by Freud (the oral, anal, phallic, genital, Oedipal and pubertal), were psychosocial stages of ego development, in which the individual had to establish new basic orientations to himself and his social world; (2) that personality development continued throughout the whole life cycle;

and (3) that each stage had a positive *as well as* a negative component.

Much about these contributions—and about Erikson's way of thinking—can be understood by looking at his scheme of life stages. Erikson identifies eight stages in the human life cycle, in each of which a new dimension of "social interaction" becomes possible—that is, a new dimension in a person's interaction with himself, and with his social environment.

Trust vs. Mistrust

The first stage corresponds to the oral stage in classical psychoanalytic theory and usually extends through the first year of life. In Erikson's view, the new dimension of social interaction that emerges during this period involves basic *trust* at the one extreme, and *mistrust* at the other. The degree to which the child comes to trust the world, other people and himself depends to a considerable extent upon the quality of the care that he receives. The infant whose needs are met when they arise, whose discomforts are quickly removed, who is cuddled, fondled, played with and talked to, develops a sense of the world as a safe place to be and of people as helpful and dependable. When, however, the care is inconsistent, inadequate and rejecting, it fosters a basic mistrust, an attitude of fear and suspicion on the part of the infant toward the world in general and people in particular that will carry through to later stages of development.

It should be said at this point that the problem of basic trust-versus-mistrust (as is true for all the later dimensions) is not resolved once and for all during the first year of life; it arises again at each successive stage of development. There is both hope and danger in this. The child who enters school with a sense of mistrust may come to trust a particular teacher who has taken the trouble to make herself trustworthy; with this second chance, he overcomes his early mistrust. On the other hand, the child who comes through infancy with a vital sense of trust can still have his sense of mistrust activated at a later stage if, say, his parents are divorced and separated under acrimonious circumstances.

This point was brought home to me in a very direct way by a four-year-old patient I saw in a court clinic. He was being seen at the court clinic because his adoptive parents, who had had him for six months, now wanted to give him back to the agency. They claimed that he was cold and unloving, took things and could not be trusted. He was indeed a cold and apathetic boy, but with good reason. About a year after his illegitimate birth, he was taken away from his mother, who had a drinking problem, and was shunted back and forth among several foster homes. Initially he had tried to relate to the persons in the foster homes, but the relationships never had a chance to develop because he was moved at just the wrong times. In the end he gave up trying to reach out to others, because the inevitable separations hurt too much.

Like the burned child who dreads the flame, this emotionally burned child shunned the pain of emotional involvement. He had trusted his mother, but now he trusted no one. Only years of devoted care and patience could now undo the damage that had been done to this child's sense of trust.

Autonomy vs. Doubt

Stage Two spans the second and third years of life, the period which Freudian theory calls the anal stage. Erikson sees here the emergence of *autonomy*. This autonomy dimension builds upon the child's new motor and mental abilities. At this stage the child can not only walk but also climb, open and close, drop, push and pull, hold and let go. The child takes pride in these new accomplishments and wants to do everything himself, whether it be pulling the wrapper off a piece of candy, selecting the vitamin out of the bottle or flushing the toilet. If parents recognize the young child's need to do what he is capable of doing at his own pace and in his own time, then he develops a sense that he is able to control his muscles, his impulses, himself and, not insignificantly, his environment—the sense of autonomy.

When, however, his caretakers are impatient and do for him what he is capable of doing for himself, they reinforce a sense of shame and doubt. To be sure, every parent has rushed a child at times and children are hardy enough to endure such lapses. It is only when caretaking is consistently overprotective and criticism of "accidents" (whether these be wetting, soiling, spilling or breaking things) is harsh and unthinking that the child develops an excessive sense of shame with respect to other people and an excessive sense of doubt about his own abilities to control his world and himself.

If the child leaves this stage with less autonomy than shame or doubt, he will be handicapped in his attempts to achieve autonomy in adolescence and adulthood. Contrariwise, the child who moves through this stage with his sense of autonomy buoyantly outbalancing his feelings of shame and doubt is well prepared to be autonomous at later phases in the life cycle. Again, however, the balance of autonomy to shame and doubt set up during this period can be changed in either positive or negative directions by later events.

It might be well to note, in addition, that too much autonomy can be as harmful as too little. I have in mind a patient of seven who had a heart condition. He had learned very quickly how terrified his parents were of any signs in him of cardiac difficulty. With the psychological acuity given to children, he soon ruled the household. The family could not go shopping, or for a drive, or on a holiday if he did not approve. On those rare occasions when the parents had had enough and defied him, he would get angry and his purple hue and gagging would frighten them into submission.

Actually, this boy was frightened of this power (as all children would be) and was really eager to give it up. When the parents and the boy came to realize this, and to recognize that a little shame and doubt were a healthy counterpoise to an inflated sense of autonomy, the three of them could once again assume their normal roles.

Initiative vs. Guilt

In this stage (the genital stage of classical psychoanalysis) the child, age four to five, is pretty much master of his body and can ride a tricycle, run, cut and hit. He can thus initiate motor activities of various sorts on his own and no longer merely responds to or imitates the actions of other children. The same holds true for his language and fantasy activities. Accordingly, Erikson argues that the social dimension that appears at this stage has *initiative* at one of its poles and *guilt* at the other.

Whether the child will leave this stage with his sense of initiative far outbalancing his sense of guilt depends to a considerable extent upon how parents respond to his self-initiated activities. Children who are given much freedom and opportunity to initiate motor play such as running, bike riding, sliding, skating, tussling and wrestling have their sense of initiative reinforced. Initiative is also reinforced when parents answer their children's questions (intellectual initiative) and do not deride or inhibit fantasy or play activity. On the other hand, if the child is made to feel that his motor activity is bad, that his questions are a nuisance and that his play is silly and stupid, then he may develop a sense of guilt over self-initiated activities in general that will persist through later life stages.

Industry vs. Inferiority

Stage Four is the age period from 6 to 11, the elementary school years (described by classical psychoanalysis as the *latency phase*). It is a time during which the child's love for the parent of the opposite sex and rivalry with the same sexed parent (elements in the so-called family romance) are quiescent. It is also a period during which the child becomes capable of deductive reasoning, and of playing and learning by rules. It is not until this period, for example, that children can really play marbles, checkers and other "take turn" games that require obedience to rules. Erikson argues that the psychosocial dimension that emerges during this period has a sense of *industry* at one extreme and a sense of *inferiority* at the other.

The term industry nicely captures a dominant theme of this period during which the concern with how things are made, how they work and what they do predominates. It is the Robinson Crusoe age in the sense that the enthusiasm and minute detail with which Crusoe describes his activities appeals to the child's own budding sense of industry. When children are encouraged in their efforts to make, do, or build practical things (whether it be to construct creepy crawlers, tree houses, or airplane models— or to cook, bake or sew), are allowed to finish their products, and are praised and rewarded for the results, then the sense of industry is enhanced. But parents who see their children's efforts at making and doing as "mischief," and as simply "making a mess," help to encourage in children a sense of inferiority.

During these elementary-school years, however, the child's world includes more than the home. Now social institutions other than the family come to play a central role in the developmental crisis of the individual. (Here Erikson introduced still another advance in psychoanalytic theory, which heretofore concerned itself only with the effects of the parents' behavior upon the child's development.)

A child's school experiences affect his industry-inferiority balance. The child, for example, with an I.Q. of 80 to 90 has a particularly traumatic school experience, even when his sense of industry is rewarded and encouraged at home. He is "too bright" to be in special classes, but "too slow" to compete with children of average ability. Consequently he experiences constant failures in his academic efforts that reinforce a sense of inferiority.

On the other hand, the child who had his sense of industry derogated at home can have it revitalized at school through the offices of a sensitive and committed teacher. Whether the child develops a sense of industry or inferiority, therefore, no longer depends solely on the caretaking efforts of the parents but on the actions and offices of other adults as well.

Identity vs. Role Confusion

When the child moves into adolescence (Stage Five—roughly the ages 12 to 18), he encounters, according to traditional psychoanalytic theory, a reawakening of the family-romance problem of early childhood. His means of resolving the problem is to seek and find a romantic partner of his own generation. While Erikson does not deny this aspect of adolescence, he points out that there are other problems as well. The adolescent matures mentally as well as physiologically and, in addition to the new feelings, sensations and desires he experiences as a result of changes in his body, he develops a multitude of new ways of looking at and thinking about the world. Among other things, those in adolescence can now think about other people's thinking and wonder about what other people think of them. They can also conceive of ideal families, religions and societies which they then compare with the imperfect families, religions and societies of their own experience. Finally, adolescents become capable of constructing theories and philosophies designed to bring all the varied and conflicting aspects of society into a working, harmonious and peaceful whole. The adolescent, in a word, is an impatient idealist who believes that it is as easy to realize an ideal as it is to imagine it.

Erikson believes that the new interpersonal dimension which emerges during this period has to do with a sense of ego identity at the positive end and a sense of role confusion at the negative end. That is to say, given the adolescent's newfound integrative abilities, his task is to bring together all of the things he has learned about himself as a son, student, athlete, friend, Scout, newspaper boy, and so on, and integrate these different images of himself into a whole that makes sense and that shows continuity with the past while preparing for the future. To the extent that the young person succeeds in this endeavor, he arrives at a sense of psychosocial identity, a sense of who he is, where he has been and where he is going.

In contrast to the earlier stages, where parents play a more or less direct role in the determination of the result of the developmental crises, the influence of parents during this stage is much more indirect. If the young person reaches adolescence with, thanks to his parents, a vital sense of trust, autonomy, initiative and industry, then his chances of arriving at a meaningful sense of ego identity are much enhanced. The reverse, of course, holds true for the young person who enters adolescence with considerable mistrust, shame, doubt, guilt and inferiority. Preparation for a successful adolescence, and the attainment of an integrated psychosocial identity must, therefore, begin in the cradle.

Over and above what the individual brings with him from his childhood, the attainment of a sense of personal identity depends upon the social milieu in which he or she grows up. For example, in a society where women are to some extent second-class citizens, it may be harder for females to arrive at a sense of psychosocial identity. Likewise at times, such as the present, when rapid social and technological change breaks down many traditional values, it may be more difficult for young people to find continuity between what they learned and experienced as children and what they learn and experience as adolescents. At such times young people often seek causes that give their lives meaning and direction. The activism of the current generation of young people may well stem, in part at least, from this search.

When the young person cannot attain a sense of personal identity, either because of an unfortunate childhood or difficult social circumstances, he shows a certain amount of *role confusion*—a sense of not knowing what he is, where he belongs or whom he belongs to. Such confusion is a frequent symptom in delinquent young people. Promiscuous adolescent girls, for example, often seem to have a fragmented sense of ego identity. Some young people seek a "negative identity," an identity opposite to the one prescribed for them by their family and friends. Having an identity as a "delinquent," or as a "hippie," or even as an "acid head," may sometimes be preferable to having no identity at all.

In some cases young people do not seek a negative identity so much as they have it thrust upon them. I remember another court case in which the defendant was an attractive sixteen-year-old girl who had been found "tricking it" in a trailer located just outside the grounds of an Air Force base. From about the age of twelve, her mother had encouraged her to dress seductively and to go out with boys. When she returned from dates, her sexually frustrated mother demanded a kiss-by-kiss, caress-by-caress description of the evening's activities. After the mother had vicariously satisfied her sexual needs, she proceeded to call her daughter a "whore" and a "dirty tramp." As the girl told me, "Hell, I have the name, so I might as well play the role."

Failure to establish a clear sense of personal identity at adolescence does not guarantee perpetual failure. And the person who attains a working sense of ego identity in adolescence will of necessity encounter challenges and threats to that identity as he moves through life. Erikson, perhaps more than any other personality theorist, has emphasized that life is constant change and that confronting problems at one stage in life is not a guarantee against the reappearance of these problems at later stages, or against the finding of new solutions to them.

Intimacy vs. Isolation

Stage Six in the life cycle is young adulthood; roughly the period of courtship and early family life that extends from late adolescence till early middle age. For this stage, and the stages described hereafter, classical psychoanalysis has nothing new or major to say. For Erikson, however, the previous attainment of a sense of personal identity and the engagement in productive work that marks this period gives rise to a new interpersonal dimension of *intimacy* at the one extreme and *isolation* at the other.

When Erikson speaks of intimacy he means much more than love-making alone; he means the ability to share with and care about another person without fear of losing oneself in the process. In the case of intimacy, as in the case of identity, success or failure no longer depends directly upon the parents but only indirectly as they have contributed to the individual's success or failure at the earlier stages. Here, too, as in the case of identity, social conditions may help or hinder the establishment of a sense of intimacy. Likewise, intimacy need not involve sexuality; it includes the relationship between friends. Soldiers who have served together under the most dangerous circumstances often develop a sense of commitment to one another that exemplifies intimacy in its broadest sense. If a sense of intimacy is not established with friends or a marriage partner, the result, in Erikson's view, is a sense of isolation—of being alone without anyone to share with or care for.

Generativity vs. Self-Absorption

This stage—middle age—brings with it what Erikson speaks of as either *generativity or self-absorption,* and stagnation. What

Erikson means by generativity is that the person begins to be concerned with others beyond his immediate family, with future generations and the nature of the society and world in which those generations will live. Generativity does not reside only in parents; it can be found in any individual who actively concerns himself with the welfare of young people and with making the world a better place for them to live and to work.

Those who fail to establish a sense of generativity fall into a state of self-absorption in which their personal needs and comforts are of predominant concern. A fictional case of self-absorption is Dickens's Scrooge in "A Christmas Carol." In his one-sided concern with money and in his disregard for the interests and welfare of his young employe, Bob Cratchit, Scrooge exemplifies the self-absorbed, embittered (the two often go together) old man. Dickens also illustrated, however, what Erikson points out: namely, that unhappy solutions to life's crises are not irreversible. Scrooge, at the end of the tale, manifested both a sense of generativity and of intimacy which he had not experienced before.

Integrity vs. Despair

Stage Eight in the Eriksonian scheme corresponds roughly to the period when the individual's major efforts are nearing completion and when there is time for reflection—and for the enjoyment of grandchildren, if any. The psychosocial dimension that comes into prominence now has *integrity* on one hand and *despair* on the other.

The sense of integrity arises from the individual's ability to look back on his life with satisfaction. At the other extreme is the individual who looks back upon his life as a series of missed opportunities and missed directions; now in the twilight years he realizes that it is too late to start again. For such a person the inevitable result is a sense of despair at what might have been.

These, then, are the major stages in the life cycle as described by Erikson. Their presentation, for one thing, frees the clinician to treat adult emotional problems as failures (in part at least) to solve genuinely adult personality crises and not, as heretofore, as mere residuals of infantile frustrations and conflicts. This view of personality growth, moreover, takes some of the onus off parents and takes account of the role which society and the person himself play in the formation of an individual personality. Finally, Erikson has offered hope for us all by demonstrating that each phase of growth has its strengths as well as its weaknesses and that failures at one stage of development can be rectified by successes at later stages.

The reason that these ideals, which sound so agreeable to "common sense," are in fact so revolutionary has a lot to do with the state of psychoanalysis in America. As formulated by Freud, psychoanalysis encompassed a theory of personality development, a method of studying the human mind and, finally, procedures for treating troubled and unhappy people. Freud viewed this system as a scientific one, open to revision as new facts and observations accumulated.

The system was, however, so vehemently attacked that Freud's followers were constantly in the position of having to defend Freud's views. Perhaps because of this situation, Freud's system became, in the hands of some of his followers and defenders, a dogma upon which all theoretical innovation, clinical observation and therapeutic practice had to be grounded. That this attitude persists is evidenced in the recent remark by a psychoanalyst that he believed psychotic patients could not be treated by psychoanalysis because "Freud said so." Such attitudes, in which Freud's authority rather than observation and data is the basis of deciding what is true and what is false, has contributed to the disrepute in which psychoanalysis is widely held today.

Erik Erikson has broken out of this scholasticism and has had the courage to say that Freud's discoveries and practices were the start and not the end of the study and treatment of the human personality. In addition to advocating the modifications of psychoanalytic theory outlined above, Erikson has also suggested modifications in therapeutic practice, particularly in the treatment of young patients. "Young people in severe trouble are not fit for the couch," he writes. "They want to face you, and they want you to face them, not as a facsimile of a parent, or wearing the mask of a professional helper, but as a kind of over-all individual a young person can live with or despair of."

Erikson has had the boldness to remark on some of the negative effects that distorted notions of psychoanalysis have had on society at large. Psychoanalysis, he says, has contributed to a widespread fatalism—"even as we were trying to devise, with scientific determinism, a therapy for the few, we were led to promote an ethical disease among the many."

Perhaps Erikson's innovations in psychoanalytic theory are best exemplified in his psycho-historical writings, in which he combines psychoanalytic insight with a true historical imagination. After the publication of "Childhood and Society," Erikson undertook the application of his scheme of the human life cycle to the study of historical persons. He wrote a series of brilliant essays on men as varied as Maxim Gorky, George Bernard Shaw and Freud himself. These studies were not narrow case histories but rather reflected Erikson's remarkable grasp of Europe's social and political history, as well as of its literature. (His mastery of American folklore, history and literature is equally remarkable.)

While Erikson's major biographical studies were yet to come, these early essays already revealed his unique psychohistory method. For one thing, Erikson always chose men whose lives fascinated him in one way or another, perhaps because of some conscious or unconscious affinity with them. Erikson thus had a sense of community with his subjects which he adroitly used (he calls it *disciplined subjectivity*) to take his subject's point of view and to experience the world as that person might.

Secondly, Erikson chose to elaborate a particular crisis or episode in the individual's life which seemed to crystallize a life-theme that united the activities of his past and gave direction to his activities for the future. Then, much as an artist might, Erikson proceeded to fill in the background of the episode and add social and historical perspective. In a very real sense Erikson's biographical sketches are like paintings which direct the viewer's gaze from a focal point of attention to background and back again, so that one's appreciation of the focal area is enriched by having pursued the picture in its entirety.

This method was given its first major test in Erikson's study of "Young Man Luther." Originally, Erikson planned only a brief study of Luther, but "Luther proved too bulky a man to be merely a chapter in a book." Erikson's involvement with

Luther dated from his youth, when, as a wandering artist, he happened to hear the Lord's Prayer in Luther's German. "Never knowingly having heard it, I had the experience, as seldom before or after, of a wholeness captured in a few simple words, of poetry fusing the esthetic and the moral; those who have suddenly 'heard' the Gettysburg Address will know what I mean."

Erikson's interest in Luther may have had other roots as well. In some ways, Luther's unhappiness with the papal intermediaries of Christianity resembled on a grand scale Erikson's own dissatisfaction with the intermediaries of Freud's system. In both cases some of the intermediaries had so distorted the original teachings that what was being preached in the name of the master came close to being the opposite of what he had himself proclaimed. While it is not possible to describe Erikson's treatment of Luther here, one can get some feeling for Erikson's brand of historical analysis from his sketch of Luther:

"Luther was a very troubled and a very gifted young man who had to create his own cause on which to focus his fidelity in the Roman Catholic world as it was then. . . . He first became a monk and tried to solve his scruples by being an exceptionally good monk. But even his superiors thought that he tried much too hard. He felt himself to be such a sinner that he began to lose faith in the charity of God and his superiors told him, 'Look, God doesn't hate you, you hate God or else you would trust Him to accept your prayers.' But I would like to make it clear that someone like Luther becomes a historical person only because he also has an acute understanding of historical actuality and knows how to 'speak to the condition' of his times. Only then do inner struggles become representative of those of a large number of vigorous and sincere young people—and begin to interest some troublemakers and hangers-on."

After Erikson's study of "Young Man Luther" (1958), he turned his attention to "middle-aged" Gandhi. As did Luther, Gandhi evoked for Erikson childhood memories. Gandhi led his first nonviolent protest in India in 1918 on behalf of some mill workers, and Erikson, then a young man of sixteen, had read glowing accounts of the event. Almost a half a century later Erikson was invited to Ahmedabad, an industrial city in western

India, to give a seminar on the human life cycle. Erikson discovered that Ahmedabad was the city in which Gandhi had led the demonstration about which Erikson had read as a youth. Indeed, Erikson's host was none other than Ambalal Sarabahai, the benevolent industrialist who had been Gandhi's host—as well as antagonist—in the 1918 wage dispute. Throughout his stay in Ahmedabad, Erikson continued to encounter people and places that were related to Gandhi's initial experiments with nonviolent techniques.

The more Erikson learned about the event at Ahmedabad, the more intrigued he became with its pivotal importance in Gandhi's career. It seemed to be the historical moment upon which all the earlier events of Gandhi's life converged and from which diverged all of his later endeavors. So captured was Erikson by the event at Ahmedabad, that he returned the following year to research a book on Gandhi in which the event would serve as a fulcrum.

At least part of Erikson's interest in Gandhi may have stemmed from certain parallels in their lives. The 1918 event marked Gandhi's emergence as a national political leader. He was forty-eight at the time, and had become involved reluctantly, not so much out of a need for power or fame as out of a genuine conviction that something had to be done about the disintegration of Indian culture. Coincidentally, Erikson's book, "Childhood and Society," appeared in 1950 when Erikson was forty-eight, and it is that book which brought him national prominence in the mental health field. Like Gandhi, too, Erikson reluctantly did what he felt he had to do (namely, publish his observations and conclusions) for the benefit of his ailing profession and for the patients treated by its practitioners. So while Erikson's affinity with Luther seemed to derive from comparable professional identity crises, his affinity for Gandhi appears to derive from a parallel crisis of generativity. A passage from "Gandhi's Truth" (from a chapter wherein Erikson addresses himself directly to his subject) helps to convey Erikson's feeling for his subject.

"So far, I have followed you through the loneliness of your childhood and through the experiments and the scruples of your youth. I have affirmed my belief in your ceaseless endeavor to perfect yourself as a man who came to feel that he was the only one available to reverse India's fate. You experimented with what to you were debilitating temptations and you did gain vigor and agility from your victories over yourself. Your identity could be no less than that of universal man, although you had to become an Indian—and one close to the masses—first."

The following passage speaks to Erikson's belief in the general significance of Gandhi's efforts:

"We have seen in Gandhi's development the strong attraction of one of those more inclusive identities: that of an enlightened citizen of the British Empire. In proving himself willing neither to abandon vital ties to his native tradition nor to sacrifice lightly a Western education which eventually contributed to his ability to help defeat British hegemony—in all of these seeming contradictions Gandhi showed himself on intimate terms with the actualities of his era. For in all parts of the world, the struggle now is for the *anticipatory development of more inclusive identities* . . . I submit then, that Gandhi, in his immense intuition for historical actuality and his capacity to assume leadership in 'truth in action,' may have created a ritualization through which men, equipped with both realism and strength, can face each other with mutual confidence."

There is now more and more teaching of Erikson's concepts in psychiatry, psychology, education and social work in America and in other parts of the world. His description of the stages of the life cycle are summarized in major textbooks in all of these fields and clinicians are increasingly looking at their cases in Eriksonian terms.

Research investigators have, however, found Erikson's formulations somewhat difficult to test. This is not surprising, inasmuch as Erikson's conceptions, like Freud's, take into account the infinite complexity of the human personality. Current research methodologies are, by and large, still not able to deal with these complexities at their own level, and distortions are inevitable when such concepts as "identity" come to be defined in terms of responses to a questionnaire.

Likewise, although Erikson's life-stages have an intuitive "rightness" about them, not everyone agrees with his formulations. Douvan and Adelson in their book, "The Adolescent Experience," argue that while his identity theory may hold true for boys, it doesn't for girls. This argument is based on findings which suggest that girls postpone identity consolidation until after marriage (and intimacy) have been established. Such postponement occurs, say Douvan and Adelson, because a woman's identity is partially defined by the identity of the man whom she marries. This view does not really contradict Erikson's, since he recognizes that later events, such as marriage, can help to resolve both current and past developmental crises. For the woman, but not for the man, the problems of identity and intimacy may be solved concurrently.

Objections to Erikson's formulations have come from other directions as well. Robert W. White, Erikson's good friend and colleague at Harvard, has a long standing (and warm-hearted) debate with Erikson over his life-stages. White believes that his own theory of "competence motivation," a theory which has received wide recognition, can account for the phenomena of ego development much more economically than can Erikson's stages. Erikson has, however, little interest in debating the validity of the stages he has described. As an artist he recognizes that there are many different ways to view one and the same phenomenon and that a perspective that is congenial to one person will be repugnant to another. He offers his stage-wise description of the life cycle for those who find such perspectives congenial and not as a world view that everyone should adopt.

It is this lack of dogmatism and sensitivity to the diversity and complexity of the human personality which help to account for the growing recognition of Erikson's contribution within as well as without the helping professions. Indeed, his psychohistorical investigations have originated a whole new field of study which has caught the interest of historians and political scientists alike. (It has also intrigued his wife, Joan, who has published pieces on Eleanor Roosevelt and who has a book on Saint Francis in press.) A recent issue of Daedalus, the journal for the American Academy of Arts and Sciences, was entirely devoted to psycho-historical and psycho-political investigations of creative leaders by authors from diverse disciplines who have been stimulated by Erikson's work.

Now in his sixty-eighth year, Erikson maintains the pattern of multiple activities and appointments which has characterized his entire career. He spends the fall in Cambridge, Mass., where he teaches a large course on "the human life cycle" for Harvard seniors. The spring semester is spent at his home in Stockbridge, Mass., where he participates in case conferences and staff seminars at the Austen Riggs Center. His summers are spent on Cape Cod. Although Erikson's major commitment these days is to his psychohistorical investigation, he is embarking on a study of preschool children's play constructions in different settings and countries, a follow-up of some research he conducted with preadolescents more than a quarter-century ago. He is also planning to review other early observations in the light of contemporary change. In his approach to his work, Erikson appears neither drawn nor driven, but rather to be following an inner schedule as natural as the life cycle itself.

Although Erikson, during his decade of college teaching, has not seen any patients or taught at psychoanalytic institutes, he maintains his dedication to psychoanalysis and views his psycho-historical investigations as an applied branch of that discipline. While some older analysts continue to ignore Erikson's work, there is increasing evidence (including a recent poll of psychiatrists and psychoanalysts) that he is having a rejuvenating influence upon a discipline which many regard as dead or dying. Young analysts are today proclaiming a "new freedom" to see Freud in historical perspective—which reflects the Eriksonian view that one can recognize Freud's greatness without bowing to conceptual precedent.

Accordingly, the reports of the demise of psychoanalysis may have been somewhat premature. In the work of Erik Erikson, at any rate, psychoanalysis lives and continues to beget life.

Bruno Bettelheim Is Dr. No
by David Dempsey

THE WORLD OF Bruno Bettelheim is a psychoanalyst's vision of hell. Inside this hell stands a therapeutic treatment center for the psychologically damned. This is the Sonia Shankman Orthogenic School for severely disturbed children, which Bettelheim has directed since 1944 on the campus at the University of Chicago. A Vienna-born disciple of Freud and one of the world's foremost authorities on childhood psychosis, he has made the school into a unique personal laboratory for the study of human behavior. His books on the emotional disorders of children have contributed a disproportionate bulk to the weighty canon of treatment in this field, and on the broader, more controversial subject of modern youth, he is an indefatigable speaker before both lay and professional audiences.

For millions of Americans who are understandably nervous about the radical young, the Bettelheim view of what ails them seems both timely and important: Many of the hippies, militants, Yippies and assorted fringe groups of the New Left, he believes, are emotionally sick. Although, unlike his patients at the school, the radical young do not realize it, their hell is no less real. What is even more disturbing to Bettelheim is that an influential segment of the adult world has elevated this sickness to the status of a "youth culture," glorifying what should properly be looked upon as a pathology.

The chaos these young people rage against, Bettelheim says, is within themselves, not the world. Changing society will not do the job, since no change is ever enough for the truly militant. "While consciously they demand freedom and participation," he has written, "unconsciously their commitment to Mao and leaders like him suggests their desperate need for controls from the outside, since without them they cannot bring order to their own inner chaos." Only by understanding the psychological motivation of these young activists, only by deglamorizing the illusory role they have invented for themselves, Bettelheim contends, can we help them.

In an age of confrontation politics, Bettelheim is counter-Spock, the Dr. No of child-care authorities. Many of youth's problems, he believes, can be traced to the indifferent, contradictory and easy-going approach that passes for "permissiveness" (a term that, he says, has very little meaning). At the University of Chicago, where he has taught for the last 30 years, Bettelheim enjoys— the word is appropriate—the reputation of being a tyrannical figure in the classroom and out. When students occupied the administration building in the spring of 1968, he turned up at a press conference, took the microphone and denounced them as paranoid. Many of the faculty were angered at this, but in the end the "revolt" failed and the ringleaders were later expelled.

Bettelheim denies that he is unsympathetic with the legitimate aspirations of the young, but insists that much of what passes for idealism is misdirected psychic energy. Society has imposed enormous frustrations on youth, and, in the title of a recent Bettelheim magazine article, made it "obsolete." The adolescent is crying for a manhood which is postponed, at great psychological cost, by the technical nature of a society that has dispensed with his services; by an educational process that "has brought incredibly large numbers to the academic life who do *not* find their self-realization through study or intellectual adventure . . ."

In his numerous public appearances—he spoke once in Boston, four times in New York City and once in Atlanta during a recent three-week span—Bettelheim tells these young people what they don't want to hear ("One should go along with the Establishment if it is halfway reasonable; any Establishment is only halfway reasonable") and the adults, by and large, what they do want to hear. In testimony before the House Special Subcommittee on Education investigating student disorders last spring, he declared that militant leaders are bright but emotionally "fixated at the age of the temper tantrum." Elsewhere he has declared: "Big in size and age, those who sit-in feel like little boys with a need to 'play big' by sitting in papa's big chair . . . they want to have a say in how things are run, not because they feel competent to do so but because they cannot bear to feel incompetent a single moment longer."

Bettelheim's popular writings have the comforting ring of old-fashioned virtues sanctioned by Freudian psychology. ". . . For self-control to develop, children must have learned to fear something before they enter society," he wrote recently. This "something," he adds, is parental authority.* Although a disciple of John Dewey, he criticizes the misapplied Deweyism that has infected many schools. "The biggest nonsense in American education today," he lectured his graduate class in education, "is for the teacher to tell her pupils, 'Look, children, it is easy.' Make it attractive, not easy. The task must be possible, and it must be meaningful. Ease has no place in it." In essence, this is the message Bettelheim directs at the adolescent young. "You have nothing to push against because everything gives way. How can you find an identity?" he asked a New York audience at a panel discussion on new life styles for youth. Bettelheim's co-panelists were Paul Goodman and Leslie Fiedler, both culture heroes of the college generation. He is at his best during such confrontations: although small of build, with an accent not unlike Dr. Strangelove's and a polished, almost totally bald head, Bettelheim is a

---

* In another context, Bettelheim has amplified this idea. "What was wrong with old-fashioned authoritarian education was not that it rested on fear," he wrote in Encounter magazine. "On the contrary, that is what was right with it. What was wrong was that it disregarded the need to modify the fear in a continuous process so that irrational anxiety would steadily give way to more rational motivation."

commanding presence on the dais. He is capable of a scathing wit and has access to an analytic nomenclature of such technical resonance that authority is exhaled with every breath.

He dresses conservatively, and although his manner is dignified it is in no sense pompous. In private gatherings, he can be a vigorous chest-puncher as he drives home his views. In public, this aggressiveness is suggested by a forceful way of speaking that belies an underlying good humor. At the youth meeting in New York, during remarks by Goodman and Fiedler, the microphone refused to work. When Bettelheim's turn came, it had been restored with such vengeance that his opening sentence all but blasted the crowd out of its chairs. "Nothing personal," he remarked.

He went on to deprecate beards and long hair ("Whenever anybody has to follow a certain style, it is a denial of his ability to live without it"), the "cool" style of life, the sex revolution and a number of other matters close to the hearts of many in the audience. Asked by a young girl if his disapproval of the sexual revolution wasn't motivated by envy, Bettelheim, who is 66, shook his head and grinned. He is not, he has insisted on other occasions, one of those men that La Rochefoucauld speaks about who give good advice simply because they are too old to set a bad example.

As an analyst, Bettelheim sees the bad examples almost exclusively, and this, his critics point out, has colored his view of the young. "Inevitably, he sees patients—the losers, as it were," says Dr. Robert Coles of Harvard. "But there are a lot of bright young radicals who are thoroughly intelligent, compassionate and decent; in fact, their values often resemble Bettelheim's, as he has stated them so beautifully in some of his books."

Bettelheim would probably not deny this, but he might ask: At what risk to the emotional well-being of those who try to reconcile their militant, often destructive behavior with decent instincts? He thinks that most adolescents are not aware of the risks, and his work with them has convinced him that the price is too high. The Orthogenic School has treated its share of "radical" teen-agers and affluent hippies; more ominously, it is now getting children born to the drug and hippie generation of young parents.

Recently, a 7-year-old girl was admitted whose behavior was so bizarre that she had been diagnosed by a number of psychiatrists as mentally retarded. Evaluation of the child by the school's staff convinced Bettelheim that this was probably not the case. "Katie" had been conceived while her parents were living in a San Francisco commune. Although both were university graduates with good jobs, they continued to practice their brand of "youth culture." The mother took a lover, who later shot himself to death in the child's presence. Until "Katie" came to the school, she had never worn a pair of shoes. Over and over, she sang a song to the tune of "Frère Jacques." The words were, "Marijuana, marijuana. . . ."

"But it wasn't marijuana the mother had been taking," Bettelheim explains. "It was LSD."

It is cases such as this that shake him. And it is because they do that he feels a duty to shake up the young. "I am not like Edgar Friedenberg or Paul Goodman or Leslie Fiedler," he says. "They have a tremendous need to be loved by the young. I have absolutely none."

The feeling is largely mutual. Although Bettelheim is much in demand at Middle Western colleges and universities and recently addressed the right-leaning Association of Student Governments, his standing among undergraduates at the more prestigious institutions is low. Not a few of them at the University of Chicago refer to him as "Dr. Brutalheim." "Just hearing his name mentioned makes me mad," a coed told me.

The Orthogenic School is at the easternmost edge of Chicago's campus, on the Midway. Originally a Universalist church and seminary, it is now a tidy complex of dormitories, lounges, dining halls and classrooms. A steeple still rises overhead. Once inside the door of the vestibule—alive with carved angels, gilt-edged cupids, playful gargoyles—there is a feeling of sanctuary. An episcopal throne at one end of the reception lounge looks across at an antique cradle, a sleek wooden hobby horse with fish's tail, a three-tiered, gimcracky doll's house. Books line the walls and upholstered furniture occupies the center area. It could be a setting for a play by Arthur Schnitzler.

While you are waiting for the curtain to go up, a little man dashes in, grabs the day's mail and exits without speaking. A few minutes later he returns to introduce himself. This is Bruno Bettelheim. Inside his office, peering across an uncluttered desk, he transfixes visitors through thick-lensed glasses. Magnified, his eyes seem to penetrate the psyche like laser beams. Later, he will relax, swivel sideways and prop one foot on the window sill, but until that happens he is taking your measure from above. Portnoy would never bring his complaint here.*

"Is there such a thing as a youth culture?" I asked.

"The idea that adolescence is God-given, that it has any special virtues, doesn't appeal to me. And I don't think we are going to cope with it intelligently by glorifying it. Adolescence is not a physiological period in one's life, like puberty, but a culturally imposed age. As a particular style of life it can only be possible if people are not part of the working force. Until 1900, almost nobody became adolescent because after the age of 14 or 15 he went to work. The first really typical adolescent was created by Richard Wagner in Siegfried, a young man utterly truthful, fearless and somewhat dumb, I may say, who fought the evil world of the Establishment. And it was very much after the Siegfried myth that the youth movement in Germany became a special culture. Now we have it all over again.

"You see, the adolescent today is someone who is grown up but still not independent economically. This leads to terrible psychological strains which didn't exist when 95 per cent of the group was fully employed and had a family. I don't think any greater wisdom is vested in youth, but there is something about Americans that makes them want to be young, and to be with the young. . . . This is really sad."

"But haven't they liberated themselves from the restrictions that

---

* Had he done so, Philip Roth's novel might never have been written; or at least not in its present form. "He uses obscenity to impress others and fools himself into thinking himself liberated," Bettelheim wrote in "Portnoy Psychoanalyzed" (Midstream, June/July, 1969). ". . . did I do the right thing [to] tell him . . . that it is time to stop being a man of letters so that, through analyzing himself, he might finally become a man?"

were imposed on them in the old days, when they *did* have to go to work at 14 and become adults too early in life? Haven't they struck a blow for freedom by insisting on being adolescents?"

"Everybody wants to strike blows for freedom. It is such a nice thing to do, you know. So what do we mean by freedom? Let's look at the long hair and the beard, shall we? So if you look at them you see that the same fashion has occurred and reoccurred. So what's new and original about that? As a matter of fact, wigs are back. So what is so great an innovation that people wear wigs? It's just the flow of fashion. Do men wear colorful dress and jewelry? Well, my God!—we are back in the 18th century. We are not yet back to lace collars, but they will come. They will come. And they will go again. Let's not mistake custom for real progress.

"Fashion always changes from restricting the body to freeing the body to restricting the body. No, it's not a freedom movement! There was no real gain of freedom in the time of the French Revolution, when women bared their breasts as they now do again. I tell you nothing is more restrictive in fashion than the freedom of the hippie. As a psychoanalyst I see girls who find it much more restrictive and inhibiting that the new morality demands that they should have sex relations without much ado, who cannot afford to admit how old-fashioned they are, how desperate for someone who doesn't *want* them to be a liberated woman.

"These conventions can be as crippling as the Victorian conventions. Actually, I think this movement has enslaved women much more than they were before. But it's a different slavery, a new one, as much as the Victorian slavery looked awfully good to women at first, when they became so glorified. The Victorian state was not simply imposed on women; it was desired by them. Then after a while they found how much they had shackled themselves, and then they objected to the shackles.

"After World War I, when I was a student at the University of Vienna, there were students who formed communes and lived there promiscuously. They were less than one-half of one per cent of the college population; nobody paid any attention to them. They were not the wave of the future. Let me give you another example. Let us say that one per cent of the University of Illinois went on the peace march. But a considerably larger group suddenly believes in astrology. Is this a blow for freedom or a regression into medieval superstition?

"For these people, the discrepancy lies in the fact that they know they are parasites on society economically. If you listen to Jerry Rubin or Paul Goodman, they are waste material. Now whether you are going to make a contribution to society or become waste material is a psychological view of yourself. It has nothing to do with external society. I think, personally, that it is highly desirable that more groups in the population, particularly the young, be permitted to experiment with a wide variety of views. I think what is evil—and I use here the religious term— is that the mass media push them into extreme positions, because that is what gets attention. The young person who is insecure is always a sucker for public attention.

"The original hippies—very sick people, very sweet people— wanted to be nothing but left alone. If they had been, most of them would have found their way back sooner or later. By becoming glorified in the public eye, being weak to begin with, they were sucked into a life that became utterly destructive to them. If adult society mistakes such quite necessary youthful experimentation with the portents of the future, then something very bad happens to society and the young people."

Had Dr. Bettelheim read about the Woodstock Festival?

"Why Woodstock? Why not Fort Lauderdale? I don't know where you went to college, but it wasn't just one Woodstock a year. It was a football trip every other weekend."

"Not for me."

"Well, not for me, either, but for thousands. And you heard the same stories that you got from the March on Washington— how wonderful that somebody shared his blanket with me; somebody shared his food with me. We had a wonderful time, we sat up all night, sang all night, drank all night. . . . Youth has a tremendous need to get together in large groups, to get intoxicated by the image of each other's presence. I cannot be too impressed by the external forms because I see the underlying need, which is the same—to escape my loneliness, my isolation, to find a reaffirmation that I am a worthwhile person by the fact that so many other people do the same things that I do.

"Group intelligence is always far inferior, you know. The individual who fights all by himself might at least come up as a genius. No guarantee; he might be a quack. What concerns me most is that suddenly the mass mind, the mob spirit, is advertised as the highest achievement of Western society, where up to very recently it was the individual struggling alone who was the culture hero. That's where progress comes from, not by 50,000 people in the same boat. . . . Let me put it this way: If you had put on a demonstration in the time of Copernicus, that the earth is flat and the center of the universe, millions would have demonstrated in favor of this position. Would that have proved anything? The merits of the case have nothing to do with how many followers it has.

"For more than 20 years I have been concerned with the creating of readers which would be suitable for underprivileged children. We still haven't solved the problem, but no mass demonstrations are going to get us those books. All the screaming that we do it wrong will not get us better ideas of how to do it right. But this is an age that wants easy solutions. Well, the militants want to change society to please themselves, without asking how society works. . . ."

Wasn't it possible that Bettelheim left no room in his scheme for the gifted militants of history—the martyrs and saints?

"I have no use for saints. They are *impossible* people; they destroy everybody around them. The sooner they go to heaven the better, because that is where they belong."

He beamed. "Would you like to see our school?"

"One cannot help another in his ascent from hell unless one has joined him there," Bettelheim has written in one of four books based on his work with disturbed children. At the school everything is done to make that journey cheerful. Furnishings, designed to Bettelheim's specifications, are a kind of updated Biedermeier. Bettelheim selected the paintings on the walls, picked out the light fixtures and chose the wallpaper and color schemes for the rooms. (Children are allowed to select the colors of their rooms only if Dr. B., as he is called by his staff, agrees that they are "happy" colors—i.e., therapeutic.) Stairways have animal figures playfully worked into the tiling—like the hallways, they are "transitional" areas and must be friendly. Dormitory rooms are replete with stuffed dragons, koala bears, penguins, boa constrictors, tigers. On each child's birthday, and again at Christmas, he is presented with a new animal of Dr. Bettelheim's choosing. It is not unusual to see half a dozen of these beasts piled up on the bed of an 18-year-old boy about to be discharged from the school to enter college.

Still churchlike in appearance, the exterior walls also illustrate the Bettelheim approach to environmental therapy. On the fringe of Chicago's South Side slums, the school is an inviting target for vandals. Some time ago, Bettelheim had a large mural painted on one of these walls. "Not one of the neighborhood kids has ever done any harm to it," he says, "although hundreds pass it daily. In working with the most asocial youngsters, I have found that the only sure way to prevent their defacing the walls is to decorate them with objects of beauty."

A member of the university's English department who has known Bettelheim for some time thinks that the private world he has created for the patients reflects in great measure his own secure childhood. "Using a little curbstone Freud, I'd say that the school is a Viennese young man's idea of heaven—bourgeois furnishings, a love of art, servants, orderliness, a house full of toys, a strong father image and all you want to eat. It worked for Bruno and it seems to work very well for these kids."

Bettelheim is quick to point out, however, that these are simply the visible symbols. The real work lies in the years of patient, one-to-one "confrontation" between counselor and child, the unraveling of the latter's tangled emotional life and the habilitation of his personality. A controlled environment helps make this possible. The school's routine is highly structured, and Bettelheim presides over it with a "father knows best" attitude, which, his staff willingly acknowledges, is usually justified. (One associate purchased a Modigliani painting a few years ago and proudly brought it in to show Dr. B. "It's a fake," he declared. And it was.)

Bettelheim was born in Vienna in 1903 and grew up there

during the great age of Freud and Rank. "At that time, there were a limited number of opportunities open to a Jew," says an Austrian-born writer now living in New York. "If you had money, you might go into business or one of the professions. If you didn't, your choice was pretty much limited to being a tailor or a zither player."

Bettelheim, whose father was a lumber dealer—he describes his family as "assimilated Jewish bourgeoisie"—had money. At the university, he combined majors in literature and art history, took his Ph.D. in esthetics, then switched to psychoanalysis. It was during his early years as a practicing analyst that he became interested in the behavior—or rather, the misbehavior—of the young.

One of the most baffling childhood disorders is autism, a condition that frequently leaves its victim mute or the possessor of an unintelligible language of his own. Most autistic children live in a private fantasy world, their relationship to others virtually nonexistent. Many do not even experience pain. It is, as Bettelheim has written, "a solipsistic way of perceiving the world," and in the nineteen-twenties, when he became aware of the disorder, autism was considered incurable.

Bettelheim was convinced, however, that it was not congenital. In 1932 he took an autistic child into his home; another followed somewhat later, and for the next six years he created "a very special environment that might undo emotional isolation in a child and build up personality." This experiment was suddenly ended in 1938, when the Nazis invaded Austria and Bettelheim was dragged off to Buchenwald. He remained there, and at Dachau, for almost two years, using his time to study the behavior of other inmates under stress. The war had not yet started, and both Gov. Herbert Lehman of New York and Mrs. Eleanor Roosevelt, who knew of Bettelheim's work, intervened with German authorities on his behalf. Released in 1939, he came to the United States and found a place on the University of Chicago faculty.

Although of Jewish origin, Bettelheim has no religious affiliation, has never been a Zionist and does not involve himself in Jewish culture as such. (Many of his friends, however, such as Saul Bellow, have strong Jewish identification.) Since making a name for himself in this country, Bettelheim has angered many Jews by being generally critical of the European Jews who stayed behind. As for the wealthy and middle class, he has written, less concern with holding on to their material possessions and more respect for themselves as individuals would have enabled most of them to escape the extermination camps. (Bettelheim's own family, with the exception of a few cousins, successfully fled to other parts of Europe or the United States.) Even those imprisoned, he adds, displayed a passive acceptance of their fate which played into their captors' hands.

A Bettelheim monograph, "Individual and Mass Behavior in Extreme Situations," written shortly after he was released, became required reading for U.S. Army officers in Europe during the war. Yet in 1946, when called to testify before a Congressional committee making preparations for the War Crimes Tribunal, Bettelheim advised against such a commission. To try men for acts committed while obeying orders, he contended, could only destroy the legitimate role of government, even if that role is abused. He has not changed his views.

In 1941, Bettelheim married a girl he had known in Vienna who, until recently, was a social worker in Chicago. The couple's three children—one daughter 27, another in college and an 18-year-old son just finishing high school—afforded Bettelheim an opportunity to raise "normal" children of his own. ("Well, the boy plays poker," a faculty member reported. "That's pretty normal, isn't it?") Bettelheim shares his findings with a group of young mothers who meet with him intermittently on the campus. At these sessions, practical child-rearing problems are discussed, and, peripherally, he offers advice on marital problems. "I've seen parents wait for a divorce till the children grow up," he remarked once, "but I've never seen the children better off for it."

Bettelheim's experiences in the concentration camps had a profound effect on his theories of human behavior. As a Freudian, he had believed that personality change was the result of slow, step-by-step processes. But in Buchenwald, he realized, men were broken in a matter of weeks. ". . . The psychoanalytic notions by which I had tried to guide my life . . . failed me at the moment when I needed them most," he wrote in his book, "The Informed

Heart." "Being placed in a particular type of environment can produce much more radical changes, and in a much shorter time."

If this were so—if massive and deliberately negative forces could destroy human personality—would it not also be possible to turn the tables and create an overwhelmingly positive environment that might serve to *create* personality? This was the hell-bent-for-heaven approach that Bettelheim adopted in 1944, when he was made director of the Orthogenic School. Although established at the turn of the century, the school had worked primarily with spastics and children with physical handicaps. They were transferred to other institutions when Bettelheim took over, and admissions were limited to severely psychotic and autistic children.

Supported in part by the university as a continuing research laboratory for developing ways of treating childhood psychosis, the school selects its students from all social backgrounds. Tuition is $8,000 a year, but public agencies and foundations supply partial or full scholarships for those unable to pay. For many youngsters who have been in other institutions, the school is a place of last resort. Applications for admission far exceed the openings available and, in Bettelheim's words, "preference is given to those whom no one else can help."

Except for a university psychiatrist who comes in once a week to interview new admissions and meet with the counselors, the school employs no medical personnel. Drugs are never used. The 30 staff members and 54 patients eat together in a common dining room and live in the same building. On Bettelheim's orders, women counselors may not wear miniskirts or slacks, the men must be clean-shaven and, needless to say, neatly shorn. "I don't want any unresolved father transferences here," he reportedly told his staff on one occasion.

Bettelheim arrives at the school about 10:30 in the morning and, except for his teaching chores and dinner at home, remains until midnight. Much of his time is spent prowling around, popping into classrooms and lounges, visiting with the children and chatting with his staff. When he enters the dining hall for lunch, a slight, reverential hush comes over the room. "He can be quite demanding, even authoritarian," says the associate director, Dr. Bert Cohler, "but he has an uncanny ability to put himself in the child's place, to know what makes him act the way he does, and to give him his own unique therapeutic environment." This may be a matter of discipline, although not until the child's emotional bonds to the school are secure enough to withstand it. (He has been known to spank a youngster.) Bettelheim believes that a patient must realize that it is he who is sick—not the outside world—before he begins to get well. "You are crazy—insane!" he may tell his students. "You can't do that if you ever expect to leave this place." To Bettelheim, only another person, not drugs or shock therapy, can lead the mentally ill back to reality.

"There is no direct confrontation available to the sick child unless somebody offers himself for the confrontation . . ." he has written. "What we have to demonstrate is that together we can make a go of it, even down there—something that he alone at this point cannot do. Hence the heart of our work is not any particular knowledge or procedure as such, but an inner attitude to life and to those caught up in its struggle, even as we are."

How effective this "inner attitude" can be is seen in the treatment of "Joey," a 9-year-old autistic who was convinced that he was run by machines. So controlling was this belief that Joey carried with him an elaborate life-support system made up of radio tubes, light bulbs and a "breathing machine." At meals, he ran imaginary wires from a wall socket to himself so that his food would be digested. His bed was rigged up with batteries, a loudspeaker and other improvised equipment to keep him alive while he slept.

Joey was allowed to play out this fantasy for years while Bettelheim and the counselors explored his infancy, largely through the innumerable drawings by which the child recalled his earliest years. Gradually, as he realized that he was not going to die, that he was an individual in his own right, Joey was able to substitute a "real" life for a mechanical one. After 11 years, he returned home and entered high school.

"Autism is a response to a catastrophic threat," Bettelheim says. It is "the conviction that one's own efforts have no power to influence the world because of the earlier conviction that the world is insensitive to one's reactions." With Freudian predictability, he traces this traumatic experience to such Oedipal situations

as parental rejection and toilet training. Since these factors cannot
be undone, the emphasis is on creating a new, benign environment until the child at last conceives of himself as a separate
"person." The daily process of creating an environment begins
the moment the child awakens in the morning, when his counselor
sits by his bed with toys, waiting to play a game. It continues on
the playground and in the classroom, as teacher and counselor
accommodate themselves to the individual child's needs. Food is
everywhere, and the child may eat at any time. Not until he is
secure is an effort made to "socialize" him and subject him to
the rules of society. At this stage, too, he begins weekly psychotherapy sessions with his counselor. Through these sessions the
treatment becomes "rational" and the child achieves some insight
into his condition; he realizes that he is sick.

As a result of such analytic positivism, Bettelheim can point
to a remarkable record during his 25-year tenure at the school.*
And it is from this well-ordered fortress that he looks in dismay
at a radical generation that is filled with self-hatred, alienated
from society and yet economically dependent upon it, roleless,
confused. "You are sick—insane!" he admonishes them. "Get
well!"

We are in his office again, and he is talking about a student
revolutionary who had been a patient at the school two years
before. "He was a very bright boy, going to one of the best
private schools in New York. At home, all he did was sit in a
dark room, in front of a TV, huddled in a blanket, eating TV
dinners. On the outside, he demonstrated. No demonstration was
too big for him, no sit-in could last long enough. It was the only
time he wasn't desperately alone. How did he come to me? In
one demonstration, the leader said they should all hold hands,
and suddenly he realized that nobody held his hand. Later, in

---

* Many graduates have gone on to college or become self-supporting.
Dr. Cohler, who earned his Ph.D. at Harvard, spent eight years at the
school as a patient. A study made two years ago of the 40 autistics who
had been discharged up to that time showed that for eight the end
results were considered "poor," for 15 "fair" and for 17 "good" or "cured."
Nine of the 17 were gainfully employed, eight were still in high school or
college. Three of five students who had finished college earned higher
degrees.

desperation, he tried to commit suicide and they brought him here. You see, the trouble with you gentlemen of the press is that you pay attention to them only as long as they make news. I pay attention to them afterward.

"Of course, it would be ridiculous to overlook the fact that there is a lot wrong in our society that should be remedied. But you see, that is the difference between the violent militant and the reformer, whose main concern is what is wrong and whose motive is an effort to set it right. The militant is more motivated by his inner anger than by the wrongs of society. . . . We need a lot more people who work hard at reforming society, but I have never yet seen anything good come out of what people did in anger.

"It has been observed that the girls among these groups are much more angry than the boys. . . . It is quite obvious that many of them are unable to accept their femininity. For example, very obese girls are way out of proportion to the frequency with which they appear in the rest of the population. Now, I think it is a good thing that they are openly angry about what they consider the wrong role into which women are forced in our society —well, it is the wrong role for them because they can't fit in. But I don't think their anger at society is the cause of their militancy.

"You might say I have been very militant in fighting for reforms in the treatment of psychotic children. I have had many confrontations. . . . But while I am quite militant in stating my opinions, I would never make any effort to force anybody else to accept them."

Bettelheim is a collector of Renaissance medals, and now he removes one from its flannel case while he talks, handling it like a talisman. I had asked him about the Freedom Riders. There was militance among them, even violence: would he not agree that changes resulted—changes in attitudes, even laws?

"Frankly, I don't think so at all. The Freedom Ride made a lot of headlines, but I am not sure that they helped the Negro to find himself. It is my conviction that what these white people did was to contribute to black separatism because they intruded on an indigenous movement and tried to create a revolutionary situation, whereas it was in the interests of the black community to push their own thing. What is necessary for the blacks is much more respect for their background and history; out of *that* the reform has to come, rather than having it imposed by people who are 'gung ho' from their inner pressures.

"It is very easy to say, 'I want a just society,' but that is not idealism. Adolescents make tremendously high moral demands on others, but nowhere is it expected that *they* should live up to the demands. This is characteristic of the person who is not yet settled in life or in society. I admired the kibbutzim because the Jews went ahead and tried to do it. To scream that other people should do things—well, idealism is when you put your ideas into practice, at some expense and hardship to yourself."

(Later that day, in a lecture on "Expectations," he will tell his class: "Our work is to pick up the pieces, to undo the damage, not to worry about the future." Bettelheim laces the 90-minute session with anecdotes—"You can ask any question you want, but you may not interrupt my stories"—moving back and forth between a chair and a lectern, gently tyrannizing his class with his *ex cathedra* manner. A legendary Bettelheim incident concerns a girl whom he observed knitting. "Do you know, Miss—," he remarked acidly, "that what you are doing is a substitute for masturbation?" Unintimidated, the student stared back. "Dr. Bettelheim," she replied, "when I knit, I knit.")

Bettelheim had stressed in his writings that new ways of rearing children in upper-middle-class homes help explain the problems of the young. Would he elaborate?

"Well, the contradictions in which these children are raised: that life is a rat race, but you be the first rat in the race! Or: I am your friend, you can tell me anything that is on your mind, but you are to respect me as a parent. You can't be a friend on an equal basis and at the same time expect to be treated as someone special. This is very similar to the 'Do anything you like as long as I don't know about it' attitude—meaning, 'I don't have to be responsible.' And children are quite keenly aware that what they are given is not freedom, but just an easy way out for the parents. This so-called trust is interpreted by the child as 'The parents don't care.'

"I have not changed my mind that you cannot raise children without moderate amounts of anxiety. I wish that some of our young people would be more afraid of the consequences of LSD; they would be much better off. On the other hand, there are many children, particularly emotionally disturbed children, who are beset by overpowering and crippling fears. This is true for our children here, so we have to do everything we can to reduce them. What I have tried to suggest is that too little fear can be as damaging as too much.

"Again, the materialistic factor in upper-middle-class America has become a contradiction for these children. Personally, I think America is quite livable. It is the liberal or left-oriented parent who says, 'This is all a sham, you know. Who needs a big car?' Well, he does—he buys one every other year! It is not affluence as such, but the inner contradiction of the parents that is so destructive; the discrepancy between the public image and the private reality. . . . I have never heard a young person who said, 'Never trust anyone over 30,' who did not have perfectly good grounds for saying it. To them, people over 30 *don't* make sense.

"How unbearable society seems is a reflection of how unbearable life is to the individual. If he rages at himself, whatever the changes in society, he will continue to rage. During the French Revolution, nothing was radical enough. More and more people had to be killed off to create the just society. In the end, they were destroyed. So it is with our militants. Nothing that is done is ever enough. They are the true believers, very intolerant of others. . . . Marcuse is a true believer, a person so insecure in his ability to flexibly adjust his judgment to the exigencies of the situation that he has had to make up his mind once and forever; no questions asked and none answered.

"You see this in the vilification—not the criticism, which may be justified, but the vilification—of American institutions by our intellectuals. This is nothing but self-hatred. Like the adolescent, there does not seem to be a place for them in our society. That is where the scientist is so different. He is needed, and you must have this feeling about your life if you are going to have self-respect. And if you don't, you substitute some rigid belief about 'society' or the idea that you are something special—an 'adolescent.' Marcuse is very popular with the radical young because he tells them they are the élite.

"Sometimes you get violence. We have a generation that, by and large, was not allowed to act out its violent tendencies in games. That, too, is part of the new child-rearing. So now they play cops and robbers with real policemen; and—believe me— this, too, is only a game. If the radical young were serious about their revolution they would understand that the police are part of the working class, an economically exploited group in our society. They would try to win them over—no revolution was ever made without their support. Our radicals don't understand this. They throw bottles at the police and call them pigs. To society, that should be very reassuring. Well, the young militants don't like to be told that, but then I am just an opinionated old man. . . ." A bony smile broke across Bettelheim's face. It was time to go to class.

Bettelheim's standing among liberal intellectuals is an ambiguous one. Admired for his books, notably his recent study of childrearing in the Israeli kibbutzim, "Children of the Dream," he is criticized for his conservative ideological bias and his strong views on deviant political behavior. "Bruno's books are definitive and marvelous, absolutely free of professional jargon," a Yale psychiatrist says. "More than any others that I know of, you can have a poetic response to them. But you can't have a poetic response to the man who wrote them."

The most popularly written of his books, "Children of the Dream" challenged Bettelheim to come to terms with his own theory of child-rearing. Elsewhere, he had insisted that the home, with its close rapport among parents and children, formed the basis of a secure and stable childhood. But in the kibbutzim children are separated from their parents in infancy, to be brought up by professional *metapalets,* or foster mothers. Even these are changed frequently as the child grows older. Yet the results, as Bettelheim discovered during his lengthy stay, were surprisingly good. The kibbutz, in effect, *was* the family, a "community of such cohesion, one where there is so high a degree of consensus on all essential issues, that it is hard to visualize how we could duplicate it in our pluralistic society."

Although the kibbutz does not produce many individualists or men of high achievement, neither does it have a delinquency problem. "The kibbutz satisfies the adolescent's longing for simple, radical, unequivocal solutions to life's problems." In a curious way, it resembles the Orthogenic School, with counselors enacting the role of *metapalets* and the general program resembling, in an obverse sense, that "society of high consensus where everyone sees the central issues of life more or less alike. . . ."

In four seminal works—"Love Is Not Enough," "Truants from Life," "The Informed Heart" and "The Empty Fortress"—Bettelheim has created a compelling psychodrama that mirrors the sanctity of human life from a reflection of its wounds. Much of his own quest for wholeness is interwoven in these books, giving them a tingling immediacy that transcends ordinary scholarship; Bettelheim's dream is not only to heal, but to understand. Beneath the crusty exterior is a molten core of humanity, and in his dedication to the psychic cripple he resembles that which he professes most to despise—a saint. "No human being is useless," he says, "although I know quite a few who feel this way."

But it is this very involvement in pathology, many of his colleagues feel, that has given him tunnel vision in looking at young people as a whole. A prominent Eastern psychologist who has worked closely with militant college students thinks that Bettelheim lacks hard evidence for his theory of militancy: "There have been about 40 studies made on this subject, and none of them bear out the thesis that student revolt is related to the adolescent revolt against parents. Bettelheim has used a few case histories to generalize about a whole group."

Harvard's Dr. Coles thinks that "either criticism or approval of student radicals must be grounded in moral or ethical terms, rather than glib psychiatric and psychoanalytic phrases, which are hopefully meant to explain things, not to judge or condemn. An analysis of the childhood experiences of any group of people will inevitably uncover sore spots and hang-ups and evidence of pathology. The real issue is whether the deeds of the young are ethical or vicious and destructive, not whether they can be traced back to 'childhood problems.'"

To a middle-aged outsider, Bettelheim's seeming inability to distinguish between paranoid militancy and a committed but rational enthusiasm for change, so typical of adolescence, gives an unduly negative emphasis to the "youth revolution." His definition of militancy leaves little room for genuinely moral and selfless motives or their effectiveness in bringing about reform. Because the individual may be "sick"—i.e., acting out his internal conflicts—does not mean that he is wrong in his indignation at specific injustice. Bettelheim distrusts the pragmatic adventures whether they be in "life styles" or political action, and he seems to have missed the revolution of rising moral expectations that has taken place in our society since World War II.

To the truly damned among the young—the window-smashers, the nihilists, the frenetic flag-wavers of the New Left—Bettelheim's warning may well apply: "You are in hell. You are crazy—insane! Get well!" Thousands of others, who agitate for a saner purpose, may simply wonder what he is talking about.

There Are No Superior Societies

by Sanche de Gramont

THERE is an endemic French illness in which the works of serious thinkers mysteriously spread beyond the small circle of initiates for whom they are intended and become the object of a cult. The thinker is afflicted with disciples he never wanted, preaching a gospel he never taught. He is hailed by worshipers who have never read a line of his work. He spends his time denying the paternity of deformed offspring bearing his name. If the movement persists he must finally imitate Marx, who denied being a Marxist.

Such was the misfortune of Jean-Paul Sartre in postwar France, when existentialism became synonymous with a life of gay abandon in St.-Germain-des-Prés. By some odd metamorphosis, his philosophy became a youth movement embodied by Juliette Greco, who sang morose existentialist songs in dank existentialist cellars, her hair existentially clouding her vision. Sartre disavowed the movement, and having survived it is not the least of his merits.

And such is the current dilemma of Claude Lévi-Strauss, an

ethnologist who has spent more than half his 59 years studying the behavior of North and South American Indian tribes. The method he uses to study the social organization of these tribes, which he calls structuralism, has flowered into a movement with many exotic blossoms. It is being applied indiscriminately to areas for which Lévi-Strauss never intended it. From an ethnological method, it has sprouted into a full-fledged philosophical doctrine whose impassioned partisans insist that all of human knowledge must be re-examined in its light.

Structuralism, as Lévi-Strauss has used it in his ethnological research, is essentially a way of answering the question, "How do you play this game?" Imagine someone who has never seen a playing card watching a rubber of bridge. By observing the way the cards are played, he should be able to reconstruct, not only the rules (or structure) of bridge, but the composition (or structure) of a deck of cards.

In the same way, the ethnologist observes how marriages are arranged within a tribe and is able to extrapolate certain laws, or structures, that govern the tribe's social organization.

"Structuralism," says Lévi-Strauss, "is the search for unsuspected harmonies. It is the discovery of a system of relations latent in a series of objects."

It is based on the idea that human behavior can be classified scientifically, like a plant or a chemical element. There is nothing arbitrary in nature. Why should there be anything arbitrary in man? There must be laws governing human behavior just as there are laws governing pollenization or cellular growth. Lévi-Strauss believes you can study a tribe the same way a biologist studies an amoeba.

The variety of experience in the life of a social group seems to defy analysis. Precisely for this reason, Lévi-Strauss chooses to study primitive societies because they are more static than our own. And within these societies, he picks what he calls "crystallized" social activities like myths, kinship laws, and cooking practices. Aside from being unchanging activities of unchanging societies, they are activities at the brink of consciousness—a member of some Brazilian tribe never stops to wonder why he cooks his meat a certain way or believes a myth about a man turning into a jaguar. This is the type of subconscious, taken-for-granted mental process which Lévi-Strauss believes lends itself best to scientific investigation.

For instance, he studied gift-giving in Polynesia, of which there were so many forms that most ethnologists had written them off as haphazard. He found that gift-giving could be broken down into four cycles with 35 subcycles. Thus, the structure of Polynesian gift-giving is the sum of all these cycles and subcycles—the law to which every known example conforms. The structure is the hidden order of human behavior.

Lévi-Strauss derived structuralism from a school of linguistics whose principal exponent is Roman Jakobson. Very simply, these linguists study the relations among words, rather than the relation of each word to the object it designates. It is not the meaning of the word which concerns them, but the patterns the words form. The structure of a language is its grammar, and through this kind of analysis, a linguist should be able to discover the grammar of a language he cannot speak, in much the same manner that a cryptographer is able to decipher a code thanks to recurring patterns of digits.

In addition, the modern linguists agree that there is a "ground plan" for all the languages of the world. Every language in every society has the same fundamental properties. Thus, Lévi-Strauss says, "just as the discovery of DNA and the genetic code led biologists to use a linguistic model to explain a natural phenomenon, I use a linguistic model to explain cultural phenomena other than language. I try to show that the basic structure of language observed by the linguists exists in a great many other activities."

Meaning, in social activities as well as in language, is thus not to be found in the designated activity but in the way it differs from other activities. He is not concerned with the story a myth tells, but in the way the symbols used in one myth become converted into another set of symbols telling the same story. This is the grammar or the code of myths. Once he has unraveled hundreds of South American myths using different symbols and sensory codes (one deals with what is heard, another with what is seen), and found that they can all be reduced to a central idea, the discovery of fire by man, he is also able to reduce the mechanism of the primitive mind to a certain number of recurring types of mental operations. In the same way, the laws governing social organization which he discovers, whether they have to do with gift-giving or marrying off one's daughter, also illustrate the workings of the human spirit.

First, he is able to abolish the distinction made by his predecessors between prelogical and logical thought, by showing that primitive peoples use either-or logical categories just as we do. Next, he infers that social organization and behavior are the result of a limited number of inherent mental categories. Just as there is a ground plan for language, there must be ground plans for other forms of collective behavior.

He sees the ground plan for kinship, for instance, as a problem in the communication of women inside a primitive society, just as an economist considers supply and demand a problem in the communication of goods and services. Instead of studying marriage and kinship in a tribe as a series of personal dramas, each the result of subjective psychological and personal factors, he studies the objective and limited number of ways a woman can pass, thanks to marriage customs, from her own family into another family.

Thus, despite Lévi-Strauss's narrow field of inquiry, there are in structuralism two ambitious implications—that the human sciences can attain the rigor and detachment of the natural sciences, and that human behavior is governed by the limitations of man's mental processes. Admirers view his work as the final panel in a triptych entitled "Contemporary Western Thought," the two other panels being occupied by Marx and Freud.

I like to imagine these Three Wise Men of Occident bent in contemplation over a South American Indian myth about a boy who steals a pet pig from his father and roasts it in the forest. Freud would conclude that the boy is symbolically killing his father because he desires his mother. Marx would say that this youthful member of the proletariat is seizing control of the methods of production in the class struggle against the landed gentry. Lévi-Strauss would find that, in cooking the pig, the primitive Indian boy had achieved the passage from nature to culture and shown that his thought processes are no different from Einstein's.

For Lévi-Strauss's contribution to the triptych is a theory of how the human mind works. Primitive man, in organizing himself into social groups, passes from a natural to a cultural state. He uses language, learns to cook his food and accepts various laws that insure the survival of the group. All these activities set him apart from the animal. Structuralism postulates that in achieving this passage from nature to culture, man obeys laws he does not invent. These laws are inherent in human nature, which is everywhere identical, since it is no more than the mechanism of the human brain. The cerebral cortex, like a computer, responds to the outside world according to a limited number of categories. The reason we think human nature is unpredictable is that we have not yet mapped the circuits.

With Lévi-Strauss, the whole humanist tradition goes down the drain. Instead of a free spirit, responsible for its decisions, we have a man responding to programed circuits called structures. The individual conscience is no longer relevant. The whole body of Western thought, from Plato to Descartes to Sartre, which held that knowledge of the world begins with knowledge of oneself, belongs in the natural-history museum, alongside the witch doctors' headdresses.

Lévi-Strauss is the advance man for an age in which the human sciences will have caught up with the natural sciences. Soon, if he is right, a psychologist will be able to chart a human life as accurately as he now measures the progress of a hungry rat sniffing its way through a labyrinth toward a piece of cheese.

History goes down the drain, too, because it is seen as merely a form of our own society's mythology, a collective delusion irrelevant to the scientific study of man. Lévi-Strauss views man, not as a privileged inhabitant of the universe, but as a passing species, like some form of plant, which will leave only a few faint traces of its passage when it becomes extinct.

The sudden popularity of structuralism has little to do with Lévi-Strauss's own specific research. It is, in part, a fad, the French intellectual's equivalent of the hula hoop. On another level, it is a reaction against centuries of rhetorical philosophers and historians, and an awareness that, today, knowledge of man cannot be divorced from the great scientific advances. Finally, it is a specific attempt to discredit Jean-Paul Sartre as an outdated thinker and relegate existentialism to the philosophical garbage can. "Today," says the critic Bernard Pingaud, "we are no longer existentialist, we are structuralist."

Structuralism has become a skeleton key to all the arts and sciences. There are structuralist novels, symphonies and paintings, connected by the tenuous link that meaning is irrelevant and that form imposes its own necessities. Samuel Beckett is hailed as a structuralist because his characters are victims of forces beyond their control. The complaint of one of Beckett's characters, "I am made of words, of the words of others," is fast becoming the structuralist motto.

One measure of the movement's extent is a singularly abstruse book called "Words and Things," which has sold 40,000 copies to date. The author, Michel Foucault, who attempts to show that thought originates with words rather than the other way around, says he was inspired by Lévi-Strauss.

To show that structuralism is an all purpose method, the magazine Communications recently published structural analyses of the James Bond novels, the death of Pope John XXIII as reported in the Paris press and 180 funny stories in the afternoon daily France-Soir. A funny story is broken down according to its structure as follows: (1) Normalization function: A husband tells his wife she should take up knitting. (2) Locutionary engagement: "I haven't time to knit," she says: "I do too much cooking." (3) Disjunctive interlocutory function: "Yes," he replies, "but you can't burn your knitting."

The result of such painstaking classification seems disappointingly tautological. A structural analysis of the French flag would doubtless lead to the discovery that it is made up of three vertical fields of color of identical width which follow one another, according to their normalization function, in the sequence red, white and blue.

Lévi-Strauss lifts his arms in a gesture of resigned helplessness and complains about the seriousness of the articles in Communications. He is at his desk in the Collège de France, an eminent institution founded in the 16th century for a small number of scholars who could, by lecturing there, escape the parochial tutelage of the Sorbonne. He holds the chair of social anthropology and delivers a minimum of 20 lectures a year. His office is decorated with Indian feather headdresses and rattan baskets. Behind his desk there is a large geological map of the United States.

The "father of structuralism" is dapper in a hound's-tooth heather sports jacket and a string tie with a tooled silver clasp. He would make an excellent model for one of the 19th-century studies in compared physiology which illustrate his book "The Savage Mind"—the transformation from fox or hooting owl to human in four or five stages with only slight alterations. A Peruvian condor would become the ethnologist's profile, narrow and aquiline, thatched with white hair.

He is horrified by the fashion for structuralism. "In the sense in which it is understood today by French opinion," he says, "I am not a structuralist. I am very much afraid that in France there is a total lack of self-criticism, an excessive sensibility to fashion and a deep intellectual instability. The best way to explain the current infatuation with structuralism is that French intellectuals and the cultured French public need new playthings every 10 or 15 years.

"Let's make one thing very clear. I have never guided nor directed any movement or doctrine. I pursue my work in almost total isolation, surrounded only by a team of ethnologists. As for the others, I don't want to name names, but to pronounce the name of structuralism in connection with certain philosophers and literary people, no matter how talented or intelligent they may be, seems to be a case of total confusion. I have the greatest admiration for the intelligence, the culture and the talent of a man like Foucault, but I don't see the slightest resemblance between what he does and what I do."

Claude Lévi-Strauss's peculiar itinerary, from the deliberate spurning of his own society to unsought notoriety in it, begins in a conventional, cultured, urban, middle-class Jewish environment. His grandfather was rabbi of Versailles. His father and two of his uncles were painters of academic portraits and landscapes.

The impact of other civilizations first struck him at the age of 6, when his father rewarded his schoolwork with a Japanese print. He was all the more tempted by other societies because he had little fondness for his own. "I have little sympathy with the century in which we are living," he has written, "for the total ascendancy of man over nature and of certain forms of humanity over others. My temperament and tastes carry me toward more modest periods where there was a certain balance between man and nature, the diverse and multiple forms of life."

The young Lévi-Strauss studied philosophy at the Sorbonne for five years, a disappointing experience. He felt his teachers were dealing in meaningless mental gymnastics, and in the esthetic contemplation of philosophical fine points, such as the consciousness of consciousness.

There was, in counterpoint to his scorn for the scholasticism of the Sorbonne (which did not prevent him from passing his exams with honors), a growing love of nature. After his parents bought a house in the Cévennes Mountains, he would disappear on 15-hour walks, forgetting time in the contemplation of a dandelion or in the search for the line of contact between two geological layers of a limestone plateau.

His "three mistresses" were Marxism, psychoanalysis and geology. From the first he learned that understanding consists in finding common properties among a variety of incidents. Freud taught him that beyond rational categories there existed forms of behavior more valid and more meaningful. In geology he had the example of a science which discovered laws amid the great tumult of nature.

He was already, says an admirer, "a structuralist without knowing it," attracted to types of thought that seek to discover human laws by studying the relations among objects. He took up law to escape an orthodox academic career, but found that a sterile discipline. He gravitated without enthusiasm toward provincial teaching posts. His chance came in 1934, when a senior professor told him about an opening in the sociology department of São Paulo University. If he was interested in ethnology, the professor said, he could visit the Indians in the suburbs on weekends.

As soon as his first teaching contract was up Lévi-Strauss made for the Brazilian interior, where he spent a year studying the Nambikwara ("pierced ear") tribe in the Mato Grosso, central Brazil's desolate savanna, followed by 10 shorter field trips, lasting from 15 days to three months, to visit other more accessible groups.

An account of his trips became the book that has most contributed to his popularity, *"Tristes Tropiques."* It is really three books in one. First, it is a return to the 18th-century genre of the philosophical traveler. He has happened on one of the few societies the white man has left untouched, and he sees it as Rousseau might have. "Their life is a daily joy," he writes in an echo of the "noble savage" theme. "I never saw a people so gay."

Elsewhere, Lévi-Strauss recounts the experience of an anthropologist who noticed that each time he left the tribe he was studying the elders began to weep. They were not weeping because they were sad to see him go, he found, but out of pity for him because he was forced to leave the only place on earth where life was worth living. The notion of a primitive happiness and innocence which we have lost forms a romantic counterpoint to his scientific investigation, which is the second level of the book.

For Lévi-Strauss is a Rousseau with a scientific background, an exact observer and a tireless collector of facts. He studies the layouts of villages, the way a chief is chosen, marriage customs and attitudes toward the dead.

And, in explanation of his title, he describes the antithesis of the lush, romantic tropics touted in brochures for Caribbean cruises. The tropics he sees are forlorn. Nature here is not plentiful. The inhabitants live on the edge of subsistence. Some tribes have yet to master the techniques of pottery-making and weaving.

Worse, these societies are doomed. Civilization—in the form of a telegraph line, rubber planters, missionaries or a government agency—intrudes and shatters the delicate balance which allowed the society to survive. *"Tristes Tropiques"* is a melancholy book, an epitaph to condemned societies.

The ethnologist is an incidental victim of these changes, since he has assigned himself the study of vanishing societies. It is with considerable anguish that Lévi-Strauss learns each year of primitive societies which have died out without yielding up the pattern of their social organization. In 1963, for instance, an ethnologist found the remote Bari tribe in the Colombian mountains, thanks to a road which had been opened up by oil prospectors. But in a matter of months, the population of the tribe was decimated by an epidemic benign to Westerners but fatal to a people who had built up no immunity.

The third layer of *"Tristes Tropiques"* contains the seeds of Lévi-Strauss's future work. He rebels against Western society's smug habit of imposing its standards on the rest of the world. He notes that so-called primitive societies represent perhaps 99 per cent of the total experience of humanity. He refutes the traditional notion that these societies are barbaric, or less rational than our own. They are merely different. There are no superior societies.

A tribe which eats roots and spiders and wears no clothes may have solved complex problems of social organization far more satisfactorily than we have. Our parochial refusal to accept cultural diversity, our criticism of those who "don't do as we do," is itself a characteristic tribal attitude.

Human societies all have more or less the same age, but they have developed unevenly. Lévi-Strauss distinguishes between progressive, acquisitive, inventive societies like our own, which he calls "hot" or "mobile" societies, and the societies which lack the gift of synthesis and the possibilities for human exchange, which he calls "cold" or "static" societies.

The cold societies are mechanical in that they do not increase the amount of energy per capita, which is one definition of technical progress. They maintain themselves in their initial state. They have no written tradition and no history in our sense of the term (which is one reason ethnologists find them ideal to study).

They are democratic and nonhierarchical. The society acts

unanimously and purges itself of dissent so that there are no disorders or minority groups.

The "hot" society is thermodynamic; it produces and consumes energy, like a steam engine. It develops through conflict and makes technological leaps which are not matched by social progress. If progress is measured by the amount of energy available per capita, Western society is miles ahead. But if the criterion were success in overcoming inhospitable geographic conditions, the Eskimos or Bedouins would rank first. And if progress were based on success in founding harmonious family and social groups, the Australian aborigines would be judged most advanced. Western society is thus not better than others, but simply more cumulative, because it has been less isolated.

Early ethnologists sought proof of the glories of their civilization in the backwardness of primitive peoples. Lévi-Strauss takes the opposite approach. Without a trace of Swiftian irony, he writes a closely reasoned defense of cannibalism in *"Tristes Tropiques."* Eating the body of an ancestor or an enemy is intended to acquire his virtue or neutralize his power. To condemn this practice on moral grounds is to believe either in physical resurrection or in a link between body and spirit, convictions identical to those in the name of which ritual cannibalism is practiced. On those grounds, why should we prefer noncannibalism to cannibalism, since we also show disregard for the sanctity of the dead in our own anatomy dissections?

A disinterested observer, says Lévi-Strauss, might distinguish cannibalistic societies—those which believe they can absorb the powers of enemies by eating them—and anthropoemic societies like our own (from the Greek *emein,* "to vomit") which expel enemies from the body politic by imprisonment or exile. Our penitentiary customs, he points out, would seem to primitive societies as barbaric as their cannibalism seems to us.

There is, however, one tradition of our society for which there is no analogous primitive institution, and that is the written tradition. Without going so far as to suggest a causal relationship, Lévi-Strauss links the origin of writing in the Eastern Mediterranean between the second and third millenniums to one of the constants of Western society, the exploitation of man by man.

Thus he considers what is usually regarded as the single most important advantage of civilized man—the ability to write—as the harbinger of bondage in Western society. For writing "seems to favor the exploitation rather than the enlightenment of mankind." Writing, which allows man to store a large body of knowledge, "made it possible to assemble workmen by the thousands and set them tasks which taxed them to the limit of their strength. If my hypothesis is correct, the primary function of writing, as a means of communication, is to facilitate the enslavement of other human beings."

Lévi-Strauss was moving toward an intuitive formulation of structuralism when the "hot" history of Western society interrupted his research. He was a liaison officer between the French and British Armies on the Maginot line when France fell in 1940. He fled to the United States, and there he met Roman Jakobson, who was already applying structuralism to linguistics. Jakobson did not invent structuralism. He improved a method introduced around 1910 by the Swiss linguist Ferdinand de Saussure, and perpetuated by the Russian school known as "formalists." But Lévi-Strauss, who has collaborated steadily with Jakobson (in 1961 they wrote a structural analysis of Baudelaire's sonnet "The Cats"), was the first to apply structuralism to ethnology.

His first structural work, "Elementary Structures of Kinship," sought one of the points of primitive man's passage from nature, where he simply responds to biological urges, to culture, where he joins in functioning social groups. Lévi-Strauss wanted to show that primitive man organizes himself, by drawing on what the natural environment provides, in a logical, coherent manner— the very opposite of an irrational, prelogical manner.

He demonstrates that the only social institution enforced to some degree by every existing social group is the prohibition of incest. The reason is not that incest biologically weakens or psychologically damages a species, but that the group derives social benefits from its prohibition. Thanks to the prohibition, each man offers to other men the women he must refuse for himself. The ensuing social benefit is the free circulation of women, similar to the circulation of goods and services in a mercantilist economy.

The bridge from nature to culture is in the priority of the social over the natural, the collective over the individual, and the organizational over the arbitrary. It assures the integration of the family in the social group and forges profitable alliances between families. Lévi-Strauss quotes conversations among Indians about the practical disadvantages of incest: "If you marry your sister you will have no brother-in-law. Who will go hunting with you? Who will help you with the planting?"

Since this early work Lévi-Strauss has been writing a series of books which explore the workings of the human mind through tribal myths. The first in the series, "Totemism Today," argued that the practice of choosing an animal or a natural object as the symbol of a family or clan was not a ridiculous superstition but part of a larger system of classification, a highly sophisticated mythical universe which he begins to explore in "The Savage Mind."

At the root of primitive thought, he says, there is a need for order. The diversity of myths, the fact that the same symbol is used in different ways by different tribes (the Pawnees relate the woodpecker to storms; the Osages, to the sun and stars), led earlier ethnologists to conclude that there could be no order in these infinitely varied and apparently arbitrary data. But this same diversity was a challenge to Lévi-Strauss. He wanted to prove that primitive thought has an inner coherence.

Lévi-Strauss's next volume in his study of myths is called "The Raw and the Cooked," but it is not, as some unsuspecting housewives have discovered, a collection of recipes. It is a study of 187 myths from 20 South American tribes, which finds another point of passage from nature to culture in the cooking of meat.

Its conclusion is simple: The myths tell us that meat exists so that man can cook it. The controlled fire used for cooking is a symbol of man's relation to the sun: If the sun were too far from the earth, the earth would rot, and if it were too close, it would burn. Cooking is an agent of passage from nature to culture just as the sun is the mediator between heaven and earth.

But the way Lévi-Strauss solves his mythological puzzle will defeat most readers. His books are possibly the greatest collection of riddles since the Sphinx. In his mythological universe, things are usually the opposite of what they seem. A myth about water turns out to be really about fire. A myth about wild pigs is really about humans who have been punished for their lack of generosity.

He pursues his analysis of myths in a book called "From Honey to Ashes," where he examines primitive man's relations to the supernatural through Indian myths about honey and tobacco.

Lévi-Strauss's latest book, called "Table Manners," will be published this year. This time he will integrate the mythology of North American Indians into his system. He will also show that "savage thought" contains a philosophy and an ethic. "Table Manners" baffled even its author, who had to reread and rewrite it three times before he decided it was coherent.

Because Lévi-Strauss aspires to the precision of the exact sciences, he is particularly sensitive to the lag of the human sciences. In the past, he believes, anthropologists "behaved like amateur botanists, haphazardly picking random samples," with the result that "we are still at the stage of discovering what a fact is. . . . It is as though cosmic physics had to base itself on the observations of Babylonian astronomers, with the difference that heavenly bodies are still with us, whereas primitive societies are vanishing fast."

An ethnologist cannot, like a physicist or a chemist, repeat his experiments in identical conditions an unlimited number of times. And yet Lévi-Strauss does not think the human sciences need remain in a position of inferiority. "It is true that ethnology is faced with the eventual disappearance of primitive societies," he says, "but this is not a threat; on the contrary, it will make us modify our line of vision and recognize our true aims.

"In studying primitive societies, the ethnologist's aim was to study a form of humanity as different and remote as possible from his own. But in our own society, there are forms of life, beliefs, types of action, which seem extremely remote to us, and I wonder whether, the more voluminous contemporary societies become, the more they tend to re-create within themselves the diversity they have destroyed elsewhere.

"This impresses me particularly in America. For instance, the religious or parareligious sects of the West Coast may seem as mysterious to an East Coast observer as primitive societies. When I read American magazines like Playboy and others, which I do with a great deal of care, curiosity and pleasure, I have the impression of witnessing a sort of ethnological understanding of a society by its own members, who are examining customs which are strange and distant, not because they are thousands of miles away, but because they are the object of a strong prohibition on the part of the society which recreates the distances.

"It is thus perfectly conceivable that ethnology represents a method of approach as eternal as humanity itself. When there is no more ethnology of primitive peoples, there will be an effort to understand man through those of his activities which, for one reason or another, are at the very limit of humanity."

In order to be equipped for this task, Lévi-Strauss believes that "the human sciences will be structuralist or they will not be at all. . . . The ethnologist, faced with thousands of societies and the incredible multiplicity of facts, must do one of two things: Either he can only describe and take inventory of all this diversity, and his work will be very estimable but it will not be scientific. Or else he will have to admit that behind this diversity there lies something deeper, something common to all its aspects. This effort to reduce a multiplicity of expressions to one language, this is structuralism. Maybe someday it will no longer be called that; I don't know and I don't care. But the effort to find a deeper and truer reality behind the multiplicity of apparent realities, that seems to me to be the condition of survival for the human sciences, whatever the undertaking is called."

Thus far, however, Lévi-Strauss has examined only fixed systems, such as marriage customs, within "cold" societies, those that do not have a changing history in our sense of the term. The historical development of man does not interest him, which helps explain both his popularity and the denunciations of his critics. Just as physicists study light either as an undulation or as an emission, says Lévi-Strauss, human phenomena may be explained historically or structurally. Both methods are valid, neither is privileged, but his only concern is with the latter.

With this in mind, an article by François Furet in the review Preuves argues that the intellectual establishment has adopted structuralism precisely because it offers an anti-history. French intellectuals, says Furet, are disenchanted with history and the left-wing ideologies which claim to be its agents, for since the end of the Algerian war these ideologies have had little relevance in France. Despite the pronouncements of General de Gaulle in both hemispheres, France no longer has much influence in world affairs. De Gaulle seems, in fact, to want to freeze history by resisting England's vocation as a Continental power, and by rekindling nostalgic 17th-century thoughts of a French Canada. Perhaps he will be remembered as the first structuralist chief of state. In any case, since history no longer seems to need France, disillusioned intellectuals feel an obscure need for a system of thought which has no need of history.

There is also something reassuring in Lévi-Strauss's insistence that Western civilization is not privileged. We have so many daily reminders of this dismal fact that he has come along with an alternative at a providential moment. We can study primitive peoples, not as amusing throwbacks to the childhood of man, but to learn from their more tranquil ways.

Because Lévi-Strauss has been so ardently taken up by part of the intellectual establishment, he has also become the object of passionate, sometimes obsessive, criticism.

There are, first of all, attempts to discredit him as an ethnologist. Critics point out that Lévi-Strauss, who advises all aspiring ethnologists to spend one year out of every three in the field, has had considerably less field experience himself, and has written only one monograph. He is the first to acknowledge this deficiency. "It is because I feel the inadequacy of my own field experience so acutely that I would like my pupils and collaborators to avoid it," he says.

Other critics view him as a man haunted by a grand design, an attempt to reduce all social activity to inherent, mechanical tendencies of the human mind. They say that he freezes and constrains man, divorcing him from life and reality, that instead of an individual capable of modifying his environment, the Lévi-Strauss man is the creature of a formal system whose life is governed by invariable structures.

This charge particularly irks Lévi-Strauss. "To accuse me of formalism," he says as though hardly believing his ears, "whereas probably no other ethnologist has been so attentive to the concrete aspects of human life! On the contrary, I try to show that it is impossible even to start interpreting a myth unless one is perfectly informed about the slightest ethnographic details of the society in which it exists. I would say that there is more concrete ethnology in my books than in any other theoretical works in the field."

Some critics become so impassioned that they portray structuralism as the machination of an unbalanced mind to subvert Western thought. Thus, the well-known sociologist Henri Lefèvre writes that one finds in Lévi-Strauss "a curious predilection, almost maniacal, almost schizophrenic, for the motionless, the diagram." He goes on to accuse structuralism of being the tool of a capitalist ideology, in that its effort to eliminate historical development is a counterrevolutionary defense of the political status quo.

Lévi-Strauss considers Lefèvre's attacks ridiculous. "I see absolutely no link between structuralism and any political system," he says. "It is exactly as if an astronomer using a telescope which only modern industry could produce were accused of justifying capitalism with his discoveries."

Lévi-Strauss dismisses the fault-finding of his minor critics handily, but in Jean-Paul Sartre he has a more evenly matched antagonist. The structural ethnologist and the existentialist philosopher have been conducting a running quarrel for seven years. It has taken on a new urgency now that Lévi-Strauss is being crowned as Sartre's successor by the intellectual establishment.

In his "Critique of Dialectical Reason," published in 1960, Sartre opened hostilities by saying that Lévi-Strauss studied men the way entomologists study ants. Sartre wrote that history is a "rational disorder." For him, historical truth exists, and meaning begins with the individual conscience. Thus, he cannot accept Lévi-Strauss's conception of a single human nature which responds to inherent laws.

In "The Savage Mind," two years later, Lévi-Strauss replied that Sartre is guilty of "intellectual cannibalism," in that he believes every form of society or thought other than our own can have a meaning only when compared with ours.

To Lévi-Strauss, Sartre describing the French Revolution in terms of the class struggle is himself worthy of an ethnological study, for he is a member of a given society repeating one of that society's myths. Lévi-Strauss contends that there is not one history but a multitude of histories, each of which cannot be more than "the interpretation which philosophers or historians give of their own mythology, and which I would consider as a variant of that mythology."

This does not invalidate history, he says, for "an astronomer knows that the straight line is an abstraction, and that in reality there are only curved lines in the universe, but that is not going to prevent him from using a plumb line when he wants to build a house. We must distinguish the action a man can have inside his own society from the way he tries to explain human phenomena in a general way. Some things which are true on the scale of our own society cease to be true on the scale of thousands of years or on the scale of humanity."

Sartre's latest counterattack appeared in a recent issue of the review L'Arc devoted to his work. In it, he placed the discussion on the political level which Lévi-Strauss has always striven to avoid.

Structuralism, he charged, is the bourgeoisie's last stand against Marxism, an attempt to set up a closed, inert system where order is privileged at the expense of change. "As it is conceived and practiced by Lévi-Strauss," he said, "structuralism has greatly contributed to the actual discredit of history, insofar as it applies itself only to already constituted systems, such as myths for example. . . . Even 'cold' societies have a history . . . but in a structuralist perspective, it is impossible to render this evolution. History appears as a purely passive phenomenon."

Let us end by giving Lévi-Strauss the last word in his dispute with Sartre. He believes that existentialism, not structuralism, is on the defensive. "In existentialism," he says, "which was so popular in the postwar years, there was something paradoxical and contradictory which had to come out in the light of day. I mean that existentialism adopted very advanced political positions whereas ideologically it represented on the contrary a conservative and even reactionary endeavor.

"Existentialism was an attempt to save philosophy, a sort of morose withdrawal before the great advance of scientific thought, a way of saying: 'No, there is still a privileged area, something which was created by man and belongs only to man'—an attempt, in short, to save humanism, whereas the nature of structuralism consists, on the one hand, in frankly accepting the dialogue with science, and, on the other hand, in recognizing that philosophy can no longer be a privileged domain but can survive only in the form of constant dialogue with scientific thought."

The Mead and Her Message

by David Dempsey

"EVERYBODY talks about Margaret Mead but nobody does anything about her," a fellow ethnologist complained, only somewhat facetiously, a short time ago. Florida's Governor Claude R. Kirk, for example, called her "this dirty old lady" (when she came to the defense of marijuana smokers at a Senate committee hearing on drug abuse). To Mrs. John Mitchell, wife of the Attorney General, she is a "spook" who just wants to get her name in the papers. Others call her "over-exposed" or "an international busybody." Unlike most of her colleagues, who bury themselves in the tribal customs of primitive man, Mead is visible, a willing plunger into modern social controversy who projects herself as a global prophetess on almost every subject that concerns the human condition. To a society troubled by its own shifting folkways, and hungry for guidance in coping with them, she is a poor man's anthropologist, a mediator between high erudition and the middlebrow mind.

Early this year, as a result of successive appearances on four major TV talk shows, Mead joined the American Federation of Television and Radio Artists—she is probably the only anthropologist in the country eligible for membership—thus guaranteeing herself about $320 for each show. Her kickoff speeches at meetings and conventions bring her from $500 to $1,000 (or nothing

From the *New York Times Magazine,* April 26, 1970, copyright © 1970 by the New York Times Company.

at all, if she decides the sponsoring organization can't afford the money); she draws a salary from two universities (Columbia and Fordham), a pension from the American Museum of Natural History, a stipend from Redbook, for which, in collaboration with Dr. Rhoda Metraux, she writes a monthly article; and royalties from numerous books that date back to 1928, when she published "Coming of Age in Samoa," which is still available in four paperback editions that sell at the merry clip of 100,000 copies a year. Her next-to-last book, "Culture and Commitment," a collection of three lectures delivered in 1969, will net her about $20,000 this year alone. Her newest, "A Way of Seeing," written with Dr. Metraux, may do even better.

Recently, she spoke in Baltimore at a conference for physicians sponsored by the Geigy Chemical Corporation. "Drinks, a free lunch and Margaret Mead—what more do you want?" one doctor remarked later. "She's a hard act to follow," he added, when a company official gave a pitch for tranquilizers. Mead has been criticized for lending her prestige to the exploitation of commercial products. Actually, she approves of mood-altering prescription drugs and in any case, she argues, why should *physicians* be denied the Mead message, whatever it may be at the moment?

During one 12-month period, from June, 1968, through May 1969, the message encompassed 43 scientific and 36 popular lectures in such widely spaced locales as London, Seoul and New Orleans. In addition, 31 television and radio broadcasts were beamed around the country and overseas to Australia, Sweden, Ireland and the Netherlands.

The distinction between scientific and popular, however, may be misleading. To a lay audience, some of Mead's talks about acculturation among the Iatmul tribe in New Guinea sound formidably scientific. ("For years, I have been able to guarantee audiences a good address by using words that aren't in the dictionary," she told a crowd at the Y.M.H.A. Poetry Center in New York.) But to a group of dues-paying anthropologists, Mead's lectures might seem too popular. "You wonder what she'll take off on next," a professor who has followed her career closely said. "We *know* what Dr. Blank will say—he's probably already distributed his paper. But we're never sure about Margaret Mead." There is a tale that she once forgot what meeting she was addressing, and delivered a talk on sex deviations among the Tchambuli to a solemn conclave of theologians. The talk was well received.

This is not surprising in view of the fact that for 42 years, ever since she described the values of adolescent lovemaking under the Samoan palm trees, the name of Margaret Mead has been identified with sex. Much of her writing, if it did not exactly anticipate the bedroom orgies implicit in the marriage manuals of today, argued that sex repression in our post-Victorian culture works against the healthy maturation of the young, and successful marriage later on. In an appearance on the "Dick Cavett Show," where she was paired off with the burlesque queen Ann Corio, it was Mead who defined the new sex morality and Miss Corio—predictably, no doubt—who stood up for strict domesticity.

"The stripteaser makes it possible for a lot of people to stay married," Mead reminded her, in defense of the profession.

"I always wanted to be a legitimate actress," Miss Corio said ruefully, "but nobody would listen to my lines. They just wanted to see them."

It must be said that Margaret Mead offers no such temptation. A short (5 feet 2 inches), sturdy woman of 69, she could pass for a Midwestern housewife who had possibly taken a few judo lessons late in life. Fluffy hair that falls over her forehead in bangs, and a pleasant, unwrinkled face belie her age. She speaks in a slightly homespun, melodious voice and, in her public appearances, presents an unassuming manner that can be in sharp contrast to the show-biz personalities with whom she frequently finds herself discussing the great issues of the day.

What is more, people really come to hear her lines. In Cambridge, Mass., when the doors were closed on a meeting restricted to Radcliffe students, hundreds of envious housewives stormed the hall and demanded to be let in. Mead finally addressed the ladies from a chair propped in the street. At Yale, when she gave a course as visiting professor in 1968, 600 undergraduates enrolled. It was the largest single class in the history of the university. (Possibly out of appreciation for this unprecedented turn-out—or maybe because it was impossible to grade 600 term papers—she gave every student an A or B.)

Except for her courses at Fordham and Columbia, Mead almost never gives the same lecture twice. Her subjects include hunger, air pollution, sex, mental hygiene, population control, women's careers, nutrition, violence, black power, drugs, primitive art, the family, military service, tribal customs, city planning, alcoholism, architecture, civil liberties and child development, to name a few. At a talk before the Wenner-Gren Foundation several years ago, Mead's sister, Mrs. Leo Rosten (now deceased), was in the audience. During the discussion period, an obscure question concerning betel-nut consumption in the Admiralty Islands brought forth a ready response. Mrs. Rosten turned to the man next to her and remarked: "I was hoping that for once someone would ask my sister a question she didn't know the answer to."

Mead's platform presence is enhanced by a flowing cape and a black lacquered, shoulder-high staff which she carries with her everywhere. Although frequently mistaken for some totemic artifact from Polynesia, the staff is, in fact, an English "thumb-stick" which Mead orders from London. Ten years ago, she broke her ankle in a fall; after a spell in a wheel chair (from which she frequently lectured), she was told by her doctor that she should use a cane. "This meant bending over and looking old," she recalls. The staff enabled her to straighten up and seem younger—no mean distinction in one's psychological view of approaching age. Although the ankle has long since healed, the thumb-stick has become a Mead panache and, like Holden Caulfield's skis, it presents certain problems when she is climbing in and out of taxis, or entering elevators. At meetings, she will sometimes wave it when she wants to be recognized from the floor.

To understand the Mead phenomenon, it is helpful to realize that the accelerated changes which society is undergoing in almost every sphere of life, and the speed with which these changes are made public through the mass media, have produced a whole new ball game for the human race. People are understandably anxious about a game in which the rules have been suddenly and drastically revised; and since anthropology is essentially a study of cultural adaptation, Mead the anthropologist has become a social umpire, calling the plays as they happen. At the same time, Mead the popularizer is an effective commentator (or "color announcer") who gives her audiences access to the new, esoteric rules in a language they can understand. It is this that irritates many scholars, who point out that Mead the commentator sometimes leads Mead the umpire astray. In substance, her critics say, she wants to influence the events she is passing judgment on. For example, she is not only a student of the generation gap, but an active proponent of it.

Mead defends her actions by pointing out that every good citizen has the obligation to apply his knowledge to the betterment of society. Scholars are not exempt, even though they are frequently unreadable. Mead's partisans trace her professional lineage to such scholar-activists as Jane Addams, who used her learning to revolutionize social work in this country. Raised in this tradition, Mead is simply an anthropologist with a mission, which the new rules of the game have made more urgent than ever.

As Mead sees it, one of the forces that have contributed to the social speed-up—television—is also making possible the enlightenment which may ultimately save us. ("For the first time, the young are seeing history being made before it is censored by their elders.") We live in a society made up of bits and pieces; the problem, she emphasizes, is how to put the fragments together again. If this sounds faintly McLuhanesque, Mead is nevertheless at pains to dissociate her views from McLuhan's. "I don't believe in retribalization," she told a New York audience recently. "You get something much worse than the original tribe. The global village is entirely new. Television is not taking us back to the tribe, but forward, away from it." Thus, although McLuhan and Mead share an overriding preoccupation with electric circuitry, there the matter ends. Whereas the former seems to be hung up on the medium, Mead is intent on pushing the message. Nevertheless, when the screen flickers out, and the national anthem has been played, one is compelled to ask: What *is* the message?

Mead's peers in anthropology are divided on this question. There are few who do not admire her as a person, yet many are unhappy at the scattershot and sometimes contradictory nature of her material. ("She illustrates the principle of *eclectic* circuitry," one of them insists.) For these critics, a career that has spanned 45 years, 12 field expeditions, a score of books and more than a thousand articles and monographs is lacking in any over-all design that might furnish a theoretical interpretation of cultural behavior. Perhaps this is another way of saying that Mead has resisted the temptation to simplify what is inherently complex. Certainly, she is no structuralist, attempting to find in society an immutable set of relationships to be classified scientifically, like plants or chemical elements. On the contrary, the "culture and personality" school of anthropology with which Mead is associated bases its work on a study of the psychological development of the individual, with all his vagaries—to the neglect, critics of this approach contend, of the political and economic factors that also influence social adaptation.

Dr. Marvin Harris, professor of anthropology at Columbia, and former head of the department there, calls Mead "a woman of rare gifts who has made few lasting theoretical contributions." The great failing of the "culture and personality" school, he adds, is that instead of providing an explanation of phenomena, it simply interprets them. As a result, "Mead has not provided the grand synthesis that might be expected from her enormous field work."

This is a harsh judgment, and inadvertently pays her the compliment of stopping just short of genius. "After all," says Prof. Ray Birdwhistell, an anthropologist who is visiting professor of communications at the University of Pennsylvania, "how many ethnologists *have* come up with a 'grand synthesis'? How many Marxes or Freuds are there in any field? Mead came close to it in her book 'Continuities in Cultural Evolution,' but apart from that she has made more contributions to information techniques, and has trained more students in sophisticated, reliable field reporting, than anyone in the business. Her method is elaborate, detailed, totally controlled."

Mead is a towering figure—more important than her work, in the opinion of Prof. Stanley Diamond of the New School. But he points out that there is hardly any technical canon in the field by which anthropologists can be judged. It is a subject replete with specializations, and one of Mead's contributions has been to bridge them for general consumption, to act as a unifying *force majeure*. As a member of numerous advisory committees, she has been influential in developing new programs, and was one of the very first anthropologists to use the camera as an adjunct to her field work.

Even those who disagree with some of Mead's theories—that the Great Russians' authoritarian behavior was the result of early swaddling, for example (a hypothesis taken up in detail by the British anthropologist Geoffrey Gorer)—respect the monumental nature of her professional writing. "No one can seriously study the South Pacific peoples without consulting her work," says Dr. Morton Klass of Barnard. "There are many ethnologists whose work has disappeared, but Mead is still very much within the body of contemporary anthropology.

"Remember that although ethnologists try to be objective, the nature of their field work is such that they cannot necessarily be a scholar in every category of the society they study. They want to get a picture of the whole culture before it dies out, and they are often working against time," Klass adds.

Although the "culture and personality" approach is no longer the vital force it once was in anthropology, Mead's influence on the younger professionals is high. Her classes at Fordham and Columbia are invariably filled. "There are three types of students who enroll," she has said. "Those who simply want to hear Margaret Mead, those who want Mead's name on their credit record, and those who are seriously interested in anthropology." To the last group, she can be a stern, but rewarding, taskmaster. Her course in field methods is considered a model for graduate students, and academia is well represented by Mead's protégés. One such, Prof. Joyce Riegelhaupt, a young anthropologist at Sarah Lawrence, thinks that her reputation remains intact because she has been willing to modify her own theories in the light of new information. "Unlike many older scholars, she is not doctrinaire," Professor Riegelhaupt says. "She is not tied down to a rigid system."

As a field researcher, Mead has always been interested in learning how children grow up in different kinds of societies, something that few of her colleagues seriously bothered with before she came on the scene. She is still deeply concerned with the acculturation of the young, but with a difference. Since the war, she says, a new world has come into being, and the youngest members of society—because they are not burdened with outmoded facts and precepts—are the ones from whom we must learn. Shifts in moral attitudes, confusion over sex roles, the Bomb, the breakdown of cities, the destruction of our natural environment, space flight, computerization, the unifying influence of television and the jet—"all these have brought about a drastic, irreversible division between the generations." This is the nub of her argument in "Culture and Commitment," a "theoretical" book which, for all its brevity, may turn out to be more of a synthesis than her critics have bargained for.

Subtitled "A Study of the Generation Gap," it is one of Mead's most satisfying works, written without the discursive slackness that flawed such earlier books as "And Keep Your Powder Dry" (1942) and "Male and Female" (1949). Here, the faint tinkle of teacups in the background is no longer heard and we are face to face with a closely reasoned argument, couched—rare for Mead—in rather abstract terms.

History, she says, has produced three broad types of cultures—postfigurative, cofigurative and prefigurative. All primitive societies are postfigurative, and until the 20th century postfigurative aspects of behavior dominated every culture. This "Papa knows best" attitude was justified because, for the most part, Papa did. In postfigurative societies "the answers to the questions: Who am I? What is the nature of my life as a member of my culture? . . . are experienced as predetermined." This gave to society an "unlabeled, unverbalized and unconscious" quality that provided great stability. But it also limited flexibility of response to change —one reason why primitive peoples, who were "locked in" by postfigurative taboos and superstition, found it hard to adjust to "civilization."

A cofigurative culture, on the other hand, is "one in which the prevailing model for members of the society is the behavior of their contemporaries." Yet, although the younger generation "take their cues from one another," the elders still remain dominant in the sense that "they set the style and define the limits within which cofiguration is expressed . . ."

In the United States, the big change appeared at the beginning of the present century. Lines of authority weakened as experienced elders were no longer able to supply the answers and determine modes of thought and behavior. Today's "youth culture," which embraces both alienation and rebellion as well as rock music and marijuana, is a product of this accelerating cofiguration, and has become institutionalized throughout our society. Style of dress, the "beat" patois, the new morality and such totems as astrology— these are the characteristic fashions which the young learn from one another, and which make up their survival kit in a seemingly hostile universe.

But they are not the symptoms of the generation gap that most interest Mead. She is convinced that the break is less a rebellion of the child against the parent than a conflict between pre-World War II and postwar cultures. We are entering, she says, "a new country," in which everyone is an immigrant, old and young alike. For the first time, the older generation—those born before the war—must learn from the younger; or at the very least, both generations must learn from the same sources. In this prefigurative society, the guidelines are all in the future. "Young people everywhere share a kind of experience that none of the elders ever have had or will have. Conversely, the older generation will never see repeated in the lives of young people their own unprecedented experience of sequentially emerging change. This break between generations is wholly new; it is planetary and universal."

In a sense, Mead has been saying this in her lectures for some time, and she seems to think that the world, in its very behavior, has at last caught up with her theories. She disclaims "belonging to the young" or wanting to be loved by them—"a temptation to be resisted at all costs"—yet there is no doubt that she uses the young as a tuning fork for her ideas, and that they, in turn, respond almost as a professional claque. Mead has become a pin-up girl (on posters advocating the legal use of marijuana) in numerous East Village coffee-houses; she is in frequent demand as a campus speaker, and is a consultant to the State Department's bureau of "youth activism." When the New York photographer Ken Heyman, who has worked with Mead on four expeditions, recently appeared at the University of California at Santa Cruz to take pictures illustrating the "generation gap," he was almost chased off the campus by students until he explained that he was working on a project with Margaret Mead. Thereupon, he was given the run of the premises. "I have traveled in 60 countries," Heyman says, "and I find that in dealing with the young, her name is a universal password—even in Russia." *

And the young are naturally pleased with Mead's attention to them; she envisions a world in which they can play an important role. True, the world is in convulsion, but this is the price of transition. Mead's philosophy is hopeful rather than apocalyptic and the intensity of commitment which characterizes modern youth is one of the props of her optimism. She herself, in recent years, has become interested in "futurology" (a discipline, strong in France, that assumes responsibility for societies that do not yet exist) and is a member of the prestige-laden Commission on the Year 2000 in this country. Paradoxically, Mead's concern with the future goes back to her involvement with the Stone Age.

Born in Philadelphia, the eldest of five children, she grew up in a highly intellectual family—her father, Edward Sherwood Mead, was a professor-economist and her mother a sociologist—where dinner-table conversation might revolve around monetary theory or the femininist movement, in which Mrs. Mead was active. A characteristic of the family was that the women képt notebooks on one another. Grandmother Mead, for example,

* But youth on the radical left will dissent from many of her interpretations. The Maoist "revolution" in China, she writes, is really an attempt to "transform the desire to destroy" into an instrument for the "preservation of the . . . Chinese Communist regime" She sees Maoism as a probably futile effort to restore in China a postfigurative culture.

recorded the emotional growing pains of her grandchildren. Margaret's mother monitored their intellectual development and Margaret herself, at the age of 8, was set to work making notes on the speech habits of her younger sisters. (When her own daughter was born, in 1939, she revived this *cahier* approach to child development and filled dozens of notebooks. To this was added a newer technique—home movies.)

After graduating from Barnard in 1923, Mead entered Columbia's department of anthropology and came under the influence of the great Franz Boas. Modern anthropology in this country can be said to date from Boas's arrival at Columbia just before the turn of the century. Previously, it had been largely an amateur's province, more involved with the specialties of folklore than with the broad investigation of culture as a scientific discipline. Mead recalls that most of the writing in the field was highly technical: "When it happened to concern the Kwakiutl or the Hopi, a good bit of it was in Kwakiutl or Hopi."

European anthropology, on the other hand, although it enjoyed an established placed in the university curriculums, suffered (as Boas saw it) from the development of broadly generalized theories that lacked field-based evidence. One influential theory, propounded by British anthropologists, held that society had evolved in a series of evolutionary steps with England standing at the pinnacle. Boas, who was German, dissented strongly from this view, and believed that cultural forms had meaning only in relation to their particular historical context. Societies were "relative" to one another, not "higher" or "lower" on some absolute scale. Some primitive cultures, although technically backward, had values that might be useful to modern man. Moreover, it was not only social organization and environment that determined cultural adaptation, but the personality of the individual within the society, his "human nature."

The person who was to strike the richest vein in this newly discovered field was Margaret Mead. When she went to Samoa in 1926 (with Boas's blessing and $1,000 of her father's money) she had never been west of Madison, Wis. For six weeks she lived in the hotel that served as an inspiration for Somerset Maugham's story "Miss Sadie Thompson" (later to become the play

"Rain"), then spent eight months in three small coastal villages on the island of Tau in the Manua archipelago. Twenty-five at the time, she was not much older than the girls she had come to observe, in order to see if "the disturbances which vex our adolescents [are] due to the nature of adolescence itself or to the civilization. Under different conditions does adolescence present a different picture?"

The answer, Mead decided, was yes; the *Sturm und Drang* associated with this age group was missing in Samoa. What she found among the young there was an easy-going way of life in which relationships were casual; conflict, as we know it, rare; the incidence of neurotic personalities, low; there was a freedom to experiment sexually without the consequent obsessions of guilt "which are so frequently a cause of maladjustment among us." In short, for a generation still climbing out of the Victorian age, she found Paradise. What is more, she gave it a measure of scientific validation.

"Coming of Age in Samoa," right from its publication, was immensely popular among students, not all of whom were studying anthropology. Its circulation was worldwide. Barnard's Dr. Klass recalls that he was an 18-year-old sailor in the Merchant Marine when a copy of the book first fell into his hands. From that moment on, he determined to become an anthropologist—and did. It is difficult to ride on a New York city bus today without seeing at least one young man or woman engrossed in "Coming of Age."

The reason is not hard to find. Here is no abstruse discussion of primitive behavior in terms of statistically enumerated culture traits. The book is descriptive; it has characters in it, with names, like a novel. Mead herself called it "this tale of another way of life." Technical matter is confined to appendixes. "I wrote it in English," she said recently, when asked to explain its popularity.*

But "Coming of Age" had another attribute which Mead herself

* *Coming of Age in Samoa* has been the subject of many critical attacks since it was published 42 years ago. Dr. Marvin Harris, for example, in *The Rise of Anthropological Theory* points out that Mead describes her Samoan girls subjectively ("high-spirited" Nito; "strong-minded" Pusa, etc.) rather than in terms of verifiable behavior—much as though she were writing *Little Women*. Yet the book has survived.

did not contemplate when she began her project. In its original draft, the book dealt only with Samoan girls and their families. Just before submitting it for publication, the author added two chapters applying her findings to life in modern society. These may well be the most important sections of the book, for they suggested that our strict attitudes toward sex might well be relaxed "without in any way accepting promiscuity." Much of what Mead called for has since come to pass. The stormy period of adolescence, however, at least in Western societies, has remained.

During the next few years, she led expeditions to the Admiralty Islands and New Guinea, studying four other tribes quite different from the Samoans. Some of her most extensive work has been done with the Manus, whom she revisited in 1953, and to whom she is affectionately known as Miss Makrit Mit. Unlike the Samoans, the Manus are not given to sensual pleasure and, in Mead's words, "emphasize the practical virtues of abstinence." (Perhaps for this reason, her study of this tribe, "Growing Up in New Guinea," never achieved as much popularity as "Coming of Age.")

In all, Mead has studied six primitive cultures—Samoan, Manu, Arapesh, Mundugumor, Tchambuli and Iatmul—in addition to the more traditional Balinese. The findings appeared in a series of books whose titles—and to some extent the contents—suggest a South Seas "Forsyte Saga": "Coming of Age in Samoa," "Growing Up in New Guinea," "Sex and Temperament in Three Primitive Societies," "Balinese Character," "New Lives for Old."

The style, like that of "Coming of Age," is often that of the novelist ("Her grandmother is very old, the muscles in her neck are stringy like uncooked pork") rather than the anthropologist, but her studies rest on a foundation of detailed and closely documented observations. What she did not do was submit her tribal subjects to Western-style anthropometric tests—or run a series of statistical surveys. Mead is intuitive. She settles in with a tribe, eating the native food (wild pigeon and dried fish, for the most part), helping nurse sick infants, and gaining the confidence of the adults while filling notebooks in her minuscule handwriting. On the Sepik River in New Guinea, she and her husband at the time, the British anthropologist Gregory Bateson, built a house without walls so that nothing that went on around them would go unobserved.

Ken Heyman recalls that on a return visit to Bali, Mead would sit on the ground and watch apparently unimportant details for hours at a time without moving. "She knows how to use her eyes —how to see," he says. "She has an uncanny perception for different cultural styles."

Her biggest asset in such a milieu is the ability to shed Western preconceptions. In the remote Bali village of Byun Gede, for example, the natives had strung light bulbs on posts and fences, although there was no electricity within miles. "Outsiders joke about this," Heyman recalls, "but Mead accepted the fact that light bulbs don't necessarily have to light up. She looks at people from inside their own culture."

Mead is so popular with the Iatmul tribe in New Guinea that her party is met at the river dock by a delegation singing, "My darling Clementine," and she herself will be carried to the village like a star quarterback after the big game. A good deal of Western technology has come to New Guinea, and on her last visit in 1967, she had hardly arrived when her hosts clamored around her to ask if she had brought a tape recorder. Told that she had, they at once offered to sing, chant and beat their log drums. The Iatmuls are well aware of her importance—a cartoon in The New Yorker some years ago showed a tribal chief passing out books to a group of preadolescent boys about to be initiated. "Rather than go into the details," he remarks, "I'm simply going to present each of you with a copy of this excellent book by Margaret Mead." (Her reputation as an authority on puberty rites is so widespread that a Brooklyn taxi driver once asked Mead if she would attend his son's *bar mizvah*. She obliged by turning up at the reception, where she helped light the candles.)

One lesson she draws from her study of primitive cultures is that each one has its own distinct psychological profile. If the Samoans were relaxed and well-adjusted, and the Manus thrifty and self-denying, the Mundugumor were found to be violent and quarrelsome; the Arapesh were nonaggressive and loved humor; the Tchambuli exemplified a matriarchy in which transvestites were common and neuroticism high. "Each society has taken a special emphasis and given it a full and integrated expression at the expense of other potentialities of the human race," Mead has written. "Primitive man, secure in a closed and ordered universe, has a dignity that we have lost. . . . But we may still ask if this homogeneity is not too dearly bought." Postfigurative man, she points out, had identity but could not change his commitment, no matter what happened to him.* Modern man can.

Mead has been spreading this gospel since the early 1940's, when she first became active in public life. In the sprawling, heterogeneous culture of her own country, she sits on numerous tribal councils, is frequently decorated (17 honorary degrees, 13 awards and citations) and has ascended to the chieftaincy of such august bodies as the World Federation for Mental Health and the American Anthropological Association. A dossier for dinner chairmen who are called upon to introduce her runs to eight closely typed pages.

Until last year, she was curator of ethnology at the American Museum of Natural History, where she still runs an office with nine assistants. One anthropologist calls it a "plantation." With one exception, the assistants are all women, most of them students or recent graduates. Some do research; one is an official Mead bibliographer. Others make arrangements for her writing and speaking assignments: The Mead schedule, set up weeks in advance, is precision-timed for maximum exposure on any given tour. A typical week (Feb. 13-20, 1970) went like this:

Friday: Conference with students in the morning; lunch with her editor at McCall's Publishing Company; thence to Fairleigh Dickinson University in Rutherford, N.J., for dinner and a talk. Driven back to Penn Station, she boarded the 3:23 A.M. train to Washington.

Saturday: An all-day conference with the State Department on the problems of radical youth. Dinner with friends, then a flight to Philadelphia, where she spent the night.

* Strictly speaking, his commitment could not be changed from within. "Civilization" has modified all primitive societies that it has come in contact with. Mead's "New Lives for Old" describes this process in the case of the Manus, who welcomed Christianity with enthusiasm. "They had never known where they came from; and were very glad to be told."

Sunday: Breakfast at the Academy of Natural Sciences with the trustees, followed by a press conference and a public lecture. In the afternoon, she spoke at a conference on environment and population at the University of Pennsylvania. Back to Washington that night.

Monday: All-day meeting with the Ekistics Society, an organization founded by the Greek architect-urbanologist Constantinos Dioxiadis to formulate a science of human settlements. (Mead also joins the society's annual floating conference on the Dioxiadis yacht in the Aegean—a session that includes sightseeing, dancing and drinking, as well as thinking.)

Tuesday: In New York, teaching at Fordham and Columbia.

Wednesday: Metroliner to Philadelphia, where she taped the "Mike Douglas Show." Then to Atlantic City to receive the American Education Award for 1970 at a banquet of the American Association of School Administrators.

Thursday: Back to New York in time for a 9:30 class. Lunch with the British scientist Nigel Calder, then to a panel on fertility control and women's careers, as moderator, at the New York Academy of Sciences.

Such whirlwind tours are by no means exceptional and they give Mead a chance to open her show on the road. She will play around with an idea for months, sounding out friends in other fields, getting audience reaction as she travels. When she thinks the package is ready, she brings it to New York as a major speech, or a series of talks on a given theme. The substance of "Culture and Commitment" was explored in various informal ways on tour. The first two sections of the book were simply transcribed from tapes; the final section was written over a weekend.

Mead is a fluent speaker, with a filing-cabinet mind that is seldom at a loss for facts. She never lectures from notes, and has a gift for putting solemn concepts into ordinary language—and, occasionally, her foot in her mouth at the same time. When she testified in favor of legalized pot at a Senate hearing last winter, critical mail so inundated her office that she was compelled to put out an explanation. It was not that pot is good for you, Mead said, in effect, but that its illegality is bad. That she has no special qualifications in the drug field did not make this distinction any more palatable to her critics.

This tendency to shoot from the hip has made her controversial, but she can be right as often as wrong. In any case, she will be provocative. At a symposium on "The Future of Cities," she explained rural migration with the comment: "At least 50 per cent of the human race doesn't want their mother-in-law within walking distance." The rural migrant, she added, "has a chance to get away from relatives."

(Such fey anthropological—as opposed to economic—explanations of human behavior are not to be dismissed lightly. Several years ago, when U.S. technical assistance to India was bogged down, Mead headed an expedition of social scientists to find out why Indian farmers were reluctant to give up their wooden plows. Her answer: because metal plows seldom needed repairing, they broke "various social relationships" with the carpenters who kept the wooden plows intact. The carpenter's wife, for example, gave a sari to the farmer's wife on feast days. It is this kind of societal analysis that has put Mead on numerous U.S. Government commissions.)

For her own part, Mead likes relatives and cannot see enough of them. She has been married twice, both times to anthropologists. A daughter, Mary Catherine Bateson (Mrs. Barkhev Kassarjian) earned her Ph.D. in linguistics and Middle East studies at Harvard, but has since drifted into anthropology, and figures as the stellar character in her mother's elaborate kinship system. Mead's sister, the former Mrs. William Steig, is a painter and her brother teaches college in California. Numerous cousins, nieces and nephews are scattered around the country, and Mead will frequently arrange her lecture schedule to visit as many of them as possible. Her loyalties to old friends are intense, and she still corresponds with people she knew in the fourth grade. All of these contacts, in addition to more recent acquaintances, help flesh out Mead's field studies on the American tribe. In essence, these form the observations that make up much of her popular writing.

"Margaret operates on the frontiers of what people are thinking about," says Dr. Metraux, who has worked with her, off and on, since 1942. She is ahead of her public—but not too far ahead. Her base camp on the frontier is furnished with the solid values of American life. (An ardent Episcopalian, Mead seldom misses a Sunday service. When the church revised its liturgy some years ago, she was put on the commission that drafted the changes.) Dr. Birdwhistell has pointed out that a good many anthropologists do not believe that modern America has a culture. Mead insists that it has, and by making hypotheses about Americans that only time can verify, she has incurred the criticism of colleagues who seek a more empirical approach. To this, Mead retorts that she is an interpreter, rather than a poll taker. She is not mapping society but exploring it.

This attitude accounts for the enormous span of her interests, for in Mead's view America is a collection of subcultures held in suspension by a common set of values. Our taboos are more sophisticated, our votive offerings and sacrifices ritualized on a higher level than primitive man's, yet they are nonetheless real. Mead has translated the tribal idiom into modern behavioral terms. She wants man to understand the cultural and psychological bases for his actions in order that he may improve the quality of his own life. Human nature is plastic, she points out, but there are "biological constraints on that plasticity, a floor below which we do not let human beings fall, so that they will not be damaged intellectually or physically. But there is no ceiling on this plasticity. This is what anthropology teaches us."

Mead's interest in "futurology" is a logical extension of her belief that man has the capacity to be better than he has ever been. "We are living in a world that no one has ever lived in before," she says, and it is here that she takes her stand. An anthropologist who likes to doodle, in discussing this aspect of her work, sketched the figure of a woman who has just lifted off from the battlements of the museum into the wild blue yonder. Her cape is flying, the thumb-stick is outstretched like a scepter. "None of us knows what really lies ahead," he mused, "not even Margaret Mead. But I assure you, if there is a committee in charge, she will be on it."

Part 4

TRENDS IN ECONOMICS

The dominant feature of modern economics is its stress on technical analysis. The consequent loss in philosophical perspective has been quite marked, as economists have concerned themselves with input-output studies, econometrics, operations research, game theory, and linear or mathematical programming. Thus economists have tended to convert themselves into technical experts who, in the pursuit of scientific truth, have been increasingly unwilling to address knotty problems of human action and behavior. If economics is defined as but one aspect of social behavior, then it may be included in a general theory of social systems and its primary task becomes the study of behavior that stems from the specifically economic.

Traditionally, economists have attended to the areas of production and distribution. But goods and services are not only commodities and performances; they are significantly related to the human actors who control them and who are controlled in turn. Overlooking these relationships results in an undue emphasis on artifacts and leads economists to dispense with ends as they pursue in great detail the problem of means. For example, by insisting that the passage from individual action to social performance is achieved via the market mechanism, economists simply evade the responsibility for elucidating ends. They fail to recognize that normative criteria and special pleading have been substituted for the realities of industrialism and an age of urbanism.

The question of goals was perhaps implicit in the theories of John Maynard Keynes. But the contrast between the two views—a study of means only and a concern with ends—is best highlighted in the economics of Milton Friedman and John Kenneth Galbraith: one a skilled technician, the other a humanist.

Came the Revolution

by John Kenneth Galbraith

THE GENERAL THEORY OF EMPLOYMENT, INTEREST, AND MONEY.
By John Maynard Keynes. 403 pp. New York: Harcourt, Brace
& World. Paper, $2.95.

*"I believe myself to be writing a book on economic theory
which will largely revolutionize—not, I suppose, at once but in
the course of the next ten years—the way the world thinks about
economic problems."*—Letter from J. M. Keynes to George Bernard Shaw, New Year's Day, 1935.

THE MOST influential book on economic and social policy so far
in this century, "The General Theory of Employment, Interest,
and Money," by John Maynard Keynes, was published 29 years
ago last February in Britain and a few weeks later in the United
States. A paperback edition is now available here for the first
time, and quite a few people who take advantage of this bargain
will be puzzled at the reason for the book's influence. Though
comfortably aware of their own intelligence, they will be unable
to read it. They will wonder, accordingly, how it persuaded so
many other people—not all of whom, certainly, were more penetrating or diligent. This was only one of the remarkable things
about this book and the revolution it precipitated.

By common, if not yet quite universal agreement, the Keynesian

From the *New York Times Book Review*, May 16, 1965, copyright © 1965
by the New York Times Company.

revolution was one of the great modern accomplishments in social design. It brought Marxism in the advanced countries to a total halt. It led to a level of economic performance that now inspires bitter-end conservatives to panegyrics of unexampled banality. Yet those responsible have had no honors and some opprobrium. For a long while, to be known as an active Keynesian was to invite the wrath of those who equate social advance with subversion. Those concerned developed a habit of reticence. As a further consequence, the history of the revolution is, perhaps, the worst told story of our era.

It is time that we knew better this part of our history and those who made it, and this is a little of the story. Much of it turns on the almost unique unreadability of "The General Theory" and hence the need for people to translate and propagate its ideas to government officials, students and the public at large. As Messiahs go, Keynes was deeply dependent on his prophets.

"The General Theory" appeared in the sixth year of the Great Depression and the fifty-third of Keynes's life. At the time Keynes, like his great contemporary Churchill, was regarded as too clear-headed and candid to be trusted. Public officials are not always admiring of men who say what the right policy should be. Their frequent need, especially in matters of foreign policy, is for men who will find persuasive reasons for the wrong policy. Keynes had foreseen grave difficulty from the reparations clauses of the Versailles Treaty and had voiced them in "The Economic Consequences of the Peace," a brilliantly polemical volume, which may well have overstated his case and which certainly was unjust to Woodrow Wilson.

Later in the twenties, in another book, he was equally untactful toward those who invited massive unemployment in Britain in order to return sterling to the gold standard at its pre-war parity with the dollar. The man immediately responsible for this effort, a highly orthodox voice in economic matters at the time, was the then Chancellor of the Exchequer, Winston Churchill, and that book was called "The Economic Consequences of Mr. Churchill."

From 1920 to 1940 Keynes was sought out by students and intellectuals in Cambridge and London; was well known in London theater and artistic circles; directed an insurance company;

made, and on occasion lost, quite a bit of money; and was an influential journalist. But he wasn't really trusted on public questions. The great public trade union which identifies trustworthiness with conformity kept him outside. Then came the Depression. There was much unemployment, much suffering. Even respectable men went broke. It was necessary, however unpleasant, to listen to the candid men who had something to say. This is the terrible punishment the gods reserve for fair weather statesmen.

It is a measure of how far the Keynesian revolution has proceeded that the central thesis of "The General Theory" now sounds rather commonplace. Until it appeared, economists, in the classical (or non-socialist) tradition, had assumed that the economy, if left to itself, would find its equilibrium at full employment. Increases or decreases in wages and in interest rates would occur as necessary to bring about this pleasant result. If men were unemployed, their wages would fall in relation to prices. With lower wages and wider margins, it would be profitable to employ those from whose toil an adequate return could not previously have been made. It followed that steps to keep wages at artificially high levels, such as might result from the ill-considered efforts by unions, would cause unemployment. Such efforts were deemed to be the principal cause of unemployment.

Movements in interest rates played a complementary role by insuring that all income would ultimately be spent. Thus, were people to decide for some reason to increase their savings, the interest rates on the now more abundant supply of loanable funds would fall. This, in turn, would lead to increased investment. The added outlays for investment goods would offset the diminished outlays by the more frugal consumers. In this fashion, changes in consumer spending or in investment decisions were kept from causing any change in total spending that would lead to unemployment.

Keynes argued that neither wage movements nor changes in the rate of interest had, necessarily, any such agreeable effect. He focused attention on the total of purchasing power in the economy —what freshmen are now taught to call aggregate demand. Wage reductions might not increase employment; in conjunction with other changes, they might merely reduce this aggregate demand.

And he held that interest was not the price that was paid to people to save but the price they got for exchanging holdings of cash, or its equivalent, their normal preference in assets, for less liquid forms of investment. And it was difficult to reduce interest beyond a certain level. Accordingly, if people sought to save more, this wouldn't necessarily mean lower interest rates and a resulting increase in investment. Instead, the total demand for goods might fall, along with employment and also investment, until savings were brought back into line with investment by the pressure of hardship which had reduced saving in favor of consumption. The economy would find its equilibrium not at full employment but with an unspecified amount of unemployment.

Out of this diagnosis came the remedy. It was to bring aggregate demand back up to the level where all willing workers were employed, and this could be accomplished by supplementing private expenditure with public expenditure. This should be the policy wherever intentions to save exceeded intentions to invest. Since public spending would not perform this offsetting role if there were compensating taxation (which is a form of saving), the public spending should be financed by borrowing—by incurring a deficit. So far as Keynes can be condensed into a few paragraphs, this is it. "The General Theory" is more difficult. There are nearly 400 pages, some of them of fascinating obscurity.

Before the publication of "The General Theory," Keynes had urged his ideas directly on President Roosevelt, most notably in a famous letter to The New York Times on Dec. 31, 1933: "I lay overwhelming emphasis on the increase of national purchasing power resulting from government expenditure which is financed by loans." And he visited F.D.R. in the summer of 1934 to press his case, although the session was no great success; each, during the meeting, seems to have developed some doubts about the general good sense of the other.

In the meantime, two key Washington officials, Marriner Eccles, the exceptionally able Utah banker who was to become head of the Federal Reserve Board, and Lauchlin Currie, a former Harvard instructor who was director of research and later an economic aide to Roosevelt (and later still a prominent victim of McCarthyite persecution), had on their own account reached conclusions similar to those of Keynes as to the proper course of fiscal policy. When "The General Theory" arrived, they took it as confirmation of the course they had previously been urging. Currie, a highly qualified economist and teacher, was also a skilled and influential interpreter of the ideas in the Washington community. Not often have important new ideas on economics entered a government by way of its central bank. Nor should conservatives worry. There is not the slightest indication that it will ever happen again.

Paralleling the work of Keynes in the thirties and rivaling it in importance, though not in fame, was that of Simon Kuznets and a group of young economists and statisticians at the University of Pennsylvania, the National Bureau of Economic Research and the U.S. Department of Commerce. They developed the now familiar concepts of National Income and Gross National Product and their components and made estimates of their amount. Included among the components of National Income and Gross National Product was the saving, investment, aggregate of disposable income and the other magnitudes of which Keynes was talking. As a result, those who were translating his ideas into action knew not only what needed to be done but how much. And many who would never have been persuaded by the Keynesian abstractions were compelled to belief by the concrete figures from Kuznets and his inventive colleagues.

However, the trumpet—if the metaphor is permissible for this particular book—that was sounded in Cambridge, England was heard most clearly in Cambridge, Mass. Harvard was the principal avenue by which Keynes's ideas passed to the United States. Conservatives worry about universities being centers of disquieting innovation. Their worries are surely exaggerated—but it has occurred.

In the late thirties, Harvard had a large community of young economists, most of them held there by the shortage of jobs that Keynes sought to cure. They had the normal confidence of their years in their ability to remake the world and, unlike less fortunate generations, the opportunity. They also had occupational indication of the need. Massive unemployment persisted year after year. It was degrading to have to continue telling the young that this was merely a temporary departure from the full employment norm, and that one need only obtain the needed wage reductions.

Paul Samuelson of M.I.T., who, almost from the outset, was the acknowledged leader of the younger Keynesian community, has compared the excitement of the young economists, on the arrival of Keynes's book, to that of Keats on first looking into Chapman's Homer. Some will wonder if economists are capable of such refined emotion, but the effect was certainly great. Here was a remedy for the despair that could be seen just beyond the Yard. It did not overthrow the system but saved it. To the non-revolutionary, it seemed too good to be true. To the occasional revolutionary, it was. The old economics was still taught by day. But in the evening, and almost every evening from 1936 on, almost everyone discussed Keynes.

This might, conceivably, have remained a rather academic discussion. As with the Bible and Marx, obscurity stimulated abstract debate. But in 1938, the practical instincts that economists sometimes suppress with success were catalyzed by the arrival at Harvard from Minnesota of Alvin H. Hansen. He was then about 50, an effective teacher and a popular colleague. But most of all he was a man for whom economic ideas had no standing apart from their use.

The economists of established reputation had not taken to Keynes. Faced with the choice between changing one's mind and proving that there is no need to do so, almost everyone opts for the latter. So it was then. Hansen had an established reputation, and he did change his mind. Though he had been an effective critic of some central propositions in Keynes's "Treatise on Money," an immediately preceding work, and was initially rather cool to "The General Theory," he soon became strongly persuaded of its importance.

He proceeded to expound the ideas in books, articles and lectures and to apply them to the American scene. He persuaded his students and younger colleagues that they should not only understand the ideas but win understanding in others and then go on to get action. Without ever seeking to do so or being quite aware of the fact, he became the leader of a crusade. In the late thirties Hansen's seminar in the new Graduate School of Public Administration was regularly visited by the Washington policymakers. Often the students overflowed into the hall. One felt that it was the most important thing currently happening in the country and this could have been the case.

The officials took Hansen's ideas, and perhaps even more his sense of conviction, back to Washington. In time there was also a strong migration of his younger colleagues and students to the capital. Among numerous others were Richard Gilbert, now a principal architect of Pakistan's economic development, who was a confidant of Harry Hopkins: Richard Musgrave, now of Princeton, who applied Keynes's and Hansen's ideas to the tax system; Alan Sweezy, now of California Institute of Technology, who went to the Federal Reserve and the W.P.A.; George Jaszi, who went to the Department of Commerce; Griffiths Johnson, who served at the Treasury, National Resources Planning Board and the White House; and Walter Salant, now of the Brookings Institution, who served in several Federal agencies. Keynes himself once wrote admiringly of this group of young Washington disciples.

The discussion that had begun in Cambridge continued through the war years in Washington. One of the leaders, a close friend of Hansen's but not otherwise connected with the Harvard group, was Gerhard Colm of the Bureau of the Budget. Colm, a German refugee who made the transition from a position of influence in Germany to one of influence in the United States in a matter of some five years, played a major role in reducing the Keynesian proposals to workable estimates of costs and quantities. Keynesian policies became central to what was called postwar planning and designs for preventing the re-emergence of massive unemployment.

Meanwhile, others were concerning themselves with a wider audience. Seymour Harris, another of Hansen's colleagues and an early convert to Keynes, became the most prolific exponent of the ideas in the course of becoming one of the most prolific scholars of modern times. He published half a dozen books on Keynes and outlined the ideas in hundreds of letters, speeches, memoranda, Congressional appearances and articles. Professor Samuelson, mentioned above, put the Keynesian ideas into what became (and remains) the most influential textbook on economics since the last great exposition of the classical system by Alfred

Marshall. Lloyd Metzler, now of the University of Chicago, applied the Keynesian system to international trade. Lloyd G. Reynolds, at a later stage, gathered a talented group of younger economists at Yale and made that university a major center of discussion of the new trends.

Nor was the Harvard influence confined to the United States. At almost the same time that "The General Theory" arrived in Cambridge, Mass., a young Canadian graduate student named Robert Bryce arrived from Cambridge, England. He had been in Keynes's seminar and had, as a result, a special license to explain what Keynes meant in his more obscure passages. With two or three other Canadian graduate students, Bryce went on to Ottawa and to a succession of senior posts culminating in his present one as Deputy Minister of Finance. Canada was perhaps the first country to commit itself to a firmly Keynesian economic policy.

Meanwhile, with the help of the academic Keynesians, a few businessmen were becoming interested. Two New England industrialists, Henry S. Dennison of the Dennison Manufacturing Company in Framingham and Ralph Flanders of the Jones and Lamson Company of Springfield, Vt. (and later United States Senator from Vermont) hired members of the Harvard group to tutor them in the ideas. Before the war they had endorsed them in a book, in which Lincoln Filene of Boston and Morris E. Leeds of Philadelphia had joined, called "Toward Full Employment." It was only slightly more readable than Keynes. In the later war years, the Committee for Economic Development, led in these matters by Flanders and the late Beardsley Ruml, and again with the help of the academic Keynesians, began explaining the ideas to businessmen.

In Washington during the war years the National Planning Association had been a center for academic discussion of the Keynesian ideas. At the end of the war Hans Christian Sonne, the imaginative and liberal New York banker, began underwriting both N.P.A., and the Keynesian ideas. With the C.E.D., in which Sonne was also influential, N.P.A. became another important instrument for explaining the policy to the larger public. (In the autumn of 1949, in an exercise of unparalleled diplomacy,

Sonne gathered a dozen economists of strongly varying views at Princeton and persuaded them to sign a specific endorsement of Keynesian fiscal policies. The agreement was later reported to the Congress in well-publicized hearings by Arthur Smithies of Harvard and Simeon Leland of Northwestern University.)

In 1946, 10 years after the publication of "The General Theory," the Employment Act of that year gave the Keynesian system the qualified but still quite explicit support of law. It recognized, as Keynes had urged, that unemployment and insufficient output would respond to positive policies. Not much was said about the specific policies but the responsibility of the Federal Government to act in some fashion was clearly affirmed. The Council of Economic Advisers became, in turn, a platform for expounding the Keynesian view of the economy and it was brought promptly into use. Leon Keyserling, as an original member and later chairman, was a tireless exponent of the ideas. And he saw at an early stage the importance of enlarging them to embrace not only the prevention of depression but the maintenance of an adequate rate of economic expansion. Thus in a decade had the revolution spread.

Those who nurture thoughts of conspiracy and clandestine plots will be saddened to know that this was a revolution without organization. All who participated felt a deep sense of personal responsibility for the ideas; there was a varying but deep urge to persuade. But no one ever responded to plans, orders, instructions, or any force apart from his own convictions. That perhaps was the most interesting single feature of the Keynesian revolution.

Something more was, however, suspected. And there was some effort at counter-revolution. Nobody could say that he preferred massive unemployment to Keynes. And even men of conservative mood, when they understood what was involved, opted for the policy—some asking only that it be called by some other name. The Committee for Economic Development, coached by Ruml on semantics, never advocated deficits. Rather it spoke well of a budget that was balanced only under conditions of high employment. Those who objected to Keynes were also invariably handicapped by the fact that they hadn't (and couldn't) read the book.

It was like attacking the original Kama Sutra for obscenity without being able to read Sanskrit. Still, where social change is involved, there are men who can surmount any handicap.

Appropriately Harvard, not Washington, was the principal object of attention. In the fifties, a group of graduates of mature years banded together in an organization called the Veritas Foundation and produced a volume called "Keynes at Harvard." It found that "Harvard was the launching pad for the Keynesian rocket in America." But then it damaged this not implausible proposition by identifying Keynesianism with socialism, Fabian socialism, Marxism, Communism, Fascism and also literary incest, meaning that one Keynesian always reviewed the works of another Keynesian. More encouragingly, the authors also reported that "Galbraith is being groomed as the new crown prince of Keynesism (sic)." Like so many others in similar situations, the authors sacrificed their chance for credibility by writing not for the public but for those who were paying the bill. The university was unperturbed, the larger public sadly indifferent. The book evidently continues to have some circulation on the more thoughtful fringes of the John Birch Society.

As a somewhat less trivial matter, another and more influential group of graduates pressed for an investigation of the Department of Economics, employing as their instrument the visiting committee that annually reviews the work of the department on behalf of the Governing Boards. The Keynesian revolution belongs to our history; so accordingly does this investigation.

It was conducted by Clarence Randall, then the exceptionally articulate head of the Inland Steel Company, with the support of Sinclair Weeks, a manufacturer, former Senator and tetrarch of the right wing of the Republican Party in Massachusetts. In due course, the committee found that Keynes was, indeed, exerting a baneful influence on the Harvard economic mind and that the department was unbalanced in his favor. As always, there was the handicap that the investigators, with one or two possible exceptions, had not read the book and were otherwise uncertain as to what they attacked. The department, including the members most skeptical of Keynes's analysis—no one accepted all of it and some very little—unanimously rejected the committee's finding.

So, as one of his last official acts before becoming High Commissioner to Germany, did President James Bryant Conant. There was much bad blood.

In ensuing years there was further discussion of the role of Keynes at Harvard and of related issues. But it became increasingly amicable, for the original investigators had been caught up in one of those fascinating and paradoxical developments with which the history of the Keynesian (and doubtless all other) revolutions is replete. Shortly after the committee reached its disturbing conclusion, the Eisenhower Administration came to power.

Mr. Randall became a Presidential assistant and adviser. Mr. Weeks became Secretary of Commerce and almost immediately was preoccupied with the firing of the head of the Bureau of Standards over the question of the efficacy of Glauber's salts as a battery additive. Having staked his public reputation against the nation's scientists and engineers on the issue (as the late Bernard De Voto put it) that a battery could be improved by giving it a laxative, Mr. Weeks could hardly be expected to keep open another front against the economists. But much worse, both he and Mr. Randall were acquiring a heavy contingent liability for the policies of the Eisenhower Administration. And these, it soon developed, had almost as strong a Keynesian coloration as the department at Harvard.

President Eisenhower's first Chairman of the Council of Economic Advisers was Arthur F. Burns of Columbia University and the National Bureau of Economic Research. Mr. Burns had credentials as a critic of Keynes. In his introduction to the 1946 annual report of the National Bureau, called "Economic Research and the Keynesian Thinking of Our Times," he had criticized a version of the Keynesian underemployment equilibrium and concluded a little heavily that "the imposing schemes for governmental action that are being bottomed on Keynes's equilibrium theory must be viewed with skepticism." Alvin Hansen had replied rather sharply.

But Burns was (and is) an able economist. If he regarded Keynes with skepticism, he viewed recessions (including ones for which he might be held responsible) with positive antipathy. In his

1955 Economic Report, he said, "Budget policies can help promote the objective of maximum production by wisely allocating resources *first between private and public uses;* second, among various government programs." (Italics added.) Keynes, reading these words carefully, would have strongly applauded. And, indeed, a spokesman for the N.A.M. told the Joint Economic Committee that they pointed "directly toward the planned and eventually the socialized economy."

After the departure of Burns, the Eisenhower Administration incurred a deficit of no less than $9.4 billions in the national income accounts in the course of overcoming the recession of 1958. This was by far the largest deficit ever incurred by an American Government in peacetime; it exceeded the *total* peacetime expenditure by F.D.R. in any year up to 1940. No Administration before or since has given the economy such a massive dose of Keynesian medicine. With a Republican Administration, guided by men like Mr. Randall and Mr. Weeks, following such policies, the academic Keynesians were no longer vulnerable. Keynes ceased to be a wholly tactful topic of conversation with such critics.

Presidents Kennedy and Johnson have continued what is now commonplace policy. Advised by Walter Heller, a remarkably skillful exponent of Keynes's ideas, they added the new device of the deliberate tax reduction to sustain aggregate demand. And they abandoned, at long last, the doubletalk by which advocates of Keynesian policies combined advocacy of measures to promote full employment and economic growth with promises of a promptly balanced budget. "We have recognized as self-defeating the effort to balance our budget too quickly in an economy operating well below its potential," President Johnson said in his 1965 report.

Now, as noted, Keynesian policies are the new orthodoxy. Economists are everywhere to be seen enjoying their new and pleasantly uncontroversial role. Like their predecessors who averted their eyes from unemployment, many are now able to ignore—often with some slight note of scholarly righteousness—the new problem, which is an atrocious allocation of resources between private wants and public needs, especially those of our cities. (In a sense, the Keynesian success has brought back an older problem of economics, that of resource allocation, in a new form.) And there is the dangerously high dependence on military spending. But these are other matters.

We have yet to pay proper respect to those who pioneered the Keynesian revolution. Everyone now takes pride in the resulting performance of the economy. We should take a little pride in the men who brought it about. It is hardly fitting that they should have been celebrated only by the reactionaries. The debt to the courage and intelligence of Alvin Hansen is especially great. Next only to Keynes, his is the credit for saving what even conservatives still call capitalism.

friedmanism, n.: Doctrine of most audacious U.S. economist; esp., theory "only money matters"

by Milton Viorst

HALF-JOCULARLY, Milton Friedman says that his favorite country in the world is Japan, because he's such a tall man there. Friedman admits unhappily to being just 5 feet 3, but adds that when he was an undergraduate he measured at least 5 feet 4½. He's been squashed down since then, he says.

But if Milton Friedman has been squashed down in height, that's surely about all. In economics, he is certainly the most irrepressible, outspoken, audacious, provocative and inventive thinker in the United States—and even at 5 feet 3, he may stand taller than all his colleagues in the profession. When the Nobel Prize is next awarded for economics, it is regarded as even money that Milton Friedman will win it.

Nonetheless, it's hard to get responsible people, whether in academia or in government, to acknowledge that they've been influenced by Friedman. He is disturbing, if only because of his contempt for the conventional economic wisdom. He is too aggressive in challenging the premises themselves of long-standing economic policy. He's just too damned radical. And, in many circles, the fact that he was tied up with Barry Goldwater during the 1964 campaign doesn't recommend him either.

Still, there is no doubt that at Harvard and M.I.T., where he is considered a heretic, to say nothing of the University of Chicago, where he is the chief luminary of the "Chicago school" of economics, his ideas have had an enormous impact. Meanwhile, down in Washington, the people who make policy have begun to realize that there might be a lot of good sense in what Milton Friedman's been saying.

Currently, the doctrines known as Friedmanism are engaged in a major assault upon the Federal Reserve System, the high church of economic orthodoxy. The Fed is the issuing authority for the nation's money. It is empowered to regulate the supply of money in circulation—usually defined as actual currency, plus checking-account balances—through such devices as the sale and purchase of Government bonds, the setting of reserve requirements for banks, or even the actual printing of bills. It also exercises certain leverage over the use of this money by influencing the interest rate at which most credit flows.

The Fed's goal is to contribute to economic stability, normally by "leaning against the wind," a wind which may be inflationary in some cases and deflationary in others. Friedmanism shares this goal but contends that the Fed has been going after it backwards.

Friedman argues that the Fed has blundered by tinkering with interest rates to stabilize the economy. Instead, the Fed should concentrate on regulating the quantity of money itself and let interest rates fall where they may. Friedman says the Fed's preoccupation with interest rates is not useless merely; it is positively harmful. In fact, he goes a step further by arguing that not only interest rates but Federal fiscal policy itself—that is, Federal spending and taxation—have a negligible impact on economic stability.

This rather extreme view—which holds that taxes, spending and interest rates do not compare in importance with the size of the money supply—has been designated, chiefly by its disgruntled opponents, as Friedman's "Only money matters" doctrine.

Friedman seized upon this doctrine in the course of preparing, with Dr. Anna Schwartz, the book called "A Monetary History of the United States," now recognized as a classic in the literature of economics. From the data he accumulated, he made the observation that economic instability over the past century has been the consequence principally of abrupt fluctuations in the money supply. During the Great Depression of the nineteen-thirties, for example, the Federal Reserve Board allowed the quantity of money in circulation to shrink by more than a third, with disastrous results. From these observations, Friedman concluded that the Fed should aim to keep the money supply stable—or have it increase (via a fixed rule laid down by Congress) at a steady percentage to keep up with economic growth.

Milton Friedman's reputation as a provocateur waxes by the moment as this doctrine makes headway in the corridors of power, particularly in the Fed, which changes chairmen this week. But because Friedman, at 57, is the reigning "monetarist" in the United States, it should by no means be assumed that his disruptive ideas stop there. His mind ranges across the entire field of economics and spills over into politics itself. To him, virtually no concept, no institution, no personality is sacrosanct.

When he was a 21-year-old graduate student at the University of Chicago, he emerged from a couple of days in a sickbed with a corrective of the work of Prof. Arthur C. Pigou of Cambridge, one of the leading economists of the day, which was published in the eminent Quarterly Journal of Economics. Ever since, he's been a gadfly, but because his capacity to nettle is matched by an indisputable scholarly brilliance, he could never quite be ignored.

Some say his most significant work is not on monetarism at all, nor on political economics, but in an abstruse book meant only for the experts called "A Theory of the Consumption Function," which showed that consumption, in the short run, tends to remain constant despite sharp fluctuations in income. Though it may be true that Friedman is at his best in technical economics, he has not become a major public figure because of his esoteric economic theories. Rather it is because he is willing to leave his ivory tower and, in behalf of ideas that are dear to him, come out scrapping.

He was born in Brooklyn of Jewish immigrant parents and raised in Rahway, N. J., where his father did sweatshop work that provided a marginal income for the family. When he reached college age, he won a scholarship to nearby Rutgers and came to the attention of a young economics professor named Arthur Burns, who recognized in him a superior mind. Friedman also came under the influence of a young professor named Homer Jones, who had brought with him from the University of Chicago certain ideas about how to rescue the country from the Depression through a selective return to laissez-faire economics.

Friedman, who at first specialized in math, acknowledges that it was Burns who steered him into economics, while it was Jones who had the greatest impact on his early intellectual development. Jones, he says, steered him to the graduate school at the University of Chicago.

But much as his brilliance was recognized, Friedman was far from an immediate success in the intellectual world. Leaving Chicago, he had difficulty getting a university position. Some academic mandarins maintained that he was more interested in being daring than thorough, and there was some truth to the charge. Others considered him excessively aggressive, a compensation, friends observed, for his small stature and uncomely visage. In at least one instance, and probably more, he was a victim of academic anti-Semitism.

So, from the mid-nineteen-thirties to the end of World War II, Friedman held a variety of Government jobs, and for a time it appeared he would end up a government statistician. Thanks to Arthur Burns, he was given a staff appointment at the National Bureau of Economic Research, where he worked full-time at scholarship from 1936 to 1940.

But apart from one year on a campus, during which he was the subject of a bitter intrafaculty fight, it was not until 1945 that he got his first teaching post, at the University of Minnesota; and only the following year that he was invited to return, with faculty status, to the University of Chicago. Apart from various visiting professorships, it is there that he has remained since.

Because he has championed economic freedom in an age when

the left has put its faith in Government intercession—whether of the Marxian or the Keynesian variety—Milton Friedman has inevitably been considered a "right-wing" economist, an impression seemingly confirmed by his association with Goldwater in 1964.

But if the term "right-wing" implies an inordinate sympathy for the vested interests of society, along with a high degree of indulgence for existing social institutions, then nothing could be further from the truth. Friedman is no Chamber of Commerce economist, and surely no Bircher. Whatever the classical foundations of his thinking, he professes ideas that are warmly social and espouses programs that are, within the framework of our time, genuinely radical. Friedman may not be a pure egalitarian, but he has no tolerance for a system of government that proclaims programs to help the poor but winds up with a structure that enriches the rich.

It's been said there is something anomalous in Friedman's denial of the responsibility of government for establishing social and economic justice—a responsibility rather commonly acknowledged by today's Jewish intellectuals. Friedman does not conceal the influence of Jewish social thought, as well as his own impoverished upbringing, on his intellectual development.

He rejects the contention that he lacks the concern common to so many Jews for humanitarian ends. But he says that Jewish intellectuals often forget that a Jewish community survived for 2,000 years in the Western world because it was able to carve out for itself a niche in the free market. So he believes that the underprivileged and the poor in our own day have far better opportunities to improve their status in a fluid, competitive system than under a paternalistic bureaucracy that preserves the status quo in the name of justice.

At the heart of the Friedman principles, then, is a deep cynicism about the processes of government, founded largely on the judgment that men are essentially incompetent or venal, if not both. In a way, the feeling goes back to Montesquieu and Jefferson during the Enlightenment, and to Lord Acton in the last century.

But if Montesquieu, Jefferson and Acton feared political tyranny, Friedman's preoccupation is chiefly with economic tyranny. He simply does not believe that a governmental system can be devised which will not be taken over by vested economic interests and exploited for the preservation and enhancement of their own wealth. He concludes, then, that individual opportunity is best served when the power of government is least.

Despite the favor he has found among many conservatives and right-wingers, Friedman has sometimes contemplated characterizing himself as a "philosophical anarchist." The term, however, is probably too strong. It is enough to say that he would organize his society on the basis of individual economic freedom, curbed by government only to the degree necessary to keep markets free, competition open and innocent bystanders unharmed.

This essentially anti-Government approach appealed strongly to Goldwater in 1964 and in the course of several meetings together he borrowed heavily from Friedman without ever accepting the Friedmanite cosmology *in toto.* Four years later Richard Nixon, though more conventional in his economic thinking, also turned occasionally to Friedman for ideas. If the press has tended to exaggerate Friedman's personal influence on both men, neither of whom he saw very often, Friedman himself makes no apologies for voting Republican and giving advice to one or the other. However different his social objectives may be from theirs, he reasons that they are more likely than liberal Democrats to build a system that approximates his ideals.

Most of Friedman's formulations on the political economy were laid out earlier in this decade in a book called "Capitalism and Freedom" (known by the wags as "Capitalism and Friedman"). Many members of the economics community regard it as a shameless political tract, unworthy of a scholar. But Friedman, while acknowledging it as a popular and not an academic work, is extremely proud of it. He has named his summer home "Capitaf" in its honor. He is pleased that it is collateral reading in economics at many colleges and that, in paperback, it sells tens of thousands of copies every year.

Many of the ideas Friedman conveys in platform talks and in the column he now writes every third week for Newsweek first appeared in "Capitalism and Freedom." Taken as a whole, it unfurls the Friedmanite cosmology. Examined in parts, it provides interesting and useful hypotheses for solving some of the country's most puzzling politico-economic problems.

Friedman's prescription for maintaining the economy vigorously competitive, thereby striking at privilege and serving the consumer, is an odd mélange of ideas previously heard from both left and right. He would abolish protective tariffs (left), oil subsidies and quotas (left), and farm-price supports (right). He would abolish corporate income taxes (right), but he would require corporations to attribute all their earnings to stockholders, who would be taxed on them at the regular rather than the capital-gains rate (left), and he would discourage amassing of great reserves as a temptation to gobbling up other companies.

He would deprive the regulatory agencies of their rate-setting powers (right), without impairing safety regulations (left), in order to encourage more price competition within such industries as securities, airlines and railroads, and he would open radio and television licenses to public bidding (left). He would repeal such codes as would require auto manufacturers to install seat belts, on the grounds that individual purchasers can make that decision (right), but he would retain such requirements as the installation of antipollution devices, on the grounds that these devices protect the rights of third parties (left).

Friedman acknowledges that in the case of natural monopolies, such as the telephone system, there is no ideal means of maintaining competition. But so great is his distrust of bureaucrats that he concludes that, in preference to a public corporation or a regulated industry, it is better to take a chance with private monopoly.

His formula for dealing with poverty is, perhaps, even more daring—though it is the one that the Government, under President Nixon, has come closest to adopting. Friedman, once asked what he thought was the best way to help the poor, replied, "Give them money." To implement this simple idea, he devised the now celebrated plan for a negative income tax, which would put money into the hands of the poor without their having to pass through a labyrinthine welfare apparatus.

But as Friedman sees it, the negative income tax would change little, unless accompanied by other basic reforms. What he proposes is to do away with the bureaucracy not only of welfare but of the war on poverty, urban renewal, Medicare, minimum wage and even Social Security itself. The Social Security system, cornerstone of the New Deal's program for social justice, particularly irritates him. Financed by a "regressive" system of taxation, it takes from the poor at a much more onerous rate than from the rich, yet rewards the rich more generously than the poor.

Similarly, Friedman says that Federal housing programs—which bulldoze away the homes of the poor while subsidizing mortgages on the homes of the rich—are basically discriminatory and unjust. As for the minimum wage, Friedman figures that it rigs the market place in favor of the upper echelons of the labor force, and drives the old and the young, whose market value is below the legal minimum, completely out of work.

Friedman is frank to admit that he does not, in principle, approve of a system that takes money from some citizens to give it to others, whether the beneficiaries are rich or poor. He feels it is an impingment on freedom and, if he had his way, the poor would be supported by private volunteer charity.

But he acknowledges that reliance on charity would be impractical, if not inhumane, and, as he sees it, the negative income tax is the best alternative. As long as it provides the poor with a livable income, while presenting them with built-in incentives to work, their buying power would assure them an adequate diet, decent medical care and suitable housing. Furthermore, he says, freed of oppressive bureaucracies, they could make their own spending decisions and, having an impact on the law of supply and demand, influence the market place to meet their needs.

Education, too, Friedman would open to the competition of the market. Like most Americans, he observes that the quality of the public schools has declined disastrously in our time, even though billions in new funds have been spent upon them.

The chief victim of this inferiority in educational opportunity, he points out, is not the rich but the poor. "Let a poor family in a slum have a gifted child," he says, "and let it set a high value on his schooling. . . . The 'good' public schools are in the high-income neighborhoods. The family might be willing to spend something in addition to what it pays in taxes to get better schooling for its child. But it can hardly afford simultaneously to move to the expensive neighborhood. . . . Our present school system, far from equalizing opportunity, very likely does just the opposite."

What Friedman wants to do is to break the virtual monopoly of the educational bureaucracy over mass schooling in the United States. To achieve this end, Friedman would grant for each school-age child a "voucher" good for a certain sum of money, preferably equal to the average per capita cost of public education. A family would then be empowered to present this voucher either at the nearest public school or at the private school of its choice, where it would serve as full or partial tuition payment. Such a system, he says, would at once encourage competent educators to build a network of private schools, which would then compete for students against the public schools—giving both a positive incentive to maintain a high level of quality.

The Government's role in this plan would be to enforce certain minimum standards, perhaps including a prohibition of racial discrimination. Otherwise, it would leave the private schools free to cater (be "responsive") to the needs and peculiarities of their student bodies.

It goes without saying that the Keynes-oriented economists of our day—and that probably includes a substantial majority—do not share Milton Friedman's faith in the competitive market, or his distrust of the processes of government. Many see even his advocacy of a fixed rule for governing the money supply, leaving to fallible men a bare minimum of discretion, as proceeding directly from ideology rather than from scholarly analysis.

"Sure, Milton has forced us to tighten up and see things in a more balanced way," said Arthur Okun, a Keynesian and former chairman of the President's Council of Economic Advisers. "But he doesn't see things in a balanced way himself. You can't buy and sell everything on the market, like honesty and racial equality. Under Milton's system, why not wives? Why not votes? Milton talks as if it's a perfect—or perfectible—marketplace, where everyone has perfect information and perfect understanding when he makes his marketplace decisions. But I think Milton's world is only a caricature."

Paul Samuelson of M.I.T. says that Friedman mixes up sequence with causation and that in his desire to be a "big swinger" on the economic stage he engages in "intellectual tightrope walking." Nonetheless, there is more than enough hard logic in Friedman's arguments to keep the Keynesians from dismissing them as hokum. And there is even some factual evidence—as in the recent successful readjustment of European exchange rates on the open market—that at least a few of his positions on economic freedom are correct.

As for Friedman's money doctrine, what the generation of economists nurtured on the teachings of Lord Keynes seemed to have forgotten is that Keynes himself had recognized a major function in the money supply. This was obscured by the lessons Keynes taught about the role of government fiscal policy in maintaining economic stability.

Friedman never claimed that he invented the money doctrine, but he did reintroduce it to the general body of economic thought, in a fashion so scholarly and persuasive that it could scarcely be ignored. Samuelson has injected more and more of Friedmanesque monetary theory into successive editions of his basic economics textbook—in use in most colleges—while denying vigorously that Friedman has had anything to do with it. Samuelson, often looked upon as Friedman's principal rival for America's first Nobel prize for economics, now readily admits that "money matters," but in common with other Keynesians he dismisses as nonsense the Friedman doctrine that "*only* money matters."

Now two of the seven members of the Fed's board of governors have aligned themselves publicly with the principles, if not with the details, of Friedman's teachings, and there is indication that perhaps one or two more have become private converts. In Congress, the prestigious Joint Economic Committee has recommended that the Fed shift to essentially Friedmanite policies, and within the President's Council of Economic Advisers, Chairman Paul McCracken has confessed to being "Friedmanesque," if not a full-fledged Friedmanite. It is now being said that opinion at the

Fed is so closely divided that future policies will be determined by the incoming chairman, Arthur Burns—who was Milton Friedman's first teacher of economics at Rutgers and is now one of his most intimate friends.

Already, the Fed has conceded the existence of Friedman, if only by beginning to publish periodic figures on the nation's money supply. One of the Federal Reserve System's 12 semi-autonomous regional banks, the St. Louis branch, has been virtually captured by Friedmanism, and researchers there have done much to substantiate the essence of Friedmanite doctrine. (The research director in St. Louis is none other than Friedman's other Rutgers mentor, Homer Jones.)

But William McChesney Martin, Jr., the Fed's chairman since 1951, is an ex-stockbroker, not a professional economist, and, according to most careful observers of the Fed, he barely perceived what Friedman was trying to convey. Besides, the members of the Fed, taken as a whole could scarcely help but react to a message that was so clearly directed against them. In his "Monetary History," published in 1963, Friedman designates the Federal Reserve System as the villain bungling the nation into economic disruptions. If Friedmanism has quietly infiltrated the Fed, Friedman himself has found no reason to change that judgment on the basis of Federal Reserve policy since.

In bringing this judgment up to date, Friedman cites the Fed's much-disputed decision to stuff a large quantity of money into the economy just after Congress, as an anti-inflationary fiscal move, passed the surtax in 1968. What followed was a vast new surge of inflation, which even many non-Friedmanites blame on the Fed.

Then, in the middle of last year, the Fed decided to reduce the rate of increase in the money supply to zero. Again and again, Friedman has argued that this policy is so drastic that it will lead directly to an economic recession. The full impact of this policy, he said, would take about six months to be felt—which makes him believe that a recession is now imminent. Friedman acknowledges a rather remote chance that he is mistaken, since economics is a science based on probability rather than mathematical certainty. But he is prepared, as are his antagonists, to consider the recession which he predicts as a fundamental test of Friedmanite doctrines.

So persuaded is Friedman of the institutional incompetence of the Fed that if he *really* had his way, he says, he would abolish it altogether. In its place, he would have Congress legislate a fixed annual rate of increase in the money supply, somewhere around 4 per cent. At the moment, he says, economists still do not know enough about the processes of the economic system to justify constant intercession, and a fixed rule could hardly be worse, and would probably be better, than the Fed's tinkering.

Arthur Burns, in testifying before the Senate Banking Committee prior to his confirmation last December, gave the first public clue on the position he takes on Friedmanism. To no one's surprise, Burns revealed himself to be far more conventional in his views than Friedman himself. He regards a reduction in Federal spending and a balanced budget as fundamental to halting inflation. He considers it important to have the Government's anti-inflationary posture appear "credible" to the business community. He does not dismiss interest rates as a significant factor in economic stability.

But Burns conceded that he saw more than a little truth in Friedman's recession forecast, and he said his "impulse" was to follow Friedman—though not with the rigid Friedmanite formula—in maintaining a relatively constant but gradually increasing supply of money in circulation. Thus it became quite clear that, after William McChesney Martin goes at the end of this week, Milton Friedman will have won a victory (though hardly an unconditional surrender), and the Fed will never again be quite so casual about whether or not "money matters."

What makes Friedman such a formidable antagonist of the Keynesians, apart from the strength of his ideas, is his skill as a debater and polemicist. Samuelson says that Friedman's style surpasses his integrity and that Friedman simply ignores arguments and evidence that are not useful to him. He maintains that Friedman's personal powers of persuasion are so great that, if he died tomorrow, most of his ideas would vanish with him. Whether or not this is wishful thinking, it is true that Friedman can be devastating on the speaker's platform. A year ago, in a celebrated debate on "Monetary vs. Fiscal Policy," Walter Heller, President Kennedy's chairman of the Council of Economic Advisers, was torn to shreds by Friedman's arguments.

Yet Friedman, if he was once considered a pushy Jewish kid from New Jersey, is now acknowledged to be unfailingly thoughtful and courteous. Desisting from the technique of withering insult, he couches his arguments, both on the platform and on paper, in the most sweetly reasonable terms, though without ever sacrificing a cutting edge. If he resorts to one tricky semantic ploy, it is in charging his opponents with failing to "prove" some contention. But since it is virtually impossible to prove anything in economics, his opponents often turn it around and use the same ploy on him.

With all of this heated back-and-forth, much of it spilling outside the boundaries of the economics community, Friedman has become something of a public figure. Though he has many distinguished followers in the Chicago School, it is he who is constantly in demand at other universities, both to lecture and to make extended visits. As a general rule, he accepts as many of these invitations as possible, for he considers them part of his responsibility. He is also called upon at far higher fees to speak before business groups, but he turns most of these down on the ground that they are a form of self-indulgence, without discernible results.

Friedman rarely refuses an invitation to testify before Congressional committees, however, and he gave a prodigious number of hours to the President's Commission on an all All-Volunteer Armed Force, since he feels very deeply that young men should not be compelled to serve as draftees and that the military services should improve salaries and other benefits to the point where they become competitive in the job market.

He has also been telephoned by President Nixon, who has solicited his advice on the prospect of a recession. All of this attention unquestionably flatters him. He enjoys the feeling of being an influential person. But he recognizes that, for reasons of temperament and conviction, he will probably never hold a Federal policy-making position. There is no reason to doubt, however, that he enjoys being an outsider, challenging, provoking and irritating the conventional-minded and forcing them to ponder the possibility that their most strongly held beliefs might require a bit of change.

But then, why should Friedman contemplate having it otherwise? At the University of Chicago, he has influenced a generation of the country's finest young economists, and students continue to vie to become his disciples. His colleagues admire him and freely admit his preeminence among them. They are the focus of his social life and his partners in Socratic discourse, his favorite pastime. He has a charming wife, Rose, herself a University of Chicago economist by training, who cooks his dinners and edits his writing. His 24-year-old son David, a University of Chicago graduate student, idolizes him and faithfully plays back his ideas, albeit in a much fiercer version. He has a light teaching schedule, which enables him to hop to Japan or London or Miami for professional meetings and, most important, to spend almost half the year in the spot he loves the most on earth, his summer home in Vermont.

Just after the war, Friedman started spending his summers in Vermont, near the cottage of his good friend, Burns. Ultimately, he and Rose bought several hundred acres on top of a mountain, a mile or so from the Connecticut River on one side and the Burns house on the other. A few years ago, they bulldozed a road to a point just beneath the summit and there built a comfortable, modern house, hexagonal in shape and with huge panes of glass that overlook the Connecticut River valley and some of New England's grandest mountains.

Here Milton Friedman and Rose normally remain from midsummer to Christmas, occasionally leaving for a trip of a few days, now and then receiving visitors, but most often isolated from the world. It is here, at a small desk between a huge stone fireplace and the panorama outside, that Friedman, in an old wool shirt and baggy pants, sits down to work. Depending on his mood, he spins new theories or prepares new polemics.

Only at the first snowfall does the routine change. Then he throws a pair of skis into a four-wheel-drive Land Rover and makes his way to a nearby chairlift. Friedman isn't as adroit a skier as he is an economist, but he plays both games the same way. He takes on the toughest mountain, then audaciously, irrepressibly, relentlessly, scrappily, fights his way through the trees and across the ice from the top to the bottom. More often than not, he arrives a bit bruised but still on his feet. Yet, with barely a moment to catch his breath, he's ready to take on the next adversary, mountain as well as man, that dares challenge him.

Not bad for a guy who's 5 feet 3.

The World Through Galbraith's Eyes

a conversation with Anthony Lewis

John Kenneth Galbraith, Paul M. Warburg Professor of Economics at Harvard, is one of America's most influential economic and political thinkers. Among his works are "American Capitalism: The Concept of Countervailing Power," "Economic Development," "The Affluent Society," and "The New Industrial State." He has been an editor of Fortune magazine, Ambassador to India (1961–63), a close adviser to President Kennedy and a critic of the Johnson Administration. In 1966 he delivered the Reith Lectures—an annual series of addresses by prominent academicians—over the British Broadcasting Corporation in England, where he held this tape-recorded conversation with Anthony Lewis, New York Times bureau chief in London.

Britain's Economy: "Each Crisis Comes as a Surprise"

LEWIS: *You write in "The Affluent Society" about the necessity for more spending in the public sector. It seems that in Britain there's a tremendous will to spend more in the public sector, but isn't the difficulty that the pie isn't large enough and that they don't seem to be able to get it large enough?*

GALBRAITH: Of course it isn't really a small pie. The pie has grown steadily and enormously in the last 20 years and even more so in the last hundred years; the wealth of Britain today is immeasurably greater in the aggregate and per capita than it was at the very peak of Victorian power.

One has only to reflect on how intolerable life would be in these small islands if there was not very substantial spending in the public sector. If the cities here were as casually managed as those in the United States—if London traffic were as casually managed as it doubtless is, say, in Indianapolis—they would be intolerable. With a dense population heavy public-sector spending becomes a matter of greater urgency even than with us.

But, of course, Britain does have problems. It seems to me that the problem of economics in Britain is very much like that of sex in the United States: Both countries have an enormous difficulty in keeping it in perspective.

LEWIS: *Just what is wrong with Britain's economy?*

GALBRAITH: First of all, it is very delicately balanced. The British have to import a great deal, which means that they have to export a great deal. It's an open, as distinct from a closed, economy. They have to maintain a very close relationship between their prices and those of other countries. They have to be competitive.

Also England is probably the most egalitarian of the non-Communist countries. This means that a very large part of the population has lower-middle-class consuming tendencies—that is, a strong propensity to spend and not to save. Governments naturally yield to the demands of these people by offering more consumption, with the result that about every two years consumption in Britain gains too much on production. There isn't enough left for export, because the domestic market is too favorable.

So then there's a balance of payments crisis. An atmosphere of crisis develops. Indeed it must develop before the Government is able to take the relatively modest action—limiting wage and price increases, increasing down payments, increasing taxation slightly—that slows the increase in consumption and presently the balance of payments becomes all right again and the process starts over.

This is the reason for my earlier suggestion that the British who gave economics to the world have never been able to get it fully in perspective. Each of these crises has come to the people of Britain as though it were a complete novelty, when in fact every one since World War II has had the same fundamental character. I would fault the present tendency of Labor party politics—as of Democratic politics in the U. S.—for being too tactical, insufficiently concerned with long-run strategy.

LEWIS: *We often hear about the British workman being stodgy and lazy, seeking protection too much in restrictive practices, and the British themselves are in an extremely self-critical mood. Do you think there is something to that?*

GALBRAITH: Absolutely not. Anybody who is intimately associated with workers always is impressed by their dislike for sustained manual labor. As I recall the days when I did manual farm labor myself, my principal memory is of wanting to do less of it.

I have no doubt whatever that part of the great impetus to mechanization and automation in the United States is the low productivity of the American worker in purely manual terms. Every employer yearns for machines instead. Of course, America also has a greater propensity to save and a larger capital supply, so it overcomes the constitutional laziness of its workers by investing in machinery, whereas the British have to struggle along with more men. Neither the French workers nor the Italian workers are models of productivity and I think that within a few years the Japanese will learn the malingering tendencies of the rest of the world. I think that the desire to escape sustained manual effort can be put down as one of the fundamental human qualities.

LEWIS: *Is there any hope of some general solution to overcome what you say is a very logical tendency not to like production-line work?*

GALBRAITH: I expect the answer lies in the automatic and mechanized enterprise where the worker performs at a console board and/or keeps watch over some dials—this is basically much more pleasant and attractive.

Modern Economy: "Planning Takes the Place of the Market "

LEWIS: *Apart from Britain's economic problems, how do you regard the modern technological economy in general?*

GALBRAITH: I have just finished a book largely on this subject. So I can be quite eloquent. The central idea in economics has always been that the individual goes into the market and, by purchasing or not purchasing, instructs the productive apparatus. And the productive apparatus, the business enterprises, come into existence in response to this process.

This has been one of the nearly unquestioned assumptions of economics. But when I was working several years ago on "The Affluent Society" I came to the conclusion that this was an assumption which, as the economy matured, could no longer be justified. In particular, there is an increasing tendency for the business firm to create the demand that it satisfies, through product variation, advertising, sales strategy. Certainly the individual still functions in the market, still instructs the productive apparatus. But, increasingly, large organizations go into the market, fix prices, and go on beyond those fixed prices to get the kind of consumer behavior they want. Our view of what a motor car should be like is not something that is inherent—it is given to us by the automobile industry.

The market is also steadily and persistently and progressively undermined by technology. While you can buy simple things in the market, you cannot buy more complex ones—you must plan. You can buy unskilled labor in the market, but it is not easy to buy highly specialized electronic engineers; you could buy pack horses in the market, but not space vehicles. With advancing technology the market becomes ever less efficient as an instrument, and its place is taken by one or another form of planning.

Now the planning of the private firm and the planning of the state tend to supplement each other. The private firm can fix minimum prices but it can't fix maximum prices, so increasingly the state comes in with wage and price guidelines. The private firm can do a lot to influence the behavior of the individual consumer, but it can't ensure that there's enough purchasing power for everything that's produced, and that's where the state comes in. The private firm is very good at handling the technology of simple products, but it can't underwrite the technology required for modern military purposes, and so the state underwrites that.

In short, in the modern planning structure public and private planning are rather rationally intermeshed.

It seems to me that one of the reasons the French and the Germans have moved ahead so rapidly in these last years is that they've been much more pragmatic about this intermeshing than the British. The French have quite clearly decided that where the Government needs to do things, it will do them. They have never been worried much by philosophical economics, have never been given to these long debates the British and we so much enjoy on the proper role of the public and private sectors.

Increasingly, these distinctions are irrelevant—as a matter of fact, meaningless. Take an aircraft firm in the United States that does 95 per cent of its business with the Government, submits to Government supervision of its expenses, gets all its specifications from the Government and works intimately with the Air Force on specifications. To decide that this firm is in the public sector is obviously to make a highly artificial distinction.

LEWIS: *If we are to plan now for this future society you are envisaging—more and more technological, more and more automated, more and more planned through both the public and the private sectors—what do you think would be the single most fundamental thing to concentrate on?*

GALBRAITH: I would say education. Trained manpower is now the decisive factor of production. One very important thing to bear in mind is that the education explosion of recent years is not some new enlightenment. It's a response to the needs of modern industrial society. To a much greater extent than we realize, education is a reflection of industrial needs.

In the last century and the early part of this century, when the new industry, the new capitalism, required hundreds of thousands of unlettered proletarians, that is what the educational system provided. Now that it requires specialists—octane engineers and personnel managers and procurement managers and public relations experts—this increasingly is what the educational system is providing.

We should worry about the educational system being shaped in this fashion. Unless we're terribly careful, humane and liberal arts are going to be submerged and we will be too preoccupied with economic goals. There is a serious problem here. It's very easy now to get money for scientific purposes, but it is very much more difficult to get funds for the larger enjoyments of life. There will be no trouble getting public money for the supersonic transport. We will try to save it on support for arts or the poverty program.

Poverty: "We'd Better Be a Little Less Calvinist"

LEWIS: *It seems to me that with all our talk about this great technological future we may tend to overlook the continuing reservoir of poor people in the United States, about which we don't seem very effective in doing anything. We've had a poverty program now for several years, but it does not seem to be living up to the dreams people had about it. What do you think about the direction of that program, and of its possibilities?*

GALBRAITH: I had something to do with drawing up the program and I've been reasonably close to it since, and I've always thought it was much better than its popular billing. My strong impression is that Sargent Shriver has done an imaginative job under very trying circumstances.

It's also my impression that the best of the programs are of enormous value. The idea behind the Job Corps—giving these youngsters a second chance after they missed out the first time and have come to realize the cost to themselves—is superb. In one form or another, it's bound to continue in the educational system. So is Head Start. And the Youth Employment program serves a very important role.

Perhaps it would have been wiser to have shucked off some of the things which were less useful. A certain amount of money, for example, was wasted on rehabilitating small farmers—this is a sink hole. Nothing much is ever accomplished there, nothing visible. And some of the community-action programs got into the hands of incompetent or corrupt local politicians or were ill-conceived. But over-all I think the effort showed that we could come to grips with poverty.

It seems to me that two fundamental things went wrong with the poverty program. First, we weren't braced as we should have been for the fact that *whenever* you spend money on behalf of the poor you get into trouble. The Government can go into West Virginia and sink $50- or $70-million into an electronic monitoring apparatus which doesn't work, and this is dismissed as a minor error. But spend $5,000 on some dead-end youngsters and you're really in trouble. Anything done on behalf of the poor arouses the passion of one dismal kind of political critic.

Second, of course, the program fell afoul of the spending pressures of the Vietnam war. This is particularly tragic. The argument here is that although personal incomes after taxes are at an all-time high, and although they're partly there because of Vietnam war spending, we must cut down on help to the poor because of Vietnam. And to some degree this is what has happened.

Sometime or other we're going to deal with this problem of poverty. The anachronism of a country as rich as the United States with a hard core of people as poor as some Americans simply can't continue. And I'm increasingly inclined to think that we'd better become a bit less Calvinist than we have been in the past. The past theory has been that the only way to cure poverty is to make everybody a productive citizen, a participant in the economy. But the people who are poor in the United States are those who are *excluded* from participating in the economy—by personal disqualification or moral disqualification or educational disqualification or physical disqualification. I'm by no means certain we can or should make everybody participants. I think that's going to take too long, and that in the interim maybe what a rich country should do is get everybody a basic income.

LEWIS: *Do you mean the negative income tax?*

GALBRAITH: Yes. The negative income tax is really a development of this idea which gives everybody a basic income but doesn't interfere with incentives—if a worker earns more he will always have some increase in total income.

LEWIS: *But is that going to be enough? Isn't there something else besides money that is lacking? Don't we need something much more dynamic than just giving to those in this vicious circle?*

GALBRAITH: I'm not suggesting that money is a total cure—but let us not underemphasize its importance. For example, about 30 per cent of the children who are in poor families—with incomes under $3,000—have no visible male parent. The family is headed by a woman. We would greatly help these families by supplying them with a standard basic income as a routine matter.

Poverty has, of course, other roots. There is a deeper community problem in Harlem, for example, associated with a sense of racial injustice, of inequality, unequal application of the law and ineffectively enforced laws, and no one should doubt it is of great urgency and great importance.

LEWIS: *Do you feel there is a lack of political leadership in this area? Do you think that the President in particular has become too distracted by Vietnam, so that the moral impulse one felt he was giving on civil rights and poverty has been allowed to wane?*

GALBRAITH: I have no doubt that this has been one of the great tragedies of the Vietnam conflict. There are a good many reasons for regretting our involvement in Vietnam apart from the neglect of the domestic problems. But that is one of the great costs—unquestionably.

There is also—and this is curious, you know—a certain state of mind which worries enormously about the problems of liberty and democracy in Saigon but which reacts with total equanimity to similar problems in Harlem or in Birmingham. I am struck by how few of the passionate defenders of Marshal Ky's somewhat guided democracy have ever opened their mouths on civil rights or in support of the poverty program.

Kennedy: "He Broke with the Clichés of Politics"

LEWIS: *Would you be willing to say a word in general about President Johnson compared with President Kennedy, especially in their reaction to Vietnam? Do you think Kennedy would have been able to stick more resolutely to these domestic questions and provide a better kind of leadership?*

GALBRAITH: Well, I think I knew the drift of President Kennedy's thinking on these general matters. I went to Saigon for him in 1961. And I could readily concoct an argument—as many have—that because he was unwilling to become involved in Laos when many people said that the whole state of the free world turned on moving troops into Vientiane, he wouldn't have gone into Vietnam. He was certainly very much worried about our commitment in Vietnam, and there was nothing willing, nothing avid, about this involvement—it was most unwelcome to him. But I wouldn't really like to make a guess. Nor do I like comparing the two Presidents.

I would say one thing: I don't think anybody could ever doubt that the legislative program President Johnson shoved through in the two years following the death of President Kennedy was an enormous achievement. No one would have respected that achievement more than President Kennedy.

The men I regret, in my less compassionate moments, are those who advised both Presidents that a few soldiers and a few planes would quickly straighten the Vietnamese out. I went to Saigon in 1961 because Kennedy had a recommendation that a division of troops should be sent in—disguised, as I recall, as flood-control workers. I think he hoped that I would advise against it and I certainly obliged.

Arthur Schlesinger used to say that foreign policy is the only field of endeavor where a man gets promoted for being wrong. Eventually the men who agreed that a little intervention would provide quick therapy got their way. They have moved ahead rapidly. So have their military needs. Now they are urging the country to avoid unnecessary criticism of the war effort. Well, one must be large-minded—and never petulant.

LEWIS: *Can you isolate the qualities President Kennedy had that made the world react so strongly to him—and that still produce a tremendous sense of respect and admiration for him now, three years later?*

GALBRAITH: I'm sure that youth had something to do with it —after all, most people in the world are young. My sense of that in 1960 was striking. I'd been accustomed to going to Washington and finding myself among my own generation or men who were older. Within three or four weeks I suddenly found myself surrounded by people who were 10 to 20 years younger and who were saying: Galbraith, he's getting rather fragile, handle him rather carefully. This wasn't entirely pleasant to the people of my generation, but I'm sure it was enormously welcome to people all around the world of the Kennedy generation.

Also it was quite clear that Kennedy had taken the full measure of the dangers, the terrors, of the nuclear age, and was determined to do something about it. Nothing was more central to his thought. I heard him say not once, but several times, that the only problem that he thought about every day, that was never off his mind, was the problem of nuclear catastrophe.

The sense that he was bringing the power of the United States to bear fully on that question was also very important in winning the response he did. Moreover, in some perceptible fashion this terror did lessen during his years. In 1960, we need to remind ourselves, the problem of fallout, the problem of strontium in the milk, got daily headlines in the newspapers. Now it is something that has receded from people's thoughts.

Finally, Kennedy broke with the clichés of politics, which people throughout the country were much more tired of than we imagined. Kennedy deeply disliked the kind of banal oratory that you hear hours on end at a national convention; he disliked the arm-waving, roistering politician trying to ingratiate himself with an imagined proletariat; and he disliked the person who debases himself in an effort to prove that he is a popular figure (although it must be conceded that there are a certain number of Democrats who find this rather easy because the debasing doesn't have to go very far). His break with an outworn style of politics was an enormous source of support and affection and reward.

It is striking how little the lesson has been learned. Just wait for the next Democratic National Convention.

Europe: "The Era of U.S. Dominance Has Ended"

LEWIS: *Do you agree with Walter Lippmann that there is a tendency for the countries of the West now to become more inward-looking and think less about cooperation with each other in great international ventures? Or is this merely a reflection of the decline of American influence in Europe?*

GALBRAITH: There's always been some impression in the State Department that we had influence in Europe because we were loved or because of our superior political system or because of our superior national character. In fact, we had influence in Europe when our help was needed and when Europe was subject to the cohesive influence of fear of the Soviets. And as Europe has ceased to need our help and as the fear of the Soviets has receded, our influence has diminished. I would attribute more of the tendencies that Lippmann mentions to this than to any recurrence of xenophobia. I don't think there's a great deal of that.

LEWIS: *But are these factors that you mention going to kill the dream of a larger Europe? Will they impede all the efforts toward organization of the West that we've made since the war?*

GALBRAITH: By no means. The idea of Europe is here to stay. It is beyond doubt that the old national units of Europe are technologically and economically obsolete, so that a much greater amount of international cooperation is inevitable. The new feature, and the feature we must recognize, is that it's not going to come about under American leadership any more.

We all got a rather biased view of the possibilities of American foreign policy from the immediate post-World War II experience when Europe badly needed American economic help and feared the forward policy of Russia. These two factors combined to give an almost unique impetus to American foreign policy, and it was pushed by very able people—Dean Acheson, Averell Harriman, Paul Hoffman, John J. McCloy—and we have been living on that capital ever since. But that era in American foreign policy is not only coming to an end, it *has come* to an end, and the great mistake of American foreign policy in these last 10 years has been the effort to keep it alive. Our reverses on the Multilateral Force, on the Kennedy grand design, on the effort to get Britain into the Common Market—all followed from this effort to recapture the glory of this earlier period.

As to the Common Market, it does not make a great deal of difference whether we urge Britain to go in or not. Britain will decide this issue on her side and France and the Continental countries on their side, and it's the better part of wisdom for us to realize that we will have very little to do with it.

Instead of lecturing Europe we must confine policy to matters on which we are ourselves involved. Thus if Britain does not make it into the Common Market, I am attracted by the idea of having another look at an association between ourselves and the Canadians and the British, if it were sensibly approached. If we're determined and there is enough merit in it to be part of our foreign policy, it is in this direction that we should be looking.

Foreign Policy: "We Suffer from a Schizophrenia"

LEWIS: *What about in the direction of East-West relations?*

GALBRAITH: There is a great deal of room here for a creative American policy, but one of the first things we have to do is escape from a kind of schizophrenia which presently characterizes our policies.

President Johnson, in my view, has taken much greater steps than he's been credited with in lowering the tension between ourselves and the Soviet Union and Eastern Europe. He's dropped that prefabricated section that used to be put into every Presidential speech, about how we are engaged in a death struggle with the Communist menace but if we are vigilant and we never let down our guard we will, of course, win out over the forces of darkness in the end and without a reduction in our standard of living. He's also taken a variety of steps in addition to sending Gronouski to Poland to indicate our desire to bring Eastern Europe closer to the Western community.

But we've still got to reconcile this part of the policy with the talk about strengthening NATO and sharing nuclear capacity and the other clichés of the State Department and the Pentagon. This is our schizophrenia: We combine the mystique of the cold war with the new policy of bridge-building to Eastern Europe and with seeking Soviet help in Vietnam or encouraging Soviet efforts in settling the India-Pakistan conflict. Nobody seems yet to have faced up to the fact there is a very substantial degree of inconsistency between a policy that assumes conflict and a policy that assumes accommodation—and sometime or other we're going to have to sort that out.

LEWIS: *Might this depend not only on us but particularly on the Germans and their ability to come out of their current political turmoil to a more moderate direction on relations with the East?*

GALBRAITH: Yes, although I think that perhaps we have difficulty in keeping the German problem in perspective. I find it difficult to react to these so-called neo-Nazi gains in Bavaria, somewhere in the range of 5 to 8 per cent. My impression is that in any Western country including our own you can get between 5 to 10 per cent of the people at any given time to vote against law, decency and constitutional order and in favor of the most prevalent current form of insanity. The more remarkable feature about Germany is the number of people who in fact consistently vote for the Christian Democrats and the Socialists.

I would think the rather more important thing is to see whether we can't find a modus vivendi for living with the divided-Germany problem. In the next few decades Germany isn't going to be reunited, and I wonder why we have to deny the existence of East Germany quite as systematically as we do.

The East: "Convergence Will Mean Greater Freedom"

LEWIS: *What reading do you have of the European Communists' willingness to deal with us, their outward-lookingness, these days?*

GALBRAITH: One major lesson of the period since World War II is that we must not overestimate the cohesive power of Communism and we must not underestimate the cohesive power of Europe. My instinct is to think that the tendency of Eastern European countries is toward Europe and that there is a growing economic pragmatism on both sides in Europe.

The nature of technology—the nature of the large organization that sustains technology and the nature of planning that technology requires—has an imperative of its own, and this is causing a greater convergence in all industrial societies. In the Eastern European societies it's leading to a decentralization of power from the state to the firm; in the Western European industrial societies it's leading to a kind of *ad hoc* planning. In fewer years than we imagine this will produce a rather indistinguishable melange of planning and market influences.

The overwhelming fact is that if you have to make steel on a large scale you have to have a massive technical complex, and there will be a certain similarity in the organization, and in the related social organization, whether that steel complex is in Novosibirsk or in Nova Huta, Poland, or in Gary, Ind.

LEWIS: *Are you suggesting that as the two societies converge, the Communist society will necessarily introduce greater political and cultural freedom?*

GALBRAITH: I'm saying precisely that. The requirements of deep scientific perception and deep technical specialization cannot be reconciled with intellectual regimentation. They inevitably lead to intellectual curiosity and to a measure of intellectual liberalism. And on our side the requirements of large organization impose a measure of discipline, a measure of subordination of the individual to the organization, which is very much less than the individualism that has been popularly identified with the Western economy.

Part 5

NEW INTELLECTUAL TRENDS

Some of the deepest tensions in the modern world stem from the conflict between thought and action, between individual and society, between matter and spirit. Neither the conflict nor the tension is new, but in an age of industrialism they have become more stressful, driving man to greater and greater extremes. Ancient truths are discarded, and the uncertainty we must confront makes us cast about for roots we cannot discover. Man loses touch with his environment and becomes so routinized that the only mood he is able to express is complete dissociation.

The cure for this malady seems to be *action;* it is not surprising that so many are prepared to lose themselves in mass movements which promise to cure all social and psychological ills. But such a response only strengthens the collective of the modern age, absorbing individuals and imposing a common objective on them all, though they manifest no common interests. Existence then becomes standardized and anonymous, clashing violently with human nature.

How does one escape this impasse? One may attempt a Faustian role, combining thought and action in a single career, reaching out to the frontiers of politics, then turning back to raise ideas to heroic levels. This has been the career of André Malraux, but such an adventure does not seem available to ordinary men. As a substitute, one can opt for the blessings of technology, in the vain hope that inanimate objects can somehow be vitalized by electricity. That is the import of McLuhanism, but it sounds the death knell of human autonomy. Or one can reject totally and unequivocally all the works and deeds of man in the belief that, like Noah after the flood, a new race of men will be spawned. Unfortunately, men are men and nothing really new in humanity has yet been created.

The Three Lives of André Malraux

by Theodore H. White

UNLESS ONE EXAMINES the hole in the green shutters carefully,
the mark looks like a rust spot. Closer up, however, it is easy
to see—the torn edges of the hole, furling back like petals of
iron, mark the passage of a bullet fired too low to hit its mark,
but aimed from the street to pass directly over the writer's desk.

In the story of any other writer, such an attempt might have
marked the man's promotion to momentary celebrity. In the story
of André Malraux, already gory with bullets and blood, the shot
of the unknown assassin was no more than a punctuation mark.
It would have been noteworthy only if it had struck home, and
then only in retrospect. For, had it done so on that winter night
of 1947, it would have ended a career that has enthralled France
for a generation—at precisely the moment when that career split
in a baffling, schizoid divergence of purpose.

In a country that reserves for its great writers a special measure
of passionate interest and devotion, André Malraux is crowded by
only two contemporaries—the aging Nobel laureate, François
Mauriac, and the owl philosopher, Jean-Paul Sartre. But André

Malraux has been able to call from his countrymen something more—a quality of excited, almost animal, fascination which neither of his two great rivals can evoke to match. And it is this that infuses the French as they look with bafflement on their new Malraux.

The dark-eyed, glossy-haired young man, taut and resonant as a violin string, who, twenty years ago, remade the French literary scene by projecting the heroes of his writing into the violence of contemporary politics, torturing and brutalizing them in the convulsions of history—that Malraux has vanished. The new, middle-aged Malraux—his dark hair still thick but receding, his eyes sunken in great hollows of darkness—is someone else. He is, in fact, two men, both new.

One is a politician, involved and tangled in the brambles of French party strife. The other is a philosopher of art—serene, remote, aloof from all matters unmeasured by eternity. This divergence, moreover, has taken place in the past five years—since, roughly, that winter season when the bullet designed for the politician passed over the desk where the philosopher was preparing that treatise on art and humanism, "Les Voix de Silence," which has become, in the first year since its publication, one of the monuments of this literary century in France.

Malraux, the politician, is a Gaullist. As such, he sits on the twenty-four-man National Council of General Charles de Gaulle's R. P. F. (Rally of the French People), in its gray, soot-smeared headquarters on the Rue Solferino on Paris' Left Bank. Within this party, Malraux has two sources of strength. One is his influence over the personality of General de Gaulle, sole commander of the party, in whose entourage of ambitious captains Malraux, the unambitious, ranks first. His second is his influence over masses of Frenchmen by his skill with words. Whoever has seen Malraux on a platform, his hands suddenly transformed into claws that tear at the air as his voice winds up with a fantastic, hypnotic eloquence to sweep an audience of thousands into frenzy, knows that in naming this man as director of his national propaganda, General de Gaulle has chosen the most effective rabble-rouser in France.

Malraux, the philosopher of art, lives in a high-roofed, white-walled studio on a tree-lined street in suburban Boulogne. Between the nervous, twitching philosopher of enormous eloquence and stupendous learning of the studio and the self-intoxicated man of the platform there seems no kinship whatsoever—until, suddenly, the studio conversation wanders off into art. Then, as Malraux talks of what men can see with their eyes, make with their fingers, grasp with their imaginations, an ecstasy grips him. He is up, almost dancing from his chair, showing the line of a painting that hangs on his wall, his hand following the curve of a Gandhara head on his piano, his fingers flickering over the strange Hopi heads his friends have brought from America, as if a current jumped the gap between the inanimate object and his own quivering consciousness.

The legend of Malraux, as it is strained out of the shreds of Paris gossip, is of a life that squirms with restless activity. Trained as an archaeologist, a student of Sanskrit, he set out for Asia at the age of 21 to search for Cambodian antiquities. There the wild, revolutionary politics of Asia sucked him in, drawing him to participation in an Annamite revolutionary movement (for which he was arrested on trumped-up charges of theft of art objects by French authorities).

From Indo-China, after his release, the turmoil of Asia carried him to China, in its days of great revolution, where he sat in the inner sanctums of Chiang Kai-shek's Nationalist party, in the days when the party was Stalin's chief ally in the Orient. From China, after the collapse of that revolution, he made his way back to Europe as a member of an archaeological expedition through Afghanistan and Persia.

Success came to Malraux with the publication of his third book, at the age of 32—the savage, magnificent and hopeless story of the Chinese Revolution, "Man's Fate," In awe, the sedate and polished literary stylists of France saw his arrival in their midst, in the words of François Mauraic, "advancing like a man with a dagger in his hand" determined to kill—and recognized him as an authentic, towering man of genius.

Malraux's literary success coincided with the decade of fascism and for the next decade his life was submerged in that struggle. He received the German and Jewish refugees who fled from Hitler in the name of France; he joined the French committee for the defense of Thaelmann, the German Communist leader; he helped found the World League Against Anti-Semitism; he flew to Berlin to protest the trial of Dimitrov under Hitler's nose; he fought in Spain as commander of the Republican aviation in the first weeks of the war.

When France herself was caught in 1939, Malraux followed the colors—he was captured as a tank commander in the campaign of 1940, escaped, joined the Resistance, was captured again, escaped again and ended by commanding a brigade of French troops in the advance across the Rhine. Out of each of his adventures, from Indo-China to the German prison camp, Malraux refined a novel—novels drenched in blood, obsessed with the savagery of men, mesmerized by the spectacle of men in the presence of death, novels all of them imbued with the mystique of revolution.

When, thus, in the chaos of post-war France, André Malraux emerged first as a Minister (of Information) in General de Gaulle's government and later as chief ornament of the general's party (which most Frenchmen set at the extreme right of the political spectrum), the shock to France was immeasurable.

The shock of France's intellectuals at Malraux's association with the Gaullists still irritates Malraux. For Malraux holds he is not of that legion of innocents betrayed by communism, the roster of the Silones, Spenders and Koestlers. Malraux makes no attempt to deny that he worked with the Communists. "But no one was fooled," says Malraux, for he was neither a member of the party nor a fellow-traveler.

He has not, insists Malraux, changed since—it is the world, and most of all the Russians, who have changed. "It happened," said Malraux several years ago, "that André Gide and myself were asked to protest to Hitler the condemnation of Dimitrov who was innocent of the Reichstag fire. And now—when Dimitrov in power hangs Petkov who is innocent—who has changed? Myself or Gide? Or Dimitrov?"

It was the Russo-German pact that widened the cleavage between Malraux and the Communists (which had begun in the Spanish civil war) into an open breach. "For I could understand the pact," says Malraux. "It was perfectly comprehensible from a Russian point of view." There was a logic, a Russian logic, to the pact to turn Germany against the Western world—"but I could not agree that Stalin had the right to pay for this logic with the blood of millions of ordinary Frenchmen whom he had doomed." It was in defeat then, and in the Resistance, that in his own words "I married France."

Between marrying France and espousing Gaullism another episode intervened. As Minister of Information in the early post-war French Cabinets, Malraux saw, from the inside, the ramshackle machinery of French politics slowly mincing down the triumph of French Liberation to the shabby despair and frustration of present French life. Men talk of how stupid and inefficient government is in France "but to know how foul it really is, one must be in it," says Malraux, "one must be married to it, and be frustrated as a man is by a wife with whom he is hopelessly coupled."

France had to be changed, therefore. And, since the only party organized technically to change France was the Communists, who wished to destroy her, another party had to be formed. This was the R.P.F., General de Gaulle's party. The R.P.F. was not conceived by Malraux, but its appeal to the nation was swollen with Malraux's ideas.

The R.P.F, says Malraux, is not a party with a philosophy of history, like the Communists or the Fascists or the Hitlerites; it is a group of men seeking a pragmatic, workable way out of France's dead-end. There are only two planks to the R.P.F.'s program. The first is that France must become great again; this is a need foreigners have difficulty in understanding, for, says Malraux, it is impossible to explain the gigantic emotional effect of a simple fact: "We were a great power—and then we simply stopped being so." The second is that France cannot become great until its present constitutional anarchy is reformed to give it a strong working executive that can attack the social misery in which millions of underprivileged Frenchmen are permanently frozen.

The R.P.F. went up over France in 1947 like the swift burst of a skyrocket—and has ever since, slowly, steadily, been falling. Its very success was its own undoing. For not only were millions of patriotic Frenchmen of the old Resistance lured to the general's banners, but after them trooped millions of the most abominable Vichyites, who had betrayed France in the war, seeking in the general a new guardian against communism. So swift was the ascent of the party, so enthusiastically did former collaborators and old-fashioned reactionaries clamber aboard its bandwagon that all the forces of France's democratic core rallied against it.

"Gaullism might have succeeded," said a Paris wit, "without General de Gaulle." Almost every Deputy of the National Assembly agreed in 1947 (and still agrees) that France's parliamentary chaos must be replaced with the firm kind of executive leadership Americans have. But the general's party seemed to offer more than a presidential executive—its radically reactionary fringe made it sound like a would-be dictatorship.

If the years since then have proved this fear false, it has brought little yield of good fortune to the Gaullists. In 1947, when they polled 40 per cent of all French votes, the Gaullists might have seized power by force. But they would not—they waited. And waiting year by year, all the while meticulously abiding by the rules of the French democracy that they denounced, they have ebbed in strength.

The ebbing of Gaullist fortunes has come as a not unrelieved sorrow to Malraux, who helped give the movement birth. For what has been lost is the far-right wing of the party and what remains under the general's standard is basically the left, or social revolutionary wing. This heightening of his own influence within what may be a fading party might oppress another man with the irony of politics, or stimulate him to greater exertions. But with Malraux the development has had a contrary effect.

More convinced than ever that France must either accept the Gaullist solution or decay, Malraux himself is far less active than formerly in the technical machinery of his party's politics. The explanation is simple: in the past few years, Malraux, the philosopher, all the while acknowledging and believing in his bowels that France must be remade, believes that it is more important now, in this generation, to begin the elaboration of that new humanism, the new and universal culture of man which this age has been first enabled to approach. Moreover, he believes that this new culture must be founded not on words, which have been demonetized and failed but on the images of art, which are the only permanence.

Malraux, an adventurer of ideas as well as of experience, is peculiarly fortunate to live in France. For France is a nation whose marketplace of ideas is crossed and recrossed by wandering men seeking truths—not little facts, but the large, all-embracing Sole Truth.

In this marketplace, Malraux has in the last year offered, as a prophet, Art. The package of his wares is the single book, "Les Voix de Silence," which in the year since its publication has sold more copies than any other book ever published on the plastic arts in France.

Even on the lips of his political enemies, Malraux's book is treated not as a book, but as an event. A reworking and rewriting of the thoughts and essays of fifteen years' reflection, all written in typical close-textured Malrauvian prose, the book's greatness rests on its illustrations and their binding thought. The 500-odd illustrations are, very simply, perhaps the greatest collection of reproductions of man's art ever put together in the covers of one work. This greatness rests not on the individual glory of each artifact of genius, but on the breadth and spread of the world from which they they were assembled.

Drawing on his wanderings around the world, Malraux has summoned from memory and knowledge illustration after illustration to set side by side—an Asian bust of the fourth century set against a French Gothic bust of the thirteenth, an early American primiive of buffalo shooting set against an impressionist masterpiece of Rousseau—to show the underlying unity of genius, the quality of kinship of man that spurts only in the contact of genius with the world and results in beauty.

The success of the book is no surprise to Malraux. For he believes he is the first to note a development that has already altered all modern life, the first stirring of what he calls the age of "universal culture." This development rests on a device as simple and prosaic as was the invention of printing—the development of new techniques of reproduction.

In our times, the reproduction by modern photography of the world's plastic masterworks, by modern recording of the world's music, by the cinema of the world's drama, has made us the first heirs to all the world's visions of genius. We are no longer limited as Frenchmen to the cathedrals and the Louvre, as Italians to the statues of Michelangelo, as Chinese to rare glimpses of the Sung paintings. We are the first generation to inherit all.

This revolution, which has escaped the attention of journalists, has not escaped the attention of ordinary people themselves, for the phenomenon is world-wide. Malraux notes that in France, the cradle of the modern arts, the Louvre reports that admissions to its galleries last year multiplied by six times the record of the last pre-war year.

The world thus sits in audience on a prodigious contrast. On the one hand, the arts of the world, stirring the roots of civilization, are bringing men to the knowledge that wood-and-stone, line-and-color seen through Chinese, American, French or Persian eyes promote a kinship that languages cannot approximate. Yet, at the same time, the politics of the world force men farther and farther from this kinship.

There was a time, says Malraux—from Michelet to Jaurès—when Frenchmen believed that the more deliberately they abandoned love of country the closer they came to humanity. Yet, today, Russia weighs upon the world, sweeping away these dreams, making men know that in abandoning their French-ness, their British-ness, their American-ness they weaken, not strengthen, their common culture. For Malraux the task of this generation, and for himself most of all, is somehow to lay the foundation for tomorrow's universal culture, which has just become possible in the teeth of world politics which threaten to destroy it.

Between these two concepts—of the art that unites and inspires, and of politics that divide and sterilize—Malraux, like all other men, is trapped.

He apportions his time between the two judiciously, but art seems to be gaining ever more on politics. Though his high faith in the need for remodeling France under the Gaullist banner has not wavered, he now limits himself to attendance at weekly meetings of the R.P.F. executive council and to less frequent visits with the general—to whom his personal devotion is unshaken.

His role as R.P.F. Director of National Propaganda is difficult to define as he pays only perfunctory attention to daily routine but can sweep the movement with a new idea whenever he wants. By far the greater part of his time is now devoted to finishing his studies on art and completing a great trilogy novel to be entitled "La Lutte avec L'Ange" ("The Struggle with the Angel").

In his own estimate there is no doubt at all how Malraux sees himself. "Write it down," he says, "the art excites me five hundred times more than the politics."

[handwritten annotations:]
technological determination
3 inventions made the middle ages
① stirrup ② horse collar ③ ____

4 ages human history

Understanding McLuhan
(in Part)

hot & cold mediums

medium as the by Richard Kostelanetz

message

MARSHALL MCLUHAN, one of the most acclaimed, most controversial and certainly most talked-about of contemporary intellectuals, displays little of the stuff of which prophets are made. Tall,
thin, middle-aged and graying, he has a face of such meager
individual character that it is difficult to remember exactly what
he looks like; different photographs of him rarely seem to capture
the same man.

By trade, he is a professor of English at St. Michael's College,
the Roman Catholic unit of the University of Toronto. Except for
a seminar called "Communication," the courses he teaches are
the standard fare of Mod. Lit. and Crit., and around the university
he has hardly been a celebrity. One young woman now in Toronto
publishing remembers that, a decade ago, "McLuhan was a bit
of a campus joke." Even now, only a few of his graduate students
seem familiar with his studies of the impact of communications
media on civilization—those famous books that have excited so
many outside Toronto.

McLuhan's two major works, "The Gutenberg Galaxy" (1962)

From the *New York Times Magazine,* January 29, 1967, copyright © 1967
by the New York Times Company.

and "Understanding Media" (1964), have won an astonishing variety of admirers. General Electric, I.B.M. and Bell Telephone have all had him address their top executives; so have the publishers of America's largest magazines. The composer John Cage made a pilgrimage to Toronto especially to pay homage to McLuhan, and the critic Susan Sontag has praised his "grasp on the texture of contemporary reality."

He has a number of eminent and vehement detractors, too. The critic Dwight Macdonald calls McLuhan's books "impure nonsense, nonsense adulterated by sense." Leslie Fiedler wrote in Partisan Review: "Marshall McLuhan . . . continually risks sounding like the body-fluids man in 'Doctor Strangelove.' "

Still the McLuhan movement rolls on. Now he has been appointed to the Albert Schweitzer Chair in the Humanities at Fordham University, effective next September. (The post, which pays $100,000 a year for salary and research expenses, is one of 10 named for Schweitzer and Albert Einstein, underwritten by New York State. Other Schweitzer Professors include Arthur Schlesinger Jr. at City University and Conor Cruse O'Brien at N.Y.U.)

What makes McLuhan's success so surprising is that his books contain little of the slick style of which popular sociology is usually made. As anyone who opens the covers immediately discovers, "Media" and "Galaxy" are horrendously difficult to read—clumsily written, frequently contradictory, oddly organized, and overlaid with their author's singular jargon. Try this sample from "Understanding Media." Good luck.

> The movie, by sheer speeding up the mechanical, carried us from the world of sequence and connections into the world of creative configuration and structure. The message of the movie medium is that of transition from lineal connections to configurations. It is the transition that produced the now quite correct observation: "If it works, it's obsolete." When electric speed further takes over from mechanical movie sequences, then the lines of force in structures and in media become loud and clear. We return to the inclusive form of the icon.

Everything McLuhan writes is originally dictated, either to his secretary or to his wife, and he is reluctant to rewrite, because, he explains, "I tend to add, and the whole thing gets out of hand." Moreover, some of his insights are so original that they evade immediate understanding; other paragraphs may forever evade explication. "Most clear writing is a sign that there is no exploration going on," he rationalizes. "Clear prose indicates the absence of thought."

The basic themes in these books seem difficult at first, because the concepts are as unfamiliar as the language, but on second (or maybe third) thought, the ideas are really quite simple. In looking at history, McLuhan espouses a position one can only call "technological determinism." That is, whereas Karl Marx, an economic determinist, believed that the economic organization of a society shapes every important aspect of its life, McLuhan believes that crucial technological inventions are the primary influence. McLuhan admires the work of the historian Lynn White Jr., who wrote in "Medieval Technology and Social Change" (1962) that the three inventions of the stirrup, the nailed horseshoe and the horse collar created the Middle Ages. With the stirrup, a soldier could carry armor and mount a charger; and the horseshoe and the harness brought more efficient tilling of the land, which shaped the feudal system of agriculture, which, in turn, paid for the soldier's armor.

Pursuing this insight into technology's importance, McLuhan develops a narrower scheme. He maintains that a major shift in society's predominant technology of communication is the crucially determining force behind social changes, initiating great transformations not only in social organization but human sensibilities. He suggests in "The Gutenberg Galaxy" that the invention of movable type shaped the culture of Western Europe from 1500 to 1900. The mass production of printed materials encouraged nationalism by allowing more rapid and wider spread of information than permitted by hand-written messages. The linear forms of print influenced music to repudiate the structure of repetition, as in Gregorian chants, for that of linear development, as in a symphony. Also, print reshaped the sensibility of Western man, for whereas he once saw experience as individual segments, as a collection of separate entities, man in the Renaissance saw life as he saw print—as a continuity, often with causal relationships. Print even made Protestantism possible, because the printed book, by enabling people to think alone, encouraged individual revelation. Finally: "All forms of mechanization emerge from movable type, for type is the prototype of all machines."

In "Understanding Media," McLuhan suggests that electric modes of communication—telegraph, radio, television, movies, telephones, computers—are similarly reshaping civilization in the 20th century. Whereas print-age man saw one thing at a time in consecutive sequence—like a line of type—contemporary man experiences numerous forces of communication simultaneously, often through more than one of his senses. Contrast, for example, the way most of us read a book with how we look at a newspaper. With the latter, we do not start one story, read it through and then start another. Rather, we shift our eyes across the pages, assimilating a discontinuous collection of headlines, subheadlines, lead paragraphs, photographs and advertisements. "People don't actually read newspapers," McLuhan says; "they get into them every morning like a hot bath."

Moreover, the electronic media initiate sweeping changes in the distribution of sensory awareness—in what McLuhan calls the "sensory ratios." A painting or a book strikes us through only one sense, the visual; motion pictures and television hit us not only visually but also aurally. The new media envelop us, asking us to participate. McLuhan believes that such a multisensory existence is bringing a return to the primitive man's emphasis upon the sense of touch, which he considers the primary sense, "because it consists of a meeting of the senses." Politically, he sees the new media as transforming the world into "a global village," where all ends of the earth are in immediate touch with one another, as well as fostering a "retribalization" of human life. "Any highway eatery with its TV set, newspaper and magazine," he writes, "is as cosmopolitan as New York or Paris."

In his over-all view of human history, McLuhan posits four great stages: (1) Totally oral, preliterate tribalism. (2) The codification by script that arose after Homer in ancient Greece and lasted 2,000 years. (3) The age of print, roughly from 1500 to

1900. (4) The age of electronic media, from before 1900 to the present. Underpinning this classification is his thesis that "societies have been shaped more by the nature of the media by which men communicate than by the content of the communication."

This approach to the question of human development, it should be pointed out, is not wholly original. McLuhan is modest enough to note his indebtedness to such works as E. H. Gombrich's "Art and Illusion" (1960), H. A. Innis's "The Bias of Communication" (1951, recently reissued with an introduction by McLuhan), Siegfried Giedion's "Mechanization Takes Command" (1948), H. J. Chaytor's "From Script to Print" (1945) and Lewis Mumford's "Technics and Civilization" (1934).

McLuhan's discussions of the individual media move far beyond the trade talk of communications professionals (he dismisses Gen. David Sarnoff, the board chairman of R.C.A., as "the voice of the current somnambulism"). Serious critics of the new media usually complain about their content, arguing, for example, that if television had more intelligent treatments of more intelligent subjects, its contribution to culture would be greater. McLuhan proposes that, instead, we think more about the character and form of the new media. His most famous epigram—"The medium is the message"—means several things.

The phrase first suggests that each medium develops an audience of people whose love for that medium is greater than their concern for its content. That is, the TV medium itself becomes the prime interest in watching television: just as some people like to read for the joy of experiencing print, and more find great pleasure in talking to just anybody on the telephone, so others like television for the mixture of kinetic screen and relevant sound. Second, the "message" of a medium is the impact of its forms upon society. The "message" of print was all the aspects of Western culture that print influenced. "The message of the movie medium is that of transition from linear connections to configurations." Third, the aphorism suggests that the medium itself—its form—shapes its limitations and possibilities for the communication of content. One medium is better than another at evoking a certain experience. American football, for example, is better on television than on radio or in a newspaper column; a bad football game on television is more interesting than a great game on radio. Most Congressional hearings, in contrast, are less boring in the newspaper than on television. Each medium seems to possess a hidden taste mechanism that encourages some styles and rejects others.

To define this mechanism, McLuhan has devised the categories of "hot" and "cool" to describe simultaneously the composition of a communications instrument or a communicated experience, and its interaction with human attention. A "hot" medium or experience has a "high definition" or a highly individualized character as well as a considerable amount of detailed information. "Cool" is "low" in definition and information; it requires that the audience participate to complete the experience. McLuhan's own examples clarify the distinction: "A cartoon is 'low' definition, simply because very little visual information is provided." Radio is usually a hot medium; print, photography, film and paintings essentially are hot media. "Any hot medium allows of less participating than a cool one, as a lecture makes for less participation than a seminar, and a book for less than a dialogue."

The terms "hot" and "cool" he also applies to experiences and people, and, pursuing his distinction, he suggests that while a hot medium favors a performer of a strongly individualized presence, cool media prefer more nonchalant, "cooler" people. Whereas the radio medium needs a voice of a highly idiosyncratic quality that is instantly recognizable—think of Westbrook Van Voorhees, Jean Shepherd, Fanny Brice—television favors people of a definition so low they appear positively ordinary. With these terms, one can then explain all sorts of phenomena previously inscrutable—such as why bland personalities (Ed Sullivan, Jack Paar) are so successful on television.

"It was no accident that Senator McCarthy lasted such a very short time when he switched to TV," McLuhan says. "TV is a cool medium. It rejects hot figures and hot issues and people from the hot press media. Had TV occurred on a large scale during Hitler's reign he would have vanished quickly." As for the 1960 Presidential debates, McLuhan explains that whereas Richard Nixon, essentially a hot person, was superior on radio, John F.

Kennedy was the more appealing television personality. (It follows that someone with as low a definition as Dwight Eisenhower would have been more successful than either.)

The ideas are not as neatly presented as this summary might suggest, for McLuhan believes more in probing and exploring— "making discoveries"—than in offering final definitions. For this reason, he will rarely defend any of his statements as absolute truths, although he will explain how he developed them. Some perceptions are considerably more tenable than others—indeed, some are patently ridiculous—and all his original propositions are arguable, so his books require the participation of each reader to separate what is wheat to him from the chaff. In McLuhanese, they offer a cool experience in a hot medium.

A typical reader's scorecard for "Media" might show that about one-half is brilliant insight; one-fourth, suggestive hypotheses; one-fourth, nonsense. Given the book's purpose and originality, these are hardly bad percentages. "If a few details here and there are wacky," McLuhan says, "it doesn't matter a hoot."

McLuhan eschews the traditional English professor's expository style—introduction, development, elaboration and conclusion. Instead, his books imitate the segmented structure of the modern media. He makes a series of direct statements. None of them becomes a thesis but all of them approach the same phenomenon from different angles. This means that one should not necessarily read his books from start to finish—the archaic habit of print-man.

The real introduction to "The Gutenberg Galaxy" is the final chapter, called "The Galaxy Reconfigured"; even McLuhan advises his readers to start there. With "Media," the introduction and the first two chapters form the best starting point; thereafter, the reader is pretty much free to wander as he wishes. "One can stop anywhere after the first few sentences and have the full message, if one is prepared to 'dig' it," McLuhan once wrote of non-Western scriptural literature; the remark is applicable to his own books.

Similarly, McLuhan does not believe that his works have only one final meaning. "My book," he says, "is not a package but part of the dialogue, part of the conversation." (Indeed, he evaluates other books less by how definitively they treat their subject—the academic standard—than by how much thought they stimulate. Thus, a book may be wrong but still great. By his own standards, "Media" is, needless to say, a masterpiece.)

Underlying McLuhan's ideas is the question of whether technology is beneficial to man. Thinkers such as the British critic F. R. Leavis have argued, on the one hand, that technology stifles the blood of life by dehumanizing the spirit and cutting existence off from nature; more materialist thinkers, on the other hand, defend the machine for easing man's burdens. McLuhan recognizes that electronic modes of communication represent, in the subtitle of "Media," "extensions of man." Whereas the telephone is an extension of the ear (and voice), so television extends our eyes and ears. That is, our eyes and ears attended John Kennedy's funeral, but our bodies stayed at home. As extensions, the new media offer both possibility and threat, for while they lengthen man's reach into his existence, they can also extend society's reach into him, for both exploitation and control.

To prevent this latter possibility, McLuhan insists that every man should know as much about the media as possible. "By knowing how technology shapes our environment, we can transcend its absolutely determining power," he says. "Actually, rather than a 'technological determinist,' it would be more accurate to say, as regards the future, that I am an 'organic autonomist.' My entire concern is to overcome the determinism that results from the determination of people to ignore what is going on. Far from regarding technological change as inevitable, I insist that if we understand its components we can turn it off any time we choose. Short of turning it off, there are lots of moderate controls conceivable." In brief, in stressing the importance of knowledge, McLuhan is a humanist.

McLuhan advocates radical changes in education, because he believes that a contemporary man is not fully "literate" if reading is his sole pleasure: "You must be literate in umpteen media to be really 'literate' nowadays." Education, he suggests, should abandon its commitment to print—merely a focusing of the visual sense—to cultivate the "total sensorium" of man—to teach us how to use all five cylinders, rather than only one. "Postliterate does not mean illiterate," writes the Rev. John Culkin, S.J., director of the Communications Center at Fordham and a veteran propagator of McLuhan's ideas about multimedia education. "It rather describes the new social environment within which print will interact with a great variety of communications media."

Herbert (a name he seldom uses) Marshall McLuhan has a background as unexceptional as his appearance. He was born in Western Canada—Edmonton, Alberta—July 21, 1911, the son of mixed Protestant (Baptist and Methodist) parents. "Both agreed to go to all the available churches and services, and they spent much of their time in the Christian Science area," he recalls. His father was a real-estate and insurance salesman who, McLuhan remembers, "enjoyed talking with people more than pursuing his business," He describes his mother, a monologist and actress, as "the Ruth Draper of Canada, but better." His brother is now an Episcopal minister in California.

After taking his B.A. and M.A. at the University of Manitoba, McLuhan followed the route of many academically ambitious young Canadians to England, where he attended Cambridge for two years. There, he remembers, the lectures of I. A. Richards and F. R. Leavis stimulated his initial interest in studying popular culture. Returning home in 1936, he took a job at the University of Wisconsin. The following year he entered the Catholic Church, and ever since, he has taught only at Catholic institutions—at St. Louis from 1937 to 1944, at Assumption in Canada from 1944 to 1946 and at St. Michael's College, a Basilian (C.S.B.) establishment, since 1946.

His field was originally medieval and Renaissance literature, and in 1942 he completed his Cambridge Ph.D. thesis on the rhetoric of Thomas Nashe, the Elizabethan writer. As a young scholar, he began his writing career, as every professor should, by contributing articles to the professional journals, and to this day, academic circles know him as the editor of a popular paperback textbook of Tennyson's poems. Moreover, his critical essays on writers as various as Gerard Manley Hopkins, John Dos Passos and Samuel Taylor Coleridge are frequently anthologized.

By the middle forties, he was contributing more personal and eccentric articles on more general subjects to several little magazines; before long, his pieces had such outrageous titles as "The Psychopathology of Time and Life." By the time his first book, "The Mechanical Bride," appeared in 1951, McLuhan had developed his characteristic intellectual style—the capacity to offer an endless stream of radical and challenging ideas.

Although sparsely reviewed and quickly remaindered, that book has come to seem, in retrospect, the first serious attempt to inspect precisely what effects mass culture had upon people and to discover what similarities existed between mass culture and élite art. Copies are so scarce that they now often bring as much as $40 secondhand. McLuhan had the foresight and self-confidence to purchase a thousand copies at remainder prices; he still gives them to friends, as well as selling them to strangers (at far below the going price). The bottom will soon drop out of the "Mechanical Bride" market, however, for Beacon Press plans to reissue it in paperback and Vanguard, its original publisher, in hardcover.

In 1953, the year after he became a full professor at St. Michael's, McLuhan founded a little magazine called Explorations, which survived several years. Along with a coeditor, the anthropologist Edmund S. Carpenter, McLuhan collected some of the best material in a paperback called "Explorations in Communication" (1960), which is perhaps the ideal introduction to his special concerns and ideas.

Though McLuhan remains a Canadian citizen, he became, in 1959, director of the Media Project of the National Association of Educational Broadcasters and the United States Office of Education. Out of that experience came a report which, in effect, was the first draft of "Understanding Media." Then, in 1963, the University of Toronto appointed McLuhan to head a newly formed Center for Culture and Technology "to study the psychic and social consequences of technology and the media."

A visitor expects the Center, so boldly announced on its letterhead, to be a sleek building with a corps of secretaries between the corridor and the thinkers. In fact, the Center is more a committee than an institution. It exists, for the present, only in McLuhan's cluttered office.

Bookcases cover the walls, with battered old editions of the English classics on the top shelves and a varied assortment of

newer books on Western civilization on the more accessible shelves
—6,000 to 7,000 volumes in all. More books and papers cover
several large tables. Buried in a corner is a ratty metal-frame
chaise longue, more suited to a porch than an office, with a thin,
lumpy green mattress haphazardly draped across it.

In temperament, the Center's head is more passive than active.
He often loses things and forgets deadlines. The one singular
feature of his indefinite face is his mouth. Only a sliver of his lips
is visible from the front, but from the side his lips appear so thick
that his slightly open mouth resembles that of a flounder. His only
visible nervous habits are tendencies to pucker his mouth and
push his chin down toward his neck before he speaks, to twirl his
glasses around his fingers when he lectures and to rub his fingers
down the palms of his hands whenever he says "tactility."

The professor is a conscientious family man. He met his wife,
Corrine, a tall and elegant Texan, in Los Angeles, where he was
doing research at the Huntington Library and she was studying at
the Pasadena Playhouse. Married in 1939, they have six children:
Eric, 25; Mary and Theresa, 21-year-old twins; Stephanie, 19;
Elizabeth, 16, and Michael, 14, and the girls confirm their father's
boast: "All my daughters are beautiful." Every Sunday he leads
his brood to mass.

They live in a three-story house with a narrow front and a
small lawn punctuated by a skinny driveway leading to a garage
in the back. The interior is modest, except for an excessive number
of books, both shelved and sprawled. McLuhan likes to read in
a reclining position, so across the top of the living-room couch,
propped against the wall, are 20 or so fat scholarly works; in-
terspersed among them are a few mysteries—his favorite light
reading. He rarely goes to the movies or watches television; most
of his own cultural intake comes via print and conversation. Talking seems his favorite recreation.

McLuhan seems pretty much like any other small-city professor
until he begins to speak. His lectures and conversation are a
singular mixture of original assertions, imaginative comparisons,
heady abstractions and fantastically comprehensive generalizations,
and no sooner has he stunned his listeners with one extraordinary
thought than he hits them with another. His phrases are more

oracular than his manner; he makes the most extraordinary statements in the driest terms.

In his graduate seminar, he asks: "What is the future of old age?" The students look bewildered. "Why," he replies to his own question, "exploration and discovery." Nearly everything he says *sounds* important. Before long, he has characterized the Batman TV show as "simply an exploitation of nostalgia which I predicted years ago." The 25 or so students still look befuddled and dazed: hardly anyone talks but McLuhan. "The criminal, like the artist, is a social explorer," he goes on. "Bad news reveals the character of change; good news does not." No one asks him to be more definite, because his talk intimidates his listeners.

He seems enormously opinionated; in fact, he conjures insights. His method demands a memory as prodigious as his curiosity. He often elevates an analogy into a grandiose generalization, and he likes to make his points with puns: "When a thing is current, it creates currency." His critics ridicule him as a communications expert who cannot successfully communicate; but too many of his listeners, say his admirers, suffer from closed minds.

The major incongruity is that a man so intellectually adventurous should lead such a conservative life; the egocentric and passionately prophetic qualities of his books contrast with the personal modesty and pervasive confidence of a secure Catholic. What explains the paradox is that "Marshall McLuhan," the thinker, is different from "H. M. McLuhan," the man. The one writes books and delivers lectures; the other teaches school, heads a family and lists himself in the phone book. It was probably H. M. who made that often-quoted remark about Marshall's theories: "I don't pretend to understand them. After all, my stuff is very difficult."

And the private H. M. will say this about the technologies his public self has so brilliantly explored: "I wish none of these had ever happened. They impress me as nothing but a disaster. They are for dissatisfied people. Why is man so unhappy he wants to change his world? I would never attempt to improve an environment—my personal preference, I suppose, would be a preliterate milieu, but I want to study change to gain power over it."

His books, he adds, are just "probes"—that is, he does not

"believe" in his work as he believes in Catholicism. The latter is faith; the books are just thoughts. "You know the faith differently from the way you 'understand' my books."

When asked why he creates books rather than films, a medium that might be more appropriate to his ideas, McLuhan replies: "Print is the medium I trained myself to handle." So, all the recent acclaim has transformed McLuhan into a bookmaking machine. Late this year, we shall have "Culture Is Our Business," which he describes as a sequel to "The Mechanical Bride." Perhaps reflecting his own idea that future art will be, like medieval art, corporate in authorship, McLuhan is producing several more books in dialogue with others. With Wilfred Watson, a former student who is now an English professor at the University of Alberta, he is completing a history of stylistic change, "From Cliché to Archetype." With Harley W. Parker, head of design at the Royal Ontario Museum, he has just finished "Space in Poetry and Painting," a critical and comparative survey of 35 pairs of poems and pictures from primitive times to the present.

In tandem with William Jovanovich, the president of Harcourt, Brace and World, McLuhan is writing "The Future of the Book," a study of the impact of xerography, and along with the management consultant Ralph Baldwin he is investigating the future of business in "Report to Management." As if that were not enough, he joined with the book designer Quentin Fiore to compile "The Medium Is the Massage," an illustrated introduction to McLuhanism that will be out this spring; the two are doing another book on the effect of automation. Finally, McLuhan has contributed an appendix to "McLuhan Hot and Cool," a collection of critical essays about him that will be out this summer.

On another front, McLuhan and Prof. Richard J. Schoeck, head of the English Department at St. Michael's, have recently produced two imaginative textbooks, "The Voices of Literature," for use in Canadian high schools. And with Professor Schoeck and Ernest J. Sirluck, dean of the graduate school at the University of Toronto, McLuhan oversees a series of anthologies of criticism being published jointly by the Toronto and Chicago University Presses. Obviously, despite the bait from the worlds of media and advertising, McLuhan is keeping at least one foot planted in academia. Only this past December he addressed the annual meeting of the Modern Language Association on the confrontation of differing sensory modes in 19th-century poetry.

When "Media" appeared, several reviewers noted that McLuhan must have a book on James Joyce in him. That task he passed on to his son Eric, who is writing a prodigious critical study of "Finnegans Wake." Among McLuhan's greatest desires is establishing the Center for Culture and Technology in its own building, with sufficient funds to support a reference library of the sensory experience of man. That is, he envisions methods of measuring all the "sensory modalities" (systems of sensory organization) in all cultures, and of recording this knowledge on coded tapes in the Center. Assistant Professor of Design Allen Bernholtz, one of McLuhan's colleagues, foresees a machine that will, following taped instructions, artificially create a sensory environment exactly similar to that of any other culture; once the subject stepped into its capsule, the machine could be programed to simulate what and how, say, a Tahitian hears, feels, sees, smells and tastes. "It will literally put you in the other guy's shoes," Bernholtz concludes. So far, the projected Center has not received anywhere near the $5-million backing it needs to begin.

Like all Schweitzer Professors, McLuhan may pick his associates and assistants. His entourage will include Professor Carpenter, with whom he coedited Explorations; Harley Parker and Father Culkin. In addition to teaching one course and directing a research project, McLuhan and his associates plan to conduct numerous dialogues and to publish a son of Explorations. "Once you get a lot of talk going," he said recently, "you have to start a magazine." Because he believes that "I can better observe America from up here," he had rejected previous lucrative offers that involved forsaking Toronto, and as Schweitzer professorships are formally extended for only one year (although they are renewable), McLuhan will officially take only a sabbatical leave from St. Michael's.

McLuhan has always been essentially a professor living in an academic community, a father in close touch with his large family and a teacher who also writes and lectures. When some V.I.P.'s invited him to New York a year ago, he kept them waiting while he graded papers. Although he does not run away from all the reporters and visitors, he does little to attract publicity. His passion is the dialogue; if the visitor can participate in the conversation, he may be lucky enough, as this writer was, to help McLuhan write (that is, dictate) a chapter of a book.

"Most people," McLuhan once remarked, "are alive in an earlier time, but you must be alive in our own time. The artist," he added, "is the man in any field, scientific or humanistic, who grasps the implications of his actions and of new knowledge in his own time. He is the man of integral awareness."

Although his intention was otherwise, McLuhan was describing himself—the specialist in general knowledge. Who would dare surmise what thoughts, what perceptions, what grand schemes he will offer next?

Marcuse Defines His New Left Line

a conversation with Jean-Louis Ferrier, Jacques Boetsch, and Françoise Giroud

In terms of day-to-day effect, Herbert Marcuse may be the most important philosopher alive. For countless young people, discontented, demonstrating or fulminating, on campus or in the streets, here and abroad, this 70-year-old scholar is the angel of the apocalypse. "Away with the world's mess," his message seems to say. "Let us have a clean, revolutionary, new start." Born in Berlin, a Social Democrat in his youth, Marcuse came to the United States in 1934 and has been a citizen since 1940. His writings, particularly "One-Dimensional Man" (1964), have made him a hero of the New Left. Three staff members of the French magazine, L'Express, Jean-Louis Ferrier, Jacques Boetsch and Françoise Giroud, found him on holiday on the Riviera. This translation by Helen Weaver of their conversation sets forth the man and his ideas.

Six months ago, sir, your name was almost unknown in France.

It came to prominence in connection with the student revolt in Berlin, then in connection with student demonstrations in America. Next it was linked with the May demonstrations here. And now, all of a sudden, your last book has become a best-seller. How do you see your own position in relation to the student uprisings all over the world?

MARCUSE: The answer is very simple. I am deeply committed to the movement of "angry students," but I am certainly not their spokesman. It is the press and publicity that have given me this title and have turned me into a rather salable piece of merchandise. I particularly object to the juxtaposition of my name and photograph with those of Che Guevara, Debray, Rudi Dutschke, etc., because these men have truly risked and are still risking their lives in the battle for a more human society, whereas I participate in this battle only through my words and my ideas. It is a fundamental difference.

Still, your words preceded the student action.

MARCUSE: Oh, there are very few students who have really read me, I think. . . .

No doubt, especially in France; but there are also very few students who have chosen a doctrine for their revolt. Can we say that for these students you are the theorist?

MARCUSE: If that is true, I am very happy to hear it. But it's more a case of encounter than of direct influence. . . . In my books, I have tried to make a critique of society—and not only of capitalist society—in terms that avoid all ideology. Even the Socialist ideology, even the Marxist ideology. I have tried to show that contemporary society is a repressive society in all its aspects, that even the comfort, the prosperity, the alleged political and moral freedom are utilized for oppressive ends.

I have tried to show that any change would require a total rejection or, to speak the language of the students, a perpetual confrontation of this society. And that it is not merely a question of changing the institutions but rather, and this is more important, of totally changing human beings in their attitudes, their instincts, their goals, and their values.

This, I think, is the point of contact between my books and the worldwide student movement.

But you feel that they did not need you to arrive at these ideas, is that right?

MARCUSE: One of the essential characteristics of the student movement is that the students apply to reality what has been taught them in the abstract through the work of the masters who have developed the great values of Western civilization. For example, the primacy of natural law over established law, the inalienable right to resist tyranny and all illegitimate authority. . . . They simply cannot comprehend why these great principles should remain on the level of ideas instead of being put into practice. And that is exactly what they are doing.

Do you mean that fundamentally this is a humanist movement?

MARCUSE: They object to that term because according to them, humanism is a bourgeois, personal value. It is a philosophy which is inseparable from a destructive reality. But in their minds there is no point in worrying about the philosophy of a few persons; the point is to bring about a radical change in the society as a whole. So they want no part of the term "humanist."

You know, of course, that here in France we are very far from that "affluent society" whose destruction you propose and which for the moment exists, for better or worse, only in the United States.

MARCUSE: I have been accused of concentrating my critique on American society, and this is quite true. I have said so myself. But this is not only because I know this country better than any other; is it because I believe or I am afraid that American society may become the model for the other capitalist countries, and maybe even for the Socialist countries. I also believe that this route can be avoided, but again, this would presuppose a fundamental change, a total break with the content of the needs and aspirations of people as they are conditioned today.

A break. . . that is, a revolution.

MARCUSE: Precisely.

Do you believe in the existence of a revolutionary impulse in the industrial societies?

MARCUSE: You know quite well that the student movement contains a very strong element of anarchy. Very strong. And this is really new.

Anarchy—new?

MARCUSE: In the revolutionary movement of the 20th century, I believe it is new. At least on this scale, it is now. This means that the students have perceived the rigidity of the traditional political organizations, their petrification, the fact that they have stifled any revolutionary impulse. So it is outside of these organizations that the revolt spontaneously occurs.

But spontaneity is not enough. It is also necessary to have an organization. But a new, very flexible kind of organization, one that does not impose rigorous principles, one that allows for movement and initiative. An organization without the "bosses" of the old parties or political groups. This point is very important. The leaders of today are the products of publicity. In the actual movement there are no leaders as there were in the Bolshevik Revolution, for example.

In other words, it is anti-Leninist?

MARCUSE: Yes. In fact, Daniel Cohn-Bendit has severely criticized Leninism-Marxism on this ground.

Does this mean that you rely on anarchism to bring about the revolution you desire?

MARCUSE: No. But I do believe that the anarchist element is a very powerful and very progressive force, and that it is necessary to preserve this element as one of the factors in a larger and more structured process.

And yet you yourself are the opposite of an anarchist.

MARCUSE: That may be true, but I wish you'd tell me why.

Isn't it because your work is dialectical? Your work is very carefully constructed. Do you think of yourself as an anarchist?

MARCUSE: No. I am not an anarchist because I cannot imagine how one can combat a society which is mobilized and organized in its totality against any revolutionary movement, against any effective opposition; I do not see how one can combat such a society, such a concentrated force—military force, police force, etc.—without any organization. It won't work.

No, it won't work. The Communists will quote you Lenin's analysis of "leftism" which, according to him, was the manifestation of "petits bourgeois overcome with rage before the horrors of capitalism . . . a revolutionary attitude which is unstable, un-

productive, and susceptible of rapidly changing into submission or apathy or going mad over some bourgeois fad or other."

MARCUSE: I do not agree. Today's left is far from the reaction of a *petite bourgeoisie* to a revolutionary party, as in Lenin's day. It is the reaction of a revolutionary minority to the established party which the Communist party has become, which is no longer the party of Lenin, but a social democratic party.

If anarchy doesn't work and if the Communist parties are no longer revolutionary, what do you hope for from the student unrest but a superficial disorder which only serves to stiffen the repression?

MARCUSE: All militant opposition takes the risk of increasing repression. This has never been a reason to stop the opposition. Otherwise, all progress would be impossible.

No doubt. But don't you think the notion of the "progress" that might result from a revolution deserves to be better defined? You denounce the subtle restraints that weigh upon the citizens of modern societies. Wouldn't a revolution result in exchanging one series of restraints for another?

MARCUSE: Of course. But there are progressive restraints and reactionary restraints. For example, restraints imposed upon the elemental aggressiveness of man, upon the instinct of destruction, the death instinct, the transformation of this elemental aggressiveness into an energy that could be used for the improvement and protection of life—such restraints would be necessary in the freest society. For example, industries would not be permitted to pollute the air, nor would the "White Citizens Council" be permitted to disseminate racism or to possess firearms, as they are in the United States today. . . . Of course there would be restraints; but they would be progressive ones.

The ones you mention are commonplace enough. The possession of firearms is forbidden in France, and in America it is a survival, not a creation of the affluent society. Let us consider freedom of expression, which means a great deal to us. In the free society which you advocate this freedom disappears, does it not?

MARCUSE: I have written that I believe it is necessary not to extend freedom of the press to movements which are obviously aggressive and destructive, like the Nazi movement. But with the exception of this special case, I am not against freedom of expression. . . .

Even when this means the propagation of racist, nationalist or colonialist ideas?

MARCUSE: Here my answer is no. I am not in favor of granting free expression to racist, anti-Semitic, neo-Nazi movements. Certainly not; because the interval between the word and the act is too brief today. At least in American society, the one with which I am familiar. You know the famous statement of Justice Holmes, that civil rights can be withdrawn in a single case: the case of immediate danger. Today this immediate danger exists everywhere.

Can't this formula be turned against you in connection with students, revolutionaries, or Communists?

MARCUSE: It always is. And my answer is always the same. I do not believe that the Communism conceived by the great Marxist theorists is, by its very nature, aggressive and destructive; quite the contrary.

But has it not become so under certain historical circumstances? Isn't there something aggressive and destructive about the Soviet policy toward Hungary in 1956, or toward Czechoslovakia today?

MARCUSE: Yes. But that isn't Communism, it is Stalinism. I would certainly use all possible restraints to oppose Stalinism, but that is not Communism.

Why do you criticize America more severely for its deviations from the democratic ideal than you do Communism for its deviations from the Communist ideal?

MARCUSE: I am just as critical of these deviations in Communist countries. However, I believe that the institutions and the whole culture of the capitalism of monopolies militate against the development of a democratic socialism.

And you believe that one day we shall see an ideal Communist society?

MARCUSE: Well, at least there is the theory. There is the whole Marxist theory. That exists. And there is also Cuba. There is China. There is the Communist policy during the heroic period of the Bolshevik Revolution.

Do you mean that Communist societies do these reprehensible things in spite of themselves? That the Soviet Union invaded Czechoslovakia in spite of herself?

MARCUSE: In spite of the idea of Communism, not in spite of the Soviet Union. The invasion of Czechoslovakia is one of the most reprehensible acts in the history of Socialism. It is a brutal expression of the policy of power that has long been practiced by the Soviet Union in political and economic competition with capitalism. I believe that many of the reprehensible things that happen in the Communist countries are the result of competitive coexistence with capitalism, while poverty continues to reign in the Communist countries.

Here you are touching upon an important point. It does not seem possible to reduce poverty without an extremely coercive organization. So once again we find that restraint is necessary.

MARCUSE: Certainly. But here, too, there can be progressive restraint. Take a country in which poverty coexists with luxury, waste, and comfort for the privileged. . . . It is necessary to curb this waste to eliminate poverty, misery and inequality. These are necessary restraints.

Unfortunately, there is no economic correlation. It is not the curbing of waste that eliminates poverty, it is production.

MARCUSE: That's true. But my point is that the restraints that certainly exist in, say, Cuba, are not the same as those that are felt in capitalist economies.

Cuba is perhaps not a very good example of a successful Socialist economy, since the country is totally dependent on daily deliveries of Soviet petroleum. If the Soviet Union were to stop those deliveries for two weeks . . .

MARCUSE: I don't know what would happen. But even under these conditions of dependence on the Soviet Union, Cuba has made tremendous progress.

In comparison with what she was that's certainly true. Have you been there?

MARCUSE: No. I can't get authorization from the Americans.

Why do you despair of all progress within the framework of the American democracy?

MARCUSE: Do you really think that democracy is making progress in the United States?

Compared with the period of "The Grapes of Wrath," yes.

MARCUSE: I disagree. Look at the elections, the candidates for the Presidency of the United States, fabricated by the huge political machines. And who can find the differences between these candidates? If that's democracy, it's a farce. The people have said nothing and they have been asked nothing.

True. But at the same time thousands of young Americans have shown in recent months that they were against the war in Vietnam, that they were willing to work to eliminate the ghettos, to act in the political sphere.

MARCUSE: This movement is encountering a more and more effective repression.

Do you feel, then, that we are witnessing a definite obstruction of American society?

MARCUSE: The answer is a little more complicated than that. There is a possibility of progress toward democracy in the United States, but only through movements that are increasingly militant and radical. Not at all within the limits of the established process. This process is a game and the American students have not lost interest in playing this game, they have lost confidence in this allegedly democratic process.

Do you believe in the possibility of revolution in the United States?

MARCUSE: Absolutely not. Not at all.

Why not?

MARCUSE: Because there is no collaboration between the students and the workers, not even on the level on which it occurred in France in May and June.

In that case, what role do you attribute to the students?

MARCUSE: They are militant minorities who can articulate the needs and aspirations of the silent masses. But by themselves they are not revolutionaries, and nobody says they are. The students know that very well.

So their only role is to reveal?

MARCUSE: Yes. And this is very interesting. Here as well as in the United States, the students can truly be called spokesmen.

And who will make the revolution in America, in Germany, in France, if the students do not make contact with the working class?

MARCUSE: I cannot imagine. In spite of everything that has been said, I still cannot imagine a revolution without the working class.

The drawback—at least from the viewpoint of revolution—is that the working class is more interested in belonging to the affluent society than in destroying it, although it also hopes to modify certain aspects of it. At least this is the case in France. Is it different in other countries?

MARCUSE: You say that in France the working class is not yet integrated but that it would like to be. . . . In the United States it is integrated and it wants to be. This means that revolution postulates first of all the emergence of a new type of man with needs and aspirations that are qualitatively different from the aggressive and repressive needs and aspirations of established societies. It is true that the working class today shares in large measure the needs and aspirations of the dominant classes, and that without a break with the present content of needs, revolution is inconceivable.

So it will not happen tomorrow, it seems. It is easier to seize power than to change the needs of men. But what do you mean by aggressive needs?

MARCUSE: For example, the need to continue the competitive struggle for existence—the need to buy a new car every two years, the need to buy a new television set, the need to watch television five or six hours a day. This is already a vital need for a very large share of the population, and it is an aggressive and repressive need.

Aggressive to watch television? But it would seem on the face of it to be a passive activity.

MARCUSE: Are you familiar with the programs on American television? Nothing but shooting. And they always stimulate the consumption that subjects people to the capitalist mode of production.

There can be a different use of television.

MARCUSE: Of course. All this is not the fault of television, the fault of the automobile, the fault of technology in general. It is the fault of the miserable use that is made of technological progress. Television could just as well be used to reeducate the population.

In what sense? To persuade people that they do not need cars or television sets or refrigerators or washing machines?

MARCUSE: Yes, if this merchandise prevents the liberation of the serfs from their "voluntary servitude."

Wouldn't this create some problems for the people who work in the factories where they make cars, refrigerators, etc?

MARCUSE: They will shut down for a week or two. Everyone will go to the country. And then the real work will begin, the work of abolishing poverty, the work of abolishing inequality, instead of the work of waste which is performed in the society of consumption. In the United States, for example, General Motors and Ford, instead of producing private cars, will produce cars for public transportation, so that public transportation can become human.

It will take a lot of television programs to persuade the working class to make a revolution that will reduce their wages, do away with their cars, and reduce their consumption. And in the meantime there is reason to fear that things may take a different turn, that all the people affected by the economic difficulties may potentially furnish a fascist mass. Doesn't fascism always come out of an economic crisis?

MARCUSE: That's true. The revolutionary process always begins with and in an economic crisis. But this crisis would offer two possibilities: the so-called neo-fascist possibility, in which the masses turn toward a regime that is much more authoritarian and repressive, and the opposite possibility, that the masses may see an opportunity to construct a free society in which such crises would be avoidable. There are always two possibilities. One cannot, for fear of seeing the first materialize, stop hoping and working for the second through the education of the masses. And not only by words, but by actions.

For the present, aren't you afraid that these actions, especially when they are violent, will produce the opposite effect, and that the society will become even more repressive in order to defend itself?

MARCUSE: Unfortunately, that is a very real possibility. But that is not sufficient reason to give up. On the contrary, we must increase the opposition, reinforce it. There will always be privileged classes which will oppose any fundamental change.

It is not the privileged classes which have manifested their op-

position in France. It is the middle class and part of the working class. The privileged classes have been content to exploit the dissatisfaction.

MARCUSE: Next you'll tell me that the revolutionary militants are responsible for the reaction. In Germany they are already saying that neo-Nazism is the result of student action.

In France, the result of the elections is incontestably the response of the majority of the country to the May movement, which frightened them.

MARCUSE: Well, we must fight that fear!

Do you think that one can fight fear with violence?

MARCUSE: Violence, I confess, is very dangerous for those who are the weakest. But first we should examine our terminology. People are always talking about violence, but they forget that there are different kinds of violence, with different functions. There is a violence of aggression and a violence of defense. There is a violence of police forces or armed forces or of the Ku Klux Klan, and there is a violence in the opposition to these aggressive manifestations of violence.

The students have said that they are opposing the violence of society, legal violence, institutionalized violence. Their violence is that of defense. They have said this, and I believe it is true.

Thanks to a kind of political linguistics, we never use the word violence to describe the actions of the police, we never use the word violence to describe the actions of the Special Forces in Vietnam. But the word is readily applied to the actions of students who defend themselves from the police, burn cars or chop down trees. This is a typical example of political linguistics, utilized as a weapon by the established society.

There has been a lot of fuss in France over the burned automobiles. But nobody gets at all excited about the enormous number of automobiles destroyed every day on the highways, not only in France but all over the world. The number of deaths in highway accidents in America is 50,000 per year.

And between 13,000 and 14,000 in France.

MARCUSE: But that doesn't count. Whereas one burned automobile is terrible, it is the supreme crime against property. But the other crime doesn't count!

How do you explain this phenomenon?

MARCUSE: Because the other crime has a function in production. It is profitable to society.

But people don't kill themselves to make a profit. How can you separate the society from the people who compose it? Society is not some special tribunal of people who meet in secret and say to each other: we are going to see to it that people kill themselves on the highways so that we can sell a lot of cars! Society is everyone, and everyone consents. You have a car yourself and you drive it. . . .

MARCUSE: But there is a very good reason for all this. It is that this society, at the stage it is at, must mobilize our aggressive instincts to an exorbitant degree to counteract the frustrations imposed by the daily struggle for existence. The little man who works eight hours a day in the factory, who does an inhuman and stupefying work, on the weekend sits behind a huge machine much more powerful than himself, and there he can utilize all his antisocial aggressiveness. And this is absolutely necessary. If this aggressiveness were not sublimated in the speed and power of the automobile, it might be directed against the dominant powers.

This seems to be what is happening in spite of the weekend traffic!

MARCUSE: No. It is only the students who are revolting and crying, "We are all German Jews!" that is, We are all oppressed.

And why do you think this diffuse oppression is more precisely experienced and formulated by the students? Why is it that the torch of revolution which seemed to be wavering, to say the least, in the industrial countries, has passed into their hands?

MARCUSE: It is because they are not integrated. This is a very interesting point. In the United States, for example, there is a vast difference in behavior between the students and teachers in the social sciences and humanities on the one hand and the natural sciences on the other. The majority comes from the first group. In France, I believe it is not the same. . . .

No, it isn't.

MARCUSE: And in the study of these sciences they have learned a great deal. The nature of power, the existence of the forces behind the facts. They have also become very much aware of what goes on in societies. And this awareness is absolutely impossible for the vast majority of the population, which is, in some sense, inside the social machine. If you will, the students are playing the role of the professional members of the intelligentsia before the French Revolution.

You know that Tocqueville denounced the role of writers in the revolution of 1789, precisely because they were on the fringe of political life, lacking experience in public life, constructing arbitrary schemata.

MARCUSE: Magnificent! And here is my answer to Tocqueville. I say that it is precisely *because* the students and intellectuals have no experience in what is today called politics that they are in the avant-garde. Because the political experience today is the experience of a game that is both faked and bloody.

Politics has always been a bloody game which kings and heads of state played among themselves. Do you mean that today it is faked because the people have the illusion of participating in this game?

MARCUSE: Yes. Who really participates in politics? Who takes part in it? Any important decision is always made by a very small minority. Take the war in Vietnam. Who really participated in that decision? A dozen people, I would say. Afterwards the Government solicits and receives the support of the population. But in the case of Vietnam, even Congress did not get a chance to learn the facts. No, the people do not participate in decisions. We do not participate. Only in secondary decisions.

But if the American Government stops the war tomorrow—they certainly will some day—won't it be as a result of public opinion? Of the revolt in public opinion?

MARCUSE: Precisely. And who is responsible for this change in public opinion?

American television.

MARCUSE: No, no! First there were the students. Opposition to the war began in the universities.

There is a slight contradiction in what you say, since you have written that this opposition is tolerated insofar as it has no power.

MARCUSE: It may have the power to alter American policy, but not the system itself. The framework of society will remain the same.

And to try to destroy this society which is guilty of violence, you feel that violence is both legitimate and desirable. Does this mean that you think it impossible to evolve peacefully and within the democratic framework toward a nonrepressive, freer society?

MARCUSE: The students have said it: a revolution is always just as violent as the violence it combats. I believe they are right.

But you still think it is possible, in spite of the judgment of Freud to whom you refer frequently in "Eros and Civilization," to create a free society. Doesn't this betray a remarkable optimism?

MARCUSE: I am optimistic, because I believe that never in the history of humanity have the resources necessary to create a free society existed to such a degree. I am pessimistic because I believe that the established societies—capitalist society in particular —are totally organized and mobilized against this possibility.

Perhaps because people are afraid of freedom?

MARCUSE: Many people are afraid of freedom, certainly. They are conditioned to be afraid of it. They say to themselves: if people only had to work, say, five hours a week, what would they do with this freedom?

This is a condition which is not related to capitalism. The whole Judeo-Christian civilization is founded on work and is the product of work.

MARCUSE: Yes and no. Look at feudal society. That was truly a Christian society and yet work was not a value in it; on the contrary.

Because there were slaves, villagers. It was very convenient for the feudal lords.

MARCUSE: There were slaves, but the system of values was altogether different. And it was within this system that the culture was created. There is no such thing as bourgeois culture. Every genuine bourgeois culture is against the bourgeoisie.

In other words, we should return to the feudal system, but with machines taking the place of the slaves?

MARCUSE: We must have machines in place of slaves, but without returning to the feudal system. It would be the end of work, and at the same time the end of the capitalist system. Marx saw this in that famous passage where he says that with technological progress and automation, man is separated from the instruments of production, is dissociated from material production, and acts simply as a free subject, experimenting with the material possibilities of the machines, etc. But this would also mean the end of an economy founded on exchange value. Because the product would no longer be worth anything as merchandise. And this is the specter that haunts the established society.

Do you regard work, effort, as a repressive value?

MARCUSE: It all depends on its purpose. Effort is not repressive by itself. Effort in art, in every creative act, in love. . . .

Would you work if you were not obliged to do so?

MARCUSE: Certainly. I work if I am not obliged to do so.

Do you consider yourself a free man?

MARCUSE: Me? I believe that nobody is free in this society. Nobody.

Have you been psychoanalyzed?

MARCUSE: Never. Do you think I need to be?

It's quite possible, but that's beside the point. What seems curious is that you have made such a thorough study of the work of Freud and his views on the inevitably repressive quality of all civilization without asking yourself about your own obstacles to the exercise of your personal freedom.

MARCUSE: I have discussed Freud only on the level of theory, not on the level of therapy.

Don't you give European civilization any credit for being able to create its own values in reaction to American civilization while at the same time appropriating the positive element in that civilization, that is, the technical progress which you yourself have said is absolutely fundamental to the liberation of man?

MARCUSE: It is almost impossible to speak of a European civilization today. Perhaps it is even impossible to speak of a Western civilization. I believe that Eastern civilization and Western civilization are assimilating each other at an ever increasing rate. And the European civilization of today has already absorbed much of American civilization. So it seems impossible to imagine a European civilization separated from the influence of America.

Except, perhaps, in a few very isolated sectors of intellectual culture. Poetry, for example.

So you think the battle is lost. That we are Americans?

MARCUSE: We mustn't say it is lost. It is possible to change, to utilize the possibilities of American civilization for the good of humanity. We must utilize everything that enables us to facilitate daily life, to make it more tolerable. . . . We could already, today, end air pollution, for example. The means exist.

What role do you envision for art in the free society of which you dream, since art is by definition denial, challenge?

MARCUSE: I am not a prophet. In the affluent society, art is an interesting phenomenon. On the one hand, it rejects and accuses the established society; on the other hand, it is offered and sold on the market. There is not a single artistic style, however avant-garde, that does not sell. This means that the function of art is problematic, to say the least. There has been talk of the end of art, and there really is among the artists a feeling that art today has no function. There are museums, concerts, paintings in the homes of the rich, but art no longer has a function. So it wants to become an essential part of reality, to change reality.

Look at the graffiti, for example. For me, this is perhaps the most interesting aspect of the events of May, the coming together of Marx and André Breton. Imagination in power: that is truly revolutionary. It is new and revolutionary to try to translate into reality the most advanced ideas and values of the imagination. This proves that people have learned an important lesson: that truth is not only in rationality, but just as much and perhaps more in the imaginary.

The imaginary is above all the only realm where man's freedom has always been complete, where nothing has succeeded in curbing it. Dreams bear witness to this.

MARCUSE: Yes. And this is why I believe that the student rebellion, whatever its immediate results, is a real turning point in the development of contemporary society.

Because the students are reintegrating the imaginary with reality?

MARCUSE: Yes. There is a graffito which I like very much which goes, "Be realists, demand the impossible." That is magnificent. And another: "Watch out, ears have walls." That is realistic!

You have no desire to go back to Germany?

MARCUSE: I don't think so. Only to give lectures. But I like the German students very much, they are terrific!

Have they succeeded any better than the others in making contact with the working class?

MARCUSE: No. Their collaboration has been even more precarious.

Is it true that in the United States you received threats from the Ku Klux Klan?

MARCUSE: They were signed Ku Klux Klan, but I don't think it was they who sent them.

Is it true that you moved out of your house following these threats?

MARCUSE: Yes. Not in a panic, but I did leave. Frankly, I wasn't afraid. My students came and surrounded the house with their cars to protect me. . . . In one sense, they were right in thinking that there was a risk.

And do you feel that your life in the United States can continue, now that your notoriety has put you in the public eye?

MARCUSE: I'm not sure, not at all sure. At the university there's no problem. But universities are always oases.

Do you think that the American university as it is set up now can be a model for the French university, for example?

MARCUSE: One must distinguish among American universities. The large universities are always sanctuaries for free thought and a rather solid education. Take mine, for example, the University of California in San Diego. This is probably the most reactionary area in the United States—a large military base, a center of so-called defense industry, retired colonels and admirals. I have no difficulty with the university, the administration, or my colleagues. But I have a great deal of difficulty at the hands of the community, the good middle-class townspeople. No problems with the students. Relations between professors and students are, I think, much more informal than here and in Germany.

In this respect, you know, there really is an egalitarian tradition in the United States. The sanctity of the professor does not exist. It is the American materialism that prevents it. The professor is a salaried man who has studied, who has learned certain things, and who teaches them; he is not at all a mythical personage identified with the Father, not at all. His political position depends upon his position in the university hierarchy. If you reach a permanent position it is practically impossible to fire you. My own situation is precarious, and I am very curious to find out whether I will be able to retain my position at the university.

What you say is very serious. If freedom of expression no longer exists in the United States, it will no longer exist anywhere . . . or perhaps in England?

MARCUSE: Yes. England may turn out to be one of the last liberal countries. The democracy of the masses is not favorable to nonconformist intellectuals. . . .

This is the crux of the matter. You have often been criticised for wanting to establish a Platonic dictatorship of the élite. *Is this correct?*

MARCUSE: There is a very interesting passage in John Stuart Mill, who was not exactly an advocate of dictatorship. He says that in a civilized society educated people must have political prerogatives to oppose the emotions, attitudes and ideas of the uneducated masses.

I have never said that it was necessary to establish a Platonic dictatorship because there is no philosopher who is capable of doing this. But to be perfectly frank, I don't know which is worse: a dictatorship of politicians, managers and generals, or a dictatorship of intellectuals.

Personally, if this is the choice, I would prefer the dictatorship of the intellectuals, if there is no possibility of a genuine free democracy. Unfortunately this alternative does not exist at present.

The dictatorship of the intellectuals must first be established to educate and reform the masses, after which, in a remote future, when people have changed, democracy and freedom will reign. Is that it?

MARCUSE: Not a true dictatorship, but a more important role for intellectuals, yes. I think that the resentment of the worker movement against the intellectuals is one of the reasons why this movement has stopped today.

The dictatorship of the intellectuals is rather disturbing, to the extent that intellectuals often become cruel because they are afraid of action.

MARCUSE: Is that really so? There is only one example in history of a cruel intellectual: Robespierre.

And Saint-Just.

MARCUSE: We must compare the cruelty of Robespierre and Saint-Just with the cruelty and the bureaucratized violence of an Eichmann. Or even with the institutionalized violence of modern societies. Nazi cruelty is cruelty as a technique of administration. The Nazis were not intellectuals. With intellectuals, cruelty and violence are always much more immediate, shorter, less cruel. Robespierre did not use torture. Torture is not an essential aspect of the French Revolution.

You know intellectuals: they are not, or are only slightly, in touch with reality. Can you imagine a society functioning under their direct government? What effect would this have on trains running on time, for example? Or on organizing production?

MARCUSE: If you identify reality with established reality you are right. But intellectuals do not or should not identify reality with established reality. Given the imagination and rationality of true intellectuals, we can expect great things. In any case, the famous dictatorship of the intellectuals has never existed.

Perhaps because an intellectual is by his very nature an individualist. Lenin said this, too. What form of dictatorship do you prefer? One that operates directly as is the case in the Soviet Union, for example, or one that adopts the mask of democracy?

MARCUSE: It is absolutely necessary not to isolate a given situation from its tendencies for development. There is a social and political repression which can foster human progress, which can lead toward a true democracy and a true freedom. And there is a repression which does the opposite. I have always said that I utterly reject Stalinian repression and the repressive policy of Communism, although I recognize that the Socialist base of these countries contains the possibility of development toward liberalization and ultimately toward a free society.

It is a question of not being too skeptical about the end. . . .

MARCUSE: I am very skeptical about the end, in both cases.

Do you think that man can be free and at the same time believe in the existence of God?

MARCUSE: The liberation of man depends neither on God nor on the nonexistence of God. It is not the idea of God which has been an obstacle to human liberation, but the use that has been made of the idea of God.

But why has this use been made of it?

MARCUSE: From the beginning, religion has been allied with the ruling strata of society. In the case of Christianity, not from the very beginning, but still, rather early on.

In short, one must belong to the ruling strata of society! That is the sad conclusion that one could cynically draw from what you say. All the rest is adventure, more or less doomed to failure. Of course, one can prefer adventure, need adventure, and dream of being Guevara, in Paris or Berlin.

MARCUSE: Guevara was not adventure; it was the alliance between adventure and revolutionary politics. If revolution does not contain an element of adventurism, it is worthless. All the rest is organization, labor unions, social democracy, the establishment. Adventure is always beyond. . . .

What you call adventurism, others call romanticism. . . .

MARCUSE: Call it what you will. Adventure is transcendence of the given reality. Those who no longer wish to contain the revolution within the framework of the given reality. Call it what you will—adventurism, romanticism, imagination—it is an element necessary to all revolution.

No doubt. But it would seem that a concrete analysis of the situation in the countries in which one wants to make a revolution is also not an entirely negligible element. Provided, of course, that one wants to bring it off, and not merely to dream. One more question. You denounce as a painful form of oppression and one from which we suffer the deprivation of solitude and silence inflicted on us by modern society. Isn't this a plague that is just as characteristic of collectivist societies?

MARCUSE: First of all, we must eliminate the concept of collectivist societies. There are many modes of collectivization. There is a collectivism that is based on true human solidarity. There is a collectivism that is based on an authoritarian regime that is imposed on people. The destruction of autonomy, silence and solitude occurs in the so-called free societies as well as in the so-called collectivist societies. The decisive problem is to determine whether the limitations imposed on the individual are imposed in order to further the domination and indoctrination of the masses, or, on the contrary, in the interest of human progress.

It would be interesting to learn which noises are the progressive ones, if only so as to bear them with a smile. Sorry . . . we were being facetious.

MARCUSE: So was I. There is no free society without silence, without the internal and external space of solitude in which individual freedom can develop. If there is neither private life, nor autonomy, nor silence, nor solitude in a Socialist society—well, it is very simple: it is not a Socialist society! Not yet.

Seven Heroes of the New Left

by Lionel Abel

"WE OF THE New Left have seven heroes," said my informant, a graduate student at the University of Buffalo.

I knew some of the heroes, but wanted his list.

"Three of them," he said, "I have to call moralists: Albert Camus, Noam Chomsky and Paul Goodman. Then, there are the three immoralists: Guevara, Debray and Frantz Fanon. And there's one professor—Herbert Marcuse."

I pointed out that Noam Chomsky, too, is a professor. "So why do you say one professor? One and one makes two."

He answered: "On the New Left, we're not so logical."

Camus, whom I had known in New York and in Paris during the late nineteen-forties and early fifties, seemed to me a very unlikely hero for New Leftists. What did they know about him? Could it be that, as Irving Howe, the socialist critic (and critic of socialism), suggested, they knew only his name? "Oh, we know something about Camus," my informant told me. "We know he was a moralist. He said a man has to be ready to say 'no' on certain occasions, and that's what we are saying now. He said 'no' to Hitler—we say 'no' to Uncle Sam."

Morally, Camus was certainly *un type très chic*. When his friend, Françoise Leibowitz, was accused of working for the Germans, Camus staked his reputation on her innocence, proved it and saved her life; also the honor of the Resistance group to which they both belonged. He was a great journalist; even today we take pleasure in the prose of the editorial columns he wrote for Combat, the Resistance paper he edited in Paris during the German occupation. To publish this underground paper, which Sartre has called the most free press France ever had, meant a daily defiance of the Gestapo, a daily risk of life. To be such a journalist one had to be a hero. Which tells us something about Camus's appeal to modern youth.

But let us not forget that this moralist was also a nationalist and that he tried to get in politics with few political ideas. In 1947, speaking at Columbia University, he announced that "40 million Frenchmen want justice," evidently meaning to distinguish the French from the rest of humanity in this regard. Also, he was lacking in realistic judgment. I remember running into him on the day I left Paris, late in 1952. "America," he said, "is the land of the atomic bomb." I answered: "You'll have one here, too, as soon as France can afford it." "Never," he replied.

I must add—this is something New Leftists may not know— that Camus defended France's effort to maintain her rule in Algeria. At Stockholm, after he received the Nobel Prize for literature, he was asked: "Why aren't you for French withdrawal from Algeria?" "Do you want me to be against my own mother?" he replied. Camus came from Oran, the Algerian city he described so brilliantly in "Carnets (1935–42)." I mention these facts not to belittle him, but to indicate that an athletic moral posture is not incompatible with political thought that is weak.

The Camus moral posture was indeed a strong one. I remember when I first met him in New York, at Dorothy Norman's (the New York hostess of the late forties). He was presented to Richard Wright, then on the point of leaving for Paris. "You'll have a good time in Paris," said Camus. "Everybody is for you. But do you intend to stay?" "I don't know," said Wright. "If I were you," Camus told him, "I wouldn't want to be in Paris while Negroes are fighting for a better life. You know, during the war

I had several chances to come to America, but I chose to stay in the underground and fight the Nazis. So I think I have a right to say to you that you shouldn't stay in France." Wright, of course, did not take Camus's good advice.

If Camus substituted a moral for a political *posture,* Noam Chomsky, distinguished for his contributions to linguistics rather than to action, seems to have substituted moral for political *ideas.* Morality has, of course, a stronger appeal in action than in thought. Nevertheless, Chomsky's article in The New York Review of Books for Feb. 23, 1967, "The Responsibility of Intellectuals," evoked the sympathy and admiration of intellectuals and students in this country and in Europe. An award recently given Chomsky by London University mentions not only his creative work in linguistics but also the fact that he has urged a more courageous political stand on his fellow intellectuals. In "The Responsibility of Intellectuals," Chomsky argued powerfully against recent justifications of our Government's policy, specifically in Asia, and certainly scored telling points against, among others, Herman Kahn, Walt Rostow and Arthur Schlesinger. However, one good article does not make a political outlook, and even this article left something to be desired. For, granted that Chomsky scored some points against Schlesinger, what are we to think of his effort to deny Schlesinger any title as an intellectual insofar as the latter, by his own admission, lied to The New York Times in 1961 about the scale of the Bay of Pigs invasion?

The only way Chomsky could have known Schlesinger had lied was that, finally, Schlesinger chose to tell the truth (also to The New York Times) almost five years later. The important point, however, is that in politics expediency cannot be excluded, even for intellectuals; and sometimes it is not expedient to tell the truth. If it is contradictory to be an intellectual and to lie, then Trotsky would have to be refused intellectual honors on the ground that he denied the existence of Lenin's will, though he knew there was one. President Johnson can hardly be a model for intellectuals, but let us not now find such a model in George Washington—or in the man of myth who never told a lie.

And Chomsky's published statements since the appearance of his much-talked-about article have been most disappointing. In the September–October, 1967, issue of Liberation, which was devoted to A. J. Muste, Chomsky objected to a remark by the Dartmouth historian Louis Morton that the American people "had every reason to rejoice" at the end of the war in the Pacific. How could this statement be tolerated, Chomsky asked; wasn't the Japanese countryside in ruins as a result of the American bombardment? But the war was over—indeed, because of the bombardment—and this is why Americans had reason to rejoice. And in "Resistance," an article in The New York Review of Books last Dec. 7, Chomsky made many violent characterizations of American policy in Asia but no attempt to explain the motives for that policy. I was struck by this because when I first became interested in politics, during the nineteen-thirties, no serious commentator on events would have failed to interpret the motives of the participants.

According to Chomsky, we are engaged in a brutal, crazy, stupid aggression against a tiny Asian country, an aggression that can be justified only if the facts are not disclosed. But what are the motives for this aggression? Is the American effort in Vietnam linked to economic imperialism, as some of the New Leftists seem to think? Or does the United States want to outflank China, as Jean-Paul Sartre suggests? Are we fighting because of some mania of our President's, or because of the ascendency of the military-industrial establishment? I should very much like to learn from some future discourse by Mr. Chomsky what he, on reflection, sees as the real motives of our Asian policy. In his essay on "The Responsibility of Intellectuals," Chomsky wrote: "Intellectuals are in a position to expose the lies of governments, *to analyze actions according to their causes and motives and often hidden intentions."* (My italics.)

I have searched through Mr. Chomsky's writing on politics to see whether he has met the responsibility he himself recognizes of analyzing our actions according to their causes and motives, and I have to report that he has not. What he has done so far—and I do not want to minimize its value—has been to expose certain lies of the Government or of individuals speaking on its behalf. Obviously, if he were to characterize the motives of the Government he could not help but disclose his own. When he restricts himself to calling the Government's policy bad, however, the only revelation he makes of his own aims is that he considers them to be good. That is how the New Left judges *its* motives—and no doubt that is why Chomsky is one of the heroes of leftist youth.

Less of a hero, though, than the famed Paul Goodman. My informant told me: "Don't think Chomsky is our favorite. We respect him, of course."

"But you have something against him?" I asked.

"Now he's beginning to speak out against us," my informant said. "In one of his last articles he spoke against civil disobedience."

I happened to have the Chomsky article with me, and I read from its closing paragraph: "We must be careful not to construct situations in which young people will find themselves induced, perhaps in violation of their basic convictions, to commit civil disobedience. Resistance must be freely undertaken."

"You see?" said my informant. "A square."

At this point I thought I should see Paul Goodman, whom I had known for years. Latterly he had come into a great reputation among the young; during the nineteen-forties and fifties only a few followed him. I was not unacquainted with his very unusual and, to me, heady admixture of wild theories and common sense. In the period when people were bent on being sensible, his wild theories could hardly interest. Now that there was wildness everywhere, it was suddenly noticed that he was sensible (in fact, he had always been), and the youth were beating a path to his door. I found myself there, too. On a gray Sunday morning I rang his bell on New York's West Side. He was affable, admitting me. I thought: "He likes to defend himself."

Why, I wanted to know, did such war resisters as Dr. Benjamin Spock and Chaplain William Sloane Coffin taunt the Government for not arresting them, then wind up calling their arrests illegal? What was the logic of this behavior?

"It's perfectly logical," said Paul. I: "Perfectly?" Paul: "No, not perfectly." I: "Then it's not logical." "Well," he said, "I really don't like Mr. Coffin too much, and I don't want to have to defend his way of expressing himself."

I asked: "Can it be that you are too irritated by the political moralizing going on now, especially among the youth?"

"Well," said Paul, "we—and by 'we' I mean from Dr. Spock to the Students for a Democratic Society—do not make any kind of distinction between the moral and the political."

"In that case," I responded, "you, Dr. Spock and the S.D.S. are responsible for a great deal of chatter in which politics and morals are completely confused."

Paul: "Well, we can't distinguish between politics and morals as long as the bombing of Vietnam goes on." [The conversation took place before United States bombing was curtailed.]

He spoke with a seriousness I could not but respect. All the same, I couldn't help asking: "You're still an Aristotelian, aren't you?" He looked surprised. "Yes, of course."

"Well," said I, "as you know, Aristotle clearly distinguished between politics and morals. Morals were what politics were for, but not the content of politics as such."

"Yes, yes, to be sure," Paul said, a little irritably. "I know the difference. But we can't make the distinction nowadays; we just can't as long as this bombing goes on."

I saw it was time to talk about something else. I was thinking of the admiration the youth have for Che Guevara, and I brought the matter up.

"The *Guevaristas,*" said Paul, "are my real problem. They are what I would call naive Leninists. They want to take power, and they go in for actions of a type they think necessary for taking power. In this very bad society, I am in favor only of the kind of actions I would want people to take in a better society. They are for clandestine, I am for open, conspiracy. They say society is bad, which it is. But I think whatever we do now should be a model for what people are to do in the future."

I gave him a *Guevarista* argument out of Trotsky: "You don't use a chair to make a chair." "Well," he replied, "we're not making something. We're acting. Making doesn't have the relation to morality that action has. As I said, I am for people meeting publicly and saying that they intend to break the law. The *Gueva-ristas* are for the clandestine planning of violent lawless deeds." I asked: "Would you call them your enemies?" He said, twisting a line from Hopkins to his purpose: "Be they my enemies, they are my friends."

When I got back to Buffalo, I looked up my informant and brought up the matter of Goodman against Guevara. I told him that Goodman had said he was in conflict with many of the youth. "Not at all," said my informant. I: "But he says he's in conflict with the *Guevaristas*." "I told you once before," said my informant, "we're not very logical." "But Paul Goodman is." "Not when he's with us! It is not possible to be logical when you're with us." I said, "You seem proud of that." "I am," he replied. Then he offered to help me: "Would you like to hear Che Guevara speak?"

With that, he took me to the room where he kept his tapes. As he set up the machine I asked how he got Guevara's voice. "It's my voice," he said. "I'm pretending to be Guevara. In fact, I'm quite proud of my accent." He turned it on.

"Amigos," said his voice from the tape, and he turned it off. *"Amigos* of Paul Goodman," he said, smiling at me as if he were Che in person, "you who are young and under his influence . . ." He turned on the tape again. *"Amigos,"* came the voice. A pause. A scratch. "Who are we fighting? The greatest power on earth. More banks, more guns, more scientists, more beaches, more tennis courts, more detectives, also more black men whose hearts are sad. This is our enemy. How shall we treat him? Shall we tell him our names? Shall we say: 'Mr. United Chase National General Electric Wall Street States, this is little me, Che Guevara, on a hillside in Bolivia. I'll even tell you which hill, so you can kill me from a helicopter Come kill me with a golden bullet winged out of Fort Knox.' No, I won't tell our enemy where I am or where you may be—not, that is, if you follow me.

"Yes, I do defend secrecy. But then, of course, I'm not very moral, not now. I haven't been since the day we were attacked in the Sierra Maestra by the *Batistas*. At my feet were a knapsack of medicine and a box of ammunition. Which would I pick up? I couldn't carry both. I picked up the ammunition; I left the medicine. I remembered this when we were by the banks of the La Plata River, the day we ate horsemeat for the first time. You know, some of our guerrillas, who were peasants, though as hungry as the rest of us, wouldn't eat their portion of horsemeat. Some of them even called the one who killed the horse a murderer, for it belonged to a peasant named Popa. It was I who defended the horse killer."

As the tape machine came to a halt, I said: "Since you can talk like Che, be Che for a moment, without the tape. How do you relate your immoralism to Goodman's moralism?" *"Amigo,"* he said, "I want there to be more Vietnams, as many Vietnams as possible. Wars without number, murders, executions, surprise raids, night attacks, bombings and burnings and beatings. Now Goodman wants to end the Vietnam war, the one going on now, and of course he and people like him will try to end the other Vietnam wars, for there are going to be many more of them. My people will make them, his people will stop them, that is our unity, that our faith."

Régis Debray is the young French intellectual with some training in philosophy who went into Bolivia (according to some) as a *Guevarista* guerrilla, was captured and sentenced to 30 years in prison for, among other things, murder. Appeals to the Bolivian Government for clemency have been made by intellectuals, European as well as American, and de Gaulle himself wrote something in the young man's favor. However, after Guevara's capture and execution by the Bolivian Army, the sentiment for young Debray has somewhat cooled: certain rather suggestive facts have come to light. For example, the Bolivian Government offered to trade Debray to Castro for a Cuban imprisoned in Cuba. Castro did not respond, but made a counter-offer: he indicated his readiness to trade 100 prisoners he held in Cuba for the corpse of Guevara. Was Guevara's corpse worth more to Castro than the life of his admirer Debray? The Italian journalist Franco Pierini, who went to Bolivia to make his own investigation of Guevara's death, interviewed the colonel commanding the Eighth Division of the Bolivian Army and quoted him as declaring that Debray told the Government of Guevara's whereabouts. Here, as published by Atlas in January, is a portion of the dialogue between Pierini and the Bolivian officer, whose answers may, of course, have been self-serving.

"When did you find out that Che Guevara was here?"

"We had our suspicions, but they were confirmed when Debray and Bustos, the French writer and Argentine painter, were arrested in April. They told us themselves."

"Did they have any choice?"

"Certainly they did. At first, I don't think they were even asked where Che was. But Debray himself based his entire defense on the fact that he wanted to interview Mr. Guevara. And Bustos, who made sketches of the guerrillas he had met, drew from memory the face of a certain Ramon, whom we all recognized to be Che."

In questioning my young friend of the New Left about Debray, I asked, "Is Debray still one of your heroes?" "Yes, of course," he said. "His book 'Revolution in the Revolution' is brilliant, and was called brilliant in a brilliant piece in a brilliant journal by none other than the brilliant Juan Bosch." "Well," I said, "I'm not asking you what you think about his book. Suppose he betrayed Che—could you still think him a hero?"

He answered: "I have to talk about Régis's book—you notice I'm calling him by his first name—this is because he's in trouble, and people are saying bad things about him. 'Revolution in the Revolution' is so important to us because it makes a clean sweep of all theories about revolution and suggests that the best way to act is to launch oneself into action, which is what we intend to do. Maybe Régis's thing turned out badly; then we have to feel sorry for his weakness, his error. But the great thing he's told us is that we should not theorize, all we should do is act. Now what does it mean to act? And what is the best way to act, that is to say, as a revolutionary? I bet you don't know."

"Well," I said, "I did look into his book."

"Ah, but you have to know how to read it. Do you know what a revolution is to Debray? It is a coordinated series of guerrilla happenings."

"Happenings?"

"I and my friends, when we take part in happenings, which is quite often, feel that we are training for those future happenings when we'll have guns and grenades. That's what Debray means to us."

"You mean he's given you some reason for taking happenings seriously?" I asked.

"That's right," he said. "And don't forget, the greatest happening of all happenings in this hemisphere was Castro, from whom Debray learned that a political program is often a handicap to a guerrilla."

"So you have no program for action?"

"You might put it that way," he said. "But to us that means merely that we can act."

"Toward what end?"

"Against Johnson, against the war and for our black brothers."

Among his black brothers in the New Left and those whites who want to go forward with black revolt, the magic name is Frantz Fanon. This Negro psychiatrist and writer was born in Martinique and died in the United States of cancer at 36. He has been called by Sartre the voice of the Third World. Two of his books, "The Wretched of the Earth" and "Black Skin, White Masks" have had a profound effect, outlining the experiences of a man educated in the refinements of French culture but driven by a need to deny the white world. In "The Wretched of the Earth," Fanon took the view that African natives had a duty to behave in precisely the way white settlers described them. Called animals, they should behave like animals. Called barbarians, they should behave barbarously. In some ways his advice to black communities was modeled on Sartre's very subtle understanding of the playwright and novelist Genet, famous also for having been a thief. Genet, a foundling, was caught stealing by his foster parents, who called him a thief. And, according to Sartre, the great act of Genet as a boy was to become exactly what his foster parents called him. Fanon, whose books abound with quotations from Sartre, took the same attitude to blacks abused by whites in Africa. We must become what we have been called, he told them.

But if Fanon was influenced by Sartre, he was also, according to his own testimony in "Black Skin, White Masks," almost destroyed by Sartre until able to answer him. Fanon explains that when he wanted to be "typically Negro, it was no longer possible." He wanted to be white, and that, he says, was a joke. And, he concludes, when he tried to reclaim what he calls his "negritude," it was snatched away from him. The argument that his effort would be unavailing he found in Sartre's essay "Orphée Noir," prefacing an anthology of new Negro poetry. Sartre had written:

"It is no coincidence that the most ardent poets of negritude are at the same time militant Marxists.

"But this does not prevent the idea of race from mingling with that of class. . . . In fact, negritude appears as the minor term in a dialectical progression: the theoretical and practical assertion of the supremacy of the white man is its thesis; negritude is here the antithesis. But this negative moment is insufficient, and the Negroes who feel it know this quite well. . . . Negritude is the root of its own destruction, it is a transition and not a conclusion."

When he read those words, Fanon said, he felt that he had been robbed of his last chance. He had sought help from a friend of the colored people, and that friend had merely pointed out the relativity of his black heritage: "For once," Fanon wrote, Sartre "had forgotten that consciousness has to lose itself in the night of the absolute. . . . A consciousness committed to experience is ignorant and has to be ignorant. . . . " And he calls Sartre's essay "a date in the intellectualization of the experience of being black."

In this conflict between Sartre and Fanon, I read the arguments between separatist militants and liberal integrationists in today's black movement, but they are stated with an intellectual depth unequaled by our own black writers. Curiously enough, having objected to Sartre's intellectual antiracism as an attack on his "negritude," Fanon went on to formulate an antiracism of his own, to which he gave extraordinary expression in the concluding chapter of "Black Skin, White Masks":

"The black man wants to be like the white man. For the black man there is only one destiny. And it is white. Long ago the black man admitted the unarguable superiority of the white man and all his efforts are aimed at achieving a white existence.

"In this world, which is already trying to disappear, do I have to pose the problem of black truth? . . .

"I as a man of color do not have the right to seek to know in what respect my race is superior or inferior to another race.

"I as a man of color do not have the right to seek ways of stamping down the pride of my former masters.

"I have no wish to be the victim of the *fraud* of a black world."

This antiracism is probably not what won Fanon the admiration of New Leftists, black or white. It turned out that my informant did not even know of "Black Skin, White Masks." He was exclusively interested in "The Wretched of the Earth," and in praising its style he quoted from Sartre's introduction. "Sartre points out," he said, "that when Fanon says Europe is done for, he says it *coldly*. Fanon doesn't care about curing Europe; he has other things to think about. In fact, if I remember rightly, Sartre put it this way: 'He doesn't give a damn whether she lives or dies.' When Fanon speaks of Europe, Sartre points out, he is not talking to Europeans.

"Fanon's style reminds me of Stokely Carmichael on television. I feel Stokely's never looking at the whites in his audience."

The point was well taken. How could Fanon talk directly to Europeans—even though speaking with a sophistication he had learned from them—when judging Europe as he does in the final pages of "The Wretched of the Earth":

"The European game has finally ended. . . . We today can do everything so long as we do not imitate Europe, so long as we are not obsessed by the desire to catch up with Europe.

"When I search for Man in the technique, in the style of Europe, I see only a succession of negations . . . an avalanche of murders.

"Two centuries ago, a former European colony decided to catch up with Europe. It succeeded so well that the United States of America became a monster in which the taints, the sickness and the inhumanity of Europe have grown to appalling dimensions."

It is the ability shown here to speak against Europe—and, incidentally, the United States—with an eloquence and spirituality comparable to the finest expressions of Europe that has won Fanon disciples among American youth. But to understand why Fanon has been thought of as an *immoralist* hero, it is necessary to turn back to his consideration of whites and Negroes in "Black

Skin, White Masks." Fanon's whole concern in this book was with matters of identity: what is the black man in a world designed by whites? We all know that for morality to operate, identity must not be a problem. Morality is meaningless for those who are undefined. Unhappily, this is a problem not only for many of our blacks, but also for increasing numbers of white youths seeking identity change; Norman Mailer characterized them as "white Negroes" in a now-famous essay in Dissent.

Professor Marcuse, who teaches philosophy at the University of California at San Diego, is lionized by our leftist youth neither as a moralist nor as an immoralist, and not for his scholarly "Revolution and Reason," an interesting work on the philosophy of Hegel. The young are attracted to Marcuse because of two recent books, "Eros and Civilization" and "One-Dimensional Man," and an essay, "Repressive Tolerance." In these writings youth has found attacks on what most of us consider to be the *good* features of modern democratic society: liberalism, tolerance and sexual permissiveness. Not, to be sure, that Marcuse is precisely in favor of illiberalism, intolerance or sexual repression.

On the contrary, Marcuse presents a Marxist critique of the repressive features of present-day society, both in the so-called capitalist and in the Soviet world; he has also taken over the Freudian critique of those repressions made necessary by efficient organization. I must add, though, that the Marxism and the Freudianism of Professor Marcuse are rather special. Marxism has always been understood to be an optimistic doctrine, imbued, as Trotsky put it, with the optimism of progress. Marcuse's Marxism is utterly pessimistic; he accepts what Marxists have said about bourgeois society in order to change society, adding only that it cannot be changed. For Marxists, change would come through the revolutionary proletariat; but in the welfare state, Marcuse points out the proletariat cannot be revolutionary.

His Freudianism is also curious. Freud's doctrine is generally —and rightly—regarded as pessimistic; some have even said Jewishly pessimistic. Marcuse's Freudianism is optimistic. Where, in Freud's view, all cultural and moral values are made possible only by the sacrifice of our sexual energies in the process known to Freudians as sublimation, Marcuse says we can achieve a kind of sublimation that does not require the sacrifice of sex. We have suffered from "surplus sublimation" in Marcuse's phrase, and he says we may look toward the possibility of a pleasant, sexually satisfying "self-sublimation."

To what purpose, though, has Professor Marcuse subverted the accepted impact of both the Freudian and the Marxian doctrines? His aim, clearly, is as harsh an indictment as possible of modern society—of what is known as "the Free World." What is his indictment? That the Free World is not free. On the political level, this means that democratic institutions today further unfreedom, not freedom. In "Repressive Tolerance," Marcuse wrote:

"According to a dialectical proposition, it is the whole which determines the truth—not in the sense that the whole is prior or superior to its parts, but in the sense that its structure and function determine every particular condition and relation. Thus, within a repressive society, even progressive movements threaten to turn into their opposite to the degree to which they accept the rules of the game. To take a most controversial case: the exercise of political rights (such as voting, letter-writing to the press, to Senators, etc., protest demonstrations with *a priori* renunciation of counterviolence) in a society of total administration serves to strengthen the administration by testifying to the existence of democratic liberties . . . in such a case, freedom (of opinion, of assembly, of speech) becomes an instrument for absolving servitude."

Unquestionably, our society is, in Marcuse's view, one of total administration; this was the position he took in his study of contemporary society and culture, "One-Dimensional Man," called by the British philosopher Alasdair MacIntyre "an essay in pessimism so profound that it is contradicted in the act of writing it." Is it true, though, that in this society the rights of free press, free speech and free assembly end up by "absolving servitude"? Many of the young who followed Marcuse thought so, and they valued him for alerting them to the "totalitarian" features of modern democracy. Will they continue to follow him? Now, I think, one may doubt it. In recent weeks, we have seen teach-ins, write-ins and protest demonstrations actually change the policy of our Government—even its foreign policy (Lenin believed that foreign policy could be changed only by revolution). Will the young continue to believe that the rights in the exercise of which they turned the country from war toward peace are treacherous appearances of freedom functioning to "absolve servitude"?

On matters sexual, as on those political, liberalism in this society turns into its opposite for Marcuse. Thus, sexual permissiveness becomes a form of repression, and—instead of the desirable "self-sublimation" postulated as possible in "Eros and Civilization"—Marcuse finds in "One-Dimensional Man" that democratic society fosters a controlled and repressive "desublimation." What is "desublimation"? The spending of our sexual desires on transient satisfactions. (How enduring, one wonders, can sexual satisfaction be in even the best of societies? For sexual satisfaction not to be fleeting, not only would society have to be better than it is, but Venus would have to be divine!) And not only, says Marcuse, are our satisfactions fleeting, but they also sap the spirit of protest. "Satisfaction . . . generates submission and weakens the rationality of protest. . . . The range of socially permissible and desirable satisfaction is greatly enlarged, but through this satisfaction the pleasure principle is reduced. . . ." He proceeds to compare the sublimated erotic literature and culture of the 17th and 18th centuries—in the 18th century, by the way, men were still burned at the stake in Paris for pederasty—with the "desublimated" sexuality and permissiveness of modern times, which Marcuse describes as "rampant in O'Neill's alcoholics and Faulkner's savages, in 'Streetcar Named Desire' and 'Cat on a Hot Tin Roof,' in 'Lolita,' in all the stories of Hollywood and New York orgies and the adventures of suburban housewives." Freed from sublimated forms, Marcuse says, sexuality "turns into a vehicle for the bestsellers of oppression."

All this reminded me, I told my informant, of "Le Très Haut" (The Almighty), a novel by the French literary critic Maurice Blanchot that had quite a vogue in Paris during the nineteen-fifties—a much finer and more sophisticated work than Orwell's "1984." The world of "Le Très Haut" has reached the end of history, and revolutions against the state are organized by state bureaucrats, which does not prevent the state, when it puts down the revolts thus incited, from putting to death its own functionaries.

I pressed my informant: "Isn't this very much like what Marcuse is trying to say? In Blanchot, the state has absorbed its very antithesis, the revolution. According to Marcuse, intolerance has absorbed tolerance, and repression permissiveness. In fact, according to Marcuse, sexual permissiveness has turned into something even worse than sublimation."

"This is what makes Marcuse so interesting and important to us," my informant said. "He enables us to say things against modern society that even the Communists didn't dare say."

I: "They at least had to pay lip service to democracy."

He: "And we are able to say it is worse than Fascism."

"But," I insisted, "haven't the events of recent days proved that democracy is a reality, and that government policy, in this country at least, can be changed, and precisely because we do enjoy the rights of free speech, a free press and free assembly?" I thought I had him, and added: "Isn't what has happened a complete refutation of the Marcuse position?"

"By no means," he said. "Do you know why the demonstrations and protest movements succeeded? Because we didn't play the rules of the game. Our movement wasn't organized democratically. We kicked the Dow people off the campus though they had every right to be there. It was our unrepressed intolerance and thorough antipermissiveness that brought our actions success. But who gave us the intellectual courage to be intolerant and unpermissive? I think Herbert Marcuse more than anyone. He is the New Left's professor."

Suggested Reading

NO ATTEMPT is made in this note to offer a complete bibliography, as any such effort would require a listing of hundreds of volumes. Rather, the purpose is to suggest some of the more easily accessible books. Several general works serve as good introductions to the field of intellectual history. These include Jacob Bronowski and Bruce Mazlish, *The Western Intellectual Tradition* (New York, 1960), Robert A. Nisbet, *Social Change and History* (New York, 1969, and Oxford paperback [abridged edition]), and Crane Brinton, *Ideas and Men* (New York, 1950). Other works of more specific concern are John H. Randall, Jr., *The Career of Philosophy* (New York, 1962, and Columbia paperback), and Suzanne K. Langer, *Mind: An Essay on Human Feeling* (Baltimore, 1967, and Johns Hopkins paperback).

A useful introduction to Vico is offered by A. R. Conigri, *Time and Idea* (London, 1953). Readers may fruitfully consult as well Vico's *New Science,* translated by Thomas G. Bergin and Max H. Fisch (New York, 1961, and Cornell paperback), and his *Autobiography,* translated by the same scholars (Ithaca, 1944). Darwin's two most important works are readily available in a Modern Library edition which combines in one volume the *Origin of Species* and *Descent of Man* (New York, 1936). G. Bradford, *Darwin* (Boston, 1926), and Paul B. Sears, *Charles Darwin: The Naturalist as a Cultural Force* (New York, 1930), are still useful. Gertrude Himmelfarb, *Darwin and the Darwinian*

Revolution (New York, 1962, and Norton paperback) is somewhat tendentious. Walter Kaufmann is the major contemporary editor and interpreter of Nietzsche. His edition of the *Basic Writings of Nietzsche* (New York, 1968) is quite helpful, as is his *Nietzsche: Philosopher, Psychologist, Antichrist* (Princeton, 1950, and Vintage paperback). Kaufmann has also edited *The Will to Power* (New York, 1967, and Vintage paperback) in an attractive volume.

The literature on Freud is enormous. Absolutely essential is Ernest Jones, *The Life and Work of Sigmund Freud* (3 volumes, New York, 1953–1957, and Anchor paperback [abridged edition]). Readers may wish to consult *The Basic Writings of Sigmund Freud* in the Modern Library edition (New York, 1938), though the translation leaves much to be desired. The Standard Edition of *The Complete Psychological Works* (London, 1953) runs to 24 volumes. A similar problem of quantity holds for Marx also. Yet readers should not forgo *Das Kapital,* the first volume of which is available in a Modern Library edition, reproduced from the old Kerr edition translated by Moore and Aveling in 1906. However, the E. and C. Paul translation (New York, 1929) is vastly superior. Franz Mehring's biography, *Karl Marx: The Story of His Life* (New York, 1935, and Ann Arbor paperback) is standard. Special focus on the philosophical side of Marxism is provided in Lloyd D. Easton and Kurt H. Guddat, eds., *Writings of the Young Marx on Philosophy and Society* (New York, 1967, and Anchor paperback), and S. Aveneri, *The Social and Political Thought of Karl Marx* (London, 1968). A splendid introduction is Sir Isaiah Berlin, *Karl Marx: His Life and Environment* (New York, 1959, and Oxford paperback).

A good introduction to Russell is Paul A. Schilpp, ed., *The Philosophy of Bertrand Russell* (New York, 1963), one of a series of useful symposia in which the subject responds to his critics. Robert E. Egner and Lester E. Denonn edited *The Basic Writings of Bertrand Russell* (New York, 1961, and Clarion paperback), a volume that effectively reveals Russell's multifaceted personality. Aside from the more technical works, a good start is Russell's *My Philosophical Development* (New York,

1959). For the positivist viewpoint, the reader may consult Richard von Mises, *Positivism* (New York, 1956, and Dover paperback), and Hans Reichenbach, *The Rise of Scientific Philosophy* (Berkeley, 1951, and California paperback). Leszek Kolakowski, *The Alienation of Reason* (New York, 1968, and Anchor paperback) offers cogent criticisms of positivism. The operationalist variant of positivism is developed in Percy W. Bridgman, *The Way Things Are* (New York, 1961). Abraham Kaplan's *The Conduct of Inquiry* (San Francisco, 1964, and Chandler paperback) is based on a modification of the positivist position. A good general discussion is Arne Naess, *Four Modern Philosophers* (Chicago, 1968, and Phoenix paperback), discussing Carnap, Wittgenstein, Heidegger, and Sartre. George Pitcher's *The Philosophy of Wittgenstein* (Englewood Cliffs, 1964) is somewhat technical.

Another of the Schilpp volumes is *The Philosophy of John Dewey* (New York, 1951). Selections from Dewey may be found in J. Ratner, ed., *Intelligence in the Modern World* (New York, 1939). Readers should find this volume accessible, as it is included in the Modern Library series. Schilpp and Maurice Friedman also edited *The Philosophy of Martin Buber* (La Salle, Ill., 1967). Several of Buber's works are available in paperback: these include *Paths in Utopia* (Boston, 1958) and *Between Man and Man* (Boston, 1955). Maurice Friedman's *Martin Buber: The Life of Dialogue* (Chicago, 1955) is an excellent introduction to Buber's variety of existentialism.

A good history of phenomenology, though somewhat on the technical side, is Herbert Spiegelberg, *The Phenomenological Movement* (2 volumes, The Hague, 1965). Maurice Friedman has edited a selection of readings on existentialism that is most useful, *The Worlds of Existentialism* (New York, 1964). Several works edited by James M. Edie are also helpful: *An Invitation to Phenomenology* (Chicago, 1965, and Quadrangle paperback), *Phenomenology in America* (Chicago, 1967, and Quadrangle paperback), and *New Essays in Phenomenology* (Chicago, 1969, and Quadrangle paperback). Sartre's basic philosophic work is *Being and Nothingness* (New York, 1956, and Washington Square paperback). A translation of the *Critique of Dialectical Reason* is not yet available, though indications of its argument are given in *Search for a Method* (New York, 1963, and Vintage paperback) and in the selections in Robert D. Cumming, ed., *The Philosophy of Jean-Paul Sartre* (New York, 1965).

With so extensive a bibliography in psychology, we can list only a few works for the writers discussed in the text. Piaget is a most prolific writer. Among the more philosophic works are *Judgment and Reasoning in the Child* (London, 1928, and Littlefield paperback); *Language and Thought of the Child* (Cleveland, 1955, and Meridian paperback); *Moral Judgment of the Child* (London, 1932); and *The Growth of Logical Thinking* (London, 1958, and Basic paperback). A good summary of Piaget's work is in John H. Flavell, *The Developmental Psychology of Jean Piaget* (Princeton, 1963). Hans G. Furth, *Piaget and Knowledge* (Englewood Cliffs, 1969) is more recent. For almost ironic insight into Skinner's views, the reader is urged to consult his novel *Walden II* (New York, 1948, and Macmillan paperback). More academic is his *Science and Human Behavior* (New York, 1963, and Free Press paperback). An excellent introduction to Bettelheim is his *The Empty Fortress* (New York, 1967). Erikson's major work is *Childhood and Society* (New York, 1950, and Norton paperback), a book that has enjoyed fifteen printings. His *Insight and Responsibility* (New York, 1964, and Norton paperback) presents lectures on the ethical implications of psychoanalysis. The idea of identity is explored in *Identity: Youth and Crisis* (New York, 1968). Nor should the reader overlook Erikson's *Young Man Luther* (New York, 1958, and Norton paperback) and his recent *Gandhi's Truth* (New York, 1969).

To understand the development of Keynes's thinking, the reader should consult David Winch, *Economics and Policy* (London, 1969), and Robert Lekachman, *The Age of Keynes* (New York, 1966, and Vintage paperback). Only then can he profit from Keynes's *General Theory of Employment, Interest, and Money* (New York, 1936, and Harbinger paperback). The development of economic thought in the last hundred years is presented in Ben B. Seligman, *Main Currents in Modern Economics* (New

York, 1962). Milton Friedman's best nontechnical work is his *Capitalism and Freedom* (Chicago, 1962, and Phoenix paperback). John Kenneth Galbraith's most important work is *The New Industrial State* (Boston, 1967, and New American Library paperback), although the reader should also consult his *The Affluent Society* (2nd edition, Boston, 1969, and New American Library paperback).

André Malraux's *Anti-Memoirs* (New York, 1968) provides insight into the tragic imagination that has characterized his work. His *Voices of Silence* (New York, 1956) offers a new conception of art in the contemporary world. Lévi-Strauss is best represented by his *Structural Anthropology* (New York, 1963, and Anchor paperback) and *The Savage Mind* (Chicago, 1966, and Phoenix paperback). The best of Margaret Mead's books are available in paperback. These include *Coming of Age in Samoa* (New York, 1949, and Dell paperback), *Growing Up in New Guinea* (New York, 1953, and Dell paperback), *Sex and Temperament in Three Primitive Societies* (New York, 1950, and Apollo paperback), *Cooperation and Competition among Primitive Peoples* (New York, 1937, and Beacon paperback), and *Male and Female* (New York, 1955, and Dell paperback). Readers interested in a broader and somewhat more historical treatment of anthropology may do well to consult Margaret Mead and R. L. Bunzel, eds., *The Golden Age of American Anthropology* (New York, 1960), a book that offers selections from Colonial writers to those who firmly established anthropology in America—Franz Boas, Paul Radin, Alfred Kroeber, and others. McLuhan's *The Medium Is the Massage,* co-authored with Quentin Fiore (New York, 1967, and New American Library paperback), should prove more than adequate. The scholarly Marcuse is represented by *Reason and Revolution* (Boston, 1960, and Beacon paperback), the apocalyptic Marcuse by *One-Dimensional Man* (Boston, 1964, and Beacon paperback). Camus' *The Rebel* (New York, 1954, and Vintage paperback) is an extraordinary work. The reader should also consult his *Resistance, Rebellion, and Death* (New York, 1961). Chomsky is best represented by *American Power and the New Mandarins* (New York, 1969, and

Vintage paperback), a volume that contains some New Leftish revisionist essays. Paul Goodman's most interesting work is *Growing Up Absurd* (New York, 1960, and Vintage paperback). Frantz Fanon's *Wretched of the Earth* (New York, 1965, and Evergreen paperback) is as upsetting as it is wrongheaded.

Index

A Note on the Editor

Ben B. Seligman was born in Newark, New Jersey, and studied at Brooklyn College, Columbia University, and the New School for Social Research. He was formerly research director of the Retail Clerks International Association and is now Professor of Economics and Director of the Labor Relations and Research Center at the University of Massachusetts. His first book, *Main Currents in Modern Economics,* published in 1962, is considered a standard in the field; he has since written *Most Notorious Victory: Man in an Age of Automation; Permanent Poverty: An American Syndrome; Economics of Dissent;* and *The Potentates: Business and Businessmen in American History,* and edited *Poverty as a Public Issue* and *Aspects of Poverty.* His articles appear frequently in scholarly journals and magazines of opinion. Mr. Seligman is now at work on a study of the philosophic foundations of economic thought.